THE WILLIAM STALLINGS BOOKS ON COMPUTER AND DATA COMMUNICATIONS TECHNOLOGY

OPERATING SYSTEMS: CONCEPTS AND EXAMPLES

A state-of-the art survey of operating system principles. Covers fundamental technology as well as contemporary design issues, such as threads, real-time systems, multiprocessor scheduling, distributed systems, and security.

HANDBOOK OF COMPUTER-COMMUNICATIONS STANDARDS VOLUME 1
THE OPEN SYSTEMS INTERCONNECTION (OSI) MODEL AND OSI-RELATED STANDARDS, SECOND EDITION

A description of the master plan for all computer-communications standards: the OSI model. The book also provides a detailed presentation of OSI-related standards at all 7 layers, including HDLC, X.25, ISO internet, ISO transport, ISO session, ISO presentation, Abstract Syntax ONE (ASN.1), and common application service elements (CASE).

HANDBOOK OF COMPUTER-COMMUNICATIONS STANDARDS VOLUME 2
LOCAL AREA NETWORK STANDARDS, SECOND EDITION

A detailed examination of all current local network standards, including logical link control (LLC, IEEE 802.2), CSMA/CD (IEEE 802.3), token bus (IEEE 802.4), token ring (IEEE 802.5), and fiber distributed data interface (FDDI, ANS X3T9.5).

HANDBOOK OF COMPUTER-COMMUNICATIONS STANDARDS VOLUME 3
THE TCP/IP PROTOCOL SUITE, SECOND EDITION

A description of the protocol standards that are mandated on all DOD computer procurements and are becoming increasingly popular on commercial local network products, including TCP, IP, FTP, SMTP, and TELNET. The network management standards, SNMP and CMOT, are also presented.

OPERATING SYSTEMS

OPERATING SYSTEMS

William Stallings

MACMILLAN PUBLISHING COMPANY
New York

MAXWELL MACMILLAN CANADA
Toronto

MAXWELL MACMILLAN INTERNATIONAL
New York   Oxford   Singapore   Sydney

Editor: John Griffin
Production Supervisor: John Travis
Production Manager: Paul Smolenski
Text Designer: Jane Edelstein
Cover Designer: Jane Edelstein
Cover Illustration: Brian Sheridan
Illustrations by Precision Graphics

This book was set in 10/12 Palatino by Waldman Graphics, and was printed and bound by R. R. Donnelley & Sons—Crawfordsville. The cover was printed by Lehigh Press Lithographers.

Macmillan Publishing Company
866 Third Avenue, New York, New York 10022

Macmillan Publishing Company is
part of the Maxwell Communication
Group of Companies.

Maxwell Macmillan Canada, Inc.
1200 Eglinton Avenue East
Suite 200
Don Mills, Ontario M3C 3N1

Library of Congress Cataloging in Publication Data

Stallings, William.
    Operating systems / William Stallings.
        p.   cm.
    Includes bibliographical references and index.
    ISBN 0-02-415481-4
    1. Operating systems, (Computers)   I. Title.
    QA76.76.063S733   1992
    005.4'3--dc20   91-10247
                                                   CIP

Printing: 1 2 3 4 5 6 7 8   Year: 2 3 4 5 6 7 8 9 0 1

Acknowledgments are on p. 683, which constitutes an extension of the copyright page.

To Tricia,
the bravest person in the world

Preface

Objectives

This book is about the concepts, structure, and mechanisms of operating systems. Its purpose is to present, as clearly and completely as possible, the nature and characteristics of modern-day operating systems.

This task is a challenging one for several reasons.

First, there is a tremendous range and variety of computer systems for which operating systems are designed. These include single-user workstations and personal computers, medium-sized shared systems, large mainframe and super-computers, and specialized machines such as real-time systems. The variety is not just in the capacity and speed of machines, but in applications and system support requirements. Second, the rapid pace of change that has always characterized computer systems continues with no letup. A number of key areas in operating-system design are of recent origin, and research into these and other new areas continues.

In spite of this variety and pace of change, certain fundamental concepts apply consistently throughout. To be sure, the application of these concepts depends on the current state of technology and the particular application requirements. The intent of this book is to provide a thorough discussion of the fundamentals of operating-system design, and to relate these to contemporary design issues and to current directions in the development of operating systems.

The object is to provide the reader with a solid understanding of the key mechanisms of modern operating systems, the types of design trade-offs and decisions involved in OS design, and the context within which the operating system functions (hardware, other system programs, application programs, interactive users).

The Process

The concept of the process is central to the study of operating systems. While all books on the subject deal with this topic, no other leading text devotes a major section to introducing and explaining the basic principles of processes.

In this book, Chapter 3 is devoted to this task. The result is a solid foundation for examining the many issues addressed in later chapters.

Recent Developments in Operating System Design

In addition to providing coverage of the fundamentals of operating systems, this book examines the most important recent developments in OS design. Among the topics covered:

- *Threads:* The concept of process is more complex and subtle than usually presented and in fact embodies two separate and potentially independent concepts: one relating to resource ownership and one relating to execution. This distinction has led to the development in some operating systems of a construct known as the thread.
- *Real time systems:* In recent years, real-time computing has come to be viewed as an important emerging discipline in computer science and engineering. The operating system, and in particular the scheduler, is perhaps the most important component of a real-time system.
- *Multiprocessor scheduling:* Traditionally, there has been little difference between the scheduling approaches taken on multiprogrammed uniprocessors and multiprocessor systems. With the increasing interest in the use of threads and in parallel programming, multiprocessor scheduling has become an area of intense study and development.
- *Distributed systems:* With the increasing availability of inexpensive yet powerful personal computers and minicomputers, there has been an increasing trend toward distributed data processing (DDP). With DDP, processors, data, and other aspects of a data processing system may be dispersed within an organization. Many of the OS design issues covered in this book take on added complexity in a distributed environment.
- *Process migration:* Process migration is the ability to move an active process from one machine to another; it has become an increasingly "hot" topic in distributed operating systems. Interest in this concept grew out of research into ways to do load balancing across multiple networked systems, although the application of the concept now extends beyond that one area. Until recently, a number of observers felt that process migration was impractical. Such assessments have proved too pessimistic. New implementations, including those in commercial products, have fueled a continuing interest and new developments in this area.
- *Security:* Security has long been a concern in the design of operating systems. However, the design approaches to security have continued to evolve as the threats to security have evolved. Examples of areas of threat that present new and more complex difficulties include viruses and attacks on distributed operating systems. An example of a new approach to coping with these threats is the concept of a trusted system.

Example Systems

This text is intended to acquaint the reader with the design principles and implementation issues of contemporary operating systems. Accordingly, a purely conceptual or theoretical treatment would be inadequate. In order to illustrate the concepts and to tie them to real-world design choices that must be made, three operating systems have been chosen as running examples:

- *OS/2:* A single-user, multitasking operating system for the IBM PS/2 and compatible systems. It is one of the few truly new operating systems that has been essentially designed from scratch (although it includes an MS-DOS compatibility mode). As such, it is in a position to incorporate in a clean fashion the latest developments in operating system technology.
- *UNIX:* A multiuser operating system, originally intended for minicomputers, but implemented on a wide range of machines from powerful microcomputers to supercomputers.
- *MVS:* The top-of-the-line operating system for IBM mainframes, and perhaps the most complex operating system ever developed. It provides both batch and timesharing capabilities.

These three systems were chosen because of their relevance and representativeness. Most personal computer operating systems on new machines are single-user multitasking systems, with OS/2 becoming the market leader. UNIX has become the dominant operating system on a wide variety of workstations and multiuser systems. MVS is the most widely used mainframe operating system. Thus, most readers will be exposed to one or more of these operating systems by the time they use this book or within a few years of doing so.

As with the technique used in the author's *Computer Organization and Architecture*, the discussion of the example systems is distributed throughout the text rather than assembled as a single chapter or appendix. Thus, during the discussion of virtual memory, the page replacement algorithm of each example system is described, and the motivation for the individual design choices is discussed. With this approach, the design concepts discussed in a given chapter are immediately reinforced with real-world examples.

Intended Audience

The book is intended for both an academic and a professional audience. As a textbook, it is intended as a one-semester undergraduate course in operating systems for computer science, computer engineering, and electrical engineering majors. It covers the topics in Subject Area 5 of the IEEE Model Program in Computer Science and Engineering and also covers the OS-related topics in CS6 and CS10 of the ACM Recommendations for the Undergraduate Program in Computer Science. It also covers all of the topics in the operating systems topic area of the ACM/IEEE Joint Computing Curricula 1991.

The book also serves as a basic reference volume and is suitable for self-study.

Plan of the Text

The organization of the chapters is as follows:

1. *Computer system overview:* Provides an overview of computer architecture and organization, with emphasis on topics that relate to operating system design.
2. *Operating system overview:* Provides an overview of the remainder of the book.
3. *Process description and control:* Presents the concept of a process and examines the data structures used by the operating system to control processes. The related concepts of threads and sessions are also discussed.
4. *Concurrency:* Examines the key aspects of concurrency on a single system, with emphasis on issues of mutual exclusion and deadlock.
5. *Memory management:* Provides a comprehensive survey of techniques for memory management.
6. *Scheduling:* Provides a comparative discussion of various approaches to process scheduling. The unique requirements of multiprocessors and real-time systems are examined.
7. *I/O management and disk scheduling:* Examines the issues involved in OS control of the I/O function. Special attention is devoted to disk I/O, which is the key to system performance.
8. *File management:* Provides an overview of file management, with an emphasis on those aspects that are usually implemented as part of the operating system or are closely tied to the operating system.
9. *Networking and distributed processing:* Examines the major trends in this area, including the OSI model, the use of network servers, and distributed operating systems.
10. *Security:* Provides a survey of threats and mechanisms for providing computer and network security.
A. *Queuing analysis:* An appendix provides a practical guide to the use of queuing analysis to model performance.

In addition, the book includes an extensive glossary, a list of frequently-used acronyms, and a bibliography. Each chapter includes problems and suggestions for further reading.

Acknowledgments

Many people have reviewed all or a portion of the manuscript for this book. I would like to especially thank the following: Umakishore Ramachandran, Georgia Institute of Technology; Margaret Reek, Rochester Institute of Technology; Anand Tripathi, University of Minnesota; Sol Shatz, University of Illinois–Chicago; Philip Krueger, The Ohio State University; Samuel Gulden, Lehigh University; E. K. Parti, U.S. Naval Academy; Armin Roeseler, AT&T Bell Labs; Charles Shub, University of Colorado–Colorado Springs; Eric Cooper,

Carnegie Mellon University; Evelyn Obaid, San Jose State University; Evan Ivie, Brigham Young University; Mark Smotherman, Clemson University; Gary Harkin, Montana State University; Rance Cleaveland, North Carolina State University; James Silver, Indiana University–Purdue University at Fort Wayne.

I would like to express my deep appreciation to Margaret Reek and Sol Shatz who contributed some of the end-of-chapter homework problems.

W.S.

Contents

CHAPTER 4 CONCURRENCY   179

CHAPTER 5 MEMORY MANAGEMENT   265

CHAPTER 6 SCHEDULING   351

OPERATING SYSTEMS

CHAPTER 1

Computer System Overview

An operating system (OS) exploits the hardware resources of one or more processors to provide a set of services to system users. The operating system also manages secondary memory and input/output (I/O) devices on behalf of its users. Accordingly, it is important to have some understanding of the underlying computer system hardware as we begin our examination of operating systems.

This chapter provides an overview of computer system hardware. In most areas, the survey is extremely brief because it is assumed that the reader is familiar with this subject. However, several areas are covered in some detail because of their importance to topics covered later in the book.

1.1

BASIC ELEMENTS

At a top level, a computer consists of processor, memory, and I/O components, with one or more modules of each type. These components are interconnected in some fashion to achieve the main function of the computer, which is to execute programs. Thus, there are four main structural elements, as follows:

- *Processor:* Controls the operation of the computer and performs its data processing functions. When there is only one processor, it is often referred to as the *central processing unit* (CPU).
- *Main memory:* Stores data and programs. This memory is typically volatile; it is also referred to as *real memory,* or *primary memory.*
- *I/O modules:* Move data between the computer and its external environment. The external environment consists of a variety of external devices, including secondary memory devices, communications equipment, and terminals.

1

• *System interconnection:* Some structure and mechanisms that provide for communication among processors, main memory, and I/O modules.

Figure 1.1 depicts these top-level components. The processor is typically in control. One of its functions is to exchange data with memory. For this purpose, it typically makes use of two internal (to the processor) registers: a memory address register (MAR), which specifies the address in memory for the next read or write; and a memory buffer register (MBR), which contains the data to be written into memory, or which receives the data read from memory. Similarly, an I/O address register (I/OAR) specifies a particular I/O device. An I/O buffer register (I/OBR) is used for the exchange of data between an I/O module and the processor.

A memory module consists of a set of locations defined by sequentially numbered addresses. Each location contains a binary number that can be interpreted as either an instruction or data. An I/O module transfers data from external devices to processor and memory, and vice versa. It contains internal buffers for temporarily holding these data until they can be sent on.

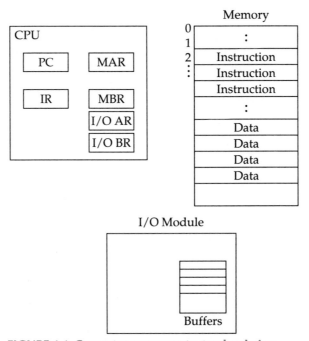

FIGURE 1.1 Computer components: top-level view

PROCESSOR REGISTERS

Within the processor, there is a set of registers that provide a level of memory that is faster and smaller than main memory. The registers in the processor serve two functions:

- *User-visible registers:* These enable the machine- or assembly-language programmer to minimize main-memory references by optimizing the use of registers. For high-level languages, an optimizing compiler will attempt to make intelligent choices of which variables to assign to registers and which to main-memory locations. Some high-level languages, such as C, allow the programmer to suggest to the compiler which variables should be held in registers.
- *Control and status registers:* These are used by the processor to control the operation of the processor and by privileged, operating-system routines to control the execution of programs.

There is not a clean separation of registers into these two categories. For example, on some machines the program counter is user visible, but on many it is not. For purposes of the following discussion, however, it is convenient to use these categories.

User-Visible Registers

A user-visible register is one that may be referenced by means of the machine language that the processor executes and that is generally available to all programs, including application programs as well as system programs. Types of registers that are typically available are data registers, address registers, and condition code registers.

Data registers can be assigned to a variety of functions by the programmer. In some cases, they are of general purpose and can be used with any machine instruction that performs operations on data. Often, however, there are restrictions. For example, there may be dedicated registers for floating-point operations.

Address registers contain main-memory addresses of data and instructions, or they contain a portion of the address that is used in the calculation of the complete address. These registers may themselves be somewhat general purpose, or they may be devoted to a particular addressing mode. Examples include the following:

- *Index register:* Indexed addressing is a common mode of addressing that involves adding an index to a base value to get the effective address.
- *Segment pointer:* With segmented addressing, memory is divided into segments, which are variable-length blocks of words. A memory reference con-

sists of a reference to a particular segment and an offset within the segment; this mode of addressing is important in our discussion of memory management in Chapter 5. In this mode of addressing, a register is used to hold the address of the base (starting location) of the segment. There may be multiple registers: for example, one for the operating system (i.e., when operating-system code is executing on the processor) and one for the currently executing application.

- *Stack pointer:* If there is user-visible stack addressing, then typically the stack is in main memory and there is a dedicated register that points to the top of the stack. This allows the use of instructions that contain no address field, such as push and pop. (See Appendix 1B for a discussion of stack processing.)

A final category of registers that is at least partially visible to the user holds **condition codes** (also referred to as *flags*). Condition codes are bits set by the processor hardware as the result of operations. For example, an arithmetic operation may produce a positive, negative, zero, or overflow result. In addition to the result itself being stored in a register or memory, a condition code is also set. The code may subsequently be tested as part of a conditional branch operation.

Condition code bits are collected into one or more registers. Usually, they form part of a control register. Generally, machine instructions allow these bits to be read by implicit reference, but they cannot be altered by the programmer.

In some machines, a procedure or subroutine call will result in automatic saving of all user-visible registers, to be restored on return. The saving and restoring is performed by the processor as part of the execution of the call and return instructions. This allows each procedure to use these registers independently. On other machines, it is the responsibility of the programmer to save the contents of the relevant user-visible registers prior to a procedure call by including instructions for this purpose in the program. Thus, the saving and restoring functions may be performed in either hardware or software, depending on the machine.

Control and Status Registers

A variety of processor registers are employed to control the operation of the processor. On most machines, most of these are not visible to the user. Some of them may be accessible by machine instructions executed in a control or operating-system mode.

Of course, different machines will have different register organizations and use different terminology. We list here a reasonable complete list of register types, with a brief description. In addition to the MAR, MBR, I/OAR, and I/OBR registers mentioned earlier, the following are essential to instruction execution:

- *Program counter (PC):* Contains the address of an instruction to be fetched.
- *Instruction register (IR):* Contains the instruction most recently fetched.

All processor designs also include a register or set of registers, often known as the program status word (PSW), which contains status information. The PSW typically contains condition codes plus other status information. Common fields and flags include the following:

- *Sign:* Contains the sign bit of the last arithmetic operation.
- *Zero:* Is set when the result of an arithmetic operation is zero.
- *Carry:* Is set if an operation resulted in a carry (addition) into or borrow (subtraction) out of a high-order bit. Used for multiword arithmetic operations.
- *Equal:* Is set if a logical compare result is equality.
- *Overflow:* Used to indicate arithmetic overflow.
- *Interrupt enable/disable:* Used to disable or enable interrupts. When interrupts are disabled, the processor ignores them. This is often desirable when the operating system is in the midst of dealing with another interrupt.
- *Supervisor:* Indicates whether the processor is executing in supervisor or user mode. Certain privileged instructions can be executed only in supervisor mode, and certain areas of memory can be accessed only in supervisor mode.

A number of other registers related to status and control may be found in a particular processor design. In addition to the PSW, there may be a pointer to a block of memory containing additional status information. In machines using multiple types of interrupts, a set of registers may be provided, with one pointer to each interrupt-handling routine. If a stack is used to implement certain functions (e.g., procedure call), then a system stack pointer is needed (see Appendix 1B). Memory-management hardware, discussed in Chapter 5, will require dedicated registers. Finally, registers may be used in the control of I/O operations.

A number of factors go into the design of the control and status register organization. One key issue is operating system support. Certain types of control information are of specific utility to the operating system. If the processor designer has a functional understanding of the operating system to be used, then the register organization can to some extent be tailored to it.

Another key design decision is the allocation of control information between registers and memory. It is common to dedicate the first (lowest) few hundred or thousand words of memory for control purposes. The designer must decide how much control information should be in more expensive, faster registers and how much in less expensive, slower main memory.

1.3

INSTRUCTION EXECUTION

The basic function performed by a computer is program execution. The program to be executed consists of a set of instructions stored in memory. The processor does the actual work by executing instructions specified in the program.

To gain a greater understanding of this function and of the way in which the major components of the computer interact to execute a program, we need to look in some detail at the elements of program execution. The simplest point of view is to consider instruction processing as consisting of two steps: The processor (1) reads (*fetches*) instructions from memory one at a time, and (2) it executes each instruction. Program execution consists of repeating the process of instruction fetch and instruction execution. The instruction execution may involve several operations and depends on the nature of the instruction.

The processing required for a single instruction is called an *instruction cycle*. Using the simplified two-step description just explained, the instruction cycle is depicted in Figure 1.2. The two steps are referred to as the *fetch cycle* and the *execute cycle*. Program execution halts only if the machine is turned off, some sort of unrecoverable error occurs, or a program instruction that halts the computer is encountered.

Instruction Fetch and Execute

At the beginning of each instruction cycle, the processor fetches an instruction from memory. In a typical processor, a register called the *program counter* (PC) is used to keep track of which instruction is to be fetched next. Unless told otherwise, the processor always increments the PC after each instruction fetch so that it will fetch the next instruction in sequence (i.e., the instruction located at the next higher memory address). So, for example, consider a computer in which each instruction occupies one 16-bit word of memory. Assume that the program counter is set to location 300. The processor will next fetch the instruc-

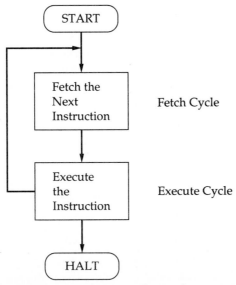

FIGURE 1.2 Basic instruction cycle

tion at location 300. On succeeding instruction cycles, it will fetch instructions from locations 301, 302, 303, and so on. This sequence may be altered, as will soon be explained.

The fetched instruction is loaded into a register in the processor known as the *instruction register* (IR). The instruction is in the form of a binary code that specifies what action the processor is to take. The processor interprets the instruction and performs the required action. In general, these actions fall into the following four categories:

- *Processor-memory:* Data may be transferred from processor to memory or from memory to processor.
- *Processor-I/O:* Data may be transferred to or from a peripheral device by transferring between the processor and an I/O module.
- *Data processing:* The processor may perform some arithmetic or logic operation on data.
- *Control:* An instruction may specify that the sequence of execution be altered. For example, the processor may fetch an instruction from location 149, which specifies that the next instruction be from location 182. The processor will remember this fact by setting the program counter to 182. Thus, on the next fetch cycle, the instruction will be fetched from location 182 rather than 150.

Of course, an instruction's execution may involve a combination of these actions.

Let us consider a simple example using a hypothetical machine that includes the characteristics listed in Figure 1.3. The processor contains a single data

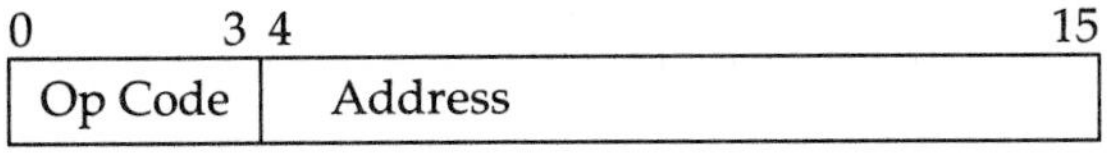

```
0        3 4                                    15
+-----------+---------------------------------+
| Op Code   | Address                         |
+-----------+---------------------------------+
```

(a) Instruction format

```
0   1                                          15
+---+-------------------------------------------+
| S | Magnitude                                 |
+---+-------------------------------------------+
```

(b) Integer format

    Program Counter (PC) = Address of Instruction
    Instruction Register (IR) = Instruction Being Executed
    Accumulator (AC) = Temporary Storage

(c) Internal CPU registers

    0001 = Load AC from Memory
    0010 = Store AC to Memory
    0101 = Add to AC from Memory

(d) Partial list of opcodes

FIGURE 1.3 Characteristics of a hypothetical machine

register, called an *accumulator* (AC). Both instructions and data are 16 bits long. Thus, it is convenient to organize memory using 16-bit locations, or words. The instruction format provides four bits for the opcode (operating code). Thus, there can be as many as $2^4 = 16$ different opcodes, and up to $2^{12} = 4096$ (4 K) words of memory can be directly addressed.

Figure 1.4 illustrates a partial program execution, showing the relevant portions of memory and processor registers. The program fragment shown adds the contents of the memory word at address 940 to the contents of the memory word at address 941 and stores the result in the latter location. Three instruc-

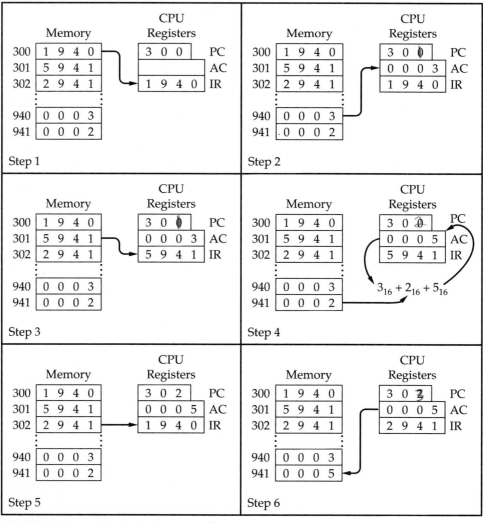

FIGURE 1.4 Example of program execution

tions, which can be described as three fetch and three execute cycles, are required:

1. The program counter (PC) contains 300, the address of the first instruction. The contents at location 300 are loaded into the instruction register (IR). Note that this process would involve the use of a memory address register (MAR) and a memory buffer register (MBR). For simplicity, these intermediate registers are ignored.
2. The first 4 bits in the IR indicate that the accumulator (AC) is to be loaded. The remaining 12 bits specify the address, which is 940.
3. The PC is incremented, and the next instruction is fetched.
4. The old contents of the AC and the contents of location 941 are added, and the result is stored in the AC.
5. The PC is incremented, and the next instruction is fetched.
6. The contents of the AC are stored in location 941.

In this example, three instruction cycles, each consisting of a fetch cycle and an execute cycle, are needed to add the contents of location 940 to the contents of 941. With a more complex set of instructions, fewer cycles would be needed. Most modern processors include instructions that contain more than one address. Thus, the execution cycle for a particular instruction may involve more than one reference to memory. Also, instead of memory references, an instruction may specify an I/O operation.

I/O Function

Thus far, we have discussed the operation of the computer as it is controlled by the processor, and we have looked primarily at the interaction of processor and memory. The discussion has only alluded to the role of the I/O component.

An I/O module (e.g., a disk controller) can exchange data directly with the processor. Just as the processor can initiate a read or write with memory, designating the address of a specific location, the processor can also read data from or write data to an I/O module. In this latter case, the processor identifies a specific device that is controlled by a particular I/O module. Thus, an instruction sequence similar in form to that of Figure 1.4 could occur, with I/O instructions rather than memory-referencing instructions.

In some cases, it is desirable to allow I/O exchanges to occur directly with memory. In such a case, the processor grants to an I/O module the authority to read from or write to memory, so that the transfer of I/O memory can occur without tying up the processor. During such a transfer, the I/O module issues read or write commands to memory, relieving the processor of responsibility for the exchange. This operation is known as *direct memory access* (DMA) and will be examined later in this chapter. For now, all that we need to know is that the interconnection structure of the computer may need to allow for direct memory–I/O interaction.

1.4

INTERRUPTS

Virtually all computers provide a mechanism by which other modules (I/O, memory) may interrupt the normal processing of the processor. Table 1.1 lists the most common classes of interrupts.

Interrupts are provided primarily as a way to improve processing efficiency. For example, most external devices are much slower than the processor. Suppose that the processor is transferring data to a printer by using the instruction cycle scheme of Figure 1.2. After each WRITE operation, the processor will have to pause and remain idle until the printer catches up. The length of this pause can be on the order of many hundreds or even thousands of instruction cycles that do not involve memory. Clearly, this is a very wasteful use of the processor.

Figure 1.5a illustrates this state of affairs for the application referred to in the preceding paragraph. The user program performs a series of WRITE calls interleaved with processing. Code segments 1, 2, and 3 refer to sequences of instructions that do not involve I/O. The WRITE calls are actually calls to an I/O program that is a system utility and that will perform the actual I/O operation. The I/O program consists of three sections:

- A sequence of instructions, labeled 4 in the figure, to prepare for the actual I/O operation. This may include copying the data to be output into a special buffer and preparing the parameters for a device command.
- The actual I/O command. Without the use of interrupts, once this command is issued, the program must wait for the I/O device to perform the requested function. The program may wait by simply repeatedly performing a test operation to determine if the I/O operation is done.
- A sequence of instructions, labeled 5 in the figure, to complete the operation. This may include setting a flag indicating the success or failure of the operation.

TABLE 1.1   Classes of Interrupts

Program	Generated by some condition that occurs as a result of an instruction execution, such as arithmetic overflow, division by zero, attempt to execute an illegal machine instruction, and reference outside a user's allowed memory space.
Timer	Generated by a timer within the processor. This allows the operating system to perform certain functions on a regular basis.
I/O	Generated by an I/O controller, to signal normal completion of an operation or to signal a variety of error conditions.
Hardware failure	Generated by a failure such as power failure or memory parity error.

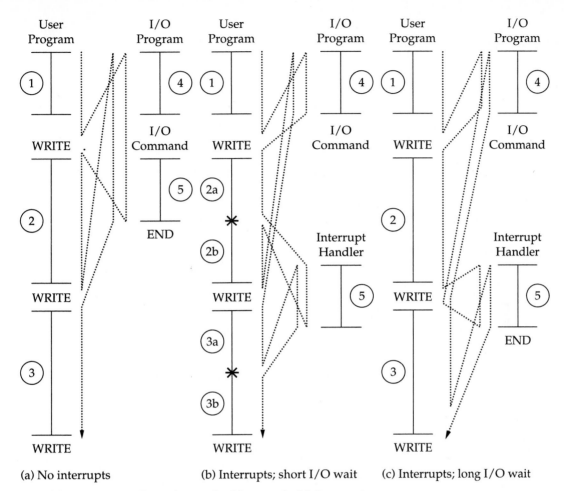

(a) No interrupts (b) Interrupts; short I/O wait (c) Interrupts; long I/O wait

FIGURE 1.5 Program flow of control without and with interrupts

Because the I/O operation may take a relatively long time to complete, the I/O program is hung up waiting for the operation to complete; hence, the user program is stopped at the point of the WRITE call for some considerable time.

Interrupts and the Instruction Cycle

With interrupts, the processor can be engaged in executing other instructions while an I/O operation is in progress. Consider the flow of control in Figure 1.5b. As before, the user program reaches a point at which it makes a system call in the form of a WRITE call. The I/O program that is invoked in this case consists only of the preparation code and the actual I/O command. After these few instructions have been executed, control returns to the user program. Meanwhile, the external device is busy accepting data from computer memory and printing it. This I/O operation is conducted concurrently with the execution of instructions in the user program.

When the external device becomes ready to be serviced, that is, when it is ready to accept more data from the processor, the I/O module for that external device sends an *interrupt request* signal to the processor. The processor responds by suspending operation of the current program, branching off to a program to service that particular I/O device, known as an *interrupt handler,* and resuming the original execution after the device is serviced. The points at which such interrupts occur are indicated by an asterisk (∗) in Figure 1.5b.

From the point of view of the user program, an interrupt is just that: an interruption of the normal sequence of execution. When the interrupt processing is completed, execution resumes (Figure 1.6). Thus, the user program does not have to contain any special code to accommodate interrupts; the processor and the operating system are responsible for suspending the user program and then resuming it at the same point.

To accommodate interrupts, an *interrupt cycle* is added to the instruction cycle, as shown in Figure 1.7. In the interrupt cycle, the processor checks to see if any interrupts have occurred, which would be indicated by the presence of an interrupt signal. If no interrupts are pending, the processor proceeds to the fetch cycle and fetches the next instruction of the current program. If an interrupt is pending, the processor suspends execution of the current program and executes an *interrupt handler* routine. The interrupt handler program is generally part of the operating system. Typically, this program determines the nature of the

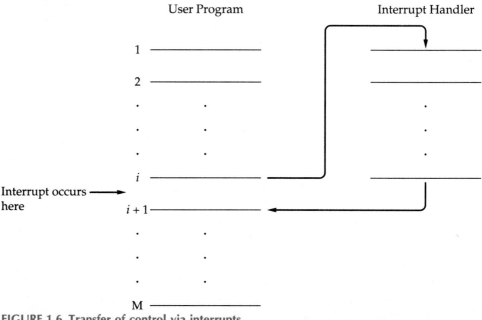

FIGURE 1.6 Transfer of control via interrupts

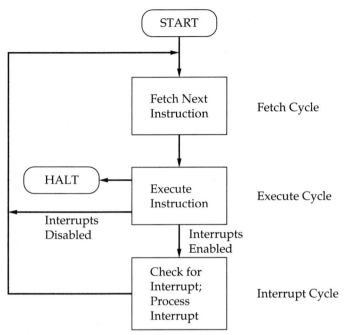

FIGURE 1.7 Instruction cycle with interrupts

interrupt and performs whatever actions are needed. For instance, in the example we have been using, the handler determines which I/O module generated the interrupt, and it may branch to a program that will write more data out to that I/O module. When the interrupt handler routine is completed, the processor can resume execution of the user program at the point of interruption.

It is clear that there is some overhead involved in this process. Extra instructions must be executed (in the interrupt handler) to determine the nature of the interrupt and to decide on the appropriate action. Nevertheless, because of the relatively large amount of time that would be wasted by simply waiting on an I/O operation, the processor can be employed much more efficiently with the use of interrupts.

To appreciate the gain in efficiency, consider Figure 1.8, which is a timing diagram based on the flow of control in Figures 1.5a and 1.5b.

Figures 1.5b and 1.8 assume that the time required for the I/O operation is relatively short: less than the time to complete the execution of instructions between WRITE operations in the user program. The more typical case, especially for a slow device such as a printer, is that the I/O operation will take much more time than executing a sequence of user instructions. Figure 1.5c indicates this state of affairs. In this case, the user program reaches the second WRITE call before the I/O operation spawned by the first call is complete. The result is that the user program is hung up at that point. When the preceding I/O operation is completed, this new WRITE call may be processed and a new

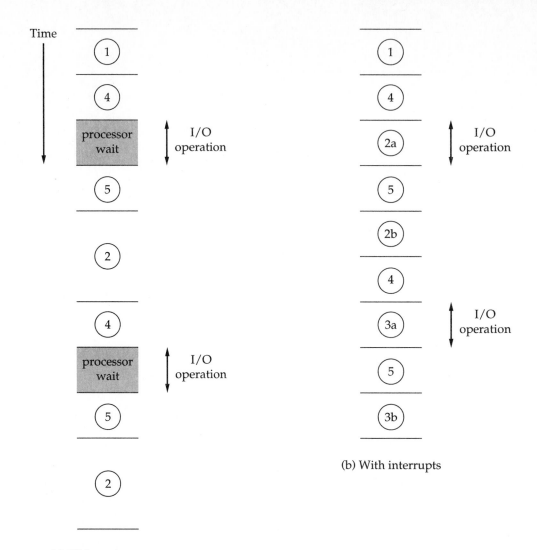

(a) Without interrupts

FIGURE 1.8 Program timing; short I/O wait

I/O operation may be started. Figure 1.9 shows the timing for this situation with and without the use of interrupts. We can see that there is still a gain in efficiency because part of the time during which the I/O operation is underway overlaps with the execution of user instructions.

Interrupt Processing

The occurrence of an interrupt triggers a number of events, both in the processor hardware and in software. Figure 1.10 shows a typical sequence. When an I/O

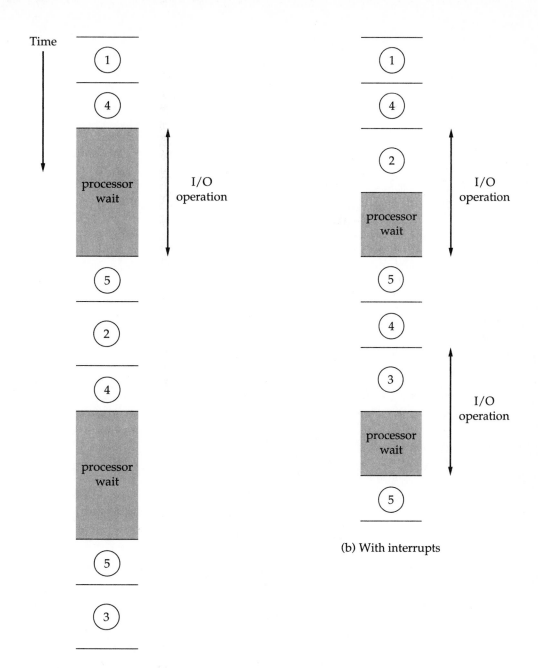

(a) Without interrupts

FIGURE 1.9 Program timing; long I/O wait

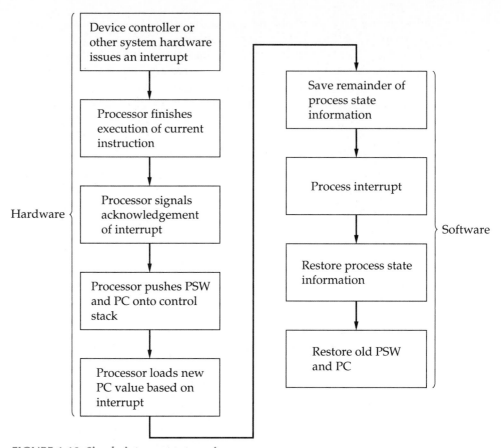

FIGURE 1.10 Simple interrupt processing

device completes an I/O operation, the following sequence of hardware events occurs:

1. The device issues an interrupt signal to the processor.
2. The processor finishes execution of the current instruction before responding to the interrupt, as indicated in Figure 1.7.
3. The processor tests for an interrupt, determines that there is one, and sends an acknowledgment signal to the device that issued the interrupt. The acknowledgment allows the device to remove its interrupt signal.
4. The processor now needs to prepare to transfer control to the interrupt routine. To begin, it needs to save information needed to resume the current program at the point of interrupt. The minimum information required is the program status word (PSW) and the location of the next instruction to be executed, which is contained in the program counter. These can be pushed onto the system control stack (see Appendix 1B).

5. The processor now loads the program counter with the entry location of the interrupt-handling program that will respond to this interrupt. Depending on the computer architecture and operating-system design, there may be a single program, one for each type of interrupt, or one for each device and each type of interrupt. If there is more than one interrupt-handling routine, the processor must determine which one to invoke. This information may have been included in the original interrupt signal, or the processor may have to issue a request to the device that issued the interrupt to get a response that contains the needed information.

Once the program counter has been loaded, the processor proceeds to the next instruction cycle, which begins with an instruction fetch. Since the instruction fetch is determined by the contents of the program counter, the result is that control is transferred to the interrupt-handling program. The execution of this program results in the following operations:

6. At this point, the program counter and PSW relating to the interrupted program have been saved on the system stack. However, other information is considered part of the "state" of the executing program. In particular, the contents of the processor registers need to be saved because these registers may be used by the interrupt handler. So, all these values, plus any other state information, need to be saved. Typically, the interrupt handler will begin by saving the contents of all registers on the stack. Other state information that must be saved is discussed in Chapter 3. Figure 1.11a shows a simple example. In this case, a user program is interrupted after the instruction at location N. The contents of all of the registers plus the address of the next instruction $(N + 1)$ are pushed onto the stack. The stack pointer is updated to point to the new top of the stack, and the program counter is updated to point to the beginning of the interrupt service routine.

7. The interrupt handler may now proceed to process the interrupt. This will include an examination of status information relating to the I/O operation or other event that caused an interrupt. It may also involve sending additional commands or acknowledgments to the I/O device.

8. When interrupt processing is complete, the saved register values are retrieved from the stack and restored to the registers (e.g., see Figure 1.11b).

9. The final act is to restore the PSW and program counter values from the stack. As a result, the next instruction to be executed will be from the previously interrupted program.

It is important to save all the state information about the interrupted program for later resumption because the interrupt handler is not a routine called from the program. Rather, the interrupt can occur at any time and therefore at any point in the execution of a user program. Its occurrence is unpredictable. Indeed, as we will see later in this section, the two programs may not have anything in common and may belong to two different users.

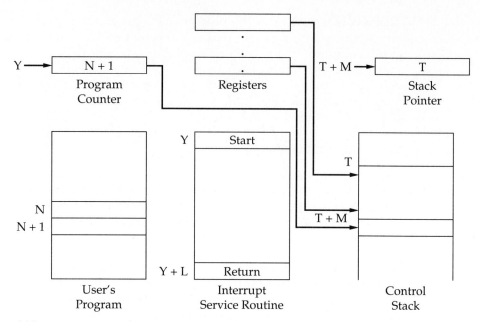

(a) Interrupt occurs after instruction at location *N*

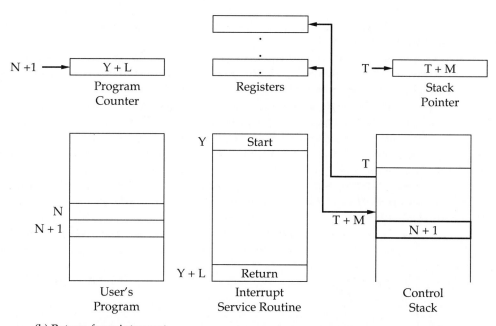

(b) Return from interrupt

FIGURE 1.11 Changes in memory and registers for an interrupt

Multiple Interrupts

The discussion so far has discussed the occurrence of only a single interrupt. Suppose, however, that multiple interrupts can occur. For example, a program may be receiving data from a communications line and printing results. The printer will generate an interrupt every time it completes a print operation. The communication line controller will generate an interrupt every time a unit of data arrives. The unit can be either a single character or a block, depending on the nature of the communications discipline. In any case, it is possible for a communications interrupt to occur while a printer interrupt is being processed.

Two approaches can be taken to dealing with multiple interrupts. The first is to disable interrupts while an interrupt is being processed. A *disabled interrupt* simply means that the processor can and will ignore that interrupt request signal. If an interrupt occurs during this time, it generally remains pending and will be checked by the processor after the processor has enabled interrupts. Thus, when a user program is executing and an interrupt occurs, interrupts are disabled immediately. After the interrupt handler routine completes, interrupts are enabled before resuming the user program, and the processor checks to see if additional interrupts have occurred. This approach is nice and simple because interrupts are handled in strict sequential order (Figure 1.12a).

The drawback to this approach is that it does not take into account relative priority or time-critical needs. For example, when input arrives from the communications line, it may need to be absorbed rapidly to make room for more input. If the first batch of input has not been processed before the second batch arrives, data may be lost.

A second approach is to define priorities for interrupts and to allow an interrupt of higher priority to cause a lower-priority interrupt handler to be itself interrupted (Figure 1.12b).

As an example of this second approach, consider a system with three I/O devices: a printer, a disk, and a communications line, with increasing priorities of 2, 4, and 5 respectively. Figure 1.13 illustrates a possible sequence. A user program begins at $t = 0$. At $t = 10$, a printer interrupt occurs; user information is placed on the system stack, and execution continues at the printer interrupt service routine (ISR). While this routine is still executing, at $t = 15$, a communications interrupt occurs. Because the communications line has higher priority than the printer, the interrupt is honored. The printer ISR is interrupted, its state is pushed onto the stack, and execution continues at the communications ISR. While this routine is executing, a disk interrupt occurs ($t = 20$). Because this interrupt is of lower priority, it is simply held and the communications ISR runs to completion.

When the communications ISR is complete ($t = 25$), the previous processor state is restored, which is the execution of the printer ISR. However, before even a single instruction in that routine can be executed, the processor honors the higher-priority disk interrupt and control transfers to the disk ISR. Only when that routine is complete ($t = 35$) is the printer ISR resumed. When that routine completes ($t = 40$), control finally returns to the user program.

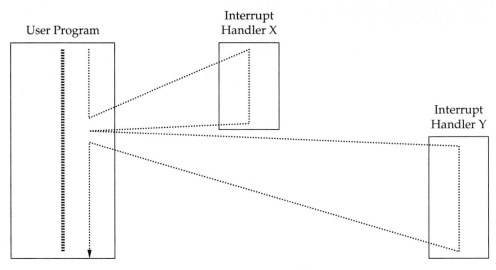

(a) Sequential interrupt processing

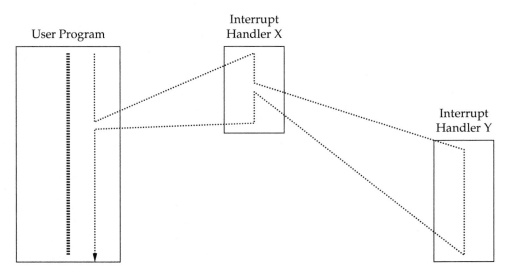

(b) Nested interrupt processing

FIGURE 1.12 Transfer of control with multiple interrupts

Multiprogramming

Even with the use of interrupts, a processor may not be used very efficiently. For example, consider again Figure 1.9b. If the time required to complete an I/O operation is much greater than the user code between I/O calls (a common situation), then the processor will be idle much of the time. A solution to this problem is to allow several user programs to be active at the same time.

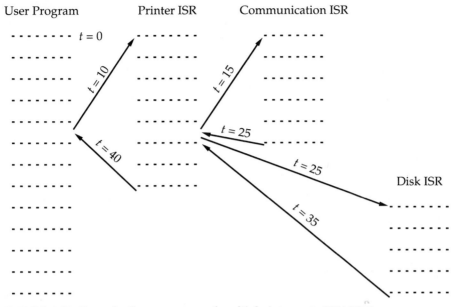

User Program   Printer ISR   Communication ISR

FIGURE 1.13 Example time sequence of multiple interrupts [TANE90]

Suppose, for example, that the processor has two programs to execute. One is simply a program for reading data from memory and putting it out on a external device; the other is some application that involves a lot of calculation. The processor can begin the output program, issue a WRITE command to the external device, and then proceed to begin execution of the other application.

When the processor is dealing with a number of programs, the sequence with which programs are executed will depend on their relative priority as well as on whether they are waiting for I/O. When a program has been interrupted and control transfers to an interrupt handler, once the interrupt handler routine has completed, control may not immediately be returned to the user program that was in execution at the time. Instead, control may pass to some other pending program with a higher priority. Eventually, when it has the highest priority, the user program that was interrupted will be resumed. This concept of multiple programs taking turns in execution is known as *multiprogramming* and is discussed further in Chapter 2.

1.5

INTERCONNECTION STRUCTURES

A computer consists of a set of components, or modules, of three basic types (processor, memory, I/O) that communicate with one another. In effect, a computer is a network of basic modules. Thus, there must be paths for connecting the modules together.

Figure 1.14 suggests the types of exchanges that are needed by indicating the major forms of input and output for each module type; as follows:

• *Memory:* Typically, a memory module will consist of N words of equal length. Each word is assigned a unique numerical address (0, 1, . . . , $N - 1$). A word of data can be read from or written into the memory. The nature of the operation is indicated by READ and WRITE control signals. The location of the operation is specified by an address.
• *I/O module:* From an internal (to the computer system) point of view, I/O is functionally similar to memory. There are two operations, READ and WRITE.

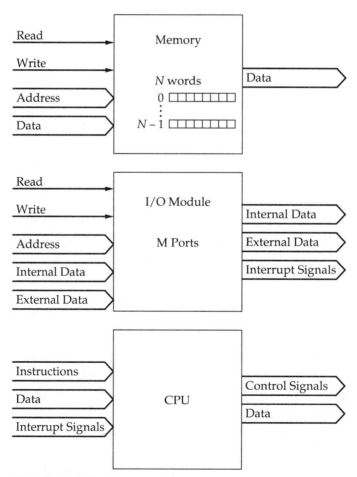

FIGURE 1.14 Computer modules

Furthermore, an I/O module may control more than one external device. We can refer to each of the interfaces to an external device as a *port* and give each a unique address (e.g., 0, 1, . . . , $M - 1$). In addition, there are external data paths for the input and output of data with an external device. Finally, an I/O module may be able to send interrupt signals to the processor.

- *Processor:* The processor reads in instructions and data, writes out data after processing, and uses control signals to control the overall operation of the system. It also receives interrupt signals.

The preceding list defines the data to be exchanged. An interconnection structure is needed that allows each component to communicate directly with each of the other components. Over the years, a number of interconnection structures have been implemented, but by far the most common is the bus structure. As an example of an interconnection structure, the remainder of this section introduces the bus structure.

A *bus* is a shared transmission medium connecting two or more modules. In computer systems, a bus consists of multiple communication pathways, or lines. Each line is capable of transmitting signals representing binary 1 and binary 0. Because the bus is shared, a signal transmitted by any one module on any one line is available for reception by all other devices attached to that line. If two devices transmit on the same line during the same time period, their signals will overlap and become garbled. Thus, some line discipline must be enforced.

A computer bus consists, typically, of from 50 to 100 separate lines. Each line is assigned a particular meaning, or function. Although there are many different bus designs, on any bus the lines can be classified into three functional groups (Figure 1.15): data, address, and control lines. In addition, there may be power distribution lines that supply power to the attached modules.

The **data lines** provide a path for moving data between system modules. These lines, collectively, are called the *data bus*. The data bus typically consists

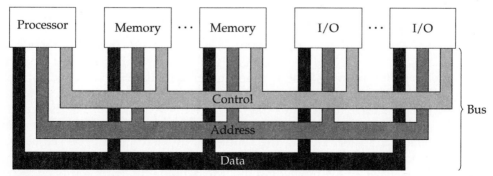

FIGURE 1.15 Bus interconnection structure

of 8, 16, or 32 lines, the number of lines being referred to as the *width* of the data bus. Because each line can carry only 1 bit at a time, the number of lines determines how many bits can be transferred at a time. The width of the data bus is a key factor in determining overall system performance. For example, if the data bus is 8 bits wide and each instruction is 16 bits long, the processor must access the memory module twice during each instruction fetch operation.

The **address lines** are used to designate the source or destination of the data on the data bus. For example, if the processor executes an instruction that references a word (8, 16, or 32 bits) of data to be read from memory, the processor puts the address of the desired word on the address lines. Clearly, the width of the address bus determines the maximum possible memory capacity of the system. Furthermore, the address lines are generally also used to address I/O ports. Typically, the higher-order bits are used to select a particular module on the bus, and the lower-order bits select a memory location or I/O port within the module. For example, on an 8-bit bus, address 01111111 and below might reference locations in a memory module (module 0) with 128 words of memory, and address 10000000 and above might refer to devices attached to an I/O module (module 1).

The **control lines** are used to control access to and the use of the data and address lines. Because the data and address lines are shared by all components, there must be a means of controlling their use. Control signals transmit both command and timing information between system modules. Timing signals indicate the validity of data and address information. Command signals specify operations to be performed. Typical control lines include the following:

- *Memory write:* Causes data on the data bus to be written into the addressed location.
- *Memory read:* Causes data from the addressed location to be placed on the data bus by the addressed memory module.
- *I/O write:* Causes data on the data bus to be output to the addressed I/O port.
- *I/O read:* Causes data from the addressed I/O port to be placed on the data bus.
- *Transfer ACK:* Indicates that data have been accepted from or placed on the data bus.
- *Bus request:* Indicates that a module needs to gain control of the bus in order to send a command or to respond to the command of another module.
- *Bus grant:* Indicates that a requesting module has been granted control of the bus by the module that asserts the bus grant line.
- *Interrupt request:* Indicates that an interrupt is pending. For example, an I/O module would assert this line to alert the processor that the I/O module had data to transfer. During the course of the instruction cycle (Figure 1.7), the processor will check this line.
- *Interrupt ACK:* Acknowledges that the pending interrupt has been recognized.
- *Clock:* Used to synchronize operations.
- *Reset:* Initializes all modules.

The operation of the bus is as follows: If one module wishes to send data to another, it must do two things: (1) obtain the use of the bus, and (2) transfer data via the bus. If one module wishes to receive data from another, it must (1) obtain the use of the bus, and (2) transfer a request to the other module over the appropriate control and address lines. It must then wait for that second module to send the data.

1.6

THE MEMORY HIERARCHY

The design constraints on a computer's memory can be summed up by three questions: How much? How fast? How expensive?

The question of how much is somewhat open-ended. If the capacity is there, it is likely that applications will be developed to use it. The question of how fast is, in a sense, easier to answer. To achieve greatest performance, the memory must be able to keep up with the processor. That is, while the processor is executing instructions, we would not want it to have to pause to wait for instructions or operands. The final question must also be considered. For a practical system, the cost of memory must be reasonable in relationship to other components.

As might be expected, there is a trade-off among the three key characteristics of memory: cost, capacity, and access time. At any given time, a variety of technologies are used to implement memory systems. Across this spectrum of technologies, the following relationships hold:

- Smaller access time, greater cost per bit
- Greater capacity, smaller cost per bit
- Greater capacity, greater access time

The dilemma facing the designer is clear. The designer would like to use memory technologies that provide for large-capacity memory, both because the capacity is needed and because the cost per bit is low. However, to meet performance requirements, the designer needs to use expensive, relatively lower-capacity memories with fast access times.

The way out of this dilemma is not to rely on a single memory component or technology but to employ a **memory hierarchy.** A traditional hierarchy is illustrated in Figure 1.16a. As one goes down the hierarchy, the following conditions occur:

1. Decreasing cost per bit
2. Increasing capacity
3. Increasing access time
4. Decreasing frequency of access of the memory by the processor

Thus, smaller, more expensive, faster memories are supplemented by larger,

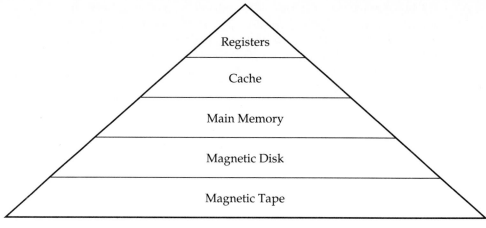

(a) Traditional memory hierarchy

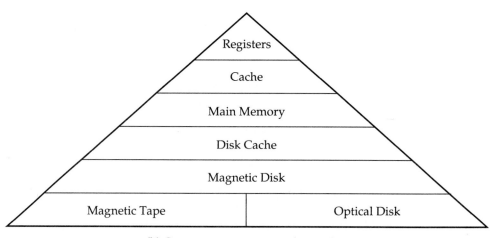

(b) Contemporary memory hierarchy

FIGURE 1.16 The memory hierarchy

cheaper, slower memories. The key to the success of this organization is the last item: decreasing frequency of access. We examine this concept in greater detail later in this chapter when we discuss the cache, and when we discuss virtual memory later in this book. A brief explanation is provided at this point.

Suppose that the processor has access to two levels of memory. Level 1 contains 1000 words and has an access time or 0.1 μs; level 2 contains 100,000 words and has an access time of 1 μs. Assume that if a word to be accessed is in level 1, then the processor accesses it directly. If it is in level 2, then the word is first transferred to level 1 and then accessed by the processor. For simplicity, we ignore the time required for the processor to determine whether the word is in level 1 or level 2. Figure 1.17 shows the general shape of the curve that

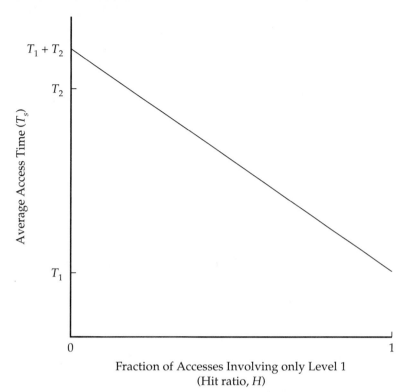

FIGURE 1.17 **Performance of a simple two-level memory**

covers this situation. As can be seen, for high percentages of level 1 access, the average total access time is much closer to that of level 1 than of level 2.

So, the strategy works in principle but only if conditions 1 through 4 apply. Figure 1.18 shows typical characteristics of alternative memory systems. This figure shows that by employing a variety of technologies, a spectrum of memory systems exist that satisfy conditions 1 through 3. Fortunately, condition 4 is also generally valid.

The basis for the validity of condition 4 is a principle known as *locality of reference* [DENN68]. During the course of execution of a program, memory references by the processor, for both instructions and data, tend to cluster. Programs typically contain a number of iterative loops and subroutines. Once a loop or subroutine is entered, there are repeated references to a small set of instructions. Similarly, operations on tables and arrays involve access to a clustered set of data words. Over a long period, the clusters in use change, but over a short period, the processor is primarily working with fixed clusters of memory references.

Accordingly, it is possible to organize data across the hierarchy such that the percentage of accesses to each succeedingly lower level is substantially less than

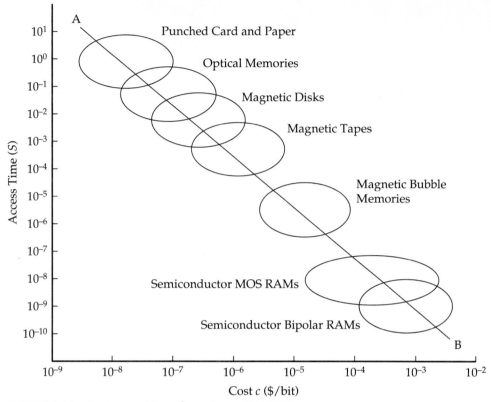

FIGURE 1.18 Memory cost/speed spectrum [HAYE88]

that of the level above. Consider the two-level example already presented. Let level 2 memory contain all program instructions and data. The current clusters can be temporarily placed in level 1. From time to time, one of the clusters in level 1 will have to be swapped back to level 2 to make room for a new cluster coming in to level 1. On average, however, most references will be to instructions and data contained in level 1.

This principle can be applied across more than two levels of memory. Consider the hierarchy shown in Figure 1.16a. The fastest, smallest, and most expensive type of memory consists of the registers internal to the processor. Typically, a processor will contain a few dozen such registers, although some machines contain hundreds of registers. Skipping down two levels, main memory, also referred to as real memory, is the principal internal memory system of the computer. Each location in main memory has a unique address, and most machine instructions refer to one or more main memory addresses. Main memory is usually extended with a higher-speed, smaller cache. The cache is not usually visible to the programmer or, indeed, to the processor. It is a device for staging the movement of data between main memory and processor registers to improve performance.

The three forms of memory just described are typically volatile and employ semiconductor technology. The use of three levels exploits the fact that semiconductor memory comes in a variety of types that differ in speed and cost. Data are stored more permanently on external mass storage devices, of which the most common are magnetic disk and tape. External, nonvolatile memory is also referred to as secondary or auxiliary memory. These are used to store program and data files and are usually visible to the programmer only in terms of files and records, as opposed to individual bytes or words. Disks are also used to provide an extension to main memory, known as *virtual storage* or *virtual memory*, which is discussed in Chapter 5.

Other forms of memory may be included in the hierarchy. For example, large IBM mainframes include a form of internal memory known as *expanded storage,* which uses a semiconductor technology that is slower and less expensive than that of main memory. Strictly speaking, this memory does not fit into the hierarchy but is a side branch: Data can be moved between main memory and expanded storage but not between expanded storage and external memory. Other forms of secondary memory include optical disks and bubble memory devices. Finally, additional levels can be effectively added to the hierarchy in software. A portion of main memory can be used as a buffer to temporarily hold data that are to be read out to disk. Such a technique, sometimes referred to as a *disk cache* (examined in detail in Chapter 7), improves performance in two ways:

• Disk writes are clustered. Instead of many small transfers of data, we have a few large transfers of data. This improves disk performance and minimizes processor involvement.
• Some data destined for write-out may be referenced by a program before the next dump to disk. In that case, the data are retrieved rapidly from the software cache rather than slowly from the disk.

Figure 1.16b shows a contemporary memory hierarchy that includes a disk cache and an optical disk as additional types of secondary memory.

Appendix 1A examines the performance implications of multilevel memory structures.

1.7

CACHE MEMORY

Although cache memory is invisible to the operating system, it interacts with other memory-management hardware. Furthermore, many of the principles used in virtual memory schemes are also applied in cache memory.

Motivation

On all instruction cycles, the processor accesses memory at least once, to fetch the instruction, and often one or more additional times, to fetch operands and/or store results. The rate at which the processor can execute instructions is clearly limited by the memory cycle time. This limitation has in fact been a significant problem because of the persistent mismatch between processor and main memory speeds. Figure 1.19, which may be considered representative, illustrates this situation.

   The figure shows that memory speed has not kept up with processor speed. What we are faced with is a trade-off among speed, cost, and size. Ideally, the main memory should be built with the same technology as that of the processor registers, giving memory cycle times comparable to processor cycle times. This has always been too expensive a strategy. The solution is to exploit the principle of locality by providing a small, fast memory between the processor and main memory, namely the cache.

Cache Principles

Cache memory is intended to give memory speed approaching that of the fastest memories available, and at the same time to provide a large memory size at the price of less expensive types of semiconductor memories. The concept is illustrated in Figure 1.20. There is a relatively large and slower main memory to-

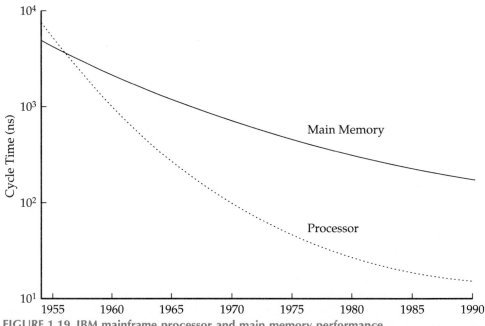

FIGURE 1.19 IBM mainframe processor and main memory performance

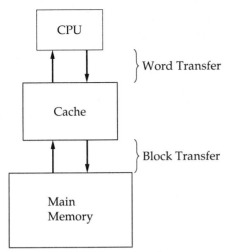

FIGURE 1.20 Cache and main memory

gether with a smaller, faster cache memory. The cache contains a copy of a portion of main memory. When the processor attempts to read a word of memory, a check is made to determine if the word is in the cache. If so, the word is delivered to the processor. If not, a block of main memory, consisting of some fixed number of words, is read into the cache and then the word is delivered to the processor. Because of the phenomenon of locality of reference, when a block of data is fetched into the cache to satisfy a single memory reference, it is likely that there will soon be references to other words in that block.

Figure 1.21 depicts the structure of a cache/main-memory system. Main memory consists of up to 2^n addressable words, with each word having a unique n-bit address. For mapping purposes, this memory is considered to consist of a number of fixed-length blocks of K words each. That is, there are $M = 2^n/K$ blocks. The cache consists of C slots of K words each, and the number of slots is considerably less than the number of main memory blocks ($C \ll M$). At any time, some subset of the blocks of memory resides in the slots in the cache. If a word in a block of memory that is not in the cache is to be read, that block is transferred to one of the slots of the cache. Since there are more blocks than slots, an individual slot cannot be uniquely and permanently dedicated to a particular block. Thus, each slot includes a tag that identifies which particular block is currently being stored. The tag is usually some number of higher-order bits of the address.

Figure 1.22 illustrates the READ operation. The processor generates the address, RA, of a word to be read. If the word is contained in the cache, it is delivered to the processor. Otherwise, the block containing that word is loaded into the cache and the word is delivered to the processor.

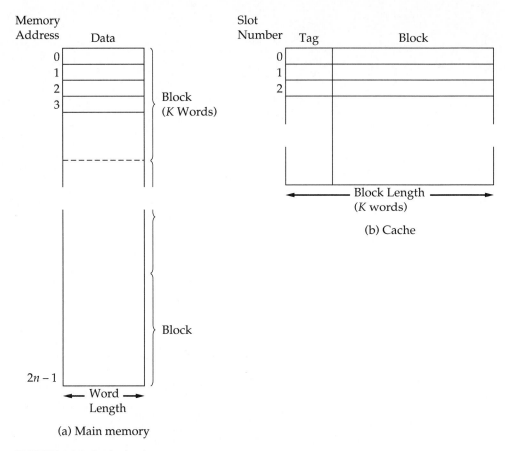

FIGURE 1.21 Cache/main-memory structure

Cache Design

A detailed discussion of cache design is beyond the scope of this book. Key elements are briefly summarized here. We will see that similar design issues must be addressed in dealing with the design of virtual memory and disk caches. These issues fall into the following categories:

• Cache size
• Block size
• Mapping function
• Replacement algorithm
• Write policy

  We have already dealt with the issue of **cache size.** It turns out that reasonably small caches can have a significant impact on performance. Another size issue is that of **block size**: the unit of data exchanged between cache and main memory. As the block size increases from very small to larger sizes, the hit ratio

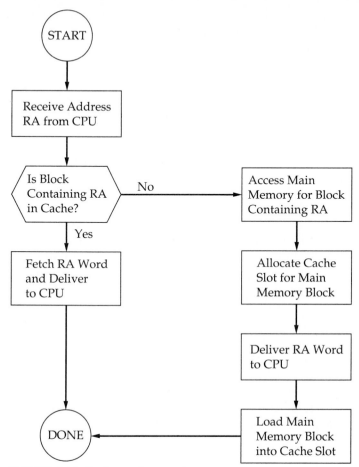

FIGURE 1.22 Cache read operation

(fraction of time that reference is found in cache) will at first increase because of the principle of locality: the high probability that data in the vicinity of a referenced word is likely to be referenced in the near future. As the block size increases, more useful data are brought into the cache. The hit ratio will begin to decrease, however, as the block becomes even bigger, and the probability of using the newly fetched data becomes less than the probability of reusing the data that must be moved out of the cache to make room for the new block.

When a new block of data is read into the cache, the **mapping function** determines which cache location the block will occupy. Two constraints affect the design of the mapping function. First, when one block is read in, another may have to be replaced. We would like to do this in such a way as to minimize the probability that we will replace a block that will be needed in the near future. The more flexible the mapping function, the more scope we have to design a replacement algorithm to maximize the hit ratio. Second, the more flexible the mapping function, the more complex is the circuitry required to search the cache to determine if a given block is in the cache.

The **replacement algorithm** chooses, within the constraints of the mapping function, which block to replace. We would like to replace that block that is least likely to be needed again in the near future. Although it is impossible to identify such a block, a reasonably effective strategy is to replace the block that has been in the cache longest with no reference to it. This policy is referred to as the *least recently used* (LRU) algorithm. Hardware mechanisms are needed to identify the least recently used block.

If the contents of a block in the cache are altered, then it is necessary to write it back to main memory before replacing it. The **write policy** dictates when the memory write operation takes place. At one extreme, the writing can occur every time the block is updated. At the other extreme, the writing occurs only when the block is replaced. The latter policy minimizes memory write operations but leaves main memory in an obsolete state. This can interfere with multiple-processor operation and with direct memory access by I/O modules.

1.8

INPUT/OUTPUT ORGANIZATION

In addition to one or more processors and a set of memory modules, the third key element of a computer system is a set of I/O modules. Each module interfaces to the system bus or other interconnection structure and controls one or more external devices. An I/O module is not simply mechanical connectors that wire a device into the system bus. Rather, the I/O module contains some "intelligence," that is, it contains logic for controlling the flow of data between the external device and the bus.

You may wonder why one does not connect external devices directly to the system bus. The reasons are as follows:

- There is a wide variety of external devices with various methods of operation. It would be impractical to incorporate the necessary logic within the processor to control a range of devices.
- The data transfer rate of external devices is often much slower than that of the memory or processor. Thus, it is impractical to use the high-speed system bus to communicate directly with an external device.
- External devices often use data formats and word lengths different from those used by the computer to which they are attached.

Thus, an I/O module is required. This module has two major functions (Figure 1.23), as follows:

- Interface to the processor and memory via the system bus or other interconnection structure.

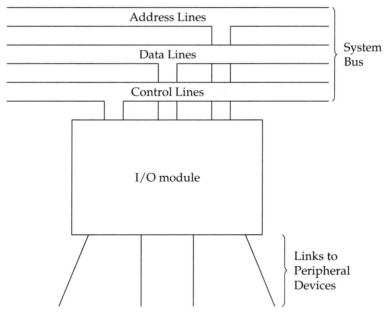

FIGURE 1.23 Generic model of an I/O module

• Interface to one or more external devices by tailored data links.

   In the remainder of this section, we provide a brief overview of external devices, followed by an overview of the structure and function of an I/O module.

External Devices

A computer system is of no use without some means of input and output. I/O operations are accomplished through a wide assortment of external devices that provide a means of exchanging data between the external environment and the computer. An external device attaches to the computer by a link to an I/O module (Figure 1.24). The link is used to exchange control, status, and data between the I/O module and the external device. An external device connected to an I/O module is often referred to as a **peripheral** device or, simply, a peripheral.

   We can broadly classify external devices into three categories:

• *Human-readable:* Suitable for communicating with the computer user
• *Machine-readable:* Suitable for communicating with equipment
• *Communication:* Suitable for communicating with remote devices

   Examples of human-readable devices are video display terminals (VDT), which generally consist of keyboard and display units, and printers. Examples

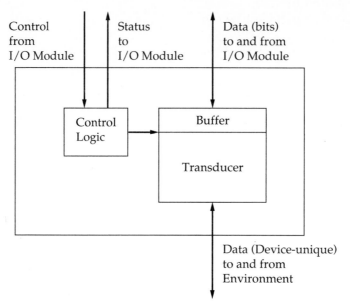

FIGURE 1.24 An external device

of machine-readable devices are magnetic disk and tape systems, and sensors and actuators, such as are used in a robotics application. Note that we are viewing disk and tape systems as I/O devices in this section, whereas previously we viewed them as memory devices. From a functional point of view, these devices are part of the memory hierarchy, and their use is appropriately considered in that context. From a structural point of view, these devices are controlled by I/O modules and are hence to be considered as part of the I/O organization. In this book discussion of both memory management and I/O involves analysis of disk and tape subsystems.

Communication devices allow a computer to exchange data with a remote device that may be a human-readable device, such as a terminal, a machine-readable device, or even another computer.

In very general terms, the nature of an external device is indicated in Figure 1.24. The interface to the I/O module is in the form of control, status, and data signals. **Data signals** are in the form of a set of bits to be sent to or received from the I/O module. **Control signals** determine the function that the device will perform, such as transmit data to the I/O module (INPUT or READ), accept data from the I/O module (OUTPUT or WRITE), report status, or perform some control function particular to the device (e.g., position a disk head). **Status signals** indicate the state of the device. Examples are READY/BUSY to show whether the device is ready for data transfer.

Control logic associated with the device controls the device's operation in response to direction from the I/O module. The **transducer** converts data from electrical to other forms of energy during output and from other forms to electrical during input. Typically, a buffer is associated with the transducer to temporarily hold data being transferred between the I/O module and the external environment; a buffer size of 8 to 16 bits is common.

I/O Module Function

An I/O module is the entity within a computer that is responsible for the control of one or more external devices and for the exchange of data between those devices and main memory and/or processor registers. Thus, the I/O module must have an interface internal to the computer (to the processor and main memory) and an interface external to the computer (to the external device).

The major functions or requirements for an I/O module fall into the following categories:

- Control and timing
- Communication with processor
- Communication with external device
- Data buffering
- Error detection

During any period, the processor may communicate with one or more external devices in unpredictable patterns, depending on the program's need for I/O. The internal resources, such as main memory and the system bus, must be shared among a number of activities, including I/O. Thus, the I/O function includes a **control and timing** requirement to coordinate the flow of traffic between internal resources and external devices. For example, the control of the transfer of data from an external device to the processor might involve the following sequence of steps:

1. The processor interrogates the I/O module to check the status of the attached device.
2. The I/O module returns the device status.
3. If the device is operational and ready to transmit, the processor requests the transfer of data by means of a command to the I/O module.
4. The I/O module obtains a unit of data (e.g., 8 or 16 bits) from the external device.
5. The data are transferred from the I/O module to the processor.

If the system employs a bus, then each of the interactions between the processor and the I/O module involves one or more bus events.

The preceding simplified scenario also illustrates that the I/O module must have the capability to engage in **communication with the processor** and with the external device. Communication with the processor involves the following:

- *Command decoding:* The I/O module accepts commands from the processor. These commands are generally sent as signals on the control bus. For example, an I/O module for a disk drive might accept the following commands: READ

SECTOR, WRITE SECTOR, SEEK track number, and SCAN record ID. The latter two commands each includes a parameter that is sent on the data bus.

- *Data:* Data are exchanged between the processor and the I/O module over the data bus.
- *Status reporting:* Because peripherals are so slow, it is important to know the status of the I/O module. For example, if an I/O module is asked to send data to the processor (READ), it may not be ready to do so because it is still working on the previous command. This fact can be reported with a status signal. Common status signals are BUSY and READY. There may also be signals to report various error conditions.
- *Address recognition:* Just as each word of memory has an address, so does each I/O device. Thus, an I/O module must recognize one unique address for each peripheral it controls.

On the other side, the I/O module must be able to **communicate with external devices**. This communication also involves commands, status information, and data (Figure 1.23).

An essential task of an I/O module is **data buffering**. The need for this function is apparent from Table 1.2. Whereas the transfer rate into and out of main memory or the processor is quite high, the rate is orders of magnitude lower for most peripheral devices. Data coming from the main memory are sent to an I/O module in a rapid burst. The data are buffered in the I/O module and then sent to the external device at its data rate. In the opposite direction, data are buffered so as not to tie up the memory in a slow transfer operation. Thus, the I/O module must be able to operate at both device and memory speeds.

TABLE 1.2   Examples of I/O Devices Categorized by Behavior, Partner, and Data Rate [HENN90]

Device	Behavior	Partner	Data Rate (KBytes/s)
Keyboard	Input	Human	0.01
Mouse	Input	Human	0.02
Voice input	Input	Human	0.02
Scanner	Input	Human	200
Voice output	Output	Human	0.6
Line printer	Output	Human	1
Laser printer	Output	Human	100
Graphics Display	Output	Human	30,000
CPU to frame buffer	Output	Human	200
Network-terminal	Input or output	Machine	0.05
Network-LAN	Input or output	Machine	200
Optical disk	Storage	Machine	500
Magnetic tape	Storage	Machine	2,000
Magnetic disk	Storage	Machine	2,000

Finally, an I/O module is often responsible for **error detection** and for sub-sequently reporting errors to the processor. One class of errors includes mechanical and electrical malfunctions reported by the device (e.g., paper jam, bad disk track). Another class consists of unintentional changes to the bit pattern as it is transmitted from device to I/O module. Some form of error-detecting code is often used to detect transmission errors. A common example is the use of a parity bit on each character of data. For example, the ASCII character occupies 7 bits of a byte. The eighth bit is set so that the total number of 1s in the byte is even (even parity) or odd (odd parity). When a byte is received, the I/O module checks the parity to determine whether an error has occurred.

I/O Module Structure

I/O modules vary considerably in complexity and the number of external devices that they control. We will attempt only a very general description here. Figure 1.25 provides a general block diagram of an I/O module. The module connects to the rest of the computer through a set of signal lines (e.g., system bus lines). Data transferred to and from the module are buffered in one or more data registers. There may also be one or more status registers that provide current status information. A status register may also function as a control register to accept detailed control information from the processor. The logic within the module interacts with the processor via a set of control lines. These are used by the processor to issue commands to the I/O module. Some of the control lines may be used by the I/O module (e.g., for gaining control of the bus and status signals). The module must also be able to recognize and generate addresses associated with the devices it controls. Each I/O module has a unique address or, if it controls more than one external device, a unique set of ad-

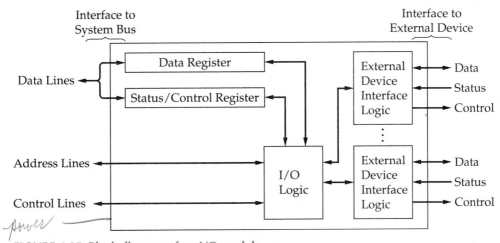

FIGURE 1.25 Block diagram of an I/O module

dresses. Finally, the I/O module contains logic specific to the interface with each device that it controls.

I/O modules allow the processor to view a wide range of devices in a simple-minded way. A spectrum of capabilities may be provided . The I/O module may hide the details of timing, formats, and the electromechanics of an external device so that the processor can function in terms of simple READ and WRITE commands and, possibly, open and close file commands. In its simplest form, the I/O module may still leave much of the work of controlling a device (e.g., rewind a tape) visible to the processor.

An I/O module that takes on most of the of the detailed processing burden, presenting a high-level interface to the processor, is usually referred to as an *I/O channel* or *I/O processor*. An I/O module that is quite primitive and requires detailed control is commonly referred to as an *I/O controller* or *device controller*. I/O controllers are commonly seen on microcomputers, whereas I/O channels are used on mainframes. Minicomputers employ a mixture.

When an I/O module is complex (I/O channel), it is usually functionally partitioned in the form of an I/O channel controlling one or more I/O controllers, each of which in turn controls one or more external devices.

1.9

I/O COMMUNICATION TECHNIQUES

The following three techniques are possible for I/O operations:

- Programmed I/O
- Interrupt-driven I/O
- Direct memory access (DMA)

Programmed I/O

When the processor is executing a program and encounters an instruction relating to I/O, it executes that instruction by issuing a command to the appropriate I/O module. With programmed I/O, the I/O module will perform the requested action and then set the appropriate bits in the I/O status register (Figure 1.25). The I/O module takes no further action to alert the processor. In particular, it does not interrupt the processor. Thus, it is the responsibility of the processor to check the status of the I/O module periodically until it finds that the operation is complete.

With this technique, the processor is responsible for extracting data from main memory for output and storing data in main memory for input. I/O software is written in such a way that the processor executes instructions that give it direct control of the I/O operation, including sensing device status, sending a read or write command, and transferring the data. Thus, the instruction set includes

I/O instructions in the following categories:

- *Control:* Used to activate an external device and tell it what to do. For example, a magnetic tape unit may be instructed to rewind or to move forward one record.
- *Test:* Used to test various status conditions associated with an I/O module and its peripherals.
- *Read, Write:* Used to transfer data between processor registers and external devices.

Figure 1.26a gives an example of the use of programmed I/O to read in a block of data from an external device (e.g., a record from tape) into memory. Data are read in one word (e.g., 16 bits) at a time. For each word that is read in, the processor must remain in a status-checking cycle until it determines that the word is available in the I/O module's data register. The flowchart shown in Figure 1.26 highlights the main disadvantage of this technique: It is a time-consuming process that keeps the processor busy needlessly.

Interrupt-Driven I/O

The problem with programmed I/O is that the processor has to wait a long time for the I/O module of concern to be ready for either reception or transmission of more data. The processor, while waiting, must repeatedly interrogate the status of the I/O module. As a result, the level of the performance of the entire system is severely degraded.

An alternative is for the processor to issue an I/O command to a module and then go on to do some other useful work. The I/O module will then interrupt the processor to request service when it is ready to exchange data with the processor. The processor then executes the data transfer as before and then resumes its former processing.

Let us consider how this works, first from the point of view of the I/O module. For input, the I/O module receives a READ command from the processor. The I/O module then proceeds to read data in from an associated peripheral. Once the data are in the module's data register, the module signals an interrupt to the processor over a control line. The module then waits until its data are requested by the processor. When the request is made, the module places its data on the data bus and is then ready for another I/O operation.

From the processor's point of view, the action for input is as follows. The processor issues a READ command. It then saves the context (e.g., program counter and processor registers) of the current program and goes off and does something else (e.g., the processor may be working on several different programs at the same time). At the end of each instruction cycle, the processor checks for interrupts (Figure 1.7). When the interrupt from the I/O module occurs, the processor saves the context of the program it is currently executing and begins to execute an interrupt-handling program that processes the interrupt. In this case, the processor reads the word of data from the I/O module

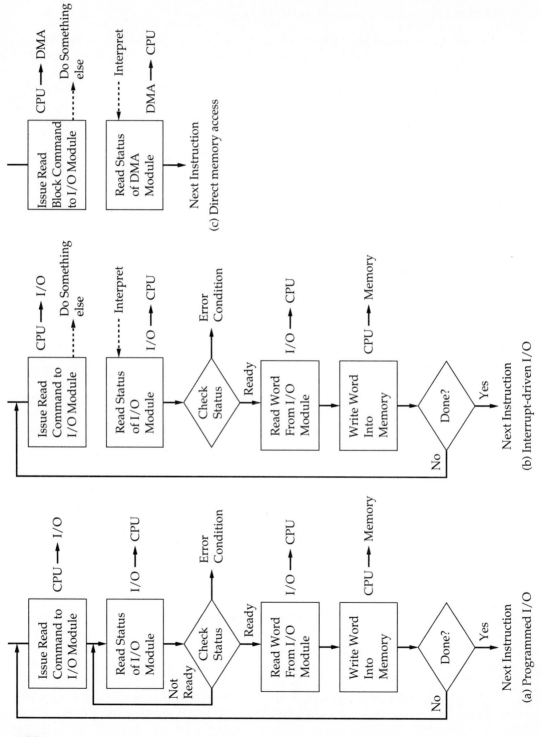

FIGURE 1.26 Three techniques for input of a block of data

(a) Programmed I/O

(b) Interrupt-driven I/O

(c) Direct memory access

and stores it in memory. It then restores the context of the program that issued the I/O command (or some other program) and resumes execution.

Figure 1.26b shows the use of interrupt I/O for reading in a block of data. Compare this to Figure 1.26a. Interrupt I/O is more efficient than programmed I/O because it eliminates needless waiting. However, interrupt I/O still consumes a lot of processor time because every word of data that goes from memory to I/O module or from I/O module to memory must pass through the processor.

Almost invariably, there will be multiple I/O modules in a computer system, so mechanisms are needed to enable the processor to determine which device caused the interrupt and to decide, in the case of multiple interrupts, which one to handle first. In some systems, there are multiple interrupt lines, so that each I/O module signals on a different line. Each line has a different priority. Alternatively, there can be a single interrupt line, but additional lines are used to hold a device address. Again, different devices are assigned different priorities.

Direct Memory Access

Interrupt-driven I/O, although more efficient than simple programmed I/O, still requires the active intervention of the processor to transfer data between memory and an I/O module, and any data transfer must traverse a path through the processor. Thus, both these forms of I/O suffer from two inherent drawbacks:

1. The I/O transfer rate is limited by the speed with which the processor can test and service a device.
2. The processor is tied up in managing an I/O transfer; a number of instructions must be executed for each I/O transfer.

When large volumes of data are to be moved, a more efficient technique is required: direct memory access (DMA). The DMA function can be performed by a separate module on the system bus, or it can be incorporated into an I/O module. In either case, the technique works as follows. When the processor wishes to read or write a block of data, it issues a command to the DMA module by sending to the DMA module the following information:

- Whether a read or write is requested
- The address of the I/O device involved
- The starting location in memory to read from or write to
- The number of words to be read or written

The processor then continues with other work. It has delegated this I/O operation to the DMA module, and that module will take care of it. The DMA module transfers the entire block of data, one word at a time, directly to or from memory, without going through the processor. When the transfer is complete, the DMA module sends an interrupt signal to the processor. Thus, the processor is involved only at the beginning and end of the transfer (Figure 1.26c).

The DMA module needs to take control of the bus in order to transfer data to and from memory. Because of this competition for bus usage, there may be times when the processor needs the bus and must wait for it. Note that this is not an interrupt; the processor does not save a context and do something else. Rather, the processor pauses for one bus cycle. The overall effect is to cause the processor to execute more slowly during a DMA transfer. Nevertheless, for a multiple-word I/O transfer, DMA is far more efficient than interrupt-driven or programmed I/O.

When the I/O module in question is a sophisticated I/O channel, the DMA concept can be taken even further. An I/O channel is a processor in its own right, with a specialized instruction set tailored for I/O. In a computer system with such devices, the processor does not execute I/O instructions. Such instructions are stored in main memory to be executed by the I/O channel itself. Thus, the processor initiates an I/O transfer by instructing the I/O channel to execute a program in memory. The program specifies the device or devices, the area or areas of memory for storage, priority, and action to be taken for certain error conditions. The I/O channel follows these instructions and controls the data transfer, reporting back to the processor at completion.

1.10

RECOMMENDED READING

[STAL90a] covers the topics of this chapter in detail. In addition, there are many other texts on computer organization and architecture. Among the more worthwhile texts are the following. [HENN90] is a comprehensive survey that emphasizes quantitative aspects of design. [HAYE88] is a very well-organized and well-written book with a particularly good discussion of the control aspects of computer systems, including a detailed discussion of microprogramming. [MANO88] emphasizes computer hardware with a detailed look at digital design and its use to implement the major feature of the processor. [TANE90] views a computer system in logical layers, from digital logic, through microprogramming, machine level, to the operating system level; this provides a unified treatment of a variety of topics. [HAMA84] provides broad coverage with many useful examples. Many books on computer architecture and operating systems provide a treatment of the basic principles of interrupts; a particularly clear and thorough account is in [BECK90].

Throughout this book, several operating systems are used as example systems to illustrate various design issues. Two of these systems were designed with particular processors in mind: IBM MVS (Multiple Virtual Storage) for the System/370 architecture and IBM OS/2 for the Intel 80286/80386 architectures. For the S/370 architecture, the following provide good coverage, in increasing order of complexity and thoroughness: [LEBA84a and b], [PRAS81], and [PRAS89]. Good coverage of the Intel architectures can be found in [MORS87], [BRUM87], and [HALL88].

1.11

PROBLEMS

1.1 The hypothetical machine of Figure 1.3 also has two I/O instructions:

0011 = Load AC (accumulator) from I/O
0111 = Store AC to I/O

In these cases, the 12-bit address identifies a particular external device. Show the program execution (using the format of Figure 1.4) for the following program:
(a) Load AC from device 5.
(b) Add contents of memory location 940.
(c) Store AC to device 6.

1.2 Consider a computer system that contains an I/O module controlling a simple keyboard/printer teletype. The following registers are contained in the CPU and are connected directly to the system bus:

INPR: Input Register, 8 bits
OUTR: Output Register, 8 bits
FGI: Input Flag, 1 bit
FGO: Output Flag, 1 bit
IEN: Interrupt Enable, 1 bit

Keystroke input from the teletype and output to the printer are controlled by the I/O module. The teletype is able to encode an alphanumeric symbol to an 8-bit word and to decode an 8-bit word into an alphanumeric symbol. The Input Flag is set when an 8-bit word enters the input register from the teletype. The Output flag is set when a word is printed.
(a) Describe how the CPU, using the first four registers listed in this problem, can achieve I/O with the teletype.
(b) Describe how the function can be performed more efficiently by also employing IEN.

1.3 A main memory system consists of a number of memory modules attached to the system bus. When a write request is made, the bus is occupied for 100 nanoseconds (ns) by the data, address, and control signals. During the same 100 ns, and for 500 ns thereafter, the addressed memory module executes one cycle accepting and storing the data. The operation of the memory modules may overlap, but only one request can be on the bus at any time.
(a) Assume that there are eight such modules connected to the bus. What is the maximum possible rate (in words per second) at which data can be stored?
(b) Sketch a graph of the maximum write rate as a function of the module cycle time, assuming eight memory modules and a bus busy time of 100 ns.

1.4 To save gates, buses are often time-multiplexed. That is, certain bus lines are used for two different functions at two different times. For example, the same lines may be used as both address lines and data lines. Consider a machine with 48-bit words, a disk with a transfer rate of 10^7 bps (bits per second), and a 600-ns memory access time. Assume that each bus transmission requires 750 ns for data bits and various control "hand-shaking" operations. How many data bits would have to be sent in each 750-ns period to stay ahead of the disk, and would time multiplexing help or hinder? What fraction of the main memory bandwidth is consumed by a disk I/O operation?

1.5 Generalize Equations 1.1 and 1.2 to n-level memory hierarchies.

1.6 Consider a memory system with the following parameters:

$Tc = 100$ ns $Cc = 0.01$ ¢/bit
$Tm = 1,200$ ns $Cm = 0.001$ ¢/bit
$H = 0.95$

(a) What is the cost of 1 megabyte (MB) of main memory?
(b) What is the cost of 1 MB of main memory using cache memory technology?
(c) Design a main memory/cache system with 1 MB of main memory whose effective access time is no more than 10% greater than the cache memory access time. What is its cost?

1.7 When multiple modules can generate interrupts, there needs to be a way for the processor to determine which module caused the interrupt. One technique is known as *vectored bus arbitration*. In this scheme, a module must first gain control of the bus by using some method of arbitration before it can raise the interrupt request line. Thus, only one module can raise that line at a time. When the processor detects the interrupt, it responds by raising the interrupt response line. The interrupting module then places a word on the data lines. This word is referred to as a *vector* and is either the address of the I/O module or some other unique identifier. In either case, the processor uses the vector as a pointer to the appropriate interrupt-handling routine.
   Why does the interrupting module place the vector on the data lines rather than on the address lines?

1.8 In virtually all systems that include DMA modules, DMA access to main memory is given higher priority than processor access to main memory. Why?

1.9 A DMA module is transferring characters to main memory from an external device transmitting at 9600 bps. The processor can fetch instructions at the rate of 1 million instructions per second. By how much will the processor be slowed down due to the DMA activity?

1.10 A computer consists of a CPU and an I/O device D connected to main memory M via a shared bus with a data bus width of one word. The CPU can execute a maximum of 10^6 instructions per second. An average instruction requires five machine cycles, three of which use the memory bus. A memory READ or WRITE operation uses one machine cycle. Suppose that the CPU is continuously executing "background" programs that require 95% of its instruction execution rate but not any I/O instructions. Now suppose that very large blocks of data are to be transferred between M and D.

(a) If programmed I/O is used and each one-word I/O transfer requires the CPU to execute two instructions, estimate the maximum I/O data-transfer rate R_{MAX} possible through D.

(b) Estimate R_{MAX} if DMA transfer is used.

1.11 Suppose a stack is to be used by the processor to manage procedure calls and returns. Can the program counter be eliminated by using the top of the stack as a program counter?

APPENDIX 1A

Performance Characteristics of Two-Level Memories

In this chapter, reference is made to a cache that acts as a buffer between main memory and processor to create a two-level internal memory. This two-level architecture provides improved performance over a comparable one-level memory by exploiting a property known as *locality*, which is explored below.

The main memory cache mechanism is part of the computer architecture; it is implemented in hardware and typically invisible to the operating system. Accordingly, this mechanism is not pursued in this book. However, there are two other instances of a two-level memory approach that also exploit locality and that are, at least partially, implemented in the operating system: virtual memory and the disk cache (Table 1.3). These two topics are explored in Chapters 5 and 7, respectively. In this appendix, we look at some of the performance characteristics of two-level memories that are common to all three approaches.

TABLE 1.3   Characteristics of Two-Level Memories

	Main Memory Cache	Virtual Memory (Paging)	Disk Cache
Typical access time ratios	5/1	1000/1	1000/1
Memory-management system	Implemented by special hardware	Combination of hardware and system software	System software
Typical block size	4 to 128 bytes	64 to 4096 bytes	64 to 4096 bytes
Access of processor to second level	Direct access	Indirect access	Indirect access

1A.1 Locality

The basis for the performance advantage of a two-level memory is a principle known as *locality of reference* [DENN68]. This principle states that memory references tend to cluster. Over a long period, the clusters in use change, but over a short period, the processor is primarily working with fixed clusters of memory references.

From an intuitive point of view, the principle of locality makes sense. Consider the following line of reasoning:

1. Except for branch and call instructions, which constitute only a small fraction of all program instructions, program execution is sequential. Hence, in most cases, the next instruction to be fetched immediately follows the last instruction fetched.
2. It is rare to have a long uninterrupted sequence of procedure calls followed by the corresponding sequence of returns. Rather, a program remains confined to a rather narrow window of procedure-invocation depth. Thus, over a short period, references to instructions tend to be localized to a few procedures.
3. Most iterative constructs consist of a relatively small number of instructions repeated many times. For the duration of the iteration, computation is therefore confined to a small contiguous portion of a program.
4. In many programs, much of the computation involves processing data structures, such as arrays or sequences of records. In many cases, successive references to these data structures will be to closely located data items.

This line of reasoning has been confirmed in many studies. For example, let us consider assertion 1. A variety of studies have been made to analyze the behavior of high-level language programs. Table 1.4 includes key results, measuring the appearance of various statement types during execution, from the following studies. The earliest study of programming language behavior, performed by Knuth [KNUT71], examined a collection of FORTRAN programs used as student exercises. Tanenbaum [TANE78] published measurements collected from over 300 procedures used in operating-system programs and written in a language that supports structured programming (SAL). Patterson

TABLE 1.4   Relative Dynamic Frequency of High-Level Language Operations

Study	[HUCK83]	[KNUT71]	[PATT82a]		[TANE78]
Language	Pascal	FORTRAN	Pascal	C	SAL
Workload	Scientific	Student	System	System	System
Assign	74	67	45	38	42
Loop	4	3	5	3	4
Call	1	3	15	12	12
IF	20	11	29	43	36
GOTO	2	9	—	3	—
Other	—	7	6	1	6

and Sequin [PATT82] analyzed a set of measurements taken from compilers and programs for typesetting, CAD, sorting, and file comparison. The programming languages C and Pascal were studied. Huck [HUCK83] analyzed four programs intended to represent a mix of general-purpose scientific computing, including fast Fourier transform and the integration of systems of differential equations. There is quite good agreement in the results of this mixture of languages and applications that branching and call instructions represent only a fraction of statements executed during the lifetime of a program. Thus, these studies confirm the foregoing assertion 1.

With respect to assertion 2, studies reported in Patterson [PATT85] provide confirmation. This is illustrated in Figure 1.27, which shows call-return behavior. Each call is represented by the line moving down and to the right, and each return by the line moving up and to the right. In the figure, a *window* with depth equal to 5 is defined. Only a sequence of calls and returns with a net movement of 6 in either direction causes the window to move. As can be seen, the executing program can remain within a stationary window for quite long periods. A study by the same group of C and Pascal programs showed that a window of depth 8 will need to shift on fewer than 1% of the calls or returns [TAMI83].

Other studies have also demonstrated the validity of assertions 3 and 4 (e.g., [DENN80b], [CHU76]).

1A.2 Operation of Two-Level Memory

The locality property can be exploited in the formation of a two-level memory. The upper-level memory (M1) is smaller, faster, and more expensive (per bit) than the lower-level memory (M2). M1 is used as a temporary store for part of the contents of the larger M2. When a memory reference is made, an attempt

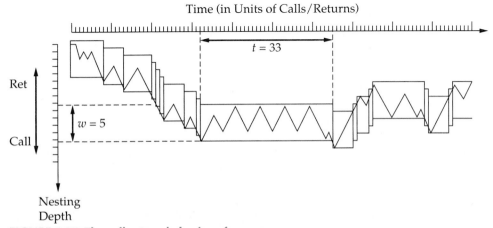

FIGURE 1.27 The call-return behavior of programs

is made to access the item in M1. If this succeeds, then a quick access is made. If not, then a block of memory locations is copied from M2 to M1 and the access then takes place via M1. Because of locality, once a block is brought into M1, there should be a number of accesses to locations in that block, resulting in fast overall service.

To express the average time to access an item, we must consider not only the speeds of the two levels of memory but also the probability that a given reference can be found in M1. This probability is known as the *hit ratio*. We have

$$T_s = H \times T_1 + (1-H) \times (T_1 + T_2)$$
$$= T_1 + (1-H) T_2$$

(1.1)

where

T_s = average (system) access time
T_1 = access time of M1 (e.g., cache, disk cache)
T_2 = access time of M2 (e.g., main memory, disk)
H = hit ratio (fraction of time reference is found in M1)

Figure 1.17 shows average access time as a function of hit ratio. As can be seen, for a high percentage of hits, the average total access time is much closer to that of M1 than M2.

1A.3 Performance

Let us look at some of the parameters relevant to an assessment of a two-level memory mechanism. First consider cost. We have

$$C_s = \frac{C_1 S_1 + C_2 S_2}{S_1 + S_2}$$

(1.2)

where

C_s = average cost per bit for the combined two-level memory
C_1 = average cost per bit of upper-level memory M1
C_2 = average cost per bit of lower-level memory M2
S_1 = size of M1
S_2 = size of M2

We would like $C_s \approx C_2$. Given that $C_1 >> C_2$, this requires $S_1 << S_2$. Figure 1.28 shows the relationship.

Next, consider access time. For a two-level memory to provide a significant performance improvement, we need to have T_s approximately equal to T_1 ($T_s \approx T_1$). Given that T_1 is much less than T_2 ($T_1 << T_2$), a hit ratio of close to 1 is needed.

So, we would like M1 to be small to hold down cost and large to improve the hit ratio and therefore the performance. Is there a size of M1 that satisfies both requirements to a reasonable extent? We can answer this question with a series of subquestions:

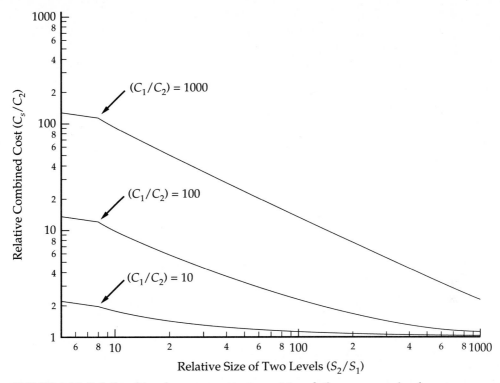

FIGURE 1.28 Relationship of average memory cost to relative memory size for a two-level memory

- What value of hit ratio is needed to satisfy the performance requirement?
- What size of M1 will assure the needed hit ratio?
- Does this size satisfy the cost requirement?

To get at this, consider the quantity T_1/T_s, which is referred to as the *access efficiency*. It is a measure of how close average access time (T_s) is to M1 access time (T_1). From Equation (1.1):

$$\frac{T_1}{T_s} = \frac{1}{H + (1 - H)\dfrac{T_2}{T_1}} \tag{1.3}$$

In Figure 1.29, we plot T_1/T_s as a function of the hit ratio H, with the quantity T_2/T_1 as a parameter. Typically, cache access time is about five to ten times faster than main memory access time (i.e., T_2/T_1 is 5 to 10), and main-memory access time is about 1000 times faster than disk access time ($T_2/T_1 = 1,000$). Thus, a hit ratio in the range of 0.8 to 0.9 would seem to be needed to satisfy the performance requirement.

We can now phrase the question about relative memory size more exactly. Is a hit ratio of 0.8 or better reasonable for $S_1 \ll S_2$? This will depend on a number

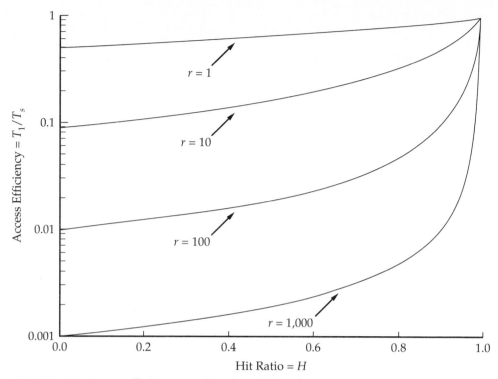

FIGURE 1.29 Access efficiency as a function of hit ratio ($R = T_2/T_1$)

of factors, including the nature of the software being executed and the details of the design of the two-level memory. The main determinant is, of course, the degree of locality. Figure 1.30 suggests the effect that locality has on the hit ratio. Clearly, if M1 is the same size as M2, then the hit ratio will be 1.0: All the items in M2 are always stored also in M1. Now, suppose that there is no locality; that is, references are completely random. In that case the hit ratio should be a strictly linear function of the relative memory size. For example, if M1 is half the size of M2, then at any time, half of the items from M2 are also in M1 and the hit ratio will be 0.5. In practice, however, there is some degree of locality in the references. The effects of moderate and strong locality are indicated in the figure.

So, if there is strong locality, it is possible to achieve high values of hit ratio even with relatively small upper-level memory size. For example, numerous studies have shown that rather small cache sizes will yield a hit ratio above 0.75, *regardless of the size of main memory* (e.g., [AGAR89a], [AGAR89b], [PRZY88], [STRE83], and [SMIT82]). A cache in the range of 1 K to 128 K words is generally adequate, whereas main memory is now typically in the multiple-megabyte range. When we consider virtual memory and disk cache, we will cite other studies that confirm the same phenomenon, namely, that a relatively small M1 yields a high value of hit ratio because of locality.

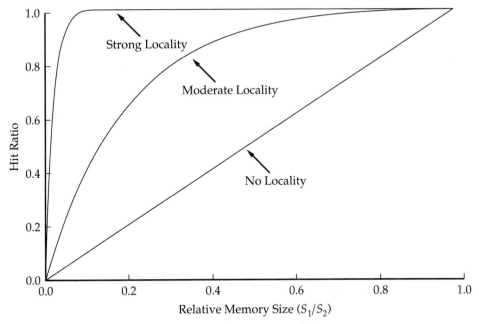

FIGURE 1.30 Hit ratio as a function of relative memory size

This brings us to the last question listed earlier: Does the relative size of the two memories satisfy the cost requirement? The answer is clearly yes. If we need only a relatively small upper-level memory to achieve good performance, then the average cost per bit of the two levels of memory will approach that of the cheaper lower-level memory.

APPENDIX 1B
Procedure Control

A common technique for controlling the execution of procedure calls and returns makes use of a stack. This appendix summarizes the basic properties of stacks and looks at their use in procedure control.

1B.1 Stack Implementation

A *stack* is an ordered set of elements, only one of which can be accessed at a time. The point of access is called the *top* of the stack. The number of elements in the stack, or length of the stack, is variable. Items may be added to or deleted from only the top of the stack. For this reason, a stack is also known as a *pushdown list* or a *last-in, first-out (LIFO) list*.

Figure 1.31 shows the two basic operations that can be performed on stacks. We begin at some point in time when the stack contains some number of ele-

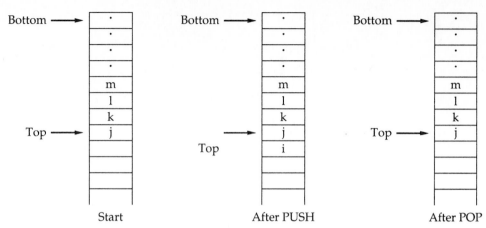

FIGURE 1.31 Basic stack operation

ments. A PUSH operation appends one new item to the top of the stack. A POP operation removes the top item from the stack. In both cases, the top of the stack moves accordingly.

The implementation of a stack requires that there be some set of locations used to store the stack elements. A typical approach is illustrated in Figure 1.32. A contiguous block of locations is reserved in main memory (or virtual memory) for the stack. Most of the time, the block is partially filled with stack elements and the remainder is available for stack growth. Three addresses are needed for proper operation, and these are often stored in processor registers:

- *Stack pointer:* Contains the address of the top of the stack. If an item is appended to the stack (PUSH) or deleted from the stack (POP), the pointer is incremented or decremented to contain the address of the new top of the stack.
- *Stack base:* Contains the address of the bottom location in the reserved block. This is the first location to be used when an item is added to an empty stack. If an attempt is made to POP when the stack is empty, an error is reported.
- *Stack limit:* Contains the address of the other end, or top, of the reserved block. If an attempt is made to PUSH when the stack is full, an error is reported.

1B.2 Procedure Calls and Returns

A common technique for managing procedure calls and returns makes use of a stack. When the processor executes a call, it places the return address on the stack. When it executes a return, it uses the address on top of the stack. Figure 1.33 illustrated the use of a stack to manage the nested procedures of Figure 1.34.

In addition to providing a return address, it is also often necessary to pass

Main Memory

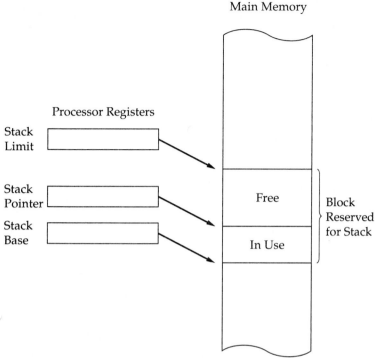

FIGURE 1.32 Typical stack organization

parameters with a procedure call. These could be passed in registers. Another possibility is to store the parameters in memory just after the Call instruction. In this case, the return must be to the location following the parameters. Both of these approaches have drawbacks. If registers are used, the called program and the calling program must be written to assure that the registers are used properly. The storing of parameters in memory makes it difficult to exchange a variable number of parameters.

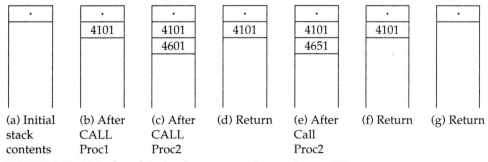

FIGURE 1.33 Use of stack to implement nested procedures of Figure 1.34

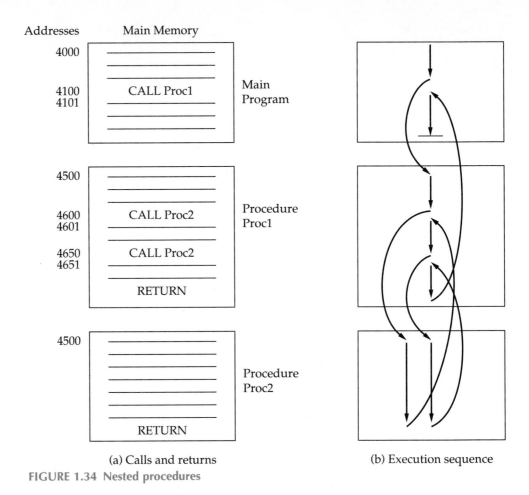

(a) Calls and returns   (b) Execution sequence

FIGURE 1.34 Nested procedures

A more flexible approach to parameter passing is the stack. When the processor executes a call, it not only stacks the return address, it stacks parameters to be passed to the called procedure. The called procedure can access the parameters from the stack. Upon return, return parameters can also be placed on the stack *under* the return address. The entire set of parameters, including return address, that is stored for a procedure invocation is referred to as a **stack frame**.

An example is provided in Figure 1.35. The example refers to procedure P in which the local variables $x1$ and $x2$ are declared, and procedure Q, which can be called by P and in which the local variables $y1$ and $y2$ are declared. In this figure, the return point for each procedure is the first item stored in the corresponding stack frame. Next is stored a pointer to the beginning of the previous frame. This is needed if a number or length of parameters to be stacked is variable.

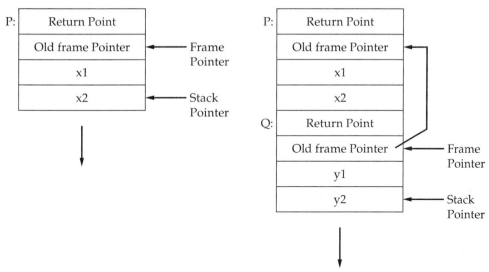

FIGURE 1.35 Stack frame growth using sample procedures P and Q [DEWA90]

1B.3 Reentrant Procedures

A useful concept, particularly in a system that supports multiple users at the same time, is that of the reentrant procedure. A *reentrant procedure* is one in which a single copy of the program code can be shared by multiple users during the same period. Reentrancy has two key aspects: The program code cannot modify itself and the local data for each user must be stored separately. A reentrant procedure can be interrupted and called by an interrupting program and still execute correctly upon return to the procedure. In a shared system, reentrancy allows more efficient use of main memory: One copy of the program code is kept in main memory, but more than one application can call the procedure.

Thus, a reentrant procedure must have a permanent part (the instructions that make up the procedure) and a temporary part (a pointer back to the calling program as well as memory for local variables used by the program). Each execution instance, called an *activation*, of a procedure will execute the code in the permanent part but must have its own copy of local variables and parameters. The temporary part associated with a particular activation is referred to as an *activation record*.

The most convenient way to support reentrant procedures is by means of a stack. When a reentrant procedure is called, the activation record of the procedure can be stored on the stack. Thus, the activation record becomes part of the stack frame that is created on procedure CALL.

CHAPTER 2

Operating Systems Overview

We begin our study of operating systems with a brief history of them. This history is interesting in itself and also provides an overview of principles of operating systems.

The chapter begins with a look at the objectives and functions of operating systems, which serves to define the requirements that an operating system design is intended to meet. Then, we look at how operating systems have evolved from primitive batch systems to sophisticated multimode, multiuser systems. The remainder of the chapter looks at the history and general characteristics of the three operating systems that serve as examples throughout the book. It is a happy coincidence that not only are these perhaps the three best examples that could be used in this book, but also among them they encompass most of the major milestones in the history of operating systems.

2.1

OPERATING SYSTEMS OBJECTIVES AND FUNCTIONS

An operating system is a program that controls the execution of application programs and acts as an interface between the user of a computer and the computer hardware. An operating system can be thought of as having three objectives or performing three functions:

- *Convenience:* An operating system makes a computer more convenient to use.
- *Efficiency:* An operating system allows the computer system resources to be used in an efficient manner.
- *Ability to evolve:* An operating system should be constructed in such a way as to permit the effective development, testing, and introduction of new system functions without at the same time interfering with service.

Let us examine these three aspects of an operating system in turn.

The Operating System as a User/Computer Interface

The hardware and software that are used in providing applications to a user can be viewed in a layered, or hierarchical, fashion, as depicted in Figure 2.1. The user of those applications is called the *end user* and generally is not concerned with the computer's architecture. Thus, the end user views a computer system in terms of an application. That application can be expressed in a programming language and is developed by an application programmer. If one were to develop an application program as a set of machine instructions that is completely responsible for controlling the computer hardware, one would be faced with an overwhelmingly complex task. To ease this task, a set of systems programs is provided. Some of these programs are referred to as *utilities,* and they implement frequently used functions that assist in program creation, the management of files, and the control of I/O devices. A programmer makes use of these facilities in developing an application, and the application, while it is running, invokes the utilities to perform certain functions. The most important system program is the operating system. The operating system masks the details of the hardware from the programmer and provides the programmer with a convenient interface for using the system. It acts as mediator, making it easier for the programmer and for application programs to access and use those facilities and services.

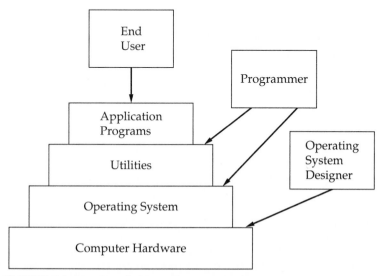

FIGURE 2.1 Layers and views of a computer system

Briefly, the operating system typically provides services in the following areas:

- *Program creation:* The operating system provides a variety of facilities and services, such as editors and debuggers, to assist the programmer in creating programs. Typically, these services are in the form of utility programs that are not actually part of the operating system but are accessible through the operating system.
- *Program execution:* A number of tasks need to be performed to execute a program. Instructions and data must be loaded into main memory, I/O devices and files must be initialized, and other resources must be prepared. The operating system handles all these tasks for the user.
- *Access to I/O devices:* Each I/O device requires its own peculiar set of instructions, or control signals, for operation. The operating system takes care of the details so that the programmer can think in terms of simple reads and writes.
- *Controlled access to files:* In the case of files, control must include an understanding of not only the nature of the I/O device (disk drive, tape drive) but also the file format on the storage medium. Again, the operating system deals with the details. Furthermore, in the case of a system with multiple simultaneous users, the operating system can provide protection mechanisms to control access to the files.
- *System access:* In the case of a shared or public system, the operating system controls access to the system as a whole and to specific system resources. The access function must provide protection of resources and data from unauthorized users and must resolve conflicts in the contention for resources.
- *Error detection and response:* A variety of errors can occur while a computer system is running. These include internal and external hardware errors, such as a memory error, or a device failure or malfunction; and various software errors, such as arithmetic overflow, attempt to access forbidden memory location, and inability of the operating system to grant the request of an application. In each case, the operating system must make the response that clears the error condition with the least impact on running applications. The response may range from ending the program that caused the error, to retrying the operation, to simply reporting the error to the application.
- *Accounting:* A good operating system collects usage statistics for various resources and monitors performance parameters such as response time. On any system, this information is useful in anticipating the need for future enhancements and in tuning the system to improve performance. On a multiuser system, the information can be used for billing purposes.

The Operating System as Resource Manager

A computer is a set of resources for the movement, storage, and processing of data and for the control of these functions. The operating system is responsible for managing these resources.

Can we say that it is the operating system that controls the movement, storage, and processing of data? From one point of view, the answer is yes: By managing the computer's resources, the operating system is in control of the computer's basic functions. But this control is exercised in a curious way. Normally, we think of a control mechanism as something external to that which is controlled or at least as something that is a distinct and separate part of that which is controlled. (For example, a residential heating system is controlled by a thermostat, which is completely distinct from the heat-generation and heat-distribution apparatus.) This is not the case with the operating system, which as a control mechanism is unusual in two respects:

- The operating system functions in the same way as ordinary computer software; that is, it is a program executed by the processor.
- The operating system frequently relinquishes control and must depend on the processor to allow it to regain control.

The operating system is, in fact, nothing more than a computer program.[1] Like other computer programs, it provides instructions for the processor. The key difference is in the intent of the program. The operating system directs the processor in the use of the other system resources and in the timing of its execution of other programs. But for the processor to do any of these things, it must cease executing the operating system program and execute other programs. Thus, the operating system relinquishes control for the processor to do some "useful" work, and then it resumes control long enough to prepare the processor to do the next piece of work. The mechanisms involved in all this should become clear as the chapter proceeds.

Figure 2.2 suggests the main resources that are managed by the operating system. A portion of the operating system is in main memory. This includes the **kernel,** or **nucleus,** which contains the most frequently used functions in the operating system and, at a given time, other portions of the operating system currently in use. The remainder of main memory contains other user programs and data. The allocation of this resource (main memory) is controlled jointly by the operating system and memory-management hardware in the processor, as we shall see. The operating system decides when an I/O device can be used by a program in execution and controls access to and use of files. The processor itself is a resource, and the operating system must determine how much processor time is to be devoted to the execution of a particular user program. In the case of a multiple-processor system, this decision must span all the processors.

---

[1]An increasing portion of a number of operating systems is committed to firmware rather than to software. This does not materially change the argument.

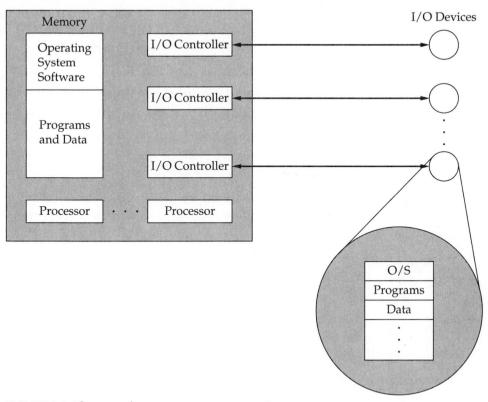

FIGURE 2.2 The operating system as a resource manager

Ease of Evolution of an Operating System

A major operating system will evolve over time for a number of reasons:

- *Hardware upgrades plus new types of hardware:* For example, early versions of UNIX and OS/2 did not employ a paging mechanism because they were run on machines without paging hardware.[2] More recent versions have been modified to exploit paging capabilities. Also, the use of graphics terminals and page-mode terminals instead of line-at-a-time scroll-mode terminals may affect operating system design. For example, such a terminal may allow the user to view several applications at the same time through "windows" on the screen. This requires more sophisticated support in the operating system.
- *New services:* In response to user demand or in response to the needs of system managers, the operating system will expand to offer new services. For ex-

---

[2]Paging is introduced briefly later in this chapter and is discussed in detail in Chapter 5.

ample, if it is found to be difficult to maintain good performance for users with existing tools, new measurement and control tools may be added to the operating system. Another example is new applications that require the use of windows on the display screen. This feature will require major upgrades to the operating system.

• *Fixes:* Alas, 'tis true, your operating system has faults that will be discovered over the course of time and fixes will need to be made. Of course, the fixes may introduce new faults . . .

The need to change an operating system on a regular basis places certain requirements on its design. An obvious statement is that the system should be modular in construction, with clearly defined interfaces between the modules, and that it should be well documented. For large programs, such as the typical contemporary operating system, what might be referred to as straightforward modularization is inadequate [DENN80a]. That is, much more must be done than simply partitioning a program into subroutines. We return to this topic later in this chapter.

THE EVOLUTION OF OPERATING SYSTEMS

In attempting to understand the key requirements for an operating system and the significance of the major features of a contemporary operating system, it is useful to consider how operating systems have evolved over the years.

Serial Processing

With the earliest computers, from the late 1940s to the mid-1950s, the programmer interacted directly with the computer hardware; there was no operating system. These machines were run from a console consisting of display lights, toggle switches, some form of input device, and a printer. Programs in machine code were loaded via the input device (e.g., a card reader). If an error halted the program, the error condition was indicated by the lights. The programmer could proceed to examine registers and main memory to determine the cause of the error. If the program proceeded to a normal completion, the output appeared on the printer.

These early systems presented two main problems:

• *Scheduling:* Most installations used a sign-up sheet to reserve machine time. Typically, a user could sign up for a block of time in multiples of a half hour or so. A user might sign up for an hour and finish in 45 minutes; this would result in wasted computer idle time. On the other hand, the user might run into problems, not finish in the allotted time, and be forced to stop before resolving the problem.

- *Setup time:* A single program, called a **job,** could involve loading the compiler plus the high-level language program (source program) into memory, saving the compiled program (object program), and then loading and linking together the object program and common functions. Each of these steps could involve mounting or dismounting tapes or setting up card decks. If an error occurred, the hapless user typically had to go back to the beginning of the setup sequence. Thus, a considerable amount of time was spent just in setting up the program to run.

This mode of operation could be termed *serial processing,* reflecting the fact that users had access to the computer in series. Over time, various system software tools were developed to attempt to make serial processing more efficient. These included libraries of common functions, linkers, loaders, debuggers, and I/O driver routines that were available as common software for all users.

Simple Batch Systems

Early machines were very expensive and therefore it was important to maximize machine use. The wasted time caused by scheduling and setup time was unacceptable.

To improve use, the concept of a batch operating system was developed. The first batch operating system (and the first operating system of any kind) was developed in the mid-1950s by General Motors for use on an IBM 701 [WEIZ81]. The concept was subsequently refined and implemented on the IBM 704 by a number of IBM customers. By the early 1960s, a number of vendors had developed batch operating systems for their computer systems. IBSYS, the IBM operating system for the 7090/7094 computers, is particularly notable because of its widespread influence on other systems.

The central idea behind the simple batch processing scheme was the use of a piece of software known as the **monitor.** With the use of this type of operating system, the user no longer has direct access to the machine. Rather, the user submits the job on cards or tape to a computer operator, who *batches* the jobs together sequentially and places the entire batch on an input device for use by the monitor. Each program is constructed to branch back to the monitor when it completes processing, at which point the monitor automatically begins loading the next program.

To understand how this scheme works, let us look at it from two points of view: that of the monitor and that of the processor. From the point of view of the monitor, it is the monitor that controls the sequence of events. For this to be so, much of the monitor must always be in main memory and available for execution (Figure 2.3). That portion is referred to as the **resident monitor**. The rest of the monitor consists of utilities and common functions that are loaded as subroutines to the user program at the beginning of any job that requires them. The monitor reads in jobs one at a time from the input device (typically

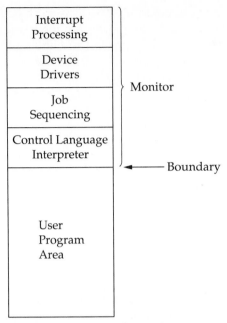

FIGURE 2.3 Memory layout for a resident monitor [SILB91]

a card reader or magnetic tape drive). As it is read in, the current job is placed in the user program area, and control is passed to this job. When the job is completed, it returns control to the monitor, which immediately reads in the next job. The results of each job are printed out for delivery to the user.

Now let us consider this sequence from the point of view of the processor. At a certain point in time, the processor is executing instructions from the portion of main memory containing the monitor. These instructions cause the next job to be read in to another portion of main memory. Once a job has been read in, the processor encounters in the monitor a branch instruction that instructs the processor to continue execution at the start of the user program. The processor then executes the instructions in the user's program until it encounters an ending or error condition. Either event causes the processor to fetch its next instruction from the monitor program. Thus, the phrase "control is passed to a job" simply means that the processor is now fetching and executing instructions in a user program, and "control is returned to the monitor" means that the processor is now fetching and executing instructions from the monitor program.

It should be clear that the monitor handles the scheduling problem. A batch of jobs is queued up, and jobs are executed as rapidly as possible, with no intervening idle time.

How about the job setup? The monitor handles this as well. With each job, instructions are included in a primitive form of **job control language** (JCL), which is a special type of programming language used to provide instructions to the monitor. Figure 2.4 shows a simple example with job input achieved by card. In this example, the user is submitting a program written in FORTRAN plus some data to be used by the program. In addition to FORTRAN and data cards, the deck includes job control instructions, which are denoted by the beginning dollar sign ($).

To execute this job, the monitor reads the $FTN card and loads the appropriate compiler from its mass storage (usually tape). The compiler translates the user's program into object code, which is stored in memory or mass storage. If it is stored in memory, the operation is referred to as "compile, load, and go." If it is stored on tape, then the $LOAD card is required. This card is read by the monitor, which regains control after the compile operation. The monitor invokes the loader, which loads the object program into memory in place of the compiler and transfers control to it. In this manner, a large segment of main memory can be shared among different subsystems, although only one such subsystem need be resident and executing at a time.

During the execution of the user program, any input instruction causes one card of data to be read. The input instruction in the user program causes an input routine that is part of the operating system to be invoked. The input routine checks to make sure that the program does not accidentally read in a JCL card. If this happens, an error occurs and control transfers to the monitor. At the successful or unsuccessful completion of the user job, the monitor will scan the input cards until it encounters the next JCL card. Thus, the system is protected against a program with too many or too few data cards.

We see that the monitor, or batch operating system, is simply a computer

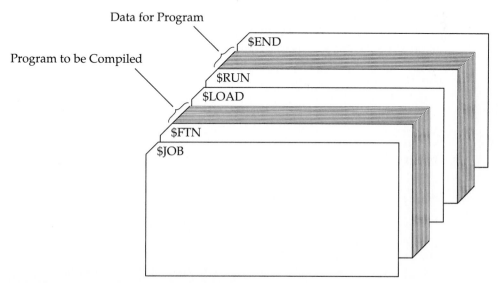

FIGURE 2.4 Card deck for a simple batch system

program. It relies on the ability of the processor to fetch instructions from various portions of main memory in order to alternately seize and relinquish control. Certain other hardware features are also desirable. They are the following:

- *Memory protection:* While the user program is executing, it must not alter the memory area containing the monitor. If such an attempt is made, the processor hardware should detect an error and transfer control to the monitor. The monitor would then abort the job, print out an error message, and load in the next job.
- *Timer:* A timer is used to prevent a single job from monopolizing the system. The timer is set at the beginning of each job. If the timer expires, an interrupt occurs, and control returns to the monitor.
- *Privileged instructions:* Certain instructions are designated as privileged and can be executed only by the monitor. If the processor encounters such an instruction while executing a user program, an error interrupt occurs. Among the privileged instructions are I/O instructions, so that the monitor retains control of all I/O devices. This prevents, for example, a user program from accidentally reading job control instructions from the next job. If a user program wishes to perform I/O, it must request that the monitor perform the operation for it. If a privileged instruction is encountered by the processor while it is executing a user program, the processor hardware considers this an error and transfers control to the monitor.
- *Interrupts:* Early computer models did not have this capability. This feature gives the operating system more flexibility in relinquishing control to and regaining control from user programs.

Of course, an operating system can be built without these features. But computer vendors quickly learned that the results are chaos, and so even relatively primitive batch operating systems were provided with these hardware features. As an aside, the world's most widely used operating system, PC-DOS/MS-DOS, has neither memory protection nor privileged I/O instructions. However, since this system is for only a single-user personal computer, the problems are less severe.

With a batch operating system, machine time alternates between execution of user programs and execution of the monitor. There have been two sacrifices: some main memory is now given over to the monitor and some machine time is consumed by the monitor. Both of these are forms of overhead. Even with this overhead, the simple batch system improves the use of the computer.

Multiprogrammed Batch Systems

Even with the automatic job sequencing provided by a simple batch operating system, the processor is often idle. The problem is that I/O devices are slow compared to the processor. Figure 2.5 details a representative calculation. The calculation concerns a program that processes a file of records and performs,

Read one record	0.0015 seconds
Execute 100 instructions	0.0001 seconds
Write one record	0.0015 seconds
TOTAL	0.0031 seconds

$$\text{Percent CPU Utilization} = \frac{0.0001}{0.0031} = 0.032 = 3.2\%$$

FIGURE 2.5 System utilization example

on average, 100 machine instructions per record. In this example, the computer spends more than 96% of its time waiting for I/O devices to finish transferring data! Figure 2.6a illustrates this situation. The processor spends a certain amount of time executing until it reaches an I/O instruction. It must then wait until that I/O instruction concludes before proceeding.

This inefficiency is not necessary. We know that there must be enough memory to hold the operating system (resident monitor) and one user program. Suppose that there is room for the operating system and two user programs. Now, when one job needs to wait for I/O, the processor can switch to the other job, which likely is not waiting for I/O (Figure 2.6b). Furthermore, we might expand memory to hold three, four, or more programs and switch among all of them (Figure 2.6c). The process is known as **multiprogramming**, or **multitasking**. It is the central theme of modern operating systems.

To illustrate the benefit of multiprogramming, let us consider an example based on one in Turner [TURN86]. Consider a computer with 256K words of available memory (not used by the operating system), a disk , a terminal, and a printer. Three programs, JOB1, JOB2, and JOB3, are submitted for execution at the same time, with the attributes listed in Table 2.1. We assume minimal processor requirements for JOB2 and JOB3 and continuous disk and printer use by JOB3. For a simple batch environment, these jobs will be executed in sequence. Thus, JOB1 completes in 5 minutes. JOB2 must wait until the 5 minutes are over and then completes 15 minutes after that. JOB3 begins after 20 minutes and completes at 30 minutes from the time it was initially submitted. The average resource use, throughput, and response times are shown in the uniprogramming column of Table 2.2. Device-by-device use is illustrated in Figure 2.7. It is evident that there is gross underuse for all resources when the times of use are averaged over the required 30-minute period.

Now suppose that the jobs are run concurrently under a multiprogramming operating system. Because there is little resource contention between the jobs, all three can run in nearly minimum time while coexisting with the others in the computer (assuming that JOB2 and JOB3 are allotted enough processor time to keep their input and output operations active). JOB1 will still require 5 minutes to complete, but at the end of that time, JOB2 will be one-third finished

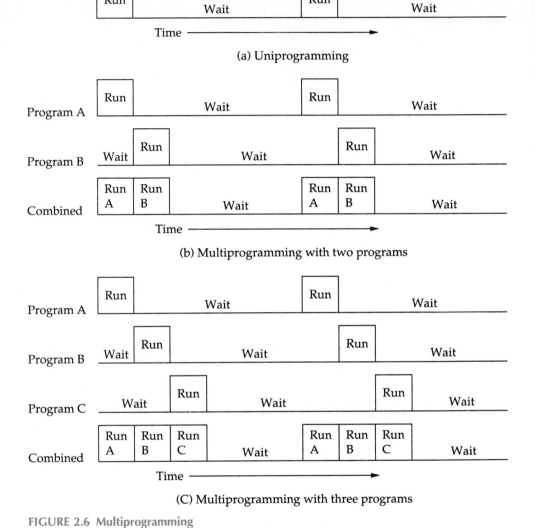

FIGURE 2.6 Multiprogramming

TABLE 2.1   Sample Program Execution Attributes

	JOB1	JOB2	JOB3
Type of job	Heavy compute	Heavy I/O	Heavy I/O
Duration	5 min	15 min	10 min
Memory required	50 K	100 K	80 K
Need disk?	No	No	Yes
Need terminal?	No	Yes	No
Need printer?	No	No	Yes

TABLE 2.2   Effects of Multiprogramming on Resource Utilization

	Uniprogramming	Multiprogramming
Processor use	17%	33%
Memory use	30%	67%
Disk use	33%	67%
Printer use	33%	67%
Elapsed time	30 min	15 min
Throughput rate	6 jobs/hr	12 jobs/hr
Mean response time	18 min	10 min

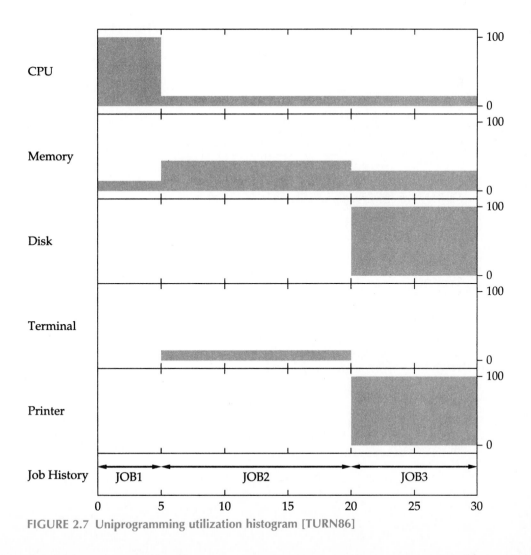

FIGURE 2.7 Uniprogramming utilization histogram [TURN86]

and JOB3 one-half finished. All three jobs will have finished within 15 minutes. The improvement is evident when one examines the multiprogramming column of Table 2.2, obtained from the histogram shown in Figure 2.8.

As with a simple batch system, a multiprogramming batch system is a program that must rely on certain computer hardware features. The most notable additional feature that is useful for multiprogramming is the hardware that supports I/O interrupts and DMA. With interrupt-driven I/O or DMA, the processor can issue an I/O command for one job and proceed with the execution of another job while the I/O is carried out by the device controller. When

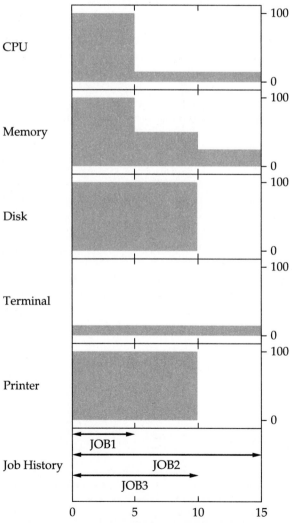

FIGURE 2.8 Multiprogramming utilization histogram [TURN86]

the I/O operation is complete, the processor is interrupted and control is passed to an interrupt-handling program in the operating system. The operating system will then pass control to another job.

Multiprogramming operating systems are fairly sophisticated compared to single-program, or **uniprogramming**, systems. To have several jobs ready to run, they must be kept in main memory, requiring some form of **memory management**. In addition, if several jobs are ready to run, the processor must decide which one to run, which requires some algorithm for scheduling. These concepts are discussed later in this chapter.

Time-Sharing Systems

With the use of multiprogramming, batch processing can be quite efficient. However, for many jobs, it is desirable to provide a mode in which the user interacts directly with the computer. Indeed, for some jobs, such as transaction processing, an interactive mode is essential.

Today, the requirement for an interactive computing facility can be, and often is, met by the use of a dedicated microcomputer. That option was not available in the 1960s, when most computers were big and costly. Instead, time sharing was developed.

Just as multiprogramming allows the processor to handle multiple batch jobs at a time, multiprogramming can be used to handle multiple interactive jobs. In this latter case, the technique is referred to as time sharing, reflecting the fact that the processor's time is shared among multiple users. The basic technique for a time-sharing system is to have multiple users simultaneously using the system through terminals, with the operating system interleaving the execution of each user program in a short burst, or quantum, of computation. Thus, if there are n users actively requesting service at one time, each user will see on the average only $1/n$ of the effective computer speed, not counting operating-system overhead. However, given the relatively slow human reaction time, the response time on a properly designed system should be comparable to that on a dedicated computer.

Both batch multiprogramming and time sharing use multiprogramming. The key differences are listed in Table 2.3.

TABLE 2.3   Batch Multiprogramming Versus Time Sharing

	Batch Multiprogramming	Time Sharing
Principal Objective	Maximize processor use	Minimize response time
Source of instructions to operating system	Job control language instructions provided with the job	Commands entered at the terminal

One of the first time-sharing operating systems to be developed was the Compatible Time-Sharing System (CTSS) [CORB63, CORB62], developed at MIT by a group known as Project MAC (Machine-Aided Cognition, Multiple-Access Computers). The system was first developed for the IBM 709 in 1961 and later transferred to an IBM 7094.

Compared to later systems, CTSS was quite primitive and its basic operation is easily explained. The system ran on a machine with 32 K 36-bit words of main memory, with the resident monitor consuming 5 K of that. When control was to be assigned to an interactive user, the user's program and data were loaded into the remaining 27 K of main memory. A system clock generated interrupts at a rate of approximately one every 0.2 seconds (sec). At each clock interrupt, the operating system regained control and could assign the processor to another user. Thus, at regular intervals, the current user would be preempted and another user loaded in. To preserve the old user's status for later resumption, the old user's programs and data were written out to disk before the new user's programs and data were read in. Subsequently, the old user's main memory space would be restored when it was next given a turn.

To minimize disk traffic, user memory was written out only when the incoming program would overwrite it. This principle is illustrated in Figure 2.9. Assume that there are four interactive users with the following memory requirements:

- JOB1: 15K
- JOB2: 20K
- JOB3: 5K
- JOB4: 10K

Initially, the monitor loads in JOB1 and transfers control to it (Figure 2.9a). Later, the monitor decides to transfer control to JOB2. Since JOB2 requires more memory than JOB1, JOB1 must be written out first, and then JOB2 can be loaded (Figure 2.9b). Next, JOB3 is loaded in to be run. However, because JOB3 is smaller than JOB2, a portion of JOB2 can remain in memory, reducing disk write time (Figure 2.9c). Later, the monitor decides to transfer control back to JOB1. An additional portion of JOB2 must be written out when JOB1 is loaded back into memory (Figure 2.9d). When JOB4 is loaded, part of JOB1 and the portion of JOB2 remaining in memory are retained (Figure 2.9e). At this point, if either JOB1 or JOB2 is activated, only a partial load will be required. In this example, it is JOB2 that runs next. This requires that JOB4 and the remaining resident portion of JOB1 be written out and that the missing portion of JOB2 be read in.

The CTSS approach was primitive compared to present-day time sharing, but it worked. It was extremely simple, which minimized the size of the monitor. Because a job was always loaded into the same locations in memory, there was no need for relocation techniques at load time (discussed later). The technique of writing out only what was necessary minimized disk activity. Running on the 7094, CTSS supported a maximum of 32 users.

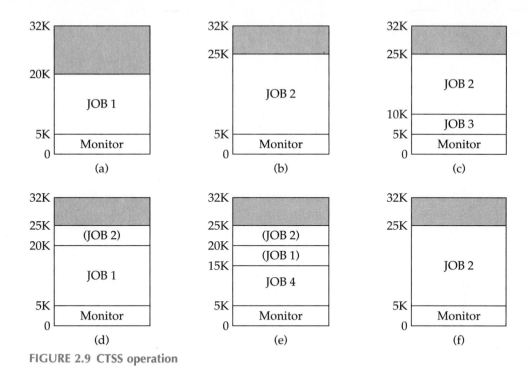

FIGURE 2.9 CTSS operation

Time sharing and multiprogramming raise a host of new problems for the operating system. If multiple jobs are in memory, then they must be protected from interfering with each other by, for example, modifying each other's data. With multiple interactive users, the file system must be protected so that only authorized users have access to a particular file. The contention for resources, such as printers and mass storage devices, must be handled. These and other problems, with possible solutions, will be encountered throughout the text.

2.3

MAJOR ACHIEVEMENTS

Operating systems are among the most complex pieces of software yet developed. This reflects the challenge of trying to meet the difficult and in some cases competing objectives of convenience, efficiency, and ability to evolve. Denning and his associates [DENN80a] propose that there have been five major intellectual achievements in the development of operating systems to date:

- Processes
- Memory management
- Information protection and security

• Scheduling and resource management
• System structure

Each achievement is characterized by principles, or abstractions, developed to meet difficult practical problems. Taken together, these five areas span the key design and implementation issues of modern operating systems. The brief review of these five areas in this section serves as an overview of much of the rest of the text.

Processes

The concept of *process* is fundamental to the structure of operating systems. This term was first used by the designers of Multics in the 1960s. It is a somewhat more general term than *job*. Many definitions have been given for the term *process*, including the following:

• A program in execution
• The "animated spirit" of a program
• That entity that can be assigned to and executed on a processor

The concept of process should become clearer as we proceed.

Three major lines of computer system development created problems in timing and synchronization that contributed to the development of the concept of the process: multiprogramming batch operation, time sharing, and real-time transaction systems. As we have seen, multiprogramming was designed to keep the processor and I/O devices, including storage devices, simultaneously busy to achieve maximum efficiency. The key mechanism is this: In response to signals indicating the completion of I/O transactions, the processor is switched among the various programs residing in main memory.

A second line of development was general-purpose time sharing. The rationale for such systems is that computer users are more productive if they can interact directly with the computer from some sort of terminal. Here, the key design objective is that the system be responsive to the needs of the individual user and yet, for cost reasons, be able to simultaneously support many users. These goals are compatible because of the relatively slow reaction time of the user. For example, if a typical user needs an average of 2 seconds of processing time per minute, then close to 30 such users should be able to share the same system without noticeable interference. Of course, the overhead of the operating system must be allowed for.

Another important line of development has been real-time transaction processing systems. In this case, a number of users are entering queries or updates against a data base. An example is an airline reservation system. The key difference between the transaction processing system and the time-sharing system is that the former is limited to one or a few applications, whereas users of a time-sharing system can engage in program development, job execution, and the use of various applications. In both cases, system response time is paramount.

The principal tool available to system programmers in developing the early multiprogramming and multiuser interactive systems was the interrupt. The activity of any job could be suspended by the occurrence of a defined event, such as an I/O completion. The processor would save some sort of context (e.g., program counter and other registers) and branch to an interrupt-handling routine, which would determine the nature of the interrupt, process the interrupt, and then resume user processing with the interrupted job or some other job.

The design of the system software to coordinate these various activities turned out to be remarkably difficult. With many jobs in progress at any one time, each of which involved numerous steps to be performed in sequence, it became impossible to analyze all the possible combinations of sequences of events. In the absence of some systematic means of coordination and cooperation among activities, programmers resorted to ad hoc methods based on their understanding of the environment that the operating system had to control. These efforts were vulnerable to subtle programming errors whose effects could be observed only when certain relatively rare sequences of actions occurred. These errors were difficult to diagnose because they needed to be distinguished from application software errors and hardware errors. Even when the error was detected, it was difficult to determine the cause because the precise conditions under which the errors appeared were very hard to reproduce. In general terms, there were four main causes of such errors [DENN80a]:

- *Improper synchronization:* It is often the case that a routine must be suspended awaiting an event elsewhere in the system. For example, a program initiates an I/O read and must wait until the data are available in a buffer before proceeding. In such cases, a signal from some other routine is required. Improper design of the signaling mechanism can result in signals being lost or duplicate signals being received.
- *Failed mutual exclusion:* It is often the case that more than one user or program will attempt to make use of a shared resource at the same time. For example, in an airline reservation system, two users may attempt to read the data base and, if a seat is available, update the data base to make a reservation. If these accesses are not controlled, an error can occur. There must be some sort of mutual exclusion mechanism that permits only one routine at a time to perform a transaction against a portion of data. The implementation of such mutual exclusion is difficult to verify as being correct under all possible sequences of events.
- *Nondeterminate program operation:* The results of a particular program normally should depend on only the input to that program and not on the activities of other programs in a shared system. But when programs share memory and their execution is interleaved by the processor, they may interfere with each other by overwriting common memory areas in unpredictable ways. Thus, the order in which various programs are scheduled may affect the outcome of any particular program.
- *Deadlocks:* It is possible for two or more programs to be hung up waiting for each other. For example, two programs may each require two I/O devices to

perform some operation (e.g., disk to tape copy). One of the programs has seized control of one of the devices, and the other program has control of the other device. Each is waiting for the other program to release the desired resource. Such a deadlock may depend on the chance timing of resource allocation and release.

What is needed to tackle these problems is a systematic way to monitor and control the various programs executing on the processor. The concept of the process provides the foundation. We can think of a process as consisting of the following three components:

- An executable program
- The associated data needed by the program (variables, work space, buffers, etc.)
- The execution context of the program

This last element is essential. The execution context includes all the information that the operating system needs to manage the process and that the processor needs to properly execute the process. Thus, the context includes the contents of the various processor registers, such as the program counter and data registers. It also includes information of use to the operating system, such as the priority of the process and whether the process is waiting for the completion of a particular I/O event.

Figure 2.10 indicates a way in which processes may be implemented. Two processes, A and B, exist in portions of main memory. That is, a block of memory is allocated to each process that contains the programs, data, and context information. Each process is recorded in a process list built and maintained by the operating system. The process list contains one entry for each process, which includes a pointer to the location of the block of memory that contains the process. The entry may also include part or all of the execution context of the process. The remainder of the execution context is stored with the process itself. The process index register contains the index into the process list of the process currently controlling the processor. The program counter points to the next instruction in that process to be executed. The base and limit registers define the region in memory occupied by the process. The program counter and all data references are interpreted relative to the base register and must not exceed the value in the limit register. This prevents interprocess interference.

In Figure 2.10, the process index register indicates that process B is executing. Process A was previously executing but has been temporarily interrupted. The content of all the registers at the moment of A's interruption were recorded in its execution context. Later, the processor can perform a context switch and resume execution of process A. The context switch consists of storing the context of B and restoring the context of A. When the program counter is loaded with a value pointing into A's program area, process A will automatically resume execution.

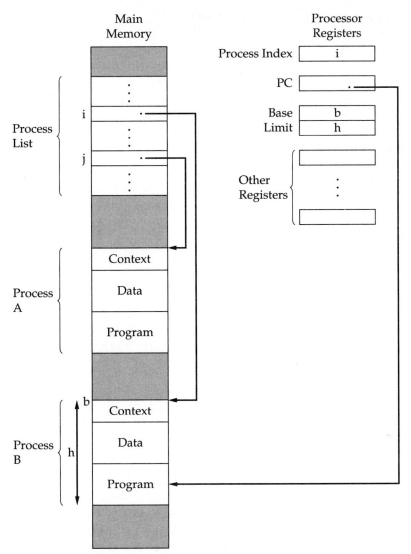

FIGURE 2.10 Typical process implementation

Thus, the process is realized as a data structure. A process can either be executing or awaiting execution. The entire "state" of the process is contained in its context. This structure allows the development of powerful techniques for ensuring coordination and cooperation among processes. New features can be designed and incorporated into the operating system (e.g., priority) by expanding the context to include any new information needed to support the feature. Throughout the book, we will see a number of examples where this process structure is employed to solve the problems raised by multiprogramming and resource sharing.

Memory Management

Users need a computing environment that supports modular programming and the flexible use of data. System managers need efficient and orderly control of storage allocation. The operating system, to satisfy these requirements, has five principal storage management responsibilities [DENN71] as follows:

- *Process isolation:* The operating system must prevent independent processes from interfering with the data and memory of each other.
- *Automatic allocation and management:* Programs should be dynamically allocated memory across the memory hierarchy as required. This process should be transparent to the programmer. Thus, the programmer is relieved of concerns relating to memory limitations, and the operating system can achieve efficiency by assigning memory to jobs only as needed.
- *Support of modular programming:* Programmers should be able to define program modules and to create, destroy, and alter the size of modules dynamically.
- *Protection and access control:* Sharing of memory at any level of the memory hierarchy creates the potential for one program to address the memory space of another program. Sometimes this is desirable, when sharing is needed by a particular application. At other times, it threatens the integrity of programs and even of the operating system itself. The operating system must allow portions of memory to be accessible in various ways by various users.
- *Long-term storage:* Many users and applications require means for storing information for extended periods.

Typically, operating systems meet these requirements with virtual memory and file system facilities. *Virtual memory* is a facility that allows programs to address memory from a logical point of view without regard to the amount of main memory physically available. When a program is executing, only a portion of the program and data may actually be maintained in main memory. Other portions of the program and data are kept in blocks on disk. We will see in later chapters that this separation of addressable memory into physical and logical views provides the operating system with a powerful tool for achieving its objectives.

The file system implements a long-term store, with information stored in named objects called *files*. The file is a convenient concept for the programmer and is a useful unit of access control and protection for the operating system.

Figure 2.11 provides a general depiction of a storage system managed by an operating system. The processor hardware, together with the operating system, provides the user with a "virtual processor" that has access to a virtual memory. This store may be a linear address space or a collection of segments, which are variable-length blocks of contiguous addresses. In either case, programming language instructions can reference program and data locations in the virtual

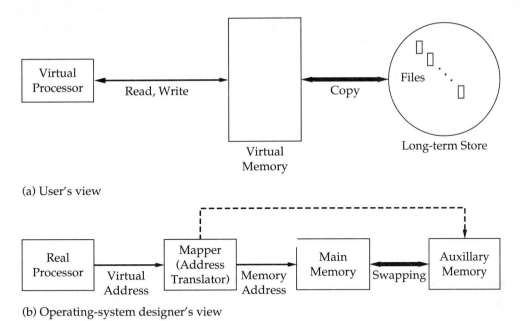

(a) User's view

(b) Operating-system designer's view

FIGURE 2.11 Two views of a storage system [DENN80]

memory. Process isolation can be achieved by giving each process a unique nonoverlapping virtual memory. Process sharing can be achieved by overlapping portions of two virtual memory spaces. Files are maintained in a long-term store. Files and portions of files may be copied into the virtual memory for manipulation by programs.

The designer's view of storage is also illustrated in Figure 2.11. Storage consists of directly addressable (by machine instructions) main memory and lower-speed auxiliary memory that is accessed indirectly by loading blocks into main memory. Address translation hardware (mapper) is interposed between the processor and memory. Programs reference locations using virtual addresses, which are mapped into real main memory addresses. If a reference is made to a virtual address not in real memory, then a portion of the contents of real memory is swapped out to auxiliary memory and the desired block of data is swapped in. During this activity, the process that generated the address reference must be suspended. It is the task of the designer to develop an address translation mechanism that generates little overhead and a storage allocation policy that minimizes the traffic between memory levels.

Information Protection and Security

The growth in the use of time-sharing systems and, more recently, computer networks has brought with it a growth in concern for the protection of information.

A publication of the National Bureau of Standards identified some of the threats that need to be addressed in the area of security [BRAN78]:

1. Organized and intentional attempts to obtain economic or market information from competitive organizations in the private sector
2. Organized and intentional attempts to obtain economic information from government agencies
3. Inadvertent acquisition of economic or market information
4. Inadvertent acquisition of information about individuals
5. Intentional fraud through illegal access to computer data banks with emphasis, in decreasing order of importance, on acquisition of funding data, economic data, law enforcement data, and data about individuals
6. Government intrusion on the rights of individuals
7. Invasion of individual rights by the intelligence community

These are examples of specific threats that an organization or an individual (or an organization on behalf of its employees) may feel the need to counter. The nature of the threat that concerns an organization will vary greatly from one set of circumstances to another. However, some general-purpose tools can be built into computers and operating systems to support a variety of protection and security mechanisms. In general, we are concerned with the problem of controlling access to computer systems and the information stored in them. Four types of overall protection policies, of increasing order of difficulty, have been identified [DENN80a]:

- *No sharing:* In this case, processes are completely isolated from each other, and each process has exclusive control over the resources statically or dynamically assigned to it. With this policy, processes often share a program or data file by making a copy of it and transferring the copy into their own virtual memory.
- *Sharing originals of program or data files:* With the use of a reentrant code (see Appendix 1B), a single physical realization of a program can appear in multiple virtual address spaces, as can read-only data files. Special locking mechanisms are required for the sharing of writable data files to prevent simultaneous users from interfering with each other.
- *Confined, or memoryless, subsystems:* In this case, processes are grouped into subsystems to enforce a particular protection policy. For example, a "client" process calls a "server" process to perform some task on data. The server is to be protected against the client's discovering the algorithm by which it performs the task, and the client is to be protected against the server's retaining any information about the task being performed.
- *Controlled information dissemination:* In some systems, security classes are defined to enforce a particular dissemination policy. Users and applications are given security clearances of a certain level, whereas data and other resources (e.g., I/O devices) are given security classifications. The security policy enforces restrictions concerning which users have access to which classifications.

This model is useful not only in the military context but in commercial applications as well.

Much of the work in security and protection as it relates to operating systems can be roughly grouped into the following three categories.

- *Access control:* Is concerned with regulating user access to the total system, subsystems, and data, and regulating process access to various resources and objects within the system.
- *Information flow control:* Regulates the flow of data within the system and its delivery to users.
- *Certification:* Relates to proving that access and flow control mechanisms perform according to their specifications and that they enforce desired protection and security policies.

Scheduling and Resource Management

A key task of the operating system is to manage the various resources available to it (main memory space, I/O devices, processors) and to schedule their use by the various active processes. Any resource allocation and scheduling policy must consider the following three factors:

- *Fairness:* Typically, we would like all processes that are competing for the use of a particular resource to be given approximately equal and fair access to that resource. This is especially so for jobs of the same class, that is, jobs of similar demands, which are charged the same rate.
- *Differential responsiveness:* On the other hand, the operating system may need to discriminate between different classes of jobs with different service requirements. The operating system should attempt to make allocation and scheduling decisions to meet the total set of requirements. The operating system should also view these decisions dynamically. For example, if a process is waiting for the use of an I/O device, the operating system may wish to schedule that process for execution as soon as possible in order to free up the device for later demands from other processes.
- *Efficiency:* Within the constraints of fairness and efficiency, the operating system should attempt to maximize throughput, minimize response time, and in the case of time sharing, accommodate as many users as possible.

The scheduling and resource management task is essentially an operations-research problem, and the mathematical results of that discipline can be applied. In addition, measurement of system activity is important to be able to monitor performance and to make adjustments.

Figure 2.12 suggests the major elements of the operating system involved in the scheduling of processes and the allocation of resources in a multiprogramming environment. The operating system maintains a number of queues, each of which is simply a list of processes waiting for some resource. The short-term

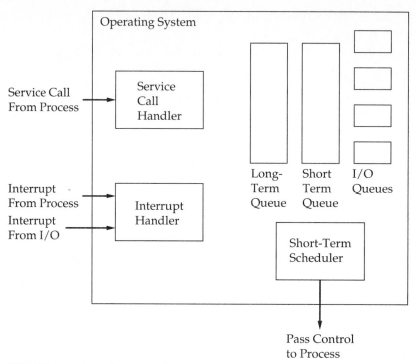

FIGURE 2.12 Key elements of an operating system for multiprogramming

queue consists of processes that are in main memory (or at least an essential minimum portion is in main memory) and are ready to run. Any one of these processes could use the processor next. It is up to the short-term scheduler, or dispatcher, to pick one. A common strategy is to give each process in the queue some time in turn; this is referred to as a *round-robin technique*. Priority levels may also be used.

The long-term queue is a list of new jobs waiting to use the system. The operating system adds jobs to the system by transferring a process from the long-term queue to the short-term queue. At that time, a portion of main memory must be allocated to the incoming process. Thus, the operating system must be sure that it does not overcommit memory or processing time by admitting too many processes to the system. There is an I/O queue for each I/O device. More than one process may request the use of the same I/O device. All processes waiting to use each device are lined up in the devices' queues. Again, the operating system must determine which process to assign to an available I/O device.

The operating system receives control of the processor at the interrupt handler if an interrupt occurs. A process may specifically invoke some operating-system service, such as an I/O device handler, by means of a service call. In this case, a service-call handler is the entry point into the operating system. In any case, once the interrupt or service call is handled, the short-term scheduler is invoked to pick a process for execution.

The foregoing description is functional only; details and modular design of this portion of the operating system differ in various systems. These general functions must be performed, however. Much of the research and development effort in operating systems has been directed at picking algorithms and data structures for this function that provide fairness, differential responsiveness, and efficiency.

System Structure

As more and more features have been added to operating systems and as the underlying hardware has become more complex and versatile, the size and complexity of operating systems has grown (Figure 2.13). The Compatible Time-Sharing System (CTSS), put into operation at MIT in 1963, consisted, at its peak, of approximately 32,000 36-bit words of storage. OS/360, introduced a year later by IBM, had more than a million machine instructions. By 1973, the Multics system, developed by MIT and Bell Laboratories, had grown to more than 20

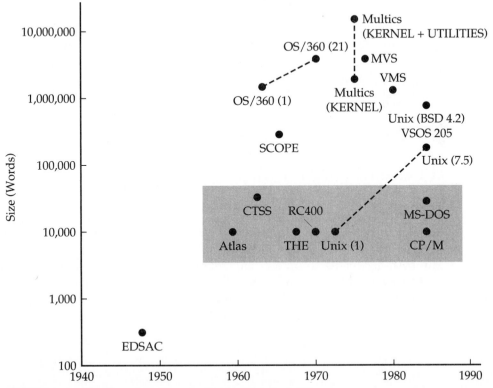

FIGURE 2.13 The size of some operating systems (words)

million instructions. It is true that more recently some simpler operating systems have been introduced for smaller systems, but these have inevitably grown more complex as the underlying hardware and users' requirements have grown. Thus, the UNIX of today is far more complex than the toylike system put together by a few talented programmers in the early 1970s, and the simple PC-DOS has given way to the rich and complex power of OS/2.

The size of a full-featured operating system and the difficulty of the task it addresses have led to three unfortunate but all too common problems. First, operating systems are chronically late in being delivered. This goes for new operating systems and for upgrades of older systems. Second, the systems have latent bugs that show up in the field and must be fixed and reworked. And finally, performance is often not what was expected.

To manage the complexity of operating systems and to overcome these problems, much attention has been given over the years to the software structure of the operating system. Certain points seem obvious. The software must be modular. This helps to organize the software development process and limits the task of diagnosing and fixing errors. The modules must have well-defined interfaces to each other, and the interfaces must be as simple as possible. Again, this eases the programming task. It also makes the task of system evolution easier. With clean, minimal interfaces between modules, one module can be changed with minimal impact on other modules.

As an example consider the VMS operating system, which runs on DEC VAX machines.[3] The VMS consists of three major subsystems:

- *I/O subsystem:* Consists of device drivers and their associated data structures, together with device-independent routines that relate to the task of controlling I/O.
- *Memory management:* The main components of this subsystem are the virtual memory facility, which allocates and controls the use of virtual memory, and the swapper, which controls the number of active processes in the system.
- *Scheduler:* Selects programs for execution and provides other process-control services. For example, it can provide one process the ability to control the execution of another.

There is actually little interaction among these three major subsystems of the operating system. In addition, each of the three components is responsible for its own section of executive data structures. When one of the other pieces of the system wishes to access such data structures, it does so through some controlled interface. Figure 2.14 shows the small amount of interaction that occurs among the three. These interactions can be summarized as follows:

- *I/O subsystem requests:* When the I/O subsystem is about to engage in an ex-

---

[3]Some of the terminology used in this discussion and the accompanying illustration has not yet been introduced but will be explored in later chapters. For now, the general structure and philosophy are all that is important.

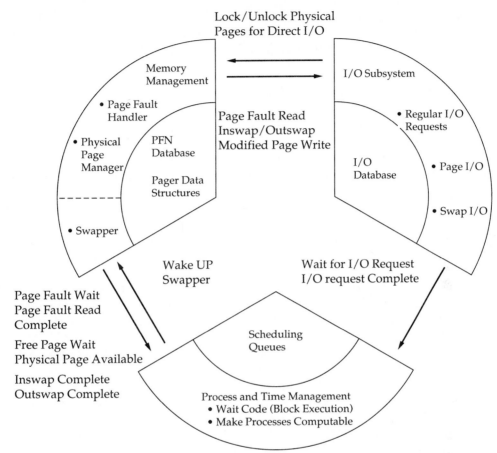

FIGURE 2.14 Interaction between components of VAX VMS kernel [KENA88]

change of data with a device, it makes a request to memory management to lock certain blocks of real memory, called *pages*, to prevent them from being swapped out or used by other processes during an I/O operation. I/O requests can result in the requesting process being placed in a wait state until the request completes. This change of process state requires that the scheduler be notified. Correspondingly, I/O completion can also cause a change in the scheduling state of a process. Again, the scheduler is notified.

- *Memory-management requests:* The virtual memory facility and the swapper both require the use of the I/O subsystem to move pages between disk and main memory. When a process needs access to a portion of its virtual memory that is not currently in main memory or if a process requires physical memory to be swapped in and none is available, the scheduler is notified to put the process in a wait state. When the memory requirement is satisfied, the scheduler is again notified.

- *Scheduler requests:* The scheduler interacts very little with the rest of the system. It functions in a passive role when cooperation with memory management or the I/O subsystem is required. One exception is that the scheduler triggers the swapper when a new process becomes eligible to be swapped into the system.

For large operating systems, which run from the hundreds of thousands to the millions of lines of code, modular programming alone has not been found to be sufficient. Instead, there has been increasing use of the concepts of hierarchical layers and information abstraction. The hierarchical structure of a modern operating system separates its functions according to their complexity, their characteristic time scale, and their level of abstraction. We can view the system as a series of levels. Each level performs a related subset of the functions required of the operating system. It relies on the next lower level to perform more primitive functions and to conceal the details of those functions. It provides services to the next higher layer. Ideally, the levels should be defined so that changes in one level do not require changes in other levels. Thus, we have decomposed one problem into a number of more manageable subproblems.

In general, lower layers deal with a far shorter time scale. Some parts of the operating system must interact directly with the computer hardware, where events can have a time scale as brief as a few billionths of a second. At the other end of the spectrum, parts of the operating system communicate with the user, who issues commands at a much more leisurely pace, perhaps one every few seconds. The use of a set of levels conforms nicely to this environment.

The way in which these principles are applied varies greatly among contemporary operating systems. However, it is useful at this point, for the purpose of gaining an overview of operating systems, to present a model of a hierarchical operating system. One proposed by Brown and his associates [BROW84] and by Denning and Brown [DENN84] is useful, although it does not correspond to any particular operating system. The model is defined in Table 2.4, and consists of the following levels:

- *Level 1:* Consists of electronic circuits, where the objects that are dealt with are registers, memory cells, and logic gates. The operation defined on these objects are actions such as clearing a register or reading a memory location.
- *Level 2:* Is the processor's instruction set. The operations at this level are those allowed in the machine-language instruction set, such as ADD, SUBTRACT, LOAD, and STORE.
- *Level 3:* Adds the concept of a procedure or subroutine, plus the call-return operations.
- *Level 4:* Introduces interrupts, which cause the processor to save the current context and invoke an interrupt-handling routine.

These first four levels are not part of the operating system but constitute the processor hardware. However, some elements of the operating system begin to

TABLE 2.4   Operating System Design Hierarchy

Level	Name	Objects	Example Operations
13	Shell	User programming environment	Statements in shell language
12	User processes	User processes	Quit, kill, suspend, resume
11	Directories	Directories	Create, destroy, attach, detach, search, list
10	Devices	External devices, such as printers, displays, and keyboards	Create, destroy, open, close, read, write
9	File system	Files	Create, destroy, open, close, read, write
8	Communications	Pipes	Create, destroy, open, close, read, write
7	Virtual memory	Segments, pages	Read, write, fetch
6	Local secondary store	Blocks of data, device channels	Read, write, allocate, free
5	Primitive processes	Primitive process, semaphores, ready list	Suspend, resume, wait, signal
4	Interrupts	Interrupt-handling programs	Invoke, mask, unmask, retry
3	Procedures	Procedures, call stack, display	Mark stack, call, return
2	Instruction set	Evaluation stack, microprogram interpreter, scalar and array data	Load, store, add, subtract, branch
1	Electronic circuits	Registers, gates, buses, etc.	Clear, transfer, activate, complement

appear at these levels, such as the interrupt-handling routines. It is at level 5 that we begin to reach the operating system proper and that the concepts associated with multiprogramming begin to appear.

- *Level 5:* The notion of a process as a program in execution is introduced at this level. The fundamental requirements on the operating system to support multiple processes include the ability to suspend and resume processes. This requires saving hardware registers so that execution can be switched from one process to another. In addition, if processes need to cooperate, then some method of synchronization is needed. One of the simplest techniques, and an important concept in operating system design, is the semaphore. The semaphore is a simple signaling technique that is explored in Chapter 4.
- *Level 6:* Deals with the secondary storage devices of the computer. At this level, the functions of positioning the read/write heads and the actual transfer of blocks of data occur. Level 6 relies on level 5 to schedule the operation and

to notify the requesting process of completion of an operation. Higher levels are concerned with the address of the needed data on the disk and provide a request for the appropriate block to a device driver at level 5.

- *Level 7:* Creates a logical address space for processes. This level organizes the virtual address space into blocks that can be moved between main memory and secondary memory. Three schemes are in common use: those using fixed-size pages, those using variable-length segments, and those using both. When a needed block is not in main memory, logic at this level requests a transfer from level 6.

Up to this point, the operating system deals with the resources of a single processor. Beginning with level 8, the operating system deals with external objects such as peripheral devices and possibly networks and computers attached to the network. The objects at these upper levels are logical, named objects that can be shared among processes on the same computer or on multiple computers.

- *Level 8:* Deals with the communication of information and messages between processes. Whereas level 5 provided a primitive signal mechanism that allowed for the synchronization of processes, this level deals with a richer sharing of information. One of the most powerful tools for this purpose is the pipe, which is a logical channel for the flow of data between processes. A *pipe* is defined with its output from one process and its input into another process. It can also be used to link external devices or files to processes. The concept is discussed in Chapter 4.
- *Level 9:* Supports the long storage of named files. At this level, the data on secondary storage is viewed in terms of abstract, variable-length entities, in contrast to the hardware-oriented view of secondary storage in terms of tracks, sectors, and fixed-size blocks at level 6.
- *Level 10:* Provides access to external devices using standardized interfaces.
- *Level 11:* Is responsible for maintaining the association between the external and internal identifiers of the system's resources and objects. The external identifier is a name that can be employed by an application or user. The internal identifier is an address or other indicator that can be used by lower levels of the operating system to locate and control an object. These associations are maintained in a directory. Entries include not only external/internal mapping but also characteristics such as access rights.
- *Level 12:* Provides a full-featured facility for the support of processes. This goes far beyond what is provided at level 5. At level 5, only the processor register contents associated with a process are maintained, plus the logic for dispatching processes. At level 12, all the information needed for the orderly management of processes is supported. This includes the virtual address space of the process, a list of objects and processes with which it may interact and the constraints of that interaction, parameters passed to the process upon creation,

and any other characteristics of the process that might be used by the operating system to control the process.

- *Level 13:* Provides an interface to the operating system for the user. It is referred to as the *shell* because it separates the user from operating-system details and presents the operating system simply as a collection of services. The shell accepts user commands or job control statements, interprets these, and creates and controls processes as needed.

This hypothetical model of an operating system provides a useful descriptive structure as well as serving as an implementation guideline. You may wish to refer back to this structure during the course of the book to observe the context of any particular design issue under discussion.

2.4

EXAMPLE SYSTEMS

This text is intended to acquaint you with the design principles and implementation issues of contemporary operating systems. Accordingly, a purely conceptual or theoretical treatment would be inadequate. To illustrate the concepts and to tie them to real-world design choices that must be made, three operating systems have been chosen as running examples:

- *OS/2:* A single-user, multitasking operating system for the IBM PS/2 and compatible systems. It is one of the few truly new operating systems that has been essentially designed from scratch (although it includes an MS-DOS compatibility mode). As such, it is in a position to incorporate in a clean fashion the latest developments in operating system technology.
- *UNIX:* A multiuser operating system originally intended for minicomputers but implemented on a wide range of machines from powerful microcomputers to supercomputers.
- *MVS (Multiple Virtual Storage):* The top-of-the-line operating system for IBM mainframes and one of the most complex operating systems ever developed. It provides both batch and time-sharing capabilities.

These three systems were chosen because of their relevance and representativeness. Most personal computer operating systems on new machines are single-user, multitasking systems, with OS/2 being the market leader. UNIX has become the dominant operating system on a wide variety of workstations and multiuser systems. MVS is the most widely used mainframe operating system.

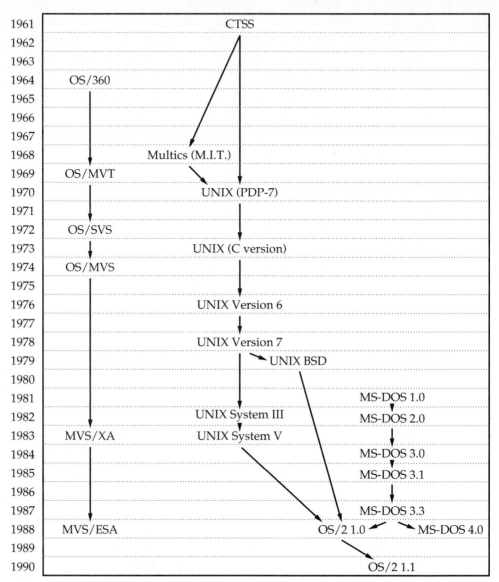

FIGURE 2.15 Operating systems over the years

Thus, most readers will have been exposed to one or more of these operating systems by the time they use this book or within a few years of doing so.

In this section we provide a brief description and history of each operating system. Figure 2.15 summarizes the historical narrative.

OS/2

History

The ancestor of OS/2 is an operating system developed by Microsoft for the first IBM personal computer and referred to as MS-DOS or PC-DOS. The initial release, MS-DOS 1.0, was released in August 1981. It consisted of 4,000 lines of assembly-language source code and ran in 8 KB of memory using the Intel 8086 microprocessor.

When IBM developed a personal computer based on a hard disk, the PC XT, Microsoft developed MS-DOS 2.0. This new version was released in 1983. It contained support for the hard disk and provided for hierarchical directories. Heretofore, a disk could contain only one directory of files, supporting a maximum of 64 files. Although this was adequate in the era of floppy disks, it was too limited for a hard disk, and the single-directory restriction was too clumsy. The new release allowed directories to contain subdirectories as well as files. The new release also contained a richer set of commands embedded in the operating system to provide functions that had to be performed by external programs provided as utilities with release 1. Among the capabilities added were several UNIX-like features, such as I/O redirection, which is the ability to change the input or output identity for a given application, and background printing. The memory-resident portion grew to 24 KB.

When IBM announced the PC AT in 1984, Microsoft introduced MS-DOS 3.0. The AT contained the Intel 80286 processor, which provided extended addressing and memory protection features. These were not used by MS-DOS. To remain compatible with previous releases, the operating system simply used the 80286 as a "fast 8086." The operating system did provide support for new keyboard and hard disk peripherals. Even so, the memory requirement grew to 36 KB. There were several notable upgrades to the 3.0 release. MS-DOS 3.1, released in 1984, contained support for networking of PCs. The size of the resident portion did not change; this was achieved by increasing the amount of the operating system that could be swapped. MS-DOS 3.3, released in 1987, provided support for the new line of IBM machines, the PS/2. Again, this release did not take advantage of the processor capabilities of the PS/2 provided by the 80286 and the 32-bit 80386 chips. The resident portion at this stage had grown to a minimum of 46 KB, with more required if certain optional extensions were selected.

By this time, MS-DOS was being used in an environment far beyond its capabilities. Nevertheless, to provide service to existing users, another upgrade was released in 1989 as MS-DOS 4.0. This is a specialized system that provides a limited form of multiprogramming, or multitasking. However, it still uses the advanced Intel chips as fast 8086s. Thus, the memory on this system is limited to 640 KB with no swapping. That is, all processes must be fully resident in main memory; there is no virtual memory support.

Meanwhile, Microsoft and IBM were at work jointly on an operating system worthy of the power of the 80286 and 80386 processors. The result is OS/2, which many observers believe is destined to become the most widely used operating system. The first release, OS/2 1.0, provides full multitasking in a single-user environment. An upgrade, OS/2 1.1, provides for a more flexible user interface with the use of windows and menus in the style of Macintosh.

Description

The OS/2 is the most important example of what has become the new wave in personal computer operating systems. The development of the OS/2 was driven by a need to exploit the tremendous power of today's 32-bit microprocessor, which rivals the mainframes and minicomputers of just a few years ago in speed, hardware sophistication, and memory capacity.

Perhaps the most significant feature of these new operating systems is that, although they are still intended for support of a single interactive user, they are multitasking operating systems. Two main developments have triggered the need for multitasking on personal computers. First, with the increased speed and memory capacity of microprocessors, together with the support for virtual memory, applications have become more complex and interrelated. A user may wish to employ a word processor, a drawing program, and a spreadsheet application simultaneously to produce a document. Without multitasking, if a user wishes to create a drawing and paste it into a word processing document, the following steps are required:

1. Open the drawing program.
2. Create the drawing and save it in a file or on a temporary clipboard.
3. Close the drawing program.
4. Open the word processing program.
5. Insert the drawing in the correct location.

If any changes are desired, the user must close the word processing program, open the drawing program, edit the graphic image, save it, close the drawing program, open the word processing program, and insert the updated image. This becomes tedious very quickly. As the services and capabilities available to users become more powerful and varied, the single-task environment becomes more clumsy and user-unfriendly. In a multitasking environment, the user opens each application as needed, *and leaves it open*. Information can be easily moved around among a number of applications. Each application has one or more open windows, and a graphical interface with a pointing device such as a mouse allows the user to quickly navigate in this environment.

A second motivation for multitasking is the growth of cooperative processing. Cooperative processing occurs when a personal computer and a mainframe are used jointly to accomplish a particular application. The two are linked together and each is assigned that portion of the job that it is suited to. Cooperative processing can also be achieved in a local area network of personal computers and servers. An application may involve one or more personal computers and one or more server devices. To provide the required responsiveness, the operating system needs to provide support sophisticated real-time communication hardware and the associated communications protocols and data transfer architectures while at the same time supporting ongoing user interaction.

Although OS/2 has grown out of the hardware evolution of IBM's personal computers and the capabilities and services of MS-DOS, its internal architecture is actually rather closer to UNIX than it is to MS-DOS. We will see many examples of this throughout the book. However, OS/2 is not simply a proprietary version of UNIX. Instead, it is a powerful, full-featured operating system with many features and design decisions that are unique to itself. Two sets of design constraints forced the designers of OS/2 to use novel techniques in a number of areas to meet the requirements imposed on the system [KOGA88]. The first set of design constraints is architectural in nature:

- Provide a way to run the vast body of existing MS-DOS applications.
- Effectively use the large physical memory that can be attached to the 80286 and 80386 processors.

These constraints are in conflict. The resolution of this conflict is a significant design achievement of OS/2.

The other set of constraints relates to the use of a small-system platform:

- Provide the features of a full-scale operating system, such as might be found on larger microcomputers and on minicomputers.
- Execute without consuming large amounts of system resources in order to fit on the machines it is intended to support.

As always with these types of constraints, the result is a compromise between complex and powerful ways of implementing features and simpler, less functional means of providing them.

Figure 2.16 shows the basic structure of OS/2, which is organized in levels. At the lowest level are the device drivers, which are system routines that interface with the peripheral devices and provide the logic for controlling the basic transfer of bits between devices and the processor. Above them comes the main body of the operating system, which provides basic system services. Above that is an application program interface, which serves as a shell for users and application programs.

One final aspect of OS/2 is worth mentioning. It has taken the concept of process to a degree of sophistication not found on most other operating systems. Actually, there are three levels of concepts used in OS/2 that relate to what is traditionally referred to as a process:

- *Thread:* A dispatchable unit of work. It is the thing that executes sequentially and is interruptable so that the processor can turn to another thread. From the point of view of scheduling and dispatching, this concept is equivalent to that of process on most other operating systems.
- *Process:* A collection of one or more threads and associated system resources

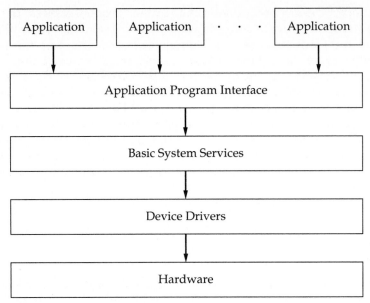

FIGURE 2.16 OS/2 structure

(such as memory, open files, and devices). This corresponds closely to the concept of a program in execution. By breaking a single application up into multiple threads, the programmer has great control over the modularity of the application and the timing of application-related events. From the point of view of the job or application, this concept is equivalent to that of process on most other operating systems.

• *Session:* A collection of one or more processes associated with a user interface (keyboard, display, mouse). This concept allows the personal computer user to open more than one application, giving each one or more windows on the screen. The operating system must keep track of which window, and therefore which session, is active, so that keyboard and mouse input are routed to the appropriate session. From the point of view of interactive user control, this concept is equivalent to that of process on most other operating systems.

The concepts of thread, process, and session will be examined in detail in Chapter 3.

UNIX System V

History

The history of UNIX is an oft-told tale and will not be repeated in great detail here. Instead, a brief summary is provided.

UNIX was initially developed at Bell Labs and became operational on a PDP-7 in 1970. Some of the people involved at Bell Labs had also participated in the time-sharing work being done at MIT's Project MAC. That project led to the development of first CTSS and then Multics. Although it is common to say that UNIX is a scaled-down version of Multics, the developers of UNIX actually claimed to be more influenced by CTSS [RITC78b]. Nevertheless, UNIX incorporated many ideas from Multics.

It is worth saying a few words about Multics. Multics was not just years but decades ahead of its time. Even by the mid-1980s, almost 20 years after it became operational, Multics had superior security features and greater sophistication in the user interface and other areas than comparable contemporary mainframe operating systems. Although the UNIX developers dropped out of the Multics project because of their sense that it was a failure, Multics was later transferred to Honeywell and went on to enjoy modest commercial success. Had Honeywell not had two other mainframe operating systems, one of which it was marketing very aggressively, Multics might have had a greater success. Nevertheless, Multics remained a Honeywell product with a small but faithful customer base until Honeywell got out of the computer business in the late 1980s. Honeywell also developed a scaled-down version of Multics to run on its minicomputer line. Its developers used the working title of "mini-Multics." One must question the judgment shown by Honeywell when they chose to market this gem of an operating system under the uninspiring name GCOS 6.

Meanwhile, work on UNIX at Bell Labs, and later elsewhere, produced a series of versions of UNIX. The first notable milestone was porting the UNIX system from the PDP-7 to the PDP-11. This was the first hint that UNIX would be an operating system for all computers. The next important milestone was the rewriting of UNIX in the programming language C. This was an unheard-of strategy at the time. It was generally felt that something as complex as an operating system, which must deal with time-critical events, had to be written exclusively in assembly language. The C implementation demonstrated the advantages of using a high-level language for most if not all of the system code. Today, virtually all UNIX implementations are written in C.

These early versions of UNIX were quite popular within Bell Labs. In 1974, the UNIX system was described in a technical journal for the first time [RITC74]. This spurred great interest in the system. Licenses for UNIX were provided to commercial institutions as well as universities. The first widely available version outside Bell Labs was Version 6, in 1976. The follow-on Version 7, released in 1978, is the ancestor of most modern UNIX systems. The most important of the non-AT&T systems to be developed was done at the University of California at Berkeley. It was called UNIX BSD and ran first on PDP and then VAX machines. AT&T continued to develop and refine the system. By 1982, Bell Labs had combined several AT&T variants of UNIX into a single system that was marketed commercially as UNIX System III. A number of features were later added to the operating system to produce UNIX System V.

This book uses UNIX System V as its UNIX example. At the time of this writing, it appears that this will become the dominant commercial version of UNIX. Furthermore, it incorporates most of the important features ever developed on any UNIX system and does so in an integrated, commercially viable fashion. System V is currently running on machines ranging from 32-bit microprocessors up to supercomputers, and it is clearly one of the most important operating systems ever developed.

Description

Figure 2.17 provides a general description of the UNIX architecture. The underlying hardware is surrounded by the operating system software. The operating system is often called the *system kernel*, or simply the *kernel*, to emphasize its isolation from the user and applications. This portion of UNIX is what we will be concerned with in our use of UNIX as an example in this book. However, UNIX comes equipped with a number of user services and interfaces that are considered part of the system. These can be grouped into the shell, other interface software, and the components of the C compiler (compiler, assembler,

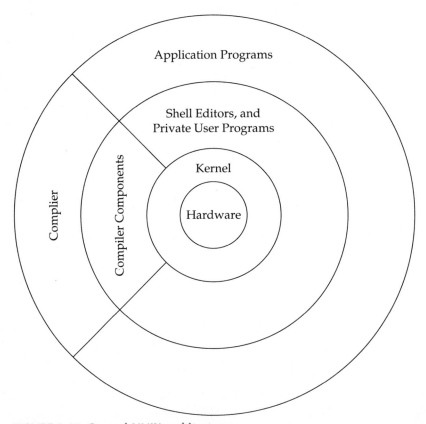

FIGURE 2.17 General UNIX architecture

loader). The layer outside of this consists of user applications and the user interface to the C compiler.

A closer look at the kernel is provided in Figure 2.18. User programs can invoke operating-system services either directly or through library programs. The system call interface is the boundary with the user and allows higher-level software to gain access to specific kernel functions. At the other end, the operating system contains primitive routines that interact directly with the hardware. Between these two interfaces, the system is divided into two main parts, one concerned with process control and the other concerned with file management and I/O. The process-control subsystem is responsible for memory manage-

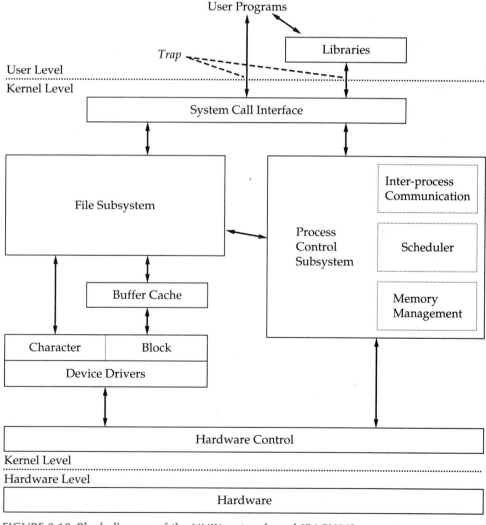

FIGURE 2.18 Block diagram of the UNIX system kernel [BACH86]

ment, the scheduling and dispatching of processes, and the synchronization and interprocess communication of processes. The file system exchanges data between memory and external devices either as a stream of characters or in blocks. To achieve this, a variety of device drivers are used. For block-oriented transfers, a disk cache approach is used: A system buffer in main memory is interposed between the user address space and the external device.

MVS

History

By 1964, IBM had a firm grip on the computer market with its 7000 series of machines. In that year, IBM announced the System/360, a new family of computer products. Although the announcement itself was no surprise, it contained some unpleasant news for current IBM customers: The 360 product line was incompatible with older IBM machines. Thus, the transition to the 360 would be difficult for the current customer base. This was a bold step by IBM but one they felt was necessary to break out of some of the constraints of the 7000 architecture and to produce a system capable of evolving with the new integrated circuit technology. The strategy paid off both financially and technically. The 360 was the success of the decade and cemented IBM as the overwhelmingly dominant computer vendor with a market share above 70%. And, with some modifications and extensions, the architecture of the 360 remains to this day, more than a quarter of a century later, the architecture of IBM's large computers.

Although the operating-system software for IBM's mainframes has changed beyond recognition from that of the initial 360 offering, its origins can be traced back to those early days. The System/360 was the industry's first planned family of computers. The family covered a wide range of performance and cost. The various models were compatible in that a program written for one model was capable of being executed by another model in the family with only a difference in the time needed to execute. Thus, the first announced operating system for the new machines, OS/360, was intended to be a single operating system that could operate on all machines in the family. However, the widening spectrum of the 360 family and the diversity of user needs forced IBM to introduce a variety of operating systems. Here, we concentrate on the line of development that led to MVS (Multiple Virtual Storage).

The original OS/360 was a multiprogramming batch system and remained so for some time. Its most complete version, MVT (Multiprogramming with a Variable number of Tasks) was released in 1969 and was the most flexible of the OS/360 variants. The memory allocation for a job was variable and need not be decided until run time. It became the most popular operating system on IBM's large 360s and early large 370s. MVT was missing some of the features present in the more advanced of its competitors' offerings, such as the ability to support multiple processors, virtual storage, and source-level debugging, but it did provide a more complete set of facilities and supporting utilities than any other contemporary operating system. In such areas as job scheduling, peripheral support, number of different systems supported, and conversion support from older systems, OS/360 was unequaled [WEIZ81].

MVT allowed only 15 jobs to run concurrently. OS/SVS (Single Virtual Storage) was introduced in 1972 as an interim operating system to take advantage of the IBM/370 architecture. The most noteworthy addition 'was support for virtual memory. With SVS, a virtual address space of 16 MB was established. However, this address space had to be shared among the operating system and all active jobs. Soon, even this amount of memory appeared inadequate.

In response to growing memory needs of application programmers, IBM introduced MVS. As with SVS, and as dictated by the 370 architecture, virtual addresses were limited to 24 bits and hence 16 MB. However, with MVS, the limit is 16 MB *per job*. That is, each job has its own dedicated virtual memory of 16 MB. The operating system maps blocks of virtual memory into real main memory and is able to keep track of the separate virtual memories for each job. Actually, each job typically gets something less than half of its assigned virtual memory; the rest is available for use by the operating system.

The 24-bit address space, even with separate virtual memories for each job, quickly became inadequate for some users. IBM extended its underlying processor to handle 31-bit addresses, a facility known as *extended addressing* (XA). To take advantage of this new hardware, a new version of MVS, known as MVS/XA, was introduced in 1983. With MVS/XA, the per-job address space grew to a maximum of 2 GB (gigabytes). This, believe it or not, is still not considered adequate for some environments and some applications. Accordingly, in what may represent the last major extension of the 370 (really the 360) architecture, IBM developed the Enterprise System Architecture (ESA) and the enhanced operating system, MVS/ESA. The same 2-GB address space per job that was available in MVS/XA is also available for programs and data. What is new is that there are up to 15 additional 2-GB address spaces for data available only to a specific job. Thus, the maximum addressable virtual memory per job is 32 GB.

Description

MVS is probably the largest and most complex operating system ever developed. It requires a minimum of 2 MB of resident storage. A more realistic configuration would require 6 MB for the operating system. The four most important factors that have determined the design of MVS are the following:

- Support of batch and interactive jobs
- Virtual storage of up to 32 GB per job or user
- Tightly coupled multiprocessing; this architecture, which is examined in Chapter 6, consists of a number of processors that share the same main memory.

• Sophisticated resource allocation and monitoring facilities to achieve efficient use of the system's large memory, multiple processors, and complex I/O channel structure.

The need to deal with multiple processors is a requirement not faced in OS/2 and UNIX System V. When there are multiple processors, each of which may execute any process, and when communication among processes running on different processors is supported, the complexity of the operating system can be significantly greater than for a single-processor machine.

Figure 2.19 gives a simplified view of the major building blocks. An outer shell contains services and interfaces visible to users and to system operators responsible for maintaining and tuning the system. In addition to a collection

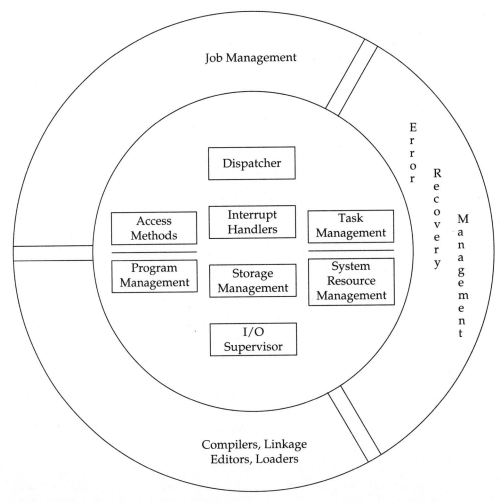

FIGURE 2.19 Simplified view of building blocks of the MVS operating system [PRAS81]

of programs needed for program creation and compilation, there is a job management subsystem with the following functions:

- Interpret operator commands (from an operator console) and route appropriate messages.
- Read job input data from and write job output data to peripheral devices.
- Allocate I/O devices to a job and notify the operator of any physical data units (e.g., tape reel, disk pack) that have to be mounted prior to the execution of a job.
- Convert the job into tasks that can be processed by task management.

Finally, the outer shell includes an elaborate management subsystem for error recovery that assures that job faults are isolated so as to not interfere with the rest of the operation and so that the fault can be diagnosed. If possible, the job or jobs affected by the error will be enabled to continue execution.

The core of the operating system consists of a set of major modules or subsystems that interact with each other, the hardware, and the outer shell. These include the following:

- *Dispatcher:* The dispatcher can be regarded as the manager of the processors. Its function is to scan the queue of ready tasks and to schedule one for execution.
- *Interrupt handlers:* The System/370 architecture supports a wide variety of interrupts. Any interrupt causes the current process to be suspended and control to pass to the appropriate handler routine.
- *Task management:* A task is essentially a process, as we have used that latter term. Task management is responsible for the creation and deletion of tasks, the control of their priorities, the management of task queues for serially reusable resources (e.g., I/O devices), and the synchronization of events.
- *Program management:* This module is responsible for linking together the necessary steps involved in the execution of a program. This module can be driven by JCL commands or in response to user requests to compile and execute a program.
- *Storage management:* This module is responsible for managing virtual and real memory.
- *System resource management:* This module is responsible for the allocation of resources among address spaces (processes).
- *Access methods:* An application program usually employs an access method in performing an I/O operation. An access method is an interface between an application program and the I/O supervisor. An access method relieves the application program from the burden of writing channel programs, building various control blocks required by the I/O supervisor, and handling termination conditions.
- *I/O supervisor:* The I/O supervisor performs initiation and completion of the I/O operation at a hardware level. It issues the Start I/O instruction, which causes an I/O channel processor to execute an I/O program from main mem-

ory, and it also handles the interrupt arising from completion of I/O operations.

It is worth saying a few words here about the system resources manager (SRM). The SRM gives MVS a degree of sophistication unique among operating systems. No other mainframe operating system, and certainly no other type of operating system, can match the functions performed by SRM.

The concept of resource includes processor, real memory, and I/O channels. In performing resource allocation, SRM accumulates statistics pertaining to the use of processor, channel, and various key data structures. Its purpose is to provide optimum performance based on performance monitoring and analysis. The installation sets forth various performance objectives, and these serve as guidance to the SRM, which dynamically modifies installation and job performance characteristics based on system use. In turn, the SRM provides reports that enable the trained operator to refine the configuration and parameter settings to improve service to the user.

One example will give the flavor of SRM activity. Real memory is divided into equal-sized blocks called frames, of which there may be many thousands. Each frame can hold a block of virtual memory, which is referred to as a *page*. SRM receives control approximately 20 times per second and inspects each and every page frame. If the page has not been referenced or changed, a counter is incremented by 1. Over a period, SRM averages these numbers to determine the average number of seconds that a page frame in the system goes untouched. The system operator can review this quantity to determine the degree of "stress" on the system. By reducing the number of active jobs allowed on the system, this average can be kept high. One useful guideline is that this average should be kept above 2 minutes to avoid major performance problems [JOHN89]. That may sound like a lot, but it isn't.

2.5

OUTLINE OF THE REMAINDER OF THE BOOK

The first two chapters have provided an overview of computer architecture and operating systems, and an introduction to the remainder of the book. This section provides a brief synopsis of the remaining chapters.

Process Description and Control

The concept of the process is central to the study of operating systems and is examined in detail in Chapter 3. Process descriptors and logical resource descriptors are defined. A discussion of the typical elements of these descriptors forms the basis for a discussion of the functions related to processes that are performed by the operating system. Process control primitives are described. A state description of processes (ready, running, blocked, etc.) is also presented. The important new concept of the thread is also examined in some detail in this chapter.

Concurrency

The two central themes of modern operating systems are multiprogramming and distributed processing. Fundamental to both these themes, and fundamental to the technology of operating system design, is concurrency. When multiple processes are executing concurrently, either actually in the case of a multiprocessor system, or virtually in the case of a single-processor multiprogramming system, issues of conflict resolution and cooperation arise. Chapter 4 examines conflict resolution mechanisms in the context of critical sections of process execution that must be controlled. Semaphores and messages are two key techniques employed in the control of critical sections by enforcing a discipline of mutual exclusion. The chapter also looks at two problems that plague all efforts to support concurrent processing: deadlock and starvation.

Memory Management

Chapter 5 deals with the management of main memory. It provides a description of the objectives of memory management in terms of the overlay problem and the need for protection and sharing. The chapter proceeds with a discussion of program loading and the concept of relocation. This leads into a discussion of segmentation. The mechanisms—hardware and software—needed to support segmentation are discussed. Then, paging and virtual memory are introduced. The chapter includes a discussion of the interplay of hardware and software; secondary memory, main memory, and cache; segmentation and paging. The objective is to show how all these objects and mechanisms can be integrated into a total memory-management scheme.

Scheduling

Chapter 6 begins with an examination of the three types of processor scheduling: long-term, medium-term, and short-term. Issues of long-term and medium-term scheduling are also examined in Chapters 3 and 5. Accordingly, the bulk of the chapter focuses on short-term scheduling issues. The various algorithms that have been tried are examined and compared. Then, scheduling issues that relate specifically to multiprocessor configurations are examined. Finally, the chapter looks at the design considerations for real-time scheduling.

I/O Management and Disk Scheduling

Chapter 7 begins with a summary of I/O aspects of computer architecture and then moves on to the requirements that I/O places on the operating system.

Various buffering strategies are examined and compared. Then, issues relating to disk I/O are explored, including disk scheduling and the use of a disk cache.

File Management

Chapter 8 discusses physical and logical organization of data. It examines the services relating to file management that a typical operating system provides for users. It then looks at the specific mechanisms and data structures that are part of a file management system.

Networking and Distributed Processing

Increasingly, computers function not in isolation but as part of a network of computers and terminals. Chapter 9 begins with an examination of the concept of a communications architecture, with special emphasis on the open systems interconnection (OSI) model. The chapter then looks at the use of servers on local area networks and the requirements that these place on an operating system. Next, the increasingly important concept of process migration is examined. The remainder of the chapter looks at key elements of distributed operating systems, including process communication using messages, and the mechanisms for mutual exclusion and the detection and prevention of deadlock.

Security

Chapter 10 begins by examining the types of threats faced by computer communication complexes. Then, the bulk of the chapter deals with specific tools that can be used to enhance security. First to be examined are traditional approaches to computer security, which are based on the protection of various computer resources, including memory and data. Next, a relatively new approach to security, trusted systems, is examined. This is followed by a discussion of network security. The main body of the chapter closes with a look at a recent and increasingly worrisome type of threat: that posed by viruses and similar mechanisms. Finally, an appendix to this chapter introduces encryption, which is a basic tool used in many security applications.

Topic Ordering

It would be natural for you to question the particular ordering of topics presented in this book. For example, the topic of scheduling (Chapter 6) is closely related to those of concurrency (Chapter 4) and the general topic of processes (Chapter 3), and it might reasonably be covered immediately after those topics.

The difficulty is that the various topics are highly interrelated. For example, in discussing virtual memory, it is useful to be able to refer to the scheduling issues related to a page fault. Of course, it is also useful to be able to refer to some memory-management issues when discussing scheduling decisions! This type of example can be repeated endlessly: A discussion of scheduling requires some understanding of I/O management and vice versa.

Figure 2.20 suggests some of the important interrelationships between topics. The bold lines indicate very strong relationships from the point of view of design and implementation decisions. On the basis of this diagram, it would appear to make sense to begin with a basic discussion of processes, which we indeed do in Chapter 3. After that, the order is somewhat arbitrary. Many treatments of operating systems bunch all the material on processes at the beginning and then deal with other topics. This is certainly valid. However, the key importance of memory management, which I believe is of equal importance to process management, has led to my decision to present this material prior to an in-depth look at scheduling.

The ideal solution is for the student, after completing Chapters 1 through 3 in series, to read and absorb Chapters 4 through 7 in parallel, and then do Chapters 8, 9, and 10 in any order. However, although the human brain may engage in parallel processing, the human student finds it impossible (and expensive) to work successfully with four copies of the same book simultaneously open to four different chapters. Given the necessity for a linear ordering, I feel that the ordering used in this book is the most effective.

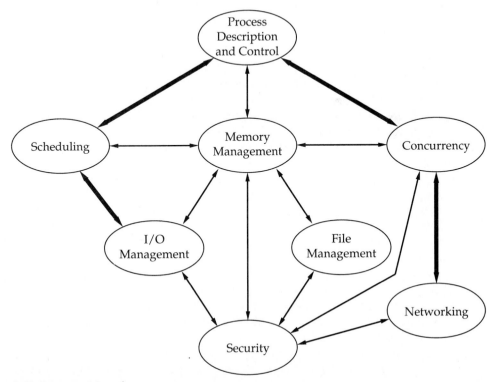

FIGURE 2.20 OS topics

2.6

RECOMMENDED READING

As in the area of computer architecture, there is a great number of books on operating systems. [SILB91] and [DEIT90] cover the basic principles using a number of important operating systems as case studies; somewhat less technical coverage is provided in [LANE89] and [MASS86]. Three books [TANE87, COME84, MILE87] take the interesting approach of providing step-by-step implementation details for small but complete UNIX-like operating systems. As I do in the present book, [DAVI87] takes the approach of providing a small number of important operating systems as running examples throughout the text. This latter book, however, emphasizes operating system services and the user interface rather than underlying mechanisms. Other books that do a good job of covering the basic principles at a technical level are [PINK89], [FINK88], and [BIC88]. [MAEK87] treats OS topics at a more advanced level.

We turn now to books devoted to our example systems. For UNIX, it sometimes seems that there as many UNIX books as there are computers running the system. At last count, Prentice-Hall alone had 84 UNIX books on its list! Virtually all these books, however, deal with the use of UNIX rather than its internal architecture and mechanisms. For UNIX System V, [BACH86] provides a definitive treatment with ample technical detail. A less detailed and more approachable reference is [SHAW87]. The student intent on a thorough investigation of System V would do well to read the latter reference first and then tackle Bach. Another book that covers UNIX internals is [ANDL90]; it provides a terse but systematic and exhaustive treatment of UNIX features and mechanisms. For the academically popular Berkeley UNIX 4.3BSD, [LEFF88] is highly recommended. Important collections of papers on UNIX were published in the July-August 1978 issue of the *Bell System Technical Journal* and the October 1984 issue of the AT&T *Bell Laboratories Technical Journal*. These were reprinted as [ATT87a and b].

Despite its relative youth, OS/2 is making a strong bid to compete with UNIX in the quantity of books. It seems as if everyone, including the parking lot attendant at Microsoft headquarters, has written about the system from their own perspective. The three best technical treatments are all done by people on the joint Microsoft–IBM development team. [LETW88] is a joy to read. It is at the same time highly technical and very approachable. Letwin, the chief architect of OS/2 for Microsoft, is at pains to explain the why as well as the how of OS/2. [KRAN88] is a good but perhaps slightly less technical treatment by three members of the IBM design team. [IACO88] is the massive (1100 pages) contribution of the leader of the IBM OS/2 design team. It is addressed to programmers with the objective of explaining the system in such a way that it can be exploited to the maximum by the programmer. Along the way, it provides a detailed exposition of OS/2 internals. As a final recommendation, the *IBM Systems Journal* No. 2, 1988, is devoted to OS/2 and contains a number of useful articles.

Alas, probably the largest and most complex, and certainly one of the most important operating systems, MVS, suffers from a dearth of explanation. One remarkable exception is [JOHN89]. This book is intended primarily for the system manager and computer-room operator, and it explains MVS from that perspective. However, in doing so, it provides a reasonable amount of technical depth on MVS. The principal achievement of this book is that it manages to provide a clear and comprehensive survey of MVS within the covers of a single book. [KATZ84] is also a technical treatment but is quite dated. The only other substantive books of which I am aware deal with MVS from a performance point of view: [PAAN86] and [SAMS90]. Finally, [LEBA84c] provides a concise but not detailed overview of MVS.

You may also wish to investigate the VMS operating system, which runs on the DEC VAX machines. This is one of the best designed, best documented, and most widely studied of operating systems. A good survey of both the VAX architecture and VMS is [LEVY89]. The definitive treatment is [KENA88], which is a model of how to document an operating system.

2.7

PROBLEMS

2.1 Suppose that we have a multiprogrammed computer in which each job has identical characteristics. In one computation period, T, for a job, half the time is spent in I/O and the other half in processor activity. Each job runs for a total of N periods. Define the following quantities:

- Turnaround time = actual time to complete a job
- Throughput = average number of jobs completed per time period T
- Processor utilization = percentage of time that the processor is active (not waiting)

Compute these quantities for one, two, and four simultaneous jobs, assuming that the period T is distributed in each of the following ways:
(a) I/O first half, processor second half
(b) I/O first and fourth quarters, processor second and third quarters

2.2 Define waiting time as the amount of time that a job spends waiting in the short-term queue (Figure 2.12). Give an equation that relates turnaround time, processor busy time, and waiting time.

2.3 An I/O-bound program is one that, if run alone, would spend more time waiting for I/O than using the processor. A processor-bound program is the opposite. Suppose a short-term scheduling algorithm favors those programs that have used little processor time in the recent past. Explain why this algorithm favors I/O-bound programs and yet does not permanently deny processor time to processor-bound programs.

2.4 A computer has a cache, main memory, and a disk used for virtual memory. If a word is in the cache, A *n*s are required to access it. If it is in main memory but not in cache, B *n*s are needed to load it into the cache, and then the reference is started again. If the word is not in main memory, C *n*s are required to fetch it from disk, followed by B *n*s to get it to the cache. If the cache hit ratio is $\frac{n-1}{n}$, and the main-memory hit ratio is $\frac{m-1}{m}$, what is the average access time?

2.5 Contrast the scheduling policies you might use when trying to optimize a time-sharing system with those policies you would use to optimize a multi-programmed batch system.

CHAPTER 3

Process Description and Control

The design of an operating system must surely reflect the requirements that it is intended to meet. And all multiprogramming operating systems, from single-user systems such as OS/2 to mainframe systems such as MVS that can support thousands of users, are built around the concept of the process. Thus, the major requirements that the operating system must meet can all be expressed with reference to processes:

- The operating system must interleave the execution of a number of processes to maximize processor use while providing reasonable response time.
- The operating system must allocate resources to processes in conformance with a specific policy (e.g., certain functions or applications are of higher priority) while at the same time avoiding deadlock.[1]
- The operating system may be required to support interprocess communication and user creation of processes, both of which may aid in the structuring of applications.

Because the process is central to all the key requirements of the operating system, we begin our detailed study of operating systems with an examination of the ways in which processes are represented and controlled by operating systems. The chapter opens with a discussion of process states, which characterize the behavior of processes. Then, we look at the data structures that are needed by the operating system to represent the state of each process and other characteristics of processes needed by the operating system to achieve its objectives. Next, we discover that the concept of process is more complex and

---

[1]Deadlock is examined in Chapter 4. In essence, a deadlock occurs if there are two processes that need the same two resources to continue and each has ownership of one. Each process will wait indefinitely for the missing resource.

subtle than originally presented and in fact embodies two separate and potentially independent concepts: one relating to resource ownership and one relating to execution. This distinction has led to the development in some operating systems of a construct known as the *thread*. Finally, we look at the ways in which our example operating systems handle the issues raised in this chapter.

3.1

PROCESS STATES

The principal function of a processor is to execute machine instructions residing in main memory. These instructions are provided in the form of programs containing sequences of instructions. As we discussed in the last chapter, for reasons of efficiency and ease of programming, a processor may interleave the execution of a number of programs over time.

Thus, from the processor's point of view, it will execute instructions from its repertoire of instructions in some sequence dictated by the changing values in the register known as the *program counter* (PC), or instruction pointer. Over time, that pointer may refer to code in different programs that are part of different applications. From the point of view of an individual program, its execution involves a sequence of instructions within that program. The execution of an individual program is referred to as a *process*, or *task*.

The behavior of an individual process can be characterized by listing the sequence of instructions that execute for that process. Such a listing is referred to as a *trace* of the process. See, for example, Hoare's rigorous treatment of traces [HOAR85]. The behavior of the processor can be characterized by showing the way in which the traces of the various processes are interleaved.

Let us consider a very simple example. Figure 3.1 shows a memory layout of three processes. To simplify the discussion, we assume no use of virtual memory; thus all three processes are represented by programs that are fully loaded in main memory. In addition, there is a small dispatcher program that moves the processor from one process to another. Figure 3.2 shows the traces of the three individual processes during the early part of their execution. The first 12 instructions executed in processes A and C are shown. Process B executes four instructions, and it is assumed that the fourth instruction invokes an I/O operation for which the process must wait.

Now let us view these traces from the processor's point of view. Figure 3.3 shows the interleaved traces resulting from the first 52 instruction cycles. We assume that the operating system allows a process to continue execution for a maximum of only six instruction cycles, after which it is interrupted; this prevents any single process from monopolizing processor time. As the figure illustrates, the first six instructions of process A are executed, followed by a time-out and the execution of some code in the dispatcher, which turns control to

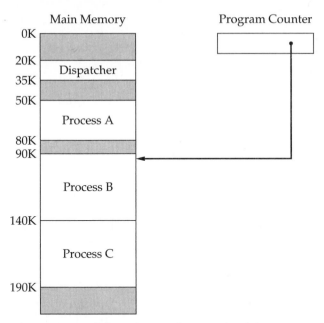

FIGURE 3.1 Snapshot of example execution (Figure 3.3) at time epoch 18

α + 0	β + 0	γ + 0
α + 1	β + 1	γ + 1
α + 2	β + 2	γ + 2
α + 3	β + 3	γ + 3
α + 4		γ + 4
α + 5	(b) Trace of	γ + 5
α + 6	Process B	γ + 6
α + 7		γ + 7
α + 8		γ + 8
α + 9		γ + 9
α + 10		γ + 10
α + 11		γ + 11

(a) Trace of
Process A

(c) Trace of
Process C

α = Starting address of program of Process A
β = Starting address of program of Process B
γ = Starting address of program of Process C

FIGURE 3.2 Traces of processes of Figure 3.1.

1	$\alpha + 0$		28	$\gamma + 5$
2	$\alpha + 1$			
3	$\alpha + 2$		---------------------Time out	
4	$\alpha + 3$		29	$\delta + 0$
5	$\alpha + 4$		30	$\delta + 1$
6	$\alpha + 5$		31	$\delta + 2$
			32	$\delta + 3$
---------------------Time out			33	$\delta + 4$
7	$\delta + 0$		34	$\delta + 5$
8	$\delta + 1$		35	$\alpha + 6$
9	$\delta + 2$		36	$\alpha + 7$
10	$\delta + 3$		37	$\alpha + 8$
11	$\delta + 4$		38	$\alpha + 9$
12	$\delta + 5$		39	$\alpha + 10$
13	$\beta + 0$		40	$\alpha + 11$
14	$\beta + 1$			
15	$\beta + 2$		---------------------Time out	
16	$\beta + 3$		41	$\delta + 0$
			42	$\delta + 1$
---------------------I/O request			43	$\delta + 2$
17	$\delta + 0$		44	$\delta + 3$
18	$\delta + 1$		45	$\delta + 4$
19	$\delta + 2$		46	$\delta + 5$
20	$\delta + 3$		47	$\gamma + 6$
21	$\delta + 4$		48	$\gamma + 7$
22	$\delta + 5$		49	$\gamma + 8$
23	$\gamma + 0$		50	$\gamma + 9$
24	$\gamma + 1$		51	$\gamma + 10$
25	$\gamma + 2$		52	$\gamma + 11$
26	$\gamma + 3$			
27	$\gamma + 4$		---------------------Time out	

δ = Starting address of dispatcher program

FIGURE 3.3 Combined trace of processes of Figure 3.1.

process B.[2] After four instructions are executed in this process, the process requests an I/O action for which it must wait. Therefore, the processor stops executing process B and moves on, via the dispatcher, to process C. After a time-out, the processor next moves back to process A. When this process times out, process B is still waiting for the I/O operation to complete, so the dispatcher moves on to process C again.

[2]The small number of instructions executed for the processes and the dispatcher are unrealistically low; they are used in this simplified example to clarify the discussion.

A Two-State Process Model

The principal responsibility of the operating system is to control the execution of processes; this includes determining the interleaving pattern that is followed and allocating resources to processes. To be able to design the operating system effectively, we need to have a clear model of the behavior of a process. The first step in designing a program to control processes is to describe the behavior that we would like the processes to exhibit.

The simplest possible model can be constructed by observing that, at any time, a process is either being executed by a processor or not. Thus, a process may be in one of two states: Running and Not-running. This is illustrated in Figure 3.4a. When the operating system creates a new process, it enters that process into the system in the Not-running state. Thus, the process exists, is known to the operating system, and is waiting for an opportunity to execute. From time to time, the currently running process will be interrupted and the dispatcher portion of the operating system will select a new process to run. The former process moves from the Running state to the Not-running state, and one of the other processes moves to the Running state.

Even with this simple model, we can already begin to appreciate some of the design elements of the operating system. Each process must be represented in some way so that the operating system can keep track of it. That is, there must be some information relating to each process, including current state and location in memory. Those processes that are not running need to be kept in some sort of queue, waiting their turn to execute. Figure 3.4b suggests a structure. There is a single queue of processes. Each entry in the queue is a pointer to a particular process. Alternatively, the queue consists of a linked list of data blocks

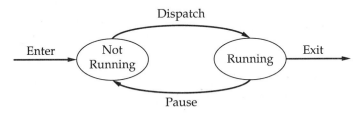

(a) State transition diagram

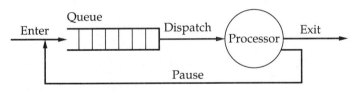

(b) Queueing diagram

FIGURE 3.4 Two-state process model

in which each block represents one process; we explore this latter implementation in the next section.

The behavior of the dispatcher can be described in terms of this queueing diagram. When a process is interrupted, it is transferred to the queue of waiting processes. Alternatively, if the process has completed or aborted, the process is discarded (exits the system). In either case, the dispatcher then selects a process from the queue to execute.

The Creation and Termination of Processes

Before attempting to refine our simple two-state model, it will be useful to discuss the creation and termination of processes; ultimately, and regardless of the model of process behavior that is used, the life of a process is bounded by its creation and termination.

Creation of Process

When a new process is to be added to those that are currently being managed by the operating system, the operating system builds the data structures that are used to manage the process (as described in Section 3.2) and allocates the address space to be used by the process. These actions constitute the creation of a new process.

Four common events lead to the creation of a process, as indicated in Table 3.1. First, in a batch environment, a process is created in response to the submission of a job. In an interactive environment, a process is created when a new user attempts to log on. In both cases, the operating system is responsible for the creation of the new process. A third occasion on which an operating system creates a process is on behalf of an application. For example, if a user requests that a file be printed, the operating system can create a process that

TABLE 3.1   Reasons for Process Creation

New batch job	The operating system is provided with a batch job control stream, usually on tape or disk. When the operating system is prepared to take on new work, it will read the next sequence of job control commands.
Interactive log on	A user at a terminal logs on to the system.
Created by OS to provide a service	The operating system can create a process to perform a function on behalf of a user program, without the user having to wait (e.g., printing).
Spawned by existing process	For purposes of modularity or to exploit parallelism, a user program can dictate the creation of a number of processes.

will manage the printing. This allows the requesting process to proceed independent of the amount of time that it takes to complete the printing task.

Traditionally, all processes were created by the operating system in a fashion that is transparent to the user or application program, and this is still commonly found with many contemporary operating systems. However, it can be useful to allow one process to cause the creation of another process. For example, an application process may create another process to receive data that the application is generating and to organize those data into a form suitable for later analysis. The new process runs in parallel to the application and is activated from time to time when new data are available. This arrangement can be very useful in structuring the application. Another example, a server process (e.g., print server, file server) may create a new process for each request that it handles. When a process is created by the operating system at the explicit request of another process, the action is referred to as *process spawning*.

When one process spawns another process, the spawning process is referred to as the *parent process* and the spawned process is referred to as the *child process*. Typically, the "related" processes will need to communicate and cooperate with each other. Achieving this cooperation is a difficult task for the programmer; this topic is discussed in Chapter 4.

Termination of Process

Table 3.2, based on the work of Pinkert and Wear [PINK89], summarizes typical reasons for process termination.

In any computer system, there must be a means for a process to indicate its completion. A batch job should include a *Halt* instruction or an explicit operating-system service call for termination. In the former case, the *Halt* instruction will generate an interrupt to alert the operating system that a process has completed. For an interactive application, the action of the user will indicate when the process is completed. For example, in a time-sharing system, the process for a particular user is to be terminated when the user logs off or turns off the terminal. On a personal computer or workstation, a user may quit an application (e.g., word processing or spreadsheet). All these actions ultimately result in a service request to the operating system to terminate the requesting process.

Additionally, a number of error and fault conditions can lead to the termination of a process. Table 3.2 lists some of the more commonly recognized conditions.[3]

Finally, in some operating systems, a process may be terminated by the process that created it or when the parent process is itself terminated.

---

[3] A forgiving operating system may, in some cases, allow the user to recover from a fault without terminating the process. For example, if a user requests access to a file and that access is denied, the operating system may simply inform the user that access is denied and allow the process to proceed.

TABLE 3.2   Reasons for Process Termination [PINK89]

Normal completion	The process executes an OS service call to indicate that it has completed running.
Time limit exceeded	The process has run longer than the specified total time limit. There are a number of possibilities for the type of time that is measured. These include total elapsed time ("wall clock time"), amount of time spent executing, and, in the case of an interactive process, the amount of time since the user last provided any input.
Memory unavailable	The process requires more memory than the system can provide.
Bounds violation	The process tries to access memory location that it is not allowed to access.
Protection error	The process attempts to use a resource or a file that it is not allowed to use, or it tries to use it in an improper fashion, such as writing to a read-only file.
Arithmetic error	The process tries a prohibited computation, such as division by zero, or tries to store numbers larger than the hardware can accommodate.
Time overrun	The process has waited longer than a specified maximum for a certain event to occur.
I/O failure	An error occurs in input or output, such as inability to find a file, failure to read or write after a specified maximum number of tries (when, for example, a defective area is encountered on a tape), or invalid operation (such as reading from the line printer).
Invalid instruction	The process attempts to execute a nonexistent instruction (often a result of branching into a data area and attempting to execute the data).
Privileged instruction	The process attempts to use an instruction reserved for the operating system.
Data misuse	A piece of data is of the wrong type or is not initialized.
Operator or OS intervention	For some reason, the operator or the operating system has terminated the process (for example, if a deadlock exists).
Parent termination	When a parent terminates, the operating system may be designed to automatically terminate all the offspring of that parent.
Parent request	A parent process typically has the authority to terminate any of its offspring.

A Five-State Model

If all processes were always ready to execute, then the queueing discipline suggested by Figure 3.4b would be effective. The queue is a first-in, first-out (FIFO) list, and the processor operates in round-robin fashion on the available processes (each process in the queue is given a certain amount of time to execute

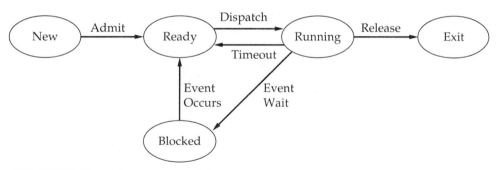

FIGURE 3.5 Five-state process model

and then returned to the queue unless blocked). However, even with the simple example that we have described, this implementation is inadequate: Some processes in the Not-running state are ready to execute, whereas others are blocked, waiting for an I/O operation to complete. Thus, using a single queue, the dispatcher could not just select the process at the oldest end of the queue. Rather, the dispatcher would have to scan the list looking for the process that is not blocked that has been in the queue the longest.

A more natural way to handle this situation is to split the Not-running state into two states: *Ready* and *Blocked*. This is shown in Figure 3.5. For good measure, we have added two additional states that will prove useful. The five states in this new diagram are the following:

- *Running:* The process that is currently being executed. For this chapter, we assume a computer with a single processor, so at most one process can be in this state at a time.
- *Ready:* Processes that are prepared to execute when given the opportunity.
- *Blocked:* A process that cannot execute until some event occurs, such as the completion of an I/O operation.
- *New:* A process that has just been created but has not yet been admitted to the pool of executable processes by the operating system.
- *Exit:* A process that has been released from the pool of executable processes by the operating system, either because it halted or because it aborted for some reason.

The New and Exit states are useful constructs for process management. The New state corresponds to a process that has just been defined. For example, if a new user attempts to log on to a time-sharing system or if a new batch job is submitted for execution, the operating system can define a new process in two stages. First, the operating system performs the necessary housekeeping chores. An identifier is associated with the process. Any tables that will be needed to manage the process are allocated and built. At this point, the process is in the New state. This means that the operating system has performed the necessary actions to create the process but has not committed itself to the execution of the process. For example, the operating system may limit the number of processes that may be in the system for reasons of performance or memory limitation.

Similarly, a process exits a system in two stages. First, a process is terminated when it reaches a natural completion point, when it aborts due to an unrecoverable error, or when another process with the appropriate authority causes the process to abort. Termination moves the process to the Exit state. At this point the process is no longer eligible for execution. However, the tables and other information associated with the job are temporarily preserved by the operating system. This provides time for auxiliary or support programs to extract any needed information. For example, an accounting program may need to record the processor time and other resources used by the process for billing purposes. A utility program may need to extract information about the history of the process for purposes related to performance or use analysis. Once these programs have extracted the needed information, the operating system no longer needs to maintain any data relating to the process, and they are deleted from the system. Table 3.3 provides more detail. Let us look at each possibility in turn:

- *Null → New:* A new process is created to execute a program. This event occurs for any of the reasons listed in Table 3.1.
- *New → Ready:* The operating system will move a process from the New state to the Ready state when it is prepared to take on an additional process. Most systems set some limit based on the number of existing processes or the amount of virtual memory committed to existing processes. The purpose of the limit is to assure that there are not so many active processes as to degrade performance.
- *Ready → Running:* When it is time to select a new process to run, the operating system chooses one of the processes in the Ready state. The issue of which process to choose is explored in Chapter 6.
- *Running → Exit:* The currently running process is terminated by the operating system if the process indicates that it has completed, or if it aborts.
- *Running → Ready:* The most common reason for this transition is that the running process has reached the maximum allowable time for uninterrupted execution; virtually all multiprogramming operating systems impose this type of time discipline. There are several other alternative causes for this transition that are not implemented in all operating systems. For example, if the operating system assigns different levels of priority to different processes, then it is possible for a process to be preempted. Suppose, for example, that process A is running at a given priority level and that process B, at a higher priority level, is blocked. If the operating system learns that the event upon which process B has been waiting has occurred, moving B to a Ready state, then it can interrupt process A and dispatch process B. Finally, a process may voluntarily release control of the processor.
- *Running → Blocked:* A process is put in the Blocked state if it requests something for which it must wait. A request to the operating system is usually in the form of a system service call, that is, a call from the running program to

TABLE 3.3 Process State Transitions

FROM	TO				
	New	Running	Ready	Blocked	Exit
	OS creates in response to job control request; Time-sharing user logs on; process creates child.				
New	X	X	X	X	X
Running	X	X	OS prepared to take on additional process.	X	X
Ready	X	Timeout; OS service request; OS preempts for higher-priority process; process releases control.	OS service request; resource request; event request.	Process completes; process aborts.	
	X	Selected by dispatcher as next process to run.	X	X	Process terminated by parent.
Blocked	X	X	Event occurs.	X	Process terminated by parent.

123

TABLE 3.4   Process States for Trace of Figure 3.3

Time Epoch	Process A	Process B	Process C
1–6	**Running**	Ready	Ready
7–12	Ready	Ready	Ready
13–18 6	Ready	**Running**	Ready
19–24 2	Ready	Blocked	Ready
25–28	Ready	Blocked	**Running**
29–34	Ready	Blocked	Ready
35–40	**Running**	Blocked	Ready
41–46	Ready	Blocked	Ready
47–52	Ready	Blocked	**Running**

a procedure that is part of the operating system code. For example, a process may request a service from the operating system that the operating system is not prepared to perform immediately. It can request a resource, such as a file or a shared section of virtual memory, that is not immediately available. Or the process may initiate an action, such as an I/O operation, that must be completed before the process can continue. When processes communicate with each other, a process may be blocked when it is waiting for another process to provide input or waiting for a message from another process.

- *Blocked → Ready:* A process in the Blocked state is moved to the Ready state when the event for which it has been waiting occurs.
- *Ready → Exit:* For clarity, this transition is not shown on the state diagram of Figure 3.5. In some systems, a parent may terminate a child process at any time. Also, if a parent terminates, all child processes associated with that parent may be terminated.
- *Blocked → Exit:* The comments under the previous item apply.

Returning to our simple example, Table 3.4 shows the movement of each process among the five states. Figure 3.6a suggests the way in which a queueing discipline might be implemented. There are now two queues: a Ready queue and a Suspend queue. As each process is admitted to the system, it is placed in the Ready queue. When it is time for the operating system to choose another process to run, it selects one from the Ready queue. In the absence of any priority scheme, this can be a simple first-in, first-out queue. When a running process is removed from execution, it is either terminated or placed in the Ready or Blocked queue, depending on the circumstances. Finally, when an event occurs, all processes in the Blocked queue that are waiting on that event are moved to the Ready queue.

This latter arrangement means that, when an event occurs, the operating system must scan the entire Blocked queue, searching for those processes waiting on that event. In a large operating system, there could be hundreds or even thousands of processes in that queue. Therefore, it would be more efficient to have a number of queues, one for each event. Then, when the event occurs, the entire list of processes in the appropriate queue can be moved to the Ready state (Figure 3.6b).

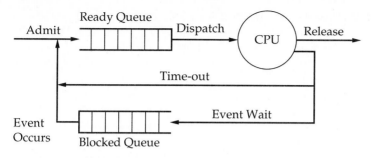

(a) Single blocked queue

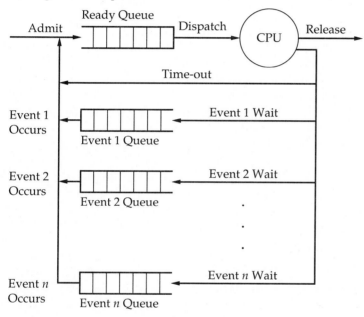

(b) Multiple blocked queues

FIGURE 3.6 Queuing model of Figure 3.5

One final refinement: If the dispatching of processes is dictated by a priority scheme, then it is convenient to have a number of Ready queues, one for each priority level. The operating system can then readily determine which is the highest-priority Ready process that has been waiting the longest.

Suspended Processes

The Need for Swapping

The three principal states that have been described (Ready, Running, Blocked) provide a systematic way of modeling the behavior of processes and guide the implementation of the operating system. Many operating systems are constructed using only these three states.

However, there is good justification for adding additional states to the model. To see the benefit of these new states, consider a system that does not employ virtual memory. Each process to be executed must be loaded fully into main memory. Thus, in Figure 3.6b, all the processes in all the queues must be resident in main memory.

Now, recall that the reason for all this elaborate machinery is that I/O activities are much slower than computation, and therefore the processor in a uniprogramming system is idle most of the time. But the arrangement of Figure 3.6b does not entirely solve the problem. It is true that in this case memory holds multiple processes and that the processor can move to another process when one process is waiting. But the processor is so much faster than I/O that it will be common for *all* the processes in memory to be waiting for I/O. Thus, even with multiprogramming, a processor could be idle most of the time.

What to do? Main memory could be expanded, and so be able to accommodate more processes. But there are two flaws in this approach. First, there is a cost associated with main memory, which although small on a per-bit basis, begins to add up as we get into the megabytes and gigabytes of storage. Second, the appetite of programs for memory has grown as fast as the cost of memory has dropped. So larger memory results in larger processes, not more processes.

Another solution is swapping, which involves moving part or all of a process from main memory to disk. When none of the processes in main memory is in the ready state, the operating system swaps one of the blocked processes out onto disk into a Suspend queue. This is a queue of existing processes that have been temporarily kicked out of main memory, or suspended. The operating system then brings in another process from the Suspend queue, or it honors a new-process request. Execution then continues with the newly arrived process.

Swapping, however, is an I/O operation, and therefore there is the potential for making the problem worse, not better. But because disk I/O is generally the fastest I/O on a system (e.g., compared to tape or printer I/O), swapping will usually enhance performance.

With the use of swapping as just described, one additional state must be added to our process behavior model (Figure 3.7a), the Suspend state. When all the processes in main memory are in the Blocked state, the operating system can suspend one process by putting it in the Suspend state and transferring it to disk. The space that is freed up in main memory can then be used to bring in another process.

When the operating system has performed a swapping-out operation, it has two choices for selecting a process to bring into main memory: It can admit a newly created process, or it can bring in a previously suspended process. It would appear that the preference should be to bring in a previously suspended process to provide it with service rather than increasing the total load on the system.

But this line of reasoning presents a difficulty. All the processes that have been suspended were in the Blocked state at the time of suspension. It clearly would not do any good to bring a Blocked process back into main memory,

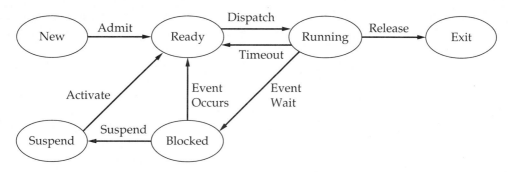

(a) With one suspend state

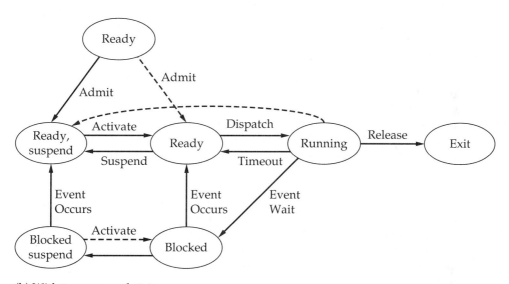

(b) With two suspend states

FIGURE 3.7 Process state transition diagrams with suspend states

since it is still not ready for execution. Recognize, however, that each process in the Suspend state was originally blocked on a particular event. When that event occurs, the process is not blocked and is potentially available for execution.

Therefore, we need to rethink this aspect of the design. There are two independent concepts here: whether a process is waiting on an event (blocked or not), and whether a process has been swapped out of main memory (suspended or not). To accommodate this two-by-two combination, we need the following four states:

- *Ready:* The process is in main memory and available for execution.
- *Blocked:* The process is in main memory and awaiting an event.

- *Blocked, suspend:* The process is in secondary memory and awaiting an event.
- *Ready, suspend:* The process is in secondary memory but is available for execution as soon as it is loaded into main memory.

Before looking at a state transition diagram that encompasses the two new Suspend states, one other point should be mentioned. The discussion so far has assumed that virtual memory is not in use and that a process is either all in main memory or all out of main memory. With a virtual memory scheme, it is possible to execute a process that is only partially in main memory. If reference is made to a process address that is not in main memory, then the appropriate portion of the process can be brought in. The use of virtual memory would appear to eliminate the need for explicit swapping because any desired address in any desired process can be moved in or out of main memory by the memory-management hardware of the processor. However, as we shall see in Chapter 5, the performance of a virtual memory system can collapse if there is a sufficiently large number of active processes, all of which are partially in main memory. Therefore, even in a virtual memory system, the operating system will need to explicitly and completely swap out processes from time to time in the interests of performance.

Let us look now, in Figure 3.7b and Table 3.5, at the State transition model that we have developed. (The dashed lines in the figure indicate possible but not necessary transitions.) Important new transitions are the following:

- *Blocked → Blocked, suspend:* If there are no Ready processes, then at least one Blocked process is swapped out to make room for another process that is not Blocked. This transition can be made even if there are ready processes available, when the operating system determines that the currently Running process or a Ready process that it would like to dispatch requires more main memory to maintain adequate performance.
- *Blocked, suspend → Ready, suspend:* A process in the Blocked, suspend state is moved to the Ready, suspend state when the event for which it has been waiting occurs. Note that this requires that the state information concerning Suspend processes must be accessible to the operating system.
- *Ready, suspend → Ready:* When there are no Ready processes in main memory, the operating system will need to bring one in to continue execution. In addition, it might be the case that a process in the Ready, suspend state has higher priority than any of the processes in the Ready state. In that case, the operating-system designer may dictate that it is more important to get at the higher-priority process than to minimize swapping.
- *Ready → Ready, suspend:* Normally, the operating system would prefer to suspend a Blocked process rather than a Ready one, since the Ready process can now be executed, whereas the Blocked process is taking up main memory space and cannot be executed. However, it may be necessary to suspend a Ready process if that is the only way to free up a sufficiently large block of

main memory. Finally, the operating system may choose to suspend a lower-priority Ready process rather than a higher-priority Blocked process if it believes that the Blocked process will be ready soon.

Several other transitions are worth considering.

- *New → Ready, suspend* and *New → Ready:* When a new process is created, it can either be added to the Ready queue or the Ready, suspend queue. In either case, the operating system needs to build some tables to be able to manage the process and allocate an address space to the process. It might be preferable for the operating system to perform these housekeeping duties at any early time, so that it can maintain a large pool of processes that are not Blocked. With this strategy, it would often be the case that there is insufficient room in main memory for a new process; hence the use of the New → Ready, suspend transition. On the other hand, it might be argued that a just-in-time philosophy, of creating processes as late as possible, reduces operating system overhead and allows the operating system to perform the process-creation duties at a time when the system is clogged with Blocked processes anyway.
- *Blocked, suspend → Blocked:* Inclusion of this transition may seem to be poor design. After all, if a process is not ready to execute and is not already in main memory, what is the point of bringing it in? One possible scenario is the following: A process terminates, freeing up some main memory. There is a process in the Blocked, suspend queue that has a higher priority than any of the processes in the Ready, suspend queue, and the operating system has reason to believe that the blocking event for that process will occur soon. Under these circumstances, it would seem reasonable to bring a Blocked process into main memory in preference to a Ready process.
- *Running → Ready, suspend:* Normally, a Running process is moved to the Ready state when its time allocation expires. If, however, the operating system is preempting the process because a higher-priority process on the Blocked, suspend queue has just become unblocked, the operating system could move the Running process directly to the Ready, suspend queue and free up some main memory.
- *Various → Exit:* Typically, a process terminates while it is running, either because it has completed or because of some fatal fault condition. However, in some operating systems, a process may be terminated by the process that created it or when the parent process is itself terminated. If this is allowed, then a process in any state can be moved to the Exit state.

Other Uses of Suspension

So far, we have equated the concept of a Suspend process with that of a process that is not in main memory. A process that is not in main memory is not immediately available for execution, whether or not it is awaiting an event.

TABLE 3.5 Process State Transitions with Suspend States

	TO						
FROM	New	Running	Ready	Blocked	Ready, Suspend	Blocked, Suspend	Exit
——	OS creates in response to job control request; time-sharing user logs on; process creates child.	X	X	X	X	X	X
New		X	OS prepared to take on additional process.	X	OS prepared to take on additional process.	X	X
Running	X		Timeout; OS service request; OS preempts for higher-priority process; process releases control.	OS service request; resource request; event request.	User requests process suspension; OS requests process suspension.	X	Process completes; process aborts.

130

Ready	Selected by dispatcher as next process to run.	X	X	OS swaps process out to free up memory.	X	Process terminated by parent
Blocked	X	Event occurs.	X	X	OS swaps process out to free up memory; OS or other process requests process suspension.	Process terminated by parent.
Ready, suspend	X	OS swaps process in.	X	X	X	Process terminated by parent.
Blocked, suspend	X	X	OS swaps process in.	Event occurs.	X	Process terminated by parent.

We can generalize this concept of a Suspend process. Let us define a Suspend process by saying that it has the following characteristics:

1. A process that is suspended is not immediately available for execution.
2. The process may or may not be waiting on an event. If it is, this Blocked condition is independent of the Suspend condition, and occurrence of the blocking event does not enable the process to be executed.
3. The process was placed in a Suspend state by an agent—either itself, a parent process, or the operating system—for the purpose of preventing its execution.
4. The process may not be removed from this state until the agent explicitly orders the removal.

Table 3.6 lists some reasons for the suspension of a process. One reason that we have discussed is the need to swap a process out to disk to enable a Ready process to be brought in, or simply to relieve the pressure on the virtual memory system so that each remaining process has more main memory available to it. The operating system may have other motivations for suspending a process. For example, an auditing or tracing process may be employed to monitor activity on the system; the process may be used to record the level of use of various resources (processor, memory, channels) and the rate of progress of the user processes in the system. The operating system, under operator control, may turn this process on and off from time to time. If the operating system detects or suspects a problem, it may suspend a process. One example of this is deadlock, which is discussed in Chapter 4. Another example: A problem is detected on a communications line, and the operator has the operating system suspend the process that is using the line while some tests are run.

Another set of reasons has to do with the actions of an interactive user. For example, if a user suspects a flaw in the program, the user may debug the program by suspending its execution, examining and modifying the program or data, and resuming execution. Or there may be a background process that

TABLE 3.6   Reasons for Process Suspension

Swapping	The operating system needs to release sufficient main memory to bring in a process that is ready to execute.
Other OS reason	The operating system may suspend a background or utility process or a process that is suspected of causing a problem.
Interactive user request	A user may wish to suspend execution of a program for purposes of debugging or in connection with the use of a resource.
Timing	A process may be executed periodically (e.g., an accounting or system monitoring process) and may be suspended while waiting for the next time interval.
Parent process request	A parent process may wish to suspend execution of a descendant to examine or modify the suspended process or to coordinate the activity of various descendants.

is collecting trace or accounting statistics, which the user may wish to be able to turn on and off.

Timing considerations may also lead to a swapping decision. For example, if a process is to be activated periodically but is idle most of the time, then it should be swapped out between uses. A program that monitors use or user activity is an example.

Finally, a parent process may wish to suspend a descendant process. For example, process A may spawn process B to perform a file read. Subsequently, process B encounters an error in the file read procedure and reports this to process A. Process A suspends process B to investigate the cause.

In all these cases, the activation of a Suspend process is requested by the agent that initially requested the suspension.

3.2 PROCESS DESCRIPTION

The operating system is the controller of events within the computer system. It is the operating system that schedules and dispatches processes for execution by the processor, that allocates resources to processes, and that responds to requests by user programs for basic services. Fundamentally, we can think of the operating system as that entity that manages the use of system resources by processes.

This concept is illustrated in Figure 3.8. In a multiprogramming environment, there are a number of processes $(P_1, \ldots P_N)$ that have been created and exist in virtual memory. During the course of its execution, each process needs to have access to certain system resources, including the processor, I/O devices, and main memory. In the figure, process P_1 is running; at least part of the process is in main memory, and it has control of two I/O devices. Process P_2 is also in main memory, but it is blocked waiting for an I/O device allocated to P_1. Process P_N has been swapped out and is therefore suspended.

The details of the management of these resources by the operating system on behalf of the processes is explored in later chapters. Here, we are concerned with a more fundamental question: What does the operating system need to be able to control processes and manage resources for them?

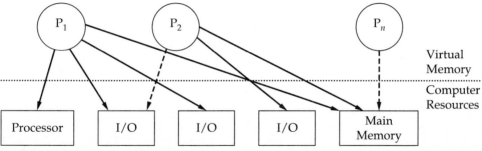

FIGURE 3.8 Processes and resources

Operating-System Control Structures

If the operating system is to manage processes and resources, then it must have information about the current status of each process and resource. The universal approach to providing this information is straightforward: The operating system constructs and maintains tables of information about each entity that it is managing. A general idea of the scope of this effort is indicated in Figure 3.9, which shows four different types of tables maintained by the operating system: memory, I/O, file, and process. Although the details will differ from one operating system to another, fundamentally, all operating systems maintain information in these four categories.

Memory tables are used to keep track of both main (real) and secondary (virtual) memory. Some of main memory is reserved for use by the operating system; the remainder is available for use by processes. Processes are maintained on secondary memory by using some sort of virtual memory or simple swapping mechanism. The memory tables must include the following information:

• The allocation of main memory to processes
• The allocation of secondary memory to processes

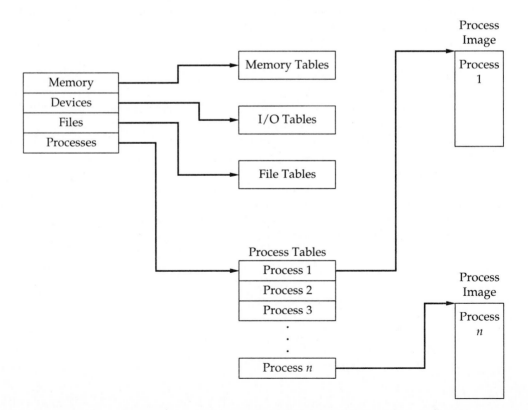

FIGURE 3.9 General structure of operating-system control tables

- Any protection attributes of segments of main or virtual memory, such as which processes may access certain shared memory regions
- Any information needed to manage virtual memory

We look at the information structures for memory management in detail in Chapter 5.

I/O tables are used by the operating system to manage the I/O devices and channels of the computer system. At any given time, an I/O device may be available or assigned to a particular process. If an I/O operation is in progress, the operating system needs to know the status of the I/O operation and the location in main memory being used as the source or destination of the I/O transfer. I/O management is examined in Chapter 7.

The operating system may also maintain **file tables**, which provide information about the existence of files, their location on secondary memory, their current status, and other attributes. Much, if not all, of this information may be maintained and used by a file-management system, in which case the operating system has little or no knowledge of files. In other operating systems, much of the detail of file management is managed by the operating system itself. This topic is explored in Chapter 7.

Finally, the operating system must maintain process tables to manage processes. The remainder of this section is devoted to an examination of the required **process tables**. Before proceeding to this discussion, two additional points should be made. First, although Figure 3.9 shows four distinct sets of tables, it should be clear that these tables must be linked or cross-referenced in some fashion. Memory, I/O, and files are managed on behalf of processes, so there must be some direct or indirect reference to these resources in the process tables. The files referred to in the file tables are accessible via an I/O device and will, at some times, be in main or virtual memory. Thus, cross-references are needed. The tables themselves must be accessible by the operating system and therefore are subject to memory management.

The second point refers to the earlier statement that the operating system creates and maintains these tables. The question of origins arises. How does the operating system know to create the tables in the first place? Clearly, the operating system must have some knowledge of the basic environment, such as how much main memory exists, what the I/O devices are, and what their identifiers are, and so on. This is an issue of configuration. That is, when the operating system is initialized, it must have access to some configuration data that define the basic environment, and these data must be created outside the operating system with human assistance.

Process Control Structures

Consider what the operating system must know if it is to manage and control a process. First, it must know where the process is located, and second, it must know the attributes of the process that are necessary for its management.

Process Location

Before we can deal with the questions of where a process is located or what its attributes are, we need to address an even more fundamental question: What is the physical manifestation of a process? At a minimum, a process must include a program or set of programs to be executed. Associated with these programs is a set of data locations for local and global variables and any defined constants. Thus, a process will consist of at least sufficient memory to hold the programs and the data of that process. In addition, the execution of a program typically involves a stack (see Appendix 1B) that is used to keep track of procedure calls and parameter passing between procedures. Finally, associated with each process are a number of attributes used by the operating system for process control. Typically, the collection of attributes is referred to as a **process control block**.[4] We can refer to this collection of program, data, stack, and attributes as the **process image** (Table 3.7).

The location of a process image depends on the memory-management scheme being used. In the simplest possible case, the process image is maintained as a contiguous block of memory. This block is maintained in secondary memory, usually disk. So that the operating system can manage the process, at least a small portion of the image containing information of use to the operating system must be maintained in main memory. To execute the process, the entire process image must be loaded into main memory. Thus, the operating system needs to know the location of each process on disk and, for each process that is in main memory, the location of the process in main memory. We saw in Chapter 2 a slightly more complex variation on this scheme—the CTSS operating system. When a process is swapped out with CTSS, part of the process image may remain in main memory. Thus, the operating system must keep track of which portions of the image of each process are still in main memory.

Most modern operating systems use some sort of memory-management scheme in which a process image consists of a set of blocks that need not be stored contiguously. Depending on the type of scheme used, these blocks may

TABLE 3.7   Typical Elements of a Process Image

User Data
> The modifiable part of the user space. May include program data, a user stack area, and programs that may be modified.

User Program
> The program to be executed.

System Stack
> Each process has one or more last-in, first-out (LIFO) system stacks associated with it. A stack is used to store parameters and calling addresses for procedure and system calls.

Process Control Block
> Information needed by the operating system to control the process (see Table 3.8).

---

[4]Other commonly used names for this data structure are task control block, process descriptor, and task descriptor.

be of variable length (called segments) or fixed length (called pages), or a combination. In any case, such schemes allow the operating system to bring in only a portion of any particular process. Thus, at any given time, a portion of a process image may be in main memory with the remainder in secondary memory.[5] Therefore, process tables maintained by the operating system must show the location of each segment and/or page of each process image.

Figure 3.9 depicts the structure of the location information in the following way. There is a primary process table with one entry for each process. Each entry contains, at least, a pointer to a process image. If the process image contains multiple blocks, then this information will be contained directly in the primary process table or by cross-reference to entries in memory tables. Of course, this depiction is generic; any given operating system will have its own way of organizing the location information.

Process Attributes

In a sophisticated multiprogramming system, a great deal of information about each process is required for process management. As was mentioned, this information can be considered to reside in a process control block. Different systems will organize this information in different ways, and we shall see several examples of this in Section 3.5. For now, let us simply try to explore the type of information that might be of use to an operating system, without considering in any detail the way in which that information is organized.

Table 3.8 lists the typical categories of information required by the operating system for each process. You may be initially somewhat surprised by the quantity of information required. As the book proceeds and a greater appreciation of the responsibilities of the operating system is gained, this list should appear more reasonable to you.

We can group the process control block information into the following three general categories:

- Process identification
- Processor state information
- Process control information

With respect to **process identification**, in virtually all operating systems, each process is assigned a unique numeric identifier. The identifier may simply be an index into the primary process table (e.g., see Figure 3.9). If there is no numeric identifier, there must be a mapping that allows the operating system to locate the appropriate tables on the basis of the process identifier. This identifier is useful in a variety of ways. Many of the other tables controlled by the operating system may use process identifiers to cross-reference process tables.

[5]This brief discussion slides over some details. In particular, all the process image for an active process is always in secondary memory. When a portion of the image is loaded into main memory, it is copied rather than moved. Thus, the secondary memory retains a copy of all segments and/or pages. However, if the main-memory portion of the image is modified, the secondary copy will be out of date until the main memory portion is copied back onto disk.

TABLE 3.8   Typical Elements of a Process Control Block

Process Identification

Identifiers
Numeric identifiers that may be stored with the process control block include:
- Identifier of this process
- Identifier of the process that created this process (parent process)
- User identifier

Processor State Information

User-Visible Registers
A user-visible register is one that may be referenced by means of the machine language that the processor executes. Typically, there are from 8 to 32 of these registers, although some RISC implementations have more than 100.

Control and Status Registers
These are a variety of processor registers that are employed to control the operation of the processor. These include:
- *Program counter:* contains the address of the next instruction to be fetched.
- *Condition codes:* result of the most recent arithmetic or logical operation (e.g., sign, zero, carry, equal, overflow).
- *Status information:* includes interrupt enabled/disabled flags, execution mode.

Stack Pointers
Each process has one or more last-in, first out (LIFO) system stacks associated with it. A stack is used to store parameters and calling addresses for procedure and system calls. The stack pointer points to the top of the stack.

Process Control Information

Scheduling and State Information
This is information that is needed by the operating system to perform its scheduling function. Typical items of information are the following:
- *Process state:* defines the readiness of the process to be scheduled for execution (e.g., running, ready, waiting, halted).
- *Priority:* One or more fields may be used to describe the scheduling priority of the process. In some systems, several values are required (e.g., default, current, highest-allowable).
- *Scheduling-related information:* This will depend on the scheduling algorithm used. Examples are the amount of time that the process has been waiting and the amount of time that the process executed the last time it was running.
- *Event:* The identity of event that process is awaiting before it can be resumed

Data Structuring
A process may be linked to other processes in a queue, ring, or some other structure. For example, all processes in a waiting state for a particular priority level may be linked in a queue. A process may exhibit a parent-child (creator-created) relationship with another process. The process control block may contain pointers to other processes to support these structures.

Interprocess Communication
Various flags, signals, and messages may be associated with communication between two independent processes. Some or all of this information may be maintained in the process control block.

TABLE 3.8   *(Continued)*

Process Control Information

Process Privileges
> Processes are granted privileges in terms of the memory that may be accessed and the types of instructions that may be executed. In addition, privileges may apply to the use of system utilities and services.

Memory Management
> This section may include pointers to segment and/or page tables that describe the virtual memory assigned to this process.

Resource Ownership and Utilization
> Resources controlled by the process may be indicated, such as opened files. A history of the use of the processor or other resources may also be included; this information may be needed by the scheduler.

For example, the memory tables may be organized in such a way as to provide a map of main memory with an indication of which process is assigned to each region of memory. Similar references will appear in I/O and file tables. When processes communicate with one another, the process identifier is used to inform the operating system of the destination of a particular communication. When processes are allowed to create other processes, identifiers are used to indicate the parent and descendants of each process.

In addition to these process identifiers, a process may be assigned a user identifier that indicates the user who is responsible for the job.

The next major collection of information is **processor state information**. This, essentially, consists of the contents of processor registers. While a process is running, of course, the information is in the registers. When a process is interrupted, all this register information must be saved so that it can be restored when the process resumes execution. The nature and number of registers involved depend on the design of the processor. Typically, the register set includes user-visible registers, control and status registers, and stack pointers. *User-visible registers* are those that are accessible to user programs and are to be used for temporary storage of data. Most processors include from 8 to 32 such registers. Some recent reduced instruction set computer (RISC) architectures have more than 100 such registers.

A variety of *control* and *status registers* are employed to control the operation of the processor. Most of these, on most machines, are not visible to the user. Some of them may be visible to machine instructions executed in a control or operating-system mode. A control register found in all processors is the program counter, or instruction register, which contains the address of the next instruction to be fetched. In addition, all processor designs include a register or set of registers, often known as the program status word (PSW), that contains status information. The PSW typically contains condition codes plus other status information.

A good example of a processor status word is that on VAX machines, shown in Figure 3.10 and Table 3.9. This structure is used by both the VAX VMS operating system and the Berkeley BSD UNIX operating systems.

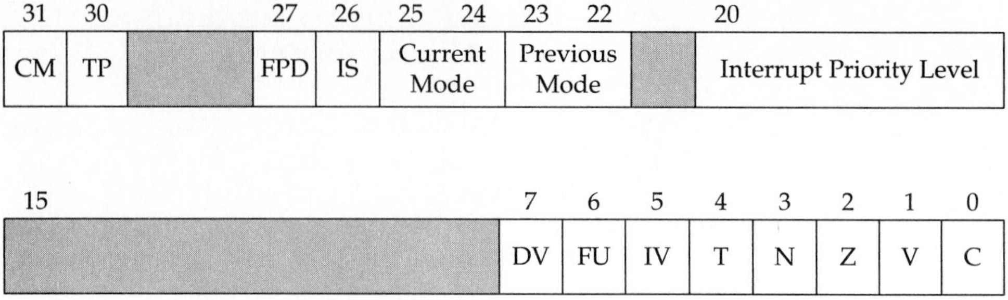

31	30		27	26	25 24	23 22		20		
CM	TP		FPD	IS	Current Mode	Previous Mode		Interrupt Priority Level		

15				7	6	5	4	3	2	1	0
				DV	FU	IV	T	N	Z	V	C

FIGURE 3.10 VAX processor status longword

TABLE 3.9   VAX Processor Status Longword Fields

Condition Codes (N, Z, V, C)
These bits reflect the result of the most recent instruction that affects them: N = negative, Z = zero, V = overflow, C = carry. These bits may be tested by a conditional branch instruction.
Trap-Enable Flags (DV, FU, IV, T)
These bits are used to enable/disable a type of interrupt called a trap: DV = decimal overflow, FU = floating underflow, IV = integer overflow, T = trace
Interrupt Priority Level (IPL)
The processor's current priority level. Only interrupts of higher priority will be acknowledged.
Previous Mode
Value of the access mode prior to the current one.
Current Mode
Current processor access mode, which determines what instructions the processor may execute and which locations in virtual memory the current instruction may access. The four modes are kernel, executive, supervisor, and user. See Problem 3.5.
Interrupt Stack (IS)
Indicates whether the processor is processing an interrupt. If so, the processor makes use of a special stack called the interrupt stack.
First Part Done (FPD)
Used with instruction that may be interrupted during execution. If FDP = 1 when the processor returns from an interrupt, it resumes the operation where it left off, rather than restarting the instruction.
Trace Pending (TP)
The trace facility allows a debugger to gain control following the execution of every instruction by using a trace interrupt. When trace interrupts are enabled, the TP bit ensures that only one trace interrupt can occur for each instruction.
Compatibility Mode (CM)
When the VAX-11 processor is in compatibility mode, it executes PDP-11 instructions rather than VAX instructions. Other members of the VAX family provide this function via software emulation.

Finally, one or more *stack registers* provide pointers to stacks used by the operating system to control program execution and to keep track of interrupts.

The third major category of information in the process control block can be called, for want of a better name, **process control information**, which is the additional information needed by the operating system to control and coordinate the various active processes. The last part of Table 3.8 indicates the scope of this information. As we examine the details of operating-system functionality in succeeding chapters, the need for the various items on this list will become clearer.

Figure 3.11 suggests the structure of process images in virtual memory. Each process image consists of a process control block, a user stack, the private address space of the process, and any other address space that the process shares with other processes. In the figure, each process image appears as a contiguous range of addresses. In an actual implementation, this may not be the case; it depends on the memory management scheme and the way in which control structures are organized by the operating system.

As indicated in Table 3.8, the process control block may contain structuring information, including pointers that allow the linking of process control blocks. Thus, the queues that were described in the preceding section could be implemented as linked lists of process control blocks. For example, the queuing structure of Figure 3.6a could be implemented as suggested in Figure 3.12.

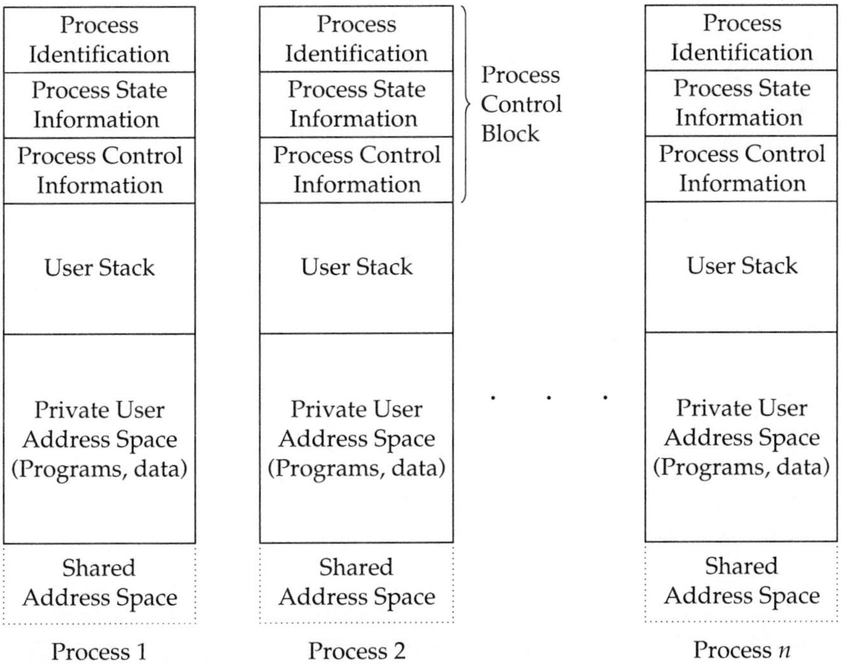

FIGURE 3.11 User processes in virtual memory

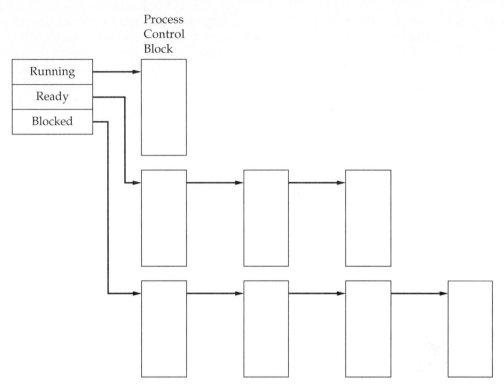

FIGURE 3.12 Process list structures

The Role of the Process Control Block

The process control block is the most important and central data structure in an operating system. Each process control block contains all the information about a process that is needed by the operating system. The blocks are read and/or modified by virtually every module in the operating system, including those involved with scheduling, resource allocation, interrupt processing, and performance monitoring and analysis. One can say that the set of process control blocks defines the state of the operating system.

This brings up an important design issue. A number of routines within the operating system will need access to information in process control blocks. The provision of direct access to these tables is not difficult. Each process is equipped with a unique ID that can be used as an index into a table of pointers to the process control blocks. The difficulty is not access but, rather, protection. There are two problems:

- A bug in a single routine, such as an interrupt handler, could damage process control blocks, which could destroy the system's ability to manage the affected processes.

- A design change in the structure or semantics of the process control block could affect a number of modules in the operating system.

These problems can be addressed by requiring all routines in the operating system to go through a handler routine, the only job of which is to protect process control blocks, and which is the sole arbiter for reading and writing these blocks. The trade-off in the use of such a routine involves performance issues and the degree to which the remainder of the system software can be trusted to be correct.

3.3

PROCESS CONTROL

Modes of Execution

Before continuing with our discussion of the way in which the operating system manages processes, we need to distinguish between the mode of processor execution normally associated with the operating system and that normally associated with user programs. Most processors support at least two modes of execution. Certain instructions can be executed only in the more privileged mode. These include reading or altering a control register, such as the program status word, primitive I/O instructions, and instructions that relate to memory management. In addition, certain regions of memory can be accessed only in the more privileged mode.

The less privileged mode is often referred to as the *user mode* because user programs typically execute in this mode. The more privileged mode is referred to as the *system mode*, *control mode*, or *kernel mode*. This last term refers to the kernel of the operating system, which is that portion of the operating system that encompasses the important system functions. Table 3.10 lists the functions typically found in the kernel of an operating system.

The reason for using two modes should be clear. It is necessary to protect the operating system and key operating-system tables, such as process control blocks, from interference by user programs. In the kernel mode, the software has complete control of the processor and all its instructions, registers, and memory. This level of control is not necessary, and for safety, is not desirable for user programs.

Two questions arise: How does the processor know in which mode it is to be executing? And how is the mode changed? As to the first question, typically there is a bit in the program status word (PSW) that indicates the mode of execution. This bit is changed in response to certain events. For example, when a user makes a call to an operating-system service, the mode is set to the kernel mode. Typically, this is done by executing an instruction that changes the mode. An example of how this is done is the Change Mode (CHM) instruction on the VAX. When the user makes a system service call or when an interrupt transfers

TABLE 3.10   Typical Functions of an Operating-System Kernel

Process Management

- Process creation and termination
- Process scheduling and dispatching
- Process switching
- Process synchronization and support for inter-process communication
- Management of process control blocks

Memory Management

- Allocation of address space to processes
- Swapping
- Page and segment management

I/O Management

- Buffer management
- Allocation of I/O channels and devices to processes

Support Functions

- Interrupt handling
- Accounting
- Monitoring

---

control to a system routine, the routine executes CHM to enter a more privileged mode and executes it again to enter a less privileged mode before returning control to the user process. If a user program attempts to execute a CHM, it will simply result in a call to the operating system, which will return an error unless the mode change is to be allowed.

Creation of Process

Earlier, in Section 3.1, we discussed the events that lead to the creation of a new process. Having discussed the data structures associated with a process, we are now in a position to briefly describe the steps involved in actually creating the process.

Once the operating system decides, for whatever reason (Table 3.1), to create a new process, it can proceed as follows:

1. Assign a unique process identifier to the new process. At this time, a new entry is added to the primary process table, which contains one entry per process.
2. Allocate space for the process. This includes all elements of the process image. Thus, the operating system must know how much space is needed for the private user address space (programs and data) and for the user stack. These values can be assigned by default on the basis of the type of process,

or they can be set on the basis of user request when the job is created. If a process is spawned by another process, the parent process can pass the needed values to the operating system as part of the process-creation request. If any existing address space is to be shared by this new process, the appropriate linkages must be set up. Finally, space for a process control block must be allocated.

3. The process control block must be initialized. The process identification portion contains the ID of this process plus other appropriate IDs, such as that of the parent process. The processor state information portion will typically be initialized with most entries zero, except for the program counter (set to the program entry point) and system stack pointers (set to define the process stack boundaries). The processor control information portion is initialized on the basis of standard default values plus attributes that have been requested for this process. For example, the process state would typically be initialized to Ready or Ready, suspend. The priority may be set by default to the lowest value unless an explicit request is made for a higher value. Initially, the process may own no resources (I/O devices, files), unless there is an explicit request for these or unless they are inherited from the parent.

4. The appropriate linkages must be set. For example, if the operating system maintains each scheduling queue as a linked list, then the new process must be put in the Ready or Ready, suspend list.

5. There may be other data structures to be created or expanded. For example, the operating system may maintain an accounting file on each process to be used subsequently for billing and/or performance assessment purposes.

Process Switching

On the face of it, the function of process switching seems to be straightforward. At some time, a running process is interrupted and the operating system assigns another process to the Running state and turns control over to that process. However, several design issues are raised. First, what events trigger a process switch? Another issue is that we must recognize the distinction between context switching and process switching. Finally, what must the operating system do to the various data structures under its control to achieve a process switch?

When to Switch Processes

A process switch may occur any time that the operating system has gained control from the currently running process. Table 3.11 suggests the possible events that may give control to the operating system.

First, let us consider system interrupts. We can distinguish, as many systems do, two kinds of system interrupts, one of which is simply referred to as an interrupt and the other as a trap. The former is caused by some sort of event that is external to and independent of the currently running process, such as the completion of an I/O operation. The latter relates to an error or exception

TABLE 3.11   Mechanisms for Interrupting the Execution of a Process [KRAK88]

Mechanism	Cause	Use
Interrupt	External to the execution of the current instruction	Reaction to an asynchronous external event
Trap	Associated with the execution of the current instruction	Handling of an error or an exceptional condition
Supervisor call	Explicit request	Call to an operating-system function

condition generated within the currently running process, such as an illegal attempt to access a file. With an ordinary **interrupt**, control is first transferred to an interrupt handler, which does some basic housekeeping and then branches to an operating-system routine that is concerned with the particular type of interrupt that has occurred. Some examples are the following:

- *Clock interrupt:* The operating system determines whether the currently running process has been executing for the maximum allowable time slice. If so, this process must be switched to a Ready state and another process dispatched.
- *I/O interrupt:* The operating system determines exactly what I/O action has occurred. If the I/O action constitutes an event for which one or more processes are waiting, then the operating system moves all the corresponding blocked processes to the Ready state (and Blocked, suspend processes to the Ready, suspend state). The operating system must then decide whether to resume execution of the process currently in the Running state or to preempt that process for a higher-priority Ready process.
- *Memory fault:* The processor encounters a virtual memory address reference for a word that is not in main memory. The operating system must bring in the block (page or segment) of memory containing the reference from secondary memory to main memory. After the I/O request is issued to bring in the block of memory, the operating system may perform a context switch to resume execution of another process; the process with the memory fault is placed in a blocked state. After the desired block is brought into memory, that process is placed in a Ready state.

With a **trap**, the operating system determines whether the error is fatal. If so, then the currently running process is moved to the Exit state and a process switch occurs. If not, then the action of the operating system will depend on the nature of the error and the design of the operating system. It may attempt some recovery procedure, or it may simply notify the user. It may do a process switch, or it may resume the currently running process.

Finally, the operating system may be activated by a **supervisor call** from the program being executed. For example, a user process is running and an instruction is executed that requests an I/O operation, such as a file open. This call results in a transfer to a routine that is part of the operating-system code.

Generally, the use of a system call results in placing the user process in the Blocked state.

Context Switching

In Chapter 1, we discussed the inclusion of an interrupt cycle as part of the instruction cycle. Recall that in the interrupt cycle the processor checks to see if any interrupts have occurred, which would be indicated by the presence of an interrupt signal. If no interrupts are pending, the processor proceeds to the fetch cycle and fetches the next instruction of the current program in the current process. If an interrupt is pending, the processor does the following:

1. It saves the context of the current program being executed.
2. It sets the program counter to the starting address of an *interrupt handler* program.

The processor now proceeds to the fetch cycle and fetches the first instruction of the interrupt handler program, which will service the interrupt.

One question that may now occur to you is: What constitutes the context that is saved? The answer is that it must include any information that may be altered by the execution of the interrupt handler and that will be needed to resume the program that was interrupted. Thus, the portion of the process control block that was referred to as processor state information must be saved. This includes the program counter, other processor registers, and stack information.

Does anything else need to be done? That depends on what happens next. The interrupt handler is typically a short program that performs a few basic tasks related to an interrupt. For example, it resets that flag or indicator that signals the presence of an interrupt. It may send an acknowledgment to the entity that issued the interrupt, such as an I/O module. And it may do some basic housekeeping relating to the effects of the event that caused the interrupt. For example, if the interrupt relates to an I/O event, the interrupt handler will check for an error condition. If an error has occurred, the interrupt handler may send a signal to the process that originally requested the I/O operation. If the interrupt is by the clock, then the handler will hand control over to the dispatcher, which will want to pass control to another process because the time slice allotted to the currently running process will have expired.

What about the other information in the process control block? If this interrupt is to be followed by a switch to another process, then some work will need to be done there. However, the key word in the previous sentence is *if*. In most operating systems, the occurrence of an interrupt does not necessarily result in a process switch. It is possible that after the interrupt handler has executed, the currently running process will resume execution. In that case, all that is necessary is to save the processor state information when the interrupt occurs and restore that information when control is returned to the program that was in progress. Typically, the saving and restoring functions are performed in hardware.

Change of Process State

It is clear, then, that the context switch is a concept distinct from that of the process switch.[6] A context switch may occur without changing the state of the process that is currently in the Running state. In that case, the context saving and subsequent restoral involve little overhead. However, if the currently running process is to be moved to another state (Ready, Blocked, etc.), then the operating system must make substantial changes in its environment. The steps involved in a full process switch are as follows:

1. Save the context of the processor, including program counter and other registers.
2. Update the process control block of the process that is currently in the Running state. This includes changing the state of the process to one of the other states (Ready; Blocked; Ready, suspend; or Exit). Other relevant fields must also be updated, including the reason for leaving the Running state and accounting information.
3. Move the process control block of this process to the appropriate queue (Ready; Blocked on Event i; Ready, suspend)
4. Select another process for execution; this topic is explored in Chapter 5.
5. Update the process control block of the process selected. This includes changing the state of this process to Running.
6. Update memory-management data structures. This may be required depending on how address translation is managed; this topic is explored in Chapter 5.
7. Restore the context of the processor to that which existed at the time the selected process was last switched out of the Running state by loading in the previous values of the program counter and other registers.

Thus, the process switch, which involves a state change, requires considerably more effort than a context switch.

Execution of the Operating System

In Chapter 2, we pointed out several intriguing facts about operating systems:

- The operating system functions in the same way as ordinary computer software; that is, it is a program executed by the processor.
- The operating system frequently relinquishes control and must depend on the processor to allow it to regain control.

If the operating system is just a collection of programs and if it is executed by the processor just like any other program, is the operating system a process? If so, how is it controlled?

---

[6]Unfortunately, some textbooks on the subject use the term *context switch* to mean *process switch*, and have no particular term for the simpler action that we have defined as a context switch.

These interesting questions have received a number of answers from operating-system designers. Figure 3.13 illustrates a range of approaches that are found in various contemporary operating systems.

Nonprocess Kernel

An approach that is quite traditional and common on many older operating systems is to execute the kernel of the operating system outside of any process (Figure 3.13a). With this approach, when the currently running process is interrupted or issues a supervisor call, the processor context of this process is saved and control is passed to the kernel. The operating system has its own region of memory to use and its own system stack for controlling procedure calls and returns. The operating system can perform any desired functions and restore the context of the interrupted process, which causes execution to resume in the interrupted user process. Alternatively, the operating system can complete the function of saving the environment of the process and proceed to

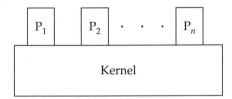

(a) Separate kernel

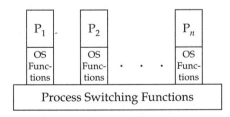

(b) OS functions execute within user processes

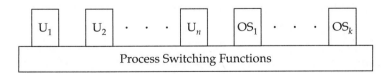

(c) OS functions execute as separate processes

FIGURE 3.13 Relationship between operating system and user processes

schedule and dispatch another process. Whether this happens depends on the reason for the interruption and the circumstances at the time.

In any case, the key point here is that the concept of process is considered to apply only to user programs. The operating system code is executed as a separate entity that operates in privileged mode.

Execution Within User Processes

An alternative that is common with operating systems on smaller machines (minicomputers and microcomputers) is to execute virtually all operating-system software in the context of a user process. The view is that the operating system is primarily a collection of routines that the user calls to perform various functions and that are executed within the environment of the user's process, as illustrated in Figure 3.13b. At any given point, the operating system is managing N process images. Each image includes not only the regions illustrated in Figure 3.11 but also program, data, and stack areas for kernel programs.

Figure 3.14 suggests a typical process image structure for this strategy. A

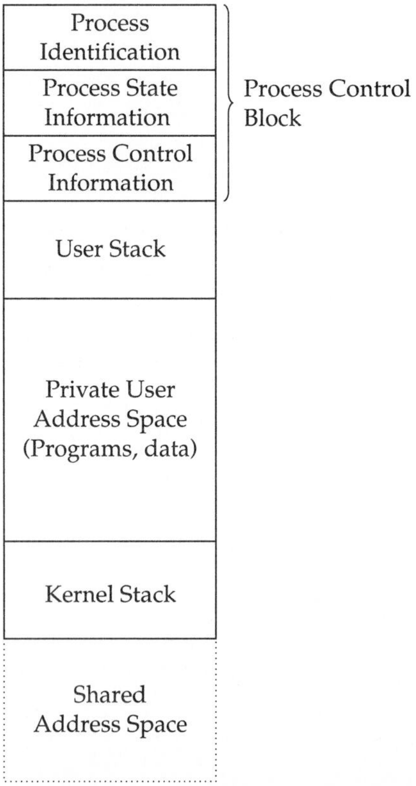

Process Identification
Process State Information
Process Control Information

Process Control Block

User Stack

Private User Address Space (Programs, data)

Kernel Stack

Shared Address Space

FIGURE 3.14 Process image: operating system executes within user process

separate kernel stack is used to manage calls and returns while the process is in kernel mode. The operating-system code and data are in the shared address space and are shared by all user processes.

When an interrupt, trap, or supervisor call occurs, the processor is placed in kernel mode and control is passed to the operating system. For this purpose, the processor context is saved and a context switch takes place to an operating-system routine. However, execution continues within the current user process. Thus, a process switch is not performed, just a context switch within the same process.

If the operating system, upon completion of its work, determines that the current process should continue to run, then a context switch resumes the interrupted program within the current process. This is one of the key advantages of this approach: A user program has been interrupted in order to employ some operating system routine, and then resumed, and all this has occurred without incurring the penalty of two process switches. If, however, it is determined that a process switch is to occur rather than returning to the previously executing program, then control is passed to a process-switching routine. This routine may or may not execute in the current process, depending on system design. At some point, however, the current process has to be placed in a non-Running state and another process designated as the Running process. During this phase, it is logically most convenient to view execution as taking place outside of all processes.

In a way, this view of the operating system is quite remarkable. Simply put, at certain times, a process will save its state information, choose another process to run from among those that are ready, and relinquish control to that process. The reason this is not an arbitrary and indeed chaotic situation is that during the critical time, the code that is executed in the user process is shared operating-system code and not user code. Because of the concept of user mode and kernel mode, the user cannot tamper with or interfere with the operating-system routines, even though they are executing in the user's process environment. This further reminds us that there is a distinction between the concepts of process and program and that the relationship between the two is not one to one. Within a process, both a user program and operating-system programs may execute, and the operating-system programs that execute in the various user processes are identical.

Process-Based Operating System

A final alternative, illustrated in Figure 3.13c, is to implement the operating system as a collection of system processes. As in the other options, the software that is part of the kernel will execute in a kernel mode. In this case, however, major kernel functions are organized as separate processes. Again, there may be a small amount of process-switching code that is executed outside of any process.

This approach has several advantages. It imposes a program design discipline that encourages the use of a modular operating system with minimal, clean interfaces between the modules. In addition, some noncritical operating-system functions are conveniently implemented as separate processes. For example, we mentioned earlier a monitor program that records the level of use of various resources (processor, memory, channels) and the rate of progress of the user processes in the system. Because this program does not provide a particular service to any active process, it can be invoked only by the operating system. As a process, the function can run at an assigned priority level and be inter-leaved with other processes under dispatcher control. Finally, implementing the operating system as a set of processes is useful in a multiprocessor or multicomputer environment in which some of the operating-system services can be shipped out to dedicated processors, thus improving performance.

3.4

PROCESSES AND THREADS

In the discussion so far, it can be seen that we have presented the concept of a process as embodying the following two characteristics:

- *Unit of resource ownership:* A process is allocated a virtual address space to hold the process image, and from time to time the process may be assigned main memory plus control of other resources, such as I/O channels, I/O devices, and files.
- *Unit of dispatching:* A process is an execution path (trace) through one or more programs. This execution may be interleaved with that of other processes. Thus, a process has an execution state (Running, Ready, etc.) and a dispatch-ing priority, and it is the entity that is scheduled and dispatched by the oper-ating system.

In most operating systems, these two characteristics are indeed the essence of a process. However, some thought should convince you that these two char-acteristics are independent and could be treated independently by the operating system. This is done in a number of operating systems, particularly some re-cently developed systems. To distinguish the two characteristics, the unit of dispatching is usually referred to as a **thread**, or **lightweight process**, whereas the unit of resource ownership is usually still referred to as a **process**, or **task**.[7]

Multiple Threads in a Single Process

The most prominent use of the concept of thread is in an arrangement in which multiple threads may exist within a single process. Something approximating this approach is taken in MVS. More explicitly, this approach is taken in OS/2,

---

[7]Alas, even this degree of consistency cannot be maintained. In MVS, the concepts of address space and task, respectively, correspond roughly to the concepts of process and thread that we describe in this section.

the Sun version of UNIX, and in an important operating system known as Mach [KIRS89, TEVA89, RASH89, WEND89]. Mach is an evolutionary extension of UNIX that is used in the Next workstation and is the basis for the Open Software Foundation version of UNIX. This subsection describes the approach taken in Mach; the techniques used in OS/2 and MVS are discussed in Section 3.5.

Mach is designed specifically to work in a multiprocessor environment, although it is also well suited to a single-processor system. In Mach, a task is defined as the unit of protection, or the unit of resource allocation. The following are associated with tasks:

- A virtual address space that holds the task image
- Protected access to processors, other processes (for interprocess communication), files, and I/O resources (devices and channels)

Within a task, there may be one or more threads, each with the following:

- A thread execution state (Running, Ready, etc.)
- A saved processor context when not running; one way to view a thread is as an independent program counter operating within a task
- An execution stack
- Some per-thread static storage for local variables
- Access to the memory and resources of its task, shared with all other threads in that task

The key benefits of threads derive from the performance implications: It takes far less time to create a new thread in an existing process than to create a brand-new task, less time to terminate a thread, and less time to switch between two threads within the same process. Thus, if there is an application or function that can be implemented as a set of related units of execution, it is far more efficient to do so as a collection of threads rather than as a collection of separate tasks.[8] Studies done by the Mach developers show that the speedup in process creation compared to a comparable UNIX implementation, which does not use threads, is a factor of 10 [TEVA87].

An example of an application that could make use of threads is a server, such as a file server on a local area network. As each new file request comes in, a new thread could be spawned for the file-management program. Because a server will handle many requests, many threads will be created and destroyed in a short period. If the server is a multiprocessor, then multiple threads within the same task can be executing simultaneously on different processors. The thread construct is also useful on a single processor to simplify the structure of a program that is logically doing several different functions. Other examples of

---

[8]It is interesting to note that similar concepts have arisen in the areas of communications protocols, computer architecture, and operating systems at about the same time. In computer architecture, the reduced instruction set computer (RISC) approach has led to improved processor speed by streamlining processor architecture. In communications protocols, the need for high-speed data transfer across computer networks has led to the development of lightweight transport protocols. These two concepts are discussed at length in [STAL90a] and [STAL91], respectively.

the effective use of threads are for a communications processing application [COOP90] and a transaction processing monitor [BERN90].

Another way in which threads provide efficiency is in communication between different executing programs. In most operating systems, communication between independent processes requires the intervention of the kernel to provide protection and the mechanisms needed for communication. However, because threads within the same task share memory and files, they can communicate with each other without invoking the kernel.

Scheduling and dispatching are done on a thread basis; hence, most of the state information dealing with execution is maintained in thread-level data structures. There are, however, several actions that affect all the threads in a task and that the operating system must manage at the task level. Suspension involves swapping the address space out of main memory. Because all threads in a task share the same address space, all threads must enter a Suspend state at the same time. Similarly, termination of a task terminates all threads within that task.

Example — Aldus PageMaker

As an example of the use of threads, consider the Aldus PageMaker application, which runs under OS/2. PageMaker is a writing, design, and production tool for desktop publishing. The thread structure, shown in Figure 3.15 [KRON90], was chosen to optimize the responsiveness of the application. Three threads are always active: an event-handling thread, a screen-redraw thread, and a service thread.

Generally, OS/2 is less responsive in managing windows if any input message requires too much processing. The OS/2 guidelines state that no message should require more than 1/10 sec. For example, calling a subroutine to print a page

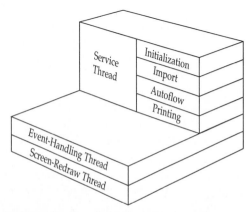

FIGURE 3.15 Thread structure for Aldus Pagemaker

while processing a print command would prevent the system from dispatching any further message to any applications, slowing performance. To meet this criterion, long user operations in PageMaker—printing, importing data, and flowing text—are performed by a service thread. Program initialization is also largely performed by the service thread, which absorbs the idle time while the user invokes the dialogue to create a new document or open an existing document. A separate thread waits on new event messages.

Synchronizing the service thread and the event-handling thread is complicated because a user may continue to type or move the mouse, which activates the event-handling thread, while the service thread is still busy. If this conflict occurs, PageMaker filters these messages and accepts only certain basic ones, such as window resize.

A message is posted from the service thread to indicate completion of its task. Until this occurs, user activity in PageMaker is restricted. The program indicates this restriction by disabling menu items and displaying a "busy" cursor. The user is free to switch to other applications, and when the busy cursor is moved to another window, it will change to the appropriate cursor for that application.

A separate thread is used for screen redraw for two reasons:

1. PageMaker does not limit the number of objects appearing on a page; thus, processing a redraw request can easily exceed the guideline of 1/10 sec.
2. Using a separate thread allows the user to abort drawing. In this case, when the user rescales a page, the redraw can proceed immediately. The program is less responsive if it finishes displaying the page at the old scale and then completely redraws at the new scale.

Dynamic scrolling—redrawing the screen as the user drags the scroll indicator—is also possible. The event-handling thread monitors the scroll bar and redraws the margin rulers (which redraw quickly and give immediate positional feedback to the user). Meanwhile, the screen-redraw thread constantly tries to redraw the page and catch up.

Implementing dynamic redraw without the use of multiple threads places a greater burden on the application to poll for messages at various points. Multithreading allows concurrent activities to be separated more naturally in the code.

Other Arrangements

As we have said, the concepts of resource allocation and dispatching unit have traditionally been embodied in the single concept of the process; that is, a one-to-one relationship between threads and processes. Recently, there has been much interest in providing for multiple threads within a single process, or a many-to-one relationship. However, as Table 3.12 shows, the other two combinations have also been investigated, namely a many-to-many relationship and even a one-to-many relationship.

TABLE 3.12   Relationship Between Threads and Processes

Threads:Processes	Description	Example Systems
1:1	Each thread of execution is a unique process with its own address space and resources.	UNIX System V
M:1	A process defines an address space and dynamic resource ownership. Multiple threads may be created and executed within that process.	OS/2, MVS, MACH
1:M	A thread may migrate from one process environment to another. This allows a thread to be easily moved among distinct systems.	Ra
M:M	Combines attributes of M:1 and 1:M cases	TRIX

Many-to-Many Relationship

The idea of having a many-to-many relationship between threads and processes has been explored in the experimental operating system TRIX [SIEB83, WARD80]. In TRIX, there are the concepts of domain and thread. A domain is a static entity consisting of an address space and "ports" through which messages may be sent and received. A thread is a single execution path, with an execution stack, processor state, and scheduling information.

As with Mach, multiple threads may execute in a single domain, providing the efficiency gains discussed earlier. However, it is also possible for a single-user activity, or application, to be performed in multiple domains. In this case, a thread exists that can move from one domain to another.

The use of a single thread in multiple domains seems primarily motivated by a desire to provide structuring tools for the programmer. For example, consider a program that makes use of an I/O subprogram. In a multiprogramming environment that allows user-spawned processes, the main program could generate a new process to handle I/O and then continue to execute. However, if the future progress of the main program depends on the outcome of the I/O operation, then the main program will have to wait for the other I/O program to finish. There are several ways to implement this application:

1. The entire program can be implemented as a single process. This is a reasonable and straightforward solution. There are drawbacks related to memory management. The process as a whole may require considerable main memory to execute efficiently, whereas the I/O subprogram requires a relatively small address space to buffer I/O and to handle the relatively small amount of program code. Because the I/O program executes in the address space of the larger program, either the entire process must remain in main

memory during the I/O operation or the I/O operation is subject to swapping. This memory-management effect would also exist if the main program and the I/O subprogram were implemented as two threads in the same address space.

2. The main program and I/O subprogram can be implemented as two separate processes. This incurs the overhead of creating the subordinate process. If the I/O activity is frequent, one must either leave the subordinate process alive, which consumes management resources, or frequently create and destroy the subprogram, which is inefficient.

3. Treat the main program and the I/O subprogram as a single activity that is to be implemented as a single thread. However, one address space (domain) can be created for the main program and one for the I/O subprogram. Thus, the thread can be moved between the two address spaces as execution proceeds. The operating system can manage the two address spaces independently, and no process creation overhead is incurred. Furthermore, the address space used by the I/O subprogram can also be shared by other simple I/O programs.

The experiences of the TRIX developers indicate that the third option has merit and may be the most effective solution for some applications.

One-to-Many Relationship

In the field of distributed operating systems (designed to control distributed computer systems), there has been interest in the concept of a thread as primarily an entity that can move among address spaces.[9] A notable example of this research is the Clouds operating system [DASG88], and especially its kernel, known as Ra [BERN89]. Another example is the Emerald system [JUL88].

A thread in Clouds is a unit of activity from the user's perspective. A process is a virtual address space with an associated process control block. Upon creation, a thread starts executing in a process by invoking an entry point to a program in that process. Threads may move from one address space to another and actually span machine boundaries (i.e., move from one computer to another). As a thread moves, it must carry with it certain information, such as the controlling terminal, global parameters, and scheduling guidance (e.g., priority).

The Clouds approach provides an effective way of insulating a user and programmer from the details of the distributed environment. A user's activity may be represented as a single thread, and the movement of that thread among machines may be dictated by the operating system for a variety of system-related reasons, such as the need to access a remote resource and to balance the load.

---

[9]The movement of processes or threads among address spaces on different machines has become a hot topic in recent years (e.g., see [ARTS89a,89b]). We explore this topic in Chapter 9.

3.5

EXAMPLES OF PROCESS DESCRIPTION AND CONTROL

UNIX System V

UNIX makes use of a simple but powerful process facility that is highly visible to the user. All processes in the system except for two basic system processes are created by user program command.

Process States

A total of nine process states are recognized by the UNIX operating system; these are listed in Table 3.13, and a state transition diagram is shown in Figure 3.16. This figure is quite similar to Figure 3.7, with the two UNIX Asleep states corresponding to the two Blocked states. The differences can be quickly summarized as follows:

- UNIX employs two Running states to indicate whether the process is executing in user mode or kernel mode.
- A distinction is made between the two states: Ready to Run, in Memory and Preempted. These are essentially the same state, as indicated by the dotted line joining them. The distinction is made to emphasize the way in which the preempted state is entered. When a process is running in kernel mode (as a result of a supervisor call, clock interrupt, or I/O interrupt), there will come a time when the kernel has completed its work and is ready to return control to the user program. At this point, the kernel may decide to preempt the current process in favor of one that is ready and of higher priority. In that

TABLE 3.13   UNIX Process States

User running	Executing in user mode.
Kernel running	Executing in kernel mode.
Ready to run, in memory	Ready to run as soon as the kernel schedules it.
Sleeping in memory	Unable to execute until an event occurs; process is in main memory.
Ready to run, swapped	Process is ready to run, but the swapper must swap the process into main memory before the kernel can schedule it to execute.
Sleeping, swapped	The process is awaiting an event and has been swapped to secondary storage.
Preempted	Process is returning from kernel to user mode, but the kernel preempts it and does a context switch to schedule another process.
Created	Process is newly created and not yet ready to run.
Zombie	Process no longer exists, but it leaves a record for its parent process to collect.

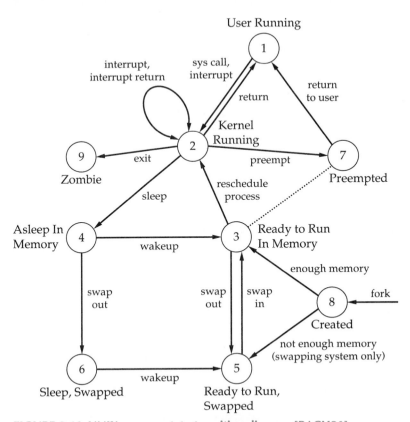

FIGURE 3.16 UNIX process state transition diagram [BACH86]

case, the current process moves to the preempted state. However, for purposes of dispatching, those processes in the preempted state and those in the Ready to Run, in Memory state form one queue.

Preemption can occur only when a process is about to move from kernel mode to user mode. While a process is running in kernel mode, it may not be preempted. This makes UNIX unsuitable for real-time processing. Chapter 6 discusses the requirements for real-time processing.

Two processes are unique in UNIX. Process 0 is a special process that is created when the system boots; in effect, it is predefined as a data structure loaded at boot time. It is the swapper process. In addition, process 0 spawns process 1, referred to as the *init* process; all other processes in the system have process 1 as an ancestor. When a new interactive user logs onto the system, it is process 1 that creates a user process for that user. Subsequently, the user program can create child processes in a branching tree, so that any particular application can consist of a number of related processes.

Process Description

A process in UNIX is a rather complex set of data structures that provide the operating system with all the information necessary to manage and dispatch processes. Table 3.14 summarizes the elements of the process image that are organized into three parts: user-level context, register context, and system-level context.

The **user-level context** contains the basic elements of a user's program and can be generated directly from a compiled object file. The user's program is separated into text and data areas; the text area is read-only and is intended to hold the program's instructions. While the process is executing, the processor uses the user stack area for procedure calls and returns and parameter passing. The shared memory area is a data area that is shared with other processes. There is only one physical copy of a shared memory area, but by the use of

TABLE 3.14   UNIX Process Image

User-Level Context

Process Text	Executable machine instructions of the program.
Process Data	Data accessible by the program of this process.
User Stack	Contains the arguments, local variables, and pointers for functions executing in user mode.
Shared Memory	Memory shared with other processes, used for interprocess communication.

Register Context

Program Counter	Address of next instruction to be executed; may be in kernel or user memory space of this process.
Processor Status Register	Contains the hardware status at the time of preemption; contents and format are hardware-dependent.
Stack Pointer	Points to the top of the kernel or user stack, depending on the mode of operation at the time of preemption.
General-Purpose Registers	Hardware-dependent.

System-Level Context

Process Table Entry	Defines state of a process; this information is always accessible to the operating system.
U (user) Area	Process control information that needs to be accessed only in the context of the process.
Pre-Process Region Table	Defines the mapping from virtual to physical addresses; also contains a permission field that indicates the type of access allowed the process: read-only, read-write, or read-execute.
Kernel Stack	Contains the stack frame of kernel procedures as the process executes in kernel mode.

virtual memory, it appears to each sharing process that the shared memory region is in its address space.

When a process is not running, the processor status information is stored in the **register context** area.

Finally, the **system-level context** contains the remaining information that the operating system needs to manage the process. It consists of a static part, which is fixed in size and stays with a process throughout its lifetime, and a dynamic part, which varies in size through the life of the process. One element of the static part is the process table entry. This is actually part of the process table maintained by the operating system, with one entry per process. The process table entry contains process control information that is accessible to the kernel at all times; hence, in a virtual memory system, all process table entries are maintained in main memory. Table 3.15 lists the contents of a process table entry. The user area, or U area, contains additional process control information that is needed by the kernel only when it is executing in the context of this process. Table 3.16 shows the contents of this table.

The distinction between the process table entry and the U area reflects the fact that the UNIX kernel always executes in the context of some process. Much of the time, the kernel will be dealing with the concerns of that process. However, some of the time, such as when the kernel is performing a scheduling algorithm preparatory to dispatching another process, it will need access to information about other processes.

TABLE 3.15   UNIX Process Table Entry

Process Status	Current state of process.
Pointers	To U area and process memory area (text, data, stack).
Process Size	Enables the operating system to know how much space to allocate the process.
User Identifiers	The real user ID identifies the user who is responsible for the running process. The effective user ID may be used by a process to gain temporary privileges associated with a particular program; while that program is being executed as part of the process, the process operates with the effective user ID.
Process Identifiers	ID of this process; ID of parent process.
Event Descriptor	Valid when a process is in a sleeping state; when the event occurs, the process is transferred to a ready-to-run state.
Priority	Used for process scheduling.
Signal	Enumerates signals sent to a process but not yet handled.
Timers	Includes process execution time, kernel resource use, and user-set timer used to send alarm signal to a process.
P-link	Pointer to the next link in the ready queue (valid if process is ready to execute).
Memory Status	Indicates whether process image is in main memory or swapped-out. If it is in memory, this field also indicates whether it may be swapped out or is temporarily locked into main memory.

TABLE 3.16   UNIX U Area

Process Table Pointer	Indicates entry that corresponds to the U area.
User Identifiers	Real and effective user IDs.
Timers	Record time that the process (and its descendants) spent executing in user mode and in kernel mode.
Signal Handler Array	For each type of signal defined in the system, indicates how the process will react to receipt of that signal (exit, ignore, execute specified user function).
Control Terminal	Indicates login terminal for this process if one exists.
Error Field	Records errors encountered during a system call.
Return Value	Contains the result of system calls.
I/O Parameters	Describe the amount of data to transfer, the address of the source (or target) data array in user space, and file offsets for I/O.
File Parameters	Current directory and current root describe the file system environment of the process.
User File Descriptor Table	Records the files the process has open.
Limit Fields	Restrict the size of the process and the size of a file it can write.
Permission Modes Fields	Masks mode settings on files the process creates.

The third static portion of the system-level context is the per-process region table, which is used by the memory-management system. Finally, the kernel stack is the dynamic portion of the system-level context. This stack is used when the process is executing in kernel mode, and it contains the information that must be saved and restored as procedure calls and interrupts occur.

Process Control

As was mentioned, UNIX System V follows the model of Figure 3.13b, in which most of the operating system executes within the environment of a user process. Thus, two modes, user and kernel, are required. Some portions of the operating system, notably the swapper, operate as separate processes, known as *kernel processes*.

Process creation in UNIX is made by means of the kernel system call, fork( ). When a process issues a fork request, the operating system performs the following functions [BACH86]:

1. It allocates a slot in the process table for the new process.
2. It assigns a unique process ID to the child process.
3. It makes a copy of the process image of the parent, with the exception of any shared memory.
4. It increments counters for any files owned by the parent, to reflect that an additional process now also owns those files.
5. It assigns the child process to a Ready to Run state.
6. It returns the ID number of the child to the parent process, and a zero value to the child process.

All this work is accomplished in kernel mode in the parent process. When the kernel has completed these functions, it can do one of the following as part of the dispatcher routine:

1. Stay in the parent process. Control returns to user mode at the point of the fork call of the parent.
2. Transfer control to the child process. The child process begins executing at the same point in the code as the parent, namely, at the return from the fork call.
3. Transfer control to another process. Both parent and child are left in the Ready to Run state.

It is perhaps difficult to visualize this method of process creation because both parent and child are executing the same passage of code. The difference is this: When the return from the fork occurs, the return parameter is tested. If the value is zero, then this is the child process, and a branch can be executed to the appropriate user program to continue execution. If the value is nonzero, then this is the parent process, and the main line of execution can continue.

OS/2

Sessions, Processes, and Threads

In OS/2, what is commonly embodied in the concept of process in other operating systems is split into three separate types of entities: session, processes, and threads (Table 3.17). This split is well tailored to the needs of an interactive graphics interface for personal computer and workstation use.

TABLE 3.17   OS/2 Process-Related Concepts

	Description	Area of Concern
Session	A collection of one or more processes associated with a user interface (keyboard, display, mouse). This concept allows the user to open more than one application, giving each application one or more windows on the screen. The operating system must keep track of which window, and therefore which session, is active, so that keyboard and mouse input are routed to the appropriate session.	Interactive user control
Process	An entity corresponding to a user job or application that owns resources, such as memory and open files.	Job or application
Thread	A dispatchable unit of work that executes sequentially and is interruptable, so that the processor can turn to another thread.	Scheduling and dispatching

The session represents an interactive user application, such as a word processing program or a spreadsheet. OS/2 supports up to 16 sessions at any time. The following four of these are reserved for use by the system:

- *DOS environment:* This session supports command-line-driven applications that run under the older DOS operating system.
- *The user shell:* This is an application program that interacts with the user and the session manager software to start, stop, and switch application sessions.
- *Detached processes:* This is a "hidden session" that never has direct access to keyboard, screen, or mouse. It contains processes spawned by applications that are detached from the application session to run in a background mode, such as an I/O operation.
- *Hard-error handler:* A hard error is a program error caused by something external to the application, such as device not ready, file-sharing violation, and hardware error. The hard-error handler is responsible for receiving such catastrophic system errors and prompting the user for recovery actions.

The user may open up to 12 application sessions. At any time, one session is in foreground mode, with other sessions in background mode. All keyboard and mouse input is directed to one of the processes of the foreground session, as dictated by the applications. When a session is in foreground mode, a process performing video output sends it directly to the hardware video buffer and thence to the user's screen. When the session is moved to the background, the hardware video buffer is saved to a logical video buffer for that session. While a session is in background, if any of the threads of any of the processes of that session execute and produce screen output, that output is directed to the logical video buffer. When the session returns to foreground, the screen is updated to reflect the current contents of the logical video buffer for the new foreground session.

This structure allows the user to have a number of applications up and running concurrently and imposes the necessary discipline so that user input goes to the appropriate application and screen output comes from the appropriate application.

Within a session, a number of processes may be created. One is the initial process for that session; any others are either direct or indirect descendants of the primary process in a parent-child relationship (Figure 3.17). The process is the entity to which resources are allocated, including main and virtual memory, open files, connections to loadable linked object code, and interprocess signals known as *semaphores* (discussed in Chapter 4). Processes provide a useful way of structuring the software of an application.

The ability of a single application to be structured as a set of processes, each with its own resource ownership attributes, is useful for large and complex applications. By providing each process with its own distinct memory and other resources, one can break the application into smaller pieces that can interact with each other only in some very well-defined ways.

Within a process, one or more threads may be assigned. These threads share

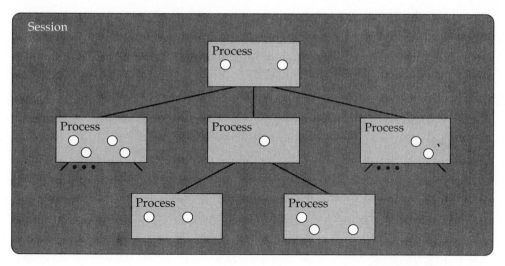

O = Thread

FIGURE 3.17 OS/2 sessions, processes, and threads

all the resources owned by the process. The thread is the unit of execution in OS/2; it is the entity that is scheduled and dispatched. The ability to structure a single process as a set of threads is also useful. Because the threads share the same resources, including memory, they can interact tightly without need for operating-system support. For example, if one thread in a process opens a file, all threads in the process can access that file without having to pass permissions around via the operating system.

Letwin gives the following four examples of the uses of threads [LETW88]:

- *Foreground and background work:* This is in the sense of directly interacting with the user, not as in foreground and background sessions. For example, in a spreadsheet program, one thread could display menus and read user input, while another thread executes user commands and updates the spreadsheet. This arrangement will often increase the perceived speed of the application by allowing the program to prompt for the next command before the previous command is complete.

- *Asynchronous processing:* Asynchronous elements in the program can be implemented as threads. For example, as a protection against power failure, you can design a word processor to write its RAM buffer to disk once every minute. A thread can be created whose sole job is periodic backup and which schedules itself directly with the operating system; there is no need for fancy code in the main program to provide for time checks or to coordinate input and output.

- *Speed execution:* A multithreaded process can compute one batch of data while reading the next batch from a device. When OS/2 is implemented on a multiprocessing system, multiple threads from the same process will actually be able to execute simultaneously.

• *Organizing programs:* Programs that involve a variety of activities or a variety of sources and destinations of input and output may be easier to design and implement using threads.

Control Structures

Several data structures are used by OS/2 to manage the processes and threads that are under its control. Sessions are managed by the session manager, which is an application-level subsystem. Thus, sessions as such are not visible to or known by the kernel of the operating system.

One key data structure is the per task data area (PTDA), of which there is one per process. Resources are allocated at the process level, and OS/2 uses the PTDA to keep track of and control these allocations. Thus, the PTDA indicates the threads, open files, semaphores, and other resources allocated to the process. In addition, there is one thread control block (TCB) for each thread in a process. The TCB contains the register set and the kernel stack of the thread, and information for thread scheduling (e.g, thread state and priority) and I/O activity. These are collected with the PTDA into a single segment (unit of memory management), which is of variable length (Figure 3.18). As threads are created and destroyed, the PDTA segment grows and shrinks accordingly.

Another important data structure is the local descriptor table (LDT). Again, there is one of these per process. This table is used primarily for memory management.

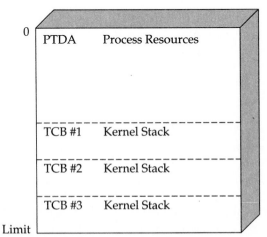

FIGURE 3.18 Per task data area (PTDA) segment [KOGA88]

Process and Thread Control

As with most operating systems, OS/2 makes use of different levels, or modes, of protection to protect the operating system code and key memory areas from less privileged application programs. In the case of OS/2, three levels of protection are provided, exploiting the four-level structure provided on the Intel microprocessors on which OS/2 runs. These levels are referred to as rings, with the innermost ring providing the greatest protection and each successive ring providing less protection.

Figure 3.19 illustrates the way in which OS/2 uses the ring structure. In ring 0 is found the kernel of the operating system, which provides basic system services, and device drivers. At the outermost ring, user applications and OS/2

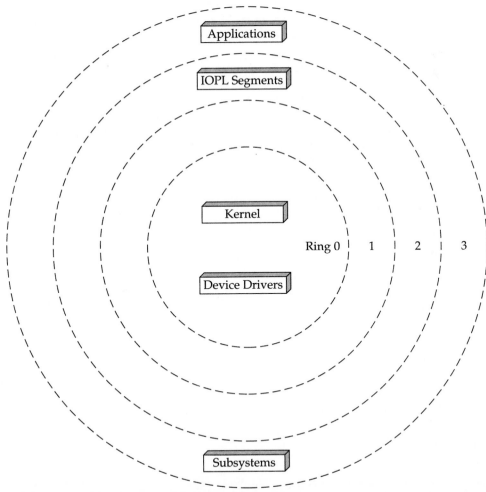

FIGURE 3.19 OS/2 protection ring usage [KOGA88]

subsystems are supported. Subsystems are system services and extensions that do not require hardware privilege. Ring 2 is used by subsystems and applications that execute instructions requiring I/O privilege. This allows these programs to do I/O operations that do not require servicing interrupts.

MVS

MVS Tasks

The MVS operating system makes use of a highly structured process environment. In MVS, virtual memory is broken up into large regions called *address spaces*. Roughly speaking, a single address space corresponds to a single application. Within that address space, a number of tasks may be generated. It is the MVS task that is the unit of dispatching.

Typically, a hundred or more address spaces exist concurrently, each of which may have many tasks. Thus, MVS is capable of, and often is, managing thousands of tasks concurrently.

Figure 3.20, based on a figure in Leban and Arnold [LEBA84], gives an example of the way in which multiple tasks are generated within an address space. The application supports inquiry transactions from a number of terminals. The program is broken up into four modules: a main program, and three programs for the three types of inquiry: customer, order, and product. When the application is loaded into the system, the address space starts out with some memory devoted to MVS, and the main program loaded (Figure 3.20a). Then, a terminal user enters a customer inquiry. As a result, Main issues a request to create a new task to execute the customer module, and this is loaded in to the address space (Figure 3.20b). While this transaction is in progress, a second terminal issues an order request, and that module is loaded in as a separate task (Figure 3.20c). Next, while both transactions are still in progress, a third terminal issues an order inquiry. The code for the order module is already in the address space and can be used by more than one task. However, each task will need its own private region of memory for local variables and stack processing, as illustrated in Figure 3.20d.

Explicitly, MVS makes use of only three task states: Ready, Active (running), and Waiting. However, an entire address space may be swapped out to secondary storage. Thus, all the tasks of that address space are suspended, as we have used that term.

Each task is represented by a task control block (TCB). In addition, there is another type of dispatchable entity, the service request. The *service request* is a "system task," of which there are two kinds. Some system tasks provide services to a specific application and are executed in the address space of that application; others are involved in interaddress space operations and do not execute in any user address space but, rather, in the system's reserved address space. These system tasks, collectively, can be considered the kernel of the MVS operating system. Each system task has its own service request block (SRB),

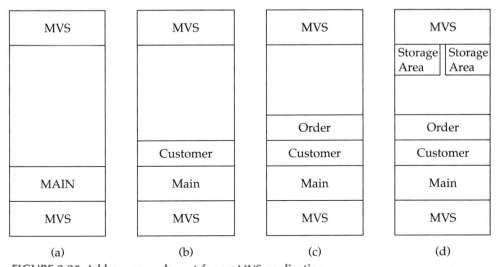

FIGURE 3.20 Address space layout for an MVS application

and the dispatcher chooses among all ready SRBs and TCBs when it is time to dispatch the next task.

Thus, two apparently modern concepts, that of threads within a process and that of the operating system as a set of processes (Figure 3.13c) are found, in their own way, in MVS.

Task-Related Control Structures

Table 3.18 lists the major controls structures that MVS uses to manage user tasks and system tasks. These structures collectively encompass much of what we have referred to as process control blocks. Global service request blocks are used to manage system tasks that do not execute within a user address space. The remaining structures are all concerned with address space management. The address space control block (ASCB) and address space extension block (ASXB) contain information about address spaces. The distinction is that the ASCB information is needed by MVS when it is executing in the system's reserved address space, whereas the ASXB contains additional information that is needed only when MVS is dealing with and executing in a specific user address space. Finally, local SRBs and TCBs contain information about dispatchable entities within an address space.

Figure 3.21 shows how these structures are organized and suggests the dispatching discipline observed by MVS. Global SRBs are maintained in a queue of descending priority in the system queue area, which is a region of main memory that cannot be swapped. Thus, global SRBs are always available in main memory. When a processor is available, MVS first searches this queue for a Ready SRB. If none are found, MVS then looks for an address space that has

TABLE 3.18   MVS Process Control Structures

Global Service Request Block (SRB)	Represents a system task that is independent of any user address space. Includes: • Address of the ASCB to which the routine will be dispatched • Entry point to routine • Address of a parameter list to be passed to routine • Priority level
Address Space Control Block (ASCB)	Contains system-wide information about an address space. That is, this is information about an address space that is needed by MVS when not executing within a particular user address space. Information includes: • Pointers to create queues of ASCBs • Whether the address space is swapped-out • Dispatching priority • Real and virtual memory allocated to this address space • Number of Ready TCBs in this address space • Pointer to ASXB
Address Space Extension Block (ASXB)	Contains information about an address space not of global interest. Includes: • Number of TCBs in this address space • Pointer to TCB dispatching queue for this address space • Pointer to local SRB dispatching queue for this address space • Pointer to interrupt handler save area
Local Service Request Block (SRB)	Represents a system task that is executed within a particular user address space. Includes: • Address of the ASCB to which the routine will be dispatched • Entry point to routine • Address of a parameter list to be passed to routine • Priority level
Task Control Block (TCB)	Represents a user program in execution. Contains information needed for managing a task within an address space. Includes: • Processor status information • Pointers to programs that are part of this task

at least one Ready TCB or SRB. For this purpose, a queue of ASCBs is maintained in the system queue area. Each address space is assigned an overall priority level; hence, the ASCBs can be arranged in descending priority.

Once an address space is selected, MVS can work with the structures in that address space, referred to as the local system queue area. MVS selects the highest-priority SRB, or failing that, the highest-priority TCB to dispatch. In

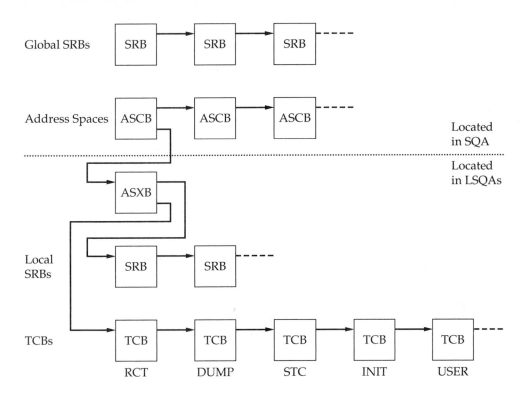

SRB = Service Request Block
ASCB = Address Space Control Block
ASXB = Address Space Extension Block
TCB = Task Control Block
SQA = System Queue Area

LSQA = Local System Queue Area
RCT = Region Control Area
STC = Started Task Control
INIT = Initiator

FIGURE 3.21 MVS dispatcher queues [PAAN86]

this example, the TCB queue structure for a batch job is shown. It consists of the following tasks:

- *Region control task:* Responsible for managing this address space on behalf of all the tasks executing in it.
- *Dump:* Responsible for dumping the address space if the address space terminates abnormally.
- *Started control task:* The TCB for the program that starts the address space.
- *Initiator:* Responsible for loading a stream of batch jobs.
- *User task:* The application itself consists of one or more user tasks.

The advantage of splitting the control information into global and local is that as much information as possible about an address space can be swapped out with the address space, thus conserving main memory.

3.6

SUMMARY

The most fundamental building block in a modern operating system is the process. The principal function of the operating system is to create, manage, and terminate processes. While processes are active, the operating system must see that each is allocated time for execution by the processor, coordinate their activities, manage conflicting demands, and allocate system resources to processes.

To perform its process-management functions, the operating system must maintain a description of each process. Each process is represented by a process image, which includes the address space within which the process executes and a process control block. The latter contains all the information that is required by the operating system to manage the process, including its current state, resources allocated to it, priority, and other relevant data.

During its lifetime, a process moves among a number of states. The most important of these are Ready, Running, and Blocked. A Ready process is one that is not currently executing but that is ready to be executed as soon as the operating system dispatches it. The Running process is that process which is currently being executed by the processor. In a multiple-processor system, more than one process can be in this state. A Blocked process is waiting for the completion of some event, such as an I/O operation.

A Running process is interrupted either by an interrupt, which is an event that occurs outside the process and which is recognized by the processor, or by executing a supervisor call to the operating system. In either case, the processor performs a context switch, transferring control to an operating-system routine. After it has completed necessary work, the operating system may resume the interrupted process or switch to some other process.

Some operating systems distinguish the concepts of process and thread, the former related to resource ownership and the latter related to program execution. This approach may lead to improved efficiency and coding convenience.

3.7

RECOMMENDED READING

All the textbooks listed in Section 2.6 cover the material of this chapter, although, curiously, none give these topics the prominence found in this book. For UNIX, OS/2, and MVS, good sources for this material are [BACH86], [IACO88], and [KATZ84], respectively. [NEHM75] is an interesting discussion of process states and the operating-system primitives needed for process dispatching.

3.8

PROBLEMS

3.1 Table 3.19 shows the process states for the VAX/VMS operating system.
(a) Can you provide a justification for the existence of so many distinct wait states?
(b) Why do the following states not have resident and swapped out versions: page fault wait, collided page wait, common event wait, free page wait, and resource wait.
(c) Draw the state transition diagram and indicate the action or occurrence that causes each transition.

3.2 Pinkert and Wear defined the following states for processes: execute (running), active (ready), blocked, and suspend [PINK89]. A process is blocked if it is waiting for permission to use a resource, and it is suspended if it is waiting for an operation to be completed on a resource it has already acquired. In many operating systems, these two states are lumped together as the Block state, and the Suspend state is defined as in this chapter. Compare the relative merits of the two sets of definitions.

TABLE 3.19   VAX/VMS Process States

Process State	Process Condition
Currently executing	Running process.
Computable (resident)	Ready and resident in main memory.
Computable (outswapped)	Ready, but swapped out of main memory.
Page fault wait	Process has referenced a page not in main memory and must wait for the page to be read in.
Collided page wait	Process has referenced a shared page that is the cause of an existing page fault wait in another process, or a private page that is currently being read in or written out.
Common event wait	Waiting for shared event flag (event flags are single-bit interprocess signalling mechanisms).
Free page wait	Waiting for a free page in main memory to be added to the collection of pages in main memory devoted to this process (the working set of the process).
Hibernate wait (resident)	Process puts itself in a wait state.
Hibernate wait (outswapped)	Hibernating process is swapped out of main memory.
Local event wait (resident)	Process in main memory and waiting for local event flag (usually I/O completion).
Local event wait (outswapped)	Process in local event wait is swapped out of main memory.
Suspended wait (resident)	Process is put into a wait state by another process.
Suspended wait (outswapped)	Suspended process is swapped out of main memory.
Resource wait	Process waiting for miscellaneous system resource.

3.3 For the seven-state process model of Figure 3.7b, draw a queueing diagram similar to that of Figure 3.6b.

3.4 Consider the state transition diagram of Figure 3.7b. Suppose that it is time for the operating system to dispatch a process and that there are processes in both the Ready state and the Ready, suspend state, and that at least one process in the Ready, suspend state has higher scheduling priority than any of the processes in the Ready state. Two extreme policies are (1) always dispatch from a process in the Ready state to minimize swapping, and (2) always give preference to the highest-priority process even though that may mean swapping when swapping is not necessary. Suggest an intermediate policy that tries to balance the concerns of priority and performance.

3.5 The VAX/VMS operating system makes use of four processor access modes to facilitate the protection and sharing of system resources among processes. The access mode determines the following:

- *Instruction execution privileges:* The instructions that the processor may execute
- *Memory access privileges:* The locations in virtual memory that the current instruction may access

The four modes are the following:

- *Kernel:* Executes the kernel of the VMS operating system, which includes memory management, interrupt handling, and I/O operations (Figure 2.14).
- *Executive:* Executes many of the operating-system service calls, including file and record (disk and tape) management routines.
- *Supervisor:* Executes other operating-system services, such as responses to user commands.
- *User:* Executes user programs, plus utilities such as compilers, editors, linkers, and debuggers.

A process executing in a less privileged mode often needs to call a procedure that executes in a more privileged mode; for example, a user program requires an operating-system service. This call is achieved by using a Change Mode(CHM) instruction, which causes an interrupt that transfers control to a routine at the new access mode. A return is made by executing the REI (return from exception or interrupt) instruction.

(a) A number of operating systems have two modes, kernel and user. What are the advantages and disadvantages of providing four modes instead of two?

(b) Can you make a case for having even more than four modes?

3.6 The VMS scheme discussed in the preceding problem is often referred to as a *ring protection structure,* as illustrated in Figure 3.22. Indeed, the simple kernel/user scheme, as described in Section 3.3, is a two-ring structure.

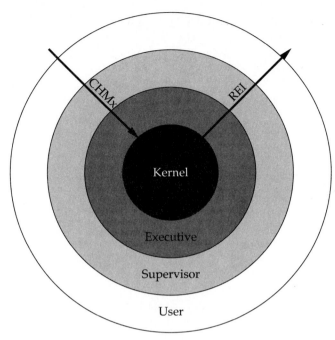

FIGURE 3.22 VAX/VMS access modes

Silberschatz, Peterson, and Galvin point out a problem with this approach [SILB91] :

> The main disadvantage of the ring (hierarchical) structure is that it does not allow us to enforce the need-to-know principle. In particular, if an object must be accessible in domain D_j but not accessible in domain D_i, then we must have $j < i$. But this means that every segment accessible in D_i is also accessible in D_j.

(a) Explain clearly the problem that is referred to in the foregoing quotation.

(b) Suggest a way that a ring-structured operating system can deal with this problem.

3.7 Figure 3.6b suggests that a process can be in only one Event queue at a time.

(a) Is it possible that you would want to allow a process to wait for more than one event at the same time? Provide an example.

(b) In that case, how would you modify the queueing structure of the figure to support this new feature?

3.8 In a number of early computers, an interrupt caused the register values to be stored in fixed locations associated with the given interrupt signal.

Under what circumstances is this a practical technique? Explain why it is inconvenient in general.

3.9 It was pointed out that two advantages of using multiple threads within a process are (1) less work is involved in creating a new thread within an existing process than in creating a new process, and (2) communication among threads within the same process is simplified. Is it also the case that a context switch between two threads within the same process involves less work than a context switch between two threads in different processes?

3.10 It was stated in Section 3.5 that UNIX is unsuitable for real-time applications because a process executing in kernel mode may not be preempted. Elaborate.

3.11 The number of process-related concepts in OS/2 can be reduced from three to two by eliminating sessions and associating the user interface (keyboard, mouse, screen) with processes. Thus, one process at a time is in foreground mode. For further structuring, processes can be broken up into threads.
(a) What benefits are lost with this approach?
(b) If you go ahead with this modification, where do you assign resources (memory, files, etc.): at the process or thread level?

3.12 A process completes its work and exits. What basic operations are needed to clean up and continue with another process?

CHAPTER 4

Concurrency

Until just a few years ago, one could safely say that the central theme of modern operating systems was multiprogramming. Today, it is more accurate to say that modern operating systems have two central themes:

- *Multiprogramming:* the management of multiple processes within a single computer system
- *Distributed processing:* the management of multiple processes executing on multiple, distributed computer systems

Fundamental to both these themes and fundamental to the technology of operating-system design is concurrency. Therefore, concurrency is a dominant topic in this text. Having presented an overview of operating systems and having introduced the concept of process, we are now in a position to examine the concept of concurrent processes, which we do in some detail in this chapter. Although the remainder of the book covers a number of other important topics in operating-system design, concurrency will play a major role in our consideration of all these topics.

The chapter begins with an introduction to the concept of concurrency and the implications of the execution of multiple concurrent processes.[1] We find that the basic requirement for support of concurrent processes is the ability to enforce mutual exclusion, that is, the ability to exclude all other processes from a course of action while one process is granted that ability. In the second section of this chapter, we look at some possible approaches to achieving mutual exclusion. All these are software solutions and require the use of a technique known as *busy-waiting.* Because of the complexity of these solutions and the undesirability of busy-waiting, we search for solutions that do not involve busy-waiting and that can be either supported by the operating system or enforced by language compilers. Next, we look at two problems that plague all efforts to support concurrent processing: deadlock and starvation. The chapter closes with an

---

[1]For simplicity, we refer in this chapter to the concurrent execution of *processes.* In fact, as we have seen in the preceding chapter, in some systems the fundamental unit of concurrency is a thread rather than a process.

examination of several classic problems in concurrency that highlight the strengths and weaknesses of various approaches discussed in the chapter.

In this chapter, the discussion is limited to a consideration of concurrency on a single system. Issues related to concurrency across multiple systems are pursued in Chapter 9.

PRINCIPLES OF CONCURRENCY

In a single-processor multiprogramming system, processes are interleaved in time to yield the appearance of simultaneous execution (Figure 4.1a). Even though actual parallel processing is not achieved and even though there is a certain amount of overhead involved in switching back and forth between processes, interleaved execution provides major benefits in processing efficiency and in program structuring. In a multiple-processor system, it is possible not only to interleave processes but to overlap them (Figure 4.1b).

At first glance, it may seem that interleaving and overlapping represent fundamentally different modes of execution and present different problems. In fact, both techniques can be viewed as examples of concurrent processing, and both present the same problems. The problems all flow from a basic characteristic of multiprogramming systems: The relative speed of execution of processes cannot be predicted. It depends on the activities of other processes, the way in which the operating system handles interrupts, and the scheduling policies of the operating system. This makes it difficult for the operating system to manage the allocation of resources optimally. In addition, it becomes very difficult to

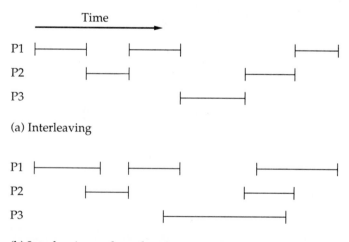

(a) Interleaving

(b) Interleaving and overlapping

FIGURE 4.1 Concurrent processes

locate a programming error because results are typically not reproducible [LEBL87, CARR89].

A Simple Example

Figure 4.2 shows the essential elements of a program that will provide a character echo function; input is obtained from a keyboard one keystroke at a time. Each input character is stored in variable *in*. It is then transferred to variable *out* and then output to the display. Now, both the input and output functions are I/O operations and are subject to interruption. However, since they are independent of each other, it is possible to execute them in parallel. The program uses the notation **parbegin, parend** to delimit operations that may be performed concurrently. The way this is dealt with by the compiler and operating system will be specific to a particular implementation. In any case, the program is informing the system that the following operations may execute concurrently. Potentially, this program will run more efficiently than a simple sequential program.

Suppose, however, that the programmer makes a mistake and writes the following fragment of code:

```
repeat
   parbegin
      out : = in;
      output (out, display);
      input (in, keyboard)
   parend
forever.
```

By mistake, the copy operation has been placed inside the concurrent portion of the program. Now the output depends on the order in which these operations are carried out. The desired result is as follows: For a sequence of input char-

```
procedure echo;
var   s, t: character;
begin
   input (in, keyboard);
   repeat
      out : = in;
      parbegin
         output (out, display);
         input (in, keyboard)
      parend
   forever
end.
```

FIGURE 4.2 Character echo program.

acters $\{c_1, c_2, c_3, \ldots\}$, we would like the exact same sequence of output characters to be generated. Suppose that the first character has been successfully read in and displayed. Thus, the input sequence is $\{c_1\}$ and the output sequence is also $\{c_1\}$. For simplicity, let us assume that the three statements inside the repeat loop can be interleaved but not overlapped. Then the following are the possible outcomes of the second iteration of the repeat loop:

out := in;	output (out, display);	input (in, keyboard)	$\rightarrow \{c_1, c_2\}$
out := in;	input (in, keyboard);	output (out, display)	$\rightarrow \{c_1, c_2\}$
output (out, display);	out := in;	input (in, keyboard)	$\rightarrow \{c_1, c_1\}$
output (out, display);	input (in, keyboard);	out := in	$\rightarrow \{c_1, c_1\}$
input (in, keyboard);	output (out, display);	out := in	$\rightarrow \{c_1, c_1\}$
input (in, keyboard);	out := in;	output (out, display)	$\rightarrow \{c_1, c_3\}$

So, there are six possible sequences, with the following three possible outcomes:

1. If the copy operation is completed before input and output, then the correct character sequence is preserved.
2. If the output operation is performed before the copy operation, then the previous character is displayed a second time and the current character is missed.
3. If the input operation is completed before the copy operation, which is in turn completed before the output operation, then the next character is displayed and the current character is missed.

Of course, this is just a single execution of the repeat loop. During the course of lengthy input, dozens or hundreds of iterations of the loop could occur, and the number of possible sequences and the number of possible erroneous outputs increases exponentially. Thus, it is unlikely that an erroneous result will be reproduced exactly, and therefore it is extremely difficult to debug concurrent programs. The programmer must resort to studying the program text. In this simple example, such an approach is feasible, but in a lengthy program with hundreds or thousands of lines of code the task is daunting.

One alternative is to provide structures and mechanisms, either in the programming language or in the operating system, that encourage the production of concurrent programs whose results are reproducible. Much of this chapter is devoted to discussing such features. However, be warned that the existence of such features does not eliminate the problem, since such features are open to misuse.

Motivation for Concurrency

In a multiprogramming environment, concurrency may arise in three different contexts:

- *Multiple applications:* Multiprogramming was invented to allow the processing time of the computer to be dynamically shared among a number of active jobs or applications.

- *Structured application:* As an extension of the principles of modular design and structured programming, some applications can be effectively implemented as a set of concurrent processes.
- *Operating system structure:* The same structuring advantages apply to the systems programmer, and we have seen that some operating systems are themselves implemented as a set of processes.

Program Structuring Alternatives

It should be clear from the discussion in preceding chapters that concurrent processing is attractive from the point of view of multiprogramming. To appreciate the programming advantages for both applications and systems programs, consider this simple problem from Conway [CONW63]:

> Read 80-column cards and print them on 125-character lines, with the following changes. After every card image an extra blank is inserted, and every adjacent pair of asterisks (**) on a card is replaced by the character ↑ .

This program is tricky to write as an ordinary sequential program. The interactions among the various elements of the program are uneven because of the conversion from a length of 80 to 125; furthermore, the length of the card image after conversion will vary depending on the number of occurrences of double asterisks. One way to improve clarity and to minimize the potential for bugs is to write the application as three separate programs. The first program reads in card images, pads each image with a blank, and writes a stream of characters to a temporary file. After all the cards have been read, the second program reads the temporary file, does the character substitution, and writes out a second temporary file. The third program reads the stream of characters from the second temporary file and prints lines of 125 characters each.

This solution is unattractive because of the overhead of I/O and temporary files. Conway proposes a new form of program structure, the coroutine, that allows the application to be written as three programs connected by one-character buffers.

Figure 4.3 highlights the difference between a coroutine and the traditional procedure or subroutine. In a traditional **procedure**, there is a master/slave relationship between the called and calling procedure. The calling procedure may execute a call from any point; the called procedure is begun at its entry point and returns to the calling procedure at the point of call. The **coroutine** exhibits a more symmetric relationship. As each call is made, execution takes up from the last active point in the called procedure. Since there is no sense in which a calling procedure is "higher" than the called, there is no return. Rather, any coroutine can pass control to any other coroutine with a resume command. The first time a coroutine is invoked, it is "resumed" at its entry point. Subsequently, the coroutine is reactivated at the point of its own last resume command. Only one coroutine in a procedure can be in execution at one time, and the transition points are explicitly defined in the code, so this is not an example of concurrent processing.

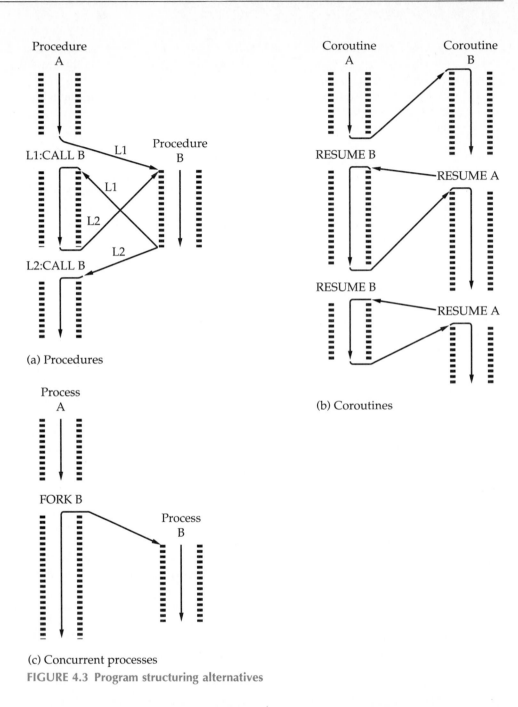

(a) Procedures

(b) Coroutines

(c) Concurrent processes

FIGURE 4.3 Program structuring alternatives

Figure 4.4 illustrates a solution to Conway's problem by using coroutines. The *read* coroutine reads the cards and passes characters through a one-character buffer, *rs*, to the *squash* coroutine. The read coroutine also passes the extra blank at the end of every card image. The *squash* coroutine need know nothing about

```
var   rs, sp: character;
          inbuf: array [1 . . 80] of character;
          outbuf: array [1 . . 125] of character;
procedure read;
begin
  repeat
    READCARD (inbuf);
    for i=1 to 80 do
      begin
        rs := inbuf [i];
        RESUME squash
      end;
    rs := " ";
    RESUME squash
  forever
end;
procedure print;
begin
  repeat
    for j = 1 to 125
      begin
        outbuf [j] := sp;
        RESUME squash
      end;
    OUTPUT (outbuf)
  forever
end;
```

```
procedure squash;
begin
  repeat
    if rs ≠ "*" then
      begin
        sp := rs;
        RESUME print
      end
    else begin
      RESUME read;
      if rs = "*" then
        begin
          sp := " ↑ ";
          RESUME print
        end
      else begin
        sp := "*";
        RESUME print;
        sp := rs;
        RESUME print
      end
    end
    RESUME read
  forever
end.
```

FIGURE 4.4 An application of coroutines.

the 80-character structure of the input; it simply looks for double asterisks and passes a stream of modified characters to the *print* coroutine via a one-character buffer, *sp*. Finally, print simply accepts an incoming stream of characters and prints it as a sequence of 125-character lines.

Note the simplicity and independence of each routine. We could go further and implement the solution as a set of three concurrent processes. This would allow us to take advantage of opportunities for concurrency, such as performing input and output at the same time. Of course, care must be taken to implement concurrency correctly.

Concurrent Processes

The structure suggested by Conway's problem fits the requirements of many system and application programs. For example, a compiler may consist of three passes: a first pass to check syntax and build a symbol table, a second pass to generate code, and a third pass to optimize. These three functions can be implemented as separate processes. Similarly, an interactive application may consist of the following parts. A *read process* accepts data from the user, encodes it into an internally meaningful form, and passes it to an analysis process. An *execute process* analyzes the data received from the input process; such analysis includes at least recognition and possibly translation and/or interpretation. The results are then passed on to a *print routine*, which formats the output and disposes of it (e.g., by writing to printer or display).

In designing a program that is to be made up of a set of cooperating processes, synchronization concerns must be addressed. For example, in the case of a three-pass compiler, or the interactive structure mentioned in the preceding paragraph, it may be that the three processes must proceed in strict time sequence for a single transaction. However, multiple transactions may pass through the program in a pipeline fashion, in which case the input process may be engaged in the second transaction while the analyze process is still working on the first transaction.

Figure 4.5 suggests a way of depicting these relationships in a precedence graph. Each node represents one instance of an operation: r_i (read module,

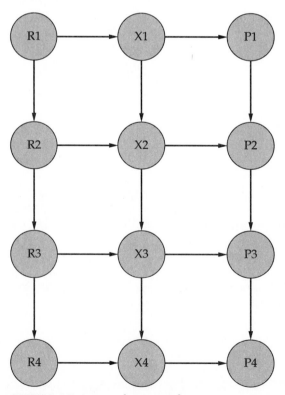

FIGURE 4.5 A precedence graph

transaction i), x_i (execute module, transaction i), and p_i (print module, transaction i).

Operating System Concerns

What design and management issues are raised by the existence of concurrency? We can list the following concerns:

1. The operating system must be able to keep track of the various active processes. This is done with the use of process control blocks and was described in Chapter 3.
2. The operating system must allocate and deallocate various resources for each active process. These resources include:

   - *Processor time:* This is the scheduling function discussed in Chapter 6.
   - *Memory:* Most operating systems use a virtual memory scheme. The topic is addressed in Chapter 5.
   - *Files:* Discussed in Chapter 8.
   - *I/O devices:* Discussed in Chapter 7.

3. The operating system must protect the data and physical resources of each process against unintended interference by other processes. This involves techniques that relate to memory, files, and I/O devices and is discussed in the appropriate chapter. A more general treatment of protection is found in Chapter 10.
4. The results of a process must be independent of the speed at which the execution is carried out relative to the speed of other concurrent processes. This is the subject of this chapter.

To understand how the issue of speed independence can be addressed, we need to look at the ways in which processes can interact.

Process Interaction

We have indicated that process concurrency can exist as a result of the multiprogramming of independent applications, of multiple-process applications, and of the use of a multiple-process structure in the operating system. With these possibilities in mind, let us consider the ways in which processes interact.

We can classify these interactions on the basis of the degree to which processes are aware of each other's existence. Table 4.1 lists three possible degrees of awareness plus the consequences of each:

- *Processes unaware of each other:* These are independent processes that are not intended to work together. The best example of this situation is the multiprogramming of multiple independent processes. These can be either batch jobs or interactive sessions, or a mixture. Although the processes are not working together, the operating system needs to be concerned about **competition** for

TABLE 4.1 Process Interaction

Degree of Awareness	Relationship	Influence that One Process Has on the Other	Potential Control Problems
Processes unaware of each other	Competition	• Results of one process independent of the action of others • Timing of process may be affected	• Mutual exclusion • Deadlock (renewable resource) • Starvation
Processes indirectly aware of each other (e.g., shared object)	Cooperation by sharing	• Results of one process may depend on information obtained from others • Timing of process may be affected	• Mutual exclusion • Deadlock (renewable resource) • Starvation • Data coherence
Processes directly aware of each other (have communication primitives available to them)	Cooperation by communication	• Results of one process may depend on information obtained from others • Timing of process may be affected	• Deadlock (consumable resource) • Starvation

resources. For example, two independent applications may both want access to the same disk or file or printer. The operating system must regulate these accesses.
• *Processes indirectly aware of each other:* These are processes that are not necessarily aware of each other by name but that share access to some object, such as an I/O buffer. Such processes exhibit **cooperation** in sharing the common object.
• *Processes directly aware of each other:* These are processes that are able to communicate with each other by name and that are designed to work jointly on some activity. Again, such processes exhibit **cooperation**.

It needs to be pointed out that conditions will not always be as clear-cut as suggested in Table 4.1. Rather, several processes may exhibit aspects of both competition and cooperation. Nevertheless, it is productive to examine separately each of the three conditions and determine its implications for the operating system.

Competition Among Processes for Resources

Concurrent processes come into conflict with each other when they are competing for the use of the same resource. In its pure form, we can describe the situation as follows. Two or more processes need to access a resource during the course of their execution. Each process is unaware of the existence of the other processes, and each is to be unaffected by the execution of the other processes. It follows from this that each process should leave the state of any resource that it uses unaffected. Examples of resources include I/O devices, memory, processor time, and the clock.

With competing processes, there is no exchange of information between the competing processes. However, the execution of one process may affect the behavior of competing processes. In particular, if two processes both wish access to a single resource, then one process will be allocated that resource by the operating system and the other one will have to wait. Therefore, the process that is denied access will be slowed down. In an extreme case, the blocked process may never get access to the resource and hence will never successfully terminate.

In the case of competing processes, three control problems must be faced. First is the need for **mutual exclusion**. Suppose two or more processes require access to a single nonsharable resource, such as a printer. During the course of execution, each process will be sending commands to the I/O device, receiving status information, sending data, and/or receiving data. We will refer to such a resource as a *critical resource* and the portion of the program that uses it as a *critical section* of the program. It is important that only one program at a time be allowed in its critical section. We cannot simply rely on the operating system to understand and enforce this restriction because the detailed requirement may not be obvious. In the case of the printer, for example, we wish any individual process to have control of the printer while it prints an entire file. Otherwise, lines from competing processes will be interleaved.

The enforcement of mutual exclusion creates two additional control problems. One is that of **deadlock**. Consider two processes, P1 and P2, and two critical resources, R1 and R2. Suppose that each process needs access to both resources to perform part of its function. Then it is possible to have the following situation: R1 is assigned by the operating system to P2, and R2 is assigned to P1. Each process is waiting for one of the two resources. Neither will release the resource that it already owns until it has acquired the other resource and performed its critical section. Both processes are deadlocked.

A final control problem is **starvation**. Suppose that three processes, P1, P2, and P3, each requires periodic access to resources R. Consider the situation in which P1 is in possession of the resource, and both P2 and P3 are delayed, waiting for that resource. When P1 exits its critical section, either P2 or P3 should be allowed access to R. Assume that P3 is granted access and that before it completes its critical section, P1 again requires access. If P1 is granted access after P3 has finished, and if P1 and P3 repeatedly grant access to each other, then P2 may indefinitely be denied access to the resource, even though there is no deadlock situation.

Control of competition inevitably involves the operating system because it is the operating system that allocates resources. In addition, the processes themselves must be able to express the requirement for mutual exclusion in some fashion, such as locking a resource prior to its use. Any solution will involve some support from the operating system, such as the provision of the locking facility. Figure 4.6 illustrates the mutual exclusion mechanism in abstract terms. There are *n* processes to be executed concurrently. Each process includes a critical section that operates on some resource R and a remainder that does not involve resource R. To enforce mutual exclusion, two functions are provided: *entercritical* and *exitcritical*. Each function takes as an argument that name of the resource that is the subject of competition. Any process that attempts to enter its critical section while another process is in its critical section, for the same resource, is made to wait.

It remains to examine specific mechanisms for providing the functions *entercritical* and *exitcritical*. For the moment, we defer this issue while we consider the other cases of process interaction.

Cooperation Among Processes by Sharing

The case of cooperation by sharing covers processes that interact with other processes without being explicitly aware of them. For example, multiple processes may have access to shared variables or to shared files or data bases. Processes may use and update the shared data without reference to other processes but know that other processes may have access to the same data. Thus, the processes must cooperate to ensure that the data they share are properly managed. The control mechanisms must ensure the integrity of the shared data.

```
program     mutualexclusion;
const  n = . . . ; (*number of processes*);
procedure P(i: integer);
begin
  repeat
    entercritical (R);
    < critical section >;
    exitcritical (R);
    < remainder >
  forever
end;
begin (* main program *)
  parbegin
    P(1);
    P(2);
    . . .
    P(n)
  parend
end.
```
FIGURE 4.6 Mutual exclusion.

Because data are held on resources (devices, memory), the control problems of mutual exclusion, deadlock, and starvation are again present. The only difference is that data items may be accessed in two different modes, reading and writing, and only writing operations must be mutually exclusive.

However, over and above these problems, a new requirement is introduced: that of data coherence. A simple example, based on one in Raynal's work, is a bookkeeping application in which various data items may be updated [RAYN86]. Suppose two items of data a and b are to be maintained in the relationship $a = b$. That is, any program that updates one value must also update the other to maintain the relationship. Now consider the following two processes:

P1: $a := a + 1;$
     $b := b + 1;$
P2: $b := 2 * b;$
     $a := 2 * a;$

If the state is initially consistent, each process taken separately will leave the shared data in a consistent state. Now consider the following concurrent execution, in which the two processes respect mutual exclusion on each individual data item (a and b):

$a := a + 1;$
$b := 2 * b;$
$b := b + 1;$
$a := 2 * a;$

At the end of this execution sequence, the condition $a = b$ no longer holds. The problem can be avoided by declaring the entire sequence in each process to be a critical section, even though strictly speaking no critical resource is involved.

Thus, we see that the concept of critical section is important in the case of cooperation by sharing. The same abstract functions of *entercritical* and *exitcritical* discussed earlier (Figure 4.6) can be used here. In this case, the argument for the functions could be a variable, a file, or any other shared object. Furthermore, if critical sections are used to provide data integrity, then there may be no specific resource or variable that can be identified as an argument. In that case, we can think of the argument as being an identifier that is shared among concurrent processes to identify critical sections that must be mutually exclusive.

Cooperation Among Processes by Communication

In the first two cases that we have discussed, each process has its own isolated environment that does not include the other processes. The interactions among processes are indirect. In both cases, there is a sharing. In the case of competition, they are sharing resources without being aware of the other processes. In the second case, they are sharing values, and although each process is not explicitly aware of the other processes, it is aware of the need to maintain data integrity. When processes cooperate by communication, however, the various processes participate in a common effort that links all the processes. The communication provides a way to synchronize, or coordinate, the various activities.

Typically, communication can be characterized as consisting of messages of some sort. Primitives for sending and receiving messages may be provided as part of the programming language or provided by the system kernel of the operating system.

Because nothing is shared between processes in the act of passing messages, mutual exclusion is not a control requirement for this sort of cooperation. However, the problems of deadlock and starvation are present. As an example of deadlock, two processes may be blocked, each waiting for a communication from the other. As an example of starvation, consider three processes, P1, P2, and P3, which exhibit the following behavior. P1 is repeatedly attempting to communicate with either P2 or P3, and P2 and P3 are both attempting to communicate with P1. A sequence could arise in which P1 and P2 exchange information repeatedly, while P3 is blocked waiting for a communication from P1. There is no deadlock because P1 remains active, but P3 is starved.

Requirements for Mutual Exclusion

The successful use of concurrency among processes requires the ability to define critical sections and enforce mutual exclusion. This is fundamental for any concurrent processing scheme. Any facility or capability that is to provide support for mutual exclusion should meet the following requirements:

1. Mutual exclusion must be enforced: Only one process at a time is allowed into its critical section among all processes that have critical sections for the same resource or shared object.
2. A process that halts in its noncritical section must do so without interfering with other processes.
3. It must not be possible for a process requiring access to a critical section to be delayed indefinitely; no deadlock or starvation can be allowed.
4. When no process is in a critical section, any process that requests entry to its critical section must be permitted to enter without delay.
5. No assumptions are made about relative process speeds or number of processes.
6. A process remains inside its critical section for a finite time only.

There are a number of ways in which the requirements for mutual exclusion can be satisfied. One way is to leave the responsibility with the processes that wish to execute concurrently. Thus, whether they are system programs or application programs, processes would be required to coordinate with one another to enforce mutual exclusion, with no support from the programming language or the operating system. We can refer to these as *software approaches*. Although software approaches are prone to high processing overhead and bugs, it is nevertheless useful to examine such approaches to gain a better understanding of the complexity of concurrent processing. This topic is covered in Section 4.2. A second approach involves the use of special-purpose machine instructions. These have the advantage of reducing overhead but nevertheless will be shown in Section 4.3 to be unattractive. A third approach is to provide some level of support within the operating system. Several of the most important such approaches are examined in Section 4.4. Finally, a number of programming languages provide features for concurrent processing, which means that the support is provided by the compiler. Because the focus of this text is on operating systems and not on programming languages, we will not examine such approaches. The interested reader can consult Axford or one of a number of other treatments of such languages [AXFO88].

4.2

MUTUAL EXCLUSION—SOFTWARE APPROACHES

Software approaches can be implemented for concurrent processes that execute on a single-processor or a multiprocessor machine with shared main memory. These approaches usually assume elementary mutual exclusion at the memory access level ([LAMP91] but see Problem 4.10). That is, simultaneous accesses (reading and/or writing) to the same location in main memory are serialized by some sort of memory arbiter, although the order in which access is granted is not specified ahead of time. Beyond this, no support at the hardware, operating-system, or programming language level is assumed.

Dekker's Algorithm

Dijkstra [DIJK65] reported an algorithm for mutual exclusion for two processes that was designed by the Dutch mathematician Dekker. Following Dijkstra, we develop the solution in stages. This approach has the advantage of illustrating most of the common bugs encountered in developing concurrent programs. As the algorithm is developed, we will also make use of some picturesque illustrations from Ben-Ari to dramatize the action [BEN82].

First Attempt

As mentioned earlier, any attempt at mutual exclusion must rely on some fundamental exclusion mechanism in the hardware. The most common of these is the constraint that only one access to a memory location can be made at a time. As a metaphor for such a memory arbiter, Figure 4.7 shows a "protocol igloo." The entrance and the igloo itself are small enough so that only one person can be in the igloo at a time. Inside, there is a blackboard on which a single value can be written.

FIGURE 4.7 An igloo for mutual exclusion

The protocol is as follows. A process (P0 or P1) that wishes to execute its critical section first enters the igloo and examines the blackboard. If its number is on the blackboard, then the process may leave the igloo and proceed to its critical section. Otherwise, it leaves the igloo and is forced to wait. From time to time, the process reenters the igloo to check the blackboard. It repeats this exercise until it is allowed to enter its critical section. This procedure is known as busy-waiting because the thwarted process can do nothing productive until it gets permission to enter its critical section. Instead, it must linger and periodically check the igloo; thus, it consumes processor time (it is busy) while waiting for its chance.

After a process has gained access to its critical section and after it has completed that section, it must return to the igloo and place the number of the other process on the board.

In formal terms, there is a shared global variable:

var   turn: 0 .. 1;

The program for process Pi:

while turn $\neq$ i **do** { nothing };
< critical section >;
turn := 1 − i;

This solution does guarantee the property of mutual exclusion. There are two drawbacks to this solution. First, processes must strictly alternate in their use of their critical section; thus, the pace of execution is dictated by the slower of the two processes. If P0 uses its critical section only once per hour, but P1 would like to use its critical section at a rate of 1000 times per hour, P1 is forced to adopt the pace of P0. A much more serious problem is that if one process fails (e.g., it is eaten by a polar bear on its way to the igloo), the other process is permanently blocked. This is true whether a process fails in its critical section or outside of it.

The foregoing construction is that of a coroutine. As was discussed earlier

(Figure 4.3b), coroutines are designed to be able to pass execution control back and forth between themselves. Although this is a useful structuring technique for a single process, it is inadequate to support concurrent processing.

Second Attempt

The problem with the first attempt is that it stores the name of the process that may enter its critical section when in fact we need state information about both processes. In effect, each process should have its own key to the critical section so that if one is eliminated by a polar bear, the other can still access its critical section. This philosophy is illustrated in Figure 4.8. Each process now has its own igloo. Each process may examine the other's blackboard but cannot alter it. When a process wishes to enter its critical section, it periodically checks the other's blackboard until it finds "false" written on it, indicating that the other process is not in its critical section. It then quickly goes to its own igloo, crawls in, and writes "true" on the blackboard. The process may now proceed to its critical section. When it leaves its critical section, it alters its blackboard to show "false."

The shared global variable now is:

var flag: **array** [0 .. 1] **of** boolean;

which is initialized to false. The protocol for process Pi:

while flag [1-i] **do** { nothing };
flag [i] : = true;
< critical section >;
flag [i] : = false;

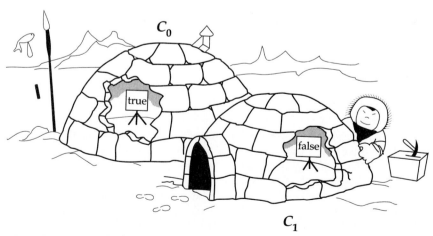

FIGURE 4.8 A two-igloo solution

This solution is, if anything, worse than the first attempt because it does not even guarantee mutual exclusion. Consider the following sequence:

P0 executes the **while** statement and finds flag [1] set to false.
P1 executes the **while** statement and finds flag [0] set to false.
P0 sets flag [0] to true and enters its critical section.
P1 sets flag [1] to true and enters its critical section.

Because both processes are now in their critical sections, the program is incorrect. The problem is that the proposed solution is not independent of relative speeds of process execution.

Third Attempt

Because a process can change its state after the other process has checked it but before the other process can enter its critical section, the second attempt failed. Perhaps we can fix this problem with a simple interchange of two lines:

flag [i] := true;
while flag [1-i] **do** { nothing };
< critical section >;
flag [i] := false;

First, let us check that mutual exclusion is guaranteed, using the point of view of process P0. Once P0 has set flag [0] to "true," P1 cannot enter its critical section until after P0 has entered and left its critical section. It could be that P1 is already in its critical section when P0 sets its flag. In that case, P0 will be blocked by the **while** statement until P1 has left its critical section. The same reasoning applies from the point of view of P1.

This guarantees mutual exclusion but creates yet another problem. If both processes set their flags to "true" before either has executed the **while** statement, then each will think that the other has entered its critical section. The result is deadlock.

Fourth Attempt

In the third attempt, a process sets its state without knowing the state of the other process. Deadlock occurs because each process can insist on its right to enter its critical section; there is no opportunity to back off from this position. We can try to fix this in a way that makes each process more deferential: It sets its flag to indicate its desire to enter its critical section but is prepared to reset the flag to defer to the other process:

flag [i] := true;
while flag [1-i] **do**
  begin
    flag [i] := false;

```
      < delay for a short time >;
      flag [i] := true
   end;
< critical section >
flag [i] := false;
```

This is close to a correct solution but is still flawed. Mutual exclusion is still guaranteed, using similar reasoning to that followed in the discussion of the third attempt. However, consider the following sequence of events:

P0 sets flag [0] to true
P1 sets flag [1] to true
P0 checks flag [1]
P1 checks flag [0]
P0 sets flag [0] to false
P1 sets flag [1] to false
P0 sets flag [0] to true
P1 sets flag [1] to true

This sequence could be extended indefinitely, and neither process could enter its critical section. Strictly speaking, this is not deadlock because any alteration in the relative speed of the two processes will break this cycle and allow one to enter the critical section. Although this is a scenario that is not likely to be sustained for very long, it is nevertheless a possible scenario. Thus, we reject the fourth attempt.

A Correct Solution

We need to be able to observe the state of both processes, which is provided by the array variable flag. But, as the fourth attempt shows, this is not enough. Some means is needed to impose some order on the activities of the two processes to avoid the problem of "mutual courtesy" that we have just observed. The variable *turn* from the first attempt can be used for this purpose; in this case the variable indicates which process has the right to insist on entering its critical region.

We can describe this solution in igloo terms with attention to Figure 4.9. There is now an "referee" igloo with a blackboard labeled "turn." When P0 wants to enter its critical section, it sets its flag to "true". It then goes and checks the flag of P1. If that is false, P0 may immediately enter its critical section. Otherwise, P0 goes to consult the referee. If it finds that *turn* = 0, then it knows that it is its turn to insist, and periodically checks P1's igloo. P1 will at some point note that it is its turn to defer and will chalk up "false" on its blackboard, allowing P0 to proceed. After P0 has used its critical section, it sets its flag to "false" to free the critical section and sets *turn* to 1 to transfer the right to insist to P1.

Figure 4.10 provides a specification of Dekker's algorithm. The proof is left as an exercise (see Problem 4.7).

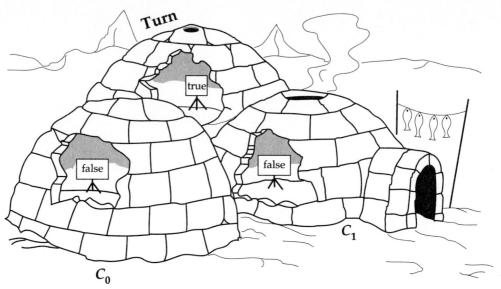

FIGURE 4.9 A three-igloo solution

Peterson's Algorithm

Dekker's algorithm solves the mutual exclusion problem but with a rather complex program that is difficult to follow and whose correctness is tricky to prove. Peterson [PETE81] has provided a simple, elegant solution. As before, the global array variable flag indicates the position of each process with respect to mutual exclusion, and the global variable *turn* resolves simultaneity conflicts. The algorithm is presented in Figure 4.11.

That mutual exclusion is preserved is easily shown. Consider process P0. Once it has set flag [0] to true, P1 cannot enter its critical section. If P1 already is in its critical section, then flag [1] = true and P0 is blocked from entering its critical section. On the other hand, mutual blocking is prevented. Suppose that P0 is blocked in its **while** loop. This means that flag [1] is true and *turn* = 1. P0 can enter its critical section when either flag [1] becomes false or turn becomes 0. Now consider the following three exhaustive cases:

1. P1 has no interest in its critical section. This case is impossible because it implies flag [1] = false.
2. P1 is waiting for its critical section. This case is also impossible because if *turn* = 1, P1 is able to enter its critical section.
3. P1 is using its critical section repeatedly and therefore monopolizing access to it. This cannot happen because P1 is obliged to give P0 an opportunity by setting *turn* to 0 before each attempt to enter its critical section.

Thus we have a simple solution to the mutual exclusion problem for two processes. Furthermore, Peterson's algorithm is easily generalized to the case of *n* processes [HOFR90].

```
var   flag: array [0 . . 1] of boolean;
      turn: 0 . . 1;
procedure P0;
begin
  repeat
    flag [0] := true;
    while flag [1] do if turn = 1 then
                    begin
                      flag [0] := false;
                        while turn = 1 do { nothing };
                      flag [0] := true
                    end;
      < critical section >;
      turn := 1;
      flag [0] := false;
      < remainder >
  forever
end;
procedure P1;
begin
  repeat
    flag [1] := true;
    while flag [0] do if turn = 0 then
                    begin
                      flag [1] := false;
                        while turn = 1 do { nothing };
                      flag [1] := true
                    end;
      < critical section >;
      turn := 0;
      flag [1] := false;
      < remainder >
  forever
end;
begin
  flag [0] := false;
  flag [1] := false;
  turn := 1;
  parbegin
    P0; P1
  parend
end.
```

FIGURE 4.10 Dekker's Algorithm.

```
var   flag: array [0 . . 1] of boolean;
      turn: 0 . . 1;
procedure P0;
begin
  repeat
    flag [0] := true;
    turn := 1;
    while flag [1] and turn = 1 do {nothing};
    < critical section >;
    flag [0] := false;
    < remainder >
  forever
end;
procedure P1;
begin
  repeat
    flag [1] := true;
    turn := 0;
    while flag [0] and turn = 0 do {nothing};
    < critical section >;
    flag [1] := false;
    < remainder >
  forever
end;
begin
  flag [0] := false;
  flag [1] := false;
  turn := 1;
  parbegin
    P0; P1
  parend
end.
```

FIGURE 4.11 Peterson's Algorithm for two processes.

4.3

MUTUAL EXCLUSION—HARDWARE SUPPORT

Interrupt Disabling

In a uniprocessor machine, concurrent processes cannot be overlapped; they can only be interleaved. Furthermore, a process will continue to run until it invokes an operating-system service or until it is interrupted. Therefore, to guarantee mutual exclusion, it is sufficient to prevent a process from being interrupted. This capability can be provided in the form of primitives defined by the system kernel for disabling and enabling interrupts. A process can then enforce mutual exclusion in the following way (compare Figure 4.6):

repeat
    < disable interrupts >;
    < critical section >;
    < enable interrupts >;
    < remainder >
forever.

Because the critical section cannot be interrupted, mutual exclusion is guaranteed. The price of this approach is high, however. The efficiency of execution could be noticeably degraded since the processor is limited in its ability to interleave programs. A second problem is that this approach will not work in a multiprocessor architecture. When the computer system includes more than one processor, it is possible (and typical) for more than one process to be executing at a time. In this case, disabled interrupts do not guarantee mutual exclusion.

Special Machine Instructions

In a multiprocessor configuration, several processors share access to a common main memory. In this case, there is not a master/slave relationship; rather, the processors behave independently in a peer relationship. There is no interrupt mechanism between processors on which mutual exclusion can be based.

At a hardware level, as was mentioned, access to a memory location excludes any other access to that same location. With this as a foundation, designers have proposed several machine instructions that carry out two actions atomically, such as reading and writing or reading and testing, of a single memory location with one instruction fetch cycle. Because these actions are performed in a single instruction cycle, they are not subject to interference from other instructions.

In this section, we look at two of the most commonly implemented instructions. Others are described in [RAYN86] and [STON90].

Test and Set Instruction

The test and set instruction can be defined as follows:

```
function testset (var i: integer): boolean;
begin
    if i = 0 then
      begin
        i := 1;
        testset := true
      end
    else testset := false
end.
```

The instruction tests the value of its argument i. If the value is 0, then it replaces it by 1 and returns true. Otherwise, the value is not changed and false is returned. The entire testset function is carried out atomically; that is, it is not subject to interruption.

Figure 4.12a shows a mutual exclusion protocol based on the use of this instruction. A shared variable *bolt* is initialized to 0. The only process that may enter its critical section is one that finds *bolt* equal to 0. All other processes attempting to enter their critical section go into a busy-waiting mode. When a process leaves its critical section, it resets *bolt* to 0; at this point one and only one of the waiting processes is granted access to its critical section. The choice of process depends on which process happens to execute the testset instruction next.

Exchange Instruction

The exchange instruction can be defined as follows:

procedure exchange (**var** r: register; **var** m: memory);
var   temp;
begin
  temp := m;
  m := r;
  r := temp
end.

The instruction exchanges the contents of a register with that of a memory location. During execution of the instruction, access to the memory location is blocked for any other instruction referencing that location.

Figure 4.12b shows a mutual exclusion protocol based on the use of this instruction. A shared variable *bolt* is initialized to 0. The only process that may enter its critical section is one that finds *bolt* equal to 0. It excludes all other processes from the critical section by setting *bolt* to 1. When a process leaves its critical section, it resets *bolt* to 0, allowing another process to gain access to its critical section.

Properties of the Machine-Instruction Approach

The use of a special machine instruction to enforce mutual exclusion has a number of advantages:

- It is applicable to any number of processes on either a single processor or multiple processors sharing main memory.
- It is simple, and therefore easy to verify.
- It can be used to support multiple critical sections; each critical section can be defined by its own variable.

```
program mutualexclusion;                        program mutualexclusion;
const n = . . . ; (*number of                   const n = . . . ; (*number of processes*);
processes*);                                     var   bolt: integer;
var   bolt: integer;                             procedure P(i: integer);
procedure P(i: integer);                         var   key_i: integer;
begin                                            begin
  repeat                                           repeat
    repeat { nothing } until testset (bolt);         key_i := 1;
    < critical section >;                            repeat exchange (key_i, bolt) until key_i = 0;
    bolt := 0;                                       < critical section >;
    < remainder >                                    exchange (key_i, bolt);
  forever                                            < remainder >
end;                                               forever
begin (* main program *)                         end;
  bolt := 0;                                      begin (* main program *)
  parbegin                                          bolt := 0;
    P(1);                                           parbegin
    P(2);                                             P(1);
    . . .                                             P(2);
    P(n)                                              . . .
  parend                                              P(n)
end.                                               parend
                                                 end.
```

(a) Test and set instruction   (b) Exchange instruction

FIGURE 4.12 Hardware support for mutual exclusion.

Some serious disadvantages are the following:

- Busy-waiting is employed. Thus, while a process is waiting for access to a critical section, it continues to consume processor time.
- Starvation is possible. When a process leaves a critical section and more than one process is waiting, the selection of a waiting process is arbitrary. Thus, some process could indefinitely be denied access.
- Deadlock is possible. Consider the following scenario on a single-processor system. Process P1 executes the special instruction (e.g., testset, exchange) and enters its critical section. P1 is then interrupted to give the processor to P2, which has higher priority. If P2 now attempts to use the same resource as P1, it will be denied access because of the mutual exclusion mechanism. Thus, it will go into a busy-waiting loop. However, P1 will never be dispatched because it is of lower priority than another ready process, P2.

Because of these drawbacks of both the software and hardware solutions, we need to look for other mechanisms.

4.4

MUTUAL EXCLUSION—OPERATING SYSTEM SUPPORT

Semaphores

The first major advance in dealing with the problems of concurrent processes came in 1965 with Dijkstra's treatise on cooperating sequential processes [DIJK65]. Dijkstra was concerned with the design of an operating system as a collection of cooperating sequential processes and with the development of efficient and reliable mechanisms for supporting cooperation. These mechanisms can just as readily be used by user processes if the processor and operating system make the mechanisms available.

The fundamental principle is this: Two or more processes can cooperate by means of simple signals, such that a process can be forced to stop at a specified place until it has received a specific signal. Any complex coordination requirement can be satisfied by the appropriate structure of signals. For signaling, special variables called *semaphores* are used. To transmit a signal via semaphore s, a process executes the primitive *signal*(s). To receive a signal via semaphore s, a process executes the primitive *wait*(s); if the corresponding signal has not yet been transmitted, the process is suspended until the transmission takes place.[2]

To achieve the desired effect, we can view the semaphore as a variable that has an integer value upon which the following three operations are defined:

1. A semaphore may be initialized to a nonnegative value.
2. The *wait* operation decrements the semaphore value. If the value becomes negative, then the process executing the *wait* is blocked.
3. The *signal* operation increments the semaphore value. If the value is not positive, then a process blocked by a *wait* operation is unblocked.

Other than these three operations, there is no way to inspect or manipulate semaphores.

Figure 4.13 suggests a more formal definition of the primitives for semaphores. The *wait* and *signal* primitives are assumed to be atomic; that is, they cannot be interrupted and each routine can be treated as an indivisible step. A more restricted version, known as the *binary semaphore*, is defined in Figure 4.14. A binary semaphore may take on only the values 0 and 1. In principle, it should be easier to implement the binary semaphore, and it can be shown that it has the same expressive power as the general semaphore (see Problem 4.14).

Mutual Exclusion

Figure 4.15 shows a straightforward solution to the mutual exclusion problem using a semaphore s (compare Figure 4.6). Let there be n processes, identified in the array $P_{(i)}$. In each process, a *wait(s)* is executed just before its critical

---

[2]In Dijkstra's original paper and in much of the literature, the letter P is used for *wait* and the letter V for *signal*; these are the initials of the Dutch words for test (*proberen*) and increment (*verhogen*).

```
type semaphore = record
                    count: integer;
                    queue: list of process
                 end;

wait(s):
    s.count := s.count − 1;
    if s.count < 0
        then begin
            place this process in s.queue;
            block this process
        end;

signal(s):
    s.count := s.count + 1;
    if s.count ≤ 0
        then begin
            remove a process P from s.queue;
            place process P on ready list
        end;
```

FIGURE 4.13 A definition of semaphore primitives.

```
type binary semaphore =    record
                            value: (0,1);
                            queue: list of process
                         end;

waitB(s):
    if s.value = 1
        then
            s.value = 0
        else begin
            place this process in s.queue;
            block this process
        end;

signalB(s):
    if s.queue is empty
        then
            s.value := 1
        else begin
            remove a process P from s.queue;
            place process P on ready list
        end;
```

FIGURE 4.14 A definition of binary semaphore primitives.

```
program mutualexclusion;
const n = . . . ; (*number of processes*);
var      s: semaphore (:= 1);
procedure P(i: integer);
begin
  repeat
  wait(s);
  < critical section >;
  signal(s);
  < remainder >
  forever
end;
begin (* main program *)
  parbegin
    P(1);
    P(2);
    . . .
    P(n)
  parend
end.
```

FIGURE 4.15 Mutual exclusion using semaphores.

section. If the value of s is negative, the process is suspended. If the value is 1, then it is decremented to 0 and the process immediately enters its critical section; since s is no longer positive, no other process will be able to enter its critical section.

The semaphore is initialized to 1. Thus, the first process that executes a *wait* will be able to immediately enter the critical section, setting the value of s to 0. Any other process attempting to enter the critical section will find it busy and will be blocked, setting the value of s to -1. Any number of processes may attempt entry; each such unsuccessful attempt results in a further decrement of the value of s. When the process that initially entered its critical section departs, s is incremented and one of the blocked processes (if any) is removed from the queue of blocked processes associated with the semaphore and put in a ready state. When it is next scheduled by the operating system, it may enter the critical section.

The mutual exclusion algorithm using semaphores can be illustrated with our igloo model (Figure 4.16). In addition to a blackboard, the igloo now has a deep freezer. A process enters to perform a *wait*. It decrements the value on the blackboard by 1. If the value now on the blackboard is nonnegative, it can enter its critical section.Otherwise, it goes into hibernation in the freezer. This clears the interior of the igloo, allowing another process to enter. When a process has completed its critical section, it enters the igloo to perform a *signal* by incrementing the blackboard value by 1. If the value is not positive, then it releases a process from the freezer.

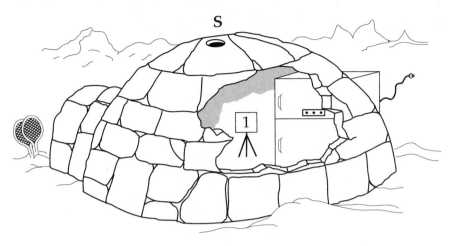

FIGURE 4.16 A semaphore igloo

The program of Figure 4.15 can equally well handle a requirement that more than one process be allowed in its critical section at a time. This requirement is met simply by initializing the semaphore to the specified value. Thus, at any time, the value of s.count can be interpreted as follows:

- s.count $\geq$ 0: s.count is the number of processes which can execute *wait*(s) without suspension (if no *signal*(s) is executed in the meantime).
- s.count < 0: the magnitude of s.count is the number of processes suspended in s.queue.

The Producer/Consumer Problem

We now examine one of the most common problems faced in concurrent processing: the producer/consumer problem. We will follow a development given in the work of Ben-Ari [BEN82]. The general statement is this: One or more producers are generating some type of data (records, characters) and placing these in a buffer. A single consumer is taking items out of the buffer one at a time. The system is to be constrained to prevent the overlap of buffer operations. That is, only one agent (producer or consumer) may access the buffer at any one time. We will look at a number of solutions to this problem to illustrate both the power and the pitfalls of semaphores.

To begin, let us assume that the buffer is infinite and consists of a linear array of elements. In abstract terms, we can define the producer function as follows:

```
producer:
repeat
   produce item v;
   b[in] := v;
   in := in + 1
forever;
```

Similarly, the consumer function takes the following form:

consumer:
repeat
   while in ≤ out **do** { nothing };
   w := b[out];
   out := out + 1;
   consume item w
forever;

Figure 4.17 illustrates the structure of buffer b. The producer can generate items and store them in the buffer at its own pace. Each time, an index (in) into the buffer is incremented. The consumer proceeds in a similar fashion but must make sure that it does not attempt to read from an empty buffer. Hence, the consumer makes sure that the producer has advanced beyond it (in > out) before proceeding.

Let us try to implement this system using binary semaphores. Figure 4.18 is a first attempt. Rather than deal with the indexes in and out, we can simply keep track of the number of items in the buffer, using the integer variable n (= in − out). The semaphore s is used to enforce mutual exclusion; the semaphore *delay* is used to force the consumer to wait if the buffer is empty.

This solution seems rather straightforward. The producer is free to add to the buffer at any time. It performs *waitB(s)* before appending and *signalB(s)* afterwards to prevent the consumer or any other producer from accessing the buffer during the append operation. Also, while in the critical section, the producer increments the value of n. If $n = 1$, then the buffer was empty just before this append, so the producer performs *signalB(delay)* to alert the consumer of this fact. The consumer begins by waiting for the first item to be produced, using *waitB(delay)*. It then takes an item and decrements n in its critical section. If the producer is able to stay ahead of the consumer (a common situation), then the consumer will rarely block on the semaphore delay, since n will usually be positive. Hence, both producer and consumer run smoothly.

There is, however, a flaw in this program. When the consumer has exhausted the buffer, it needs to reset the *delay* semaphore so that it will be forced to wait until the producer has placed more items in the buffer. This is the purpose of

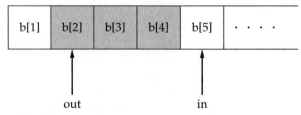

FIGURE 4.17 Infinite buffer for the producer/ consumer problem

```
program    producerconsumer;
var        n: integer;
           s: (*binary*) semaphore (:= 1);
           delay: (*binary*) semaphore (:= 0);
procedure producer;
begin
  repeat
    produce;
    waitB(s);
    append;
    n := n + 1;
    if n=1 then signalB(delay);
    signalB(s)
  forever
end;
procedure consumer;
begin
  waitB(delay);
  repeat
    waitB(s);
    take;
    n := n - 1;
    signalB(s);
    consume;
    if n=0 then waitB(delay)
  forever
end;
begin (*main program*)
  n := 0;
  parbegin
    producer; consumer
  parend
end.
```

FIGURE 4.18 An incorrect solution to the infinite-buffer producer/consumer problem using binary semaphores.

the statement: **if** $n = 0$ **then** *waitB*(delay). Consider the scenario outlined in Table 4.2. In line 6, the consumer fails to execute the *waitB* operation. The consumer did indeed exhaust the buffer and set n to 0 (line 4), but the producer has incremented n before the consumer can test it in line 6. The result is a *signalB* not matched by a prior *waitB*. The value of -1 for n in line 9 means that the consumer has consumed an item from the buffer that does not exist. It would not do to simply move the conditional statement inside the critical section of the consumer because this could lead to deadlock (e.g., at line 3).

TABLE 4.2   Possible Scenario for the Program
of Figure 4.19

	Action	n	delay
1	Initially	0	0
2	Producer: critical section	1	1
3	Consumer: waitB(delay)	1	0
4	Consumer: critical section	0	0
5	Producer: critical section	1	1
6	Consumer: **if** n=0 **then** waitB(delay)	1	1
7	Consumer: critical section	0	1
8	Consumer: **if** n=0 **then** waitB(delay)	0	0
9	Consumer: critical section	-1	0

A fix for the problem is to introduce an auxiliary variable that can be set in the consumer's critical section for later use, as is shown in Figure 4.19. A careful trace of the logic should convince you that deadlock cannot now occur.

A somewhat cleaner solution can be obtained if general semaphores (also called *counting semaphores*) are used, as shown in Figure 4.20. The variable n is now a semaphore. Its value still is equal to the number of items in the buffer. Suppose, now, that in transcribing this program, a mistake is made and the operations *signal(s)* and *signal(n)* are interchanged. This would require that the *signal(n)* operation be performed in the producer's critical section without interruption by the consumer or another producer. Would this affect the program? No, because the consumer must wait for both semaphores before proceeding in any case.

Now suppose that the *wait(n)* and *wait(s)* operations are accidentally reversed. This produces a serious, indeed a fatal, flaw. If the consumer ever enters its critical section when the buffer is empty (n.count = 0), then no producer can ever append to the buffer and the system is deadlocked. This is a good example of the subtlety of semaphores and the difficulty of producing correct designs.

Finally, let us add a new and realistic restriction to the producer/consumer problem: namely, that the buffer is finite. The buffer is treated as a circular storage (Figure 4.21), and pointer values must be expressed modulo the size of the buffer. The producer and consumer functions can be expressed as follows (variable *in* and *out* are initialized to 0):

producer:
repeat
   produce item v;
     while ((in + 1) **mod** n = out) **do** { nothing };
   b[in] := v;
   in = (in + 1) **mod** n
forever;

```
program    producerconsumer;
var        n: integer;
           s: (*binary*) semaphore (:= 1);
           delay: (*binary*) semaphore (:= 0);
procedure producer;
begin
  repeat
    produce;
    waitB(s);
    append;
    n := n + 1;
    if n = 1 then signalB(delay);
    signalB(s)
  forever
end;
procedure consumer;
var   m: integer; (* a local variable *);
begin
  waitB(delay);
  repeat
    waitB(s);
    take;
    n := n - 1;
    m := n;
    signalB(s);
    consume;
    if m = 0 then waitB(delay)
  forever
end;
begin (*main program*)
  n := 0;
  parbegin
    producer; consumer
  parend
end.
```

FIGURE 4.19 A correct solution to the infinite-buffer producer/consumer problem using binary semaphores.

```
consumer:
repeat
  while in = out do { nothing };
  w := b[out];
  out = (out + 1) mod n;
  consume item w
forever;
```

```
program    producerconsumer;
var        n: semaphore (:= 0);
           s: semaphore (:= 1);
procedure producer;
begin
  repeat
    produce;
    wait(s);
    append;
    signal(s):
    signal(n)
  forever
end;
procedure consumer;
begin
  repeat
    wait(n);
    wait(s);
    take;
    signal(s);
    consume
  forever
end;
begin (*main program*)
  parbegin
    producer; consumer
  parend
end.
```

FIGURE 4.20 A solution to the infinite-buffer producer/consumer problem using semaphores.

Figure 4.22 shows a solution using general semaphores. The semaphore *e* has been added to keep track of the number of empty spaces.

Implementation of Semaphores

As was mentioned earlier, it is imperative that the *wait* and *signal* operations be implemented as atomic primitives. One obvious way is to implement them in hardware or firmware. Failing this, a variety of schemes has been suggested. The essence of the problem is one of mutual exclusion: Only one process at a time may manipulate a semaphore with either a *wait* or *signal* operation. Thus, any of the software schemes, such as Dekker's algorithm or Peterson's algorithm, could be used, entailing a substantial processing overhead. Another alternative is to use one of the hardware-supported schemes for mutual exclusion. For example, Figure 4.23a shows the use of a test and set instruction. In this

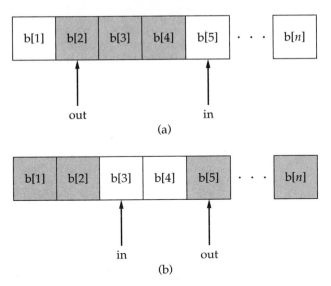

FIGURE 4.21 Finite circular buffer for the producer/ consumer problem

implementation, the semaphore is again of type **record**, as in Figure 4.13 but now includes a new integer component, *s.flag*. Admittedly, this involves a form of busy-waiting. However, the *wait* and *signal* operations are relatively short, so the amount of busy-waiting involved should be minor.

For a single-processor system, it is possible to simply inhibit interrupts for the duration of a *wait* or *signal* operation, as suggested in Figure 4.23b. Once again, the relatively short duration of these operations means that this approach is reasonable.

Messages

When processes interact with one another, two fundamental requirements must be satisfied: synchronization and communication. Processes need to be synchronized to enforce mutual exclusion; cooperating processes may need to exchange information. One approach to providing both of these functions is message passing. Message passing has the further advantage in that it lends itself to implementation in distributed systems as well as in shared-memory multiprocessor and uniprocessor systems.

Message-passing systems come in many forms. In this section, we provide a general introduction that discusses features typically found in such systems. The actual function of message passing is normally provided in the form of a pair of primitives:

- *send (destination, message)*
- *receive (source, message)*

```
program   boundedbuffer;
const     sizeofbuffer = . . .;
var       s: semaphore (: = 1);
          n: semaphore (: = 0);
          e: semaphore (: = sizeofbuffer);
procedure producer;
begin
  repeat
    produce;
    wait(e);
    wait(s);
    append;
    signal(s);
    signal(n)
  forever
end;
procedure consumer;
begin
  repeat
    wait(n);
    wait(s);
    take;
    signal(s);
    signal(e);
    consume
  forever
end;
begin (*main program*)
  parbegin
    producer; consumer
  parend
end.
```

FIGURE 4.22 A solution to the bounded-buffer producer/consumer problem using semaphores.

This is the minimum set of operations needed for processes to engage in message passing. A process sends information in the form of a *message* to another process designated by a *destination*. A process receives information by executing the *receive* primitive, indicating the *source* of the sending process and the *message*.

Design issues relating to message-passing systems are listed in Table 4.3; in the remainder of this section, we examine each of these issues in turn.

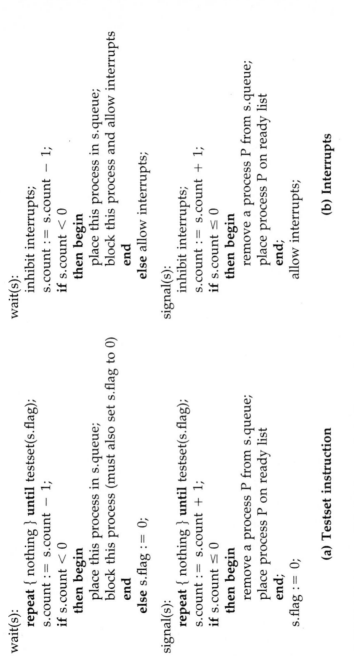

```
wait(s):
    repeat { nothing } until testset(s.flag);
    s.count := s.count − 1;
    if s.count < 0
        then begin
            place this process in s.queue;
            block this process (must also set s.flag to 0)
        end
    else s.flag := 0;

signal(s):
    repeat { nothing } until testset(s.flag);
    s.count := s.count + 1;
    if s.count ≤ 0
        then begin
            remove a process P from s.queue;
            place process P on ready list
        end;
    s.flag := 0;
```

(a) Testset instruction

```
wait(s):
    inhibit interrupts;
    s.count := s.count − 1;
    if s.count < 0
        then begin
            place this process in s.queue;
            block this process and allow interrupts
        end
    else allow interrupts;

signal(s):
    inhibit interrupts;
    s.count := s.count + 1;
    if s.count ≤ 0
        then begin
            remove a process P from s.queue;
            place process P on ready list
        end;
        allow interrupts;
```

(b) Interrupts

FIGURE 4.23 Two possible implementations of semaphores.

TABLE 4.3   Design Characteristics of
Message Systems for Interprocessor
Communication and Synchronization

Synchronization	Format
Send	Content
blocking	Length
nonblocking	fixed
Receive	variable
blocking	**Queuing Discipline**
nonblocking	FIFO
test for arrival	Priority
Addressing	
Direct	
send	
receive	
explicit	
implicit	
Indirect	
static	
dynamic	
ownership	

Synchronization

The communication of a message between two processes implies some level of synchronization between the two: The receiver cannot receive a message until it has been sent by another process. In addition, we need to specify what happens to a process after it issues a *send* or *receive* primitive.

Consider the *send* primitive first. When a *send* primitive is executed in a process, there are two possibilities: Either the sending process is blocked until the message is received, or it is not. Similarly, when a process issues a *receive* primitive, there are two possibilities:

1. If a message has previously been sent, the message is received and execution continues.
2. If there is no waiting message then, either (a) the process is blocked until a message arrives, or (b) the process continues to execute, abandoning the attempt to receive.

Thus, both the sender and receiver can be blocking or nonblocking. The following three combinations are common, although any particular system will usually have only one or two combinations implemented:

- *Blocking send, blocking receive:* Both the sender and receiver are blocked until the message is delivered; this is sometimes referred to as a *rendezvous*. This combination allows for tight synchronization between processes.
- *Nonblocking send, blocking receive:* Although the sender may continue on, the

receiver is blocked until the requested message arrives. This is probably the most useful combination. It allows a process to send one or more messages to a variety of destinations as quickly as possible. A process that must receive a message before it can do useful work needs to be blocked until such a message arrives. An example is a server process that exists to provide a service or resource to other processes.

• *Nonblocking send, nonblocking receive:* Neither party is required to wait.

The nonblocking *send* is the most natural for many concurrent programming tasks. For example, if it is used to request an output operation, such as printing, it allows the requesting process to issue the request in the form of a message and then carry on. One potential danger of the nonblocking *send* is that an error can lead to a situation in which a process repeatedly generates messages. Because there is no blocking to discipline the process, these messages can consume system resources, including processor time and buffer space, to the detriment of other processes and the operating system. Also, the nonblocking *send* places the burden on the programmer to determine that a message has been received: Processes must employ reply messages to acknowledge receipt of a message.

For the *receive* primitive, the blocking version appears to be the most natural for many concurrent programming tasks. Generally, a process that requests a message will need the expected information before proceeding. However, if a message is lost, which can happen in a distributed system, or if a process fails before it sends an anticipated message, a receiving process can be blocked indefinitely. This problem can be solved by the use of the nonblocking *receive*. However, the danger of this approach is that if a message is sent after a process has already executed a matching *receive*, the message will be lost. Other possible approaches are to allow a process to test whether a message is waiting before issuing a *receive* and to allow a process to specify more than one source in a *receive* primitive. The latter approach is useful if a process is waiting for messages from more than one source and can proceed if any of these messages arrive.

Addressing

Clearly, it is necessary to have a way of specifying in the *send* primitive which process is to receive the message. Similarly, most implementations allow a receiving process to indicate the source of a message to be received.

The various schemes for specifying processes in *send* and *receive* primitives fall into two categories: direct addressing and indirect addressing. With **direct addressing**, the *send* primitive includes a specific identifier of the destination process. The *receive* primitive can be handled in one of two ways. One possibility is to require that the process explicitly designate a sending process. Thus, the process must know ahead of time from which process a message is expected. This is often effective for cooperating concurrent processes. In other cases, however, it is impossible to specify the anticipated source process. An example is a printer-server process, which will accept a print request message from any other process. For such applications, a more effective approach is the use of implicit addressing. In this case, the *source* parameter of the *receive* primitive possesses a value returned when the receive operation has been performed.

The other general approach is **indirect addressing**. In this case, messages are not sent directly from sender to receiver but to a shared data structure consisting of queues that can temporarily hold messages. Such queues are generally referred to as *mailboxes*. Thus, for two processes to communicate, one process sends a message to the appropriate mailbox and the other process picks up the message from the mailbox.

A strength of the use of indirect addressing is that by decoupling the sender and receiver, it allows for greater flexibility in the use of messages. The relationship between senders and receivers can be one-to-one, many-to-one, one-to-many, or many-to-many. A one-to-one relationship allows a private communications link to be set up between two processes, which insulates their interaction from erroneous interference from other processes. A many-to-one relationship is useful for client-server interaction; one process provides service to a number of other processes. In this case, the mailbox is often referred to as a *port* (Figure 4.24). A one-to-many relationship allows for one sender and mul-

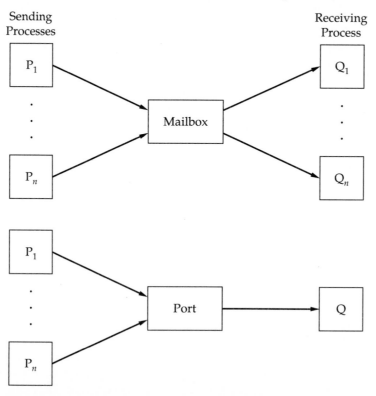

FIGURE 4.24 Indirect process communication [BIC88]

tiple receivers; it is useful for applications in which a message or some information is to be broadcast to a set of processes.

The association of processes to mailboxes can be either static or dynamic. Ports are often statically associated with a particular process; that is, the port is created and assigned to the process permanently. Similarly, a one-to-one relationship is typically defined statically and permanently. When there are many senders, the association of a sender to a mailbox may occur dynamically. Primitives such as *connect* and *disconnect* may be used for this purpose.

A related issue has to do with the ownership of a mailbox. In the case of a port, it is typically owned by and created by the receiving process. Thus, when the process is destroyed, the port is also destroyed. For the general mailbox case, the operating system may offer a create-mailbox service. Such mailboxes can be viewed as being owned by the creating process, in which case they terminate with the process; or they can be viewed as being owned by the operating system, in which case an explicit command is required to destroy the mailbox.

Message Format

The format of the message depends on the objectives of the messaging facility and whether the facility runs on a single computer or on a distributed system. For some operating systems, designers have preferred short, fixed-length messages to minimize processing and storage overhead. If a large amount of data is to be passed, the data can be placed in a file and the message then simply references that file. A more flexible approach is to allow variable-length messages.

Figure 4.25 shows a typical message format for operating systems that support variable-length messages. The message is divided into two parts: a header, which contains information about the message, and a body, which contains the

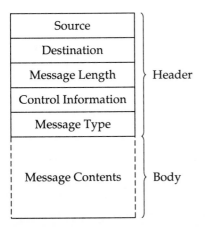

FIGURE 4.25 Typical message format

actual contents of the message. The header may contain an identification of the source and intended destination of the message, a length field, and a type field to discriminate among various types of messages. There may also be additional control information, such as a pointer field so that a linked list of messages can be created; a sequence number, to keep track of the number and order of messages passed between source and destination; and a priority field.

Queuing Discipline

The simplest queuing discipline is first-in, first-out, but this may not be sufficient if some messages are more urgent than others. An alternative is to allow the specifying of message priority on the basis of message type or by designation by the sender. Another alternative is to allow the receiver to inspect the message queue and select which message to receive next.

Mutual Exclusion

Figure 4.26 shows one way in which message passing can be used to enforce mutual exclusion (compare Figures 4.6, 4.12, and 4.15). We assume the use of

```
program    mutualexclusion;
const  n = . . . ; (*number of processes*);
procedure P(i: integer);
var msg: message;
begin
  repeat
    receive (mutex, msg);
    < critical section >;
    send (mutex, msg);
    < remainder >
  forever
end;
begin (*main program*)
  create_mailbox (mutex);
  send (mutex, null);
  parbegin
    P(1);
    P(2);
    . . .
    P(n)
  parend
end.
```

FIGURE 4.26 Mutual exclusion using messages.

the blocking *receive* primitive and the nonblocking *send* primitive. A set of concurrent processes shares a mailbox, *mutex*, which can be used by all processes to send and receive. The mailbox is initialized to contain a single message with null content. A process wishing to enter its critical section first attempts to receive a message. If the mailbox is empty, then the process is blocked. Once a process has acquired the message, it performs its critical section and then places the message back in the mailbox. Thus, the message functions as a token that is passed from process to process. This solution assumes that if more than one process performs the receive operation concurrently, then:

- If there is a message, it is delivered to only one process and the others are blocked, or
- If the message queue is empty, all messages are blocked. When a message is available, only one blocked process is activated and given the message.

These assumptions are true of virtually all message-passing facilities.

As another example of the use of message passing, Figure 4.27 is a solution to the bounded-buffer producer/consumer problem. Using the basic mutual-exclusion power of message passing, the problem could have been solved with an algorithmic structure similar to that of Figure 4.22. Instead, the program of Figure 4.27 takes advantage of the ability of message passing to be used to pass data in addition to signals. Two mailboxes are used. As the producer generates data, it sends the data as messages to the mailbox *mayconsume*. As long as there is at least one message in that mailbox, the consumer can consume. Hence, *mayconsume* serves as the buffer; the data in the buffer are organized as a queue of messages. The "size" of the buffer is determined by the global variable *capacity*. Initially, the mailbox *mayproduce* is filled with a number of null messages equal to the capacity of the buffer. The number of messages in *mayproduce* shrinks with each production and grows with each consumption.

This approach is quite flexible. There may be multiple producers and consumers as long as all have access to both mailboxes. The system may even be distributed, with all producer processes and the *mayproduce* mailbox at one site and all the consumer processes and the *mayconsume* mailbox at another.

4.5

DEADLOCK

Maekawa, Oldehoeft, and Oldehoeft define deadlock as the *permanent* blocking of a set of processes that either compete for system resources or communicate with each other [MAEK87]. Unlike other problems in concurrent process management, there is no efficient solution in the general case. In this section, we examine the nature of the deadlock problem, and then look at some of the more common approaches to dealing with that problem.

```
const
  capacity = . . .;   {buffering capacity}
  null = . . .;       {empty message}
var   i: integer;
procedure producer;
  var pmsg: message;
  begin
    while true do
      begin
        receive (mayproduce, pmsg);
        pmsg := produce;
        send (mayconsume, pmsg)
      end
  end;
procedure consumer;
  var csmg: message;
  begin
    while true do
      begin
        receive (mayconsume, cmsg);
        consume (csmg);
        send (mayproduce, null)
      end
  end;

{parent process}
begin
  create_mailbox (mayproduce);
  create_mailbox (mayconsume);
  for i = 1 to capacity do send (mayproduce, null);
  parbegin
    producer;
    consumers
  parend
end.
```

FIGURE 4.27 A solution to the bounded-buffer producer/consumer problem using messages [MILE87].

All deadlocks involve conflicting needs for resources by two or more processes. Figure 4.28 illustrates this conflict in an abstract way in the case of two processes and two resources. The two axes of the diagram represent the progress of the two processes in terms of instructions executed. The joint progress of the two processes is therefore represented by a sequence of discrete points in this space. A horizontal or vertical line represents an interval of time in which only one process is executing (interleaving); a diagonal line corresponds to simultaneous execution (overlap). Assume that there is a point in the execution of each process at which exclusive use of both resources R1 and R2 are required to continue. In the example, process P1 reaches a point at which it has acquired resource R1, and process P2 reaches a point at which it has acquired resource R2, and each process requests the other resource. This is a point of deadlock.

Reusable Resources

Two general categories of resources can be distinguished: reusable and consumable. A reusable resource is one that can be safely used by only one process at a time and is not depleted by that use. Processes obtain resource units that they

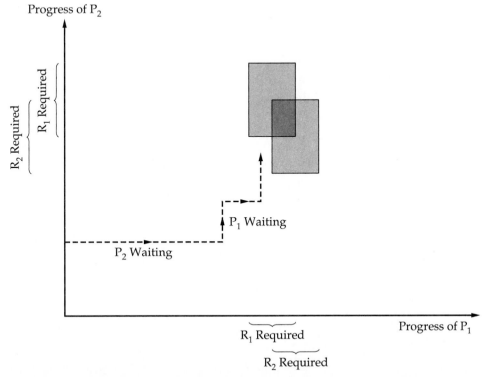

FIGURE 4.28 Joint progress of processes P₁ and P₂ [COFF71]

later release for reuse by other processes. Examples of reusable resources include processors, I/O channels, main and secondary memory, devices, and data structures such as files, data bases, and semaphores.

As an example of deadlock involving reusable resources, consider two processes that compete for exclusive access to a disk file D and a tape drive T. The programs engage in the following repetitive operations:

P1	P2
repeat	**repeat**
...	...
Request (D);	Request (T);
...	...
Request (T);	Request (D);
...	...
Release (T);	Release (D);
...	...
Release (D);	Release (T);
...	...
forever	**forever**

Deadlock occurs if each process holds one resource and requests the other. It may appear that this is a programming error rather than a problem for the operating-system designer. However, we have seen that concurrent program design is challenging. Such deadlocks do occur, and the cause is often embedded in complex program logic, making detection difficult. One strategy for dealing with such a deadlock is to impose constraints on system design concerning the order in which resources are requested.

Another example of deadlock with a reusable resource has to do with requests for main memory. Suppose the space available for allocation is 200 KB, and that the following sequence of requests occur:

P1	P2
...	...
Request 80K bytes;	Request 70K bytes;
...	...
Request 60K bytes;	Request 80K bytes;

Deadlock occurs if both processes progress to their second request. If the amount of memory to be requested is not known ahead of time, it is difficult to deal with this type of deadlock by means of constraints on system design. The best way to deal with this particular problem is to, in effect, eliminate the possibility by using virtual memory, which is discussed in Chapter 5.

Consumable Resources

A consumable resource is one that can be created (produced) and destroyed (consumed). Typically, there is no limit on the number of consumable resources of a particular type. An unblocked producing process may release any number of such resources. When a resource is acquired by a process, the resource ceases to exist. Examples of consumable resources are interrupts, signals, messages, and information in I/O buffers.

As an example of deadlock involving consumable resources, consider the following pair of processes:

P1	**P2**
...	...
Receive (P2, M);	Receive (P1, Q);
...	...
Send (P2, N);	Send (P1, R);

Deadlock occurs if the Receive is blocking. Once again, a design error is the cause of the deadlock. Such errors may be quite subtle and difficult to detect. Furthermore, it may take a rare combination of events to cause the deadlock; thus a program could be in use for a considerable period, even years, before the problem became evident.

There is no single effective strategy that can deal with all types of deadlock. Table 4.4 summarizes the key elements of the most important approaches that have been developed: detection, prevention, and avoidance. We examine each of these in turn.

The Conditions for Deadlock

Three conditions of policy must be present for it to be possible for a deadlock to occur:

1. *Mutual exclusion.* Only one process may use a resource at a time.
2. *Hold-and-wait.* A process may hold allocated resources while awaiting assignment of others.
3. *No preemption.* No resource can be forcibly removed from a process holding it.

In many ways these conditions are quite desirable. For example, mutual exclusion is needed to ensure consistency of results and the integrity of a data base. Similarly, preemption cannot be done arbitrarily and, especially when data resources are involved, must be supported by a rollback recovery mechanism, which restores a process and its resources to a suitable previous state from which the process can eventually repeat its actions.

Deadlock *can* exist with these three conditions but may not exist with *only* these three conditions. For deadlock actually to take place, a fourth condition is required:

4. *Circular wait.* A closed chain of processes exists, such that each process holds at least one resource needed by the next process in the chain (e.g., Figure 4.29).

The first three conditions listed are necessary but not sufficient for a deadlock to exist. The fourth condition is, actually, a potential consequence of the first

TABLE 4.4 Summary of Deadlock Detection, Prevention, and Avoidance Approaches for Operating Systems [ISLO80]

Principle	Resource Allocation Policy	Different Schemes	Major Advantages	Major Disadvantages
Prevention	Conservative; undercommits resources.	Requesting all resources at once.	• Works well for processes that perform a single burst of activity. • No preemption necessary.	• Inefficient • Delays process initiation.
		Preemption	• Convenient when applied to resources whose state can be saved and restored easily.	• Preempts more often than necessary. • Subject to cyclic restart.
		Resource ordering	• Feasible to enforce via compile-time checks. • Needs no run-time computation since problem is solved in system design.	• Preempts without much use. • Disallows incremental resource requests.
Detection	Very liberal; requested resources are granted where possible.	Invoke periodically to test for deadlock.	• Never delays process initiation. • Facilitates on-line handling.	• Inherent preemption losses.
Avoidance	Selects midway between that of detection and prevention.	Manipulate to find at least one safe path.	• No preemption necessary.	• Future resource requirements must be known. • Processes can be blocked for long periods.

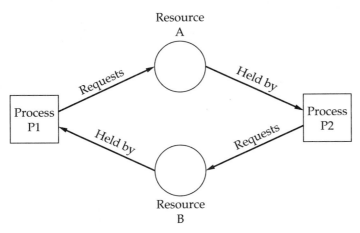

FIGURE 4.29 Circular wait

three. That is, given that the first three conditions exist, a sequence of events may occur that lead to an unresolvable circular wait. The unresolvable circular wait is in fact a definition of deadlock. The circular wait listed as condition 4 is unresolvable because the first three conditions hold. Thus, the four conditions taken together constitute necessary and sufficient conditions for deadlock.[3]

Deadlock Prevention

The strategy of deadlock prevention is, simply put, to design a system in such a way that the possibility of deadlock is excluded *a priori*. Methods for preventing deadlock are of two classes. An indirect method is to prevent the occurrence of one of the three necessary conditions listed earlier (conditions 1 through 3). A direct method is to prevent the occurrence of a circular wait (condition 4). We now examine techniques related to each of the four conditions.

Mutual Exclusion

In general, the first of the four conditions listed above cannot be disallowed. If access to a resource requires mutual exclusion, then mutual exclusion must be supported by the operating system. Some resources, such as files, may allow multiple accesses for reads, but only exclusive access for writes. Even in this case, deadlock can occur if more than one process requires write permission.

---

[3]Virtually all textbooks simply list these four conditions as the conditions needed for deadlock, but such a presentation obscures some of the subtler issues [SHUB90]. Condition 4, the circular wait condition, is fundamentally different from the other three conditions. Conditions 1 through 3 are policy decisions, whereas condition 4 is a circumstance that might occur depending on the sequencing of requests and releases by the involved processes. Linking circular wait with the three necessary conditions leads to inadequate distinction between prevention and avoidance.

Hold-and-wait

The hold-and-wait condition can be prevented by requiring that a process request all its required resources at one time, and blocking the process until all requests can be granted simultaneously. This approach is inefficient in two ways. First, a process may be held up for a long time waiting for all its resource requests to be filled, when in fact it could have proceeded with only some of the resources. And second, resources allocated to a process may remain unused for a considerable period, during which time they are denied to other processes.

No Preemption

The no-preemption condition can be prevented in several ways. First, if a process holding certain resources is denied a further request, that process must release its original resources and if necessary request them again, together with the additional resource. Alternatively, if a process requests a resource that is currently held by another process, the operating system may preempt the second process and require it to release its resources. This latter scheme would prevent deadlock only if no two processes possessed the same priority.

This approach is practical only when applied to resources whose state can be easily saved and restored later, as is the case with a processor.

Circular Wait

The circular wait condition can be prevented by defining a linear ordering of resource types. If a process has been allocated resources of type R, then it may subsequently request only those resources of types following R in the ordering.

To see that this strategy works, let us associate an index with each resource type. Then, resource R_i precedes R_j in the ordering if $i < j$. Now suppose that two processes, A and B are deadlocked because A has acquired R_i and requested R_j, and B has acquired R_j and requested R_i. This condition is impossible because it implies $i < j$ and $j < i$.

As with hold-and-wait prevention, circular wait prevention may be inefficient, slowing down processes and denying resource access unnecessarily.

Deadlock Detection

Deadlock prevention strategies are very conservative; they solve the problem of deadlock by limiting access to resources and by imposing restrictions on processes. At the opposite extreme, deadlock detection strategies do not limit resource access or restrict process actions. With deadlock detection, requested resources are granted to processes whenever possible. Periodically, the operating system performs an algorithm that allows it to detect the circular wait condition described in item 4 earlier and illustrated in Figure 4.29. Any algorithm for detecting cycles in directed graphs can be used (e.g., [LEIB89]).

A check for deadlock can be made as frequently as each resource request, or less frequently, depending on how likely it is for a deadlock to occur. Checking at each resource request has two advantages: It leads to early detection, and the algorithm is relatively simple because it is based on incremental changes to the state of the system. On the other hand, such frequent checks consume considerable processor time.

Once deadlock has been detected, some strategy is needed for recovery. The following are possible approaches, listed in order of increasing sophistication:

1. Abort all deadlocked processes. This is, believe it or not, one of the most common solutions, if not the most common, adopted in operating systems.
2. Back up each deadlocked process to some previously defined checkpoint, and restart all processes. This requires that rollback and restart mechanisms be built into the system. The risk in this approach is that the original deadlock will recur. However, the nondeterminancy of concurrent processing will usually ensure that this does not happen.
3. Successively abort deadlocked processes until deadlock no longer exists. The order in which processes are selected for abortion should be on the basis of some criterion of minimum cost. After each abortion, the detection algorithm must be reinvoked to see whether deadlock still exists.
4. Successively preempt resources until deadlock no longer exists. As in item 3, a cost-based selection should be used, and reinvocation of the detection algorithm is required after each preemption. A process that loses a resource because of preemption must be rolled back to a point before its acquisition of that resource.

For items 3 and 4, the selection criterion could be one of the following. Choose the process with the:

• Least amount of processor time consumed so far
• Least number of lines of output produced so far
• Most estimated time remaining
• Least total resources allocated so far
• Lowest priority

Some of these quantities are easier to measure than others. Estimated time remaining is particularly suspect. Also, other than by means of the priority measure, there is no indication of the "cost" to the user, as opposed to the cost to the system as a whole.

Deadlock Avoidance

Another approach to solving the deadlock problem, which differs subtly from deadlock prevention, is deadlock avoidance.[4] In deadlock prevention, we constrain resource requests to prevent at least one of the four conditions of deadlock

---

[4] The term *avoidance* is a bit confusing. In fact, one could consider the strategies discussed in this subsection to be examples of deadlock prevention because they indeed prevent the occurrence of a deadlock.

from occurring. This is either done indirectly by preventing one of the three necessary policy conditions (mutual exclusion, hold-and-wait, no preemption), or directly by preventing circular wait. This leads to inefficient use of resources and inefficient execution of processes. Deadlock avoidance, on the other hand, allows the three necessary conditions but makes judicious choices to assure that the deadlock point is never reached. Avoidance therefore allows more concurrency than prevention does. With deadlock avoidance, a decision is made dynamically whether the current resource allocation request will, if granted, potentially lead to a deadlock. Deadlock avoidance thus requires knowledge of future requests for process resources.

In this subsection, we describe the following two approaches to deadlock avoidance:

- Do not start a process if its demands might lead to deadlock.
- Do not grant an incremental resource request to a process if this allocation might lead to deadlock.

Process Initiation Denial

Consider a system of n processes and m different types of resources. Let us define the following vectors and matrices:

$$\text{Resource} = \begin{pmatrix} R_1 \\ \vdots \\ R_m \end{pmatrix} \qquad \text{Total amount of each resource in the system}$$

$$\text{Available} = \begin{pmatrix} AV_1 \\ \vdots \\ AV_m \end{pmatrix} \qquad \text{Total amount of each resource not allocated to a process}$$

$$\text{Claim} = \begin{pmatrix} C_{11} & \cdots & C_{n1} \\ \vdots & & \vdots \\ C_{1m} & \cdots & C_{nm} \end{pmatrix} = (C_{1*} \cdots C_{n*}) \qquad \begin{array}{l} \text{Requirement of each process} \\ \text{for each resource} \end{array}$$

$$\text{Allocation} = \begin{pmatrix} A_{11} & \cdots & A_{n1} \\ \vdots & & \vdots \\ A_{1m} & \cdots & A_{nm} \end{pmatrix} = (A_{1*} \cdots A_{n*}) \qquad \text{Current allocation}$$

The matrix Claim gives the maximum requirement of each process for each resource. That is, C_{ij} = requirement of process i for resource j. This information must be declared in advance by a process for deadlock avoidance to work. Similarly, A_{ij} = current allocation of resource j to process i. The following relationships can be seen to hold:

$$1. \ \sum_{k=1}^{n} A_{k*} + \text{Available} = \text{Resource} \qquad \begin{array}{l} \text{All resources are either allocated or} \\ \text{available.} \end{array}$$

2. For all k, $C_{k*} \leq$ Resource

No process can claim more than the total amount of resources in the system.

3. For all k, $A_{k*} \leq C_{k*}$

No process is allocated more resources of any type than the process originally claimed to need.

With these quantities defined, we can define a deadlock avoidance policy that refuses to start a new process if its resource requirements might lead to deadlock. Start a new process P_{n+1} only if

$$\text{Resource} \geq \sum_{k=1}^{n} C_{k*} + C_{(n+1)*}$$

That is, a process is started only if the maximum claim of all current processes plus those of the new process can be met. This strategy is hardly optimal, since it assumes the worst: that all processes will make their maximum claims together.

Resource Allocation Denial

The strategy of resource allocation denial, referred to as the **banker's algorithm**, was first proposed by Dijkstra [DIJK65].[5] Let us begin by defining the concepts of state and safe state. Consider a system with a fixed number of processes and a fixed number of resources. At any time a process may have zero or more resources allocated to it. The **state** of the system is simply the current allocation of resources to processes. Thus, the state consists of the two vectors, Resource and Available, and the two matrices, Claim and Allocation, defined earlier. A **safe state** is a state in which there is at least one order in which all the processes can be run to completion without resulting in a deadlock. An **unsafe state** is, of course, a state that is not safe.

The following example illustrates these concepts. Figure 4.30a shows the state of a system consisting of four processes and three resources. The total amount of resources R1, R2, and R3 are 9, 3, and 6 units, respectively. In the current state, allocations have been made to the four processes, leaving 1 unit of resource 2 and 1 unit of resource 3 available. The question is: Is this a safe state? To answer this question, we ask an intermediate question: Can any of the four processes be run to completion with the resources available? That is, can the difference between the current allocation and the maximum requirement for any process be met with the available resources? Clearly, this is not possible

---

[5]Dijkstra used this name because of the analogy of this problem to one that occurs in banking when customers wish to borrow money. The customers correspond to processes, and the money to be borrowed corresponds to resources. Stated as a banking problem: The bank has a limited reserve of money to lend, and a list of customers, each with a line of credit. A customer may choose to borrow against the line of credit a portion at a time, and there is no guarantee that the customer will make any repayment until after having taken out the maximum amount of loan. The banker can refuse a loan to a customer if there is a risk that the bank will have insufficient funds to make further loans that will permit the customers to repay eventually.

for P1, which has only 1 unit of R1 and requires 2 more units of R1, 2 units of R2, and 2 units of R3. However, by assigning 1 unit of R3 to process P2, P2 has its maximum required resources allocated and can run to completion. Let us assume that this is accomplished. When P2 completes, its resources can be returned to the pool of available resources. The resulting state is shown in Figure 4.30b. Now, we can ask again if any of the remaining processes can be completed. In this case, each of the remaining processes could be completed. Suppose we choose P1, allocate the required resources, complete P1, and return all of P1's resources to the available pool. We are left in the state shown in Figure 4.30c. Next, we can complete P3, resulting in the state of Figure 4.30d. Finally,

	P1	P2	P3	P4
R1	3	6	3	4
R2	2	1	1	2
R3	2	3	4	2

Claim matrix

	P1	P2	P3	P4
R1	1	6	2	0
R2	0	1	1	0
R3	0	2	1	2

Allocation matrix

R1	0
R2	1
R3	1

Available vector

(a)

	P1	P2	P3	P4
R1	3	0	3	4
R2	2	0	1	2
R3	2	0	4	2

Claim matrix

	P1	P2	P3	P4
R1	1	0	2	0
R2	0	0	1	0
R3	0	0	1	2

Allocation matrix

R1	6
R2	2
R3	3

Available vector

(b)

	P1	P2	P3	P4
R1	0	0	3	4
R2	0	0	1	2
R3	0	0	4	2

Claim matrix

	P1	P2	P3	P4
R1	0	0	2	0
R2	0	0	1	0
R3	0	0	1	2

Allocation matrix

R1	7
R2	2
R3	3

Available vector

(c)

	P1	P2	P3	P4
R1	0	0	0	4
R2	0	0	0	2
R3	0	0	0	2

Claim matrix

	P1	P2	P3	P4
R1	0	0	0	0
R2	0	0	0	0
R3	0	0	0	2

Allocation matrix

R1	9
R2	3
R3	4

Available vector

(d)

FIGURE 4.30 Determination of a safe state.

we can complete P4. At this point, all the processes have been run to completion. Thus, the state defined by Figure 4.30a is a safe state.

These concepts suggest a deadlock avoidance strategy, which is to ensure that the system of processes and resources be always in a safe state. To achieve this, the following strategy is used: When a process makes a request for a set of resources, assume that the request is granted, update the system state accordingly, and then determine if the result is a safe state. If so, grant the request and if not, block the process until it is safe to grant the request.

Consider the state defined by the matrix of Figure 4.31a. Suppose P2 makes a request for 1 unit of R1 and 1 unit of R3. If we assume the request is granted, then the resulting state is that of Figure 4.30a. We have already seen that this is a safe state; therefore, it is safe to satisfy the request. However, returning to the state of Figure 4.31a, suppose that P1 makes the request for 1 unit each of R1 and R3. Now, if we assume the request is granted, we are left in the state of Figure 4.31b. Question: Is this a safe state? The answer is no because each process will need at least 1 additional unit of R1, and there are none available. Thus, on the basis of deadlock avoidance, the request by P1 should be denied and P1 should be blocked.

It is important to point out that Figure 4.31b is not a deadlocked state. It merely has the potential for deadlock. It is possible, for example, that if P1 were run from this state it would subsequently release 1 unit of R1 and 1 unit of R3 before later needing these resources again. If that happened, the system would return to a safe state. Thus, the deadlock avoidance strategy does not predict deadlock with certainty; it merely anticipates the possibility of deadlock and assures that there is never such a possibility.

Figure 4.32, based on a version in Krakowiak and Beeson, gives an abstract version of the deadlock avoidance logic [KRAK88]. The main algorithm is shown

	P1	P2	P3	P4
R1	3	6	3	4
R2	2	1	1	2
R3	2	3	4	2

Claim matrix

	P1	P2	P3	P4
R1	1	5	2	0
R2	0	1	1	0
R3	0	1	1	2

Allocation matrix

R1	1
R2	1
R3	2

Available vector

(a)

	P1	P2	P3	P4
R1	3	6	3	4
R2	2	1	1	2
R3	2	3	4	2

Claim matrix

	P1	P2	P3	P4
R1	2	5	2	0
R2	0	1	1	0
R3	1	1	1	2

Allocation matrix

R1	0
R2	1
R3	1

Available vector

(b)

FIGURE 4.31 Determination of an unsafe state.

in part b of the figure. With the state of the system defined by the data structure *state, request* [*] is a vector defining the resources requested by process *i*. First, a check is made to assure that the request does not exceed the original claim of the process. If the request is valid, the next step is to determine if it is possible to fulfil the request, that is, there are sufficient resources available. If it is not possible, then the process is suspended. If it is possible, the final step is to determine if it is safe to fulfill the request. To do this, the resources are tentatively assigned to process *i* from *newstate*. Then, a test for safety is made using the algorithm in Figure 4.32c.

Deadlock avoidance has the advantage that it is not necessary to preempt and rollback processes as in deadlock detection, and it is less restrictive than deadlock prevention. However, it does have a number of disadvantages and restrictions on its use as follows:

- The maximum resource requirement for each process must be stated in advance.
- The processes under consideration must be independent; that is, the order in which they execute must be unconstrained by any synchronization requirements.
- There must be a fixed number of resources to allocate and a fixed number of processes.

An Integrated Deadlock Strategy

As Table 4.4 suggests, there are strengths and weaknesses in all the strategies for dealing with deadlock. Rather than attempting to design an operating system facility that employs only one of these strategies, it might be more efficient to use different strategies in different situations. Silberschatz, Peterson, and Galvin suggest one approach [SILB91]:

- Group resources into a number of different resource classes.
- Use the linear ordering strategy defined earlier for the prevention of circular wait to prevent deadlocks between resource classes.
- Within a resource class, use the algorithm that is most appropriate for that class.

As an example of this technique, consider the following classes of resources:

- *Swappable space:* Blocks of memory on secondary storage for use in swapping processes.
- *Process resources:* Assignable devices, such as tape drives, and files.
- *Main memory:* Assignable in pages or segments to processes.
- *Internal resources:* Such as I/O channels.

The order in which these classes of resources are listed represents the order in which resources are assigned. The order is a reasonable one, considering the

```
type state =    record
                   resource, available; array [0 . . . m − 1] of integer;
                   claim, allocated; array [0 . . . n − 1, 0 . . . m − 1] of integer
                end
```

(a) global data structures

```
if alloc [i,*] + request [*] > claim [i,*] then
   <error>                      --total request > claim
else
   if request [*] > available [*] then
      <suspend process>
   else                         --simulate allocation
      <define newstate by:
      allocation [i,*] := allocation [i,*] + request [*]
      available [*] := available [*] − request [*] >
   end;
   if safe (newstate) then
      <carry out allocation>
   else
      <restore original state>;
      <suspend process>
   end
end.
```

(b) resource allocation algorithm

```
function safe (state: S): boolean;
var   currentavail: array [0 . . . m − 1] of integer;
      rest: set of process;
begin
currentavail := available;
rest := {all processes};
possible := true;
while possible do
   find a P_k in rest such that
      claim [k,*] − alloc [k,*] <currentavail;
   if found then               --simulate execution of P
      currentavail := currentavail + allocation [k,*];
      rest := rest − {P_k}
   else
      possible := false
   end
end;
safe := (rest = null)
end.
```

(c) test for safety algorithm (banker's algorithm)

FIGURE 4.32 Deadlock avoidance logic.

sequence of steps that a process may following during its lifetime. Within each class, the following strategies could be used:

- *Swappable space:* Prevention of deadlocks, by requiring that all the required resources be allocated at one time, may be used, as in the hold-and-wait prevention strategy, for prevention of deadlocks. This strategy is reasonable if the maximum storage requirements are known, which is often the case. Deadlock avoidance is also a possibility.
- *Process resources:* Avoidance will often be effective in this category because it is reasonable to expect processes to declare ahead of time the resources that they will require in this class. Prevention by means of resource ordering within this class is also possible.
- *Main memory:* Prevention by preemption appears to be the most appropriate strategy for main memory. When a process is preempted, it is simply swapped to secondary memory, freeing space to resolve the deadlock.
- *Internal resources:* Prevention by means of resource ordering can be used.

4.6

CLASSIC PROBLEMS IN CONCURRENCY

In dealing with the design of synchronization and concurrency mechanisms, it is useful to be able to relate the problem at hand to known problems and to be able to test any solution in terms of its ability to solve these known problems. In the literature, several problems have assumed importance and appear frequently, both because they are examples of common design problems and because of their educational value. One such problem is the producer/consumer problem, which has already been explored. In this section, we look at two other classic problems: the readers/writers problem, and the dining philosophers problem.

Readers/Writers Problem

The readers/writers problem is defined as follows: There is a data area shared among a number of processes. The data area could be a file, a block of main memory, or even a bank of processor registers. There are a number of processes that only read the data area (readers) and a number that only write to the data area (writers). The following conditions must be satisfied:

1. Any number of readers may simultaneously read the file.
2. Only one writer at a time may write to the file.
3. If a writer is writing to the file, no reader may read it.

Before proceeding, let us distinguish this problem from two others: the general mutual-exclusion problem and the producer/consumer problem. In the readers/writers problem, readers do not also write to the data area, nor do writers read the data area. A more general case, which includes this case, is to allow any of the processes to read or write to the data area. In that case, we can declare any portion of a process that accesses the data area to be a critical section and impose the general mutual-exclusion solution. The reason for being concerned with the more restricted case is that more efficient solutions are possible for this case and that the less efficient solutions to the general problem are unacceptably slow. For example, suppose that the shared area is a library catalog. Ordinary users of the library read the catalog to locate a book. One or more librarians are able to update the catalog. In the general solution, every access to the catalog would be treated as a critical section, and users would be forced to read the catalog one at a time. This would clearly impose intolerable delays. At the same time, it is important to prevent writers from interfering with each other, and it is also required to prevent reading while writing is in progress to prevent the access of incorrect information.

Can the producer/consumer problem be considered simply a special case of the readers/writers problem with a single writer (the producer) and a single reader (the consumer)? The answer is no. The producer is not just a writer. It must read queue pointers to determine where to write the next item, and it must determine if the buffer is full. Similarly, the consumer is not just a reader since it must adjust the queue pointers to show that it has removed a unit from the buffer.

We now examine two solutions to the problem.

Readers Have Priority

Figure 4.33a is a solution using semaphores, showing one instance each of a reader and a writer; the solution does not change for multiple readers and writers. The writer process is simple. The semaphore *wsem* is used to enforce mutual exclusion. So long as one writer is accessing the shared data area, no other writers and no readers may access it. The reader process also makes use of *wsem* to enforce mutual exclusion. However, to allow multiple readers, we require that when there are no readers reading, the first reader that attempts to read should wait for *wsem*. When there is already at least one reader reading, subsequent readers need not wait before entering. The global variable *readcount* is used to keep track of the number of readers, and the semaphore x is used to assure that *readcount* is updated properly.

Writers Have Priority

In the previous solution, readers have priority. Once a single reader has begun access to the data area, it is possible for readers to retain control of the data area so long as there is at least one reader in the act of reading. Therefore writers are subject to starvation.

Figure 4.33b shows a solution that guarantees no new readers are allowed

```
program readersandwriters;
var   readcount: integer;
      x, wsem: semaphore (:= 1);
procedure reader;
begin
  repeat
    wait (x);
      readcount := readcount + 1;
      if readcount = 1 then wait (wsem);
    signal (x);
    READUNIT;
    wait (x);
      readcount := readcount - 1;
      if readcount = 0 then signal (wsem);
    signal (x)
  forever
end;
procedure writer;
begin
  repeat
    wait (wsem);
      WRITEUNIT;
    signal (wsem)
  forever
end;
begin
  readcount := 0;
  parbegin
    reader;
    writer
  parend
end.
```

FIGURE 4.33a A solution to the readers/writers problem using semaphores; readers have priority.

access to the data area once at least one writer has declared a desire to write. For writers, the following semaphores and variables are added to the ones already defined:

- A semaphore *rsem* that inhibits all readers while there is at least one writer desiring access to the data area.
- A variable *writecount* that controls the setting of *rsem*.
- A semaphore *y* that controls the updating of *writecount*.

For readers, one additional semaphore is needed. A long queue must not be allowed to build up on *rsem*, otherwise writers will not be able to jump the

```
program readersandwriters;
var   readcount, writecount: integer;
      x, y, z, wsem, rsem: semaphore (: = 1);
procedure reader;
begin
  repeat
    wait (z);
      wait (rsem);
        wait (x);
          readcount := readcount + 1;
          if readcount = 1 then wait (wsem);
        signal (x);
      signal (rsem);
    signal (z);
    READUNIT;
    wait (x);
      readcount := readcount − 1;
      if readcount = 0 then signal (wsem);
    signal (x)
  forever
end;
procedure writer;
begin
  repeat
    wait (y);
      writecount := writecount + 1;
      if writecount = 1 then wait (rsem);
    signal (y);
    wait (wsem);
      WRITEUNIT;
    signal (wsem);
    wait (y);
      writecount := writecount − 1;
      if writecount = 0 then signal (rsem);
    signal (y)
  forever
end;
begin
  readcount, writecount := 0;
  parbegin
    reader;
    writer
  parend
end.
```

FIGURE 4.33b A solution to the readers/writers problem using semaphores; writers have priority.

queue. Therefore, only one reader is allowed to queue on *rsem*, with any additional readers queuing on semaphore *z* immediately before waiting for *rsem*. Table 4.5 summarizes the possibilities.

An alternative solution, which gives writers priority and which is implemented using message passing, is shown in Figure 4.34, which is based on an algorithm in the work of Theaker and Brookes [THEA83]. In this case, there is a controller process that has access to the shared data area. Other processes wishing to access the data area send a request message to the controller, are granted access with an "OK" reply message, and indicate completion of access with a "finished" message. The controller is equipped with three mailboxes, one for each type of message that it may receive.

The controller process services write request messages before read request messages in order to give writers priority. In addition, mutual exclusion must be enforced. To do this, the variable *count* is used and is initialized to some number greater than the maximum possible number of readers. In this example, we use a value of 100. The action of the controller can be summarized as follows:

- If *count* > 0, then no writer is waiting and there may or may not be readers active. Service all "finished" messages first to clear active readers. Then service write requests and then read requests.
- If *count* = 0, then the only request outstanding is a write request. Allow the writer to proceed and wait for a "finished" message.
- If *count* < 0, then a writer has made a request and is being made to wait to clear all active readers. Therefore, only "finished" messages should be serviced.

TABLE 4.5   State of the Process Queues for Program of Figure 4.33b

Readers only in the system	• wsem set • no queues
Writers only in the system	• wsem and rsem set • writers queue on wsem
Both readers and writers with read first	• wsem set by reader • rsem set by writer • all writers queue on wsem • one reader queues on rsem • other readers queue on z
Both readers and writers with write first	• wsem set by writer • rsem set by writer • writers queue on wsem • one reader queues on rsem • other readers queue on z

```
procedure readeri;
var rmsg: message;
begin
   repeat
      rmsg := i;
      send (readrequest, rmsg);
      receive (mboxi, rmsg);
      READUNIT;
      rmsg := i;
      send (finished, rmsg)
   forever
end;

procedure writerj;
var rmsg: message;
begin
   repeat
      rmsg := i;
      send (writerequest, rmsg);
      receive (mboxj, rmsg);
      WRITEUNIT;
      rmsg := i;
      send (finished, rmsg)
   forever
end;

procedure controller;
begin
   repeat
      if count > 0 do begin
         if not empty (finished) then begin
            receive (finished, msg);
            count := count + 1
         end
         else if not empty (writerequest) then begin
            receive (writerequest, msg);
            writer.id := msg.id;
            count := count - 100
         end
         else if not empty (readrequest) then begin
            receive (readrequest, msg);
            count := count - 1;
            send (msg.id, "OK")
         end
      end;
      if count = 0 do begin
         send (writer.id, "OK");
         receive (finished, msg);
         count := 100
      end;
      while count < 0 do begin
         receive (finished, msg);
         count := count + 1
      end
   forever
end.
```

FIGURE 4.34 A solution to the readers/writers problem using message-passing.

Dining Philosophers Problem

In those days and in that place, there were five philosophers living together. The life of each philosopher consisted principally of thinking and eating, and through years of thought, all the philosophers had agreed that the only food that contributed to their thinking efforts was spaghetti.

The eating arrangements were simple (Figure 4.35): a round table on which was set a large serving bowl of spaghetti, five plates, one for each philosopher, and five forks. A philosopher wishing to eat would go to his or her assigned place at the table and, using the two forks on either side of the plate, take and eat some spaghetti. The problem: Devise a ritual (algorithm) that will allow the philosophers to eat. The algorithm must satisfy mutual exclusion (no two philosophers can use the same fork at the same time) while avoiding deadlock and starvation (in this case, the term has literal as well as algorithmic meaning!).

This problem, due to Dijkstra, may not seem important or relevant in itself. However, it does illustrate basic problems in deadlock and starvation. Furthermore, attempts to develop solutions reveal many of the difficulties in concurrent programming (e.g., see [GING90]). Accordingly, this problem is a standard test case for testing approaches to synchronization.

Figure 4.36 suggests a solution that uses semaphores. Each philosopher picks up first the fork on the left and then the fork on the right. After the philosopher has finished eating, the two forks are replaced on the table. This solution, alas, leads to deadlock: If all the philosophers are hungry at the same time, they all sit down, they all pick up the fork on their left, and they all reach out for the

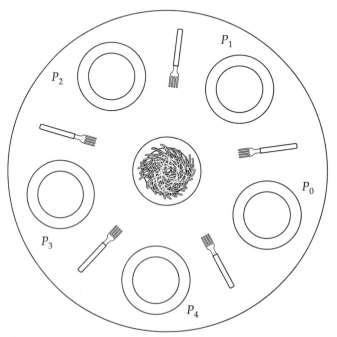

FIGURE 4.35 Dining arrangement for philosophers

```
program    diningphilosophers;
var        fork: array [0 . . . 4] of semaphore (:= 1);
           i: integer;
procedure philospher (i: integer);
begin
  repeat
    think;
    wait (fork[i]);
    wait (fork [(i+1) mod 5]);
    eat;
    signal (fork [(i+1) mod 5]);
    signal (fork[i])
  forever
end;
begin
  parbegin
    philospher (0);
    philosopher (1);
    philosopher (2);
    philosopher (3);
    philosopher (4)
  parend
end.
```

FIGURE 4.36 A first solution to the dining philosophers problem.

other fork, which isn't there. In this undignified position, all philosophers starve.

To overcome the risk of deadlock, we could buy five additional forks (a more sanitary solution!) or teach the philosophers to eat spaghetti with just one fork. As another approach, we could consider adding a footman who allows only four philosophers at a time into the dining room. With at most four seated philosophers, at least one philosopher will have access to two forks. Figure 4.37 shows such a solution, again using semaphores. This solution is free of deadlock and starvation.

4.7

EXAMPLE SYSTEMS

UNIX System V

UNIX provides a variety of mechanisms for interprocessor communication and synchronization. Here, we look at the most important of these:

- Pipes
- Messages

```
program   diningphilosophers;
var       fork: array [0 . . . 4] of semaphore (:= 1);
          room: semaphore (:= 4);
          i: integer;
procedure philospher (i: integer);
begin
  repeat
    think;
    wait (room);
    wait (fork[i]);
    wait (fork [(i+1) mod 5]);
    eat;
    signal (fork [(i+1) mod 5]);
    signal (fork[i]);
    signal (room)
  forever
end;
begin
  parbegin
    philosopher (0);
    philosopher (1);
    philosopher (2);
    philosopher (3);
    philosopher (4);
  parend
end.
```

FIGURE 4.37 A second solution to the dining philosophers problem.

- Shared memory
- Semaphores
- Signals

Pipes, messages, and shared memory provide a means of communicating data across processes, whereas semaphores and signals are used to trigger actions by other processes.

Pipes

One of the most significant contributions of UNIX to the development of operating systems is the pipe. Inspired by the concept of coroutines [RITC84], a pipe is a circular buffer allowing two processes to communicate on the producer/consumer model. Thus, it is a first-in, first-out queue written by one process and read by another.

When a pipe is created, it is given a fixed size in bytes. When a process attempts to write into the pipe, the write request is immediately executed if there is sufficient room; otherwise, the process is blocked. Similarly, a reading process is blocked if it attempts to read more bytes than are currently in the pipe; otherwise, the read request is immediately executed. The operating system enforces mutual exclusion: that is, only one process can access a pipe at a time.

There are two types of pipes: named and unnamed. Only related processes can share unnamed pipes, whereas unrelated processes can share only named pipes.

Messages

A message is a block of text with an accompanying type. UNIX provides *msgsnd* and *msgrcv* system calls for processes to engage in message passing. Associated with each process is a message queue, which functions like a mailbox.

The message sender specifies the type of message with each message sent, and this can be used as a selection criterion by the receiver. The receiver can either retrieve messages in first-in, first-out (FIFO) order or by type. A process will suspend when trying to send a message to a full queue. A process will also suspend when trying to read from an empty queue. If a process attempts to read a message of a certain type and fails, the process is not suspended.

Shared Memory

The fastest form of interprocess communication provided in UNIX is shared memory, which is a common block of virtual memory shared by multiple processes. Processes read and write shared memory using the same machine instructions they use to read and write other portions of their virtual memory space. Permission is read-only or read-write for a process, determined on a per-process basis. Mutual exclusion constraints are not part of the shared memory facility but must be provided by the processes using the shared memory.

Semaphores

The semaphore system calls in UNIX System V are a generalization of the *wait* and *signal* primitives defined in this chapter, in that several operations can be done simultaneously and the increment and decrement operations can be values greater than 1. The kernel does all the requested operations atomically; no other process may access the semaphore until all operations are done.

A semaphore consists of the following elements:

- Current value of the semaphore
- Process ID of the last process to operate on the semaphore
- Number of processes waiting for the semaphore value to be greater than its current value
- Number of processes waiting for the semaphore value to be zero

Associated with the semaphore are queues of processes suspended on that semaphore.

Semaphores are actually created in sets, with a semaphore set consisting of one or more semaphores. There is a *semctl* system call that allows all the semaphore values in the set to be set at the same time. In addition, there is a *semop* system call that takes as an argument a list of semaphore operations, each defined on one of the semaphores in a set. When this call is made, the kernel performs the indicated operations one at a time. For each operation, the actual function is specified by the value *sem_op*. The following are the possibilities.

* If *sem_op* is positive, the kernel increments the value of the semaphore and awakens all processes waiting for the value of the semaphore to increase.
* If *sem_op* is 0, the kernel checks the semaphore value. If 0, it continues with the other operations on the list; otherwise, it increments the number of processes waiting for this semaphore to be 0 and suspends the process on the event that the value of the semaphore equals 0.
* If *sem_op* is negative and its absolute value is less than or equal to the semaphore value, the kernel adds *sem_op* (a negative number) to the semaphore value. If the result is 0, the kernel awakens all processes waiting for the value of the semaphore to equal 0.
* If *sem_op* is negative and its absolute value is greater than the semaphore value, the kernel suspends the process in the event that the value of the semaphore increases.

This generalization of the semaphore provides considerable flexibility in performing process synchronization and coordination.

Signals

A signal is a software mechanism that informs a process of the occurrence of asynchronous events. A signal is similar to a hardware interrupt but does not employ priorities. That is, all signals are treated equally; signals that occur at the same time are presented to a process one at a time, with no particular ordering.

Processes may send each other signals, or the kernel may send signals internally. A signal is delivered by updating a field in the process table for the process to which the signal is being sent. Since each signal is maintained as a single bit, signals of a given type cannot be queued. A signal is processed just after a process wakes up to run, or whenever the process is preparing to return from a system call. A process may respond to a signal by performing some default action (e.g., termination), executing a signal handler function or ignoring the signal.

Table 4.6 lists the signals defined for UNIX System V.

TABLE 4.6 UNIX Signals

Value	Name	Description
01	SIGHUP	hang up; sent to process when kernel assumes that the user of that process is doing no useful work
02	SIGINT	interrupt
03	SIGQUIT	quit; sent by user to induce halting of process and production of core dump
04	SIGILL	illegal instruction
05	SIGTRAP	trace trap; triggers the execution of code for process tracing
06	SIGIOT	IOT instruction
07	SIGEMT	EMT instruction
08	SIGFPT	floating point exception
09	SIGKILL	kill; terminate process
10	SIGBUS	bus error
11	SIGSEGV	segmentation violation; process attempts to access location outside its virtual address space
12	SIGSYS	bad argument to system call
13	SIGPIPE	write on a pipe that has no readers attached to it
14	SIGALARM	alarm clock; issue when a process wishes to receive a signal after a period of time
15	SIGTERM	software termination
16	SIGUSR1	user defined signal 1
17	SIGUSR2	user defined signal 2
18	SIGCLD	death of a child
19	SIGPWR	power failure

OS/2

As with UNIX, OS/2 provides a variety of mechanisms for interprocessor communication and synchronization. Here, we look at the most important of these:

- Pipes
- Shared memory
- Queues
- Semaphores
- Signals

Pipes, shared memory, and queues provide a means of communicating data across processes, whereas semaphores and signals are used to trigger actions by other processes.

Pipes

OS/2 supports two types of pipes: anonymous pipes and named pipes. Anonymous pipes in OS/2 are virtually identical to unnamed pipes in UNIX: They provide a byte-stream FIFO buffer between two related processes. Named pipes in OS/2 differ from those in UNIX in the following ways:

- Named pipes in OS/2 can be used in byte-stream mode, as in UNIX. In addition, named pipes in OS/2 support the message mode, in which processes read and write streams of messages. In this mode, the reader asks for the next message, rather than the next n bytes. Thus, the pipe functions as a mailbox for message passing.
- Named pipes are full duplex, actually consisting of two pipes going in opposite directions between a pair of processes.

Shared Memory

Shared memory is similar to the facility available in UNIX. Memory may be shared on a segment basis, and it is up to the using processes to synchronize access. Two types of shared memory are supported. With giveaway shared memory, a current owner gives access to one of its segments to another process. With named shared memory, access to a particular segment is requested by name.

Queues

A queue is a more powerful and flexible means of passing data than the pipe. It is actually a structured shared-memory facility. This makes it more efficient than a pipe because data are not moved from a producer to a consumer; rather, both share a buffer in which data are read and written.

Queue elements are messages that may be read from the queue with (producer/consumer model) or without (readers/writers model) being destroyed. A process can read queue elements in FIFO order, LIFO order, or priority order.

Semaphores

OS/2 provides two kinds of semaphores: RAM semaphores and system semaphores. Both types of semaphores provide the same interface to processes for manipulation. In addition to *wait* and *signal* primitives, which are those of traditional semaphores, the OS/2 semaphore facility supports a *muxsemwait* primitive, which allows a thread to wait for a variety of events and wake up whenever one of those events occurs.

A RAM semaphore is a 4-byte data structure kept in a RAM location accessible to all threads that use it. System semaphores use a data structure that is kept in system memory outside the address space of any process. Thus, access to system semaphores is much slower. In compensation, system semaphores provide the following features not available in RAM semaphores:

- System semaphores are general semaphores, also known as counting semaphores, whereas RAM semaphores are binary.
- A system semaphore can be declared exclusive, which means that only the thread that set the semaphore can clear it.
- System semaphores support mechanisms that prevent deadlock by terminat-

ing programs. Other processes are never left waiting for a terminated process because the operating system manages the system semaphore.

Signals

The OS/2 signal mechanism is similar but not identical to the UNIX signal mechanism. OS/2 supports six signals (Table 4.7): three common signals sent by the operating system and three general-purpose signals sent by one process to another. The common signals are CTRL-C and CTRL-BREAK, which are sent in response to keyboard activity, and Terminate, sent in response to a request to terminate a process. When any of these signals is received, the default action is to terminate the process, although the user can specify an alternative signal-handling routine. The three general-purpose signals can be used for any inter-process coordination purpose. There is no default action for these signals; it is up to the user to specify a signal-handling routine.

MVS

MVS provides two facilities for enforcing mutual exclusion with respect to the use of resources: enqueing and locking. Enqueuing is concerned with user-controlled resources such as files, whereas locking is concerned with MVS system resources.

ENQUE

The ENQUE facility is used to regulate access to shared data resources. The requested resource may be an entire disk volume, one or more files, records within a file, program control blocks, or any work areas within main storage. A process (an address space) requests shared control if the resource is to be read only, and exclusive control if the data might be modified. Table 4.8 indicates the rules used by MVS to determine the action when an ENQUE request is issued. In essence, the scheme conforms to the readers/writers model, giving priority to writers.

In addition to an outright request for access, the user may specify that the availability of the resource is to be tested but that control of the resource is not requested, or the user may specify that control of the resource is to be assigned

TABLE 4.7   OS/2 Signals

Value	Signal	Default Action
1	CTRL-C	Terminate Process
3	Terminate	Terminate Process
4	CTRL-BREAK	Terminate Process
5	User Flag A	Ignore
6	User Flag B	Ignore
7	User Flag C	Ignore

TABLE 4.8   Decision Table for MVS ENQUE facility

	Resource Status at Time of Request		
Request Type	Free	Shared	Exclusive
Shared	Honored	Honored unless exclusive request is queued	Queued
Exclusive	Honored	Queued	Queued

to the requester only if the resource is immediately available. These options may be used to prevent deadlock or to notify the operator that there is a problem.

Locks

Locks enforce mutual exclusion for access to system resources by MVS routines. A lock is simply an area in common virtual storage, and is usually kept permanently in main memory. It contains bits to indicate whether the lock is in use and, if so, who owns the resource. Locks come in two classes and two types. The classes are:

- *Global:* Across all address spaces
- *Local:* Across all tasks in a single address space

The types are:

- *Spin:* The processor executes a test-and-set type of instruction waiting for the lock; this is busy-waiting.
- *Suspend:* The task waiting is suspended.

Spin locks are used for critical sections that run for only a short time. A suspend lock implies a long critical section and the profitability of suspending a denied process and then dispatching another process. Local locks are always suspend locks, whereas there are both spin and suspend global locks.

To prevent deadlocks, locks are arranged in a hierarchy; this is the strategy discussed earlier to prevent the circular-wait condition. Table 4.9 shows the hierarchy of locks in MVS. A processor may request only locks higher in the hierarchy than locks it currently holds.

A detailed, though somewhat dated, discussion of MVS locks can be found in [KATZ84].

4.8

SUMMARY

The two central themes of modern operating systems are multiprogramming and distributed processing. Fundamental to both these themes, and fundamental to the technology of operating system design, is concurrency. When multiple

TABLE 4.9   MVS Locks

Lock Name	Category	Type	Description (See note 1.)
RSMGL	Global	Spin	Real storage management global lock—serializes RSM global resources.
VSMFIX	Global	Spin	Virtual storage management fixed subpools lock— serializes VSM global/ queues.
ASM	Global	Spin	Auxiliary storage management lock—serializes ASM resources on an address space level.
ASMGL	Global	Spin	Auxiliary storage management global lock— serializes ASM resources on a global level.
RSMST	Global	Spin	Real storage management steal lock—serializes RSM control blocks on an address space level when it is not known which address space locks are currently held.
RSMCM	Global	Spin	Real storage management common lock— serializes RSM common area resources (such as page table entries).
RSMXM	Global	Spin	Real storage management cross memory lock— serializes RSM control blocks on an address space level when serialization is needed to a second address space.
RSMAD	Global	Spin	Real storage management address space lock— serializes RSM control blocks on an address space level.
RSM	Global	Spin	Real storage management lock (shared/ exclusive)—serializes RSM functions and resources on a global level.
VSMPAG	Global	Spin	Virtual storage management pageable subpools lock—serializes the VSM work area for VSM pageable subpools.
DISP	Global	Spin	Global dispatcher lock—serializes the ASVT and the ASCB dispatching queue.
SALLOC	Global	Spin	Space allocation lock—serializes receiving routines that enable a processor for an emergency signal or malfunction alert.
IOSYNCH	Global	Spin	I/O supervisor synchronization lock—serializes, using a table of lockwords, IOS resources.
IOSUCB	Global	Spin	I/O supervisor unit control block lock—serializes access and updates to the UCBs. There is one IOSUCB lock per UCB.
SRM	Global	Spin	System resources management lock—serializes SRM control blocks and associated data.
TRACE	Global	Spin	Trace lock (shared/exclusive)—serializes the system trace buffer.
CPU	Global	Spin	Processor lock—provides system-recognized (legal) disablement. (See note 2.)

TABLE 4.9   (*Continued*)

Lock Name	Category	Type	Description (See note 1.)
CMSSMF	Global	Suspend	System management facilities cross memory services lock—serializes SMF functions and control blocks. (See note 3.)
CMSEQDQ	Global	Suspend	ENQ/DEQ cross memory services lock—serializes ENQ/DEQ functions and control blocks. (See note 3.)
CMS	Global	Suspend	General cross memory services lock—serializes on more than one address space where this serialization is not provided by one or more of the other global locks. The CMS lock provides global serialization when enablement is required. (See note 3.)
CML	Local	Suspend	Local storage lock—serializes functions and storage within an address space other than the home address space. There is one CML lock per address space. (See note 4.)
LOCAL	Local	Suspend	Local storage lock—serializes functions and storage within a local address space. There is one LOCAL lock per address space. (See note 4.)

Notes:
1. All locks are listed hierarchical order, with RSMGL being the highest lock in the hierarchy. (See also notes 2, 3, and 4.)
2. The CPU lock has no hierarchy in respect to the other spin type locks. However, once obtained, no suspend locks can be obtained.
3. The cross memory services locks (CMSSMF, CMSEQDQ, and CMS) are equal to each other in the hierarchy.
4. The CML and LOCAL locks are equal to each other in the hierarchy.

processes are executing concurrently, either actually in the case of a multiprocessor system or virtually in the case of a single-processor multiprogramming system, issues of conflict resolution and cooperation arise.

Concurrent processes may interact in a number of ways. Processes that are unaware of each other may nevertheless compete for resources, such as processor time and access to I/O devices. Processes may be indirectly aware of one another because they share access to a common object, such as a block of main memory or a file. And processes may be directly aware of each other and cooperate by the exchange of information. The key issues that arise in these interactions are mutual exclusion and deadlock.

Mutual exclusion is a condition in which there is a set of concurrent processes, only one of which is able to access a given resource or perform a given function at any time. Mutual-exclusion techniques can be used to resolve conflicts, such as competition for resources, and to synchronize processes so that they can cooperate. An example of the latter is the producer/consumer model, in which one process is putting data into a buffer and one or more processes are extracting data from that buffer.

A number of software algorithms for providing mutual exclusion have been developed, of which the best known is Dekker's algorithm. The software approach is likely to have high processing overhead, and the risk of logical errors (bugs) is high. A second approach to supporting mutual exclusion involves the use of special-purpose machine instructions. This approach reduces overhead, but because it uses busy-waiting, it is still inefficient.

Another approach to supporting mutual exclusion is to provide features within the operating system. Two of the most common techniques are semaphores and message facilities. Semaphores are used for signaling among processes and can be readily used to enforce a mutual-exclusion discipline. Messages are useful for the enforcement of mutual exclusion and also provide an effective means of interprocess communication.

Deadlock is the blocking of a set of processes that either compete for system resources or communicate with each other. The blockage is permanent unless the operating system takes some extraordinary action, such as killing one or more processes or forcing one or more processes to backtrack. Deadlock may involve reusable resources or consumable resources. A consumable resource is one that is destroyed when it is acquired by a process; examples include messages and information in I/O buffers. A reusable resource is one that is not depleted or destroyed by use, such as an I/O channel or a region of memory.

There are three general approaches to dealing with deadlock: prevention, detection, and avoidance. Deadlock prevention guarantees that deadlock will not occur, by assuring that one of the necessary conditions for deadlock is not met. Deadlock detection is needed if the operating system is always willing to grant resource requests; periodically, the operating system must check for deadlock and take action to break the deadlock. Deadlock avoidance involves the analysis of each new resource request to determine if it could lead to deadlock and granting it only if deadlock is not possible.

4.9

RECOMMENDED READING

Despite its age, [HANS73], which is still in print, provides one of the best treatments of concurrency in an operating-system textbook. It has the further advantage of containing a number of problems with worked-out solutions. [BEN82] provides a very clear and even entertaining discussion of concurrency, mutual exclusion, semaphores, and other related topics. A more formal treatment, expanded to include distributed systems, is contained in [BEN90]. [AXFO88] is another readable and useful treatment; it also contains a number of problems with worked-out solutions. [RAYN86] is a comprehensive and lucid collection of algorithms for mutual exclusion, covering software (e.g., Dekker) and hardware approaches as well as semaphores and messages. [HOAR85] is a very readable classic that presents a formal approach to defining sequential processes and concurrency. [LAMP86] is a lengthy formal treatment of mutual exclusion. [RUDO90] is a useful aid in understanding concurrency.

The classic paper on deadlocks, [HOLT72], is still well worth a read, as is [COFF71]. Another good survey is [ISLO80]. [ZOBE88] is an exhaustive annotated bibliography up to the date of its publication.

4.10

PROBLEMS

4.1 Figure 4.4 shows a solution to Conway's problem using coroutines. Rewrite the solution using ordinary procedures.

4.2 Consider a concurrent program with two processes, P and Q, shown below. A, B, C, D, and E are arbitrary atomic (indivisible) statements. Assume that the main program (not shown) does a **parbegin** of the two processes.

```
procedure P;        procedure Q;
begin               begin
   A;                  D;
   B;                  E;
   C;               end.
end.
```

Show all the possible interleavings of the execution of the foregoing two processes (show this by giving execution "traces" in terms of the atomic statements).

4.3 Consider the following program:

```
const n = 50;
var tally: integer;
procedure total;
var count: integer;
begin
   for count := 1 to n do tally := tally + 1
end;
```

```
begin (* main program *)
  tally := 0;
  parbegin
    total; total
  parend;
  writeln (tally)
end.
```

(a) Determine the proper lower bound and upper bound on the final value of the shared variable *tally* output by this concurrent program. Assume processes can execute at any relative speed and that a value can be incremented only after it has been loaded into a register by a separate machine instruction.

(b) Suppose that an arbitrary number of these processes are permitted to execute in parallel under the assumptions of part (a). What effect will this modification have on the range of final values of *tally*?

4.4 Is busy-waiting always less efficient (in terms of using processor time) than a blocking wait? Explain.

4.5 Consider the following program:

```
var    blocked: array [0 . . 1] of boolean;
       turn: 0 .. 1;
procedure P (id: integer);
begin
  repeat
    blocked[id] := true;
    while turn ≠ id do
      begin
        while blocked[1 − id] do { nothing };
        turn := id
      end;
    < critical section >
    blocked[id] := false;
    < remainder >
  until false
end;
begin
  blocked[0] := false; blocked[1] := false;
  turn := 0;
  parbegin
    P(0); P(1)
  parend
end.
```

This is a software solution to the mutual-exclusion problem proposed in [HYMA66]. Find a counter example that demonstrates that this solution is incorrect. It is interesting to note that even the *Communications of the ACM* was fooled on this one.

4.6 Consider the following precedence graph:

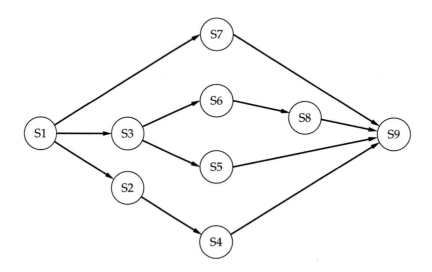

(a) Express the graph as a concurrent program using **fork, join,** and **quit** primitives. The program should permit maximum parallelism.

(b) Express the graph as a concurrent program using the **parbegin/parend** concurrent statement. The program should again permit maximum parallelism.

(c) Suppose an edge from node S3 to node S4 were added. What effect would this have on the programs developed in parts (a) and (b)?

4.7 Prove the correctness of Dekker's algorithm.

(a) Prove that mutual exclusion is enforced. Hint: Show that when P*i* enters its critical section that the following expression is true:

flag [*i*] **and** (**not** flag [1 − *i*])

(b) Prove that deadlock is avoided. Hint: Consider the following cases: (1) a single process is attempting to enter the critical section; (2) both processes are attempting to enter the critical section, and (2a) turn = 0 and flag [0] = false, and (2b) turn = 0 and flag [0] = true.

4.8 Peterson's algorithm can be generalized to provide mutual exclusion among N processes. Assume two global arrays, *q* and *turn*. The initial values of the N elements of *q* and the N − 1 elements of *turn* are all 0. Each process maintains private variable *j* and *k*, used as array indexes. The algorithm for the process *i* is as follows:

global integer arrays *q* [N], *turn* [N − 1]
repeat

```
1  for j=1 to N-1 do
2     q [i]=j;
3     turn [j]=i;
4     L: for k=1 to i−1, i+1 to N
5             if ((q [k] ≥ j) and (turn [j] = i)) goto L;
6     q [i] = n;
```

critical section of process i;

```
7  q [i] = 0;
```

remainder section of process i
until false

It is convenient to think of the value of the local variable j as the "stage" of the algorithm at which process i executes. The global array q indicates the stage of each process. When a process enters its critical phase, it passes to stage N (the statement $q [i] = N$ provides this. Actually this statement exists only to simplify the language used in the proof and is unnecessary for the correctness of the algorithm.)

If $q [x] > q [y]$, we say that process x precedes (is in front of) process y.

We would like to show that this algorithm provides:

- Mutual exclusion
- Deadlock freedom
- No starvation

To do so, prove the following lemmas:

(a) Lemma 1: A process that precedes all others can advance at least one stage.

Hint: Let process i find, when it starts line 4, that

$$j = q [i] > q [k] \qquad \text{for all } k \neq i \tag{1}$$

(b) Lemma 2: When a process passes from stage j to stage $j+1$, exactly one of the following claims holds:

- It precedes all other processes, or
- It is not alone at stage j.

Hint: Let process i be about to advance $q [i]$ and consider whether equation (1) is true or not.

(c) Lemma 3: If there are (at least) two processes at stage j, there is (at least) one process at each stage k, $1 \leq k \leq j - 1$

Hint: Prove by induction on j.

(d) Lemma 4: The maximal number of processes that can be at stage j is $N - j + 1, 1 \leq j \leq N - 1$.

Hint: This is simple arithmetic.

(e) On the basis of Lemmas 1 through 4, show that the algorithm provides mutual exclusion, deadlock freedom, and no starvation.

4.9 Another software approach to mutual exclusion is Lamport's **bakery algorithm** [LAMP74], so-called because it is based on the practice in bakeries and other shops of every customer receiving a numbered ticket on arrival, allowing each to be served in turn. The algorithm is as follows:

```
var   choosing: array [0..n−1] of boolean;
      number: array [0..n−1] of integer;
repeat
   choosing [i] := true;
   number [i] := 1 + max(number[0], number[1], ..., number[n−1]);
   choosing [i] := false;
   for j := 0 to n−1 do
      begin
         while choosing[j] do { nothing };
         while number[j] ≠ 0 and (number[j],j) < (number[i],i) do { nothing };
      end;
      < critical section >;
      number [i] := 0;
      < remainder >;
forever.
```

The arrays *choosing* and *number* are initialized to false and 0 respectively. The *i*th element of each array may be read and written by process *i* but only read by other processes. The notation $(a, b) < (c, d)$ is defined as:

$(a < c)$ or $(a = c$ and $b < d)$

(a) Describe the algorithm in words.
(b) Show that this algorithm avoids deadlock.
(c) Show that it enforces mutual exclusion.
(d) If there is always at least one process holding a ticket number while the maximum is being computed, then the values in *number* become indeterminately large. Modify the algorithm to eliminate this problem. Hint: Let the maximum value of any element in the array be $2n − 1$.

4.10 Demonstrate that the following software approaches to mutual exclusion do not depend on elementary mutual exclusion at the memory access level:
(a) The bakery algorithm
(b) Peterson's algorithm

4.11 When a special machine instruction is used to provide mutual exclusion in the fashion of Figure 4.12, there is no control over how long a process must wait before being granted access to its critical section. Devise an algorithm that uses the testset instruction but that guarantees that any process waiting to enter its critical section will do so within $n − 1$ turns, where n is the number of processes that may potentially require access to the critical section and a "turn" is an event consisting of one process leaving the critical section and another process being granted access.

4.12 Assume that at time 5 no system resources are being used except for the processor and memory. Now consider the following events:

At time 5,   P1 executes a command to read from disk unit 3.
At time 15,   P4's time slice expires.
At time 18,   P7 executes a command to write to disk unit 3.
At time 20,   P3 executes a command to read from disk unit 2.
At time 24,   P4 executes a command to write to disk unit 3.
At time 28,   P2 requests to execute a Wait operation on a semaphore *Buf* with value 2.
At time 33,   an interrupt occurs from disk unit 2: P3's read is complete.
At time 34,   P3 requests to execute a Wait operation on semaphore *Buf*.
At time 36,   an interrupt occurs from disk unit 3: P1's read is complete.
At time 38,   P8 terminates.
At time 40,   an interrupt occurs from disk unit 3. P4's write is complete.
At time 44,   P4 requests to execute a Wait operation on a semaphore *Cnt* with value 0.
At time 48,   an interrupt occurs from disk unit 3. P7's write is complete.

Identify those processes that are known to be in a Wait state (not the Ready state) and tell which event each identified process is waiting for:
(a) At time 22
(b) At time 37
(c) At time 47

4.13 Consider the following definition of semaphores:
wait(s):

if s.count > 0
  then
      s.count := s.count − 1
  else begin
      place this process in s.queue;
      block
  end;

signal(s):

if there is at least one process suspended on semaphore s
  then begin
          remove a process P from s.queue;
          place process P on ready list
      end
  else
      s.count := s.count + 1
  end;

Compare this set of definitions with that of Figure 4.13. Note one difference: With the foregoing definition, a semaphore can never take on a negative value. Is there any difference in the effect of the two sets of definitions when used in programs? That is, could you substitute one set for the other without altering the meaning of the program?

4.14 It should be possible to implement general semaphores by using binary semaphores. We can use the operations WaitB and SignalB and two binary semaphores, delay and mutex. Consider the following:

```
procedure Wait( var s: semaphore );
  begin
  WaitB(mutex);
  s := s − 1;
  if s < 0 then begin
    SignalB(mutex); WaitB(delay)
    end
  else  SignalB(mutex)
  end;
procedure Signal( var s: semaphore );
  begin
    WaitB(mutex);
    s := s + 1;
    if s ≤ 0 then SignalB(delay);
    SignalB(mutex)
  end.
```

Initially, s is set to the desired semaphore value. Each Wait operation decrements s, and each Signal operation increments s. The binary semaphore mutex, which is initialized to 1, assures that there is mutual exclusion for the updating of s. The binary semaphore delay, which is initialized to 0, is used to suspend processes.

There is a flaw in the preceding program. Demonstrate the flaw and propose a change that will fix it. Hint: All that you need to do is move a single line of the program.

4.15 Consider the solution to the infinite-buffer producer/consumer problem defined in Figure 4.19. Suppose we have the (common) case in which the producer and consumer are running at roughly the same speed. The scenario could be as follows:

- Producer: append; signal; produce; . . . ; append; signal; produce; . . .
- Consumer: consume; . . . ; take; wait; consume; . . . ; take; wait; . . .

The producer always manages to append a new element to the buffer and signal during the consumption of the previous element by the consumer. The producer is always appending to an empty buffer, and the consumer is always taking the sole item in the buffer. Although the consumer never blocks on the semaphore, a large number of calls to the semaphore mechanism is made, creating considerable overhead.

Construct a new program that will be more efficient under these circumstances. Hints: Allow n to have the value −1, which is to mean that not only is the buffer empty but the consumer has detected this fact and is going to block until the producer supplies fresh data. The solution does not require the use of the local variable m found in Figure 4.19.

4.16 Consider Figure 4.22. Would the meaning of the program change if the following were interchanged?
(a) wait(e); wait(s)
(b) signal(s); signal(n)
(c) wait(n); wait(s)
(d) signal(s); signal(e)

4.17 Figure 4.4 shows a solution to Conway's problem using coroutines.
(a) The program does not address the termination condition. Assume that the I/O routine READCARD returns the value true if it has placed an 80-character image in *inBuf*; otherwise it returns false. Modify the program to include this contingency. Note that the last printed line may therefore contain fewer than 125 characters.
(b) Rewrite the solution as a set of three processes, using semaphores.

4.18 In the subsection on the producer/consumer problem, note that our definitions allow at most $n - 1$ entries in the buffer.
(a) Why is this?
(b) Modify the algorithm to remedy this deficiency.

4.19 Suggest a way to implement message passing for a shared-memory multiprocessor system using semaphores. Hint: Make use of a shared buffer area to hold mailboxes, each one consisting of an array of message slots.

4.20 Suggest a way to implement semaphores using message passing. Hint: Introduce a separate synchronization process.

4.21 (a) Three processes share 4 resource units that can be reserved and released only one at a time. Each process needs a maximum of 2 units. Show that a deadlock cannot occur.
(b) N processes share M resource units that can be reserved and released only one at a time. The maximum need of each process does not exceed M, and the sum of all maximum needs is less than $M + N$. Show that a deadlock cannot occur.

4.22 This exercise demonstrates the subtlety of the dining philosophers problem and the difficulty of writing correct programs that use semaphores. The following solution, in C, to the dining philosophers problem is found in Tanenbaum's text [TANE87]:

```
#define N              5             /* number of philosophers */
#define LEFT           (i-1) mod N   /* number of i's left neighbor */
#define RIGHT          (i+1) mod N   /* number of i's right neighbor */
#define THINKING       0             /* philosopher is thinking */
#define HUNGRY         1             /* philosopher is trying to get forks */
#define EATING         2             /* philosopher is eating */
typedef int semaphore;               /* semaphores are a special kind of int */
int state[N];                        /* array to keep track of everyone's state */
semaphore mutex = 1;                 /* mutual exclusion for critical regions */
semaphore s[N];                      /* one semaphore per philosopher */
```

```
philosopher (i)
int i;                                    /* philosopher number, 0 to N−1 */
{
    while (TRUE) {                        /* repeat forever */
            think( );                     /* philosopher is thinking */
            take_forks(i);                /* acquire two forks or block */
            eat( );                       /* yum-yum, spaghetti */
            put_forks(i);                 /* put both forks back on table */
    }
}

take_forks(i)
int i;                                    /* philosopher number, 0 to N-1 */
{
    wait(mutex);                          /* enter critical region */
    state[i] = HUNGRY;                    /* record fact that philosopher i is hungry */
    test(i);                              /* try to acquire 2 forks */
    signal(mutex);                        /* exit critical region */
    wait(s[i])'                           /* block if forks were not acquired */
}

put_forks(i)
int i;                                    /* philosopher number, 0 to N-1 */
{
    wait(mutex);                          /* enter critical region */
    state[i] = HUNGRY;                    /* philosopher has finished eating */
    test(LEFT);                           /* see if left neighbor can now eat */
    test(RIGHT);                          /* see if right neighbor can now eat */
    signal(mutex);                        /* exit critical region */
}

test(i)
int i;                                    /* philosopher number, 0 to N-1 */
{
    if (state[i] = =HUNGRY && state[LEFT] != EATING && state[RIGHT] !=EATING) {
        state[i] = EATING;
        signal(s[i]);
    }
}
```

(a) Describe in words the way in which this solution works.

(b) Tanenbaum states: "The solution . . . is correct and also allows the maximum parallelism for an arbitrary number of philosophers." Although this solution prevents deadlock, it is not correct because starvation is possible. Demonstrate this by counterexample. Hint: Consider the case of five philosophers. Assume that these are gluttonous philosophers: They spend almost no time thinking. As soon as a philosopher has finished one bout of eating, he is almost immediately hungry. Then consider a configuration in which two of the philosophers are currently eating and the other three are blocked and hungry.

4.23 Suppose that there are two types of philosophers. One type always picks up his left fork first (a "lefty"), and the other type always picks up his right fork first (a "righty"). The behavior of a lefty is defined in Figure 4.36. The behavior of a righty is as follows:

```
begin
   repeat
      think;
      wait ( fork[ (i+1) mod 5] );
      wait ( fork[i]);
      eat;
      signal ( fork[i]);
      signal ( fork[ (i+1) mod 5] )
   forever
end;
```

Prove the following:

(a) Any seating arrangement of lefties and righties with at least one of each avoids deadlock.

(b) Any seating arrangement of lefties and righties with at least one of each prevents starvation.

CHAPTER 5

Memory Management

In a uniprogramming system, main memory is divided into two parts: one part for the operating system (resident monitor, kernel) and one part for the program currently being executed. In a multiprogramming system, the "user" part of memory must be further subdivided to accommodate multiple processes. The task of subdivision is carried out dynamically by the operating system and is known as **memory management**.

Effective memory management is vital in a multiprogramming system. If only a few processes are in memory, then for much of the time all the processes will be waiting for I/O and the processor will be idle. Thus, memory needs to be allocated efficiently to pack as many processes into memory as possible.

We begin this chapter with a look at the requirements that memory management is intended to satisfy. Next, we approach the technology of memory management by looking at a variety of simple schemes that have been used. Our focus is the requirement that a program must be loaded into main memory in order to be executed. This discussion serves to introduce some of the fundamental principles of memory management.

After analyzing the shortcomings of these simple techniques, we are ready to move on to a discussion of virtual memory. An analysis of this topic is complicated by the fact that memory management is an intimate and complex interrelationship between processor hardware and operating-system software. Accordingly, we focus first on the hardware aspect of memory management, introducing the concepts of paging, segmentation, and combined paging and segmentation. We are then in a position to look at the issues involved in the design of a virtual memory service in operating systems. This discussion, as usual, is followed by a look at our three example systems.

5.1

MEMORY MANAGEMENT REQUIREMENTS

While surveying the various mechanisms and policies associated with memory management, it is well to keep in mind the requirements that memory management is intended to satisfy. [LIST88] suggests five requirements:

- Relocation
- Protection
- Sharing
- Logical Organization
- Physical Organization

Relocation

In a multiprogramming system, the available main memory is generally shared among a number of processes. Typically, it is not possible for the programmer to know in advance which other programs will be resident in main memory at the time of execution of a program. In addition, we would like to be able to swap active processes in and out of main memory to maximize processor use by providing a large pool of ready processes to execute. Once a program has been swapped out to disk, it would be quite limiting to declare that when it is next swapped back in it must be placed in the same main memory region as before.

Thus, we cannot know ahead of time where a program should be placed, and we must allow that the program may be moved about in main memory as a result of swapping. These facts raise some technical concerns related to addressing, as illustrated in Figure 5.1, which depicts a process image. For simplicity, let us assume that the process image occupies a contiguous region of main memory. Clearly, the operating system will need to know the location of process control information and of the execution stack, as well as the entry point to begin execution of the program for this process. Since the operating system is managing memory and is responsible for bringing this process into main memory, these addresses are easy to come by. In addition, however, the processor must deal with memory references within the program. Branch instructions must contain an address to reference the instruction to be executed next. Data-reference instructions must contain the address of the byte or word of data referenced. Somehow, the processor hardware and operating-system software must be able to translate the memory references found in the code of the program into actual physical memory addresses that reflect the current location of the program in main memory.

Protection

Each process should be protected against unwanted interference by other processes, whether accidental or intentional. Thus, programs in other processes should not be able to reference memory locations in a process, for reading or writing purposes, without permission. In one sense, satisfaction of the relocation requirement increases the difficulty of satisfying the protection requirement. Because the location of a program in main memory is unknown, it is impossible to check absolute addresses at compile time to assure protection. Furthermore, most programming languages allow the dynamic calculation of

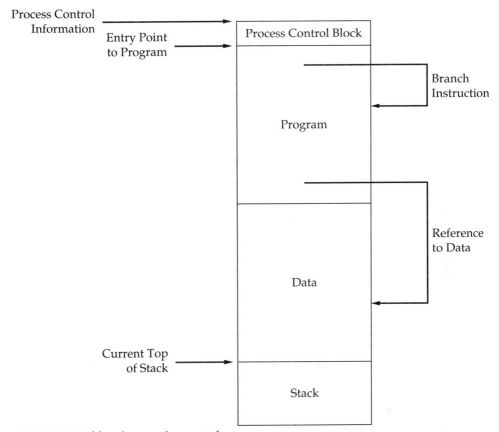

FIGURE 5.1 Addressing requirements for a process

addresses at run time, for example, by computing an array subscript or a pointer into a data structure. Hence, all memory references generated by a process must be checked at run time to ensure that they refer only to the memory space allocated to that process. Fortunately, as we shall see, mechanisms that support relocation also form the base for satisfying the protection requirement.

The process image layout of Figure 5.1 illustrates the protection requirement. Normally, a user process cannot access any portion of the operating system, either program or data. Again, a program in one process usually cannot branch to an instruction in another process. And without special arrangement a program in one process cannot access the data area of another process. The processor must be able to abort such instructions at the point of execution.

Note that, in terms of our example, the memory protection requirement must be satisfied by the processor (hardware) rather than the operating system (software). This is because the operating system cannot anticipate all the memory references that a program will make. Even if such anticipation were possible, it would be prohibitively time-consuming to screen each program in advance for possible memory-reference violations. Thus, it is possible to assess only the permissibility of a memory reference (data access or branch) at the time of execution of the instruction making the reference. To accomplish this, the processor hardware must have that capability.

Sharing

Any protection mechanisms that are implemented must have the flexibility to allow several processes to access the same portion of main memory. For example, if a number of processes are executing the same program, it is advantageous to allow each process to access the same copy of the program rather than have its own separate copy. Processes that are cooperating on some task may need to share access to the same data structure. The memory-management system must therefore allow controlled access to shared areas of memory without compromising essential protection. Again, we shall see that the mechanisms used to support relocation form the base for sharing capabilities.

Logical Organization

Almost invariably, main memory in a computer system is organized as a linear, or one-dimensional, address space that consists of a sequence of bytes or words. Secondary memory, at its physical level, is similarly organized. Although this organization closely mirrors the actual machine hardware, it does not correspond to the way in which programs are typically constructed. Most programs are organized into modules, some of which are unmodifiable (read-only, execute-only) and some of which contain data that may be modified. If the operating system and computer hardware can effectively deal with user programs and data in the form of modules of some sort, then a number of advantages can be realized, as follows:

1. Modules can be written and compiled independently, with all references from one module to another resolved by the system at run time.
2. With modest additional overhead, different degrees of protection (read-only, execute-only) can be given to different modules.
3. It is possible to introduce mechanisms by which modules can be shared among processes. The advantage of providing sharing on a module level is that this corresponds to the user's way of viewing the problem, and hence it is easy for the user to specify the sharing that is desired.

The tool that most readily satisfies these requirements is segmentation, which is one of the memory-management techniques explored in this chapter.

Physical Organization

As we discussed in Section 1.6, computer memory is organized into at least two levels: main memory and secondary memory. Main memory provides fast access at relatively high cost. In addition, main memory is volatile; that is, it does not provide permanent storage. Secondary memory is slower and cheaper than main memory, and it is usually not volatile. Thus, secondary memory of large capacity can be provided to allow for long-term storage of programs and data, while a smaller main memory holds programs and data currently in use.

In this two-level scheme, the organization of the flow of information between main and secondary memory is a major system concern. The responsibility for this flow could be assigned to the individual programmer, but this is impractical and undesirable for two reasons:

1. The main memory available for a program plus its data may be insufficient. In that case, the programmer must engage in a practice known as *overlaying*, in which the program and data are organized in such a way that various modules can be assigned the same region of memory, with a main program responsible for switching the modules in and out as needed. Even with the aid of compiler tools, overlay programming wastes programmer time.
2. In a multiprogramming environment, the programmer does not know at the time of coding how much space will be available or where that space will be.

It is clear, then, that the task of moving information between the two levels of memory should be a system responsibility. This task is the essence of memory management.

5.2

LOADING PROGRAMS INTO MAIN MEMORY

The core task of any memory management system is to bring programs into main memory for execution by the processor. In almost all modern multiprogramming systems, this task involves a sophisticated scheme known as *virtual memory*. Virtual memory is in turn based on the use of one or both of two basic techniques: segmentation and paging. Before we can look at these virtual memory techniques, we must prepare the ground by looking at simpler techniques that do not involve virtual memory (Table 5.1). One of these techniques, par-

TABLE 5.1   Memory Management Techniques

Technique	Description	Strengths	Weaknesses
Fixed Partitioning	Main memory is divided into a number of static partitions at system generation time. A process may be loaded into a partition of equal or greater size.	Simple to implement; little operating-system overhead.	Inefficient use of memory due to internal fragmentation; number of active processes is fixed.

TABLE 5.1 *(Continued)*

Technique	Description	Strengths	Weaknesses
Dynamic Partitioning	Partitions are created dynamically, so that each process is loaded into a partition of exactly the same size as that process.	No internal fragmentation; more efficient use of main memory.	Inefficient use of processor due to the need for compaction to counter external fragmentation.
Simple Paging	Main memory is divided into a number of equal-size frames. Each process is divided into a number of equal-size pages of the same length as frames. A process is loaded by loading all of its pages into available, not necessarily contiguous, frames.	No external fragmentation.	A small amount of internal fragmentation.
Simple Segmentation	Each process is divided into a number of segments. A process is loaded by loading all of its segments into dynamic partitions that need not be contiguous.	No internal fragmentation.	Need for compaction.
Virtual Memory Paging	As with simple paging, except that it is not necessary to load all of the pages of a process. Nonresident pages that are needed are brought in later automatically.	No external fragmentation; higher degree of multiprogramming; large virtual process space.	Overhead of complex memory management.
Virtual Memory Segmentation	As with simple segmentation, except that it is not necessary to load all of the segments of a process. Nonresident segments that are needed are brought in later automatically.	No internal fragmentation, higher degree of multiprogramming; large virtual address space; protection and sharing support.	Overhead of complex memory management.

titioning, has been used in several variations in some now-obsolete operating systems. The other two techniques, simple paging and simple segmentation, are not used by themselves. However, it will clarify the discussion of virtual memory if we look first at these two techniques without considering virtual memory.

Fixed Partitioning

In most schemes for memory management, we can assume that the operating system occupies some fixed portion of main memory and that the rest of main memory is available for use by multiple processes. The simplest scheme for managing this available memory is to partition it into regions with fixed boundaries.

Partition Sizes

Figure 5.2 shows examples of two alternatives for fixed partitioning. One possibility is to make use of equal-size partitions. In this case, any process whose size is less than or equal to the partition size can be loaded into any available partition. If all partitions are full and no resident process is in the Ready or Running state, the operating system can swap a process out of any of the partitions and load in another process so that there is some work for the processor.

There are two difficulties with the use of equal-size fixed partitions:

- A program may be too big to fit into a partition. In this case, the programmer must design the program with the use of overlays so that only a portion of the program need be in main memory at any one time. When a module is needed that is not present, the user's program must load that module into the program's partition, overlaying whatever programs or data are there.
- Main memory use is extremely inefficient. Any program, no matter how small, occupies an entire partition. In our example, there may be a program that occupies less than 128 KB of memory; yet, it takes up a 512 K partition whenever it is swapped in. This phenomenon, in which there is wasted space internal to a partition due to the fact that the block of data loaded is smaller than the partition, is referred to as **internal fragmentation**.

Both problems can be lessened, though not solved, by using unequal-size partitions, as shown in Figure 5.2b. In this example, programs as large as 1 MB can be accommodated without overlays. Partitions smaller than 512 K allow smaller programs to be accommodated with less inefficiency.

Placement Algorithm

With the use of equal-size partitions, the placement of processes in memory is trivial. As long as there is any available partition, a process can be loaded into

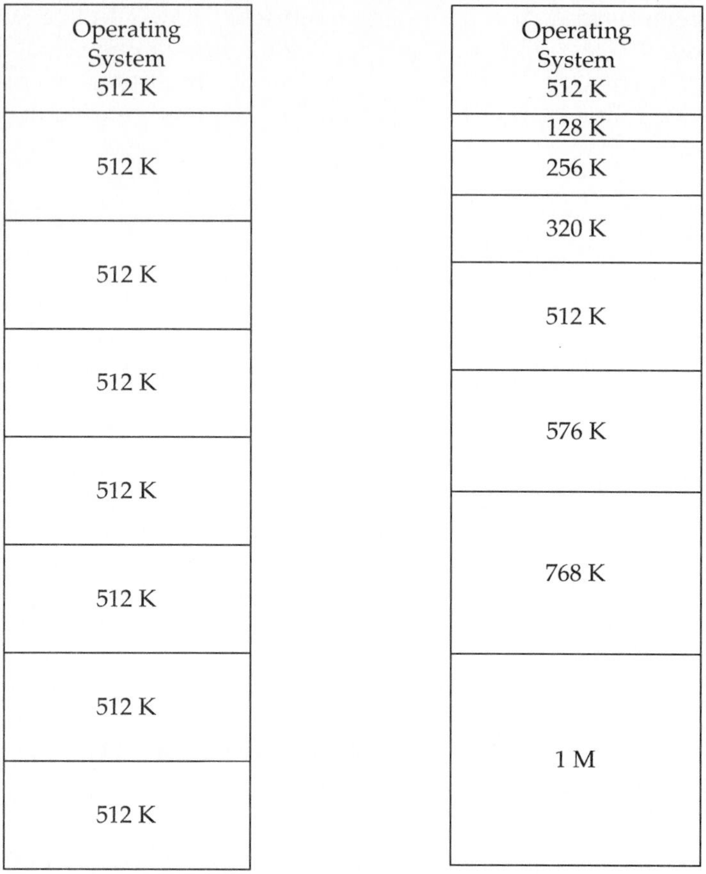

(a) Equal-size partitions   (b) Unequal-size partitions

FIGURE 5.2 Example of fixed partitioning of a 4-MByte memory

that partition. Because all partitions are of equal size, it does not matter which partition is used. If all partitions are occupied with processes that are not ready to run, then one of these processes must be swapped out to make room for a new process. Which one to swap out is a scheduling decision; this topic is explored in Chapter 6.

With unequal-size partitions, there are two possible ways to assign processes to partitions. The simplest way is to assign each process to the smallest partition within which it will fit.[1] In this case, a scheduling queue is needed for each partition, to hold swapped-out processes destined for that partition (Figure 5.3a). The advantage of this approach is that processes are always assigned in such a way as to minimize wasted memory within a partition.

---

[1]This assumes that one knows the maximum amount of memory that a process will require. This is not always the case. If it is not known how large a process may become, the only alternatives are an overlay scheme or the use of virtual memory.

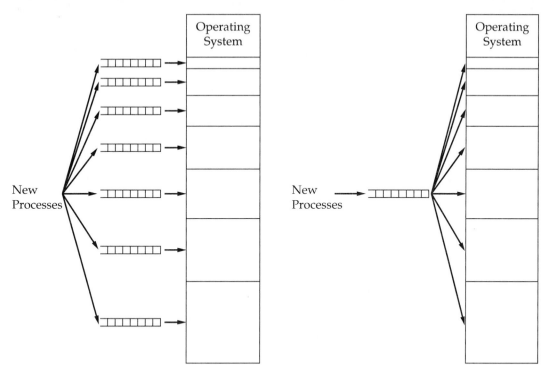

(a) One process queue per partition   (b) Single process queue

FIGURE 5.3 Memory assignment for fixed partitioning

However, although this technique seems optimum from the point of view of an individual partition, it is not optimum from the point of view of the system as a whole. In Figure 5.2b, for example, consider a case in which there are no processes with a size between 768 K and 1 M at a certain time. In that case, the 768 K partition will remain unused, even though some smaller process could have been assigned to it. Thus, a preferable approach would be to employ a single queue for all processes (Figure 5.3b). When it is time to load a process into main memory, the smallest available partition that will hold the process is selected. If all partitions are occupied, then a swapping decision must be made. Preference may be given to the swapping out of the smallest partition that will hold the incoming process. It is also possible to consider other factors, such as priority and a preference for swapping out blocked processes versus ready processes.

The use of unequal-size partitions provides a degree of flexibility to fixed partitioning. In addition, both types of fixed-partitioning schemes are relatively simple and require minimal operating-system software and processing overhead. However, there are the following disadvantages:

• The number of partitions specified at the time of system generation limits the number of active (not suspended) processes in the system.

- Because partition sizes are preset at the time of system generation, small jobs do not use partition space efficiently. In an environment in which the main storage requirement of all jobs is known beforehand, this may be reasonable, but in most cases, it is an inefficient technique.

The use of fixed partitioning is almost unknown today. One example of a successful operating system that did use this technique was an early IBM mainframe operating system, OS/MFT (Multiprogramming with a Fixed Number of Tasks).

Dynamic Partitioning

To overcome some of the difficulties with fixed partitioning, an approach known as *dynamic partitioning* was developed. Again, this approach has largely been supplanted by more sophisticated memory-management techniques. An important operating system that used this technique was IBM's mainframe operating system, OS/MVT (Multiprogramming with a Variable Number of Tasks).

With dynamic partitioning, the partitions used are of variable length and number. When a process is brought into main memory, it is allocated exactly as much memory as it requires and no more. An example, using 1 MB of main memory, is shown in Figure 5.4. Initially, main memory is empty except for the operating system (Figure 5.4a). The first three processes are loaded in, starting where the operating system ends, and occupying just enough space for each process (Figures 5.4b, c, and d). This leaves a "hole" at the end of memory that is too small for a fourth process. At some point, none of the processes in memory is ready. The operating system therefore swaps out process 2 (Figure 5.4e), which leaves sufficient room to load a new process, process 4 (Figure 5.4f). Since process 4 is smaller than process 2, another small hole is created. Later, a point is reached at which none of the processes in main memory is ready, but process 2 in the Ready-suspend state is available. Because there is insufficient room in memory for process 2, the operating system swaps process 1 out (Figure 5.4g) and swaps process 2 back in (Figure 5.4h).

As this example shows, this method starts out well, but eventually it leads to a situation in which there are a lot of small holes in memory. As time goes on, memory becomes more and more fragmented, and memory use declines. This phenomenon is called **external fragmentation**, referring to the fact that the memory that is external to all partitions becomes increasingly fragmented. This is in contrast to internal fragmentation, referred to earlier.

One technique for overcoming external fragmentation is **compaction**: From time to time, the operating system shifts the processes so that they are contiguous and so that all the free memory is together in one block. For example, in Figure 5.4h, compaction results in a block of free memory of length 256 K. This may well be sufficient to load in an additional process. The difficulty with compaction is that it is a time-consuming procedure, wasteful of processor time. Compaction implies the need for a dynamic relocation capability. That is, it

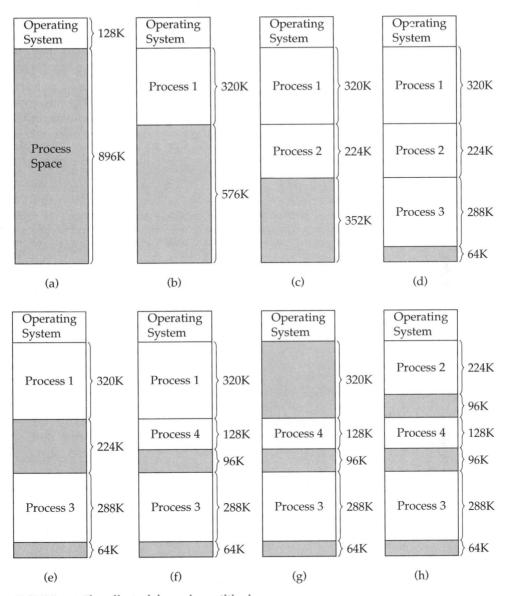

FIGURE 5.4 The effect of dynamic partitioning

must be possible to move a program from one region to another in main memory without invalidating the memory references in the program (see Appendix 5A).

Placement Algorithm

Because memory compaction is time-consuming, it behooves the operating-system designer to be clever in deciding how to assign processes to memory (how to plug the holes). When it is time to load or swap a process into main memory and if there is more than one free block of memory of sufficient size, then the operating system must decide which free block to allocate.

Three placement algorithms that can be considered are best-fit, first-fit, and next-fit. All are limited to choosing among free blocks of main memory that are equal to or larger than the process to be brought in. Best-fit chooses the block that is closest in size to the request. First-fit begins to scan memory from the beginning and chooses the first available block that is large enough. Next-fit begins to scan memory from the location of the last placement and chooses the next available block that is large enough.

Figure 5.5a shows an example memory configuration after a number of placement and swapping-out operations. The last block that was used was a 22 KB block from which a 14 KB partition was created. Figure 5.5b shows the difference between the best-, first-, and next-fit placement algorithms in satisfying a 16 KB allocation request. Best-fit will search the entire list of available blocks and make use of the 18 KB block, leaving a 2 KB fragment. First-fit results in a 6 KB fragment, and next-fit results in a 20 KB fragment.

Which of these approaches is best will depend on the exact sequence of process swappings that occurs and the size of those processes. However, some general comments can be made (also, see [BREN89], [SHOR75] and [BAYS77]). The first-fit algorithm is not only the simplest but usually the best and fastest as well. The next-fit algorithm tends to produce slightly worse results than the first-fit. The next-fit algorithm will more frequently lead to an allocation from a free block at the end of memory. The result is that the largest block of free memory, which usually appears at the end of the memory space, is quickly broken up into small fragments. Thus, compaction may be required more frequently with next-fit. On the other hand, the first-fit algorithm may litter the front end with small free partitions that need to be searched over on each subsequent first-fit pass. The best-fit algorithm, despite its name, is usually the worst performer. Because this algorithm looks for the smallest block that will satisfy the requirement, it guarantees that the fragment left behind is as small as possible. Although each memory request always wastes the smallest amount of memory, the result is that main memory is quickly littered by blocks too small to satisfy requests for memory allocation. Thus, memory compaction must be done more frequently than with the other algorithms.

Replacement Algorithm

In a multiprogramming system using dynamic partitioning, there will come a time when all of the processes in main memory are in a blocked state and there is insufficient memory, even after compaction, for an additional process. To avoid wasting processor time waiting for an active process to become unblocked, the operating system will swap one of the processes out of main memory to make room for a new process or for a process in a Ready, suspend state. Therefore, the operating system must choose which process to replace. Because the

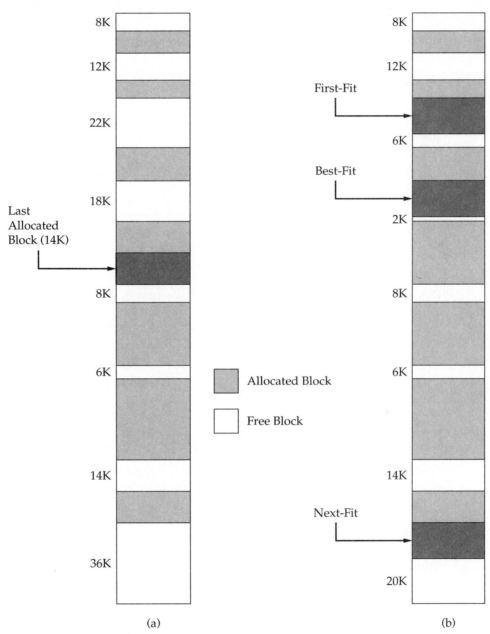

FIGURE 5.5 Example memory configuration before and after allocation of a 16-KByte block

topic of replacement algorithms will be covered in some detail with respect to various virtual memory schemes, we will defer a discussion of replacement algorithms until then.

Relocation

Before we consider ways of dealing with the shortcomings of partitioning, we must clear up one loose end, which relates to the placement of processes in memory. When the fixed partition scheme of Figure 5.3a is used, we can expect that a process will always be assigned to the same partition. That is, the partition that is selected when a new process is loaded will always be used to swap that process back into memory after it has been swapped out. In that case, a simple relocating loader, such as is described in Appendix 5A, can be used: When the process is first loaded, all relative memory references in the code are replaced by absolute main memory addresses determined by the base address of the loaded process.

In the case of equal-size partitions and in the case of a single-process queue for unequal-size partitions, a process may occupy different partitions during the course of its life. When a process image is first created, it is loaded into some partition in main memory. Later, the process may be swapped out; when it is subsequently swapped back in, it may be assigned to a partition different from the previous one. The same is true for dynamic partitioning. Observe in Figures 5.4c and 5.4h that process 2 occupies two different regions of memory on the two occasions when it is brought in. Furthermore, when compaction is used, processes are shifted while they are in main memory.

Now, consider that a process in memory includes instructions plus data. The instructions will contain memory references of the following two types:

- Addresses of data items, used in load and store instructions and some arithmetic and logical instructions.
- Addresses of instructions, used for branching and call instructions.

But now we see that these addresses are not fixed! They change each time a process is swapped in or shifted. To solve this problem, a distinction is made among several types of addresses. A **logical address** is a reference to a memory location independent of the current assignment of data to memory; a translation must be made to a physical address before the memory access can be achieved. A **relative address** is particular example of logical address, in which the address is expressed as a location relative to some known point, usually the beginning of the program. A **physical address**, or absolute address, is an actual location in main memory.

Programs that employ relative addresses in memory are loaded using dynamic run-time loading (see Appendix 5A for a discussion). This means that all the memory references in the loaded process are relative to the origin of the program. Thus, a means is needed in hardware of translating relative addresses to physical main memory addresses at the time of execution of the instruction that contains the reference.

Figure 5.6 shows the way in which this address translation is typically accomplished. When a process is assigned to the Running state, a special processor register, sometimes called the base register, is loaded with the starting address in the main memory of the process. There is also a bounds register that indicates

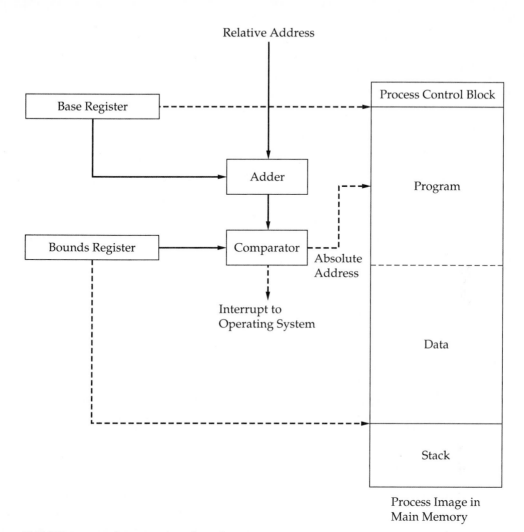

FIGURE 5.6 Hardware support for relocation

the ending location of the program; these values must be set when the program is loaded into memory or when the process image is swapped in. During the course of execution of the process, relative addresses are encountered. These include the contents of the instruction register, instruction addresses that occur in branch and call instructions, and data addresses that occur in load and store instructions. Each such relative address goes through two steps of manipulation by the processor. First, the value in the base register is added to the relative address to produce an absolute address. Second, the resulting address is compared to the value in the bounds register. If the address is within bounds, then the instruction execution may proceed. Otherwise, an interrupt is generated to the operating system, which must respond to the error in some fashion.

The scheme of Figure 5.6 allows programs to be swapped in and out of memory during the course of execution. It also provides a measure of protection: Each process image is isolated by the contents of the base and bounds registers and is safe from unwanted access by other processes.

Simple Paging

Both unequal fixed-size and variable-size partitions are inefficient in the use of memory; the former results in internal fragmentation, the latter in external fragmentation. Suppose, however, that main memory is partitioned into equal fixed-size chunks that are relatively small and that each process is also divided into small fixed-size chunks of the same size. Then the chunks of a process, known as **pages**, can be assigned to available chunks of memory, known as **frames**, or page frames. We show in this subsection that the wasted space in memory for each process is internal fragmentation consisting of only a fraction of the last page of a process. There is no external fragmentation.

Figure 5.7 shows an example of the use of pages and frames. At a given time, some of the frames in memory are in use and some are free. A list of free frames is maintained by the operating system. Process A, stored on disk, consists of four pages. When it is time to load this process, the operating system finds four free frames and loads the four pages of process A into the four frames (Figure 5.7b). Process B, consisting of three pages, and process C, consisting of four pages, are subsequently loaded. Subsequently, process B is suspended and is swapped out of main memory. Later, all the processes in main memory are blocked, and the operating system needs to bring in a new process, process D, which consists of five pages.

Now suppose, as in this example, that there are not sufficient unused contiguous frames to hold the process. Does this prevent the operating system from loading D? The answer is no, because we can once again use the concept of logical address. A simple base address register will no longer suffice. Rather, the operating system maintains a **page table** for each process. The page table shows the frame location for each page of the process. Within the program, each logical address consists of a page number and an offset within the page. Recall that in the case of simple partition, a logical address is the location of a word relative to the beginning of the program; the processor translates that into a physical address. With paging, the logical-to-physical address translation is still done by processor hardware. Now, the processor must know how to access the page table of the current process. Presented with a logical address (page number, offset), the processor uses the page table to produce a physical address (frame number, offset).

Continuing our example, the five pages of process D are loaded into frames 4, 5, 6, 11, and 12. Figure 5.8 shows the various page tables at this time. A page table contains one entry for each page of the process, so that the table is easily indexed by the page number (starting at page 0). Each page table entry contains the number of the frame in main memory, if any, that holds the corresponding

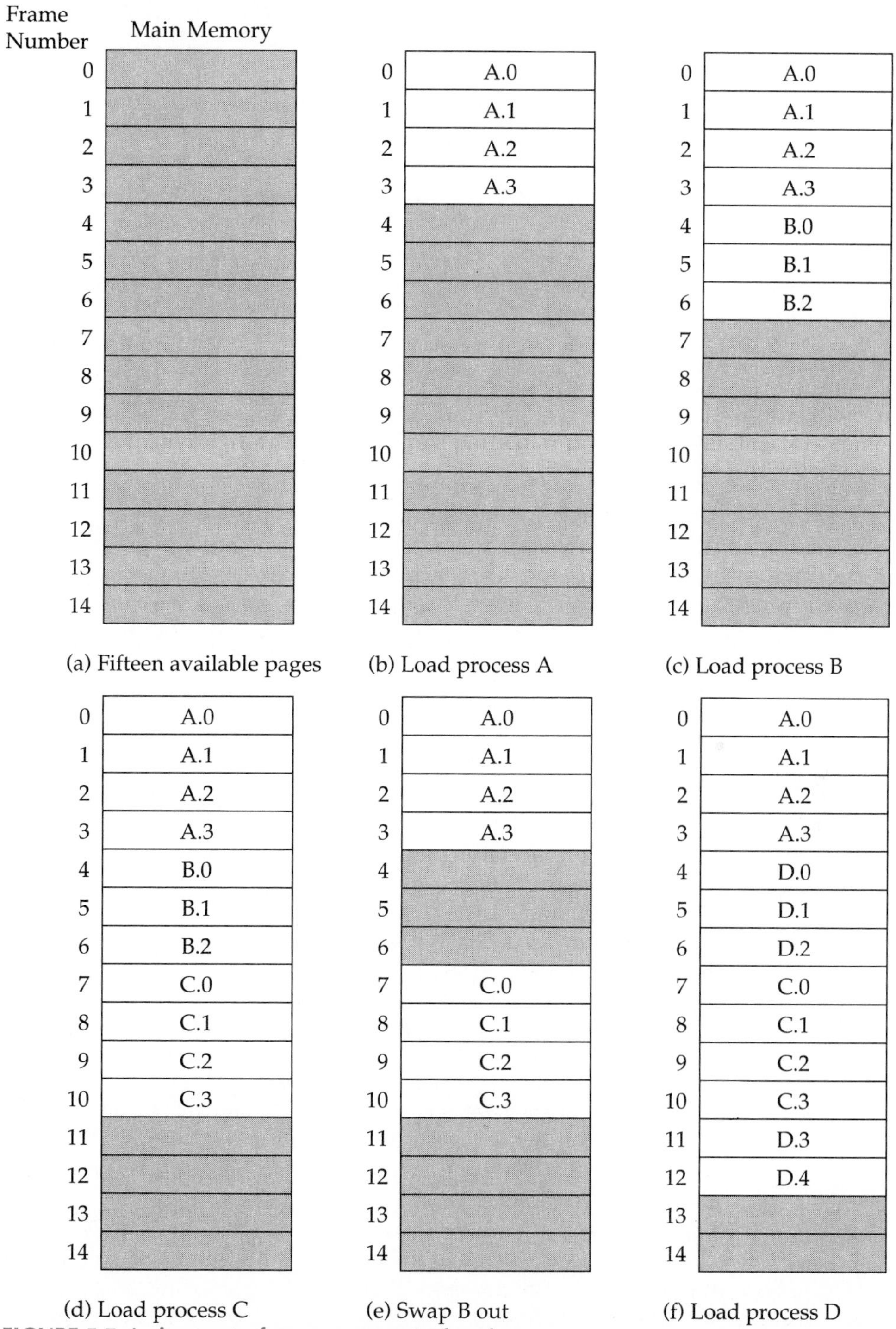

Frame Number — Main Memory

Frame Number	Main Memory
0	
1	
2	
3	
4	
5	
6	
7	
8	
9	
10	
11	
12	
13	
14	

(a) Fifteen available pages

0	A.0
1	A.1
2	A.2
3	A.3
4	
5	
6	
7	
8	
9	
10	
11	
12	
13	
14	

(b) Load process A

0	A.0
1	A.1
2	A.2
3	A.3
4	B.0
5	B.1
6	B.2
7	
8	
9	
10	
11	
12	
13	
14	

(c) Load process B

0	A.0
1	A.1
2	A.2
3	A.3
4	B.0
5	B.1
6	B.2
7	C.0
8	C.1
9	C.2
10	C.3
11	
12	
13	
14	

(d) Load process C

0	A.0
1	A.1
2	A.2
3	A.3
4	
5	
6	
7	C.0
8	C.1
9	C.2
10	C.3
11	
12	
13	
14	

(e) Swap B out

0	A.0
1	A.1
2	A.2
3	A.3
4	D.0
5	D.1
6	D.2
7	C.0
8	C.1
9	C.2
10	C.3
11	D.3
12	D.4
13	
14	

(f) Load process D

FIGURE 5.7 Assignment of process pages to free frames

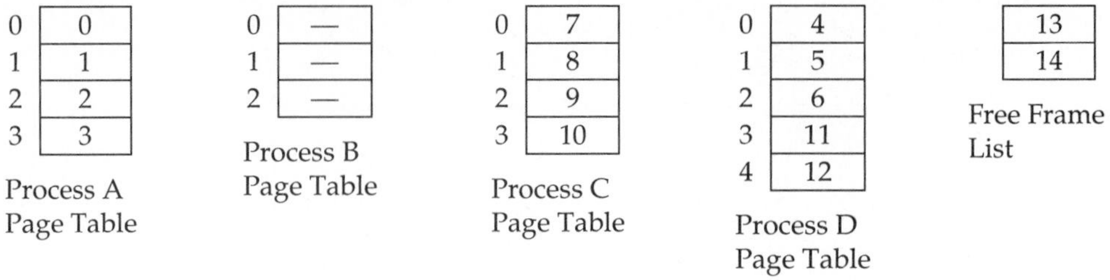

0	0
1	1
2	2
3	3

Process A
Page Table

0	—
1	—
2	—

Process B
Page Table

0	7
1	8
2	9
3	10

Process C
Page Table

0	4
1	5
2	6
3	11
4	12

Process D
Page Table

13
14

Free Frame
List

FIGURE 5.8 Data structures for the example of Figure 5.7 at time epoch (f)

page. In addition, the operating system maintains a single free-frame list of all frames in main memory that are currently unoccupied and available for pages.

Thus, we see that simple paging, as described here, is similar to fixed partitioning. The differences are that with paging the partitions are rather small, a program may occupy more than one partition, and these partitions need not be contiguous.

To make this paging scheme convenient, let us dictate that the page size, and hence the frame size, must be a power of 2. In this case, the relative address, which is defined with reference to the origin of the program, and the logical address, expressed as a page number and offset, are the same. An example is shown in Figure 5.9. In this example, 16-bit addresses are used, and the page size is 1K = 1024 bytes. The relative address, 1502, is 0000010111011110 in binary form. With a page size of 1 K, an offset field of 10 bits is needed, leaving 6 bits for page number. Thus, a program can consist of a maximum of $2^6 = 64$ pages of 1 KB each. As Figure 5.9b shows, relative address 1502 corresponds to an offset of 478 (0111011110) on page 1 (000001), which yields the same 16-bit number, 0000010111011110.

The consequences of using a page size that is a power of 2 are twofold. First, the logical addressing scheme is transparent to the programmer, the assembler, and the linker. Each logical address (page number, offset) of a program is identical to its relative address. Second, it is a relatively easy matter to implement a function in hardware to perform dynamic address translation at run time. Consider an address of $n + m$ bits, in which the leftmost n bits are the page number and the rightmost m bits are the offset. In our example (Figure 5.9b), $n = 6$ and $m = 10$. The following steps are needed for address translation:

* Extract the page number as the leftmost n bits of the logical address.
* Use the page number as an index into the process page table to find the frame number, k.
* The starting physical address of the frame is $k \times 2^m$, and the physical address of the referenced byte is that number plus the offset. This physical address need not be calculated; it is easily constructed by concatenating the frame number to the offset.

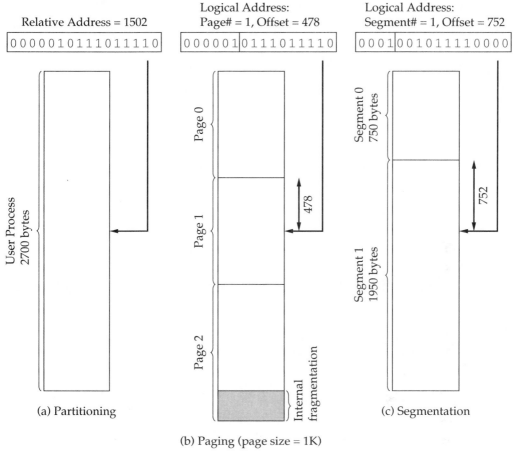

Relative Address = 1502

| 0 0 0 0 0 1 0 1 1 1 0 1 1 1 1 0 |

Logical Address:
Page# = 1, Offset = 478

| 0 0 0 0 0 1 | 0 1 1 1 0 1 1 1 1 0 |

Logical Address:
Segment# = 1, Offset = 752

| 0 0 0 1 | 0 0 1 0 1 1 1 1 0 0 0 0 |

User Process 2700 bytes

(a) Partitioning

Page 0

Page 1

Page 2

478

Internal fragmentation

(b) Paging (page size = 1K)

Segment 0 750 bytes

Segment 1 1950 bytes

752

(c) Segmentation

FIGURE 5.9 Logical addresses

In our example, we have the logical address 0000010111011110, which is page number 1, offset 478. Suppose that this page is residing in main memory frame 5 = binary 000110. Then the physical address is frame number 5, offset 478 = 0001100111011110 (Figure 5.10a).

To summarize, with simple paging, main memory is divided into many small equal-size frames. Each process is divided into frame-size pages; smaller processes require fewer pages, larger processes require more. When a process is brought in, all its pages are loaded into available frames and a page table is set up. This approach solves many of the problems inherent in partitioning.

Simple Segmentation

An alternative way in which the user program can be subdivided is by segmentation. In this case, the program and its associated data are divided into a

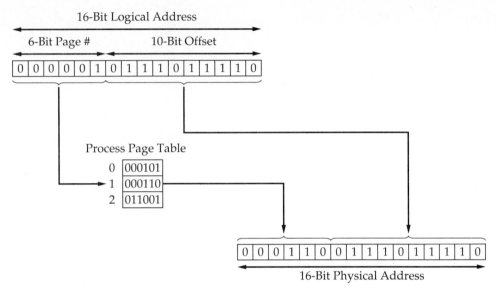

(a) Paging

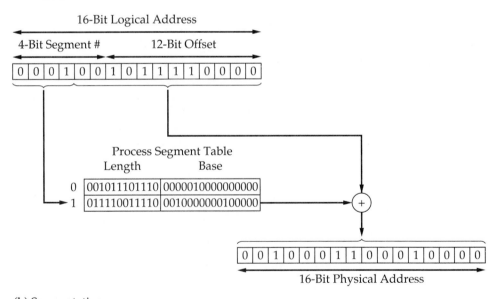

(b) Segmentation

FIGURE 5.10 Examples of logical-to-physical address translation

number of **segments**. It is not required that all segments of all programs be of the same length, although there is a maximum segment length. As with paging, a logical address using segmentation consists of two parts, in this case a segment number and an offset.

Because of the use of unequal-size segments, segmentation is similar to dynamic partitioning. In the absence of an overlay scheme or the use of virtual memory, it would be required that all of a program's segments be loaded into memory for execution. The difference, compared to dynamic partitioning, is that with segmentation a program may occupy more than one partition, and these partitions need not be contiguous. Segmentation eliminates internal fragmentation, but like dynamic partitioning it suffers from external fragmentation. However, because a process is broken up into a number of smaller pieces, the external fragmentation should be less.

Whereas paging is invisible to the programmer, segmentation is usually visible and is provided as a convenience for organizing programs and data. Typically, the programmer or compiler assigns programs and data to different segments. For purposes of modular programming, the program or data may be further broken down into multiple segments. The principal inconvenience of this service is that the programmer must be aware of the maximum size limitation on segments.

Another consequence of unequal-size segments is that there is no simple relationship between logical addresses and physical addresses. Analogous to paging, a simple segmentation scheme would make use of a segment table for each process and a list of free blocks of main memory. Each segment table entry would have to give the starting address in main memory of the corresponding segment. The entry should also provide the length of the segment to assure that invalid addresses are not used. When a process enters the Running state, the address of its segment table is loaded into a special register used by the memory-management hardware. Consider an address of $n + m$ bits, in which the leftmost n bits are the segment number and the rightmost m bits are the offset. In our example (Figure 5.9c), $n = 4$ and $m = 12$. Thus, the maximum segment size is $2^{12} = 4096$. The following steps are needed for address translation:

- Extract the segment number as the leftmost n bits of the logical address.
- Use the segment number as an index into the process segment table to find the starting physical address of the segment.
- Compare the offset, expressed in the rightmost m bits, to the length of the segment. If the offset is greater than the length, the address is invalid.
- The desired physical address is the sum of the starting physical address of the segment plus the offset.

In our example, we have the logical address 0001001011110000, which is segment number 1, offset 752. Suppose that this segment is residing in main memory starting at physical address 0010000000100000. Then the physical address is 0010000000100000 + 001011110000 = 0010001100010000.

To summarize, with simple segmentation, a process is divided into a number of segments that need not be of equal size. When a process is brought in, all its segments are loaded into available regions of memory and a segment table is set up.

5.3

VIRTUAL MEMORY—HARDWARE AND CONTROL STRUCTURES

When we compare simple paging and simple segmentation on the one hand, with fixed and dynamic partitioning on the other, we see the foundation for a fundamental breakthrough in memory management. Two characteristics of paging and segmentation are the keys to this breakthrough:

1. All memory references within a process are logical addresses that are dynamically translated into physical addresses at run time. This means that a process may be swapped in and out of main memory such that it occupies different regions of main memory at different times during the course of execution.
2. A process may be broken up into a number of pieces (pages or segments) and these pieces need not be contiguously located in main memory during execution. The combination of dynamic run-time address translation and the use of a page or segment table permits this.

Now we come to the breakthrough. *If these two characteristics are present, then it is not necessary that all the pages or all the segments of a process be in main memory during execution.* If the piece (segment or page) that holds the next instruction to be fetched and the piece that holds the next data location to be accessed are in main memory, then at least for a time execution may proceed.

Let us consider how this may be accomplished. For now, we can talk in general terms, and we will use the term *piece* to refer to either page or segment, depending on whether paging or segmentation is employed. Suppose that it is time to bring a new process into memory. The operating system begins by bringing in only one or a few pieces, including the piece that contains the start of the program. We will refer to that portion of a process that is actually in main memory at any time as the **resident set** of the process. As the process executes, things proceed smoothly as long as all memory references are to locations that are in the resident set. Using the segment or page table, the processor always is able to determine whether this is so. If the processor encounters a logical address that is not in main memory, it generates an interrupt indicating a memory access fault. The operating system puts the interrupted process in a blocking state and takes control. For the execution of this process to proceed later, the operating system will need to bring into main memory the piece of the process that contains the logical address that caused the access fault. For this purpose, the operating system issues a disk I/O Read request. After the I/O request has been issued, the operating system can dispatch another process to run while the disk I/O is performed. Once the desired piece has been brought into main memory and the I/O interrupt isssued, control is given back to the operating system, which places the affected process back into a Ready state.

Now, it may immediately occur to you to question the efficiency of this maneuver, in which a process may be executing and have to be interrupted for no other reason than that you have failed to load in all the needed pieces of the process. For now, let us defer consideration of this question with the assurance that efficiency is possible. Instead, let us ponder the implications of our new strategy. There are two implications, the second more startling than the first, and both lead to improved system utility:

1. More processes may be maintained in main memory. Because we are going to load only some of the pieces of any particular process, there is room for more processes. This leads to more efficient use of the processor because it is more likely that at least one of the more numerous processes will be in a Ready state at any particular time.

2. It is possible for a process to be larger than all the main memory. One of the most fundamental restrictions in programming is lifted. Without the scheme we have been discussing, a programmer must be acutely aware of how much memory is available. If the program being written is too large, the programmer must devise ways to structure the program into pieces that can be loaded separately in some sort of overlay strategy. With virtual memory based on paging or segmentation, that job is left to the operating system and the hardware. As far as the programmer is concerned, he or she is dealing with a huge memory, the size associated with disk storage. The operating system automatically loads pieces of that process into main memory as required.

Because a process executes only in main memory, that memory is referred to as **real memory**. But a programmer or user perceives a potentially much larger memory—that which is allocated on disk. This latter is referred to as **virtual memory**. Virtual memory allows for very effective multiprogramming and relieves the user of the unnecessarily tight constraints of main memory.

Locality and Virtual Memory

The benefits of virtual memory are attractive. The question is: Will such a scheme work? At one time, there was considerable debate on this point, but the experience with numerous operating systems has demonstrated beyond doubt that virtual memory does work. Accordingly, it has become an essential component of most contemporary operating systems.

To understand what the key issue is and why virtual memory was a matter of much debate, let us consider again the task of the operating system with respect to virtual memory. Consider a large process consisting of a long program plus a number of arrays of data. Over any short period, execution may be confined to a small section of the program (e.g., a subroutine) and access to perhaps only one or two arrays of data. If this is so, then it would clearly be wasteful to load in dozens of pieces for that process when only a few pieces will be used before the program is suspended and swapped out. We can make better use of memory by loading in just a few pieces. Then, if the program branches to an instruction or if it references a data item on a piece not in main memory, a fault is triggered. This tells the operating system to bring in the desired piece.

Thus, at any one time, only a few pieces of any given process are in memory, and therefore more processes can be maintained in memory. Furthermore, time is saved because unused pieces are not swapped in and out of memory. However, the operating system must be clever about how it manages this scheme. In the steady state, practically all the main memory will be occupied with process pieces, so that the processor and operating system will have direct access to as many processes as possible. Thus, when the operating system brings one piece in, it must throw another out. If it throws out a piece just before it is about to be used, then it will just have to go get that piece again almost immediately. Too much of this leads to a condition known as **thrashing**: The processor spends most of its time swapping pieces rather than executing user instructions. The avoidance of thrashing was a major research area in the 1970s and led to a variety of complex but effective algorithms. In essence, the operating system tries to guess, on the basis of recent history, which pieces are least likely to be used in the near future.

The foregoing reasoning is based on belief in the principle of locality, which was introduced in Chapter 1 (see especially Appendix 1A). To summarize, the principle of locality states that program and data references within a process tend to cluster. Hence, the assumption that only a few pieces of a process will be needed over a short period is valid. Also, it should be possible to make intelligent guesses about which pieces of a process will be needed in the near future, thus avoiding thrashing.

One way to confirm the principle of locality is to look at the performance of processes in a virtual memory environment. Figure 5.11 is a rather famous diagram that dramatically illustrates the principle of locality [HATF72]. Note that during the lifetime of the process references are confined to a subset of pages.

Thus, we see that the principle of locality suggests that a virtual memory scheme may work. For virtual memory to be practical and effective, two ingredients are needed. First, there must be hardware support for the paging and/or segmentation scheme to be employed. And second, the operating system must include software for managing the movement of pages and/or segments between secondary memory and main memory. In this section, we examine the hardware aspect, as well as looking at the necessary control structures that are created and maintained by the operating system but are used by the memory-management hardware. An examination of the operating-system issues is provided in the next section.

Paging

The term *virtual memory* is usually associated with systems that employ paging, although virtual memory based on segmentation is also used and is discussed next. The use of paging to achieve virtual memory was first reported for the Atlas computer [KILB62] and soon came into widespread commercial use.

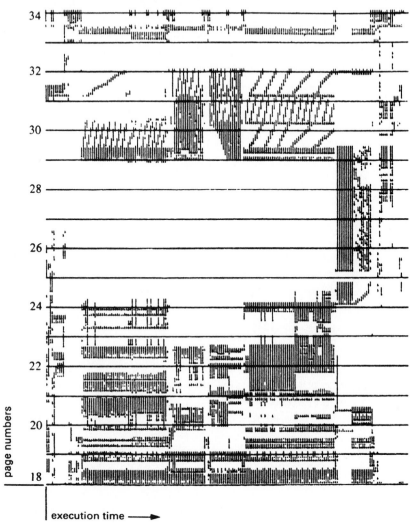

page numbers

execution time ⟶

FIGURE 5.11 Paging behavior

In the discussion of simple paging, we indicated that each process has its own page table and that when all its pages are loaded into main memory, the page table for a process is created and loaded into main memory. Each page table entry contains the frame number of the corresponding page in main memory. The same device, a page table, is needed when we consider a virtual memory scheme based on paging. Again, it is typical to associate a unique page table with each process. In this case, however, the page table entries become more complex (Figure 5.12a). Because only some of the pages of a process may be in main memory, a bit is needed in each page table entry to indicate whether

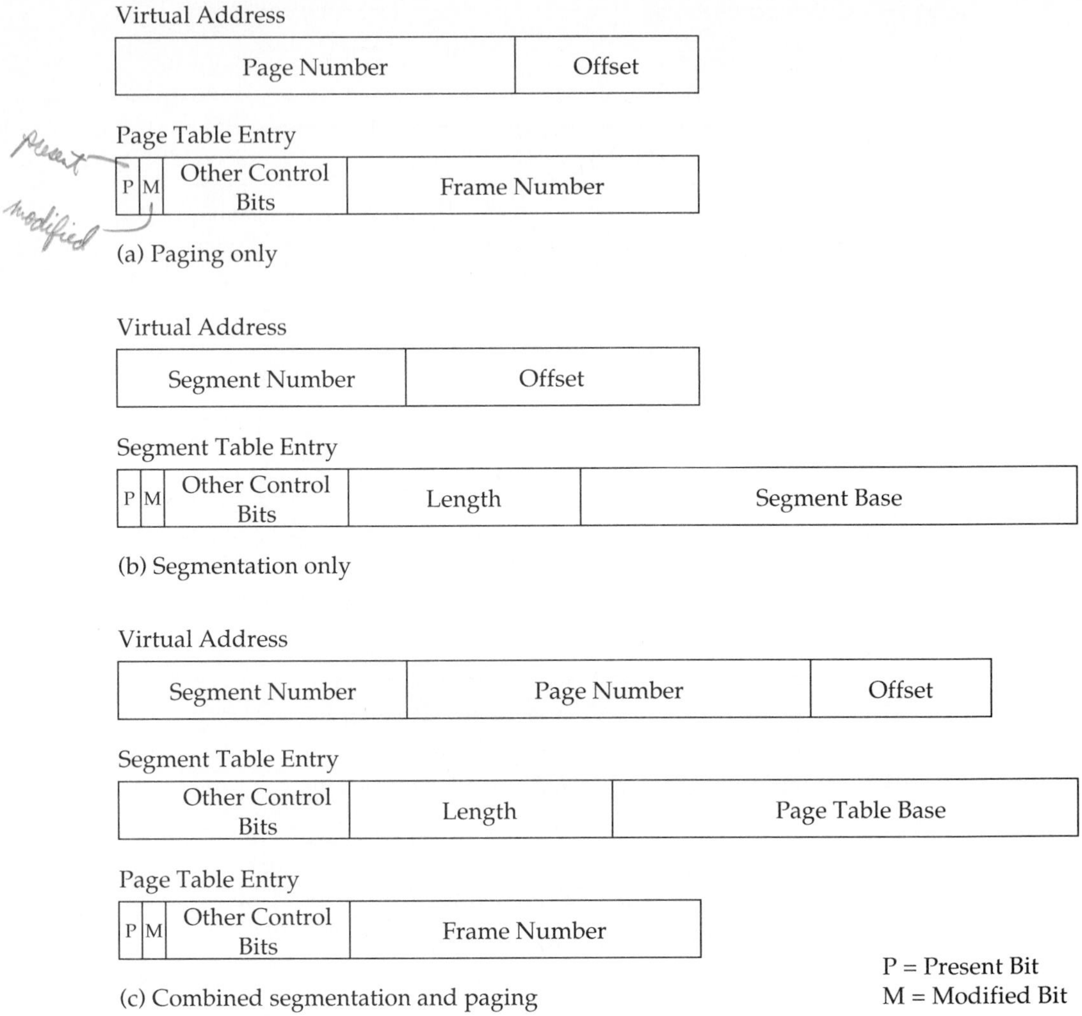

Virtual Address

Page Number	Offset

Page Table Entry

Present

modified

P	M	Other Control Bits	Frame Number

(a) Paging only

Virtual Address

Segment Number	Offset

Segment Table Entry

P	M	Other Control Bits	Length	Segment Base

(b) Segmentation only

Virtual Address

Segment Number	Page Number	Offset

Segment Table Entry

Other Control Bits	Length	Page Table Base

Page Table Entry

P	M	Other Control Bits	Frame Number

P = Present Bit
M = Modified Bit

(c) Combined segmentation and paging

FIGURE 5.12 Typical memory-management formats

the corresponding page is present (P) in main memory or not. If the bit indicates that the page is in memory, then the entry also includes the frame number of that page.

Another control bit needed in the page table entry is a modify (M) bit to indicate whether the contents of the corresponding page have been altered since the page was last loaded into main memory. If there has been no change, then it is not necessary to write the page out when it comes time to replace the page in the frame that it currently occupies. Other control bits may also be present. For example, if protection or sharing is managed at the page level, then bits for that purpose will be required. We will see several examples of page table entries later in this chapter.

Page Table Structure

Thus, the basic mechanism for reading a word from memory involves the translation by using a page table of a virtual, or logical, address that consists of page number and offset, into a physical address that consists of frame number and offset. Because the page table is of variable length, depending on the size of the process, we cannot expect to hold it in registers. Instead, it must be in main memory to be accessed. Figure 5.13 suggests a hardware implementation of this scheme. When a particular process is running, a register holds the starting address of the page table for that process. The page number of a virtual address is used to index that table and look up the corresponding frame number. This is combined with the offset portion of the virtual address to produce the desired real address.

Let us consider the number of page table entries required. In most systems, there is one page table per process. But each process can occupy huge amounts of virtual memory. For example, in the VAX architecture [LEVY89], each process can have up to $2^{31} = 2$ GB of virtual memory. Using $2^9 = 512$-byte pages, that means that as many as 2^{22} page table entries are required *per process*. Clearly, the amount of memory devoted to page tables alone could be unacceptably high. To overcome this problem, most virtual memory schemes store page tables

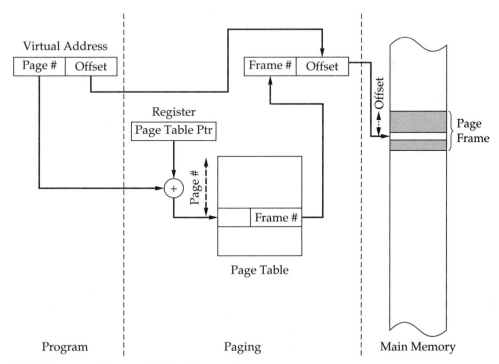

FIGURE 5.13 Address translation in a paging system

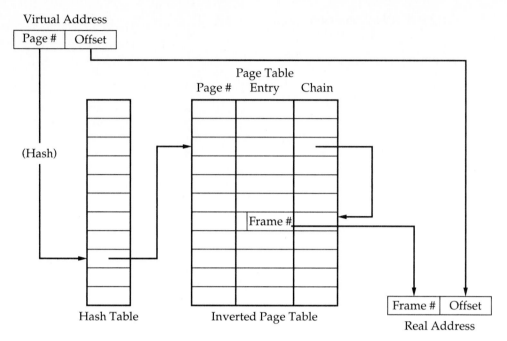

FIGURE 5.14 Inverted page table structure

in virtual memory rather than in real memory. This means that page tables are subject to paging just as other pages are. When a process is running, at least a part of its page tables must be in main memory, including the page table entry of the currently executing page. Some processors use a two-level scheme to organize large page tables. In this scheme, there is a page directory in which each entry points to a page table. Thus, if the length of the page directory is X and if the maximum length of a page table is Y, then a process can consist of up to $X \times Y$ pages. Typically, the maximum length of a page table is restricted to be equal to one page. We will see an example of this two-level approach when we consider the Intel 80386 later in this chapter.

An alternative approach to the use of one- or two-level page tables is the use of an **inverted page table** structure (Figure 5.14). This approach is used on IBM's AS/400 [SCHL89, CORA88] and IBM's RISC System/6000 workstation [WATE86, CHAN88, CHAN90a]. An implementation of the Mach operating system on the RT-PC also uses this technique [RASH88].

In this approach, the page number portion of a virtual address is mapped into a hash table using a simple hashing function.[2] The hash table contains a pointer to the inverted page table, which contains the page table entries. With this structure, there is one entry in the hash table and inverted page table for

[2]See Appendix 5B for a discussion of hashing.

each real memory page rather than one per virtual page. Thus, a fixed proportion of real memory is required for the tables regardless of the number of processes or virtual pages supported. Since more than one virtual address may map into the same hash table entry, a chaining technique is used for managing the overflow. The hashing technique results in chains that are typically short—between one and two entries.

Translation Lookaside Buffer

In principle, then, every virtual memory reference can cause two physical memory accesses: one to fetch the appropriate page table entry and one to fetch the desired data. Thus, a straightforward virtual memory scheme would have the effect of doubling the memory access time. To overcome this problem, most virtual memory schemes make use of a special cache for page table entries, usually called a **translation lookaside buffer** (TLB). This cache functions in the same way as a memory cache (see Chapter 1) and contains those page table entries that have been most recently used. The organization of the resulting paging hardware is illustrated in Figure 5.15. Given a virtual address, the processor will first examine the TLB. If the desired page table entry is present (a TLB hit), then the frame number is retrieved and the real address is formed.

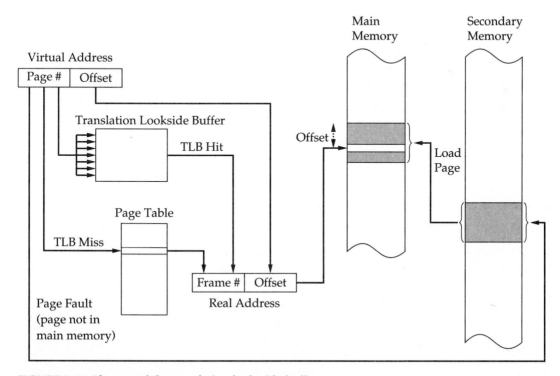

FIGURE 5.15 The use of the translation lookaside buffer

If the desired page table entry is not found (a TLB miss), then the processor uses the page number to index the process page table and examine the corresponding page table entry. If the present bit is set, then the page is in main memory, and the processor can retrieve the frame number from the page table entry to form the real address. The processor also updates the TLB to include this new page table entry. Finally, if the present bit is not set, then the desired page is not in main memory and a memory access fault, called a **page fault**, is issued. At this point, we leave the realm of hardware and invoke the operating system, which loads the needed page and updates the page table.

Figure 5.16 is a flowchart that shows the use of the TLB. The flowchart shows that if the desired page is not in main memory, a page fault interrupt causes the page fault handling routine to be invoked. To keep the flowchart simple, the fact that the operating system may dispatch another process while disk I/O is underway is not shown. By the principle of locality, most virtual memory references will be to locations in recently used pages. Therefore, most references will involve page table entries in the cache. Studies of the VAX TLB have shown that this scheme can significantly improve performance [CLAR85, SATY81].

There are a number of additional details concerning the actual organization of the TLB. Because the TLB contains only some of the entries in a full page table, we cannot simply index into the TLB on the basis of page number. Instead, each entry in the TLB must include the page number as well as the complete page table entry. The processor is equipped with hardware that allows it to simultaneously interrogate a number of TLB entries to determine if there is a match on page number. This technique is referred to as *associative mapping* and is contrasted with the direct mapping, or indexing, used for lookup in the page table in Figure 5.17. The designer of the TLB also must consider the way in which entries are organized in the TLB and which entry to replace when a new entry is brought in. These issues must be considered in any hardware cache design. This topic is not pursued here; you may consult a treatment of cache design for further details (e.g., [STAL90a]).

Finally, the virtual memory mechanism must interact with the cache system (not the TLB cache, but the main memory cache). This is illustrated in Figure 5.18. A virtual address will generally be in the form of a page number, offset. First, the memory system consults the TLB to see if the matching page table entry is present. If it is, the real (physical) address is generated by combining the frame number with the offset. If not, the entry is accessed from a page table. Once the real address is generated, which is in the form of a tag[3] and a remainder, the cache is consulted to see if the block containing that word is present. If so, it is returned to the CPU. If not, the word is retrieved from main memory.

You should be able to appreciate the complexity of the CPU hardware involved in a single memory reference. The virtual address is translated into a real address. This involves reference to a page table entry, which may be in the

---

[3]See Figure 1.21. Typically, a tag is just the leftmost few bits of the real address. Again, for a more detailed discussion of caches, see [STAL90a].

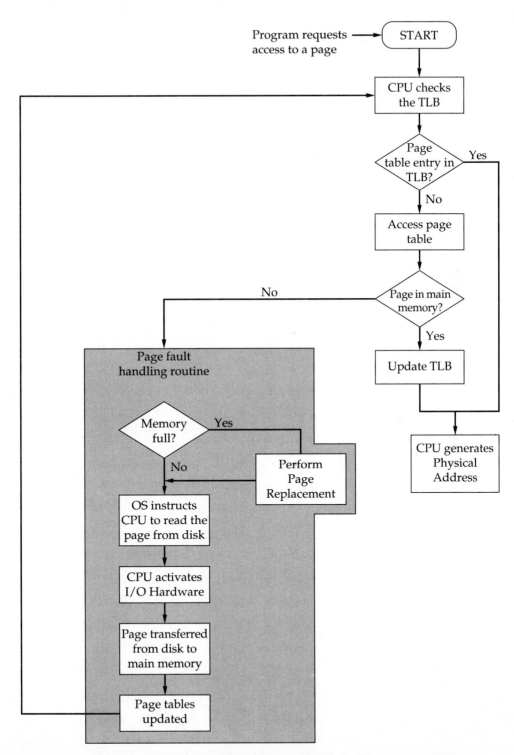

FIGURE 5.16 Operation of paging and translation lookaside buffer (TLB) [FURH87]

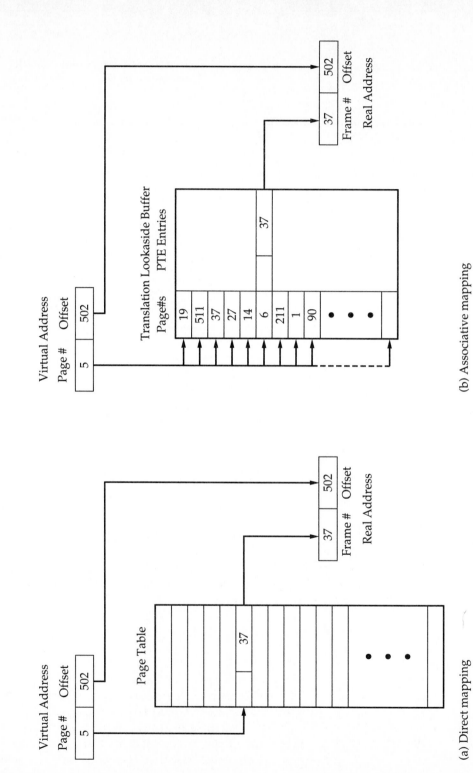

(a) Direct mapping

(b) Associative mapping

FIGURE 5.17 Direct versus associative lookup for page table entries

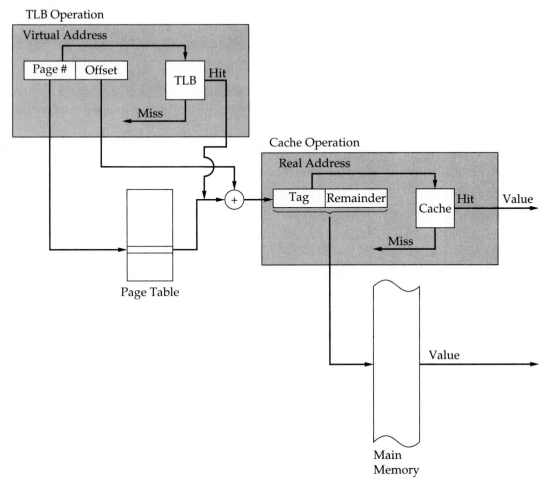

FIGURE 5.18 Translation lookaside buffer and cache operation

TLB, in main memory, or on disk. The referenced word may be in cache, main memory, or on disk. In the latter case, the page containing the word must be loaded into main memory and its block loaded into the cache. In addition, the page table entry for that page must be updated.

Page Size

An important hardware design decision is the size of page to be used. There are several factors to consider. One is internal fragmentation. Clearly, the smaller the page size, the less the amount of internal fragmentation. To optimize the use of main memory, we would like to reduce internal fragmentation. On the other hand, the smaller the page, the greater the number of pages required per process. More pages per process means larger page tables. For large pro-

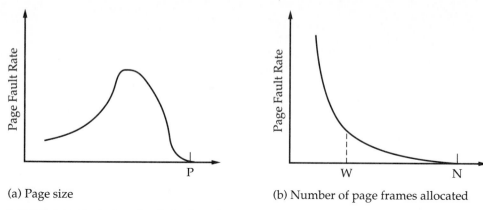

(a) Page size   (b) Number of page frames allocated

FIGURE 5.19 Typical paging behavior of a program

grams in a heavily multiprogrammed environment, this may mean that a large portion of the page tables of active processes must be in virtual memory, not in main memory. Thus, there may be a double page fault for a single reference to memory: first to bring in the needed portion of the page table and second to bring in the process page. Another factor is that the physical characteristics of most secondary-memory devices, which are rotational, favor a larger page size for more efficient block transfer of data.

Complicating these matters is the effect of page size on the rate at which page faults occur. This behavior is depicted in general terms in Figure 5.19a and is based on the principle of locality. If the page size is very small, then ordinarily a relatively large number of pages will be available in main memory for a process. After a time, the pages in memory will all contain portions of the process near recent references. Thus, the page fault rate should be low. As the size of the page is increased, each individual page will contain locations further and further from any particular recent reference. Thus, the effect of the principle of locality is weakened and the page fault rate begins to rise. Eventually, however, the page fault rate will begin to fall as the size of a page approaches the size of the entire process (point P in the diagram). When a single page encompasses the entire process, there will be no page faults.

TABLE 5.2   Example Page Sizes

Computer	Page Size	Units
Atlas	512	48-bit word
Honeywell-Multics	1024	36-bit word
IBM 370 family	2048 or 4096	8-bit byte
IBM 370/XA and 370/ESA	4096	8-bit byte
VAX family	512	8-bit byte
IBM AS/400	512	8-bit byte
Intel 80386 (IBM PS/2)	4096	8-bit byte
Motorola 68030 (Macintosh)	4096	8-bit byte

A further complication is that the page fault rate is also determined by the number of frames allocated to a process. Figure 5.19b shows that, for a fixed page size, the fault rate drops as the number of pages maintained in main memory grows. Thus, a software policy (the amount of memory to allocate to each process) affects a hardware design decision.

Table 5.2 indicates the page sizes used on some machines.

Segmentation

Virtual Memory Implications

Segmentation allows the programmer to view memory as consisting of multiple address spaces or segments. With virtual memory, the programmer need not be concerned about the memory limitations imposed by main memory. Segments may be of unequal, indeed dynamic, size. Memory references consist of a (segment number, offset) form of address.

This organization has a number of advantages to the programmer over a nonsegmented address space:

1. It simplifies the handling of growing data structures. If the programmer does not know ahead of time how large a particular data structure will become, it is necessary to guess unless dynamic segment sizes are allowed. With segmented virtual memory, the data structure can be assigned its own segment, and the operating system will expand or shrink the segment as needed. If a segment that needs to be expanded is in main memory and there is insufficient room, the operating system may move the segment to a larger area of main memory if it is available or swap it out. In the latter case, the enlarged segment would be swapped back in at the next opportunity.
2. It allows programs to be altered and recompiled independently, without requiring the entire set of programs to be relinked and reloaded. Again, this is accomplished using multiple segments.
3. It lends itself to sharing among processes. A programmer can place a utility program or a useful table of data in a segment that can be referenced by other processes.
4. It lends itself to protection. Since a segment can be constructed to contain a well-defined set of programs or data, the programmer or system administrator can assign access privileges in a convenient fashion.

Organization

In the discussion of simple segmentation, we indicated that each process has its own segment table and that when all its segments are loaded into main memory, the segment table for a process is created and loaded into main memory. Each segment table entry contains the starting address of the corresponding segment in main memory, as well as the length of the segment. The same device, a segment table, is needed when we consider a virtual memory scheme based on segmentation. Again, it is typical to associate a unique segment table with each process. In this case, however, the segment table entries become more complex (Figure 5.12b). Because only some of the segments of a process may be in main memory, a bit is needed in each segment table entry to indicate whether the corresponding segment is present in main memory. If the bit indicates that the segment is in memory, then the entry also includes the starting address and length of that segment.

Another control bit needed in the segmentation table entry is a modify bit to indicate whether the contents of the corresponding segment have been altered since the segment was last loaded into main memory. If there has been no change, then it is not necessary to write the segment out when it comes time to replace the segment in the frame that it currently occupies. Other control bits may also be present. For example, if protection or sharing is managed at the segment level, then bits for that purpose will be required. We will see several examples of segment table entries later in this chapter.

Thus, the basic mechanism for reading a word from memory involves the translation of a virtual, or logical, address, consisting of segment number and offset, into a physical address by using a segment table. Because the segment table is of variable length, depending on the size of the process, we cannot expect to hold it in registers. Instead, it must be in main memory to be accessed. Figure 5.20 suggests a hardware implementation of this scheme. When a par-

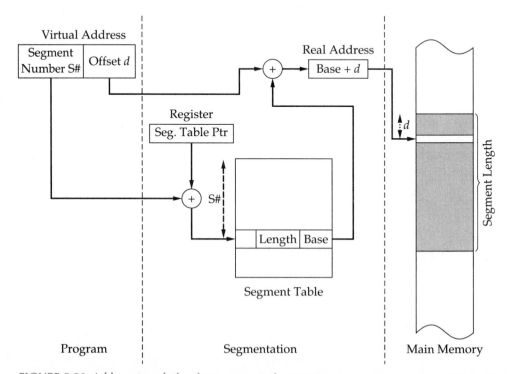

FIGURE 5.20 Address translation in a segmentation system

ticular process is running, a register holds the starting address of the segment table for that process. The segment number of a virtual address is used to index that table and look up the corresponding main memory address for the start of the segment. This is added to the offset portion of the virtual address to produce the desired real address.

Combined Paging and Segmentation

Both paging and segmentation have their strengths. Paging, which is transparent to the programmer, eliminates external fragmentation and thus provides efficient use of main memory. In addition, because the pieces that are moved in and out of main memory are of fixed equal size, it is possible to develop sophisticated memory-management algorithms that exploit the behavior of programs, as we shall see. Segmentation, which is visible to the programmer, has the strengths listed earlier, including the ability to handle growing data structures, modularity, and support for sharing and protection. To combine the advantages of both, some systems are equipped with processor hardware and operating-system software to provide both.

In a combined paging/segmentation system, a user's address space is broken up into a number of segments at the discretion of the programmer. Each segment is in turn broken up into a number of fixed-size pages, which are equal in length to a main memory frame. If a segment is less than a page in length, the segment occupies just one page. From the programmer's point of view, a logical address still consists of a segment number and a segment offset. From the system's point of view, the segment offset is viewed as a page number and page offset for a page within the specified segment.

Figure 5.21 suggests a structure to support combined paging/segmentation. Associated with each process is a segment table and a number of page tables, one per process segment. When a particular process is running, a register holds the starting address of the segment table for that process. Presented with a virtual address, the processor uses the segment number portion to index into the process segment table to find the page table for that segment. Then, the page number portion of the virtual address is used to index the page table and look up the corresponding frame number. This is combined with the offset portion of the virtual address to produce the desired real address.

Figure 5.12c suggests the segment table entry and page table entry formats. As before, the segment table entry contains the length of the segment. It also contains a base field, which now refers to a page table. The present and modified bits are not needed because these matters are handled at the page level. Other control bits may be used for purposes of sharing and protection. The page table entry is essentially the same as that used in a pure paging system. Each page number is mapped into a corresponding frame number if the page is present in main memory. The modified bit indicates whether this page needs to be written back out when the frame is allocated to another page. And there may be other control bits dealing with protection or other aspects of memory management.

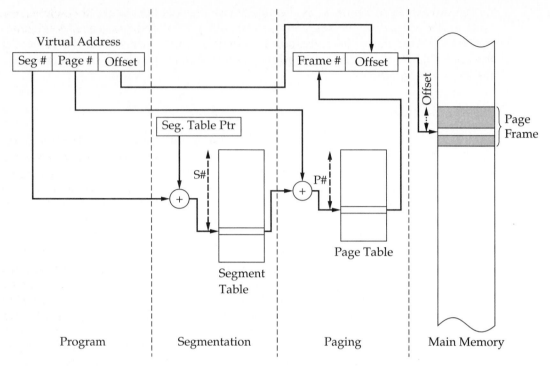

FIGURE 5.21 Address translation in a segmentation/paging system

Protection and Sharing

Segmentation lends itself to the implementation of protection and sharing policies. Since each segment table entry includes a length as well as a base address,
a program cannot inadvertently access a main memory location beyond the
limits of a segment. To achieve sharing, it is possible for a segment to be referenced in the segment tables of more than one process. The same mechanisms
are, of course, available in a paging system. However, in this case, the page
structure of programs and data is not visible to the programmer, making the
specification of protection and sharing requirements more awkward.

More sophisticated mechanisms can also be provided. A common scheme is
to use a ring-protection structure of the type we referred to in Chapter 3. In
this scheme, lower-numbered, or inner, rings enjoy greater privilege than
higher-number, or outer, rings. Figure 5.22 illustrates the types of protection
that can be enforced in such a system. Typically, ring 0 is reserved for kernel
functions of the operating system with applications at a higher level. Some
utilities or operating-system services may occupy an intermediate ring. Basic
principles of the ring system are the following:

1. A program may access only data that reside on the same ring, or a less
   privileged ring.
2. A program may call services residing on the same, or a more privileged ring.

Figure 5.23 shows the kind of restrictions that may be enforced with the use of a ring structure.

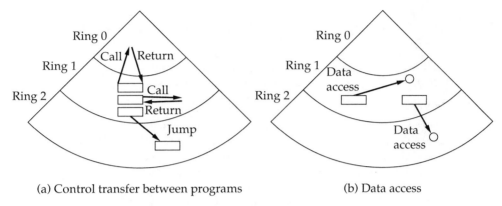

(a) Control transfer between programs　　　　　(b) Data access

FIGURE 5.22 Ring protection conventions [FURH87]

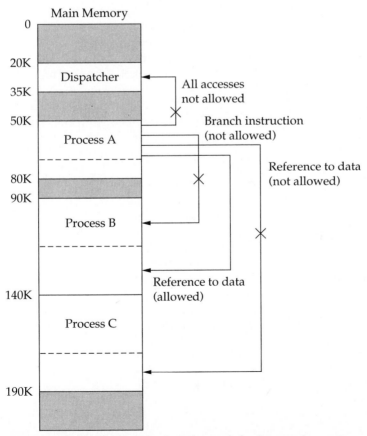

FIGURE 5.23 Fundamental protection and sharing requirements

VIRTUAL MEMORY—OPERATING SYSTEM SOFTWARE

The design of the memory management portion of an operating system depends on three fundamental areas of choice:

• Whether or not to use virtual memory techniques
• The use of paging or segmentation or both
• The algorithms employed for various aspects of memory management

The choices made in the first two areas depend on the hardware platform available. Thus, earlier UNIX implementations did not provide virtual memory because the processors on which the system ran did not support paging or segmentation. Neither of these techniques is practical without hardware support for address translation and other basic functions.

Two additional comments about the first two items in the above list: First, with the exception of operating systems for some of the older personal computers, such as MS-DOS, and for specialized systems, all important operating systems provide virtual memory. Hence, we emphasize the topic of virtual memory in this chapter. Second, pure segmentation systems are becoming increasingly rare. When segmentation is combined with paging, most of the memory-management issues confronting the operating-system designer are in the area of paging.[4] Thus, we can concentrate in this section on the issues associated with paging.

The choices in the third area (algorithms) are the domain of operating-system software and are the subject of this section. Table 5.3 lists the key design elements that are examined. In each case, the key issue is one of performance: We

TABLE 5.3   Operating-System Policies for Virtual Memory

Fetch Policy	**Resident Set Management**
Demand	Resident set size
Prepaging	Fixed
	Variable
Placement Policy	Replacement Scope
	Global
Replacement Policy	Local
Basic Algorithms	
Optimal	**Cleaning Policy**
Least recently used (LRU)	Demand
First-in, first-out (FIFO)	Precleaning
Clock	
Page Buffering	**Load Control**
	Degree of multiprogramming

[4]Protection and sharing are usually dealt with at the segment level in a combined segmentation/paging system. We deal with these issues in later chapters.

would like to minimize the rate at which page faults occur. Page faults cause considerable software overhead. At a minimum, the operating system must make a decision concerning which resident page or pages to replace, and the I/O of exchanging pages is incurred. Then the operating system must schedule another process to run during the page I/O, causing a process switch. Accordingly, we would like to arrange matters so that, during the time that a process is executing, the probability of referencing a word on a missing page is minimized. In all the areas referred to in Table 5.3, there is no definitive policy that works best. As we shall see, the task of memory management in a paging environment is fiendishly complex. Furthermore, the performance of any particular set of policies depends on main memory size, the relative speed of main and secondary memory, the size and number of processes competing for resources, and the execution behavior of individual programs. This latter characteristic depends on the nature of the application, the programming language and compiler employed, the style of the programmer who wrote it, and for an interactive program, the dynamic behavior of the user. Thus, you must expect no final answers here or anywhere. For smaller systems, the operating-system designer should attempt to choose a set of policies that seems "good" over a wide range of conditions, based on the current state of knowledge. For larger systems, particularly mainframes, the operating system should be equipped with monitoring and control tools that allow the site manager to tune the operating system to get "good" results based on site conditions.

Fetch Policy

The fetch policy is concerned with determining when a page should be brought into main memory. The two common alternatives are demand paging and prepaging. With **demand paging**, a page is brought into main memory only when a reference is made to a location on that page. If the other elements of memory-management policy are good, the following should happen. When a process is first started, there will be a flurry of page faults. As more and more pages are brought in, the principle of locality suggests that most future references will be to pages that have recently been brought in. Thus, after a time, matters should settle down and the number of page faults should drop to a very low level.

With **prepaging**, pages other than the one demanded by a page fault are brought in. The attraction of this strategy is based on the characteristics of most secondary memory devices, such as disks, which have seek times and rotational latency. If the pages of a process are stored contiguously in secondary memory, then it is more efficient to bring in a number of contiguous pages at one time rather than bringing them in one at a time over an extended period. Of course, this policy is ineffective if most of the extra pages that are brought in are not referenced.

The prepaging policy could be employed either when a process first starts up, in which case the programmer would somehow have to designate desired pages, or every time a page fault occurs. This latter course would seem preferable because it is invisible to the programmer. However, the utility of pre-paging has not been established [MAEK87].

One final point about prepaging: Prepaging should not be confused with swapping. When a process is swapped out of memory and put in a suspended state, all its resident pages are moved out. When the process is resumed, all the pages that were previously in main memory are returned to main memory. This policy is followed by most operating systems.

Placement Policy

The placement policy is concerned with determining where in real memory a process piece is to reside. This policy is of interest in a pure segmentation system, and policies such as best-fit, first-fit, and so on, which were discussed under dynamic partitioning, come into play. However, for a uniprocessor system that uses either pure paging or paging combined with segmentation, placement is irrelevant because the address translation hardware and the main memory access hardware can perform their functions for any page/frame combination with equal efficiency.

There is one area in which placement does become a concern, and this is a subject of recent research and development. On a so-called nonuniform memory access (NUMA) multiprocessor, the distributed, shared memory of the machine can be referenced by any processor on the machine, but the cost of accessing a particular physical location varies with the distance between the processor and the memory module. Thus, performance depends heavily on the extent to which data reside close to the processes that use them [BOLO89, COX89]. Thus, an automatic placement strategy is needed to assign pages to the memory module that provides the best performance.

Replacement Policy

In most operating-system texts, the treatment of memory management includes a section entitled "replacement policy," which deals with the selection of a page in memory to be replaced when a new page must be brought in. This topic is sometimes difficult to explain because several interrelated concepts are involved, as follows:

- The number of page frames to be allocated to each active process
- Whether the set of pages to be considered for replacement should be limited to those of the process that caused the page fault or encompass all the page frames in main memory
- Among the set of pages considered, the particular page that should be selected for replacement

We shall refer to the first two concepts as *resident set management*, which is dealt with in the next subsection, and reserve the term *replacement policy* for the third concept, which is discussed in the this subsection.

The area of replacement policy is probably the most studied of any area of memory management over the past twenty years. When all the frames in main memory are occupied and it is necessary to bring in a new page to satisfy a page fault, replacement policy is concerned with selecting a page currently in memory to be replaced. All the policies have as their objective that the page that is removed should be the page least likely to be referenced in the near future. Because of the principle of locality, there is a high correlation between recent referencing history and near-future referencing patterns. Thus, most policies try to predict future behavior on the basis of past behavior. One trade-off that must be considered is that the more elaborate and sophisticated the replacement policy, the greater the hardware and software overhead to implement it.

Frame Locking

One restriction on replacement policy needs to be mentioned before we look at various algorithms: Some of the frames in main memory may be locked. When a frame is locked, the page currently stored in that frame may not be replaced. Much of the kernel, as well as key control structures, of the operating system is held on locked frames. In addition, I/O buffers and other time-critical areas may be locked into main memory frames. Locking is achieved by associating a lock bit with each frame. This bit may be kept in a frame table as well as being included in the current page table.

Basic Algorithms

Regardless of the resident set management strategy (discussed in the next subsection), there are certain basic algorithms that are used for the selection of a page to replace. Replacement algorithms that have been considered in the literature include:

- Optimal
- Least recently used (LRU)
- First-in, first-out (FIFO)
- Clock

The **optimal** policy selects for replacement that page for which the time to the next reference is the longest. It can be shown that this algorithm results in the fewest number of page faults [BELA66]. Clearly, this algorithm is impossible to implement because it would require the operating system to have perfect knowledge of future events. However, it does serve as a standard against which to judge other algorithms.

Figure 5.24 gives an example of the optimal policy. The example assumes a fixed frame allocation for this process of three frames. The execution of the process requires reference to five distinct pages. The page address stream

Page Address Stream

| 2 | 3 | 2 | 1 | 5 | 2 | 4 | 5 | 3 | 2 | 5 | 2 |

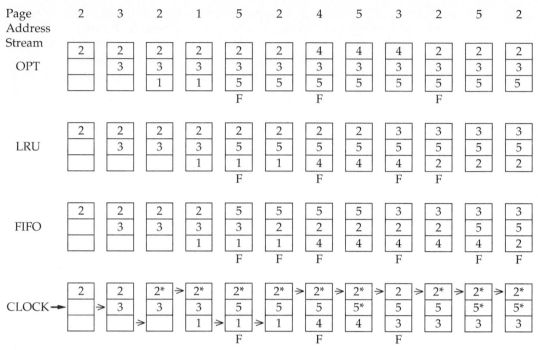

FIGURE 5.24 Behavior of four page replacement algorithms (based on [HAYE88])

formed by executing the program is:

2 3 2 1 5 2 4 5 3 2 5 2

which means that the first page referenced is 2, the second page referenced is 3, and so on. The optimal policy produces three page faults after the frame allocation has been filled.

The **least recently used (LRU)** policy replaces the page in memory that has not been referenced for the longest time. By the principle of locality, this should be the page least likely to be referenced in the near future. And in fact, the LRU policy does nearly as well as the optimal policy. The problem with this approach is the difficulty in implementation. One approach would be to tag each page with the time of its last reference; this would have to be done at each memory reference, both instruction and data. Even if the hardware would support such a scheme, the overhead would be tremendous. Alternatively, one could maintain a stack of page references, again an expensive prospect.

Figure 5.24 shows an example of the behavior of LRU, using the same page address stream as for the optimal policy example. In this case, there are four page faults.

The **first-in, first-out (FIFO)** policy treats the page frames allocated to a process as a circular buffer, and pages are removed in round-robin style. All that is required is a pointer that circles through the page frames of the process.

This is therefore one of the simplest page replacement policies to implement. The logic behind this choice, other than its simplicity, is that one is replacing the page that has been in memory the longest: A page fetched into memory a long time ago may have now fallen out of use. This reasoning will often be wrong because there will often be regions of program or data that are heavily used throughout the life of a program. Those pages will be repeatedly paged in and out by the FIFO algorithm.

Continuing our example in Figure 5.24, the FIFO policy results in six page faults. Note that LRU recognizes that pages 2 and 5 are referenced more frequently than other pages, whereas FIFO does not.

Whereas the LRU policy does nearly as well as an optimal policy, it is difficult to implement and imposes significant overhead. On the other hand, the FIFO policy is very simple to implement but performs relatively poorly. Over the years, operating-system designers have tried a number of other algorithms to approximate the performance of LRU while imposing little overhead. Many of these algorithms are variants of a scheme referred to as the **clock policy**.

The simplest form of clock policy requires the association of an additional bit with each frame, referred to as the *use bit*. When a page is first loaded into a frame in memory, the use bit for that frame is set to zero. When the page is subsequently referenced (after the reference that generated the page fault), its use bit is set to 1. For the page replacement algorithm, the set of frames that are candidates for replacement (this process: local scope; all of main memory: global scope) is considered to be a circular buffer with which a pointer is associated. When a page is replaced, the pointer is set to indicate the next frame in the buffer. When it is time to replace a page, the operating system scans the buffer to find a frame with a use bit set to 0. Each time it encounters a frame with a use bit of 1, it resets that bit to 0. If any of the frames in the buffer have a use bit of 0 at the beginning of this process, the first such frame encountered is chosen for replacement. If all the frames have a use bit of 1, then the pointer will make one complete cycle through the buffer, setting all the use bits to 0, and stop at its original position, replacing the page in that frame. We can see that this policy is similar to FIFO, except that any frame with a use bit of 1 is passed over by the algorithm. The policy is referred to as a clock policy because we can visualize the page frames as laid out in a circle. A number of operating systems have employed some variation of this simple clock policy, for example Multics [CORB68].

The behavior of the clock policy is illustrated in Figure 5.24. The presence of an asterisk indicates that the corresponding use bit is equal to 1, and the arrow indicates the current position of the pointer. Thus, in the third time unit, page 2 is referenced and its use bit is set. In the fourth time unit, a page is loaded into the third frame, and the pointer is positioned at the first frame. However, because the use bit for that frame is set, that frame will not be used for replacement in the fifth time frame. Note that the clock policy is adept at protecting frames 2 and 5 from replacement. In fact, in this example, the clock policy outperforms LRU. In general, this is not the case.

Figure 5.25 shows the results of an experiment reported in [BAER80], which compares the four algorithms that we have been discussing; it is assumed that the number of page frames assigned to a process is fixed. The results are based on the execution of 0.25×10^6 references in a FORTRAN program, using a page size of 256 words. Baer ran the experiment with frame allocations of 6, 8, 10, 12, and 14 frames. The differences among the four policies are most striking at small allocations, with FIFO being over a factor of 2 worse than optimal. Almost identical results have been reported in [FINK88], again showing a maximum spread of about a factor of 2. Finkel's approach was to simulate the effects of various policies on a synthesized page-reference string of 10,000 references selected from a virtual space of 100 pages. To approximate the effects of the principle of locality, an exponential distribution for the probability of referencing a particular page was imposed. Finkel observes that some people might be led to conclude that there is little point in elaborate page-replacement algorithms when only a factor of 2 is at stake. But he notes that this difference will have a noticeable effect either on main memory requirements (to avoid degrading operating-system performance) or operating-system performance (to avoid enlarging main memory).

The clock algorithm has also been compared to these other algorithms when a variable allocation and either global or local replacement scope is used. (See the discussion of replacement policy under "Replacement Scope" below) [CARR81, CARR84]. Again, the clock algorithm was found to closely approximate the performance of LRU.

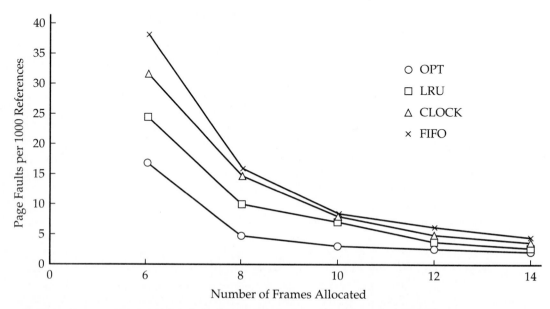

FIGURE 5.25 Comparison of fixed-allocation, local page replacement algorithms

The clock algorithm can be made more powerful by increasing the number of bits that it employs.[5] In all processors that support paging, a modify bit is associated with every page in main memory and hence with every frame of main memory. This bit is needed so that when a page has been modified, it is not replaced until it has been written back into secondary memory. We can exploit this bit in the clock algorithm in the following way. If we take the use and modify bits into account, each frame falls into one of the following four categories:

- Not accessed recently, not modified ($u = 0$; $m = 0$)
- Accessed recently, not modified ($u = 1$; $m = 0$)
- Not accessed recently, modified ($u = 0$; $m = 1$)
- Accessed recently, modified ($u = 1$; $m = 1$)

With this classification, the clock algorithm performs as follows:

1. Beginning at the current position of the pointer, scan the frame buffer. During this scan, make no changes to the use bit. The first frame encountered with ($u = 0$; $m = 0$) is selected for replacement.
2. If step 1 fails, scan again, looking for frame with ($u = 0$; $m = 1$). The first such frame encountered is selected for replacement. During this scan, set the use bit to 0 on each frame that is bypassed.
3. If step 2 fails, the pointer should have returned to its original position and all the frames in the set will have a use bit of 0. Repeat step 1 and, if necessary, step 2. This time, a frame will be found for the replacement.

This strategy is used in the Macintosh virtual memory scheme [GOLD89], illustrated in Figure 5.26. The advantage of this algorithm over the simple clock algorithm is that pages that are unchanged are given preference for replacement. Since a page that has been modified must be written out before being replaced, there is an immediate savings of time.

Page Buffering

Although LRU and the clock policies are superior to FIFO, they both involve complexity and overhead not suffered with FIFO. In addition, there is the related issue that the cost of replacing a page that has been modified is greater than for one that has not been because the former must be written back out to secondary memory.

An interesting strategy that can improve paging performance and allow the use of a simpler page-replacement policy is page buffering. The VAX/VMS approach is representative. VMS makes use of a variable-allocation, local-replacement strategy (see discussion of replacement scope, below). The page-replacement algorithm is simple FIFO. To improve performance, a replaced page is not

---

[5]On the other hand, if we reduce the number of bits employed to zero, the clock algorithm degenerates to FIFO.

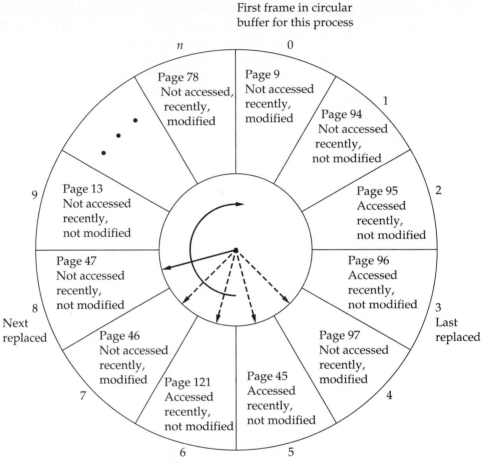

FIGURE 5.26 The clock page-replacement algorithm [GOLD89]

lost but is assigned to one of two lists: the free page list if the page has not been modified, or the modified page list if it has. Note that the page is not physically moved about in main memory; instead, the entry in the page table for this page is removed and placed in either the free or modified page list.

The free page list is a list of page frames available for reading in pages. VMS tries to keep some small number of frames free at all times. When a page is to be read in, the page frame at the head of the list is used, destroying the page that was there. When an unmodified page is to be replaced, it remains in memory and its page frame is added to the tail of the free page list. Similarly, when a modified page is to be written out and replaced, its page frame is added to the tail of the modified page list.

The important aspect of these maneuvers is that the page to be replaced remains in memory. Thus, if the process references that page, it is returned to the resident set of that process at little cost. In effect, the free and modified page lists act as a cache of pages. The modified page list serves another useful function: Modified pages are written out in clusters rather than one at a time. This significantly reduces the number of I/O operations and therefore the amount of disk access time.

A simpler version of page buffering is implemented in the Mach operating system [RASH88]. In this case, no distinction is made between modified and unmodified pages.

Resident Set Management

Resident Set Size

With paged virtual memory, it is not necessary and indeed may not be possible to bring all the pages of a process into main memory to prepare it for execution. Thus, the operating system must decide how many pages to bring in, that is, how much main memory to allocate to a particular process. Several factors come into play:

- The smaller the amount of memory allocated to a process, the more processes that can reside in main memory at any one time. This increases the probability that the operating system will find at least one Ready process at any given time and hence reduces the time lost due to swapping.
- If a relatively small number of pages of a process are in main memory, then, despite the principle of locality, the rate of page faults will be rather high (see Figure 5.19b).
- Beyond a certain size, additional allocation of main memory to a particular process will have no noticeable effect on the page fault rate for that process because of the principle of locality.

With these factors in mind, two sorts of policies are to be found in contemporary operating systems. A **fixed-allocation** policy gives a process a fixed number of pages within which to execute. That number is decided at initial load time (process creation time) and may be determined on the basis of the type of process (interactive, batch, type of application) or on the basis of guidance from the programmer or system manager. With a fixed-allocation policy, whenever a page fault occurs in the execution of a process, one of the pages of that process must be replaced by the needed page.

A **variable-allocation** policy allows the number of page frames allocated to a process to be varied over the lifetime of the process. Ideally, a process that is suffering persistent high levels of page faults, indicating that the principle of locality holds in only a weak form for that process, will be given additional page frames in order to reduce the page fault rate; whereas a process with an exceptionally low page fault rate, indicating that the process is quite well behaved from a locality point of view, will be given a reduced allocation with the hope that this will not noticeably increase the page fault rate. The use of a variable-allocation policy relates to the concept of replacement scope, as explained below.

The variable-allocation policy appears to be the more powerful one. However, the difficulty with this approach is that it requires the operating system to assess the behavior of active processes. This inevitably requires software overhead in the operating system and is dependent on hardware mechanisms provided by the processor platform.

Replacement Scope

The scope of a replacement strategy can be categorized as global or local. Both types of policies are activated by a page fault when there are no free page frames. In selecting a page to replace, a **local replacement policy** chooses among only the resident pages of the process that generated the page fault. A **global replacement policy** considers all pages in main memory to be candidates for replacement, regardless of which process owns a particular page. Although it happens that local policies are easier to analyze, there is no convincing evidence that they perform better than global policies, which are attractive because of their simplicity of implementation and minimal overhead [CARR84, MAEK87].

There is a relationship between replacement scope and resident set size (Table 5.4). A fixed resident set implies a local replacement policy: To hold the size of a resident set fixed, a page that is removed from main memory must be replaced by another page from the same process. A variable allocation policy can clearly employ a global replacement policy: The replacement of a page from one process in main memory with that of another causes the allocation of one process to grow by one page and that of the other to shrink by one page. We shall also see that variable allocation and local replacement are a valid combination. In the remainder of this subsection, we examine these three combinations.

Fixed Allocation, Local Scope

For this case, we have a process that is running in main memory with a fixed number of pages. When a page fault occurs, the operating system must choose which page from among the currently resident pages for this process is to be replaced. Replacement algorithms such as those discussed in the preceding subsection can be used.

With a fixed-allocation policy, it is necessary to decide ahead of time the amount of allocation to give to a process. This decision can be made on the basis of the type of application and the amount requested by the program. The drawback to this approach is twofold: If allocations tend to be too small, then there will be a high page fault rate, causing the entire multiprogramming system to run slowly. If allocations tend to be unnecessarily large, then there will be too few programs in main memory and there will either be considerable processor idle time or considerable time spent in swapping.

TABLE 5.4   Resident Set Management

	Local Replacement	Global Replacement
Fixed Allocation	Number of frames allocated to process is fixed. Page to be replaced is chosen from among the frames allocated to that process.	Not possible.
Variable Allocation	The number of frames allocated to a process may be changed from time to time, to maintain the working set of the process. Page to be replaced is chosen from among the frames allocated to that process.	Page to be replaced is chosen from all available frames in main memory; this causes the size of the resident set of processes to vary.

Variable Allocation, Global Scope

This combination is perhaps the easiest to implement and has been adopted in a number of operating systems. At any given time, there are a number of processes in main memory, each with a certain number of frames allocated to it. Typically, the operating system also maintains a list of free frames. When a page fault occurs, a free frame is added to the resident set of a process and the page is brought in. Thus, a process experiencing page faults will gradually grow in size, which should help reduce overall page faults in the system.

The difficulty with this approach is in the replacement choice. When there are no free frames available, the operating system must choose a page currently in memory to replace. The selection is made from among all the frames in memory, except for locked frames such as those of the kernel. Using any of the policies discussed in the preceding subsection, the page selected for replacement can belong to any of the resident processes; there is no discipline to determine which process should lose a page from its resident set. Therefore, the selection of the process that suffers the reduction in resident set size may not be optimum.

One way to counter the potential performance problems of a variable-allocation, global-scope policy is to use page buffering. In this way, the choice of which page to replace becomes less significant because the page may be reclaimed if it is referenced before the next time a block of pages is overwritten.

Variable Allocation, Local Scope

Another approach to variable allocation attempts to overcome the problems of a global-scope strategy. A variable-allocation, local-scope strategy can be summarized as follows:

1. When a new process is loaded into main memory, allocate to it a certain number of page frames on the basis of application type, program request,

or other criteria. Use either prepaging or demand paging to fill up the allocation.
2. When a page fault occurs, select the page to replace from among the resident set of the process that suffers the fault.
3. From time to time, reevaluate the allocation provided to the process, and increase or decrease it to improve overall performance.

With this strategy, the decision to increase or decrease a resident set size is a deliberate one and is based on an assessment of the likely future demands of active processes. Because of this evaluation, such a strategy is more complex than a simple global replacement policy. However, it may yield better performance.

The key elements of the variable-allocation, local-scope strategy are the criteria used to determine resident set size and the timing of changes. One specific strategy that has received much attention in the literature is known as the **working set strategy**. Although a true working set strategy would be difficult to implement, it is useful to examine it as a baseline for comparison.

The working set is a concept introduced and popularized by Denning [DENN68, DENN70, DENN80b]; it has had a profound impact on virtual memory management design. The working set with parameter Δ for a process at virtual time t, $W(t, \Delta)$, is the set of pages of that process that have been referenced in the last Δ virtual time units. We use the concept of virtual time to mean the time that elapses while the process is actually in execution. We can think of virtual time as being measured in instruction cycles, with each executed instruction equaling one time unit.

Let us consider each of the two variables of W. The variable Δ is a window of time over which the process is observed. The working set size will be a nondecreasing function of the window size. This result is illustrated in Figure 5.27, which shows a sequence of page references for a process. The dots indicate time units in which the working set does not change. Note that the larger the working set, the more infrequent the page faults. This outcome can be expressed in the following relationship:

$$W(t, \Delta + 1) \supseteq W(t, \Delta)$$

The working set is also a function of time. If a process executes over Δ time units and uses only a single page, then $|W(t, \Delta| = 1$. A working set can also grow as large as the number of pages n of the process if many different pages are rapidly addressed and if the window size allows. Thus,

$$1 \leq |W(t, \Delta| \leq \min (\Delta, n)$$

Figure 5.28 indicates the way in which the working set size can vary over time for a fixed value of Δ. For many programs, periods of relatively stable working set sizes alternate with periods of rapid change. When a process first begins executing, it gradually builds up to a working set as it references new pages. Eventually, by the principle of locality, the process should stabilize on a certain set of pages. Subsequent transient periods reflect a shift of the program

Sequence of Page References	Window Size			
	2	3	4	5
24	24	24	24	24
15	15 24	15 24	15 24	15 24
18	18 15	18 15 24	18 15 24	18 15 24
23	23 18	23 18 15	23 18 15 24	23 18 15 24
24	24 23	24 23 18	•	•
17	17 24	17 24 23	17 24 23 18	17 24 23 18 15
18	18 17	18 17 24	•	•
24	24 18	•	•	•
18	18 24	•	•	•
17	17 18	•	•	•
17	17	•	•	•
15	15 17	15 17 18	15 17 18 24	•
24	24 15	24 15 17	•	•
17	17 24	•	•	•
24	24 17	•	•	•
18	18 24	18 24 17	•	•

FIGURE 5.27 Working set of process as defined by window size [BACH86]

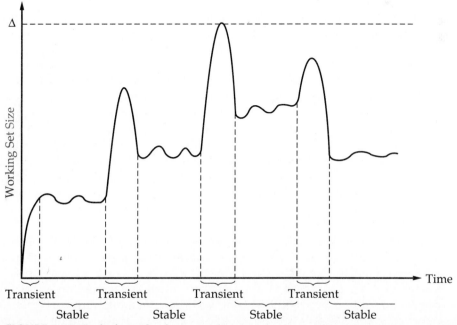

FIGURE 5.28 Typical graph of true working set size [MAEK87]

to a new locality. During the transition phase, some of the pages from the old locality remain within the window, Δ, causing a surge in the size of the working set as new pages are referenced. As the window slides past these page references, the working set size declines until it contains only those pages from the new locality.

This concept of a working set can be used to guide the following strategy for resident set size:

1. Monitor the working set of each process.
2. Periodically remove from the resident set of a process those pages that are not in its working set.
3. A process may execute only if its working set is in main memory, that is, if its resident set includes its working set.

This strategy is appealing because it takes an accepted principle, the principle of locality, and exploits it to achieve a memory-management strategy that should minimize page faults. Unfortunately, there are a number of problems with the working set strategy, as follows:

1. The past does not always predict the future. Both the size and the membership of the working set will change over time (e.g, see Figure 5.28).
2. A true measurement of working set for each process is impractical. It would be necessary to time-stamp every page reference for every process using the virtual time of that process and then maintain a time-ordered queue of pages for each process.
3. The optimal value of Δ is unknown and in any case would vary.

Nevertheless, the spirit of this strategy is valid, and a number of operating systems attempt to approximate a working set strategy. One way to do this is to focus not on the exact page references but on the page fault rate of a process. As Figure 5.19b illustrates, the page fault rate falls as we increase the resident set size of a process. The working set size should fall at a point on this curve such as indicated by W in the figure. Therefore, rather than monitor the working set size directly, we can achieve comparable results by monitoring the page fault rate. The line of reasoning is as follows: If the page fault rate for a process is below some minimum threshold, the system as a whole can benefit by assigning a smaller resident set size to this process (because more page frames are available for other processes) without harming the process (by causing it to incur increased page faults). If the page fault rate for a process is above some maximum threshold, the process can benefit from an increased resident set size (by incurring fewer faults) without degrading the system.

An algorithm that follows this strategy is the **page fault frequency (PFF)** algorithm [CHU72, GUPT78]. The algorithm requires a use bit to be associated with each page in memory. The bit is set to 1 when that page is accessed. When a page fault occurs, the operating system notes the virtual time since the last page fault for that process; this could be done by maintaining a counter of page references, for example. A threshold F is defined. If the amount of time since the last page fault is less than F, then a page is added to the resident set of the process. Otherwise, discard all pages with a use bit of 0 and shrink the resident set accordingly. At the same time, reset the use bit on the remaining pages of the process to 0. The strategy can be refined by using two thresholds: an upper threshold that is used to trigger a growth in the resident set size and a lower threshold that is used to trigger a contraction in the resident set size.

The time between page faults is the reciprocal of the page fault rate. Although it would seem to be better to maintain a running average of the page fault rate, the use of a single time measurement is a reasonable compromise that allows decisions about resident set size to be based on page fault rate. If such a strategy is supplemented with page buffering, the resulting performance should be quite good.

Nevertheless, there is a major flaw in the PFF approach, which is that it does not perform well during the transient periods when there is a shift to a new locality. With PFF, no page ever drops out of the resident set before F virtual time units have elapsed since it was last referenced. During interlocality transitions, the rapid succession of page faults causes the resident set of a process to swell before the pages of the old locality are expelled; the sudden peaks of memory demand may produce unnecessary process deactivations and reactivations, with the corresponding undesirable switching and swapping overheads.

An approach that attempts to deal with the phenomenon of interlocality transition with a similar relatively low overhead to that of PFF, is the **variable-interval sampled working set (VSWS)** policy [FERR83]. The VSWS policy evaluates the working set of a process at sampling instances based on elapsed virtual time. At the beginning of a sampling interval, the use bits of all the resident pages for the process are reset. At the end, only the pages that have been referenced during the interval will have their use bit set; these pages are retained in the resident set of the process throughout the next interval, and the others are discarded. Thus, the resident set size can decrease only at the end of an interval. During each interval, any faulted pages are added to the resident set; thus, the resident set remains fixed or grows during the interval.

The VSWS policy is driven by the following three parameters:

M   The minimum duration of the sampling interval
L   The maximum duration of the sampling interval
Q   The number of page faults that are allowed to occur
      between sampling instances

The VSWS policy is as follows:

1. If the virtual time since the last sampling instance reaches L, then suspend the process and scan the use bits.
2. If, prior to an elapsed virtual time of L, Q page faults occur:
   (a) If the virtual time since the last sampling instance is less than M, then wait until the elapsed virtual time reaches M to suspend the process and scan the use bits.

(b) If the virtual time since the last sampling instance is greater than or equal to M, suspend the process and scan the use bits.

The parameter values are to be selected so that the sampling will normally be triggered by the occurrence of the Qth page fault after the last scan (case 2b). The other two parameters (M and L) provide boundary protection for exceptional conditions. The VSWS policy tries to reduce the peak memory demands caused by abrupt interlocality transitions by increasing the sampling frequency, hence the rate at which unused pages drop out of the resident set when the paging rate increases. Experience with this technique in the Bull mainframe operating system, GCOS 8, indicates that this approach is as simple to implement as PFF and is more effective [PIZZ89].

Cleaning Policy

A cleaning policy is the opposite of a fetch policy; it is concerned with determining when a modified page should be written out to secondary memory. Two common alternatives are demand cleaning and precleaning. With **demand cleaning**, a page is written out to secondary memory only when it has been selected for replacement. A **precleaning** policy writes modified pages before their page frames are needed, so that pages can be written out in batches.

There is a danger in following either policy to the full. With precleaning, a page is written out but remains in main memory until the page replacement algorithm dictates that it be removed. Precleaning allows the writing of pages in batches, but it makes little sense to write out hundreds or thousand of pages only to find that the majority of them have been modified again before they are replaced. The transfer capacity of secondary memory is limited and should not be wasted with unnecessary cleaning operations.

On the other hand, with demand cleaning, the writing of a dirty page is coupled to, and precedes, the reading in of a new page. This technique may minimize page writes, but it means that a process that suffers a page fault may have to wait for two page transfers before it can be unblocked. This may decrease use of the processor.

A better approach incorporates page buffering, which allows the adoption of the following policy: Clean only pages that are replaceable, but decouple the cleaning and replacement operations. With page buffering, replaced pages can be placed on two lists: modified and unmodified. The pages on the modified list can periodically be written out in batches and moved to the unmodified list. A page on the unmodified list is either reclaimed if it is referenced or lost when its frame is assigned to another page.

Load Control

Load control is concerned with determining the number of processes that will be resident in main memory, which has been referred to as the multiprogramming level. The load control policy is critical in effective memory management.

If too few processes are resident at any one time, then there will be many occasions when all processes are blocked and much time will be spent in swapping. On the other hand, if too many processes are resident, then on average the size of the resident set of each process will be inadequate and frequent faulting will occur. The result is a condition known as *thrashing*.

Multiprogramming Level

Thrashing is illustrated in Figure 5.29. As the multiprogramming level increases from a small value, one would expect to see processor use rise, since there is less chance that all resident processes are blocked. However, a point is reached at which the average resident set is inadequate. At this point, the number of page faults rises dramatically, and processor use collapses.

There are a number of ways to get at this problem. A working set or page fault frequency algorithm implicitly incorporates load control. Only those processes whose resident set is sufficiently large are allowed to execute. In providing the required resident set size for each active process, the policy automatically and dynamically determines the number of active programs.

Another approach, suggested by Denning and his colleagues [DENN80b], is known as the "L=S criterion," which adjusts the multiprogramming level so that the mean time between faults equals the mean time required to process a page fault. Performance studies indicate that this is the point at which processor use attains a maximum. A policy with similar effect, proposed in [LERO76], is the "50% criterion," which attempts to keep the use of the paging device at approximately 50%. Again, performance studies indicate that this is a point of maximum processor use.

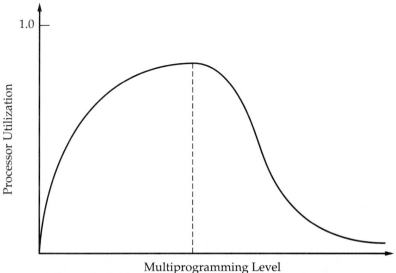

FIGURE 5.29 Multiprogramming effects

Another approach is to adapt the clock page-replacement algorithm described earlier (Figure 5.26). [CARR84] describes a technique using a global scope that involves monitoring the rate at which the pointer scans the circular buffer of frames. If the rate is below a given lower threshold, one or both of two circumstances is indicated:

1. Few page faults are occurring, resulting in few requests to advance the pointer.
2. For each request, the average number of frames scanned by the pointer is small, indicating that there are many resident pages not being referenced and that they are readily replaceable.

In both cases, the multiprogramming level can safely be increased. On the other hand, if the pointer scan rate exceeds an upper threshold, either a high fault rate or difficulty in locating replaceable pages is indicated, which implies that the multiprogramming level is too high.

Process Suspension

If the degree of multiprogramming is to be reduced, one or more of the currently resident processes must be suspended (swapped out). [CARR84] lists the following six possibilities:

- *Lowest priority process:* This alternative implements a scheduling policy decision and is unrelated to performance issues.
- *Faulting process:* The reasoning is that there is a greater probability that the faulting task does not have its working set resident, and performance would suffer least by suspending it. In addition, this choice has an immediate payoff because it blocks a process that is about to be blocked anyway, and it eliminates the overhead of a page replacement and I/O operation.
- *Last process activated:* This is the process least likely to have its working set resident.
- *Process with the smallest resident set:* This process requires the least future effort to reload. However, it penalizes programs with small locality.
- *Largest process:* This alternative obtains the most free frames in an overcommitted memory, making additional deactivations unlikely soon.
- *Process with the largest remaining execution window:* In most process scheduling schemes, a process may run for only a certain quantum of time before being interrupted and placed at the end of the Ready queue. This process approximates a shortest-processing-time-first scheduling discipline.

As in so many other areas of operating-system design, the policy to choose is a matter of judgment and depends on many other design factors in the operating system as well as the characteristics of the programs being executed.

5.5

EXAMPLES OF MEMORY MANAGEMENT

System/370 and MVS

Address Space Structure

The IBM System/370 architecture uses a two-level memory structure and refers to the two levels as segments and pages, although the segmentation approach lacks many of the features described earlier in this chapter. For the basic 370 architecture, the page size may be either 2 KB or 4 KB, and the segment size is fixed at either 64 KB or 1 MB. For the 370/XA and 370/ESA architectures, the page size is 4 KB and the segment size is 1 MB. In this discussion, we refer primarily to the XA-ESA structure.

Figure 5.30a depicts the format for a virtual address. The byte index specifies one of 4 KB within a page; the page index specifies one of 256 pages within a segment; and the segment index identifies one of 2048 user-visible segments. Thus, the user sees a virtual address space of 2^{31} bytes (2 GB) of virtual storage.

Figure 5.31 shows the evolution of address space structures for the 370 architecture. The original 370 family, which supported the original MVS operating

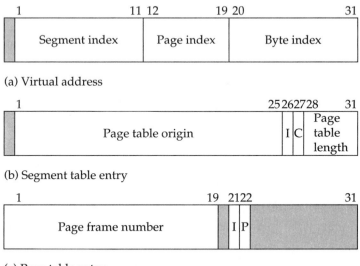

(a) Virtual address

(b) Segment table entry

(c) Page table entry

(d) Page frame table entry

FIGURE 5.30 IBM system 370/XA and 370/ESA memory management formats

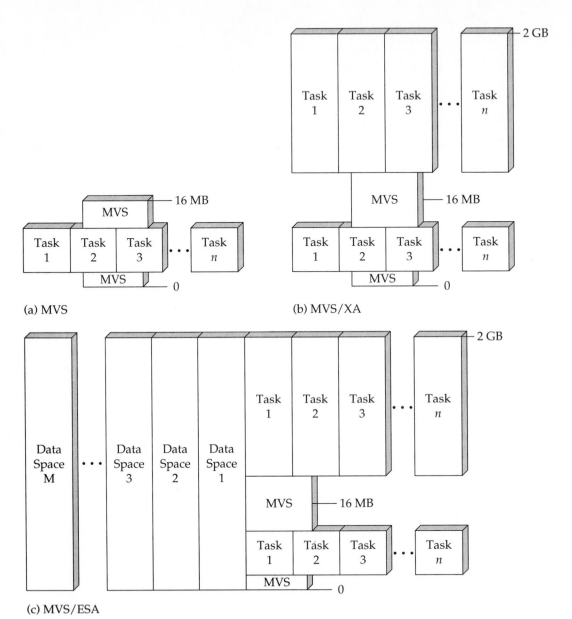

FIGURE 5.31 MVS address space structure

system, employed 24-bit addresses, allowing a virtual address space of 16 MB. Any job or application could be assigned up to the 16 MB of virtual memory. Part of the address space is reserved for MVS programs and data structures. Within a given address space, one or more tasks may be activated. As we mentioned earlier, this corresponds to the concept of multiple threads within a single process.

Eventually, IBM discovered that for two reasons the 24-bit address structure was inadequate for many customers and applications. First, applications were becoming more complex and involved the use of larger data structures. And second, the growth in MVS was such that it came to occupy anywhere from one-half to three-fourths of the user's virtual address space.[6] The result was that available virtual address space was shrinking as user requirements were expanding! Thus, IBM modified the basic architecture to provide extended addressing (XA). The resulting architecture is called System 370/XA, which supports MVS/XA. This architecture supports the 31-bit address scheme depicted in Figure 5.30a. Each application or job now has 2 GB of virtual address space available. This space is divided into two regions divided by the 16-MB line. Below this line, the space dedicated to MVS remains, and the remainder is available for one or more programs. Above this line, some additional space is also reserved for MVS, with the remainder available for programs whose requirements exceed the amount available below the line. Thus, a single task may employ user space above and below the line.

The latest version of the System 370 architecture and the corresponding MVS are referred to as Enterprise System Architecture (ESA) [PLAM89], which represents a further step by IBM to satisfy the seemingly insatiable need for virtual storage by large-scale applications. System 370/ESA employs the same addressing structure as XA, allowing an address space of 2 GB for MVS support programs and data, and for user programs. In addition, a program may address up to 15 additional 2-GB address spaces for data only, giving a total virtual address space for a single application of 16 terabytes (TB) (2^{44} bytes).

Hardware and Control Structures

To manage storage, segment and page tables are used, as in Figure 5.23. There is one segment table for each virtual address space. Thus, each virtual address space contains a number of segments, with one entry in the segment table per segment.

The format for a segment table entry is shown in Figure 5.30b. The 25-bit page table origin points to the page table for that segment; six zero bits are appended to the 25-bit field to form a 31-bit real address. The page table length indicates the number of entries in the page table ($= 16 \times$ PTL). The segment-invalid (I) bit is set when some malfunction or unrecoverable error occurs and indicates that the segment is unavailable. The common (C) bit indicates whether this segment is private to an address space or is shared by several address spaces. In the latter case, segment and page table entries relating to this segment may remain in the translation lookaside buffer after this address space is swapped out.

---

[6]This was so even though much of MVS is not located in the user's virtual address space.

Each page table entry (Figure 5.30c) includes an invalid (I) bit that indicates whether the corresponding page is in real memory. If it is, the page frame number gives the location of the page; 12 bits are appended to the right of this number to form the real address. The protection (P) bit, when set, prevents Writes but allows Reads to the corresponding page.

For 370/XA, address translation proceeds as in Figure 5.23. In addition, a translation lookaside buffer holds recently referenced segment and page table entries.

For 370/ESA, additional logic is needed. In the 370 machine instruction set, virtual memory references are made through the general-purpose registers (GPR). Associated with each of the 370's 16 general-purpose 32-bit registers is an access register (AR). When a GPR is used as a base register for an operand location, the corresponding AR specifies the address space in which the operand is located. Thus, it is possible for a different virtual address space to be associated with each GPR. By changing the contents of an AR, many different virtual address spaces may be accessed.

The ESA option is activated by a bit in the program status word. When it is in use, two sorts of translation are needed to calculate a real address. Figure 5.32 illustrates the mechanism. The example makes use of a 370 instruction type that is used for indexing. The first operand is a register. The second operand is a virtual location referenced by the sum of a 12-bit displacement plus the contents of a base register and an index register, both of which are from the pool of general-purpose registers. The 4-bit base register designation (B2) is also used to refer to one of 16 address space registers. The contents of that address space register is used as input to a translation process involving several tables

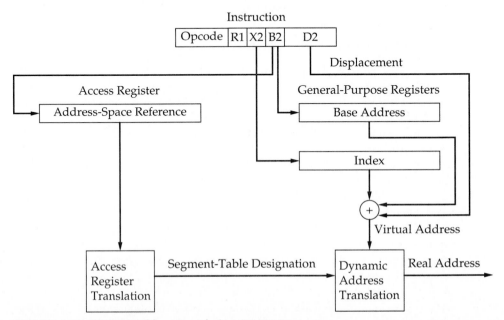

FIGURE 5.32 370/ESA address translation [PLAM89]

that results in the real address of the segment table for a particular address space. This table, plus the virtual address, serve as input to the dynamic address translation mechanism (Figure 5.23) that ultimately yields the real address.

Operating-System Considerations

MVS makes use of the hardware features just described for memory management. MVS employs a global page replacement strategy. The system maintains a list of page frames that are available. When a new page must be brought in, a page frame from this list is used. When the number of available frames drops below a certain threshold, the operating system performs a page-stealing operation by converting a number of active pages to available pages. The decision to steal a particular page is based on the activity history of each page currently residing in a real storage frame. Pages that have not been accessed for a relatively long time are good candidates for page stealing. In essence, a least-recently-used policy is followed.

To implement this policy, MVS makes use of two sources of information: a storage key associated with each frame, and a page frame table. The storage key is a control field associated with each frame of real memory. Two bits of that key that are relevant for page replacement are the reference bit and the change bit. The reference bit is set to 1 when any address within the frame is accessed for Read or Write, and it is set to 0 when a new page is loaded into the frame. The change bit is set to 1 when a Write operation is performed on any location within the frame. The page frame table contains an entry for each frame of real memory. Each entry contains the following fields (Figure 5.30d):

* *Address space identifier:* Identifies the owner address space for that frame.
* *Segment number, page number:* Virtual page occupying this frame.
* *Available frame:* Indicates whether the frame is available or occupied.
* *Unreferenced interval count (UIC):* Indicates how long it has been since a program referenced this frame.

Once per second, MVS checks the reference bit for every single frame in real memory. If the reference bit is not on (the frame has not been referenced), the system increments the UIC for that frame. If the reference bit is on, MVS resets the reference bit and sets UIC to 0. When it is necessary to steal pages, MVS selects those frames with the longest UIC for replacement. This replacement policy can be modified by a technique known as *storage isolation*, which requires that each address space maintain a specified minimum number of pages. Thus, a page frame may not be stolen from an address space if stealing it causes the number of its pages to fall below the minimum for that address space.

OS/2

OS/2 was originally implemented on the Intel 80286 processor, which supports segmentation but not paging. The more recent 80386 and 80486 processors support both paging and segmentation. Early releases of OS/2 will run on the newer processors but do not make use of the paging hardware. More recent releases of OS/2 do provide both paging and segmentation. In this subsection, we examine the facilities available on the 80386 and 80486.

Address Spaces

The 80386 includes hardware for both segmentation and paging. Both mechanisms can be disabled, allowing the user to choose from four distinct views of memory:

- *Unsegmented unpaged memory:* In this case, the virtual address is the same as the physical address, which is useful, for example, in low-complexity, high-performance controller applications.
- *Unsegmented paged memory:* Here memory is viewed as a paged linear address space. Protection and management of memory are done by paging. This view of memory is favored by some operating systems—for example, UNIX.
- *Segmented unpaged memory:* Here memory is viewed as a collection of logical address spaces. The advantages of this view over a paged approach is that it affords protection down to the level of a single byte if necessary. Furthermore, unlike paging, it guarantees that the translation table needed (the segment table) is on-chip when the segment is in memory. Hence, segmented unpaged memory results in predictable access times.
- *Segmented paged memory:* Segmentation is used to define logical memory partitions subject to access control, and paging is used to manage the allocation of memory within the partitions. Operating systems such as OS/2 favor this view.

Segmentation

When segmentation is used, each virtual address (called a logical address in the 80386 documentation) consists of a 16-bit segment reference and a 32-bit offset. Two bits of the segment reference deal with the protection mechanism, leaving 14 bits for specifying a particular segment. Thus, with unsegmented memory, the user's virtual memory is $2^{32} = 4$ GB. With segmented memory, the total virtual memory space as seen by a user is $2^{46} = 64$ TB. The physical address space employs a 32-bit address for a maximum of 4 GB.

The amount of virtual memory can actually be larger than the 64 TB: The 80386's interpretation of a virtual address depends upon which process is currently active. One-half of the virtual address space (8 K segments × 4 GB) is global, shared by all processes; the remainder is local and is distinct for each process.

Associated with each segment are two forms of protection: privilege level and access attribute. There are four **privilege levels** from most protected (level 0) to least protected (level 3). The privilege level associated with a data segment is its *classification*; the privilege level associated with a program segment is its *clearance*. An executing program may access only those data segments for which its clearance level is lower than (more privileged) or equal to (same privilege) the privilege level of the data segment.

The hardware does not dictate how these privilege levels are to be used; use depends on the operating-system design and implementation. It was intended that privilege level 1 would be used for most of the operating system, and level 0 would be used for that small portion of the operating system devoted to memory management, protection, and access control, leaving two levels for applications. In many systems, applications reside at level 3, with level 2 being unused. Specialized application subsystems that must be protected because they implement their own security mechanisms are good candidates for level 2. Some examples are data base management systems, office automation systems, and software engineering environments.

In addition to regulating access to data segments, the privilege mechanism limits the use of certain instructions. Some instructions, such as those that deal with memory-management registers, can be executed only in level 0. I/O instructions can be executed only up to a certain level that is designated by the operating system; typically this is level 1.

The **access attribute** of a data segment specifies whether Read/Write or Read-only accesses are permitted. For program segments, the access attribute specifies Read/Execute or Read-only access.

The address translation mechanism for segmentation involves mapping a **virtual address** into what is referred to as a **linear address**. The format of the virtual address (Figure 5.33a) includes the following fields:

- *Table indicator (TI):* Indicates whether the global segment table or a local segment table should be used for translation.
- *Segment number:* Is the number of the segment. This serves as an index into the segment table.
- *Offset:* The offset of the addressed byte within the segment.
- *Requested privilege level (RPL):* The privilege level requested for this access.

Each entry in a segment table consists of 64 bits, as shown in Figure 5.33c. The fields are defined in Table 5.5.

Paging

Segmentation is an optional feature and may be disabled. When segmentation is in use, addresses used in programs are virtual addresses and are converted into linear addresses, as just described. When segmentation is not in use, linear addresses are used in programs. In either case, the next subsequent step is to convert that linear address into a real 32-bit address.

To understand the structure of the linear address, you need to know that the 80386 paging mechanism is actually a two-level table lookup operation. The first level is a **page directory**, which contains up to 1024 entries. This splits the 4-GB linear memory space into 1024 page groups, each with its own **page table** and each 4 MB in length. Each page table contains up to 1024 entries; each entry

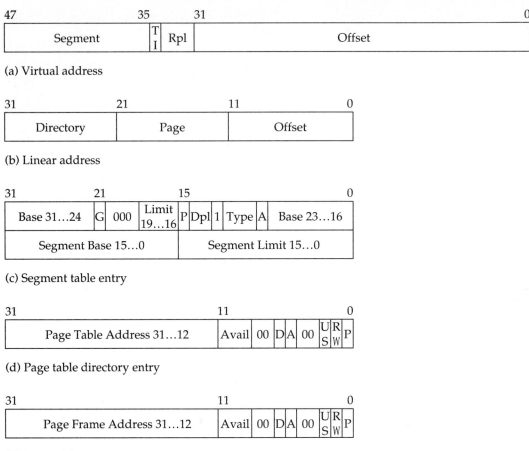

FIGURE 5.33 80386 memory management formats

corresponds to a single 4-KB page. Memory management has the option of using one page directory for all processes, one page directory for each process, or some combination of the two. The page directory for the current task is always in main memory. Page tables may be in virtual memory.

Figure 5.33 shows the formats of entries in page directories and page tables, and the fields are defined in Table 5.5. Note that access control mechanisms can be provided on a page or page group basis.

The 80386 makes use of a translation lookaside buffer that can hold 32 page table entries. Each time that the page directory is changed, the buffer is cleared.

Figure 5.34 illustrates the combination of segmentation and paging mechanisms. For clarity, the translation lookaside buffer and memory cache mechanisms are not shown.

TABLE 5.5　80386 Memory-Management Parameters

Segment Table Entry

Limit

Defines the size of the segment. The processor interprets the limit field in one of two ways, depending on the granularity bit: in units of one byte, up to a limit of 1 MB, or in units of 4 KB, up to a limit of 4 GB.

Base

Defines the starting address of the segment within the 4-GB linear address space.

Accessed bit (A)

Set whenever the segment is accessed. An operating system that uses segmented nonpaged memory may use this bit to monitor frequency of segment usage for memory management purposes. In a paged system, this bit is ignored.

Type

Distinguishes between various kinds of segments and indicates the access attributes.

Descriptor privilege level (DPL)

Specifies the privilege level of the segment referred to by this segment table entry (segment descriptor).

Segment present bit (P)

Used for nonpaged systems. It indicates whether the segment is present in main memory. For paged systems, this bit is always set to 1.

Granularity bit (G)

Indicates whether the Limit field is to be interpreted in units of 1 byte or 4 KB.

Page Table Directory Entry and Page Table Entry

Page Frame Address

Provides the physical address of the page in memory if the present bit is set. Since page frames are aligned on 4 K boundaries, the bottom 12 bits are zero, and only the top 20 bits are included in the entry.

Page Table Address

Provides the physical address of a page table in memory if the present bit is set.

Present bit (P)

Indicates whether the page table or page is in main memory.

Accessed bit (A)

This bit is set to 1 by the processor in both levels of page tables when a Read or Write operation to the corresponding page occurs.

Dirty bit (D)

This bit is set to 1 by the processor when a Write operation to the corresponding page occurs.

User/Supervisor bit (US)

Indicates whether the page is available only to the operating system (supervisor level) or is available to both operating system and applications (user level).

Read/Write bit (RW)

For user-level pages, indicates whether the page is Read-only access or Read/Write access for user-level programs.

Available bits (AVAIL)

Available for systems programmer use.

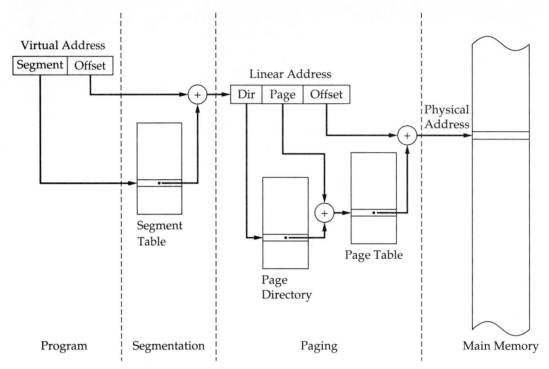

FIGURE 5.34 80386 memory address translation mechanism

UNIX System V

Because UNIX is intended to be machine-independent, its memory-management scheme varies from one system to the next. Earlier versions of UNIX simply used variable partitioning with no virtual memory scheme. Most current implementations make use of paged virtual memory.

For paged virtual memory, UNIX V makes use of a number of data structures that, with minor adjustment, are machine-independent (Figure 5.35 and Table 5.6):

- *Page table:* Typically, there is one page table per process, with one entry for each page in virtual memory for that process.
- *Disk block descriptor:* Associated with each page of a process is an entry in this table that describes the disk copy of the virtual page.
- *Page frame data table:* Describes each frame of real memory and is indexed by frame number.
- *Swap-use table:* There is one swap-use table for each swap device, with one entry for each page on the device.

Most of the fields defined in Table 5.6 are self-explanatory. A few warrant further comment. The Age field in the page table entry is similar to the UIC

Page Frame Number		Age	Copy on Write	Modi-fy	Refe-rence	Valid	Pro-tect

(a) Page table entry

Swap Device Number	Device Block Number	Type of Storage

(b) Disk block descriptor

Page State	Reference Count	Logical Device	Block Number	Pfdata Pointer

(c) Page frame data table entry

Reference Count	Page/Storage Unit Number

(a) Swap-use table entry

FIGURE 5.35 UNIX System V memory management formats

field used by MVS. However, the number of bits and the frequency of update of this field are implementation-dependent. Therefore, there is no universal UNIX use of this field for page replacement policy.

The Type of Storage field in the disk block descriptor is needed for the following reason. When an executable file is first used to create a new process, only a portion of the program and data for that file may be loaded into real memory. Later, as page faults occur, new portions of the program and data are loaded. It is only at the time of first loading that virtual memory pages are created and assigned to locations on one of the devices to be used for swapping. At that time, the operating system is told whether it needs to clear (set to 0) the locations in the page frame before the first loading of a block of the program or data.

The page frame data table is used for page replacement. Several pointers are used to create lists within this table. All the available frames are linked together in a list of free frames available for bringing in pages. When the number of available pages drops below a certain threshold, the kernel will steal a number of pages to compensate. All the containing pages that are on the same swap device and in the same device block are linked together in a list referred to as a *hash queue*. The term *hash* is used to refer to the fact that the identity of the list is derived directly from the device and block number. Such lists are useful for blocking page I/O operations.

TABLE 5.6   UNIX System V Memory-Management Parameters

Page Table Entry

Page frame number
Refers to frame in real memory.

Age
Indicates how long the page has been in memory without being referenced. The length and contents of this field are processor-dependent.

Copy on write
Set when more than one process shares a page. If one of the processes writes into the page, a separate copy of the page must first be made for all other processes that share the page. This feature allows the copy operation to be deferred until necessary and avoided in cases where it turns out not to be necessary.

Modify
Indicates page has been modified.

Reference
Indicates page has been referenced. This bit is set to zero when the page is first loaded and may be periodically reset by the page replacement algorithm.

Valid
Indicates page is in main memory.

Protect
Indicates whether Write operation is allowed.

Disk Block Descriptor

Swap device number
Logical device number of the secondary device that holds the corresponding page. This allows more than one device to be used for swapping.

Device block number
Block location of page on swap device.

Type of storage
Storage may be swap unit or executable file. In the latter case, there is an indication as to whether the virtual memory to be allocated should be cleared first.

Page Frame Data Table Entry

Page State
Indicates whether this frame is available or has an associated page. In the latter case, the status of the page is specified: on swap device, in executable file, or DMA in progress.

Reference count
Number of processes that reference the page.

Logical device
Logical device that contains a copy of the page.

Block number
Block location of the page copy on the logical device.

Pfdata pointer
Pointer to other pfdata table entries on a list of free pages and on a hash queue of pages.

TABLE 5.6 (*Continued*)

Swap-Use Table Entry

Reference count
   Number of page table entries point to a page on the swap device.
Page/storage unit number
   Page identifier on storage unit.

5.6

SUMMARY

One of the most important and most complex tasks of an operating system is memory management. Memory management involves treating main memory as a resource to be allocated to and shared among a number of active processes. To efficiently use the processor and the I/O facilities, it is desirable to maintain as many processes in main memory as possible. In addition, it is desirable to free programmers from size restrictions in program development.

The way to address both of these concerns is to use virtual memory. With virtual memory, all address references are logical references that are translated at run time to real addresses. This use allows a process to be located anywhere in main memory and for that location to change over time. Virtual memory also allows a process to be broken up into pieces. These pieces need not be contiguously located in main memory during execution, and indeed it is not even necessary for all the pieces of the process to be in main memory during execution.

Two basic approaches to providing virtual memory are paging and segmentation. With paging, each process is divided into relatively small, fixed size pages. Segmentation provides for the use of pieces of varying size. It is also possible to combine segmentation and paging in a single memory-management scheme.

A virtual memory-management scheme requires both hardware and software support. The hardware support is provided by the processor. The support includes dynamic translation of virtual addresses to physical addresses and the generation of an interrupt when a referenced page or segment is not in main memory. Such an interrupt triggers the memory-management software in the operating system.

A number of design issues relate to operating-system support for memory management:

• *Fetch policy:* Process pages can be brought in on demand, or a prepaging policy can be used; the latter clusters the input activity by bringing in a number of pages at once.
• *Placement policy:* With a pure segmentation system, an incoming segment must be fit into an available space in memory.

- *Replacement policy:* When memory is full, a decision must be made as to which page or pages are to be replaced.
- *Resident set management:* The operating system must decide how much main memory to allocate to a particular process when that process is swapped in. This can be a static allocation made at process creation time, or it can change dynamically.
- *Cleaning policy:* Modified process pages can be written out at the time of replacement, or a precleaning policy can be used; the latter clusters the output activity by writing out a number of pages at once.
- *Load control:* Load control is concerned with determining the number of processes that will be resident in main memory at any given time.

5.7

RECOMMENDED READING

All the books recommended in Section 2.6 provide coverage of memory management.

Because partitioning has been supplanted by virtual memory techniques, most books offer only cursory coverage of partitioning. Two of the more complete and interesting treatments are in [MILE87] and [HORN89]. A thorough discussion of partitioning strategies is to be found in [KNUT73]

As might be expected, virtual memory receives good coverage in most books on operating systems. [MAEK87] provides a good summary of various research areas. [CARR84] provides an excellent in-depth examination of performance issues. [KUCK78] and [BAER80] provide some interesting analytic and simulation results. The classic paper, [DENN70], is still well worth a read. An interesting contribution is [HAGM89], which argues that, at least for workstations, virtual memory may no longer be desirable because of the growth in the size of main memory and the growth in the disparity between main memory and secondary memory access time. [DEWA90] provides a detailed presentation of the 80386 virtual memory facility.

It is a sobering experience to read [IBM86], which gives a detailed account of the tools and options available to a site manager in optimizing the virtual memory policies of MVS. The document illustrates the complexity of the problem.

The topics of linking and loading are covered in many books on program development, computer architecture, and operating systems. A particularly detailed treatment is [[BECK90]. The discussion in Appendix 5A is organized along the lines of [SCHN85], which provides a basic and clear introduction. [KURZ84] examines the topic from the point of view of the implications for the design of operating systems and job management. [PINK89] provides a good summary with emphasis on the steps that precede linking and loading in the creation of an object module. [DAVI87] provides a detailed description of the linking and loading functions of MVS. The topic of dynamic linking, with particular reference to the Multics approach, is covered in [BIC88] and [KRAK88]. [IACO88] provides a detailed discussion of the use of dynamic linking in OS/2.

5.8

PROBLEMS

5.1 In Section 2.3, we listed five objectives of memory management, and in Section 5.1, we listed five requirements. Argue that each list encompasses all the concerns addressed in the other.

5.2 Consider a dynamic partitioning scheme. Show that on average the memory contains half as many holes as partitions.

5.3 During the course of execution of a program, the processor will increment the contents of the instruction register (program counter) by one word after each instruction fetch but will alter the contents of that register if it encounters a branch or call instruction that causes execution to continue elsewhere in the program. Now consider Figure 5.6. There are two alternatives with respect to instruction addresses:

(a) Maintain a relative address in the instruction register and do the dynamic address translation using the instruction register as input. When a successful branch or call is encountered, the relative address generated by that branch or call is loaded into the instruction register.

(b) Maintain an absolute address in the instruction register. When a successful branch or call is encountered, dynamic address translation is employed and the results are stored in the instruction register.

Which approach is preferable?

5.4 A process references five pages, A, B, C, D, and E, in the following order:

A; B; C; D; A; B; E; A; B; C; D; E

Assume that the replacement algorithm is first-in, first-out and find the number of page transfers during this sequence of references starting with an empty main memory with 3 and 4 page frames.

5.5 The IBM RISC System/6000 uses the following virtual address format:

segment id	page number	offset

To access the page table, a hash value is computed consisting of the exclusive-or of the segment-id and page-number fields. How effective do you think this algorithm is in producing a hash table with minimum overflow?

5.6 Construct a diagram similar to that of Figure 5.18 to show the combined operation of segmentation, paging, translation lookaside buffer, and cache.

5.7 In the VAX, user page tables are located at virtual addresses in the system space. What is the advantage of having user page tables in virtual rather than main memory? What is the disadvantage?

5.8 Suppose the program statement

for i **in** 1 . . . n **do** A[i] := B[i] + C[i] **endfor**

is executed in a memory with page size of 1000 words. Let $n = 1000$. Using a machine that has a full range of register-to-register instructions and employs index registers, write a hypothetical machine language program to implement the preceding statement. Then show the sequence of page references during execution.

5.9 To implement the various placement algorithms discussed in the section on dynamic partitioning, a list of the free blocks of memory must be kept. For each of the three methods discussed (best-fit, first-fit, next-fit), what is the average length of the search?

5.10 Another placement algorithm for dynamic partitioning is referred to as worst-fit. In this case, the largest free block of memory is used for bringing in a process. Discuss the pros and cons of this method compared to first-, next-, and best-fit. What is the average length of the search for worst-fit?

5.11 The segmentation approach used on the System/370 seems to lack many of the potential advantages of segmentation. Which advantages does it lack? What is the benefit of segmentation for the 370?

5.12 For System/370 memory management, suggest an approach for determining which page frames are least-recently-used (LRU), making use of only the reference bit associated with each frame of real memory.

5.13 Assume that we have a computer with a 3-address instruction for adding the contents of two addressed memory locations and depositing the sum in a third addressed memory location. In assembly form, the instruction looks like this:

ADD A, B, C,   /* (A) + (B) —> (C) */

If the instruction occupies three words and if all addresses are direct (i.e., the effective addresses are part of the instruction itself), what is the minimum number of page frames that this instruction requires to be guaranteed of proper execution. Explain your answer.

5.14 A key to the performance of the VSWS resident set management policy is the value of Q. Experience has shown that, with a fixed value of Q for a process, there are considerable differences in page fault frequencies at various stages of execution. Furthermore, if a single value of Q is used for different processes, dramatically different frequencies of page faults occur. These differences strongly indicate that a mechanism that would dynamically adjust the value of Q during the lifetime of a process would improve the behavior of the algorithm. Suggest a simple mechanism for this purpose.

5.15 Derive the formula for overflow with chaining in Table 5.8.

5.16 When virtual memory was first implemented, main memories were very small compared to today, and applications were often larger than main memory. Memory technology has changed dramatically since that time, with multi-megabyte systems in personal computers being common. As main memory sizes grow into the gigabyte range in the not too distant future, while disk access times are not showing a corresponding increase, will virtual memory still be a viable memory management scheme? Discuss why or why not.

5.17 Discuss the hardware support requirements for the inverted page table structure. How does this approach affect sharing?

APPENDIX 5A

Loading and Linking

The first step in the creation of an active process is to load a program into main memory and create a process image (Figure 5.36). Figure 5.37 depicts a scenario typical for most systems. The application consists of a number of compiled or

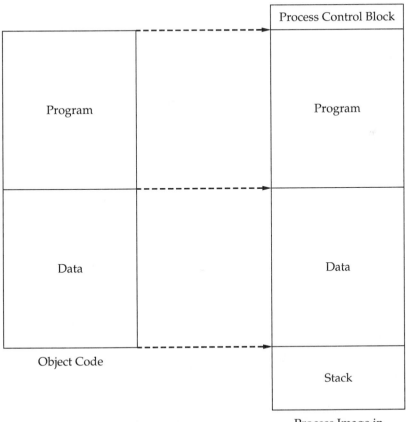

FIGURE 5.36 The loading function

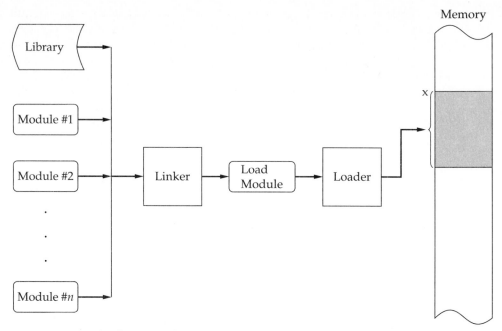

FIGURE 5.37 A loading scenario

assembled modules in object-code form that are linked together to resolve any references between modules. At the same time, references to library routines are resolved. The library routines themselves may be incorporated into the program or referenced as shared code that must be supplied by the operating system at run time. In this appendix, we summarize the key features of linkers and loaders. For clarity in the presentation, we begin with a description of the loading task when a single program module is involved; no linking is required.

5A.1 Loading

In Figure 5.37, the loader places the load module in main memory, starting at location x. In loading the program, the addressing requirement illustrated in Figure 5.1 must be satisfied. In general, three approaches can be taken:

- Absolute loading
- Relocatable loading
- Dynamic run-time loading

Absolute Loading

An absolute loader requires that a given load module always be loaded into the same location in main memory. Thus, in the load module presented to the loader, all address references must be to specific, or absolute, main memory addresses. For example, if x in Figure 5.37 is location 1024, then the first word in a load module destined for that region of memory has address 1024.

The assignment of specific address values to memory references within a program can be done either by the programmer or at compile or assembly time (Table 5.7a). There are several disadvantages to the former approach. First, every programmer would have to know the intended assignment strategy for placing modules into main memory. Second, if any modifications are made to the program that involve insertions or deletions in the body of the module, then all the addresses will have to be altered. Accordingly, it is preferable to

TABLE 5.7   Address Binding

(a) Loader

Binding Time	Function
Programming time	All actual physical addresses are directly specified by the programmer in the program itself.
Compile or assembly time	The program contains symbolic address references, and these are converted to actual physical addresses by the compiler or assembler.
Load time	The compiler or assembler produces relative addresses. The loader translates these to absolute addresses at the time of program loading.
Run time	The loaded program retains relative addresses. These are converted dynamically to absolute addresses by processor hardware.

(b) Linker

Linkage Time	Function
Programming time	No external program or data references are allowed. The programmer must place into the program the source code for all subprograms that are referenced.
Compile or assembly time	The assembler must fetch the source code of every subroutine that is referenced, and assemble them as a unit.
Load module creation	All object modules have been assembled using relative addresses. These modules are linked together and all references are restated relative to the origin of the final load module.
Load time	External references are not resolved until the load module is to be loaded into main memory. At that time, referenced dynamic link modules are appended to the load module, and the entire package is loaded into main or virtual memory.
Run time	External references are not resolved until the external call is executed by the processor. At that time, the process is interrupted and the desired module is linked to the calling program.

allow memory references within programs to be expressed symbolically, and then resolve those symbolic references at the time of compilation or assembly. This is illustrated in Figure 5.38b. Every reference to an instruction or item of data is initially represented by a symbol. In preparing the module for input to an absolute loader, the assembler or compiler will convert all these references to specific addresses (in this example, for a module to be loaded starting at location 1024).

Relocatable Loading

The disadvantage of binding memory references to specific addresses prior to loading is that the resulting load module can be placed in only one region of main memory. However, when many programs share main memory, it may not be desirable to decide ahead of time into which region of memory a particular module should be loaded. It is better to make that decision at load time. Thus, we need a load module that can be located anywhere in main memory.

To satisfy this new requirement, the assembler or compiler produces not actual main memory addresses (absolute addresses) but addresses that are relative to some known point, such as the start of the program. This technique is illustrated in Figure 5.38c. The start of the load module is assigned the relative

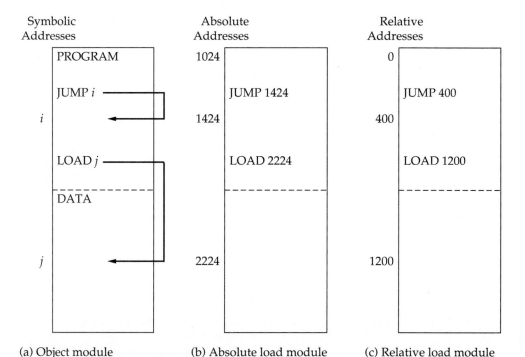

(a) Object module   (b) Absolute load module   (c) Relative load module

FIGURE 5.38 Absolute and relocatable load modules

address 0, and all other memory references within the module are expressed relative to the beginning of the module.

With all memory references expressed in relative format, it becomes a simple task for the loader to place the module in the desired location. If the module is to be loaded beginning at location x, then the loader must simply add x to each memory reference as it loads the module into memory. To assist in this task, the load module must include information that tells the loader where the address references are and how they are to be interpreted (usually relative to the program origin but also possibly relative to some other point in the program, such as the current location). This set of information is prepared by the compiler or assembler and is usually referred to as the *relocation dictionary*.

Dynamic Run-Time Loading

Relocating loaders are common and provide obvious benefits relative to absolute loaders. However, in a multiprogramming environment, even one that does not depend on virtual memory, the relocatable loading scheme is inadequate. We have referred to the need to swap process images in and out of main memory to maximize the use of the processor. To maximize main memory use, we would like to be able to swap the process image back into different locations at different times. Thus, a program once loaded may be swapped out to disk and then swapped back in at a different location. This procedure would be impossible if memory references had been bound to absolute addresses at the initial load time.

The alternative is to defer the calculation of an absolute address until it is actually needed at run time. For this purpose, the load module is loaded into main memory with all memory references in relative form (Figure 5.38c). It is not until an instruction is actually executed that the absolute address is calculated. To assure that this function does not degrade performance, it must be done by special processor hardware, rather than software. This hardware is described in Section 5.2.

Dynamic address calculation provides complete flexibility. A program can be loaded into any region of main memory. Subsequently, the execution of the program can be interrupted and the program can be swapped out of main memory to be swapped back in at a different location later.

5A.2 Linking

The function of a linker is to take as input a collection of object modules and produce a load module that consists of an integrated set of program and data modules to be passed to the loader. In each object module, there may be address references to locations in other modules. Each such reference can be expressed only symbolically in an unlinked object module. The linker creates a single load module that is the contiguous joining of all the object modules. Each intra-module reference must be changed from a symbolic address to a reference to a location within the overall load module. For example module A in Figure 5.39a contains a procedure invocation of module B. When these modules are combined in the load module, this symbolic reference to module B is changed to a specific reference to the location of the entry point of B within the load module.

Linkage Editor

The nature of the address linkage will depend on the type of load module to be created and when the linkage occurs (Table 5.7b). If, as is usually the case, a relocatable load module is desired, then linkage is usually done in the following fashion. Each compiled or assembled object module is created with references relative to the beginning of the object module. All these modules are put together into a single relocatable load module along with all references relative to the origin of the load module. This module can be used as input for relocatable loading or dynamic run-time loading.

A linker that produces a relocatable load module is often referred to as a *linkage editor*. Figure 5.39 illustrates the linkage editor function.

Dynamic Linker

As with loading, it is possible to defer some linkage functions. The term *dynamic linking* is used to refer to the practice of deferring the linkage of some external modules until after the load module has been created. Thus, the load module contains unresolved references to other programs. These references can be resolved either at load time or run time.

For **load-time dynamic linking**, the following steps occur. The load module (application module) to be loaded is read into memory. Any reference to an external module (target module) causes the loader to find the target module, load it, and alter the reference to a relative address in memory from the beginning of the application module. There are several advantages to this approach over what might be called static loading, as follows:

- It becomes easier to incorporate changed or upgraded versions of the target module, which may be an operating-system utility or some other general-purpose routine. With static linking, a change to such a supporting module would require the relinking of the entire application module. Not only is this inefficient, it may be impossible in some circumstances. For example, in the personal computer field, most commercial software is released in load module form; source and object versions are not released.
- Having target code in a dynamic link file paves the way for automatic code sharing. The operating system can recognize that more than one application is using the same target code because it loaded and linked that code. It can use that information to load a single copy of the target code and link it to both applications rather than having to load one copy for each application.
- It becomes easier for independent software developers to extend the functionality of a widely used operating system such as OS/2. A developer can

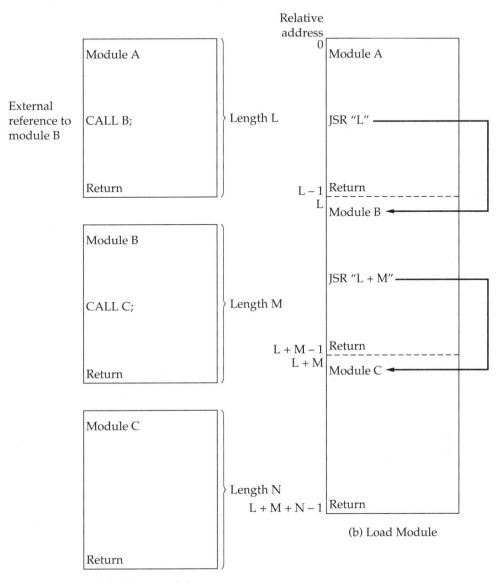

(a) Object modules

FIGURE 5.39 The linking function

come up with a new function that may be useful to a variety of applications and package it as a dynamic link module.

With **run-time dynamic linking**, some of the linking is postponed until execution time. External references to target modules remain in the loaded program. When a call is made to the absent module, the operating system locates the module, loads it, and links it to the calling module.

We have seen that dynamic loading allows an entire load module to be moved around; however, the structure of the module is static, being unchanged throughout the execution of the process and from one execution to the next. However, in some cases, it is not possible to determine prior to execution which object modules will be required. This situation is typified by transaction-processing applications, such as an airline reservation system or a banking application. The nature of the transaction dictates which program modules are required, and they are loaded as appropriate and linked with the main program. The advantage of the use of such a dynamic linker is that it is not necessary to allocate memory for program units unless those units are referenced. This capability is used in support of segmentation systems.

One additional refinement is possible: An application need not know the names of all the modules or entry points that may be called. For example, a charting program may be written to work with a variety of plotters, each of which is driven by a different driver package. The application can learn the name of the plotter that is currently installed on the system from another process or by looking it up in a configuration file, which allows the user of the application to install a new plotter that didn't even exist at the time that the application was written.

APPENDIX 5B

Hash Tables

Consider the following problem. A set of N items is to be stored in a table. Each item consists of a label plus some additional information, which we can refer to as the value of the item. We would like to be able to perform a number of ordinary operations on the table, such as insertion, deletion, and searching for a given item by label.

If the labels of the items are numeric, in the range 0 to M, then a simple solution would be to use a table of length M. An item with label i would be inserted into the table at location i. As long as items are of fixed length, table lookup is trivial and involves indexing into the table on the basis of the numeric label of the item. Furthermore, it is not necessary to store the label of an item in the table, since this is implied by the position of the item. Such a table is known as a **direct-access table**.

If the labels are nonnumeric, then it is still possible to use a direct-access approach. Let us refer to the items as $A[1], \ldots A[N]$. Each item $A[i]$ consists of a label, or key, k_i and a value v_i. Let us define a mapping function $I(k)$ such that $I(k)$ takes a value between 1 and M for all keys and $I(k_i) \neq I(k_j)$ for any i and j. In this case, a direct access table with the length of the table equal to M can also be used.

The one difficulty with these schemes occurs if $M \gg N$. In this case, the proportion of unused entries in the table is large, which is an inefficient use of memory. An alternative would be to use a table of length N and store the N items (label plus value) in the N table entries. In this scheme, the amount of memory is minimized, but there is now a processing burden to do table lookup. Several possibilities follow:

- *Sequential search:* This brute-force approach is time-consuming for large tables.
- *Associative search:* With the proper hardware, all the elements in a table can be searched simultaneously. This approach is not of general purpose and cannot be applied to any and all tables of interest.
- *Binary search:* If the labels or the numeric mapping of the labels are arranged in ascending order in the table, then a binary search is much quicker than a sequential search (Table 5.8), and requires no special hardware.

The binary search looks promising for table lookup. The major drawback with this method is that adding new items is not usually a simple process and requires reordering of the entries. Therefore, binary search is usually used only for reasonably static tables that are seldom changed.

We would like to avoid the memory penalties of a simple direct-access approach and the processing penalties of the alternatives just listed. The most frequently used method to achieve this compromise is **hashing**. Hashing, which was developed in the 1950s, is simple to implement and has two advantages. First, it can find most items with a single seek, as in direct accessing, and second, insertions and deletions can be handled without added complexity.

The hashing function can be defined as follows. Assume that up to N items are to be stored in a **hash table** of length M, with $M \geq N$ but not much larger than N. To insert an item in the table, take the following steps:

I1. Convert the label of the item to a near-random number n between 0 and $M - 1$. For example, if the label is numeric, a popular mapping function is to divide the label by M and take the remainder as the value of n.

I2. Use n as the index into the hash table.

TABLE 5.8 Average Search Length for One of N Items in a Table of Length M

Technique	Search Length
Direct	1
Sequential	$\dfrac{M + 1}{2}$
Binary	$\log_2 M$
Hash (open)	$\dfrac{2 - \dfrac{N}{M}}{2 - \dfrac{2N}{M}}$
Hash (overflow with chaining)	$1 + \dfrac{N - 1}{2M}$

(a) If the corresponding entry in the table is empty, store the item (label and value) in that entry.

(b) If the entry is already occupied, then store the item in an overflow area, as discussed below.

To perform table lookup of an item whose label is known, use the following routine:

L1. Convert the label of the item to a near-random number n between 0 and $M - 1$, using the same mapping function as for insertion.

L2. Use n as the index into the hash table.

(a) If the corresponding entry in the table is empty, then the item has not previously been stored in the table.

(b) If the entry is already occupied and the labels match, then the value can be retrieved.

(c) If the entry is already occupied and the labels do not match, then continue the search in the overflow area.

Hashing schemes differ in the way in which the overflow is handled. One common technique is referred to as the **open hash** technique and is commonly used in compilers. In this approach, preceding rule I2(b) becomes:

• If the entry is already occupied, set $n = n + 1 \pmod{M}$ and go back to step I2(a).

Rule L2(c) is modified accordingly.

Figure 5.40a is an example. In this case, the labels of the items to be stored are numeric, and the hash table has eight positions ($M = 8$). The mapping function is to take the remainder upon division by 8. The figure assumes that the items were inserted in ascending numerical order, although this is not necessary. Thus, items 50 and 51 map into positions 2 and 3, respectively, and because these positions are empty, they are inserted there. Item 74 also maps into position 2, but because it is not empty, position 3 is tried. This is also occupied, so the position 4 is ultimately used.

It is not easy to determine the average length of the search for an item in an open hash table because of the clustering effect. An approximate formula was obtained by Schay and Spruth [SCHA62]:

$$\text{Average search length} = \frac{2 - r}{2 - 2r}$$

where $r = N/M$. Note that the result is independent of table size and depends only on how full the table is. The surprising result is that with the table 80% full, the average length of the search is still around 3.

Even so, a search length of 3 may be considered long, and the open hash table has the additional problem that it is not easy to delete items. A more attractive approach, which provides searches of shorter lengths (Table 5.8) and allows deletions as well as additions, is **overflow with chaining**. This technique is illustrated in Figure 5.40b. In this case, there is a separate table into which overflow entries are inserted. This table includes pointers that pass down the chain of entries associated with any position in the hash table. In this case, the average search length, assuming randomly distributed data, is:

$$\text{Average search length} = 1 + \frac{N - 1}{2M}$$

For large values of N and M, this value approaches 1.5 for $N = M$. Thus, this technique provides for compact storage with rapid lookup.

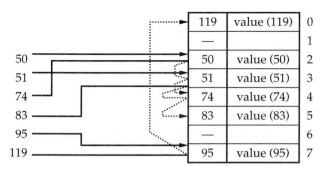

(a) Open hash

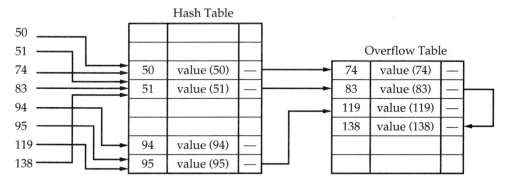

(b) Overflow with chaining

FIGURE 5.40 Hashing

CHAPTER 6

Scheduling

In a multiprogramming system, multiple processes are maintained in main memory. Each process alternates between using the processor and waiting for I/O to be performed or for some other event to occur. The processor keeps busy by executing one process while the others wait.

The key to multiprogramming is scheduling. In fact, four types of scheduling are typically involved (Table 6.1). One of these, I/O scheduling, is more conveniently addressed in Chapter 7, where I/O is discussed. The remaining three types of scheduling, which are types of processor scheduling, are addressed in this chapter.

The chapter begins with an examination of the three types of processor scheduling, showing the way in which they are related. We see that long-term scheduling and medium-term scheduling are driven primarily by performance concerns related to the degree of multiprogramming. These issues are dealt with to some extent in Chapter 3 and in more detail in Chapter 5. Thus, the remainder of this chapter concentrates on short-term scheduling. Section 6.2 looks at the various algorithms that may be used in making the short-term scheduling decision. Then, the issues raised by the availability of more than one processor are examined. Next, the special design considerations of real-time processing are examined. Then, as usual, our example systems are discussed.

TABLE 6.1 Types of Scheduling

Long-term scheduling	The decision to add to the pool of processes to be executed
Medium-term scheduling	The decision to add to the number of processes that are partially or fully in main memory
Short-term scheduling	The decision as to which available process will be executed by the processor
I/O scheduling	The decision as to which process's pending I/O request shall be handled by an available I/O device

6.1

TYPES OF SCHEDULING

The aim of processor scheduling is to assign processes to be executed by the processor or processors over time in a way that meets system objectives such as response time, throughput, and processor efficiency. In many systems, this scheduling activity is broken down into three separate functions: long-, medium-, and short-term scheduling. The names suggest the relative frequency with which these functions are performed.

Figure 6.1 relates the scheduling functions to the process state transition diagram. Long-term scheduling is performed when a new process is created. The creation of a new process results from a decision to add a new process to the set of currently active processes. Medium-term scheduling is a part of the swapping function and results from a decision to add a process to those that are at least partially in main memory and therefore available for execution. Short-term scheduling is the actual decision of which Ready process to execute next. Figure 6.2 reorganizes the state transition diagram to suggest the nesting of scheduling functions.

Scheduling affects the performance of the system because it determines which processes will wait and which will progress. This point of view is presented in Figure 6.3, which shows the queues involved in the state transitions of a process. Fundamentally, scheduling is a matter of managing queues to minimize queuing delay and to optimize performance in a queuing environment.

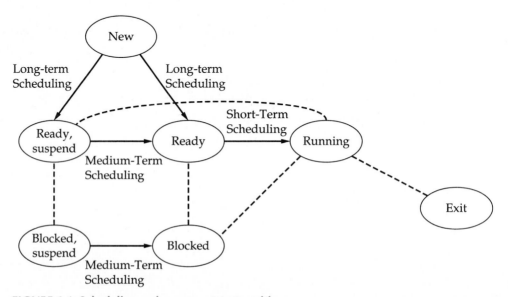

FIGURE 6.1 Scheduling and process state transitions

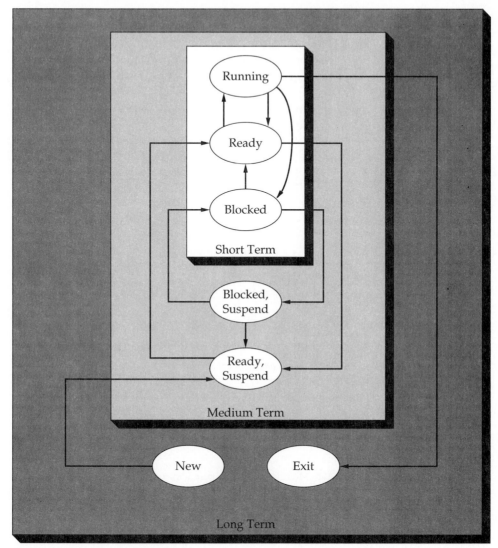

FIGURE 6.2 Levels of scheduling

Long-Term Scheduling

The long-term scheduler determines which programs are admitted to the system for processing. Thus, it controls the degree of multiprogramming. Once admitted, a job or user program becomes a process and is added to the queue for the short-term scheduler. In some systems, a newly created process begins in a swapped-out condition, in which case it is added to a queue for the medium-term scheduler.

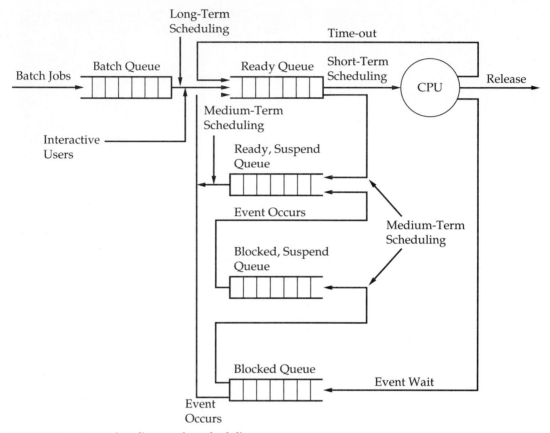

FIGURE 6.3 Queueing diagram for scheduling

In a batch system or for the batch portion of a general-purpose operating system, newly submitted jobs are routed to disk and held in a batch queue. The long-term scheduler creates processes from the queue when it can. Two decisions are involved here. First, the scheduler must decide that the operating system can take on one or more additional processes. Second, the scheduler must decide which job or jobs to accept and turn into processes. Let us briefly consider these two decisions.

The decision about when to create a new process is generally driven by the degree of multiprogramming. The more processes that are created, the smaller is the percentage of time that each process can be executed. Thus, the long-term scheduler may limit the degree of multiprogramming to provide satisfactory service to the current set of processes. Each time a job terminates, the scheduler may make the decision to add one or more new jobs. Additionally, if the fraction of time that the processor is idle exceeds a certain threshold, the long-term scheduler may be invoked.

The decision as to which job to admit next can be on a simple first-come, first-served (FCFS) basis, or it can be a tool to manage system performance. The criteria used may include priority, expected execution time, and I/O requirements. For example, if the information is available, the scheduler may attempt to keep a mix of processor-bound and I/O-bound processes.[1] Also, in an attempt to balance I/O use, the decision may be made depending on which I/O resources are to be requested.

For interactive programs in a time-sharing system, a process request is generated when a user attempts to connect to the system. Time-sharing users are not simply queued up and kept waiting until the system can accept them. Rather, the operating system accepts all authorized comers until the system is saturated, using some predefined measure of saturation. At that point, a connection request is met with a message indicating that the system is full and the user should try again later.

Medium-Term Scheduling

Medium-term scheduling is part of the swapping function. The issues involved are discussed in Chapters 3 and 5. Typically, the swapping-in decision is based on the need to manage the degree of multiprogramming. On a system that does not use virtual memory, memory management is also an issue. Thus, the swapping-in decision will consider the memory requirements of the swapped-out processes.

Short-Term Scheduling

The long-term scheduler executes relatively infrequently and makes the coarse-grained decision of whether or not to take on a new process, and which one to take. The medium-term scheduler is executed somewhat more frequently to make a swapping decision. The short-term scheduler, also known as the *dispatcher*, executes most frequently and makes the fine-grained decision of which process to execute next.

The short-term scheduler is invoked whenever an event occurs that may lead to the suspension of the current process or that may provide an opportunity to preempt to the currently running process in favor of another. Examples of such events include the following:

- Clock interrupts
- I/O interrupts
- Operating-system calls
- Signals

---

[1] A process is regarded as processor bound if it mainly performs computational work and occasionally uses I/O devices. A process is regarded as I/O bound if it spends more time in using I/O devices than using the processor.

6.2

SCHEDULING ALGORITHMS

Short-Term Scheduling Criteria

The main objective of short-term scheduling is to allocate processor time in such a way as to optimize one or more aspects of system behavior. Generally, a set of criteria is established against which various scheduling policies may be evaluated.

The commonly used criteria can be categorized along two dimensions. First, we can make a distinction between user-oriented and system-oriented criteria. **User-oriented** criteria relate to the behavior of the system as perceived by the individual user or process. An example is response time in an interactive system. *Response time* is the elapsed time between the submission of a request until the response begins to appear as output. This quantity is visible to the user and is naturally of interest to the user. We would like a scheduling policy that provides "good" service to various users. In the case of response time, a threshold may be defined of, say, 2 sec. Then a goal of the scheduling mechanism should be to maximize the number of users who experience an average response time of 2 sec or less.

Other criteria are **system-oriented**. That is, the focus is on effective and efficient use of the processor. An example is *throughput*, which is the rate at which processes are completed. Throughput is certainly a worthwhile measure of system performance and one that we would like to maximize. However, it focuses on system performance rather than on service provided to the user. Thus, it is of concern to a system administrator but not to the user population.

Whereas user-oriented criteria are important on virtually all systems, system-oriented criteria are generally of minor importance on single-user systems. On a single-user system, it probably is not important to achieve high use of the processor or high throughput so long as the responsiveness of the system to user applications is acceptable.

Other dimensions along which criteria can be classified are those that are performance-related and those that are not directly performance-related. **Performance-related** criteria are quantitative and generally can be readily measured. Examples include response time and throughput. Criteria that are **not performance related** are either qualitative in nature or cannot readily be measured and analyzed. An example of such a criterion is predictability. We would like for the service provided to users to exhibit the same characteristics over time, independent of other work being performed by the system. To some extent, this criterion can be measured by calculating variances as a function of workload. However, this method is not nearly so straightforward as measuring throughput or response time as a function of workload.

Table 6.2 summarizes key scheduling criteria. These are interdependent, and it is impossible to optimize all of them simultaneously. For example, providing

TABLE 6.2   Scheduling Criteria

User-Oriented, Performance-Related Criteria

Response time
For an interactive process, this is the interval of time from the submission of a request until the response begins to be received. Often a process can begin producing some output to the user while continuing to process the request. Thus, this is a better measure than turnaround time from the user's point of view. The scheduling discipline should attempt to achieve low response time and to maximize the number of interactive users receiving acceptable response time.

Turnaround time
This is the interval of time between the submission of a process and its completion. Includes actual execution time plus time spent waiting for resources, including the processor. This is an appropriate measure for a batch job.

Deadlines
When process completion deadlines can be specified, the scheduling discipline should subordinate other goals to that of maximizing the percentage of deadlines met.

User-Oriented, Other Criteria

Predictability
A given job should run in about the same amount of time and at about the same cost regardless of the load on the system. A wide variation in response time or turnaround time is distracting to users. It may signal a wide swing in system workloads or the need for system tuning to cure instabilities.

System-Oriented, Performance-Related Criteria

Throughput
The scheduling policy should attempt to maximize the number of processes completed per unit of time. This is a measure of how much work is being performed. This clearly depends on the average length of a process, but is also influenced by the scheduling policy, which may affect utilization.

Processor Utilization
This is the percentage of time that the processor is busy. For an expensive shared system, this is a significant criterion. In single-user systems and in some other systems, such as real-time systems, this criterion is less important than some of the others.

System-Oriented, Other Criteria

Fairness
In the absence of guidance from the user or other system-supplied guidance, processes should be treated the same, and no process should suffer starvation.

Enforcing Priorities
When processes are assigned priorities, the scheduling policy should favor higher-priority processes.

Balancing Resources
The scheduling policy should keep the resources of the system busy. Processes that will underuse stressed resources should be favored. This criterion also involves medium-term and long-term scheduling.

good response time may require a scheduling algorithm that switches between processes frequently, thus increasing the overhead of the system and reducing throughput. Thus, the design of a scheduling policy involves compromising among competing requirements; the relative weights given the various requirements will depend on the nature and use of the system.

A final point: In most interactive operating systems, whether single-user or time-shared, adequate response time is the critical requirement. Because of the importance of this requirement and because the definition of adequacy will vary from one application to another, the topic is explored further in an appendix to this chapter.

Let us now examine some alternative scheduling policies. For the remainder of this section, we will assume that there is only a single processor.

The Use of Priorities

One important aspect of scheduling is the use of priorities. In many systems, each process is assigned a priority, and the scheduler will always choose a process of higher priority over one of lower priority.

Figure 6.4 illustrates the use of priorities. For clarity, the queuing diagram is simplified, ignoring the existence of multiple blocked queues and of suspended states (compare with Figure 3.6a). Instead of a single Ready queue, we provide

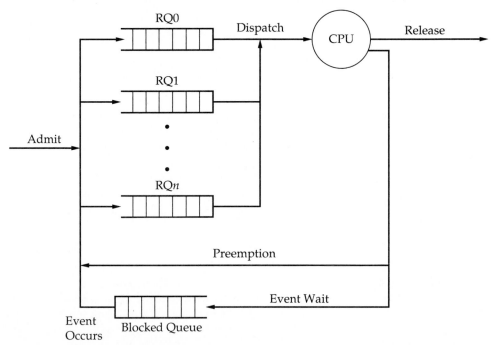

FIGURE 6.4 Priority scheduling

a set of queues in descending order of priority: RQ0, RQ2, . . . RQn, with priority[RQi] > priority[RQj] for $i < j$. When a scheduling selection is to be made, the scheduler will start at the highest priority Ready queue (RQ0). If there are one or more processes in the queue, a process is selected using some scheduling policy. If RQ0 is empty, then RQ1 is examined, and so on.

One problem with a pure priority scheduling scheme is that lower-priority processes may suffer starvation. This problem will happen if there is always a steady supply of higher-priority ready processes. To overcome this problem, the priority of a process can change with its age or execution history. We give one example of this later on.

Alternative Scheduling Policies

Table 6.3 presents some summary information about the various scheduling policies that are examined in this subsection. The first two characteristics are based on the approach suggested in [RUSC77], which classifies scheduling policies in terms of selection function and decision mode. The **selection function** determines which process, among ready processes, is selected next for execution. The function may be based on priority, resource requirements, or on the execution characteristics of the process. In the latter case, the following three quantities are significant:

w = time spent in system so far, waiting and executing
e = time spent in execution so far
s = total service time required by the process, including e

For example a selection function $f(w) = w$ indicates a first-in, first-out (FIFO) discipline.

The **decision mode** specifies the instants in time at which the selection function is exercised. There are two general categories:

• *Nonpreemptive:* In this case, once a process is in the running state, it continues to execute until it terminates or blocks itself to wait for I/O or by requesting some operating-system service.
• *Preemptive:* The currently running process may be interrupted and moved to the Ready state by the operating system. The decision to preempt may be performed when a new process arrives, when an interrupt occurs that places a blocked process in the Ready state, or periodically on the basis of a clock interrupt.

Preemptive policies incur greater overhead than nonpreemptive ones but may provide better service to the total population of processes because they prevent any one process from monopolizing the processor for very long. In addition, the cost of preemption may be kept relatively low by using efficient context-switching mechanisms (as much help from hardware as possible) and by providing a large main memory to keep a high percentage of programs in main memory.

TABLE 6.3 Characteristics of Various Scheduling Policies

	FCFS	Round Robin	SPN	SRT	HRRN	Feedback
Selection function	max [w]	constant	min [s]	min [$s - e$]	$\max\left(\dfrac{w + s}{s}\right)$	(see text)
Decision mode	Nonpreemptive	Preemptive (at time quantum)	Nonpreemptive	Preemptive (at arrival)	Nonpreemptive	Preemptive (at time quantum)
Throughput	Not emphasized	May be low if quantum is too small	High	High	High	Not emphasized
Response time	May be high, especially if there is a large variance in process execution times	Provides good response time for short processes	Provides good response time for short processes	Provides good response time	Provides good response time	Not emphasized
Overhead	Minimum	Low	Can be high	Can be high	Can be high	Can be high
Effect on processes	Penalizes short processes; penalizes I/O-bound processes	Fair treatment	Penalizes long processes	Penalizes long processes	Good balance	May favor I/O-bound processes
Starvation	No	No	Possible	Possible	No	Possible

w = time spent in system so far, waiting and executing
e = time spent in execution so far
s = total service time required by the process, including e

As we describe the various scheduling policies, we will use the following set of processes as a running example:

Process	Arrival Time	Service Time
1	0	3
2	2	6
3	4	4
4	6	5
5	8	2

We can think of these processes as batch jobs, with the service time being the total execution time required. Alternatively, we can consider them to be ongoing processes that require alternate use of the processor and I/O in a repetitive fashion. In this latter case, the service times represent the processor time required in one cycle. In either case, in terms of the queuing model (see Appendix 6A), this quantity corresponds to the service time.

First-Come, First-Served

The simplest scheduling policy is first-come, first-served (FCFS), or first-in, first-out (FIFO). As each process becomes ready, it joins the Ready queue. When the current running process ceases to execute, the oldest process in the Ready queue is selected for running.

Figure 6.5 shows the execution pattern for our example for one cycle, and Table 6.4 provides some key results. First, the finish time of each process is determined. From it, we can determine the turnaround time. In terms of the queuing model, the turnaround time is the queuing time, or total time, that the item spends in the system (waiting time plus service time). A more useful figure is the normalized turnaround time, which is the ratio of turnaround time to service time. This value indicates the relative delay experienced by a process. Typically, the longer the process execution time, the greater the absolute amount of delay that can be tolerated. The minimum possible value for this ratio is 1.0; increasing values correspond to a decreasing level of service.

FCFS performs much better for long processes than short ones. Consider the following example, based on one in [FINK88]:

Process	Arrival Time	Service Time (T_s)	Start Time	Finish Time	Turn-around Time (T_q)	T_q/T_s
A	0	1	0	1	1	1
B	1	100	1	101	100	1
C	2	1	101	102	100	100
D	3	100	102	202	199	1.99
Mean					100	26

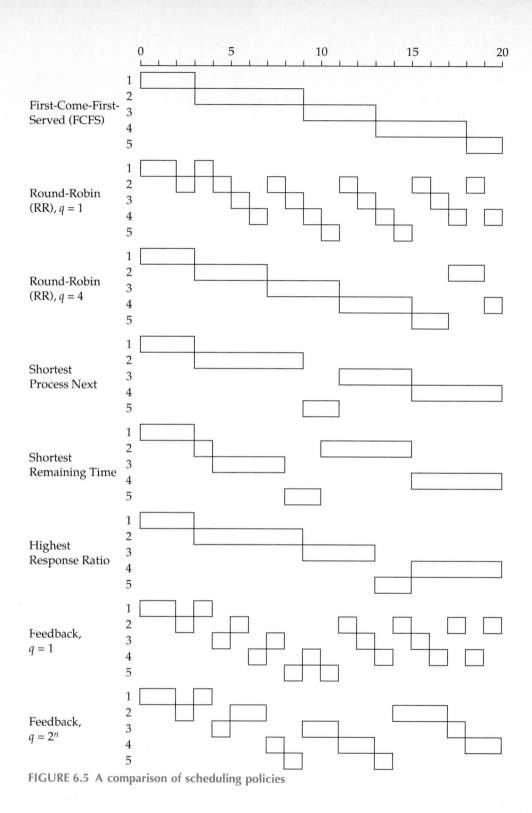

FIGURE 6.5 A comparison of scheduling policies

TABLE 6.4   A Comparison of Scheduling Policies

							Mean
	Process	1	2	3	4	5	
	Arrival Time	0	2	4	6	8	
	Service Time (Ts)	3	6	4	5	2	
FCFS	Finish Time	3	9	13	18	20	
	Turnaround time (Tq)	3	7	9	12	12	8.60
	Tq/Ts	1.00	1.17	2.25	2.40	6.00	2.56
RR q = 1	Finish Time	4	19	17	20	15	
	Turnaround time (Tq)	4	17	13	14	7	11.00
	Tq/Ts	1.33	2.83	3.25	2.80	3.50	2.74
RR q = 4	Finish Time	3	19	11	20	17	
	Turnaround time (Tq)	3	17	7	14	9	10.00
	Tq/Ts	1.00	2.83	1.75	2.80	4.50	2.58
SPN	Finish Time	3	9	15	20	11	
	Turnaround time (Tq)	3	7	11	14	3	7.60
	Tq/Ts	1.00	1.17	2.75	2.80	1.50	1.84
SRT	Finish Time	3	15	8	20	10	
	Turnaround time (Tq)	3	13	4	14	2	7.20
	Tq/Ts	1.00	2.17	1.00	2.80	1.00	1.59
HRRN	Finish Time	3	9	13	15	20	
	Turnaround time (Tq)	3	7	9	9	12	8.00
	Tq/Ts	1.00	1.17	2.25	1.80	6.00	2.44
FB q = 1	Finish Time	4	20	16	19	11	
	Turnaround time (Tq)	4	18	12	13	3	10.00
	Tq/Ts	1.33	3.00	3.00	2.60	1.50	2.29
FB q = 2**n	Finish Time	4	17	18	20	14	
	Turnaround time (Tq)	4	15	14	14	6	10.60
	Tq/Ts	1.33	2.50	3.50	2.80	3.00	2.63

The normalized waiting time for process C is intolerable: The total time that it is in the system is 100 times the required processing time. Such a long wait will happen whenever a short process arrives just behind a long process. On the other hand, even in this extreme example, long processes do not fare poorly. Process D has a turnaround time that is almost double that of C, but its normalized waiting time is under 2.0.

Another difficulty with FCFS is that it tends to favor CPU-bound processes over I/O-bound processes. Consider that there is a collection of processes, one of which mostly uses the CPU (CPU-bound) and a number of which favor I/O (I/O-bound). When a CPU-bound process is running, all the I/O-bound processes must wait. Some of these may be in I/O queues (blocked state) but may move back to the Ready queue while the CPU-bound process is executing. At this point, most or all of the I/O devices may be idle even though there is potential work for them to do. When the currently running process leaves the

Running state, the Ready I/O-bound processes quickly move through the Running state and become blocked on I/O events. If the CPU-bound process is also blocked, the processor becomes idle. Thus, FCFS may result in inefficient use of both the processor and the I/O devices.

FCFS is not an attractive alternative on its own for a single-processor system. However, it is often combined with a priority scheme to provide an effective scheduler. Thus, the scheduler may maintain a number of queues, one for each priority level, and dispatch within each queue on a first-come, first-served basis within each queue. One example of such a system is discussed later in the subsection "Feedback Scheduling."

Round-Robin

A straightforward way to reduce the penalty that short jobs suffer with FCFS is to use preemption based on a clock. The simplest such policy is the round-robin. A clock interrupt is generated at periodic intervals. When the interrupt occurs, the currently running process is placed in the Ready queue and the next ready job is selected on an FCFS basis. This technique is also known as **time-slicing** because each process is given a slice of time before being preempted.

With the round-robin policy, the principal design issue is the length of the time quantum, or slice, to be used. If the quantum is very short, then short processes will move through the system relatively quickly. On the other hand, there is processing overhead involved in handling the clock interrupt and performing the scheduling and dispatching function. Thus, very short time quanta should be avoided. One useful guide is that the time quantum should be slightly greater than the time required for a typical interaction. If it is less, then most processes will require at least two time quanta. Figure 6.6 illustrates the effect this requirement has on response time. In the limiting case of a time quantum that is longer than the longest-running process, the round-robin degenerates to FCFS.

Figure 6.5 and Table 6.4 show the results for our example using time quanta of 1 and 4 time units respectively. Note that process 5, which is the shortest job, enjoys significant improvement in both cases. Figure 6.7 shows the results as a function of the size of the time quantum. In this particular case, the size of the time quantum has little impact. However, in general, care must be taken in choosing its value.

The round-robin is particularly effective in a general-purpose time-sharing system or transaction-processing system. One drawback to round-robin is its relative treatment of processor-bound and I/O-bound processes. Generally, an I/O-bound process has a shorter processor burst (amount of time spent executing between I/O operations) than a processor-bound process. If there is a mix of processor-bound and I/O-bound processes, then the following will happen: An I/O-bound process uses a processor for a short period and then is blocked for I/O; it waits for the I/O operation to complete and then joins the Ready

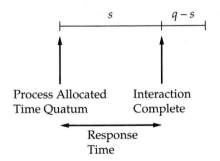

(a) Time quantum greater than typical interaction

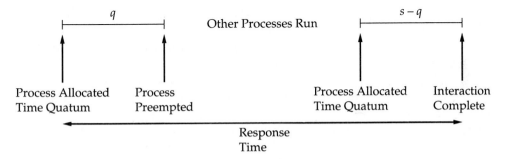

(b) Time quantum less than typical interaction

FIGURE 6.6 Effect of size of preemption time quantum

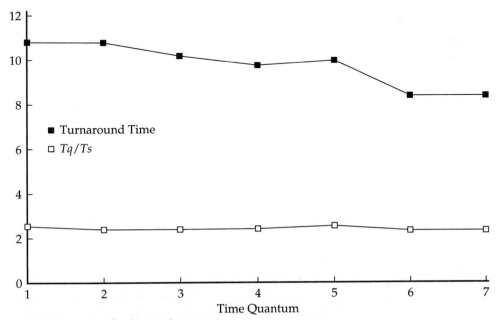

FIGURE 6.7 Round robin performance

queue. On the other hand, a processor-bound process generally uses a complete time quantum when executing and immediately returns to the Ready queue. Thus, processor-bound processes tend to receive an unfair portion of processor time, which results in poor performance of I/O-bound processes, poor use of I/O devices, and an increase in the variance of response time.

[HALD91] suggests a refinement to round-robin that he refers to as a virtual round-robin (VRR) and that avoids this unfairness. Figure 6.8 illustrates the scheme. New processes arrive and join the Ready queue, which is managed on an FCFS basis. When a running process times out, it is returned to the Ready queue. When a process is blocked for I/O, it joins an I/O queue. So far, this is as usual. The new feature is an FCFS auxiliary queue to which processes are moved after being released from an I/O wait. When a dispatching decision is to be made, processes in the auxiliary queue get preference over those in the main Ready queue. When a process is dispatched from the auxiliary queue, it runs no longer than a time equal to the basic time quantum minus the total time spent running since it was last selected from the main Ready queue. Performance studies by the authors indicate that this approach is indeed superior to round-robin in terms of fairness.

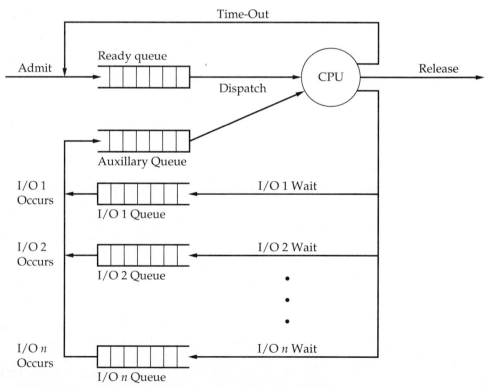

FIGURE 6.8 Queuing diagram for virtual round robin scheduler

Shortest Process Next

Another approach to reducing the bias in favor of long processes inherent in FCFS is the shortest process next (SPN) policy, which is a nonpreemptive policy in which the process with the shortest expected processing time is selected next. Thus, a short process will jump to the head of the queue past longer jobs.

Figure 6.5 and Table 6.4 show the results for our example. Note that process 5 receives service much earlier than under FCFS. Overall performance is also significantly improved in terms of response time. However, the variability of response times is increased, especially for longer processes, and thus predictability is reduced.

One difficulty with the SPN policy is the need to know or at least estimate the required processing time of each process. For batch jobs, the system may require the programmer to estimate the value and supply it to the operating system. If the programmer's estimate is substantially under the actual running time, the system may abort the job. In a production environment, the same jobs run frequently and statistics may be gathered. For interactive processes, the operating system may keep a running average of each burst for each process. The simplest calculation would be the following:

$$S_{n+1} = \frac{1}{n} \sum_{i=0}^{n} T_i \tag{1}$$

where

T_i = processor execution time for the ith instance of this process (total
      execution time for batch job; processor burst time for interactive job)
S_i = predicted value for the ith instance
S_0 = predicted value for first instance; not calculated

To avoid recalculating the entire summation each time, we can rewrite equation (1) as:

$$S_{n+1} = \frac{1}{n} T_n + \frac{n-1}{n} S_n \tag{2}$$

Note that this formulation gives equal weight to each instance. Typically, we would like to give greater weight to more recent instances because they are more likely to reflect future behavior. Thus, a common technique for predicting a future value on the basis of a time series of past values is to use an *exponential average*:

$$S_{n+1} = \alpha T_n + (1 - \alpha)S_n \tag{3}$$

Compare with equation (2). By using a constant value of α, independent of the number of past observations, we have a circumstance in which all past values are considered, but the more distant ones have less weight. To see this more clearly, consider the following expansion of equation (3):

$$S_{n+1} = \alpha T_n + (1 - \alpha)\alpha T_{n-1} + \ldots + (1 - \alpha)^i T_{n-i} + \ldots + (1 - \alpha)^n S_0 \tag{4}$$

Because both α and $(1 - \alpha)$ are less than 1, each successive term in the preceding equation is smaller. The size of the coefficient as a function of its position in the expansion is shown in Figure 6.9. Figure 6.10 compares simple averaging with exponential averaging (using two values of α). In both cases, we start out with an estimate of $S_0 = 0$, which gives greater priority to new processes. Note that exponential averaging tracks changes in process behavior faster than does simple averaging.

A risk in using SPN is the possibility of starvation for longer processes as long as there is a steady supply of shorter processes. On the other hand, although SPN reduces the bias in favor of longer jobs, it still is not desirable for a time-sharing or transaction-processing environment because of the lack of preemption. Looking back at our worst-case analysis described in the discussion of FCFS, processes A, B, C, and D will still execute in the same order, heavily penalizing the short process C.

Shortest Remaining Time

The policy of the shortest remaining time (SRT) is a preemptive version of SPN in which the scheduler always chooses the process that has the shortest expected remaining processing time. When a new process joins the Ready queue, it may in fact have a shorter remaining time than the currently running process.

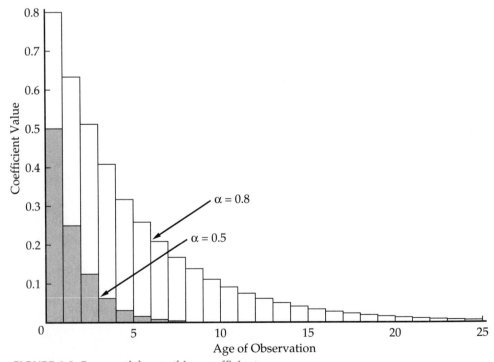

FIGURE 6.9 Exponential smoothing coefficients

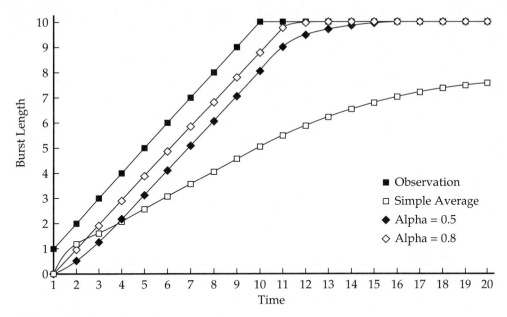

(a) Increasing Function

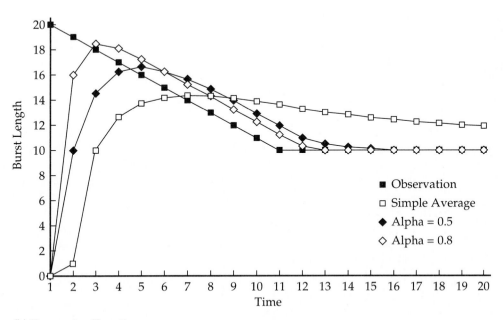

(b) Decreasing Function

FIGURE 6.10 Use of exponential averaging

Accordingly, the scheduler may preempt whenever a new process becomes ready. As with SPN, the scheduler must have an estimate of processing time to perform the selection function, and there is a risk of starvation of longer processes.

SRT does not have the bias in favor of long processes found in FCFS. Unlike round-robin, no additional interrupts are generated and overhead is therefore reduced. On the other hand, elapsed service times must be recorded, which contributes to overhead. SRT should also give superior turnaround time performance to SPN because a short job is given immediate preference to a running longer job.

Note that in our example, the three shortest processes all receive immediate service, yielding a normalized turnaround time for each of 1.0.

Highest Response Ratio Next

In Table 6.4, we have used the normalized turnaround time, which is the ratio of turnaround time to actual service time, as a figure of merit. For each individual process, we would like to minimize this ratio, and we would like to minimize the average value over all processes. Although this is an *a posteriori* measure, we can approximate it with an *a priori* measure as a selection criterion in a nonpreemptive scheduler. Specifically, consider the following response ratio (RR):

$$\text{RR} = \frac{w + s}{s}$$

where

w = time spent waiting for the processor
s = expected service time

If the process with this value is dispatched immediately, the RR is equal to the normalized turnaround time. Note that the minimum value of RR is 1.0, which occurs when a process first enters the system.

Thus, our scheduling rule becomes: When the current process completes or is blocked, choose the ready process with the greatest value of RR. This approach is attractive because it accounts for the age of the process. Although shorter jobs are favored (a smaller denominator yields a larger ratio), aging without service increases the ratio so that a longer process will eventually get past competing shorter jobs.

As with SRT and SPN, the expected service time must be estimated before using the technique of highest response ratio next (HRRN).

Feedback

If we have no indication of the relative length of various processes, then none of SPN, SRT, and HRRN can be used. Another way of establishing a preference

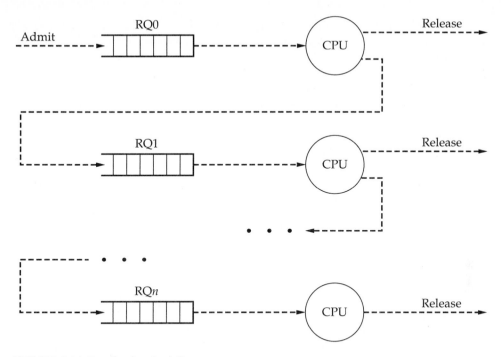

FIGURE 6.11 Feedback scheduling

for shorter jobs is to penalize jobs that have been running longer. In other words, if we cannot focus on the time remaining to execute, let us focus on the time spent in execution so far.

The way to do this is as follows. Scheduling is done on a preemptive basis, and a dynamic priority mechanism is used. When a process first enters the system, it is placed in RQ0 (see Figure 6.4). When it returns to the Ready state after its first execution, it is placed in RQ1. After each subsequent execution, it is demoted to the next lower-priority queue. A shorter process will complete quickly, without migrating very far down the hierarchy of Ready queues. A longer process will gradually drift downward. Thus, newer, shorter processes are favored over older, longer processes. Within each queue, except the lowest-priority queue, a simple FCFS mechanism is used. Once in the lowest-priority queue, a process cannot go lower but is returned to this queue repeatedly until it completes execution. Thus, this queue is treated in round-robin fashion.

Figure 6.11 illustrates the feedback scheduling mechanism by showing the path that a process follows through the various queues.[2] This approach is known as *multilevel feedback*, meaning that the operating system allocates the processor to a process, and when the process blocks or is preempted, feeds it back into one of several priority queues.

---

[2]Dotted lines are used to emphasize that this is a time sequence diagram rather than a static depiction of possible transitions, such as Figure 6.4.

There are a number of variations on this scheme. A simple version is to perform preemption in the same fashion as for round-robin: at periodic intervals. Our example shows this (Figure 6.5 and Table 6.4) for a quantum of one time unit. Note that in this case, the behavior is the similar to round robin with a time quantum of one.

One problem with the simple scheme just outlined is that the turnaround time of longer processes can stretch out alarmingly. Indeed, it is possible for starvation to occur if new jobs are regularly entering the system. To compensate for this, we can vary the preemption times according to the queue: A process schedule from RQ1 is allowed to execute for 1 time unit and then is preempted; a process scheduled from RQ2 is allowed to execute 2 time units; and so on. In general, a process scheduled from RQ_i is allowed to execute 2^i time units before preemption. This scheme is illustrated in Figure 6.5 and Table 6.4.

Even with the allowance for greater time allocation at lower priority, a longer process may still suffer starvation. A possible remedy is to promote a process to a higher-priority queue after it spends a certain amount of time waiting for service in its current queue.

Performance Comparison

Clearly, the performance of various scheduling policies is a critical factor in the choice of a scheduling policy. However, it is impossible to make definitive comparisons because relative performance will depend on a variety of factors, including the probability distribution of service times of the various processes, the efficiency of the scheduling and context switching mechanisms, and the nature of the I/O demand and the performance of the I/O subsystem. Nevertheless, we attempt in what follows to draw some general conclusions.

Queueing Analysis

In this section, we make use of basic queuing formulas, making the common assumptions of Poisson arrivals and exponential service times. A summary of these concepts is found in Appendix A.

First, we make the observation that any scheduling discipline that chooses the next item to be served independent of service time obeys the following relationship:

$$\frac{t_q}{s} = \frac{1}{1 - \rho}$$

where

t_q = turnaround time; total time in system, waiting plus execution
s = average service time; average time spent in running state
ρ = processor use

In particular, a priority-based scheduler, in which the priority of each process is assigned independent of expected service time, provides the same average turnaround time and average normalized turnaround time as a simple FCFS discipline. Furthermore, the presence or absence of preemption makes no differences in these averages.

With the exception of round-robin and FCFS, the various scheduling disciplines considered so far do make selections on the basis of expected service time. Unfortunately, it turns out to be quite difficult to develop closed analytic models of these disciplines. However, we can get an idea of the relative performance of such scheduling algorithms compared to FCFS by considering priority scheduling in which priority is based on service time.

If scheduling is done on the basis of priority and if processes are assigned to a priority class on the basis of service time, then differences do emerge. Table 6.5 shows the formulas that result when we assume two priority classes, with different service times for each class. These results can be generalized to any number of priority classes (e.g., see [MART72] for a summary of these formulas). Note that the formulas differ for nonpreemptive versus preemptive scheduling. In the latter case, it is assumed that a lower-priority process is immediately interrupted when a higher-priority process becomes ready.

TABLE 6.5   Formulas for Single-Server Queues with Two Priority Categories

Assumptions: 1. Poisson arrival rate.
2. Priority j items are serviced before priority $(j + 1)$ items.
3. No item is interrupted while being served.
4. First-in, first-out dispatching for items of equal priority.
5. No items leave the queue (lost calls delayed).

(a) General Formulas

$$\lambda = \lambda_1 + \lambda_2$$

$$\rho_1 = \lambda_1 s_1; \; \rho_2 = \lambda_2 s_2$$

$$\rho = \rho_1 + \rho_2$$

$$s = \frac{\lambda_1}{\lambda} s_1 + \frac{\lambda_2}{\lambda} s_2$$

$$t_q = \frac{\lambda_1}{\lambda} t_{q1} + \frac{\lambda_2}{\lambda} t_{q2}$$

(b) No interrupts; exponential service times

$$t_{q1} = 1 + \frac{\rho_1 t_{s1} + \rho_2 t_{s2}}{1 - \rho_1}$$

$$t_{q2} = 1 + \frac{t_{q1} - 1}{1 - \rho}$$

(c) Preemptive-resume queuing discipline; exponential service times

$$t_{q1} = 1 + \frac{\rho_1 t_{s1}}{1 - \rho_1}$$

$$t_{q2} = 1 + \frac{1}{1 - \rho_1}\left(\rho_1 t_{s1} + \frac{\rho t_s}{1 - \rho}\right)$$

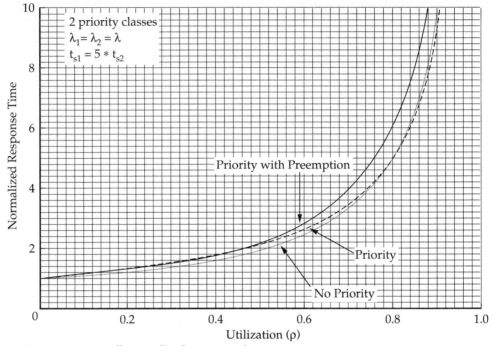

FIGURE 6.12 Overall normalized response times

As an example, let us consider the case of two priority classes, with an equal number of process arrivals in each class, and with the average service time for the lower priority class being five times that of the upper-priority class. Thus, we wish to give preference to shorter processes. Figure 6.12 shows the overall result. By giving preference to shorter jobs, we improve the average normalized turnaround time. As might be expected, the improvement is greatest with the use of preemption. Notice, however, that overall performance is not much affected.

However, significant differences emerge when we consider the two priority classes separately. Figure 6.13 shows the results for the higher-priority, shorter processes. For comparison, the upper line on the graph assumes that priorities are not used but that we are simply looking at the relative performance of that half of all processes that have the shorter processing time. The other two lines assume that these processes are assigned a higher priority. When the system is run using priority scheduling without preemption, the improvements are significant. They are even more significant when preemption is used.

Figure 6.14 shows the same analysis for the lower-priority, longer processes. As expected, such processes suffer a performance degradation under priority scheduling.

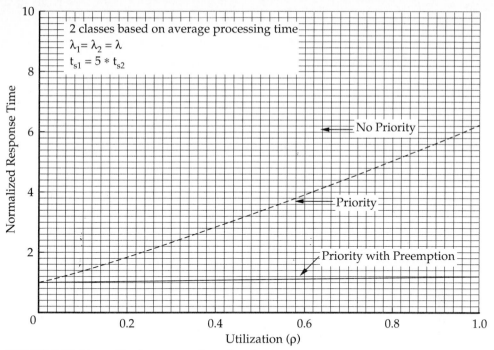

FIGURE 6.13 Normalized response times for shorter processes

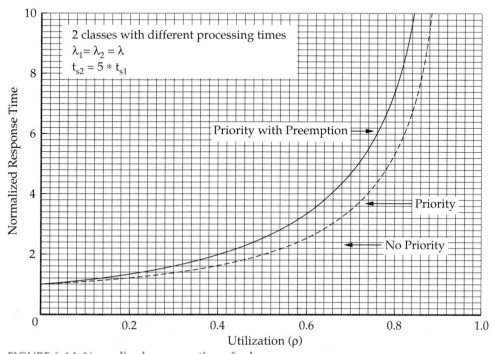

FIGURE 6.14 Normalized response times for longer processes

Simulation Modeling

Some of the difficulties of analytic modeling are overcome by using discrete-event simulation, which allows a wide range of policies to be modeled. The disadvantage of simulation is that the results for a given run apply to only that particular collection of processes under that particular set of assumptions. Nevertheless, useful insights can be gained.

The results of one such study are reported in [FINK88]. The simulation involved 50,000 processes with an arrival rate of $\lambda = 0.8$ and an average service time of $s = 1$. Thus, the assumption is that the processor use is $\rho = \lambda s = 0.8$. Note, therefore, that we are measuring only one point of use.

To present the results, processes are grouped into service-time percentiles, each of which has 500 processes. Thus, the 500 processes with the shortest service time are in the first percentile; with these eliminated, the 500 remaining processes with the shortest service time are in the second percentile; and so on. This grouping allows us to view the effect of various policies on processes as a function of the length of the process.

Figure 6.15 shows the normalized turnaround time, and Figure 6.16 shows the average waiting time. Looking at the turnaround time, we can see that the performance of FCFS is very unfavorable, with one-third of the processes having a normalized turnaround time greater than 10 times the service time. Furthermore, these are the shortest processes. On the other hand, the absolute waiting

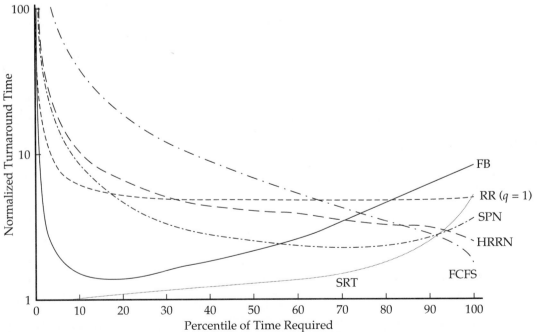

FIGURE 6.15 Simulation results for normalized turnaround time

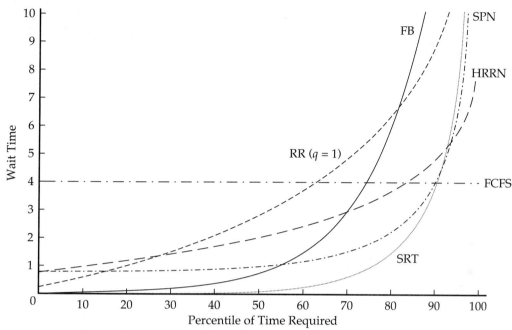

FIGURE 6.16 Simulation results for waiting time

time is uniform, as is to be expected, because scheduling is independent of service time. The figures show round-robin using a quantum of 1 time unit. Except for the shortest processes, which execute in less than 1 quantum, the RR yields a normalized turnaround time of about 5 for all processes, treating all fairly. Shortest process next (SPN) performs better than round-robin, except for the shortest processes. Shortest remaining time (SRT), the preemptive version of SPN, performs better than SPN except for the longest 7% of all processes. We have seen that among nonpreemptive policies FCFS favors long processes and SPN favors short ones. Highest response ratio next (HRRN) is intended to be a compromise between these two effects, and this is indeed confirmed in the figures. Finally, the figure shows feedback scheduling with a fixed, uniform quantum in each priority queue. As expected, feedback (FB) performs quite well for short processes.

Fair-Share Scheduling

All the scheduling algorithms discussed so far treat the collection of Ready processes as a single pool of processes from which to select the next Running process. This pool may be broken down by priority but is otherwise homogeneous.

However, in a multiuser system, if individual user applications or jobs may be organized as multiple processes (or threads), then there is a structure to the collection of processes that is not recognized by a traditional scheduler. From the user's point of view, the concern is not how a particular process performs but, rather, how the user's set of processes that constitute a single application perform. Thus, it would be attractive to make scheduling decisions on the basis of these process groupings. This approach is generally known as *fair-share scheduling* (FSS). Furthermore, the concept can be extended to groups of users, even if each user is represented by a single process. For example, in a time-sharing system, we might wish to consider all the users from a given department to be members of the same group. Scheduling decisions could then be made that attempt to give each group similar service. Thus, if a large number of people from one department log on to the system, we would like to see response time degradation primarily affect members of that department rather than users from other departments.

The term **fair share** implies the scheduler's philosophy. Each user is assigned a weighting of some sort that defines that user's share of system resources as a fraction of the total usage of those resources. In particular, each user is assigned a share of the processor. Such a scheme should operate in a more or less linear fashion, so that if user A has twice the weighting of user B, then in the long run, user A should be able to do twice as much work as user B. The objective of a fair-share scheduler is to monitor usage so as to give fewer resources to users who have had more than their fair share and more to those who have had less than their fair share.

A number of proposals have been made for fair-share schedulers [HENR84, KAY88, LARM75, WOOD86]. In this section, we describe the scheme proposed in [HENR84] and implemented on a number of UNIX systems. FSS considers the execution history of a related group of processes, along with the individual execution history of each process in making scheduling decisions. The system divides the user community into a set of fair-share groups and allocates a fraction of the processor resource to each group. Thus, there might be four groups, each having 25% of the processor's use. In effect, each fair-share group is provided with a virtual system that runs proportionally slower than a full system.

Scheduling is done on the basis of priority, which takes into account the underlying priority of the process, its recent CPU usage, and the recent CPU usage of the group to which the process belongs. The higher the numerical value of the priority, the lower the priority. The following formulas apply for process j in group k:

$$P_j(i) = \text{Base}_j + \frac{\text{CPU}_j(i-1)}{2} + \frac{\text{GCPU}_k(i-1)}{4 \times W_k}$$

$$\text{CPU}_j(i) = \frac{U_j(i-1)}{2} + \frac{\text{CPU}_j(i-1)}{2}$$

$$\text{GCPU}_k(i) = \frac{\text{GU}_k(i-1)}{2} + \frac{\text{GCPU}_k(i-1)}{2}$$

where

Time	Proc A Priority	CPU	Group	:	Proc B Priority	CPU	Group	:	Proc C Priority	CPU	Group
0	60	0	0	:	60	0	0	:	60	0	0
		1	1	:				:			
		2	2	:				:			
		⋮	⋮	:				:			
		60	60	:				:			
1	90	30	30	:	60	0	0	:	60	0	0
				:		1	1	:			1
				:		2	2	:			2
				:		⋮	⋮	:			⋮
				:		60	60	:			60
2	74	15	15	:	90	30	30	:	75	0	30
		16	16	:				:			
		17	17	:				:			
		⋮	⋮	:				:			
		75	75	:				:			
3	96	37	37	:	74	15	15	:	67	0	15
				:			16	:		1	16
				:			17	:		2	17
				:			⋮	:		⋮	⋮
				:			75	:		60	75
4	78	18	18	:	81	7	37	:	93	30	37
		19	19	:				:			
		20	20	:				:			
		⋮	⋮	:				:			
		78	78	:				:			
5	98	39	39	:	70	3	18	:	76	15	18

Figure 6-17 Example of Fair Share Scheduler—Three Processes, Two Groups [BPCH86.]

$P_j(i)$ = Priority of process j at beginning of interval i

$Base_j$ = Base priority of process j

$U_j(i)$ = CPU use of process j in interval i

$GU_k(i)$ = Total CPU use of all processes in group k during interval i

$CPU_j(i)$ = Exponentially weighted average CPU use of process j through interval i

$GCPU_k(i)$ = Exponentially weighted average total CPU use of group k through interval i

W_k = Weighting assigned to group k, with the constraint that $0 \le Wk \le 1$ and $\sum_k W_k = 1$.

Each process is assigned a base priority that drops as the process uses the CPU and as the group to which the process belongs uses the CPU. In both cases, a running average of CPU use is kept by using an exponential average, with $\alpha = 0.5$. In the case of the group use, the average is normalized by dividing by the weight of that group. The greater the weight assigned to the group, the less its use affects its priority.

Figure 6.17 is an example in which process A is in one group and process B and process C are in a second group, with each group having a weighting of 0.5. Assume that all processes are CPU-bound and are usually ready to run. All processes have a base priority of 60. CPU use is measured as follows: The processor is interrupted 60 times per 1 sec; during each interrupt, the CPU usage field of the currently running process is incremented, as is the corresponding group CPU field. Once per second, priorities are recalculated.

In the figure, process A is scheduled first. At the end of 1 sec, it is preempted. Processes B and C now have the higher priority, and process B is scheduled. At the end of the second time unit, process A has the highest priority. Note that the pattern repeats: The kernel schedules the processes in order: A, B, A, C, A, B, and so on. Thus, 50% of the CPU is allocated to process A, which constitutes one group, and 50% to processes B and C, which constitute another group.

6.3

MULTIPROCESSOR SCHEDULING

When a computer system contains more than a single processor, several new issues are introduced into the design of the scheduling function. We begin with a brief overview of multiprocessors and then look at the rather different considerations when scheduling is done at the process level and the thread level.

We can classify multiprocessor systems as follows:

- *Loosely coupled multiprocessor:* Consists of a collection of relatively autonomous systems, each processor having its own main memory and I/O channels. We address this type of configuration in Chapter 9.
- *Functionally specialized processors:* Such as an I/O processor. In this case, there is a master, general-purpose processor; specialized processors are controlled by the master processor and provide services to it. Issues relating to I/O processors are addressed in Chapter 7.
- *Tightly coupled multiprocessing:* Consists of a set of processors that share a common main memory and are under the integrated control of an operating system.

Our concern in this section is with the last category and specifically with issues relating to scheduling.

The Evolution of Tightly Coupled Multiprocessors

Multiprocessor architecture has been around for many years. The first commercially available system was the Burroughs D825, available in 1960, which included up to four processors. Until recently, the main purpose of multiple processors was to provide improved performance and reliability for multiprogramming:

- *Performance:* A single multiprocessor running a multiprogramming operating system should offer improved performance over a comparable uniprocessor system and may be more cost effective than multiple uniprocessor systems.
- *Reliability:* In a tightly coupled multiprocessor, if the processors function as peers, the failure of a processor merely results in degraded performance rather than complete loss of service.

Although it was in principle possible to run applications that involved parallel processing on a multiprocessor, this mode of execution was not common. Rather, the emphasis was on providing a system that was logically equivalent to a multiprogrammed uniprocessor with improved performance and reliability. This type of system is still the dominant form for commercial multiprocessors.

In recent years, there has been increasing interest in developing applications that involve multiple processes or threads; we refer to such applications as **parallel applications**. One advantage of this approach, as we discussed in Chapter 3, is that the design of the software may be simplified compared to constructing the application as a sequential program. Another advantage is that, on a multiprocessor, it is possible to run portions of the application simultaneously on different processors to achieve improved performance. This use of multiprocessors considerably complicates the scheduling function, as we shall see.

Granularity

A good way of characterizing multiprocessors and placing them in context with other architectures is to consider the synchronization granularity, or frequency of synchronization, among processes in a system. We can distinguish five categories of parallelism that differ in the degree of granularity. These categories are summarized in Table 6.6, which is adapted from [GEHR87] and [WOOD89].

Independent Parallelism

With independent parallelism, there is no explicit synchronization among processes. Each represents a separate, independent application or job. A typical use of this type of parallelism is in a time sharing system. Each user is performing a particular application, such as word processing or using a spreadsheet. The multiprocessor provides the same service as a multiprogrammed uniprocessor. Since more than one processor is available, average response time to the users will be less.

TABLE 6.6   Synchronization Granularity and Processes

Grain Size	Description	Synchronization Interval (Instructions)
Fine	Parallelism inherent in a single instruction stream	<20
Medium	Parallel processing or multitasking within a single application	20–200
Coarse	Multiprocessing of concurrent processes in a multiprogramming environment	200–2000
Very Coarse	Distributed processing across network nodes to form a single computing environment	2000–1M
Independent	Multiple unrelated processes	(N/A)

It is possible to achieve a similar performance gain by providing each user with a personal computer or workstation. If any files or information are to be shared, then the individual systems must be hooked together into a distributed system supported by a network. This approach is examined in Chapter 9. On the other hand a single, multiprocessor shared system in many instances is more cost-effective than a distributed system, allowing economies of scale in disks and other peripherals.

Coarse-Grained and Very-Coarse-Grained Parallelism

With coarse-grained and very-coarse-grained parallelism, there is synchronization among processes but at a very gross level. This kind of situation is easily handled as a set of concurrent processes running on a multiprogrammed uniprocessor and can be supported on a multiprocessor with little or no change to user software.

A simple example of an application that can exploit the existence of a multiprocessor is given in [WOOD89]. The authors have developed a program that takes a specification of files needing recompilation to rebuild a piece of software and determines which of these compiles (usually all of them) can be run simultaneously. The program then spawns one process for each parallel compile. Woodbury et al. report that the speedup on a multiprocessor will actually exceed what would be expected by simply adding up the number of processors in use. This result is caused by synergies in the disk buffer caches (a topic explored in Chapter 7) and by the sharing of the compiler code, which is loaded into memory only once.

In general, any collection of concurrent processes that need to communicate or synchronize can benefit from the use of a multiprocessor architecture. In the case of very infrequent interaction among processes, a distributed system can provide good support. However, if the interaction is somewhat more frequent, then the overhead of communication across the network may negate some of the potential speedup. In that case, the multiprocessor organization provides the most effective support.

Medium-Grained Parallelism

We saw in Chapter 3 that a single application can be effectively implemented as a collection of threads within a single process. In this case, the potential parallelism of an application must be explicitly specified by the programmer. Typically, there will need to be rather a high degree of coordination and interaction among the threads of an application, leading to a medium-grain level of synchronization.

Whereas independent, very coarse-grained and coarse-grained parallelism can be supported on either a multiprogrammed uniprocessor or a multiprocessor with little or no impact on the scheduling function, we need to reexamine scheduling when dealing with the scheduling of threads. Because the various threads of an application interact so frequently, scheduling decisions concerning one thread may affect the performance of the entire application. We return to this issue later in this section.

Fine-Grained Parallelism

Fine-grained parallelism represents a much more complex use of parallelism than is found in the use of threads. Although much work has been done on highly parallel applications, this is so far a specialized and fragmented area, with many different approaches. A good survey is [ALMA89].

Design Issues

Three interrelated issues are related to the scheduling on a multiprocessor:

- The assignment of processes to processors
- The use of multiprogramming on individual processors
- The actual dispatching of a process

In looking at these three issues, it is important to keep in mind that the approach taken will depend in general on the degree of granularity of the applications and on the number of processors available.

Assignment of Processes to Processors

If we assume that the architecture of the multiprocessor is uniform, in the sense that no processor has a particular physical advantage with respect to access to main memory or to I/O devices, then the simplest approach is to treat the processors as a pooled resource and assign processes to processors on demand. The question then arises as to whether the assignment should be static or dynamic.

If a process is permanently assigned to one processor from activation until its completion, then a dedicated short-term queue is maintained for each processor. An advantage of this approach is that there may be less overhead in the scheduling function because the processor assignment is made once and for all.

Also, the use of dedicated processors allows a strategy known as *group* or *gang scheduling*, which is discussed later.

A disadvantage of static assignment is that one processor can be idle, with an empty queue, while another processor has a backlog. To prevent this situation, a common queue can be used. All processes go into one global queue and are scheduled to any available processor. Thus, over the life of a process, the process may be executed on different processors at different times. In a tightly coupled, shared-memory architecture, the context information for all processes will be available to all processors, and therefore the cost of scheduling a process will be independent of the identity of the processor on which it is scheduled.

Regardless of whether processes are dedicated to processors, some means is needed to assign processes to processors. Two approaches have been used: master/slave and peer. In master/slave architecture, key kernel functions of the operating system always run on a particular processor. The other processors may execute only user programs. The master is responsible for scheduling jobs. Once a process is active, if the slave needs service (e.g., an I/O call), it must send a request to the master and wait for the service to be performed. This approach is quite simple and requires little enhancement to a uniprocessor multiprogramming operating system. Conflict resolution is simplified because one processor has control of all memory and I/O resources. The disadvantages of this approach are two: (1) a failure of the master brings down the whole system, and (2) the master can become a performance bottleneck.

In peer architecture, the operating system can execute on any processor, and each processor does self-scheduling from the pool of available processes. This approach complicates the operating system. The operating system must ensure that two processors do not choose the same process and that the processes are not somehow lost from the queue. Techniques must be employed to resolve and synchronize competing claims to resources.

There are, of course, a spectrum of approaches between these two extremes. One can provide a subset of processors dedicated to kernel processing instead of just one. Another approach is to simply manage the difference between the needs of kernel processes and other processes on the basis of priority and execution history.

The Use of Multiprogramming on Individual Processors

When each process is statically assigned to a processor for the duration of its lifetime, a new question arises: Should that processor be multiprogrammed? Your first reaction may be to wonder why the question needs to be asked; it would appear particularly wasteful to tie a processor up with a single process when that process may frequently be blocked waiting for I/O or because of concurrency/synchronization considerations.

In the traditional multiprocessor, which is dealing with coarse-grained or independent synchronization granularity (see Table 6.6), it is clear that each individual processor should be able to switch among a number of processes to achieve high use and therefore better performance. However, when we deal with medium-grained applications running on a multiprocessor with many processors, the situation is less clear. When many processors are available, it is no longer paramount that every single processor be busy as much as possible. Rather, we are concerned to provide the best performance, on average, for the applications. An application that consists of a number of threads may run poorly unless all its threads are available to run simultaneously.

Process Dispatching

The final design issue related to multiprocessor scheduling is the actual selection of a process to run. We have seen that on a multiprogrammed uniprocessor the use of priorities or of sophisticated scheduling algorithms based on past usage may improve over a simple-minded FIFO strategy. When we look to multiprocessors, these complexities may be unnecessary or even counterproductive. In the case of traditional process scheduling, a simpler approach may be more effective and have less overhead. In recent developments in thread scheduling, new issues come into play that may be more important than priorities or execution histories. We address each of these topics in turn.

Process Scheduling

In most traditional multiprocessor systems, processes are not dedicated to processors. Rather, there is a single queue for all processors, or if some sort of priority scheme is used, there are multiple queues based on priority, all feeding in to the common pool of processors. In any case, we can view the system as being a multiserver queuing architecture.

Consider the case of a dual processor system in which each processor of the dual processor system has half the processing rate of the processor in the single processor system. [SAUE81] reports a queuing analysis that compares FCFS scheduling to round-robin and to shortest remaining time. In the case of round-robin, it is assumed that the time quantum is large compared to context-switching overhead and small compared to mean service time. The results depend critically on the variability that is seen in service times. A common measure of variability is the coefficient of variation, C_s, defined by

$$C_s = \frac{\sigma_s}{s}$$

where

σ_s = standard deviation of service time
s = mean service time

A ratio of 1 would correspond to an exponential service time. However, processor service time distributions are usually more variable than that; C_s values of 10 or more are not unusual.

Figure 6.18a compares round-robin throughput to FCFS throughput as a function of C_s. Note that the difference in scheduling algorithms is much smaller in the dual processor case. With two processors, a single process with long service time is much less disruptive in the FCFS case; other processes can use the other processor. Similar results are shown in Figure 6.18b.

The study in [SAUE81] repeated this analysis under a number of assumptions about degree of multiprogramming, mix of I/O-bound versus CPU-bound processes, and the use of priorities. The general conclusion is that the specific scheduling discipline is much less important with two processors than with one. It should be evident that this conclusion is made even stronger by increases in the number of processors. Thus, a simple FCFS discipline or the use of FCFS within a static priority scheme may suffice for a multiple-processor system.

Thread Scheduling

Threads have become increasingly common in new languages and operating systems. As we have seen, in the use of threads the concept of execution is separated from the rest of the definition of a process. An application can be implemented as a set of threads that cooperate and execute concurrently in the same address space.

On a uniprocessor, threads can be used as a program-structuring aid and to overlap I/O with processing. Because of the minimal penalty in doing a thread switch compared to a process switch, these benefits are realized at little cost. However, the full power of threads becomes evident in a multiprocessor system where threads can be used to exploit true parallelism in an application. If the various threads of an application are simultaneously run on separate processors, dramatic gains in performance are possible. However, it can be shown that for applications that require significant interaction among threads (medium-grained parallelism) small differences in thread management and scheduling can have a significant performance impact [ANDE89]. There is active research in the area of thread scheduling on multiprocessors. The discussion here provides an overview of key issues and approaches.

Among the many proposals for multiprocessor thread scheduling and processor assignment, the following four general approaches stand out:

- *Self-scheduling:* Processes are not assigned to a particular processor. A global queue of Ready threads is maintained, and each processor when idle selects a thread from the queue. This is sometimes called *load sharing* to distinguish it from load-balancing schemes in which work is allocated on a more permanent basis [FEIT90a].
- *Gang scheduling:* A set of related threads is scheduled to run on a set of processors at the same time, on a one-to-one basis.
- *Dedicated processor assignment:* This is the opposite of the self-scheduling approach and provides implicit scheduling defined by the assignment of threads to processors. For the duration of the program execution, each program is allocated a number of processors equal to the number of threads in the pro-

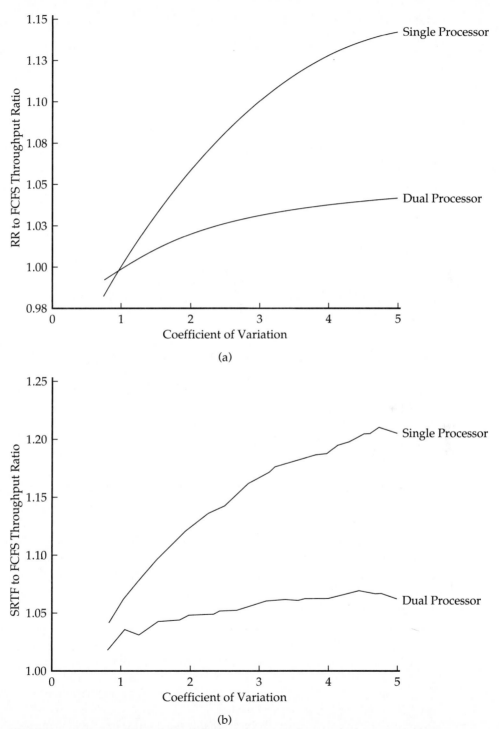

FIGURE 6.18 Comparison of scheduling performance for one and two processors

gram. When the program terminates, the processors return to the general pool for possible allocation to another program.

• *Dynamic scheduling:* The number of threads in a program can be altered during the course of execution.

Self-Scheduling

Self-scheduling is perhaps the simplest approach and the one that carries over most directly from a uniprocessor environment. It has the following several advantages:

• The load is distributed evenly across the processors, assuring that no processor is idle while work is available to do.
• No centralized scheduler is required. When a processor is available, the scheduling routine of the operating system is run on that processor to select the next thread.
• The global queue can be organized and accessed using any of the schemes discussed in Section 6.2, including priority-based schemes and schemes that consider execution history or anticipated processing demands,

[LEUT90] analyzes three different version of self-scheduling:

• *First-come, first-served (FCFS):* When a job arrives, each of its threads is placed consecutively at the end of the shared queue. When a processor becomes idle, it picks the next ready thread, which it executes until completion or blocking.
• *Smallest number of threads first:* The shared Ready queue is organized as a priority queue, with highest priority given to threads from jobs with the smallest number of unscheduled threads. Jobs of equal priority are ordered according to which job arrives first. As with FCFS, a scheduled thread is run to completion or blocking.
• *Preemptive smallest number of threads first:* Highest priority is given to jobs with the smallest number of incomplete threads. An arriving job with a smaller number of threads than an executing job will preempt threads belonging to the scheduled job.

Using simulation models, Leutenegger and Vernon report that, over a wide range of job characteristics, FCFS is superior to the other two policies. Furthermore, they find that some form of gang scheduling, discussed in the next subsection, is generally superior to self-scheduling.

Several disadvantages of self-scheduling are the following:

• The central queue occupies a region of memory that must be accessed in a manner that enforces mutual exclusion. Thus, it may become a bottleneck if many processors look for work at the same time. When there is only a small number of processors, this is unlikely to be a noticeable problem. However, when the multiprocessor consists of dozens or even hundreds of processors, the potential for bottleneck is real.
• Preempted threads are unlikely to resume execution on the same processor.

If each processor is equipped with a local cache, the caching becomes less efficient.

- If all threads are treated as a common pool of threads, it is unlikely that all the threads of a program will gain access to processors at the same time. If a high degree of coordination is required between the threads of a program, the process switches involved may seriously compromise performance.

Despite the potential disadvantages of self-scheduling, it is one of the most commonly used schemes in current multiprocessors.

A refinement of the self-scheduling technique is used in the Mach operating system [BLAC90, WEND89]. The operating system maintains a local run queue for each processor and a shared global run queue. The local run queue is used by threads that have been temporarily bound to a specific processor. A processor examines the local run queue first to give bound threads absolute preference over unbound threads. As an example of the use of bound threads, one or more processors could be dedicated to running processes that are part of the operating system. Another example: The threads of a particular application could be distributed among a number of processors; with the proper additional software, this strategy provides support for gang scheduling, which is discussed next.

Gang Scheduling

The concept of scheduling a set of processes simultaneously on a set of processors predates the use of threads. [JONE80] refers to the concept as *group scheduling* and cites the following benefits:

- If closely related processes execute in parallel, synchronization blocking may be reduced, less process switching may be necessary, and performance will increase.
- Scheduling overhead may be reduced because a single decision affects a number of processors and processes at one time.

On the Cm* multiprocessor, the term *coscheduling* is used [GEHR87]. Coscheduling is based on the concept of scheduling a related set of tasks, called a *task force*. The individual elements of a task force tend to be quite small and are hence close to the idea of a thread.

The term *gang scheduling* has been applied to the simultaneous scheduling of the threads that make up a single process [FEIT90b]. It is necessary for medium-grained to fine-grained parallel applications whose performance severely degrades when any part of the application is not running while other parts are ready to run. It is also beneficial for any parallel application, even one that is not quite so sensitive to performance. The need for gang scheduling is widely recognized, and implementations exist on a variety of multiprocessor operating systems.

One obvious way in which gang scheduling improves the performance of a single application is that process switches are minimized. Suppose one thread of a process is executing and reaches a point at which it must synchronize with

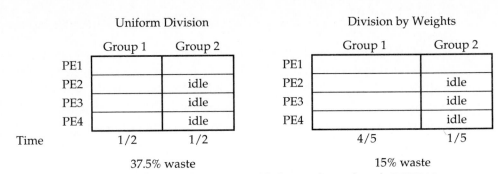

FIGURE 6.19 Example of scheduling groups with four and one threads [FEIT90]

another thread of the same process. If that other thread is not running but is in a ready queue, the first thread is hung up until a process switch can be made on some other processor to bring in the needed thread. In an application with tight coordination among threads, such switches dramatically reduce performance. The simultaneous scheduling of cooperating threads can also save time in resource allocation. For example, multiple gang-scheduled threads can access a file without the additional overhead of locking during a Seek, Read/Write operation.

The use of gang scheduling creates a requirement for processor allocation. One possibility is the following. Suppose that we have N processors and M applications, each of which has N or fewer threads. Then, each application could be given 1/M of the available time on the N processors, using time slicing. [FEIT90a] notes that this strategy can be inefficient. Consider an example in which there are two applications, one with four threads and one with one thread. Using uniform time allocation wastes 37.5% of the processing resource because when the single-thread application runs, three processors are left idle (see Figure 6.19). If there are several one-thread applications, these could all be fit together to increase processor use. If that option is not available, an alternative to uniform scheduling is scheduling that is weighted by the number of threads. Thus, the four-thread application could be given four-fifths of the time and the one-thread application given only one-fifth of the time, reducing the processor waste to 15%.

Dedicated Processor Assignment

An extreme form of gang scheduling, suggested in [TUCK89], is to dedicate a group of processors to an application for the duration of the application. That is, when an application is scheduled, each of its threads is assigned a processor that remains dedicated to that thread until the application runs to completion.

This approach would appear to be extremely wasteful of processor time. If a thread of an application is blocked waiting for I/O for synchronization with another thread, then that thread's processor remains idle: There is no multiprogramming of processors. Several observations can be made in defense of this strategy:

1. In a highly parallel processor, with tens or hundreds of processors, each of which represents a small fraction of the cost of the system, processor use is no longer so important as a metric for effectiveness or performance.
2. The total avoidance of process switching during the lifetime of a program should result in a substantial speedup of that program.

Both [TUCK89] and [ZAHO90] report analyses that support statement 2. Figure 6.20 shows the results of one experiment [TUCK89]. The authors ran two applications, a matrix multiplication and a fast Fourier transform (FFT) calculation, on a system with 16 processors. Each application breaks its problem into a number of tasks, which are mapped onto the threads executing that application. The programs are written in such a way as to allow the number of threads used to vary. In essence, a number of tasks are defined and queued by an application. Tasks are taken from the queue and mapped onto the available threads by the application. If there are fewer threads than tasks, then leftover tasks remain queued and are picked up by threads as they complete their assigned tasks. Clearly, not all applications can be structured in this way, but many numerical problems and some other applications can be dealt with in this fashion.

Figure 6.20 shows the speedup for the applications as the number of threads executing the tasks in each application is varied from one to 24. For example, we see that when both applications are started simultaneously with 24 threads each, the speedup obtained compared to using a single thread for each application is 2.8 for matrix multiplication and 2.4 for FFT. The figure shows that the

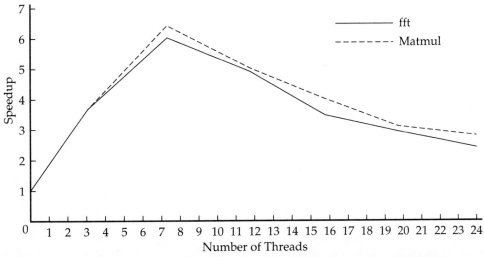

FIGURE 6.20 Application speedup as a function of number of processes [TUCK 89]

performance of both applications worsens considerably when the number of threads in each application exceeds eight, and thus the total number of processes in the system exceeds the number of processors. Furthermore, the larger the number of threads, the worse the performance gets because there is a greater frequency of thread preemption and rescheduling. This excessive preemption results in inefficiency from many sources, including time spent waiting for a suspended thread to leave a critical section, time wasted in process switching, and inefficient cache behavior.

The authors conclude that an effective strategy is to limit the number of active threads to the number of processors in the system. If most of the applications are either single-thread applications or can use the task-queue structure, an effective and reasonably efficient use of the processor resources will be provided.

Both dedicated processor assignment and gang scheduling attack the scheduling problem by addressing the issue of processor allocation. One can observe that the processor allocation problem on a multiprocessor more closely resembles the memory allocation problem on a uniprocessor than the scheduling problem on a uniprocessor. The issue is how many processors to assign to a program at any given time, which is analogous to how many page frames to assign to a given process at any time. [GEHR87] proposes the term *activity working set*, analogous to a virtual memory working set, as the minimum number of activities (threads) that must be scheduled simultaneously on processors for the application to make acceptable progress. As with memory management schemes, the failure to schedule all the elements of an activity working set can lead to *processor thrashing*, which occurs when the scheduling of threads whose services are required induces the descheduling of other threads whose services will soon be needed. Similarly, *processor fragmentation* refers to a situation in which some processors are left over when others are allocated, and the leftover processors are either insufficient in number or unsuitably organized to support the requirements of waiting applications. Gang scheduling and dedicated processor allocation are meant to avoid these problems.

Dynamic Scheduling

For some applications, it is possible to provide language and system tools that permit the number of threads in the process to be altered dynamically to allow the operating system to adjust the load to improve use.

[ZAHO90] proposes an approach in which both the operating system and the application are involved in making scheduling decisions. The operating system is responsible for partitioning the processors among the jobs. Each job uses the processors currently in its partition to execute some subset of its runnable tasks by mapping these tasks to threads. An appropriate decision about which subset to run, as well as which thread to suspend when a process is preempted, is left to the individual applications (perhaps through a set of run-time library routines). This approach may not be suitable for all applications. However, some applications could default to a single thread whereas others could be programmed to take advantage of this particular feature of the operating system.

In this approach, the scheduling responsibility of the operating system is primarily limited to processor allocation and proceeds according to the following policy. When a job requests one or more processors (either when the job arrives for the first time or because its requirements change):

1. If there are idle processors, use them to satisfy the request.
2. Otherwise, if the job making the request is a new arrival, allocate it a single processor by taking one away from any job currently allocated more than one processor.
3. If any portion of the request cannot be satisfied, it remains outstanding until either a processor becomes available for it or the job rescinds the request (e.g., if there is no longer a need for the extra processors).

Upon release of one or more processors (including job departure):

4. Scan the current queue of unsatisfied requests for processors. Assign a single processor to each job in the list that currently has no processors (i.e., to all waiting new arrivals). Then, scan the list again, allocating the rest of the processors on a FCFS basis.

Analyses reported in [ZAHO90] and [MAJU88] suggest that for applications that can take advantage of dynamic scheduling, this approach is superior to gang scheduling or dedicated processor assignment. However, the overhead of this approach may negate this apparent performance advantage. Experience with actual systems is needed to prove the worth of dynamic scheduling.

6.4

REAL-TIME SCHEDULING

Background

In recent years, real-time computing has come to be viewed as an important emerging discipline in computer science and engineering. The operating system, and in particular the scheduler, is perhaps the most important component of a real-time system. Examples of current applications of real-time systems include control of laboratory experiments, process control plants, robotics, air traffic control, telecommunications, and military command and control systems. Next-generation systems will include the autonomous landrover, controllers of robots with elastic joints, systems found in intelligent manufacturing, the space station, and undersea exploration.

Real-time computing may be defined as that type of computing in which the correctness of the system depends not only on the logical result of the computation but also on the time at which the results are produced. We can define a real-time system by defining what is meant by a real-time process, or task.[3] In general, in a real-time system, some of the tasks are real-time tasks, and they have a certain degree of urgency to them. Such tasks are attempting to control or react to events that take place in the outside world. Because these events occur in "real time," a real-time task must be able to keep up with the events with which it is concerned. Thus, it is usually possible to associate a deadline with a particular task when the deadline specifies either a start time or a completion time. Such a task may be classified as hard or soft. A **hard real-time task** must meet its deadline; otherwise it will cause undesirable damage or a fatal error to the system. A **soft real-time task** has an associated deadline, which is desirable but not mandatory; it still makes sense to schedule and complete the task even if it has passed its deadline.

Another characteristic of real-time tasks is whether they are periodic or aperiodic. An **aperiodic task** has a deadline by which it must finish or start, or it may have a constraint on both start and finish time. In the case of a **periodic task**, the requirement may be stated as "once per period T" or "exactly T units apart."

Real-Time Preemption

The basic characteristics of current real-time operating systems include the following [STAN89]:

- Fast context switch
- Small size (with its associated minimal functionality)
- Ability to respond to external interrupts quickly
- Multitasking with interprocess communication tools such as semaphores, signals, and events
- Use of special sequential files that can accumulate data at a fast rate
- Preemptive scheduling based on priority
- Minimization of intervals during which interrupts are disabled
- Primitives to delay tasks for a fixed amount of time and to pause/resume tasks
- Special alarms and timeouts

The heart of a real-time system is the short-term task scheduler. In designing such a scheduler, fairness and minimizing average response time are not important. What is important is that all hard real-time tasks complete (or start) by their deadline and that as many as possible soft real-time tasks also complete (or start) by their deadline.

---

[3]As usual, terminology poses a problem because various words are used in the literature with varying meanings. It is common for a particular process to operate under real-time constraints of a repetitive nature. That is, the process lasts for a long time and during that time performs some repetitive function in response to real-time events. Let us, in this section, refer to an individual function as a task. Thus, the process can be viewed as progressing through a sequence of tasks. At any given time, the process is engaged in a single task, and it is the process/task that must be scheduled.

Most contemporary real-time operating systems are unable to deal directly with deadlines. Instead, they are designed to be as responsive as possible to real-time tasks so that when a deadline approaches, a task can be quickly scheduled. From this point of view, real-time applications typically require deterministic response times in the several-millisecond to submillisecond span under a broad set of conditions; leading-edge applications—in simulators for military aircraft for example—often have constraints in the range of 10 to 100 microseconds (μsec) [ATLA89].

Figure 6.21 illustrates a spectrum of possibilities. In a preemptive scheduler that uses simple round-robin scheduling, a real-time task would be added to the Ready queue to await its next time slice, as illustrated in Figure 6.21a. The scheduling time would generally be unacceptable for real-time applications. Alternatively, in a nonpreemptive scheduler, we could use a priority scheduling mechanism, giving real-time tasks higher priority. A real-time task that is ready would be scheduled as soon as the current process blocks or runs to completion (Figure 6.21b). This could lead to a delay of several seconds if a slow low-priority task were executing at a critical time. Again, this approach is not acceptable. A more promising approach is to combine priorities with clock-based interrupts. Preemption points occur at regular intervals. When a preemption point occurs, the currently running task is preempted if a higher-priority task is waiting, including the preemption of tasks that are part of the operating-system kernel. Such a delay may be on the order of several milliseconds (msec) (Figure 6.21c). Although this last approach may be adequate for some real-time applications, it does not suffice for more demanding applications, in which cases, the approach that is taken is sometimes referred to as *immediate preemption*. In immediate preemption, the operating system responds to an interrupt almost immediately unless the system is in a critical-code lockout section. Scheduling delays for a real-time task can then be reduced to 100 μsec or less.

Deadline Scheduling

Most contemporary real-time operating systems are designed with the objective of starting real-time tasks as rapidly as possible, and hence they emphasize rapid interrupt handling and task dispatching. In fact, this is not a particularly useful metric in evaluating real-time operating systems. Real-time applications are generally not concerned with sheer speed but with completing (or starting) tasks at the most valuable times, neither too early or too late, despite dynamic resource demands and conflicts, processing overloads, and hardware or software faults. It follows that priorities provide a crude tool and do not capture the requirement, "completion (or initiation) at the most valuable time."

In recent years, there have been a number of proposals for more powerful and appropriate approaches to real-time task scheduling. All these are based on having additional information about each task. In its most general form, the following information about each task might be used:

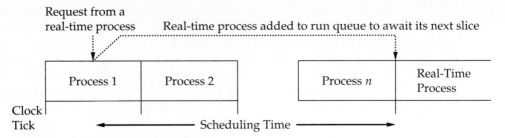

(a) Round-robin preemptive scheduler

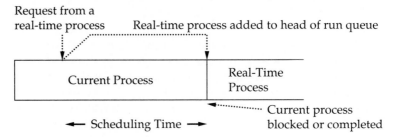

(b) Priority-driven non-preemptive scheduler

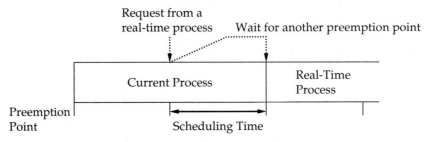

(c) Priority-driven, preemptive scheduler on preemption points

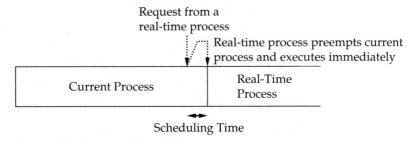

(d) Immediate preemptive scheduler

FIGURE 6.21 Scheduling of a real-time process

- *Ready time:* Time at which task becomes ready for execution. In the case of a repetitive or periodic task, this is actually a sequence of times that is known in advance. In the case of an aperiodic task, this time may be known in advance, or the operating system may be aware only when the task is actually ready.
- *Starting deadline:* Time by which a task must begin.
- *Completion deadline:* Time by which task must be completed. The typical real-time application has either starting deadlines or completion deadlines but not both.
- *Processing time:* The time required to execute the task to completion. In some cases, this time is supplied. In others, the operating system measures an exponential average. For still other scheduling systems, this information is not used.
- *Resource requirements:* The set of resources (other than the processor) required by the task while it is executing.
- *Priority:* Measures relative importance of the task. Hard real-time tasks may have an "absolute" priority, with the system failing if a deadline is missed. If the system is to continue to run no matter what, then both hard and soft real-time tasks may be assigned relative priorities as a guide to the scheduler.
- *Subtask structure:* A task may be decomposed into a mandatory subtask and an optional subtask. Only the mandatory subtask has a hard deadline.

There are several dimensions to the real-time scheduling function when deadlines are taken into account: which task to schedule next, and what sort of preemption is allowed. It can be shown, for a given preemption strategy, and using either starting or completion deadlines, that a policy of scheduling the task with the earliest deadline minimizes the fraction of tasks that miss their deadlines [HONG89, PANW88]. This conclusion holds both for single-processor and multiprocessor configurations.

The other critical design issue is that of preemption. When starting deadlines are specified, then a nonpreemptive scheduler makes sense. In this case, it would be the responsibility of the real-time task to block itself after completing the mandatory or critical portion of its execution, allowing other real-time starting deadlines to be satisfied. This fits the pattern of Figure 6.21b. For a system with completion deadlines, a preemptive strategy (Figure 6.21c or d) is most appropriate. For example, if task X is running and task Y is ready, there may be circumstances in which the only way to allow both X and Y to meet their completion deadlines is to preempt X, execute Y to completion, and then resume X to completion.

As an example of scheduling tasks with completion deadlines, taken from [FALK88], consider a system that collects and processes data from two sensors, A and B. The deadline for collecting data from sensor A must be met every 20 msec, and that for B every 50 msec. It takes 10 msec, including operating-system overhead, to process each sample of data from A and 25 msec to process each sample of data from B. The computer is capable of making a scheduling decision every 10 msec. Suppose, under these circumstances, we attempted to

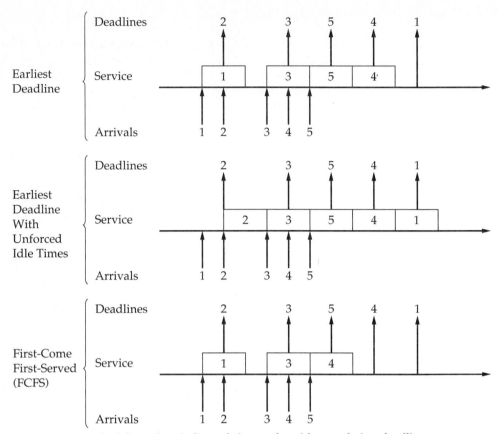

FIGURE 6.22 Scheduling of periodic real-time tasks with completion deadlines

use a priority scheduling scheme. The first two timing diagrams in Figure 6.22 show the result. If A has higher priority, B is given only 20 msec of processing time by the time its deadline is reached, and thus fails. If B is given higher priority, then A will miss its first deadline. The final timing diagram shows the use of earliest deadline scheduling. By scheduling to give priority at any preemption point to the task with the nearest deadline, all system requirements can be met.

Now consider a scheme for dealing with starting deadlines. A straightforward scheme is always to schedule the Ready task with the earliest deadline and let that task run to completion. An example of how this policy schedules a set of aperiodic tasks is shown in the first diagram of Figure 6.23. Note that although task 2 requires immediate service, the service is denied. This is the risk in dealing with aperiodic tasks, especially with starting deadlines. A refinement of the policy will improve performance if deadlines can be known in advance of the time that a task is ready. This policy, referred to as *earliest deadline with unforced idle times*, operates as follows: Always schedule the eligible task with the earliest deadline and let that task run to completion. An eligible task may

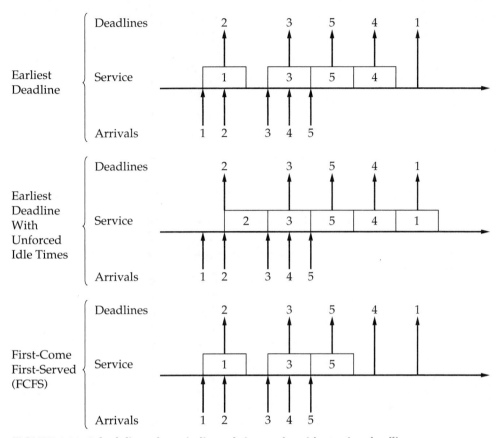

FIGURE 6.23 Scheduling of aperiodic real-time tasks with starting deadlines

not be ready, and this may result in the processor's remaining idle even though there are Ready tasks. This behavior is illustrated in the second diagram of Figure 6.23. Note that the system refrains from scheduling task 1 even though that is the only Ready task. The result is that, even though the processor is not used to maximum efficiency, all scheduling requirements are met. Finally, for comparison, the FCFS policy is shown. In this case, tasks 2 and 5 do not meet their deadlines.

6.5

EXAMPLE SYSTEMS

UNIX System V

The UNIX scheduler employs multilevel feedback using round-robin within each of the priority queues. The system makes use of 1-sec preemption. That is, if a running process does not block or complete within 1 sec, it is preempted.

Priority is based on process type and execution history. The following formulas apply:

$$P_j(i) = \text{Base}_j + \frac{\text{CPU}_j(i-1)}{2} + \text{nice}_j$$

$$\text{CPU}_j(i) = \frac{U_j(i-1)}{2} + \frac{\text{CPU}_j(i-1)}{2}$$

where

$P_j(i)$ = Priority of process j at beginning of interval i; lower values equal higher priorities

Base_j = Base priority of process j

$U_j(i)$ = CPU use of process j in interval i

$\text{CPU}_j(i)$ = Exponentially weighted average CPU use of process j through interval i

nice_j = user-controllable adjustment factor

The priority of each process is recomputed once per second, at which time a new scheduling decision is made. The purpose of the base priority is to divide all processes into fixed bands of priority levels. The *CPU* and *nice* components are restricted to prevent a process from migrating out of its assigned band (assigned by the base priority level). These bands are used to optimize access to block devices (e.g., disk) and to allow the operating system to respond quickly to system calls. In decreasing order of priority, the bands are:

• Swapper
• Block I/O device control
• File manipulation
• Character I/O device control
• User processes

This hierarchy should provide the most efficient use of the I/O devices. Within the user process band, the use of execution history tends to penalize CPU-bound processes at the expense of I/O-bound processes. Again, this should improve efficiency. Coupled with the round-robin preemption scheme, the scheduling strategy is well equipped to satisfy the requirements for general-purpose time sharing.

An example of process scheduling is shown in Figure 6.24. Processes A, B, and C are created at the same time and have base priorities of 60 (we will ignore the nice value). The clock interrupts the system 60 times per second and increments a counter for the running process. The example assumes that none of the processes block themselves and that no other processes are ready to run. Compare this with Figure 6.17.

OS/2

The scheduling objectives for OS/2 are quite different from those of UNIX. UNIX is concerned with giving fair, responsive service to a community of users who

Time	Proc A Priority	Proc A Cpu Count	:	Proc B Priority	Proc B Cpu Count	:	Proc C Priority	Proc C Cpu Count
0	60	0	:	60	0	:	60	0
		1	:			:		
		2	:			:		
		.	:			:		
		60	:			:		
1	75	30	:	60	0	:	60	0
			:		1	:		
			:		2	:		
			:		.	:		
			:		60	:		
2	67	15	:	75	30	:	60	0
			:			:		1
			:			:		2
			:			:		.
			:			:		60
3	63	7	:	67	15	:	75	30
		8	:			:		
		9	:			:		
		.	:			:		
		67	:			:		
4	76	33	:	63	7	:	67	15
			:		8	:		
			:		9	:		
			:		.	:		
			:		67	:		
5	68	16	:	76	33	:	63	7

FIGURE 6-24 Example of UNIX Process Scheduling [BACH86]

share the system. OS/2 is designed to be as responsive as possible to the needs of a single user in a highly interactive environment. As with UNIX, OS/2 implements a preemptive scheduler with multiple-priority levels and round-robin scheduling within each level. In the case of OS/2, dynamic priority variation changes the priority of threads on the basis of their current activity. By means of a configuration parameter, the user has control over the length of the time quantum used for time slicing.

Priorities in OS/2 are organized into four bands, or classes, in descending order (Figure 6.25):

- Time-critical class
- Foreground class

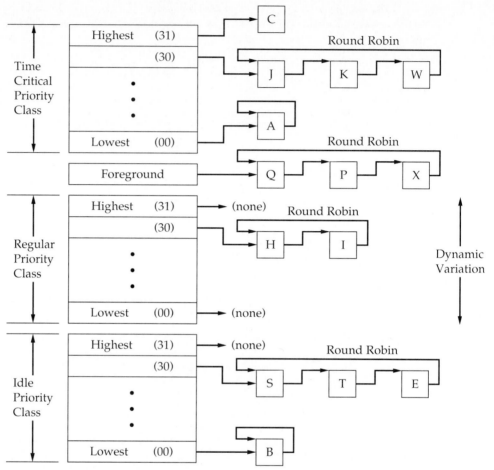

FIGURE 6.25 OS/2 dispatching priorities [IACO88]

- Regular class
- Idle class

Each of these bands contains 32 priority levels, with the exception of the foreground band, which consists of a single level. Threads requiring immediate attention are in the **time-critical class**, which includes functions such as communications and real-time tasks. The OS/2 session manager runs in the lowest time-critical priority level.

The **foreground class** is occupied by the threads of the currently controlling application. This is the application that is seen by the user as the active window on the screen.

Most user threads are in the **regular class**. This is the only class within which threads dynamically migrate from one priority level to another on the basis of recent CPU usage and I/O activity.

Finally, relatively unimportant threads are in the **idle class**.

Except for kernel threads, priorities are established by application programs that are based on the urgency of their work. [IACO88] gives the example of a point-of-sale system. For this application, there could be a process that is performing some critical work, such as looking up a price for a cash register transaction. At the same time, the system could be running lower-priority tasks, such as generating sales reports for the home office. In this scenario, the threads of the price lookup process should have higher priority than those of the sales report.

MVS

Recall from Section 3.5 that the process environment of MVS consists of the following controllable entities (see Figure 3.21):

- *Global service request block (global SRB):* Used to manage a system task that does not execute within a user address space. A global SRB represents a system task involved in interaddress space operations.
- *Address space control block (ASCB) and address space extension block (ASXB):* Used to manage an address space that corresponds roughly to a single application or job. The work within each address space consists of a set of system tasks and users' tasks.
- *Service request block (SRB):* Used to manage a system task that does execute within a user address space, which corresponds to a service request issued by one of the tasks in the address space.
- *Task control block (TCB):* Represents one of the tasks within an address space.

Tasks represented by SRBs are nonpreemptive; if such a task is interrupted, it receives control after the interruption has been processed. In contrast, a task controlled by a TCB is preemptive. If it is interrupted, control passes to the dispatcher when the interruption handling completes; the dispatcher may then select some other task to run.

Global SRBs are maintained in a queue of descending priority in the system queue area, which is a region of main memory that cannot be swapped. Thus, global SRBs are always available in main memory. When a processor is available, MVS first searches this queue for a ready SRB. If none are found, MVS then looks for an address space that has at least one ready TCB or SRB. For this purpose, a queue of ASCBs is maintained in the system queue area. Each address space is assigned an overall priority level; hence, the ASCBs can be arranged in descending priority. Once an address space is selected, MVS can work with the structures in that address space, which is referred to as the local system queue area. MVS selects the highest-priority SRB, or failing that, the highest-priority TCB to dispatch.

Dispatching priorities in MVS exist at 256 levels, and GSRBs are dispatched above the highest defined level. Within a given dispatching priority level, address spaces are in a FCFS queue. Dispatching priorities are organized into sets, or bands, of 16 levels each. Typically, an address space is assigned to a band and stays within that band. Within each band, the upper six levels are individually specifiable as **fixed priorities**, and the lower 10 levels form a **mean-time-to-wait (MTTW) group**. Within the MTTW group, address space priorities are determined by the average time between waits in each address space. Those waits of shorter intervals (usually for I/O completion) have higher priorities; those with long stretches of CPU use without intervening I/O activity have lower priorities.

When an address space is created, it is assigned to a **performance group**, which dictates the priority that that address space will enjoy. An address space in a performance group is considered to go through a sequence of **performance periods**. Performance periods allow a transaction, or any job, to be managed differently as it ages. The measure of that aging is accumulated service, and the means of changing management parameters is the passage from one performance period to the next. When a performance group is defined, one or more performance periods can be specified. Each performance period is characterized by a duration and a priority. An address space begins in period 1 and remains at the priority level specified for that period until it has exhausted the processing time for that period. Then it moves to a lower priority in period 2 for the duration of that period. The duration in each performance period is specified in terms of service units. A service unit is an interval of CPU time differing by basic CPU model, number of processors, and operating-system environment; it ranges between 1 and 11 msec of processor time.

Thus, the overall workload is broken down into performance groups—first, on the basis of similar types (transaction, batch, subsystem) or address spaces, and second, according to priorities established for the various workload constituents. Then, within an address space, a breakdown is established on the basis of expected duration of transactions. For example, a time-sharing address space might be defined as follows:

- Period 1: Highest priority and a duration of 1000 service units
- Period 2: Next highest priority and a duration of 4000 service units
- Period 3: Lowest priority and unlimited duration

With this structure, we would expect trivial commands to complete within period 1, giving the best service with highest probability of access to the system. Longer commands would exhaust the allocation in period 1 and run to completion in period 2, still giving reasonably good service. The commands in this category would be somewhat more complex than the shortest commands and fewer of these commands would be running concurrently. Finally, the longest commands, which might trigger a compile or an application program, would run at still lower service.

6.6

SUMMARY

The operating system must make three types of scheduling decisions with respect to the execution of processes. Long-term scheduling determines when new processes are admitted to the system. Medium-term scheduling is part of the swapping function and determines when a program is brought partially or fully into main memory so that it is may be executed. Short-term scheduling determines which Ready process will be executed next by the processor. This chapter focuses on the issues relating to short-term scheduling.

A variety of criteria is used in designing the short-term scheduler. Some of these criteria relate to the behavior of the system as perceived by the individual user (user-oriented), whereas others view the total effectiveness of the system in meeting the needs of all users (system-oriented). Some of the criteria relate specifically to some quantitative measure of performance, whereas others are more qualitative in nature. From a user's point of view, response time is generally the most important characteristic of a system, whereas from a system point of view, throughput or processor utilization is important.

A variety of algorithms has been developed for making the short-term scheduling decision among all Ready processes, including the following:

- *First-come, first-served:* Select the process that has been waiting the longest for service.
- *Round-robin:* Use time slicing to limit any running process to a short burst of processor time, and rotate among all Ready processes.
- *Shortest process next:* Select the process with the shortest expected processing time, and do not preempt the process.
- *Shortest remaining time:* Select the process with the shortest expected remaining process time. A process may be preempted when another process becomes ready.
- *Highest response ratio next:* Base the scheduling decision on an estimate of normalized turnaround time.
- *Feedback:* Establish a set of scheduling queues and allocate processes to queues on the basis of execution history and other criteria.

The choice of scheduling algorithm depends on expected performance and on implementation complexity.

With a tightly coupled multiprocessor, multiple processors have access to the same main memory. In this configuration, the scheduling structure is somewhat more complex. For example, a given process may be assigned to the same processor for its entire life, or it may be dispatched to any processor each time it enters the Running state. Performance studies suggest that the differences among various scheduling algorithms are less significant in a multiprocessor system.

Finally, a real-time process or task is one that is executed in connection with some process or function or set of events external to the computer system and that must meet one or more deadlines to interact effectively and correctly with the external environment. A real-time operating system is one that must manage real-time processes. In this context, the traditional criteria for choosing a scheduling algorithm do not apply. Rather, the key factor is the meeting of deadlines. Algorithms that rely heavily on preemption and on reacting to relative deadlines are appropriate in this context.

RECOMMENDED READING

Virtually every textbook on operating systems covers scheduling. Particularly good treatments can be found in [MILE87], [FINK88], and [SILB91]. Rigorous queuing analyses of various scheduling policies are presented in [KLEI76], [STUC85], and [CONW67].

Surveys of current work on multiprocessors can be found in [TABA90], [ALMA89], [GEHR88], and [DESR87]. [WEND89] is an interesting discussion of approaches to multiprocessor scheduling.

[ZHAO89] is a special issue on real-time operating systems, containing nine papers on the subject. Another collection of papers is to be found in [STAN88]. Analyses of deadline scheduling of real-time tasks can be found in [HONG89] and [PANW88].

Good descriptions of the scheduling strategies for UNIX System V, OS/2, and MVS can be found in [BACH86], [IACO88], and [SAMS90], respectively.

PROBLEMS

6.1 Consider the following set of processes:

Process Name	Arrival Time	Processing Time
1	0	3
2	1	5
3	3	2
4	9	5
5	12	5

Perform the same analysis as depicted in Table 6.4 and Figure 6.5 for this set.

6.2 Repeat Problem 6.1 for the following set:

Process Name	Arrival Time	Processing Time
A	0	1
B	1	100
C	2	1
D	3	100

6.3 Prove that, among nonpreemptive scheduling algorithms, SPN provides the minimum average waiting time.

6.4 Assume the following burst-time pattern for a process: 6, 4, 6, 4, 13, 13,

13, and assume that the initial guess is 10. Produce a plot similar to those of Figure 6.10.

6.5 Consider the following pair of equations as an alternative to equation (3):

$$S_{n+1} = \alpha T_n + (1 - \alpha)S_n$$
$$X = MIN(Ubound, MAX(Lbound, (\beta S_{n+1})))$$

where Ubound and Lbound are prechosen upper and lower bounds on the estimated value of T. The value of X is used in the shortest process next algorithm instead of the value of S_{n+1}. What functions do α and β perform, and what is the effect of higher and lower values of each?

6.6 In a nonpreemptive uniprocessor system, the Ready queue contains three jobs at time t immediately after the completion of a job. These jobs arrived at times t_1, t_2, and t_3 with estimated execution times of r_1, r_2, and r_3 respectively. Figure 6.26 shows the linear increase of their response ratios over time. Use this example to find a variant of response ratio scheduling, known as **minimax response ratio** scheduling, which minimizes the maximum response ratio for a given batch of jobs, ignoring further arrivals. (Hint: Decide first which job to schedule as the last one.)

6.7 Prove that the minimax response ratio algorithm of the preceding problem minimizes the maximum response ratio for a given batch of jobs. (Hint: Focus attention on the job that will achieve the highest response ratio and all jobs executed before it. Consider the same subset of jobs scheduled in any other order, and observe the response ratio of the job that is executed as the last one among them. Notice that this subset may now be mixed with other jobs from the total set.)

6.8 Define Response time R as the average total time a process spends waiting and being served. Show that for FIFO, with mean service time s, $R = s/(1 - \rho)$.

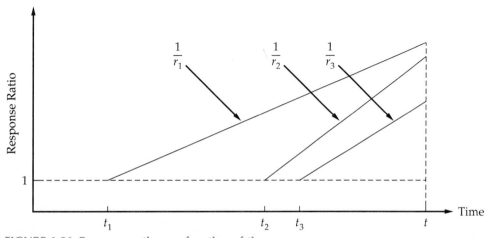

FIGURE 6.26 Response ratio as a function of time

6.9 A processor is multiplexed at infinite speed among all processes present in a Ready queue with no overhead. (This is an idealized model of round-robin scheduling among Ready processes and uses time slices that are very small compared to the mean service time.) Show that for Poisson input from an infinite source with exponential service times, the mean response time R_x of a process with service time x is given by: $R_x = x/(1 - \rho)$. (Hint: Review the queuing equations in Appendix A. Then consider the mean queue size q in the system upon arrival of the given process.)

6.10 In a queuing system, new jobs must wait for a while before being served. While a job waits, its priority increases linearly with time from zero at a rate α. A job waits until its priority reaches the priority of the jobs in service; then, it begins to share the processor equally with other jobs in service using round-robin while its priority continues to increase at a slower rate β. The algorithm is referred to as selfish round-robin because the jobs in service try (in vain) to monopolize the processor by increasing their priority continuously. Use Figure 6.27 to show that the mean response time R_x for a job of service time x is given by:

$$R_x = \frac{s}{1 - \rho} + \frac{x - s}{1 - \rho'}$$

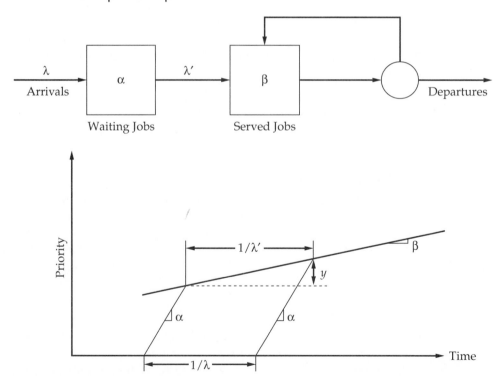

FIGURE 6.27 Selfish round robin

where

$$\rho = \lambda s \quad \rho' = \rho\left(1 - \frac{\beta}{\alpha}\right) \quad 0 \le \beta \le \alpha$$

assuming that arrival and service times are exponentially distributed with means $1/\lambda$ and s, respectively. (Hint: Consider the total system and the two subsystems separately.)

6.11 An interactive system using round-robin scheduling and swapping tries to give guaranteed response to trivial requests as follows: After completing a round-robin cycle among all Ready processes, the system determines the time slice to allocate to each Ready process for the next cycle by dividing a maximum response time by the number of processes requiring service. Is this a practical policy?

6.12 Which type of process is generally favored by a multilevel feedback queuing scheduler—a processor-bound process or an I/O-bound process? Briefly explain why.

6.13 In priority-based process scheduling, the scheduler gives control to a particular process only if no other process of higher priority is currently in the Ready state. Assume that no other information is used in making the process scheduling decision. Also assume that process priorities are established at process creation time and do not change. In a system operating with such assumptions, why would using Dekker's solution to the mutual exclusion problem be "dangerous?" Explain this by telling *what* undesired event could occur and *how* it could occur.

APPENDIX 6A

Response Time

Response time is the time it takes a system to react to a given input. In an interactive transaction, it may be defined as the time between the last keystroke by the user and the beginning of the display of a result by the computer. For different types of applications, a slightly different definition is needed. In general, it is the time it takes for the system to respond to a request to perform a particular task.

Ideally, one would like the response time for any application to be short. However, it is almost invariably the case that shorter response time imposes greater cost. This cost comes from two sources:

- *Computer processing power:* The faster the computer, the shorter the response time. Of course, increased processing power means increased cost.
- *Competing requirements:* Providing rapid response time to some processes may penalize other processes.

Thus the value of a given level of response time must be assessed versus the cost of achieving that response time.

Table 6.7, based on [MART88], lists six general ranges of response times. Design difficulties are faced when a response time of less than 1 sec is required.

That rapid response time is the key to productivity in interactive applications has been confirmed in a number of studies [SHNE84, THAD81, GUYN88]. These studies show that when a computer and a user interact at a pace that ensures that neither has to wait on the other, productivity increases significantly, the cost of the work done on the computer therefore drops, and quality tends to improve. It used to be widely accepted that a relatively slow response, up to 2 sec, was acceptable for most interactive applications because the person

---

TABLE 6.7   Response Time Ranges [MART88]

Greater than 15 seconds

This rules out conversational interaction. For certain types of applications, certain types of users may be content to sit at a terminal for more than 15 seconds waiting for the answer to a single simple inquiry. However, for a busy person, captivity for more than 15 seconds seems intolerable. If such delays will occur, the system should be designed so that the user can turn to other activities and request the response at some later time.

Greater than 4 seconds

These are generally too long for a conversation requiring the operator to retain information in short-term memory (the operator's memory, not the computer's!). Such delays would be very inhibiting in problem-solving activity and frustrating in data entry activity. However, after a major closure, delays of from 4 to 15 seconds can be tolerated.

2 to 4 seconds

A delay longer than 2 seconds can be inhibiting to terminal operations that demand a high level of concentration. A wait of 2 to 4 seconds at a terminal can seem surprisingly long when the user is absorbed and emotionally committed to complete what he or she is doing. A delay in this range may be acceptable after a minor closure has occurred.

Less than 2 seconds

When the terminal user has to remember information throughout several responses, the response time must be short. The more detailed the information remembered, the greater the need for responses of less than 2 seconds. For elaborate terminal activities, 2 seconds represents an important response-time limit.

Subsecond response time

Certain types of thought-intensive work, especially with graphics applications, require very short response times to maintain the user's interest and attention for long periods.

Decisecond response time

A response to pressing a key and seeing the character displayed on the screen or clicking a screen object with a mouse needs to be almost instantaneous—less than 0.1 second after the action. Interaction with a mouse requires extremely fast interaction if the designer is to avoid the use of alien syntax (one with commands, mnemonics, punctuation, etc.)

was thinking about the next task [MILL68]. However, it now appears that productivity increases when rapid response times are achieved.

The results reported on response time are based on an analysis of on-line transactions. A transaction consists of a user command from a terminal and the system's reply. It is the fundamental unit of work for on-line system users. It can be divided into two time sequences:

- *User response time*: The time span between the moment a user receives a complete reply to one command and enters the next command. People often refer to this as *think time*.
- *System response time:* The time span between the moment the user enters a command and the moment a complete response is displayed on the terminal.

As an example of the effect of reduced system response time, Figure 6.28 shows the results of a study carried out on engineers using a computer-aided design graphics program for the design of integrated circuit chips and boards [SMIT83]. Each transaction consists of a command by the engineer that alters in some way the graphic image being displayed on the screen. The results show that the rate of transactions increases as system response time falls and rises dramatically once system response time falls below 1 sec. What is happening is that as the system response time falls, so does the user response time, a result of the effects of short-term memory and human attention span.

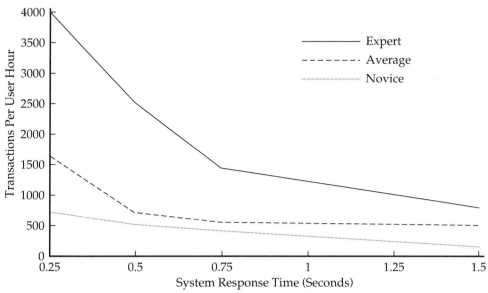

FIGURE 6.28 Response-time results for high-function graphics

CHAPTER 7

I/O Management and Disk Scheduling

Perhaps the messiest aspect of operating-system design is input/output (I/O). Because there is such a wide variety of devices and so many applications of those devices, it is difficult to develop a general, consistent solution.

We begin this chapter with a brief discussion of I/O devices and the organization of the I/O functions. These topics, which generally come within the scope of computer architecture, set the stage for an examination of I/O from the point of view of the operating system.

The next section examines operating-system design issues, including design objectives and the way in which the I/O function can be structured. Next, the key area of I/O buffering is examined. One of the basic I/O services provided by the operating system is a buffering function, which improves overall performance.

The last major section of the chapter is devoted to magnetic disk I/O. In contemporary systems, this form of I/O is the most important and is key to the performance as perceived by the user. We begin by developing a model of disk I/O performance, and then we examine several techniques that can be used to enhance performance.

An appendix to this chapter summarizes characteristics of secondary storage devices, including magnetic disk, magnetic tape, and optical memory.

7.1

I/O DEVICES

As was mentioned in Chapter 1, external devices that engage in I/O with computer systems can be roughly grouped into three categories:

- *Human-readable:* Suitable for communicating with the computer user. Examples include video display terminals, consisting of display, keyboard, and perhaps other devices such as a mouse; and printers.

413

- *Machine-readable:* Suitable for communicating with electronic equipment. Examples are disk and tape drives, sensors, controllers, and actuators.
- *Communication:* Suitable for communicating with remote devices. Examples are digital line drivers and modems.

There are great differences across classes and even substantial differences within each class. Among the key differences are the following:

- *Data rate:* There may be differences of several orders of magnitude between the data transfer rates. Table 7.1, which reproduces Table 1.2, gives some examples.
- *Application:* The use to which a device is put has an influence on the software and policies in the operating system and supporting utilities. For example, a disk used for files requires the support of file-management software. A disk used as a backing store for pages in a virtual memory scheme depends on the use of virtual memory hardware and software. Furthermore, these applications have an impact on disk-scheduling algorithms (discussed later in this chapter). As another example, a terminal may be used by an ordinary user or a system administrator. These uses imply different levels of privilege and perhaps different priorities in the operating system.
- *Complexity of control:* A printer requires a relatively simple control interface. A disk is much more complex. The effect of these differences on the operating system is filtered to some extent by the complexity of the I/O module that controls the device, as discussed in the next section.
- *Unit of transfer:* Data may be transferred as a stream of bytes or characters (e.g., a terminal) or in larger blocks (e.g., a disk).

TABLE 7.1   Examples of I/O Devices Categorized by Behavior, Partner, and Data Rate [HENN90]

Device	Purpose	Partner	Data Rate (KBytes/sec)
Keyboard	Input	Human	0.01
Mouse	Input	Human	0.02
Voice input	Input	Human	0.02
Scanner	Input	Human	200
Voice output	Output	Human	0.6
Line printer	Output	Human	1
Laser printer	Output	Human	100
Graphics display	Output	Human	30,000
CPU to frame buffer	Output	Human	200
Network-terminal	Input or output	Machine	0.05
Network-LAN	Input or output	Machine	200
Optical disk	Storage	Machine	500
Magnetic tape	Storage	Machine	2,000
Magnetic disk	Storage	Machine	2,000

- *Data representation:* Different data encoding schemes are used by different devices, including differences in character code and parity conventions.
- *Error conditions:* The nature of errors, the way in which they are reported, their consequences, and the available range of responses differ widely from one device to another.

This diversity makes a uniform and consistent approach to I/O, both from the point of view of the operating system and from the point of view of user processes, difficult to achieve.

7.2

ORGANIZATION OF THE I/O FUNCTION

Section 1.9 summarized three techniques for performing I/O:

- *Programmed I/O:* The processor issues an I/O command on behalf of a process to an I/O module; that process then busy-waits for the operation to be complete before proceeding.
- *Interrupt-driven I/O:* The processor issues an I/O command on behalf of a process, continues to execute subsequent instructions, and is interrupted by the I/O module when the latter has completed its work. The subsequent instructions may be in the same process if it is not necessary for that process to wait for the completion of the I/O. Otherwise, the process is suspended pending the interrupt, and other work is performed.
- *Direct memory access (DMA):* A DMA module controls the exchange of data between main memory and an I/O module. The processor sends a request for the transfer of a block of data to the DMA module and is interrupted only after the entire block has been transferred.

Table 7.2 indicates the relationship among these three techniques. In most computer systems, DMA is the dominant form of transfer that must be supported by the operating system. In this section, we elaborate on some of the considerations in the use of DMA.

The Evolution of the I/O Function

As computer systems have evolved, there has been a pattern of increasing complexity and sophistication of individual components. Nowhere is this more

TABLE 7.2   I/O Techniques

	No Interrupts	Use of Interrupts
I/O-to-memory transfer through processor	Programmed I/O	Interrupt-driven I/O
Direct I/O-to-memory transfer		Direct memory access (DMA)

evident than in the I/O function. The evolutionary steps can be summarized as follows:

1. The processor directly controls a peripheral device. This is seen in simple microprocessor-controlled devices.
2. A controller or I/O module is added. The processor uses programmed I/O without interrupts. With this step, the processor becomes somewhat divorced from the specific details of external device interfaces.
3. The same configuration as step 2 is used, but now interrupts are employed. The processor need not spend time waiting for an I/O operation to be performed, thus increasing efficiency.
4. The I/O module is given direct control of memory via DMA. It can now move a block of data to or from memory without involving the processor, except at the beginning and end of the transfer.
5. The I/O module is enhanced to become a separate processor with a specialized instruction set tailored for I/O. The central processor unit (CPU) directs the I/O processor to execute an I/O program in main memory. The I/O processor fetches and executes these instructions without CPU intervention. This allows the CPU to specify a sequence of I/O activities and to be interrupted only when the entire sequence has been performed.
6. The I/O module has a local memory of its own and is, in fact, a computer in its own right. With this architecture, a large set of I/O devices can be controlled with minimal CPU involvement. A common use for such an architecture has been to control communications with interactive terminals. The I/O processor takes care of most of the tasks involved in controlling the terminals.

As one proceeds along this evolutionary path, more and more of the I/O function is performed without CPU involvement. The central processor is increasingly relieved of I/O-related tasks, improving performance. With the last two steps (5 and 6), a major change occurs with the introduction of the concept of an I/O module capable of executing a program.

A note about terminology: For all the modules described in steps 4 through 6, the term direct memory access (DMA) is appropriate because all these types involve direct control of main memory by the I/O module. Also, the I/O module in step 5 is often referred to as an **I/O channel**, and that in step 6 as an **I/O processor**. Each term is on occasion applied to both situations, however. In the latter part of this section, we use the term *I/O channel* to refer to both types of I/O modules.

Direct Memory Access

Figure 7.1 indicates in general terms the DMA logic. The DMA unit is capable of mimicking the CPU and, indeed, of taking over control of the system from the CPU in order to transfer data to and from memory over the system bus. Typically, the DMA module must use the bus only when the CPU does not

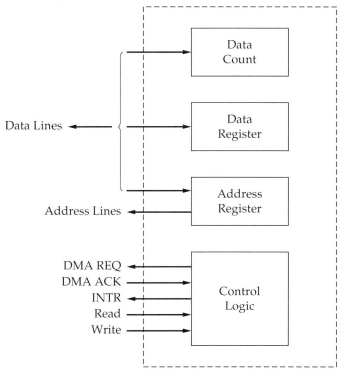

FIGURE 7.1 Typical DMA block diagram

need it, or it must force the CPU to temporarily suspend operation. The latter technique is more common and is referred to as *cycle stealing* because the DMA unit in effect steals a bus cycle.

Figure 7.2 shows where in the instruction cycle the CPU may be suspended. In each case, the CPU is suspended just before it needs to use the bus. The DMA unit then transfers one word and returns control to the CPU. Note that this is not an interrupt; the CPU does not save a context and do something else. Rather, the CPU pauses 1 bus cycle. The overall effect is to cause the CPU to execute more slowly. Nevertheless, for a multiple-word I/O transfer, DMA is far more efficient than interrupt-driven or programmed I/O.

The DMA mechanism can be configured in a variety of ways. Some possibilities are shown in Figure 7.3. In the first example, all modules share the same system bus. The DMA module, acting as a surrogate CPU, uses programmed I/O to exchange data between memory and an I/.O module through the DMA module. This configuration, although it may be inexpensive, is clearly inefficient: As with CPU-controlled programmed I/O, each transfer of a word consume 2 bus cycles.

The number of required bus cycles can be cut substantially by integrating the DMA and I/O functions. As Figure 7.3b shows, this means that there is a path

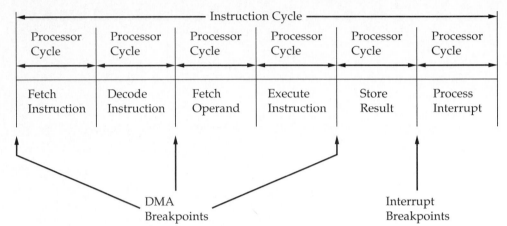

FIGURE 7.2 DMA and interrupt breakpoints during an instruction cycle

between the DMA module and one or more I/O modules that does not include the system bus. The DMA logic may actually be a part of an I/O module, or it may be a separate module that controls one or more I/O modules. This concept can be taken one step further by connecting I/O modules to the DMA module by using an I/O bus (Figure 7.3c). This reduces the number of I/O interfaces in the DMA module to one and provides for an easily expandable configuration. In all these cases (Figures 7.3b and 7.3c), the system bus that the DMA module shares with the CPU and main memory is used by the DMA module only to exchange data with memory and to exchange control signals with the CPU. The exchange of data between the DMA and I/O modules takes place off the system bus.

Characteristics of I/O Channels

The I/O channel is an extension of the DMA concept. An I/O channel has the ability to execute I/O instructions, which gives it complete control over I/O operations. In a computer system with such devices, I/O instructions are stored in main memory and are to be executed by a special-purpose processor in the I/O channel itself. Thus, the CPU initiates an I/O transfer by instructing the I/O channel to execute a program in memory. The program will specify the device or devices, the area or areas of memory for reading or writing, priority, and actions to be taken for certain error conditions.

Two types of I/O channels are common, as illustrated in Figure 7.4. A **selector channel** controls multiple high-speed devices and, at any one time, is dedicated to the transfer of data with one of those devices. Thus, the I/O channel selects one device and effects the data transfer. Each device, or a small set of devices, is handled by a **controller**, or I/O module, that is much like the I/O modules

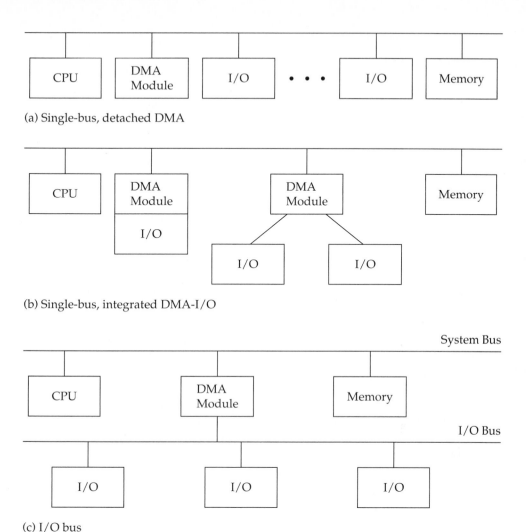

(a) Single-bus, detached DMA

(b) Single-bus, integrated DMA-I/O

(c) I/O bus

FIGURE 7.3 Possible DMA configurations

described earlier. Thus, the I/O channel serves in place of the CPU in controlling these I/O controllers. A **multiplexor channel** can handle I/O with multiple devices concurrently. For low-speed devices, a **byte multiplexor** accepts or transmits characters as fast as possible to multiple devices. For example, the resultant character stream from three devices with different data rates and individual streams $A_1A_2A_3A_4 \ldots$, $B_1B_2B_3B_4 \ldots$, $C_1C_2C_3C_4 \ldots$ might be $A_1B_1C_1A_2C_2A_3B_2C_3A_4$, and so on. For high-speed devices, a **block multiplexor** interleaves blocks of data from several devices.

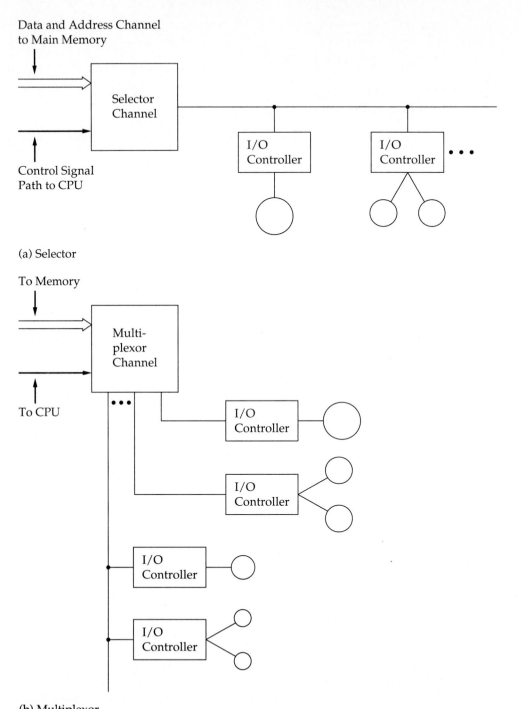

(a) Selector

(b) Multiplexor

FIGURE 7.4 I/O channel architecture

7.3

OPERATING-SYSTEM DESIGN ISSUES

Design Objectives

Two objectives are paramount in designing the I/O facility: efficiency and generality. **Efficiency** is important because I/O operations often form a bottleneck in a computing system. Looking again at Table 7.1, we see that most I/O devices are extremely slow compared with main memory and the processor. One way to tackle this problem is to use multiprogramming, which, as we have seen, allows some processes to be waiting on I/O operations while another process is executing. However, even with the vast size of main memory in today's machines, it will still often be the case that I/O is not keeping up with the activities of the processor. Swapping is used to bring in additional Ready processes to keep the processor busy, but this in itself is an I/O operation. Thus, a major effort in I/O design has been schemes for improving the efficiency of the I/O. The area that has received the most attention, because of its importance, is disk I/O, and much of this chapter is devoted to a study of disk I/O efficiency.

The other major objective is **generality**. In the interests of simplicity and freedom from error, it is desirable to handle all devices in a uniform manner. This statement applies both to the way in which processes view I/O devices and the way in which the operating system manages I/O devices and operations. Because of the diversity of device characteristics, it is difficult in practice to achieve true generality. What can be done is to use a hierarchical, modular approach to the design of the I/O function. This approach hides most of the details of device I/O in lower-level routines so that processes and upper levels of the operating system see devices in terms of general functions, such as Read, Write, Open, Close, Lock, Unlock. We turn now to a discussion of this approach.

Logical Structure of the I/O Function

In Chapter 2, in the discussion of system structure, we emphasized the hierarchical nature of modern operating systems. The hierarchical philosophy is that the functions of the operating system should be separated according to their complexity, their characteristic time scale, and their level of abstraction. Following this approach leads to an organization of the operating system into a series of levels. Each level performs a related subset of the functions required of the operating system. It relies on the next lower level to perform more primitive functions and to conceal the details of those functions. It provides services to the next-higher layer. Ideally, the levels should be defined so that changes in one level do not require changes in other levels. Thus, we have decomposed one problem into a number of more manageable subproblems.

In general, lower layers deal with a far shorter time scale. Some parts of the operating system must interact directly with the computer hardware, where events can have a time scale as brief as a few billionths of a second. At the other end of the spectrum, parts of the operating system communicate with the user, who issues commands at a much more leisurely pace, perhaps one every few seconds. The use of a set of levels conforms nicely to this environment.

Applying this philosophy specifically to the I/O facility leads to the type of organization suggested by Figure 7.5 (compare Table 2.4). The details of the organization depend on the type of device and the application. The three most important logical structures are presented in the figure. Of course, a particular

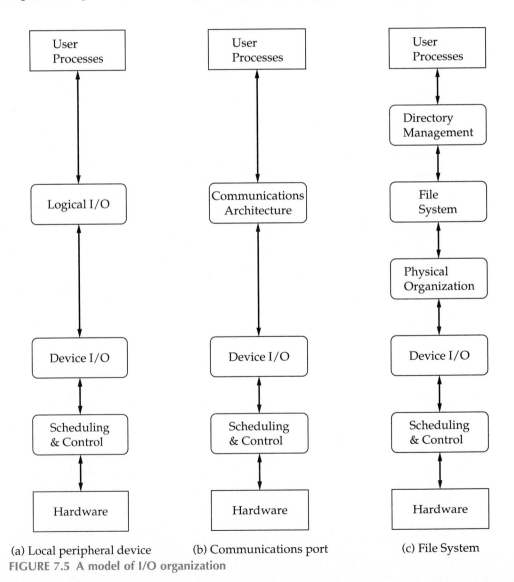

(a) Local peripheral device   (b) Communications port   (c) File System

FIGURE 7.5 A model of I/O organization

operating system may not conform exactly to these structures. However, the general principles are valid and most operating systems approach I/O in approximately this way.

Let us consider the simplest case first, that of a local peripheral device that communicates in a simple fashion, such as by a stream of bytes or records (Figure 7.5a). The levels involved are the following:

- *Logical I/O:* The logical I/O module deals with the device as a logical resource and is not concerned with the details of actually controlling the device. The logical I/O module is concerned with managing general I/O functions on behalf of user processes, allowing them to deal with the device in terms of a device identifier and simple commands such as Open, Close, Read, and Write.
- *Device I/O:* The requested operations and data (buffered characters, records, etc.) are converted into appropriate sequences of I/O instructions, channel commands, and controller orders. Buffering techniques may be used to improve use.
- *Scheduling and control:* The actual queuing and scheduling of I/O operations occurs at this level, as does the control of the operations. Thus, interrupts are handled at this level and I/O status is collected and reported. This is the level of software that actually interacts with the I/O module and hence the device hardware.

For a communications device, the I/O structure (Figure 7.5b) looks much the same as that just described. The principal difference is that the logical I/O module is replaced by a communications architecture, which may itself consist of a number of layers. For example, the well-known open-system interconnection (OSI) architecture consists of seven layers. Communications architectures are discussed in Chapter 9.

Figure 7.5c shows a representative structure for managing I/O on a secondary storage device that supports a file system. The three levels not previously discussed are the following:

- *Directory management:* At this level, symbolic file names are converted to identifiers that either reference the file directly or indirectly through a file descriptor or index table. This level is also concerned with user operations that affect the directory of files, such as Add, Delete, and Reorganize.
- *File system:* This level deals with the logical structure of files and with the operations that can be specified by users, such as Open, Close, Read, and Write. Access rights are also managed at this level.
- *Physical organization:* Just as virtual memory addresses must be converted into physical main memory addresses, taking into account the segmentation and paging structure, logical references to files and records must be converted to physical secondary storage addresses, taking into account the physical track and sector structure of the file. Allocation of secondary storage space and main storage buffers is generally treated at this level as well.

Because of the importance of the file system, we will spend some time in this chapter and the next in looking at its various components. The discussion in this chapter focuses on the lower three layers, and the upper two layers are examined in Chapter 8.

I/O BUFFERING

Suppose that a user process wishes to read blocks of data from a tape one at a time, with each block having a length of 100 bytes. The data are to be read into a data area within the user process at virtual location 1000 to 1099. The simplest way would be to execute an I/O command (something like Read Block[1000, tape]) to the tape unit and then wait for the data to become available. The waiting could either be busy-waiting (continuously test the device status), or more practically, process suspension on an interrupt.

There are two problems with this approach. First, the program is hung up waiting for the relatively slow I/O to complete. The second problem is that this approach to I/O interferes with swapping decisions by the operating system. Virtual locations 1000 to 1099 must remain in main memory during the course of the block transfer. Otherwise, some of the data may be lost. If paging is being used, at least the page containing the target locations must be locked into main memory. Thus, although portions of the process may be paged out to disk, it is impossible to completely swap the process out, even if this is desired by the operating system. Notice also that there is a risk of single-process deadlock. If a process issues an I/O command, is suspended awaiting the result, and then is swapped out prior to the beginning of the operation, then the process is blocked waiting for the I/O event, and the I/O operation is blocked waiting for the process to be swapped in. To avoid this deadlock, the user memory involved in the I/O operation must be locked in main memory immediately after the I/O request is issued, even though the I/O operation is queued and may not be executed for some time.

The same considerations apply to an output operation. If a block is being transferred from a user process area directly to an I/O module, then the process is blocked during the transfer and the process may not be swapped out.

To avoid these overheads and inefficiencies, it is sometimes convenient to perform input transfers in advance of requests being made and to perform output transfers some time after the request is made. This technique is known as *buffering*. In this section, we look at some of the buffering schemes that are supported by operating systems to improve the performance of the system.

In discussing the various approaches to buffering, it is sometimes important to make a distinction between two types of I/O devices: block-oriented and stream-oriented. **Block-oriented** devices store information in blocks that are usually of a fixed size, and transfers are made a block at a time. Generally, it is possible to reference data by their block number. Disks and tapes are examples of block-oriented devices. **Stream-oriented** devices transfer data in and out as

a stream of bytes; they have no block structure. Terminals, printers, communications ports, mouse and other pointing devices, and most other devices that
are not secondary storage are stream-oriented.

Single Buffer

The simplest type of support that the operating system can provide is single
buffering (Figure 7.6b). When a user process issues an I/O request, the operating
system assigns a buffer in the system portion of main memory to the operation.

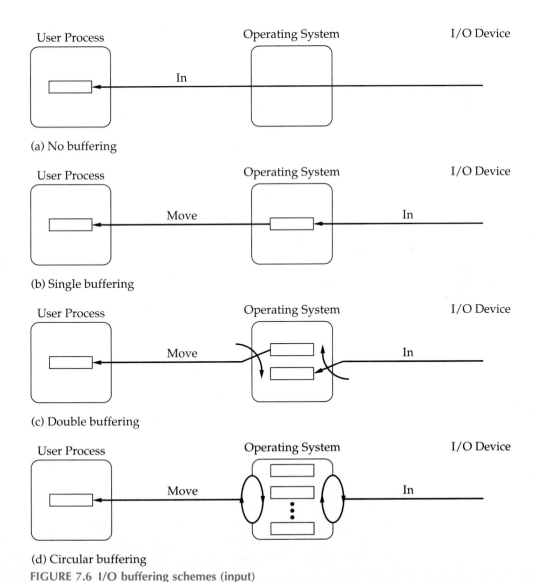

(a) No buffering

(b) Single buffering

(c) Double buffering

(d) Circular buffering

FIGURE 7.6 I/O buffering schemes (input)

For block-oriented devices, the single buffering scheme can be described as follows. Input transfers are made to the system buffer. When the transfer is complete, the process moves the block into user space and immediately requests another block. This is called *reading ahead*, or *anticipated input*; it is done in the expectation that the block will eventually be needed. For many types of computation, this is a reasonable assumption most of the time. Only at the end of a sequence of processing will a block be read in unnecessarily.

This approach will generally provide a speedup compared to the lack of system buffering. The user process can be processing one block of data while the next block is being read in. The operating system is able to swap the process out because the input operation is taking place into system memory rather than into user process memory. This technique does, however, complicate the logic in the operating system. The operating system must keep track of the assignment of system buffers to user processes. The swapping logic is also affected: If the I/O operation involves the same disk that is used for swapping, it hardly makes sense to queue disk Writes to the same device for swapping the process out. This attempt to swap the process and release main memory will itself not begin until after the I/O operation finishes, at which time swapping the process to disk may no longer be appropriate.

Similar considerations apply to block-oriented output. When data are being transmitted to a device, they are first copied from the user space into the system buffer, from which they will ultimately be written. The requesting process is now free to continue or to be swapped as necessary.

[KNUT73] suggests a crude but informative performance comparison between single buffering and no buffering. Suppose that T is the time required to input one block and that C is the computation time that intervenes between input requests. Without buffering, the execution time per block is essentially $T + C$. With a single buffer, the time is max $[C, T] + M$, where M is the time required to move the data from the system buffer to user memory. In most cases, this latter quantity is substantially less than the former.

For stream-oriented I/O, the single buffering scheme can be used in a line-at-a-time fashion or a byte-at-a-time fashion. Line-at-a-time operation is appropriate for scroll-mode terminals (sometimes called *dumb* terminals). With this form of terminal, user input is one line at a time, with a carriage return signaling the end of a line, and output to the terminal is similarly one line at a time. A line printer is another example of such a device. Byte-at-a-time operation is used on forms-mode terminals, when each keystroke is significant, and for many other peripherals, such as sensors and controllers.

In the case of line-at-a-time I/O, the buffer can be used to hold a single line. The user process is suspended during input, awaiting the arrival of the entire line. For output, the user process can place a line of output in the buffer and continue processing. It need not be suspended unless it has a second line of output to send before the buffer is emptied from the first output operation. In the case of byte-at-a-time I/O, the interaction between the operating system and the user process follows the producer/consumer model discussed in Chapter 4.

Double Buffer

An improvement over single buffering can be had by assigning two system buffers to the operation (Figure 7.6c). A process now transfers data to (or from) one buffer while the operating system empties (or fills) the other. This technique is known as **double buffering** or **buffer swapping**.

For block-oriented transfer, we can roughly estimate the transfer time as max [C, T]. It is therefore possible to keep the block-oriented device going at full speed if $C < T$. On the other hand, if $C > T$, double buffering ensures that the process will not have to wait for I/O. In either case, an improvement over single buffering is achieved. Again, this improvement comes at the cost of increased complexity.

For stream-oriented input, we again are faced with the two alternative modes of operation. For line-at-a-time I/O, the user process need not be suspended for input or output unless the process runs ahead of the double buffers. For byte-at-a-time operation, the double buffer offers no particular advantage over a single buffer of twice the length. In both cases, the producer/consumer model is followed.

Circular Buffer

A double-buffer scheme should smooth out the flow of data between an I/O device and a process. If the performance of a particular process is the focus of our concern, then we would like for the I/O operation to be able to keep up with the process. Double buffering may be inadequate if the process performs rapid bursts of I/O. In this case, the problem can often be alleviated by using more than two buffers.

When more than two buffers are used, the collection of buffers is itself re-ferred to as a *circular buffer* (Figure 7.6d), with each individual buffer being one unit in the circular buffer. This is simply the bounded-buffer producer/consumer model studied in Chapter 4.

The Utility of Buffering

Buffering is a technique that smooths out peaks in I/O demand. However, no amount of buffering will allow an I/O device to keep pace indefinitely with a process when the average demand of the process is greater than the I/O device can service. Even with multiple buffers, all the buffers will eventually fill up and the process will have to wait after processing each chunk of data. However, in a multiprogramming environment, when there is a variety of I/O activity and a variety of process activity to service, buffering is one tool that can increase the efficiency of the operating system and the performance of individual processes.

DISK I/O

Over the past 30 years, the increase in the speed of processors and main memory has far outstripped that of disk access, with processor and main memory speeds increasing by about two orders of magnitude compared to one order of magnitude for disk. The result is that disks are currently at least four orders of magnitude slower than main memory. This gap is expected to continue into the foreseeable future. Thus, the performance of disk storage subsystems is of vital concern, and much research has gone into schemes for improving that performance. In this section, we highlight some of the key issues and look at the most important approaches. Because the performance of the disk system is tied closely to issues of file design, the discussion continues in Chapter 8.

Disk Performance Parameters

The actual details of disk I/O operation depend on the computer system, the operating system, and the nature of the I/O channel and disk controller hardware. A general timing diagram of disk I/O transfer is shown in Figure 7.7.

When the disk drive is operating, the disk is rotating at constant speed. To read or write, the head must be positioned at the desired track and at the beginning of the desired sector on that track. Track selection involves moving the head in a movable-head system or electronically selecting one head on a fixed-head system. On a movable-head system, the time it takes to position the head at the track is known as **seek time**. In either case, once the track is selected, the disk controller waits until the appropriate sector rotates to line up with the head. The time it takes for the beginning of the sector to reach the head is known as **rotational delay**, or rotational latency. The sum of the seek time if any and the rotational delay is the **access time**, the time it takes to get into position to read or write. Once the head is in position, the Read or Write operation is then performed as the sector moves under the head; this is the data transfer portion of the operation.

In addition to the access time and transfer time, several queuing delays are normally associated with a disk I/O operation. When a process issues an I/O request, it must first wait in a queue for the device to be available. At that time,

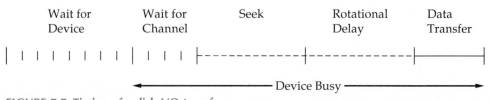

FIGURE 7.7 Timing of a disk I/O transfer

the device is assigned to the process. If the device shares a single I/O channel or a set of I/O channels with other disk drives, then there may be an additional wait for the channel to be available. At that point, the Seek is performed to begin disk access.

In some large mainframe systems, a technique known as rotational positional sensing (RPS) is used. This works as follows. When the Seek command has been issued, the channel is released to handle other I/O operations. When the Seek is completed, the device determines when the data will rotate under the head. As that sector approaches the head, the device tries to reestablish the communication path back to the host. If either the control unit or the channel is busy with another I/O, then the reconnection attempt fails and the device must rotate one whole revolution before it can attempt to reconnect, which is called an RPS miss. This is an extra delay element that must be added to the time line of Figure 7.7.

Seek Time

Seek time is the time required to move the disk arm to the required track. It turns out that this is a difficult quantity to pin down. The Seek time consists of two key components: the initial startup time and the time taken to traverse the cylinders that have to be crossed once the access arm is up to speed. The traversal time is, unfortunately, not a linear function of the number of tracks. We can approximate Seek time with the linear formula:

$$T_s = m \times n + s$$

where

T_s = estimated seek time
n = number of tracks traversed
m = constant that depends on the disk drive
s = startup time

For example, an inexpensive Winchester disk on a personal computer might be approximated by $m = 0.3$ msec and $s = 20$ msec, whereas a larger, more expensive disk drive might have $m = 0.1$ msec and $s = 3$ msec.

Rotational Delay

Disks, other than floppy disks, typically rotate at 3600 rpm, which is one revolution per 16.7 msec. Thus, on the average, the rotational delay will be 8.3 msec. Floppy disks rotate much more slowly, typically between 300 and 600 rpm. Thus, the average delay will be between 100 and 200 msec.

Transfer Time

The transfer time to or from the disk depends on the rotation speed of the disk in the following fashion:

$$T = \frac{b}{rN}$$

where

T = transfer time
b = number of bytes to be transferred
N = number of bytes on a track
r = rotation speed in revolutions per second

Thus, the total average access time can be expressed as

$$T_a = T_s + \frac{1}{2r} + \frac{b}{rN}$$

where T_s is the average seek time.

A Timing Comparison

Having defined the preceding parameters, let us look at two I/O operations that illustrate the danger of relying on average values. Consider a typical disk with an advertised average Seek time of 20 msec, a transfer rate of 1 MB/s, and 512-byte sectors with 32 sectors per track. Suppose that we wish to read a file consisting of 256 sectors for a total of 128 KB. We would like to estimate the total time for the transfer.

First, let us assume that the file is stored as compactly as possible on the disk. That is, the file occupies all the sectors on eight adjacent tracks (8 tracks × 32 sectors/track = 256 sectors). This is known as *sequential organization*. Now, the time to read the first track is as follows:

Average seek	20	msec
Rotational delay	8.3	msec
Read 32 sectors	16.7	msec
	45	msec

Suppose that the remaining tracks can now be read with essentially no Seek time. That is, the I/O operation can keep up with the flow from the disk. Then, at most, we need to deal with rotational delay for each succeeding track. Thus, each successive track is read in 8.3 + 16.7 = 25 msec. To read the entire file:

Total time = 45 + 7 × 25 = 220 msec = 0.22 sec

Now let us calculate the time required to read the same data using random access rather than sequential access; that is, access to the sectors is distributed randomly over the disk. For each sector, we have:

Average seek	20	msec
Rotational delay	8.3	msec
Read 1 sector	0.5	msec
	28.8	msec

Total time = 256 × 28.8 = 7373 msec = 7.37 sec

It is clear that the order in which sectors are read from the disk has a tremendous effect on I/O performance. In the case of file access in which multiple sectors are read or written, we have some control over the way in which sectors of data are deployed, and we have something to say on this subject in the next chapter. However, even in the case of a file access, in a multiprogramming environment, there will be multiple I/O requests competing for the same disk. Thus, it is worthwhile to examine ways in which the performance of disk I/O can be improved over performance that is achieved with purely random access to the disk. In the remainder of this section, we examine two of the most popular strategies, the use of disk scheduling and the disk cache. In the next chapter, we examine file organization and storage issues that affect performance.

Disk Scheduling Policies

If we examine the example in the previous section, we see that the reason for the difference in performance can be traced to Seek time. If sector access requests involve selection of tracks at random, then the performance of the disk I/O system will be as poor as possible. To improve matters, we need to reduce the average time spent on Seeks.

Consider the typical situation in a multiprogramming environment, in which the operating system maintains a queue of requests for each I/O device. So, for a single disk, there will be a number of I/O requests (Reads and Writes) from various processes in the queue. If we select items from the queue in random order, then we can expect that the tracks to be visited will occur randomly, giving the worst possible performance. This **random scheduling** is useful as a benchmark against which to evaluate other techniques.

The simplest form of scheduling would be first-in, first-out (FIFO) scheduling, which simply means that we process items from the queue in sequential order. This strategy has the advantage of being fair because every request is honored and the requests are honored in the order received. Figure 7.8a illustrates the disk arm movement with FIFO compared with three other policies. In this example, we assume a disk with 200 tracks and that the disk request queue has random requests in it. The requested tracks, in the order received, are: 55, 58, 39, 18, 90, 160, 150, 38, 184. Table 7.3a tabulates the results.

With FIFO, if there are only a few processes that require access and if many of the requests are to clustered file sectors, then we can hope for good performance. However, this technique will often approach random scheduling in performance if there are many processes competing for the disk. Thus, it may be profitable to consider a more sophisticated scheduling policy. A number of these are listed in Table 7.4, and will now be considered.

Priority

With a system based on priority (PRI), the control of the scheduling is outside the control of disk management software. Such an approach is not intended to optimize disk use but to meet other objectives within the operating system.

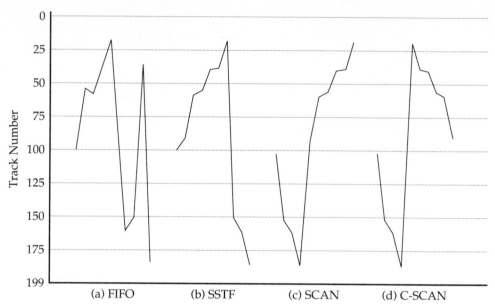

FIGURE 7.8 Comparison of disk scheduling algorithms (see Table 7.3)

Short batch jobs and interactive jobs are often given higher priority than longer jobs that require longer computation. This practice allows a lot of short jobs to be flushed through the system quickly and may provide good interactive response time. However, longer jobs may have to wait excessively long times. Furthermore, such a policy could lead to countermeasures on the part of users who may split their jobs into smaller pieces to beat the system. This type of policy tends to be poor for data base systems.

Last-In, First-Out

Surprisingly, a policy of always taking the most recent request has some merit. In transaction processing systems, giving the device to the most recent user should result in little or no arm movement for moving through a sequential file. Taking advantage of this locality improves throughput and reduces queue lengths. As long as a job can actively use the file system, it is processed as fast as possible. However, if the disk is kept busy because of a large workload, there is the distinct possibility of starvation. Once a job has entered an I/O request in the queue and fallen back from the head of the line, the job can never regain the head of the line unless the queue in front of it empties.

FIFO, priority, and (last-in, first-out) LIFO scheduling are based solely on attributes of the queue or the requestor. If the current track position is known to the scheduler, then scheduling based on the requested item can be employed. We examine these policies next.

TABLE 7.3 Comparison of Disk Scheduling Algorithms

(a) FIFO (starting at track 100)		(b) SSTF (starting at track 100)		(c) SCAN (starting at track 100, in the direction of increasing track number)		(d) C-SCAN (starting at track 100, in the direction of increasing track number)	
Next Track Accessed	Number of Tracks Traversed	Next Track Accessed	Number of Tracks Traversed	Next Track Accessed	Number of Tracks Traversed	Next Track Accessed	Number of Tracks Traversed
55	45	90	10	150	50	150	50
58	3	58	32	160	10	160	10
39	19	55	3	184	24	184	24
18	21	39	16	90	94	18	166
90	72	38	1	58	32	38	20
160	70	18	20	55	3	39	1
150	10	150	132	39	16	55	16
38	112	160	10	38	1	58	3
184	146	184	24	18	20	90	32
Average seek length:	55.3	Average seek length:	27.5	Average seek length:	27.8	Average seek length:	35.8

TABLE 7.4   Disk Scheduling Algorithms [WIED87]

Name	Description	Remarks
Selection according to requestor:		
RSS	Random scheduling	For analysis and simulation
FIFO	First-in, first-out	Fairest of them all
PRI	Priority by process	Control outside of disk queue management
LIFO	Last-in, first-out	Maximize locality and resource utilization
Selection according to requested item:		
SSTF	Shortest service time first	High use, small queues
SCAN	Back and forth over disk	Better service distribution
C-SCAN	One way with fast return	Lower service variability
N-step-SCAN	SCAN of N records at a time	Service guarantee
FSCAN	N-step-SCAN with N = queue size at beginning of SCAN cycle	Load-sensitive

Shortest Service Time First

The policy of shortest service time first (SSTF) is to select the disk I/O request that requires the least movement of the disk arm from its current position. Thus, we always choose to incur the minimum Seek time. Of course, always choosing the minimum Seek time does not guarantee that the average Seek time over a number of arm movements will be minimum. However, this choice should provide better performance than FIFO. Since the arm can move in two directions, a random tie-breaking algorithm may be used to resolve cases of equal distances.

Figure 7.8b and Table 7.3b show the performance of SSTF on the same example as was used for FIFO.

SCAN

With the exception of FIFO, all the policies described so far can leave some request unfulfilled until the entire queue is emptied. That is, there may always be new requests arriving that will be chosen before an existing request. A simple alternative that prevents this sort of starvation is the SCAN algorithm.

With SCAN, the arm is required to move in one direction only, satisfying all outstanding requests en route, until it reaches the last track in that direction or until there are no more requests in that direction. This latter refinement is sometimes referred to as the LOOK policy. The service direction is then reversed and the scan proceeds in the opposite direction, again picking up all requests in order.

Figure 7.8c and Table 7.3c illustrate the SCAN policy. As can be seen, the SCAN policy behaves almost identically with the SSTF policy. Indeed, if we had assumed that the arm was moving in the direction of lower track numbers at the beginning of the example, then the scheduling pattern would have been identical for SSTF and SCAN. However, this is a static example in which no new items are added to the queue. Even when the queue is dynamically changing, SCAN will be similar to SSTF unless the request pattern is unusual.

Note that the SCAN policy is biased against the area most recently traversed. Thus, it does not exploit locality as well as SSTF or even LIFO does.

It is not difficult to see that the SCAN policy favors jobs whose requests are for tracks nearest to both innermost and outermost cylinders and that it favors the latest-arriving jobs. The first problem can be avoided via the C-SCAN policy, whereas the second problem can be addressed by the N-step-SCAN policy.

C-SCAN

The C-SCAN policy restricts scanning to one direction only. Thus, when the last track has been visited in one direction, the arm is returned to the opposite end of the disk and the scan begins again, which reduces the maximum delay experienced by new requests. With SCAN, if the expected time for a scan from inner track to outer track is t, then the expected service interval for sectors at the periphery is $2t$. With C-SCAN, the interval is on the order of $t + s_{max}$, where s_{max} is the maximum seek time.

Figure 7.8d and Table 7.3d illustrate C-SCAN behavior.

N-step-SCAN and FSCAN

With SSTF, SCAN, and C-SCAN, it is possible that the arm may not move for a considerable time. For example, if one or a few processes have high access rates to one track, they can monopolize the entire device by repeated requests to that track. High-density multisurface disks are more likely to be affected by this characteristic than are lower-density disks and/or disks with only one or two surfaces. To avoid this "arm stickiness," the disk Request queue can be segmented, with one segment at a time being processed completely. Two examples of this approach are N-step-SCAN and FSCAN.

The N-step-SCAN policy segments the disk Request queue into subqueues of length N. Subqueues are processed one at a time, using SCAN. While a queue is being processed, new requests must be added to some other queue. If fewer than N requests are available at the end of a scan, then all of them are processed with the next scan. With large values of N, the performance of N-step-SCAN approaches that of SCAN; with a value of $N = 1$, the FIFO policy is adopted.

The FSCAN policy uses two subqueues. When a scan begins, all the requests are in one of the queues, with the other being empty. During the scan, all new requests are put into the queue that was initially empty. Thus, service of new requests is deferred until all the old requests have been processed.

Table 7.4 summarizes the various disk scheduling algorithms.

Disk Cache

In Section 1.7 and Appendix 1A, we summarized the principles of cache memory. The term *cache memory* is usually used to apply to a memory that is smaller and faster than main memory and that is interposed between main memory and the processor. Such a cache memory reduces average memory access time by exploiting the principle of locality.

The same principle can be applied to disk memory. Specifically, a disk cache is a buffer in main memory for disk sectors. The cache contains a copy of some of the sectors on the disk. When an I/O request is made for a particular sector, a check is made to determine if the sector is in the disk cache. If so, the request is satisfied via the cache. If not, the requested sector is read into the disk cache from the disk. Because of the phenomenon of locality of reference, when a block of data is fetched into the cache to satisfy a single I/O request, it is likely that there will be future references to that same block.

Design Considerations

Several design issues are of interest. First, when an I/O request is satisfied from the disk cache, the data in the disk cache must be delivered to the requesting process. Delivery can be made either by transferring the block of data within main memory from the disk cache to memory assigned to the user process, or simply by using a shared memory capability and passing a pointer to the appropriate slot in the disk cache. The latter approach saves the time of a memory-to-memory transfer and also allows shared access by other processes using the readers/writers model described in Chapter 4.

A second design issue has to do with the replacement strategy. When a new sector is brought into the disk cache, one of the existing blocks must be replaced. This is the identical problem presented in Chapter 5, where the requirement was for a page replacement algorithm. A number of algorithms have been tried. The most commonly used algorithm is the least recently used (LRU) algorithm, in which the block that has been in the cache longest with no reference to it is replaced. Logically, the cache consists of a stack of blocks, with the most recently referenced block being on the top of the stack. When a block in the cache is referenced, it is moved from its existing position on the stack to the top of the stack. When a block is brought in from secondary memory, the block that is on the bottom of the stack is removed, pushing the incoming block onto the top of the stack. Naturally, it is not necessary actually to move these blocks around in main memory; a stack of pointers can be associated with the cache.

Another possibility is the least frequently used (LFU) algorithm, in which that block in the cache that has experienced the fewest references is replaced. LFU could be implemented by associating a counter with each block. When a block is brought in, it is assigned a count of 1; with each reference to the block, its count is incremented by 1. When replacement is required, the block with the smallest count is selected. Intuitively, it might seem the LFU is more appropriate than LRU because more information about each block is used in the selection process.

A simple LFU algorithm has the following problem. It may be that certain blocks are referenced relatively infrequently overall, but when they are referenced, there are short intervals of repeated re-references due to locality, thus building up high reference counts. After such an interval is over, the reference count may be misleading and not reflect the probability that the block will soon be referenced again. Thus, the effect of locality may actually cause the LFU algorithm to make poor replacement choices.

To overcome this difficulty with LFU, a technique known as *frequency-based replacement* is proposed in [ROBI90]. For clarity, let us first consider a simplified version, illustrated in Figure 7.9a. The blocks are logically organized in a stack, as with the LRU algorithm. A certain portion of the top part of the stack is set aside as a *new section*. When there is a cache hit, the referenced block is moved to the top of the stack. If the block was already in the new section, its reference count is not incremented; otherwise it is incremented by 1. Given a sufficiently large new section, this procedure results in the reference counts for blocks that are repeatedly re-referenced within a short interval remaining unchanged. On a miss, the block with the smallest reference count that is not in the new section is chosen for replacement; the least recently used such block is chosen in the event of a tie.

The authors report that this strategy achieved only slight improvement over LRU. The problem consists of the following:

1. Once a cache miss occurs, a new block with a count of 1 is brought into the new section.
2. The count remains at 1 as long as the block remains in the new section.
3. Eventually the block ages out of the new section, with its count still at 1.

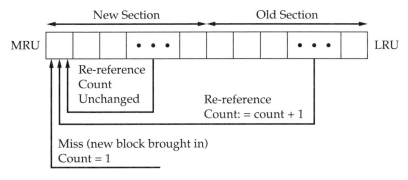

(a) Use of the new section

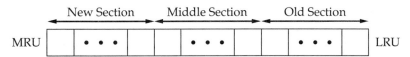

(b) Use of three sections

FIGURE 7.9 Frequency-based replacement

4. If the block is not now re-referenced fairly quickly, it is very likely to be replaced because it necessarily has the smallest reference count of those blocks that are not in the new section. In other words, there does not seem to be a sufficiently long interval for blocks aging out of the new section to build up their reference counts even if they have been relatively frequently referenced.

A further refinement addresses this problem: Divide the stack into three sections: new, middle, and old (Figure 7.9b). As before, reference counts are not incremented on blocks in the new section. However, only blocks in the old section are eligible for replacement. Assuming a sufficiently large middle section, this allows relatively frequently referenced blocks a chance to build up their reference counts before becoming eligible for replacement. Simulation studies reported in [ROBI90] indicate that this refined policy is significantly better than simple LRU or LFU.

Regardless of the particular replacement strategy, the replacement can take place on demand or it can be preplanned. In the former case, a sector is replaced only when the slot is needed. In the latter case, a number of slots are released at a time. The reason for this latter approach is related to the need to write back sectors. If a sector is brought into the cache and only read, then when it is replaced, it is not necessary to write it back out to the disk. However, if the sector has been updated, then it is necessary to write it back out before replacing it. In this latter case, it makes sense to cluster the writing and to order the writing to minimize Seek time.

Performance Considerations

The same performance considerations discussed in Appendix 1A apply here. The issue of cache performance is reduced to a question of whether a given miss ratio can be achieved. This will depend on the locality behavior of the disk references, the replacement algorithm, and other design factors. Principally, however, the miss ratio is a function of the size of the disk cache. Figure 7.10 summarizes results from several studies using LRU, one for a UNIX system running on a VAX [OUST85] and one for IBM mainframe operating systems [SMIT85]. Figure 7.11 shows results for simulation studies of the frequency-based replacement algorithm. A comparison of the two figures points out one of the risks of this sort of performance assessment. The figures appear to show that LRU outperforms the frequency-based replacement algorithm. However, when identical reference patterns using the same cache structure are compared, the frequency-based replacement algorithm is superior. Thus, the exact sequence of reference patterns plus related design issues such as block size will have a profound influence on the performance achieved.

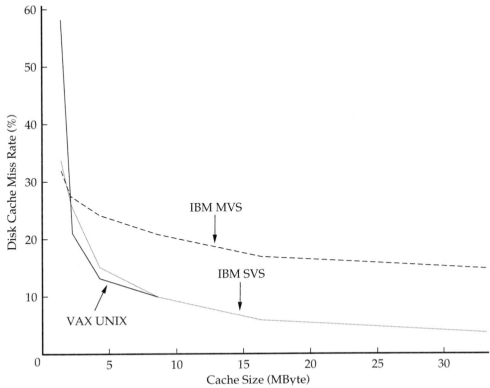

FIGURE 7.10 Some disk cache performance results using LRU

EXAMPLE SYSTEMS

UNIX System V

In UNIX, each individual I/O device is associated with a *special file*, which is managed by the file system and is read and written in the same manner as are user data files. This provides a clean, uniform interface to users and processes. To read from or write to a device, Read and Write requests are made for the special file associated with the device.

Figure 7.12 illustrates the logical structure of the I/O facility. The file subsystem manages files on secondary storage devices. In addition, it serves as the process interface to devices because devices are treated as files.

There are two types of I/O in UNIX: buffered and unbuffered. Buffered I/O passes through system buffers, whereas unbuffered I/O involves the DMA facility, with the transfer taking place directly between the I/O module and the

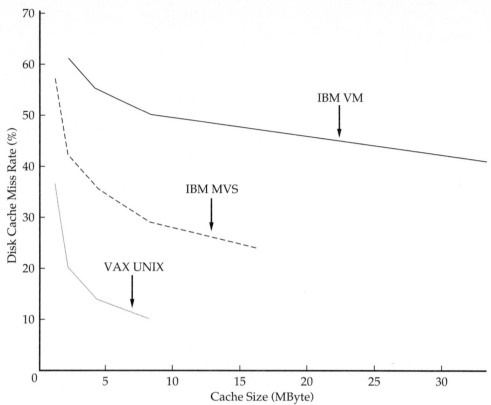

FIGURE 7.11 Disk cache performance using frequency-based replacement [ROBI90]

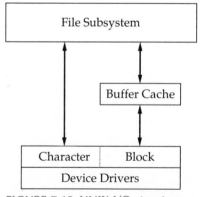

FIGURE 7.12 UNIX I/O structure

process I/O area. For buffered I/O, two types of buffers are used: system buffer caches and character queues.

Buffer Cache

The buffer cache in UNIX is essentially a disk cache. I/O operations with disk are handled through the buffer cache. The data transfer between the buffer cache and the user process space always occurs using DMA. Because both the buffer cache and the process I/O area are in main memory, the DMA facility is used in this case to perform a memory-to-memory copy. This does not use up any processor cycles, but it does consume bus cycles.

To manage the buffer cache, three lists are maintained:

* *Free list:* List of all slots in the cache (a slot is referred to as a buffer in UNIX; each slot holds one disk sector) that are available for allocation
* *Device list:* List of all buffers currently associated with each disk
* *Driver I/O queue:* List of buffers that are actually undergoing or waiting for I/O on a particular device

All buffers should be on the free list or on the driver I/O queue list. Once a buffer is associated with a device, it remains associated with the device even if it is on the free list, until it is actually reused and becomes associated with another device. These lists are maintained as pointers associated with each buffer rather than as physically separate lists.

When a reference is made to a physical block number on a particular device, the operating system first checks to see if the block is in the buffer cache. To minimize the search time, the device list is organized as a hash table, using a technique similar to the overflow with chaining technique discussed in Appendix 5A (Figure 5.40b). Figure 7.13 depicts the general organization of the buffer cache. There is a hash table of fixed length which contains pointers into the buffer cache. Each reference to a (device#, block#) maps into a particular entry in the hash table. The pointer in that entry points to the first buffer in the chain. A hash pointer associated with each buffer points to the next buffer in the chain for that hash table entry. Thus, for all (device#, block#) references that map into the same hash table entry, if the corresponding block is in the buffer cache, then that buffer will be in the chain for that hash table entry. Thus, the length of the search of the buffer cache is reduced by a factor on the order of N, where N is the length of the hash table.

For block replacement, an LRU algorithm is used: After a buffer has been allocated to a disk block, it cannot be used for another block until all other buffers have been used more recently. The free list preserves this LRU order.

Character Queue

Block-oriented devices, such as disk and tape, can be effectively served by the buffer cache. A different form of buffering is appropriate for character-oriented

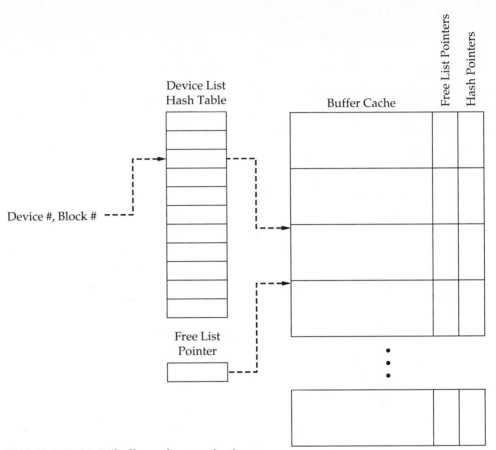

FIGURE 7.13 UNIX buffer cache organization

devices such as terminals and printers. A character queue is either written by the I/O device and read by the process or written by the process and read by the device. In both cases, the producer/consumer model introduced in Chapter 4 is used. Thus, character queues may be read only once; as each character is read, it is effectively destroyed. This is in contrast to the buffer cache, which may be read multiple times and hence follows the readers/writers model (also discussed in Chapter 4).

Unbuffered I/O

Unbuffered I/O, which is simply DMA between device and process space, is always the fastest method for a process to perform I/O. A process that is performing unbuffered I/O is locked in main memory and cannot be swapped out. This condition reduces the opportunities for swapping by tying up part of main memory, thus reducing the overall system performance. Also, the I/O device is tied up with the process for the duration of the transfer, making it unavailable for other processes.

UNIX Devices

UNIX recognizes the following five types of devices:

* Disk drives
* Tape drives
* Terminals
* Communication lines
* Printers

Table 7.5 shows the types of I/O suited to each type of device. Disk drives are heavily used in UNIX, are block-oriented, and have the potential for reasonably high throughput. Thus, I/O for these devices tends to be unbuffered or via buffer cache. Tape drives are functionally similar to disk drives and use similar I/O schemes.

Because terminals involve relatively slow exchange of characters, terminal I/O typically makes use of the character queue. Similarly, communication lines require serial processing of bytes of data for input or output and are best handled by character queues. Finally, the type of I/O used for a printer generally depends on its speed. Slow printers normally use the character queue, whereas a fast printer may employ unbuffered I/O. A buffer cache can be used for a fast printer. However, because data going to a printer are never reused, the overhead of the buffer cache is unnecessary.

OS/2

OS/2 is designed for an environment quite different from that of UNIX or MVS. OS/2 is a single-user system but is equipped with the capability to support a sophisticated array of I/O devices over a wide range of speeds. To provide good performance for the user and to accommodate future I/O devices, OS/2 provides a rich architecture for the support of I/O.

TABLE 7.5   Device I/O in UNIX

Device	Unbuffered I/O	Buffer Cache	Character Queue
Disk drive	X	X	
Tape drive	X	X	
Terminals			X
Communication lines			X
Printers	X		X

In OS/2, an application can be developed through any of the following mechanisms to use I/O:

- File system interface
- I/O control (IOCtl) interface
- Subsystem interfaces for video, keyboard, and mouse
- Character device monitor mechanism
- I/O privilege level (IOPL) code segment mechanism

Figure 7.14 shows this architecture, and Table 7.6 shows which of these mechanisms are appropriate for which devices.

File System Interface

The file system supports I/O for a variety of real and virtual devices, including files, character devices, and pipes. The file system allows the application to enforce mutual exclusion or to provide sharing. A process can perform file system I/O either by use of Read and Write function calls to the operating system or by using a thread to perform the I/O while other threads in the process perform other functions.

The file system does not guarantee the order in which I/O requests from a particular process will be completed. For example, if an application includes a buffer for the I/O and that segment has been swapped out, then other threads of the application process could issue I/O requests that the file system could

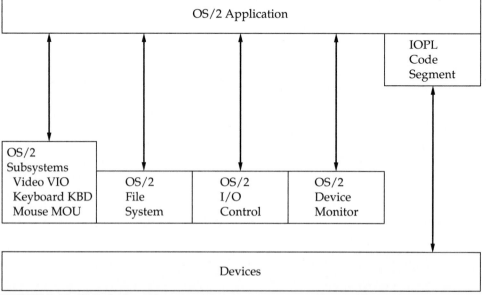

FIGURE 7.14 OS/2 device I/O structure

TABLE 7.6   Performing I/O in OS/2 [KRAN88]

Commonly Used Devices	I/O Interfaces/Mechanisms				
	File System	Subsystem	I/O Control	Monitor	IOPL
Disk	yes	File System	yes	no	no
Diskette	yes	File System	yes	no	no
Screen	yes	VIO	no	no	yes
Keyboard	yes	KBD	yes	yes	no
Mouse	yes	MOU	yes	yes	no
Printer	yes	Spooler	yes	yes	no
Async Comm	yes	no	yes	no	no
Speaker	no	(DosBeep)	no	no	yes
Clock	yes	Timer Services	no	no	no

respond to. Also, the disk device driver uses a SCAN disk scheduling technique, which causes disk requests to be reordered before processing.

The file system can be used to perform I/O to character devices as well as to secondary storage. In the case of character devices, a producer/consumer model is used, similar to the philosophy of UNIX.

I/O Control Interface

The IOCtl supports device-specific control functions over a large number of devices. In general, this interface is used to control the settable parameters of a device or device driver.

Subsystem Interfaces

Subsystem interfaces provide a powerful facility for applications to control the user interface devices: screen, keyboard, mouse. The use of subsystem interfaces facilitates the control of the user interface on a per-session basis. When a session is in the foreground, a process of that session performing video (screen) output sends it directly to the hardware video buffer. When the session is moved to the background, the hardware video buffer is saved to a logical video buffer for that session. While the session is in the background, video output from a process of that session is directed to the logical video buffer. When the user returns the session to the foreground, the subsystem copies its logical video buffer to the hardware video buffer. Keyboard and mouse inputs are always directed to one of the processes in the foreground session.

Character Device Monitor Mechanism

The character device monitor mechanism is a general-purpose method for dealing with device data. The monitor allows an application to intercept the flow of data to and from a device and to perform services on behalf of other applications. Thus, when an application wishes to perform I/O to the device, it actually is interfaced to the monitor. The monitor, in turn, controls the device I/O. The monitor consists of a high-priority thread that controls two private buffers, one for input and one for output. Data from the device are routed to the input buffer. The monitor can then examine, modify, insert, and/or delete characters before passing on the input to an application. A similar sequence occurs on output.

IOPL Code Segment Mechanism

The IOPL code segment is a facility that allows an application to perform I/O directly to a device without going through any system I/O software. This direct control has the advantage of being faster than I/O that involves intermediate system code. Thus, for very high-speed peripherals the direct I/O method is attractive.

MVS

MVS is designed to provide a layered I/O facility that allows programmers to ignore the many details of I/O operations or to bypass or add to some phases of the I/O operation. Figure 7.15 illustrates the logical structure of I/O within MVS. A typical I/O sequence involves the following steps:

1. The user program begins an I/O operation by issuing an OPEN macro instruction for a target I/O device and then requesting input or output, using a macro such as GET, PUT, READ, or WRITE. An I/O macro instruction invokes an operating-system service known as an **access method**. The access method interprets the command and determines which system resources are required. The user could bypass the access method, but this would require the user program to deal with the I/O operation in much greater detail and at a finer-grained level of control.

2. MVS access methods fall into three categories: conventional access methods, telecommunications access methods, and the virtual storage access method (VSAM). Table 7.7 summarizes the access methods available with MVS. With an access method, the program is insulated from I/O details and need be concerned only with using the proper access method to meet its needs.

3. To request the movement of data, either the access method or the user program presents information about the operation to the EXCP (execute channel program) processor. EXCP translates this information into a format understandable to the channel subsystem and invokes the I/O supervisor (IOS). Essentially, EXCP is a program that creates an I/O supervisor block (IOSB) for use by the IOS. The IOSB contains the instructions to the IOS and the main memory addresses involved in the transfer.

4. IOS places the request for I/O on the queue for the chosen I/O device and initiates the channel subsystem. The channel subsystem is initiated by is-

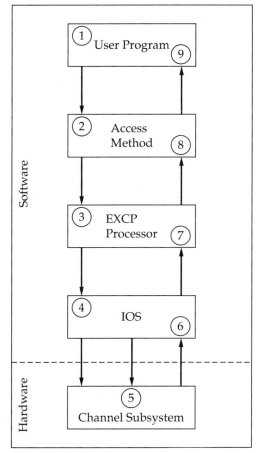

FIGURE 7.15 MVS I/O services

suing a start I/O command that references the channel program in main memory. The CPU is now free to do other work until the channel subsystem indicates that the I/O operation has completed.

5. The channel subsystem is a separate processor that can read and execute channel commands, or instructions, in main memory. It selects the best channel path for data transmission between main memory and the device, and controls the movement of data. When I/O is completed, the subsystem issues an interrupt to the CPU.

6. IOS evaluates the interrupt and returns control to EXCP.

7. EXCP updates various tables to indicate the result of the I/O operation and passes control to the dispatcher.

8. The dispatcher reactivates the access method to respond to the completion of the I/O request.

9. The access method returns control to the user program, together with any required status information.

TABLE 7.7   MVS Access Methods

Conventional Access Methods

Basic Sequential Access Method (BSAM)
Records in a file are sequentially organized. BSAM provides the ability to read and write only physical records and only in sequence.

Queued Sequential Access Method (QSAM)
Records in a file are sequentially organized. With QSAM, logical records can be grouped together and stored in larger physical records (blocks). QSAM handles the blocking and deblocking of logical records and performs buffered I/O.

Basic Direct Access Method (BDAM)
BDAM allows input and output of individual blocks by specifying the physical track and record number.

Indexed Sequential Access Method (ISAM)
One or more fields, called keys, in a record uniquely identify that record. Records can be accessed either directly, by supplying a key, or sequentially in key order.

Basic Partitioned Access Method (BPAM)
The file is grouped into independent collections of records, called *members*. All the records in a member have the same attributes, such as logical record length and block size. A directory holds the name and location of each member. BPAM maintains and accesses the directory. Once a member is located using BPAM, records are accessed using BSAM or QSAM.

Virtual Storage Access Methods

Virtual Storage Access Method (VSAM)
This access method is specifically designed to take advantage of the virtual memory hardware and MVS virtual memory software. It supports both direct and sequential access and provides greater performance and flexibility than other file access methods.

Telecommunication Access Methods

Basic Telecommunication Access Method (BTAM)
BTAM provides a simple capability for transmitting data in the form of messages to and from remote terminals.

Telecommunication Access Method (TCAM)
Supports a wider variety of terminals than BTAM. Allows an application to perform its own message routing, message editing, and error checking.

Virtual Telecommunication Access Method (VTAM)
VTAM is the access method used to support the system network architecture (SNA). It provides a powerful terminal-handling capacity in the context of a full communications architecture.

Much of the I/O activity involves only the channel subsystem and not the main processor. Thus, the MVS I/O architecture provides a facility that is both powerful and efficient.

7.7

SUMMARY

The computer system's interface to the outside world is its I/O architecture. This architecture is designed to provide a systematic means of controlling interaction with the outside world and to provide the operating system with the information it needs to manage I/O activity effectively.

The I/O function is generally broken up into a number of layers, with lower layers dealing with details that are closer to the physical functions to be performed, and higher layers dealing with I/O in a logical and generic fashion. The result is that changes in hardware parameters need not affect most of the I/O software.

A key aspect of I/O is the use of buffers that are controlled by I/O utilities rather than by application processes. Buffering smooths out the differences between the internal speeds of the computer system and the speeds of I/O devices. The use of buffers also decouples the actual I/O transfer from the address space of the application process, which allows the operating system more flexibility in performing its memory-management function.

The aspect of I/O that has the greatest impact on overall system performance is disk I/O. Accordingly, there has been greater research and design effort in this area than in any other kind of I/O. Two of the most widely used approaches to improving disk I/O performance are disk scheduling and the disk cache.

At any time, there may be a queue of requests for I/O on the same disk. It is the object of disk scheduling to satisfy these requests in a way that minimizes the mechanical Seek time of the disk and hence improves performance. The physical layout of pending requests plus considerations of locality come into play.

A disk cache is a buffer, usually kept in main memory, that functions as a cache of disk blocks between disk memory and the rest of main memory. Because of the principle of locality, the use of a disk cache should substantially reduce the number of block I/O transfers between main memory and disk.

7.8

RECOMMENDED READING

A worthwhile survey of disk technology is [SIER90]. Good discussions of disk I/O management can be found in [SILB91] and [DEIT90]. [WIED87] contains an excellent discussion of disk performance issues, including those relating to disk scheduling. More general discussions of I/O can be found in most books on computer architecture, such as [STAL90a] and [HENN90].

7.9

PROBLEMS

7.1 Perform that same type of analysis as that of Table 7.3 for the following sequence of disk track requests: 27, 129, 110, 186, 147, 41, 10, 64, 120. Assume that the disk head is initially positioned over track 100 and is moving in the direction of decreasing track number. Do the same analysis, but now assume that the disk head is moving in the direction of increasing track number.

7.2 Consider a disk with N tracks numbered from 0 to $(N - 1)$ and assume that requested sectors are distributed randomly and evenly over the disk. We want to calculate the average number of tracks traversed by a Seek.

(a) First, calculate the probability of a Seek of length j when the head is currently positioned over track t. Hint: This is a matter of determining the total number of combinations, recognizing that all track positions for the destination of the Seek are equally likely.

(b) Next, calculate the probability of a Seek of length K. Hint: This involves the summing over all possible combinations of movements of K tracks.

(c) Calculate the average number of tracks traversed by a Seek, using the formula for expected value:

$$E[x] = \sum_{i=0}^{N} i \times P_r[x = i]$$

(d) Show for large values of N the average number of tracks traversed by a Seek approach $N/3$.

7.3 In Chapter 5, we introduced the concept of page buffering, which is simply a cache strategy for virtual memory pages. Would a system that employs page buffering have no need for a disk cache of the type described in this chapter? And vice versa?

7.4 The following equation was suggested both for cache memory and disk cache memory:

$$T_S = T_C + M \times T_D$$

Generalize this equation to a memory hierarchy with N levels instead of just 2.

7.5 For the frequency-based replacement algorithm, define F_{new}, F_{middle}, and F_{old} as the fraction of the cache that comprises the new, middle, and old sections, respectively. Clearly, $F_{new} + F_{middle} + F_{old} = 1$. Characterize the policy when:

(a) $F_{old} = 1 - F_{new}$
(b) $F_{old} = 1/(\text{cache size})$

7.6 What is the transfer rate of a 9-track magnetic tape unit whose tape speed is 120 inches per second and whose tape density is 1600 linear bits per inch?

7.7 Assume a 2400-foot tape reel; an interrecord gap of 0.6 in., where the tape stops midway between Reads; that the rate of tape speed increase or decrease during gaps is linear; and that other characteristics of the tape are the same as in problem 7.6. Data on the tape are organized in physical records, with each physical record containing a fixed number of user-defined units, called *logical records*.
(a) How long will it take to read a full tape of 120-byte logical records blocked 10/physical record?
(b) Same, blocked 30?
(c) How many logical records will the tape hold with each of the preceding two blocking factors?
(d) What is the effective overall transfer rate for each of the blocking factors (a) and (b)?
(e) What is the capacity of the tape?

7.8 Calculate how much disk space (in sectors, tracks, and surfaces) will be required to store the logical records read in problem 7.7b if the disk is a fixed sector of 512 bytes per sector, with 96 sectors per track, 110 tracks per surface, and eight usable surfaces. Ignore any file header record(s) and track indexes, and assume that records cannot span two sectors.

7.9 Consider the disk system described in problem 7.8, and assume that the disk rotates at 360 rpm. A processor reads one sector from the disk using interrupt-driven I/O, with one interrupt per byte. If it takes 2.5 μs to process each interrupt, what percentage of the time will the processor spend handling I/O (disregard Seek time).

7.10 Repeat problem 7.9 using DMA, and assume one interrupt per sector.

7.11 A 32-bit computer has two selector channels and one multiplexor channel. Each selector channel supports two magnetic disks and two magnetic tape units. The multiplexor channel has two line printers, two card readers, and ten VDT terminals connected to it. Assume the following transfer rates:

Disk drive	800 KB/sec
Magnetic tape drive	200 KB/sec
Line printer	6.6 KB/sec
Card reader	1.2 KB/sec
VDT	1 KB/sec

Estimate the maximum aggregate I/O transfer rate in this system.

APPENDIX 7A

Secondary Storage Devices

7A.1 Magnetic Disk

A disk is a circular platter constructed of metal or of plastic coated with a magnetizable material. Data are recorded on and later retrieved from the disk by a conducting coil named the **head**. During a Read or Write operation, the head is stationary while the platter rotates beneath it.

The Write mechanism is based on the fact that electricity flowing through a coil produces a magnetic field. Pulses are sent to the head, and magnetic patterns are recorded on the surface below, with different patterns for positive and negative currents. The Read mechanism is based on the fact that a magnetic field moving relative to a coil produces an electrical current in the coil. When the surface of the disk passes under the head, it generates a current of the same polarity as the one already recorded.

Data Organization and Formatting

The head is a relatively small device capable of reading to or writing from a portion of the platter rotating beneath it. This gives rise to the organization of data on the platter in a concentric set of rings, called **tracks**. Each track is the same width as the head. There are typically 500 to 2000 tracks per surface.

Figure 7.16 depicts this data layout. Adjacent tracks are separated by **gaps**, which prevents, or at least minimizes, errors caused by the misalignment of the head or simply by interference of magnetic fields. To simplify the electronics, the same number of bits are typically stored on each track. Thus, the **density**, in bits per linear inch, increases in moving from the outermost track to the innermost track (this same phenomenon is present on a phonograph record).

Data are transferred to and from the disk in **blocks**. Typically, the block is smaller than the capacity of the track. Accordingly, data are stored in block-size regions known as **sectors** (Figure 7.16). There are typically between 10 and 100 sectors per track, and these may be of either fixed or variable length. To avoid imposing unreasonable precision requirements on the system, adjacent sectors are separated by intratrack (interrecord) gaps.

Some means is needed to locate sector positions within a track. Clearly, there must be some starting point on the track and a way of identifying the start and end of each sector. These requirements are handled by means of control data recorded on the disk. Thus, the disk is formatted with some extra data used only by the disk drive and not accessible to the user.

An example of disk formatting is shown in Figure 7.17. In this case, each track contains 30 fixed-length sectors of 600 bytes each. Each sector holds 512 bytes of data plus control information useful to the disk controller. The ID field is a unique identifier, or address, used to locate a particular sector. The SYNCH byte is a special bit pattern that delimits the beginning of the field. The track

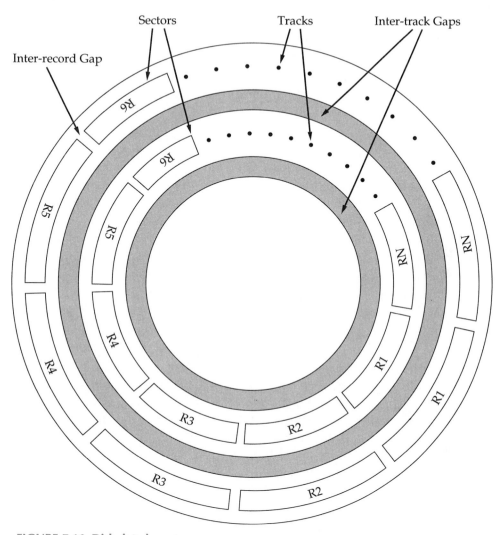

FIGURE 7.16 Disk data layout

number identifies a track on a surface. The head number identifies a head, since this disk has multiple surfaces (explained presently). The ID and data fields each contain an error-detecting code.

Physical Characteristics

Table 7.8 lists the major characteristics that differentiate among the various types of disks. First, the head may either be fixed or movable with respect to the radial direction of the platter. In a **fixed-head disk**, there is one Read/Write head per track. All the heads are mounted on a rigid arm that extends across all tracks

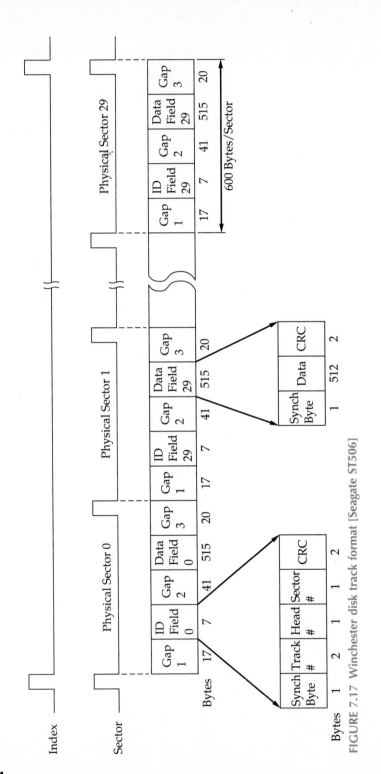

FIGURE 7.17 Winchester disk track format [Seagate ST506]

TABLE 7.8   Physical Characteristics of Disk Systems

Head Motion	Platters
Fixed Head (one per track)	Single-Platter
Movable Head (one per surface)	Multiple-Platter
Disk Portability	**Head Mechanism**
Nonremovable disk	Contact (floppy)
Removable disk	Fixed gap
Sides	Aerodynamic gap (Winchester)
Single-Sided	
Double-Sided	

(Figure 7.18a). In a **movable-head disk**, there is only one Read/Write head (Figure 7.18b). Again, the head is mounted on an arm. Because the head must be able to be positioned above any track, the arm can be extended or retracted for this purpose.

The disk itself is mounted in a disk drive, which consists of the arm, a shaft that rotates the disk, and the electronics needed for input and output of binary data. A **nonremovable disk** is permanently mounted in the disk drive. A **removable disk** can be removed and replaced with another disk. The advantage of the latter type is that unlimited amounts of data are available with a limited number of disk systems. Furthermore, such a disk may be moved from one computer system to another.

On most disks, the magnetizable coating is applied to both sides of the platter, which is then referred to as **double-sided**. Some less expensive disk systems use **single-sided** disks.

Some disk drives accommodate **multiple platters** stacked vertically about an inch apart (Figure 7.19). Multiple arms are provided. The platters come as a unit known as a **disk pack**.

Finally, the head mechanism provides a classification of disks into three types. Traditionally, the Read/Write head has been positioned a fixed distance above the platter, allowing an air gap. At the other extreme is a head mechanism that actually comes into physical contact with the medium during a Read or Write operation. This mechanism is used with the **floppy disk**, which is a small, flexible platter and the least expensive type of disk.

To understand the third type of disk, we need to comment on the relationship between data density and the size of the air gap. The head must generate or sense an electromagnetic field of sufficient magnitude to write and read properly. The narrower the head is, the closer it must be to the platter surface to function. A narrower head means narrower tracks and therefore greater data density, which is desirable. However, the closer the head is to the disk, the greater the risk of error from impurities or imperfections. To push the technology further, the Winchester disk was developed. Winchester heads are used in sealed drive assemblies that are almost free of contaminants. They are designed

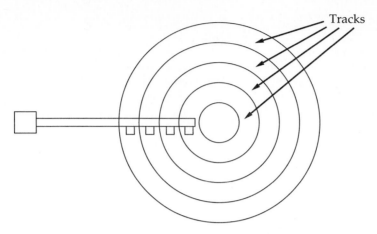

(a) Fixed head

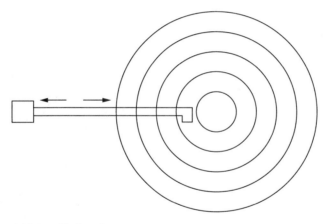

(a) Movable head

FIGURE 7.18 Fixed and movable head disks

to operate closer to the disk's surface than do conventional rigid disk heads, thus allowing greater data density. The head is actually an aerodynamic foil that rests lightly on the platter's surface when the disk is motionless. The air pressure generated by a spinning disk is enough to make the foil rise above the surface. The resulting noncontact system can be engineered to use narrower heads that operate closer to the platter's surface than do conventional rigid disk heads.[1]

---

[1]As a matter of historical interest, the term *Winchester* was originally used by IBM as a code name for the 3340 disk model prior to its announcement. The 3340 was a removable disk pack with the heads sealed within the pack. The term is now applied to any sealed-unit disk drive with aerodynamic head design. The Winchester disk is commonly found built in to personal computers and workstations, where it is referred to as a *hard disk*.

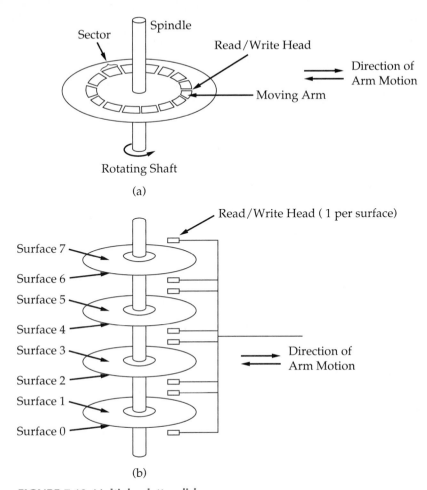

FIGURE 7.19 Multiple-platter disk

7A.2 Magnetic Tape

Tape systems use the same reading and recording techniques as disk systems do. The medium is a flexible mylar tape coated with magnetic oxide. The tape and the tape drive are similar to those of a home tape recorder system.

Data on tape are stored one byte at a time, with either 7 or 9 bits used for each character (Figure 7.20). Normally, one of the 7 or 9 bits is a parity bit. Each bit position across the width of a head is called a **track**. As with the disk, data are read and written in contiguous blocks, called **physical records**, on a tape. Blocks on the tape are separated by gaps, called **interrecord gaps**. Also, as with the disk, the tape is formatted to assist in locating physical records.

A tape drive is referred to as a **sequential-access** device. If the tape head is positioned at record 1, to read physical record n, it is necessary to read physical records 1 through $n - 1$, one at a time. If the head is currently positioned beyond the desired record, it is necessary to rewind the tape a certain distance and then begin reading forward. Unlike the disk, the tape is in motion only during a Read or Write operation.

In contrast to the tape, a disk drive is referred to as a **direct-access** device. This name reflects the fact that a disk drive need not read all sectors on a disk sequentially to get to the desired one. It must wait for only the intervening sectors within one track and can make successive accesses to any track.

Historically, magnetic tape was the first kind of secondary memory. It is still widely used as the member of the memory hierarchy of lowest cost and slowest speed.

7A.3 Optical Memory

In 1983, one of the most successful consumer products of all time was introduced: the compact disk (CD) digital audio system [GUTE88]. The CD is a nonerasable disk that can store more than 60 min of audio information on one side. The huge commercial success of the CD enabled the development of low-cost optical-disk storage technology that now promises to revolutionize the storage of computer data. In the past few years, a variety of optical-disk systems has been introduced (Table 7.9). Three of these systems are increasingly being used in computer applications: CD-ROM, WORM, and the erasable optical disk. We will briefly review each of these.

CD-ROM

Both the audio CD and the CD-ROM (compact disk read-only memory) share a similar technology. The main difference is that CD-ROM players are more rugged and have error-correction devices to ensure that data are properly transferred from disk to computer. Both types of disk are also made the same way. The disk is formed from a resin, such as polycarbonate, and coated with a highly

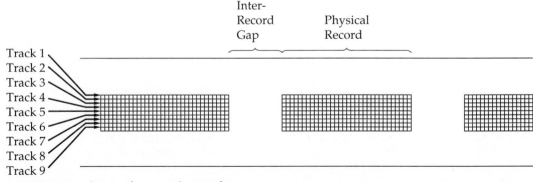

FIGURE 7.20 Nine-track magnetic tape format

reflective surface, usually aluminum. Digitally recorded information (either music or computer data) is imprinted as a series of microscopic pits on the reflective surface. This is done first with a finely focused, high-intensity laser to create a master disk. The master is used in turn to make a die to stamp out copies. The pitted surface of the copies is protected against dust and scratches by a top coat of clear lacquer.

Information is retrieved from a CD or CD-ROM by a low-powered laser housed in an optical-disk player, or drive unit. The laser shines through the clear protective coating while a motor spins the disk past it. The intensity of the reflected light of the laser changes as it encounters a pit. This change is detected by a photosensor and converted into a digital signal.

A pit near the center of a rotating disk travels past a fixed point (such as a laser beam) more slowly than does a pit on the outside rim, so some way must be found to compensate for the variation in speed so that the laser can read all the pits at the same rate. This can be done—as it is on magnetic disks—by increasing the spacing between bits of information recorded in segments of the disk. The information can then be scanned at the same rate by rotating the disk at a fixed speed, known as the **constant angular velocity (CAV)**. Figure 7.21 shows the layout of a disk using CAV. The disk is divided into a number of pie-shaped sectors and into a series of concentric tracks. The advantage of using

TABLE 7.9   Optical Disk Products

CD
  Compact Disk. A nonerasable disk that stores digitized audio information. The standard system uses 12-cm disks and can record more than 60 min of uninterrupted playing time.
CD-ROM
  Compact Disk Read-Only Memory. A nonerasable disk used for storing computer data. The standard system uses 12-cm disks and can hold more than 550 MB.
CD-I
  Compact Disk Interactive. A specification based on the use of CD-ROM. It describes methods for providing audio, video, graphics, text, and machine-executable code on CD-ROM.
DVI
  Digital Video Interactive. A technology for producing digitized, compressed representation of video information. The representation can be stored on CD or other disk media. Current systems use CDs and can store about 20 min of video on one disk.
WORM
  Write-Once, Read-Many. A disk that is more easily written than CD-ROM, making single-copy disks commercially feasible. As with CD-ROM, after the Write operation is performed, the disk is read-only. The most popular size is 5.25-in., which can hold from 200 to 800 MB of data.
Erasable Optical Disk
  A disk that uses optical technology but that can be easily erased and rewritten. Both 3.25-in. and 5.25-in. disks are in use. A typical capacity is 650 MB.

CAV is that individual blocks of data can be directly addressed by track and sector. To move the head from its current location to a specific address, it takes only a short movement of the head to a specific track and a short wait for the proper sector to spin under the head. The disadvantage of CAV is that the amount of data that can be stored on the long outer tracks is the same as that which can be stored on the short inner tracks.

Because putting less information on the outside of a disk wastes space, the CAV method is not used on CDs and CD-ROMs. Instead, information is packed evenly across the disk in segments of the same size, and these segments are scanned at the same rate by rotating the disk at a variable speed. The pits are then read by the laser at a **constant linear velocity (CLV)**. Because the amount of data per track is not constant across the disk, addresses are expressed in the manner used for CDs, that is, in units of 0 to 59 min, 0 to 59 sec, and 0 to 74 blocks. This information is carried at the beginning of each block. At 60 min (the usual limit), the CD-ROM can hold 270,000 blocks, each of which contains

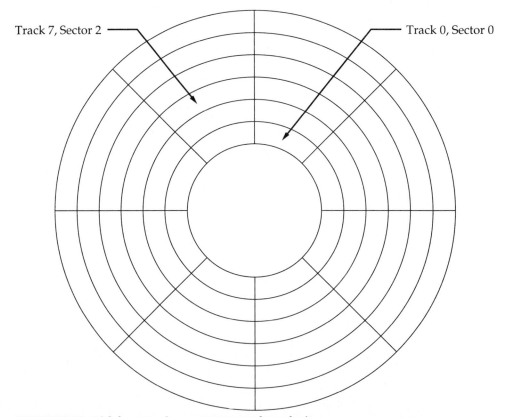

FIGURE 7.21 Disk layout using constant angular velocity

2048 bytes of user data, for a total of 553 MB, the equivalent of more than 1300 5.25-in. floppy disks. The format of a CD-ROM block is shown in Figure 7.22. The format consists of the following fields:

- *Sync:* The sync field identifies the beginning of a block. It consists of a byte of all zeros, 10 bytes of all ones, and a byte of all zeros.
- *Header:* The header contains the block address and the mode byte. Mode 0 specifies a blank data field; mode 1 specifies the use of an error-correcting code and 2048 bytes of data; mode 2 specifies 2336 bytes of user data with no error-correcting code.
- *Data:* User data.
- *Auxiliary:* Additional user data in mode 2. In mode 1, the auxiliary is a 288-byte error-correcting code.

Figure 7.23 indicates the layout used for CDs and CD-ROMs. Data are arranged sequentially along a spiral track. With the use of CLV, random access becomes more difficult. Locating a specific address involves moving the head to the general area, adjusting the rotation speed and reading the address, and then making minor adjustments to find and access the specific sector.

CD-ROM is appropriate for the distribution of large amounts of data to a large number of users. Because of the expense of the initial writing process, it is not appropriate for individualized applications. Compared with traditional magnetic disks, the CD-ROM has three major advantages:

- The information storage capacity is much greater on the optical disk.
- The optical disk together with the information stored on it can be mass replicated inexpensively—unlike a magnetic disk. The data base on a magnetic disk has to be reproduced by copying one disk at a time, using two disk drives.
- The optical disk is removable, allowing the disk itself to be used for archival storage. Most magnetic disks are nonremovable. The information on it must first be copied to tape before the disk drive/disk can be used to store new information.

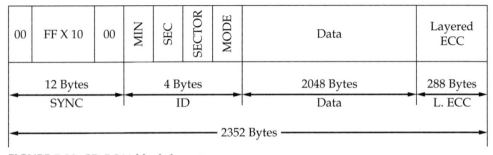

FIGURE 7.22 CD-ROM block format

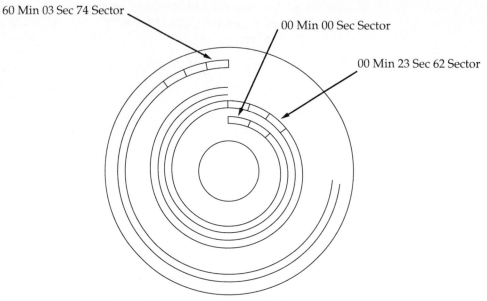

60 Min 03 Sec 74 Sector

00 Min 00 Sec Sector

00 Min 23 Sec 62 Sector

FIGURE 7.23 Disk layout using constant linear velocity

The disadvantages of CD-ROM are as follows:

• It is read-only and cannot be updated.
• It has an access time much longer than that of a magnetic disk drive, as much
  as half a second.

WORM

To accommodate applications in which only one or a small number of copies of
a set of data is needed, the write-once, read-many (WORM) CD has been developed. For the WORM CD, a disk is prepared in such a way that it can be
subsequently written once with a laser beam of modest intensity. Thus, with a
somewhat more expensive disk controller than is used for CD-ROM, the customer can write once as well as read the disk. To provide for more rapid access,
the WORM uses constant angular velocity at the sacrifice of some capacity.

A typical technique for preparing the disk is to use a high-powered laser to
produce a series of blisters on the disk. When the preformatted medium is
placed in a WORM drive, a low-powered laser can produce just enough heat
to burst the prerecorded blisters. During a disk-read operation, a laser in the
WORM drive illuminates the disk's surface. Because the burst blisters provide
higher contrast than the surrounding area does, they are easily recognized by
simple electronics.

The WORM optical disk is attractive for archival storage of documents and
files. It provides a permanent record of large volumes of user data.

Erasable Optical Disk

The most recent development in computer optical disks is the erasable optical disk, which can be repeatedly written and overwritten, as can any magnetic disk. Although a number of approaches have been tried, the only technology that has proven commercially feasible is the magneto-optical system. In this system, the energy of a laser beam is used together with a magnetic field to record and erase information by reversing the magnetic poles in a small area of a disk coated with a magnetic material. The laser beam heats a specific spot on the medium, and a magnetic field can change the orientation of that spot while its temperature is elevated. Because the polarization process does not cause a physical change in the disk, the process can be repeated many times. For reading the disk, the direction of magnetism can be detected by polarized laser light. Polarized light reflected from a particular spot will change its degree of rotation, depending on the magnetic field's orientation.

   The erasable optical disk has the obvious advantage over CD-ROM and WORM that it can be rewritten and thus used as a true secondary storage. As such, it competes with the magnetic disk. The principal advantages of the erasable optical disk compared to the magnetic disk are the following:

- *High capacity:* A 5.25-in. optical disk can hold about 650 MB of data. The most advanced Winchester disks can carry less than half that amount.
- *Portability:* The optical disk can be removed from the drive.
- *Reliability:* The engineering tolerances for the optical disk are much less severe than for high-capacity magnetic disks. Thus, they exhibit higher reliability and longer life.

As with WORM, the erasable optical disk uses constant angular velocity.

CHAPTER 8

File Management

In most applications, the file is the central element. Whatever the objective of the application, it involves the generation and use of information. With the exception of real-time applications and some other specialized applications, the input to the application is by means of a file, and in virtually all applications, output is saved in a file for long-term storage and for later access by the user and by other programs.

Files have a life outside of any individual application that uses them for input and output. Users wish to be able to access files, save them, and maintain the integrity of their contents. To aid in these objectives, virtually all computer systems provide separate file-management systems. Typically, such a system consists of system utility programs that run as privileged applications. However, at the very least, a file-management system needs special services from the operating system; at the most, the entire file-management system is considered part of the operating system. Thus, it is appropriate to consider at least the basic elements of file management in this book.

In this chapter, we examine those basic elements. We begin with an overview of files and file-management systems. This is followed by a look at alternative organizations of files. Although file organization is generally beyond the scope of the operating system, it is essential to have a general understanding of the alternatives in order to appreciate some of the design trade-offs involved in file management. The remainder of the chapter looks at other topics in file management, as outlined in Section 8.1.

OVERVIEW

Files

Four terms are in common use when discussing files:

* Field
* Record
* File
* Database

A **field** is the basic element of data. An individual field contains a single value, such as an employee's last name, a date, or the value of a sensor reading. It is characterized by its length and data type (e.g., ASCII string, decimal). The content of a field is provided by a user or a program. Depending on the file design, fields may be of fixed or variable length. In the latter case, the field often consists of two or three subfields: the actual value to be stored, the name of the field, and in some cases the length of the field. In other cases of variable-length fields, the length of the field is indicated by the use of special demarcation symbols between fields. Most file systems do not support variable-length fields.

A **record** is a collection of related fields that can be treated as a unit by some application programs. For example, an employee record would contain such fields as name, Social Security number, job classification, date of hire, and so on. Again, depending on design, records may be of fixed or variable length. A record is of variable length if some of its fields are of variable length or if the number of fields may vary. In the latter case, each field is usually accompanied by a field name. In either case, the entire record usually includes a length field.

A **file** is a collection of similar records. The file is treated as a single entity by users and applications and may be referenced by name. Files have unique file names and may be created and deleted. Restrictions on access control usually apply at the file level. That is, in a shared system, users and programs are granted or denied access to entire files. In some more sophisticated systems, such controls are enforced at the record or even the field level.

A **database** is a collection of related data. The essential aspects of a database are that the relationships that exist among elements of data are explicit and that the database is designed for use by a number of different applications. A database may contain all the information related to an organization or project, such as a business or a scientific study. The database itself consists of one or more types of files. Usually, there is a separate database management system, although that system may make use of some file-management programs.

Users and applications wish to make use of files. Typical operations that must be supported include the following [LIVA90]:

* *Retrieve_All:* Retrieve all the records of a file. This operation will be required for an application that must process all the information in the file at one time.

For example, an application that produces a summary of the information in the file would need to retrieve all records. This operation is often equated with the term *sequential processing* because all the records are accessed in sequence.

- *Retrieve_One:* This operation requires the retrieval of just a single record. Interactive, transaction-oriented applications need this operation.
- *Retrieve_Next:* This operation requires the retrieval of the record that is "next" in some logical sequence to the most recently retrieved record. Some interactive applications, such as filling in forms, may require such an operation. A program that is performing a search may also use this operation.
- *Retrieve_Previous:* Similar to retrieve next, but in this case the record that is "previous" to the currently accessed record is retrieved.
- *Insert_One:* Insert a new record into the file. It may be necessary that the new record fit into a particular position to preserve a sequencing of the file.
- *Delete_One:* Delete an existing record. Certain linkages or other data structures may need to be updated to preserve the sequencing of the file.
- *Update_One:* Retrieve a record, update one or more of its fields, and rewrite the updated record back into the file. Again, it may be necessary to preserve sequencing when using this operation. If the length of the record has changed, the update operation is generally more difficult than if length is preserved.
- *Retrieve_Few:* Retrieve a number of records. For example, an application or user may wish to retrieve all records that satisfy a certain set of criteria.

The nature of the operations that are most commonly performed on a file influences the way the file is organized, as discussed in Section 8.2.

File Management Systems

A file-management system is that set of system software that provides services to users and applications related to the use of files. Typically, the only way that a user or application may access files is through the file-management system. This relieves the user or programmer of the necessity of developing special-purpose software for each application and provides the system with a means of controlling its most important asset. [GROS86] suggests the following objectives for a file-management system:

- To meet the data-management needs and requirements of the user, which include storage of data and the ability to perform the operations listed earlier
- To guarantee, to the extent possible, that the data in the file are valid
- To optimize performance, both from the system point of view in terms of overall throughput and from the user's point of view in terms of response time
- To provide I/O support for a variety of types of storage device
- To minimize or eliminate the potential for lost or destroyed data
- To provide a standardized set of I/O interface routines
- To provide I/O support for multiple users in the case of multiple-user systems.

With respect to the first point, meeting user requirements, the extent of those requirements depends on the variety of applications and the environment in which the computer system will be used. For an interactive, general-purpose system, the following constitute a minimal set of requirements [WATS70]:

1. Each user should be able to create, delete, and change files.
2. Each user may have controlled access to other users' files.
3. Each user may control what types of accesses are allowed to the user's files.
4. Each user should be able to restructure the user's files in a form appropriate to the problem.
5. Each user should be able to move data between files.
6. Each user should be able to back up and recover the user's files in case of damage.
7. Each user should be able to access the user's files by a symbolic name.

These objectives and requirements should be kept in mind throughout our discussion of file-management systems.

File System Architecture

One way of getting a feel for the scope of file management is to look at a depiction of a typical software organization, as shown in Figure 8.1. Of course, different systems will be organized differently, but this organization is reasonably representative. At the lowest level, **device drivers** communicate directly

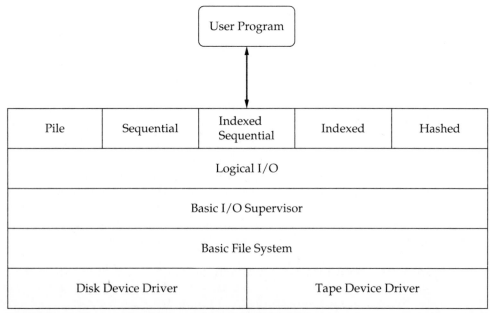

FIGURE 8.1 File system software architecture [GROS86].

with peripheral devices or their controllers or channels. A device driver is responsible for starting I/O operations on a device and processing the completion of an I/O request. In file operations, the typical devices controlled are disk and tape drives. Device drivers are usually considered to be part of the operating system.

The next level is referred to as the **basic file system**, or the **physical I/O** level, which is the primary interface with the environment outside of the computer system. It deals with blocks of data that are exchanged with disk or tape systems. Thus, it is concerned with the placement of those blocks on the secondary storage device and with the buffering of those blocks in main memory. It does not understand the content of the data or the structure of the files involved. The basic file system is often considered part of the operating system.

The **basic I/O supervisor** is responsible for all file I/O initiation and termination. At this level, control structures are maintained that deal with device I/O, scheduling, and file status. The basic I/O supervisor is concerned with the selection of the device on which file I/O is to be performed, on the basis of which file has been selected. It is also concerned with scheduling disk and tape accesses to optimize performance. I/O buffers are assigned and secondary memory is allocated at this level. The basic I/O supervisor is part of the operating system.

Logical I/O is that part of the file system that allows users and applications to access records. Thus, whereas the basic file system deals with blocks of data, the logical I/O module deals with file records. Logical I/O provides a general-purpose record I/O capability and maintains basic data about files.

Finally, the level of the file system closest to the user is usually termed the **access method**. It provides a standard interface between applications and the file systems and devices that hold the data. Different access methods reflect different file structures and different ways of accessing and processing the data. Some of the most common access methods are shown in Figure 8.1, and they are briefly described in Section 8.2.

Functions of File Management

Another way of viewing the functions of a file system is shown in Figure 8.2. Let us follow this diagram from left to right. Users and application programs interact with the file system by means of commands for creating and deleting files and for performing operations on files. Before performing any operation, the file system must identify and locate the selected file. This requires the use of some sort of directory to describe the location of all files plus their attributes. In addition, most shared systems enforce user access control: Only authorized users are allowed to access particular files in particular ways. The basic operations that a user or application may perform on a file are performed at the record level. The user or application views the file as having some structure that organizes the records, such as a sequential structure (e.g., personnel records are stored alphabetically by last name). Thus, to translate user com-

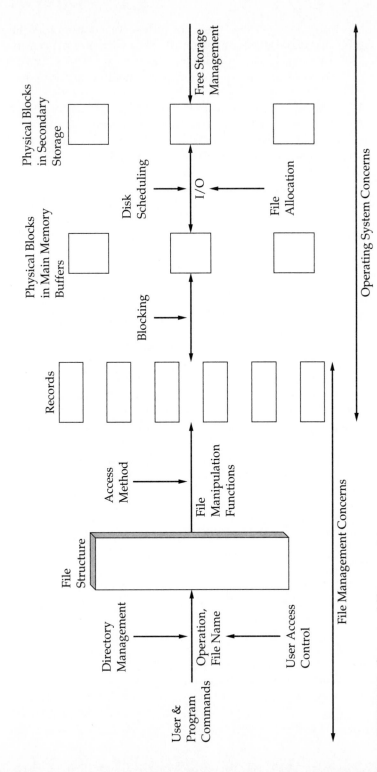

FIGURE 8.2 Elements of file management.

mands into specific file manipulation commands, the access method appropriate to this file structure must be employed.

Whereas users and applications are concerned with records, I/O is done on a block basis. Thus, the records of a file must be blocked for output and unblocked after input. To support block I/O of files, several functions are needed. The secondary storage must be managed. This involves allocating files to free blocks on secondary storage and managing free storage so as to know what blocks are available for new files and growth in existing files. In addition, individual block I/O requests must be scheduled; this issue was dealt with in Chapter 7. Both disk scheduling and file allocation are concerned with optimizing performance. As might be expected, these functions therefore need to be considered together. Furthermore, the optimization will depend on the structure of the files and the access patterns. Accordingly, developing an optimum file-management system from the point of view of performance is an exceedingly complicated task.

Figure 8.2 suggests a division between what might be considered the concerns of the file-management system as a separate system utility and the concerns of the operating system, with the point of intersection being record processing. This division is arbitrary; various approaches are taken in various systems.

As was mentioned, disk scheduling was dealt with in Chapter 7. In the remainder of this chapter, we look at some of the other design issues suggested in Figure 8.2. We begin with a discussion of file organization and access methods. Although this topic is beyond the scope of what is usually considered the concerns of the operating system, it is impossible to assess the other file-related design issues without an appreciation of file organization and access. Next, we look at the concept of file directories, which are often managed by the operating system on behalf of the file-management system. The remaining topics deal with the physical I/O aspects of file management and are properly treated as aspects of operating-system design. One such issue is the way in which logical records are organized into physical blocks. Finally, there are the related issues of file allocation of secondary storage and the management of free secondary storage.

8.2

FILE ORGANIZATION AND ACCESS

A file consists of a collection of records. One of the key elements of file system design is the way in which these records are organized, or structured. In this section, we use the term *file organization* to refer to the logical structuring of the records as determined by the way in which they are accessed. The physical organization of the file on secondary storage depends on the blocking strategy and the file allocation strategy, issues dealt with later in this chapter.

In choosing a file organization, several criteria are important:

- Rapid access for effective information retrieval
- Ease of update to aid in having up-to-date information
- Economy of storage to reduce storage costs
- Simple maintenance to reduce cost and potential for error
- Reliability to assure confidence in the data

The relative priority of these criteria will depend on the applications that will use the file. For example, if a file is to be processed only in batch mode, with all the records accessed every time, then rapid access for retrieval of a single record is of minimal concern. A file stored on CD-ROM will never be updated, and so ease of update is not an issue.

These criteria may conflict. For example, for economy of storage, there should be minimum redundancy in the data. On the other hand, redundancy is the primary means of increasing the speed of access to data. An example of this is the use of indexes.

The number of alternative file organizations that have been implemented or just proposed is unmanageably large, even for a book devoted to file systems. In this brief survey, we outline five fundamental organizations. Most structures used in actual systems either fall into one of these categories or can be implemented with a combination of these organizations. The five organizations, depicted in Figure 8.3, are the following:

- The pile
- The sequential file
- The indexed-sequential file
- The indexed file
- The direct, or hashed, file

Table 8.1 summarizes relative performance aspects of these five organizations.

The Pile

The least complicated form of file organization may be termed the *pile*. Data are collected in the order in which they arrive. Each record consists of one burst of data. The purpose of the pile is simply to accumulate the mass of data and save it. Records may have different fields, or they may have similar fields in different orders. Thus, each field should be self-describing, including a field name as well as a value. The length of each field must be implicitly indicated by delimiters, explicitly included as a subfield, or known as default for that field type.

Because there is no structure to the pile file, record access is by exhaustive search. That is, if we wish to find a record that contains a particular field with a particular value, it is necessary to examine each record in the pile until the desired record is found or the entire file has been searched. If we wish to find all records that contain a particular field or contain that field with a particular value, then the entire file must be searched.

Pile files are encountered when data are collected and stored before processing or when data are not easy to organize. This type of file uses space well

TABLE 8.1 Grades of Performance for Five Basic File Methods [WIED87]

File Method	Use of Available Space		Update		Retrieval		
	Record Size Variable	Record Size Fixed	Record Size Equal	Record Size Greater	Single Record	Subset	Exhaustive
Pile	A	B	A	E	E	D	B
Sequential	F	A	D	F	F	D	A
Indexed sequential	F	B	B	D	B	D	B
Indexed	B	C	C	C	A	B	D
Hashed	F	B	B	F	B	F	E

A = Excellent, well suited to this purpose $\approx O(r)$
B = Good $\approx O(o \times r)$
C = Adequate $\approx O(r \log n)$
D = Requires some extra effort $\approx O(n)$
E = Possible with extreme effort $\approx O(r \times n)$
F = Not reasonable for this purpose $\approx O(n^{>1})$

where
r = size of the result
o = number of records that overflow
n = number of records in file

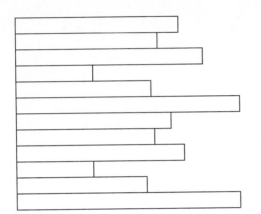

Variable-length records
Variable set of fields
Chronological order

(a) Pile file

Key field

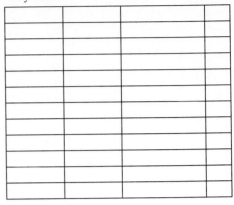

Fixed-length records
Fixed set of fields in fixed order
Sequential order based on key field

(b) Sequential file

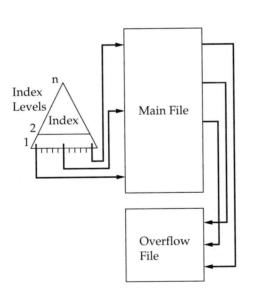

(c) Indexed sequential file

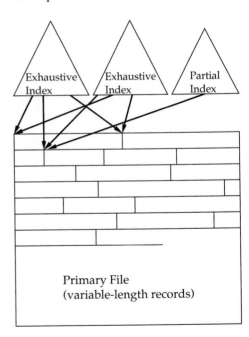

(d) Indexed file

FIGURE 8.3 Common file organizations.

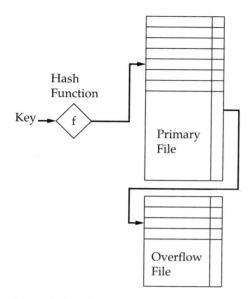

(e) Hash file

FIGURE 8.3 *(continued)*

when the stored data vary in size and structure. Pile files are perfectly adequate for exhaustive searches, and are easy to update. However, beyond these limited uses, this type of file is unsuitable for most applications.

The Sequential File

The most common form of file structure is the sequential file. In this type of file, a fixed format is used for records. All records are of the same length, consisting of the same number of fields of fixed length in a particular order. Because the length and position of each field are known, only the values of fields need to be stored; the field name and the length for each field are attributes of the file structure.

One particular field, usually the first field in each record, is referred to as the **key field**. The key field uniquely identifies the record; thus, key values for different records are always different. Furthermore, the records are stored in key sequence: alphabetical order for a text key and numerical order for a numerical key.

Sequential files are typically used in batch applications and are generally optimum for such applications if they involve the processing of all the records (e.g., a billing or payroll application). The sequential file organization is the only one that is easily stored on tape as well as on disk.

For interactive applications that involve queries or updates of individual records, the sequential file provides poor performance. Access requires the sequential search of the file for a key match. If the entire file, or a large portion of the file, can be brought into main memory at one time, more efficient search techniques are possible. Nevertheless, considerable processing and delay are encountered to access a record in a large sequential file. Additions to the file also present problems. Typically, a sequential file is stored in simple sequential ordering of the records within blocks. That is, the physical organization of the file on tape or disk directly matches the logical organization of the file. In this case, the usual procedure is to place new records in a separate pile file, called a *log file* or *transaction file*. Periodically, a batch update is performed that merges the log file with the master file to produce a new file in correct key sequence.

An alternative is to physically organize the sequential file as a linked list. One or more records are stored in each physical block. Each block on disk contains a pointer to the next block. The insertion of new records involves pointer manipulation but does not require that the new records occupy a particular physical block position. Thus, some added convenience is obtained at the cost of additional processing and overhead.

The Indexed Sequential File

The most popular approach to overcoming the disadvantages of the sequential file is the indexed sequential file. The indexed sequential file maintains the key characteristic of the sequential file: Records are organized in sequence based on a key field. Two features are added: an index to the file to support random access, and an overflow file. The index provides a lookup capability to quickly reach the vicinity of a desired record. The overflow file is similar to the log file used with a sequential file, but it is integrated so that records in the overflow file are located by following a pointer from their predecessor record.

In the simplest indexed sequential structure, a single level of indexing is used. The index in this case is a simple sequential file. Each record in the index file consists of two fields: a key field, which is the same as the key field in the main file, and a pointer into the main file. To find a specific field, the index is searched to find the highest key value that is equal to or precedes the desired key value. The search continues in the main file at the location indicated by the pointer.

To see the effectiveness of this approach, consider a sequential file with 1 million records. To search for a particular key value will require on average 500,000 record accesses. Now, suppose that an index containing 1000 entries is constructed, with the keys in the index more or less evenly distributed over the main file. Now, it will take on average 500 accesses to the index file followed by 500 accesses to the main file to find the record. The average search length is reduced from 500,000 to 1000!

Additions to the file are handled in the following manner. Each record in the main file contains an additional field not visible to the application, which is a pointer to the overflow file. When a new record is to be inserted into the file, it is added to the overflow file. The record in the main file that immediately precedes the new record in logical sequence is updated to contain a pointer to the new record in the overflow file. If the immediately preceding record is itself in the overflow file, then the pointer in that record is updated. As with the sequential file, the indexed sequential file is occasionally merged with the overflow file in batch mode.

The indexed sequential file greatly reduces the time required to access a single record without sacrificing the sequential nature of the file. To process the entire file sequentially, the records of the main file are processed in sequence until a pointer to the overflow file is found. Then accessing continues in the overflow file until a null pointer is encountered, at which time accessing of the main file is resumed where it was left off.

To provide even greater efficiency in access, multiple levels of indexing can be used. Thus, the lowest level of index file is treated as a sequential file and a higher-level index file is created for that file. Consider again a file with 1 million records. A lower-level index with 10,000 entries is constructed. A higher-level index into the lower-level index of 100 entries can then be constructed. The search begins at the higher-level index (average length = 50 accesses) to find an entry point into the lower-level index. This index is then searched (average length = 50) to find an entry point into the main file, which is then searched (average length = 50). Thus, the average length of search has been reduced from 500,000 to 1000 to 150.

The Indexed File

The indexed sequential file retains one limitation of the sequential file: Effective processing is limited to that which is based on a single field of the file. When it is necessary to search for a record on the basis of some other attribute than the key field, both forms of sequential file are inadequate. In some applications, this flexibility is desirable.

To achieve this flexibility, a structure is needed that employs multiple indexes, one for each type of field that may be the subject of a search. In the general indexed file, the concept of sequentiality and a single key are abandoned. Records are accessed only through their indexes. The result is that there is now no restriction on the placement of records so long as a pointer in at least one index refers to that record. Furthermore, records of variable length can be employed.

Two types of indexes are used. An exhaustive index contains one entry for every record in the main file. The index itself is organized as a sequential file for ease of searching. A partial index contains entries to records where the field of interest exists. With records of variable length, some records will not contain all fields. When a new record is added to the main file, all the index files must be updated.

Indexed files are used mostly in applications where timeliness of information is critical and where data are rarely processed exhaustively. Examples are airline reservation systems and inventory control systems.

The Direct, or Hashed, File

The direct, or hashed, file exploits the capability found on disks to directly access any block of a known address. As with sequential and indexed sequential files, a key field is required in each record. However, there is no concept of sequential ordering here.

The direct file makes use of hashing on the key value. This function was explained in Appendix 5B. Figure 5.40b shows the type of hashing organization with an overflow file that is typically used in a hash file.

Direct files are often used where very rapid access is required, where records of fixed length are used, and where records are always accessed one at a time. Examples are directories, pricing tables, schedules, and name lists.

8.3

FILE DIRECTORIES

Contents

Associated with any file management system and collection of files is a file directory. The directory contains information about the files, including attributes, location, and ownership. Much of this information, especially that concerned with storage, is managed by the operating system. The directory is itself a file, owned by the operating system and accessible by various file-management routines. Although some of the information in directories is available to users and applications, information is generally provided indirectly by system routines. Thus, users cannot directly access the directory even in read-only mode.

Table 8.2 suggests the information typically stored in the directory for each file in the system. From the user's point of view, the directory provides a mapping between file names that are known to users and applications, and the files themselves. Thus, each file entry includes the name of the file. Virtually all systems deal with different types of files and different file organizations, and this information is also provided. An important category of information about each file concerns its storage, including its location and size. In shared systems, it is also important to provide information that is used to control access to the file. Typically, one user is the owner of the file and may grant certain access privileges to other users. Finally, usage information is needed to manage the current use of the file and to record the history of its usage.

Structure

The way in which the information of Table 8.2 is stored differs widely among various systems. Some of the information may be stored in a header record associated with the file; this reduces the amount of storage required for the directory, making it easier to keep all or much of the directory in main memory

TABLE 8.2   Information Elements of a File Directory

Basic Information

File Name   Name as chosen by creator (user or program). Must be unique
                       within a specific directory.
File Type   For example: text, binary, load module, etc.
File Organization For systems that support different organizations

Address Information

Volume   Indicates device on which file is stored
Starting Address   Starting physical address on secondary storage
                       (e.g., cylinder, track, and block number on disk)
Size Used   Current size of the file in bytes, words, or blocks
Size Allocated   The maximum size of the file

Access Control Information

Owner   User who is assigned control of this file. The owner may be
                       able to grant or deny access to other users and to change
                       these privileges.
Access Information A simple version of this element would include the user's name
                       and password for each authorized user.
Permitted Actions Controls reading, writing, executing, transmitting over a
                       network.

Usage Information

Date Created   When file was first placed in directory
Identity of Creator   Usually but not necessarily the current owner
Date Last Read Access   Date of the last time a record was read
Identity of Last Reader User who did the reading
Date Last Modified   Date of the last update, insertion, or deletion
Identity of Last Modifier User who did the modifying
Date of Last Backup   Date of the last time the file was backed up on another storage
                             medium
Current Usage   Information about current activity on the file, such as process or
                             processes that have the file open, whether it is locked by a
                             process, and whether the file has been updated in main
                             memory but not yet on disk

to improve speed. Some key elements, of course, must be in the directory; typically, these include the name, address, size, and organization.

The simplest form of structure for a directory is that of a list of entries, one for each file. This structure could be represented by a simple sequential file, with the name of the file serving as the key. In some earlier single-user systems, this technique has been used. However, it is inadequate when multiple users share a system and even for single users with many files.

To understand the requirements for a file structure, it is well to consider the types of operations that may be performed on the directory:

- *Search:* When a user or application references a file, the directory must be searched to find the entry corresponding to that file.
- *Create file:* When a new file is created, an entry must be added to the directory.
- *Delete file:* When a file is deleted, an entry must be removed from the directory.
- *List directory:* All or a portion of the directory may be requested. Generally, this request is made by a user and results in a listing of all files owned by that user, plus some of the attributes of each file (e.g., type, access control information, usage information)

The simple list is not well suited to supporting these operations. Consider the needs of a single user. The user may have many types of files, including word processing text files, graphic files, spreadsheets, and so on. The user may like to have these organized by project, by type, or in some other convenient way. If the directory is a simple sequential list, it provides no help in organizing the files and forces the user to be careful not to use the same name for two different types of files. The problem is much worse in a shared system. Unique naming becomes a serious problem. Furthermore, it is difficult to conceal portions of the overall directory from users when there is no inherent structure in the directory.

A start in solving these problems would be to go to a two-level scheme in which there is one directory for each user and a master directory. The master directory has an entry for each user directory, providing address and access control information. Each user directory is a simple list of the files of that user. This arrangement means that names must be unique only within the collection of files of a single user, and that the file system can easily enforce access restriction on directories. However, it still provides users with no help in structuring collections of files.

A more powerful and flexible approach, and one that is almost universally adopted, is the hierarchical, or tree-structured, directory (Figure 8.4). As before, there is a master directory, which has under it a number of user directories. Each of these user directories in turn may have subdirectories and files as entries. This is true at any level: That is, at any level, a directory may consist of entries for subdirectories and/or entries for files.

It remains to say how each directory and subdirectory is organized. The simplest approach, of course, is to store each directory as a sequential file. When directories may contain a very large number of entries, such an organization may lead to unnecessarily long search times. In that case, a hashed structure is to be preferred.

Naming

Users need to be able to refer to a file by a symbolic name. Clearly, each file in the system must have a unique name in order that file references be unambig-

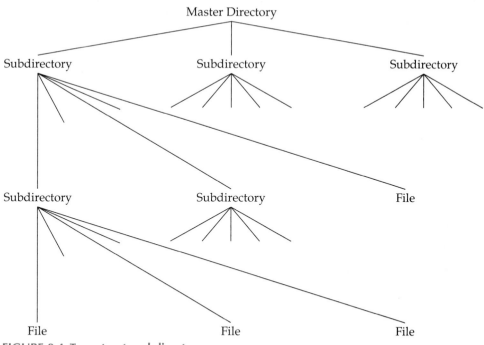

FIGURE 8.4 **Tree-structured directory.**

uous. On the other hand, it is an unacceptable burden on users to require that they provide unique names, especially in a shared system.

The use of a tree-structured directory minimizes the difficulty in assigning unique names. Any file in the system can be located by following a path from the root, or master, directory down various branches until the file is reached. The series of directory names, culminating in the file name itself, constitutes a **path name** for the file. As an example, the file in the lower left-hand corner of Figure 8.5 has the path name /User B/Word/UnitA/ABC. The slash is used to delimit names in the sequence. The name of the master directory is implicit because all paths start at that directory. It is perfectly acceptable to have several files with the same file name as long as they have unique path names. Thus, there is another file in the system with the file name ABC, but it has the path name /User B/Draw/ABC.

Although the path name facilitates the selection of file names, it would be awkward for a user to have to spell out the entire path name every time a reference is made to a file. Typically, an interactive user or a process has associated with it a current directory, often referred to as the **working directory**. Files are then referenced relative to the working directory. For example, if the working directory for user B is "Word," then the path name UnitA/ABC is sufficient to identify the file in the lower left-hand corner of Figure 8.5. When an interactive user logs on, or when a process is created, the default for the

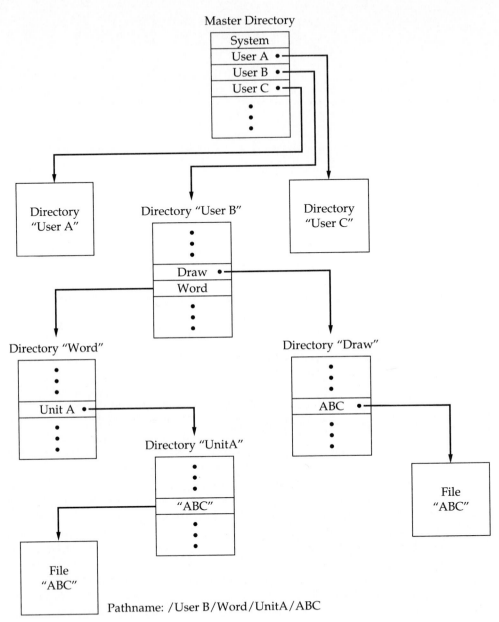

FIGURE 8.5 Example of tree-structured directory.

working directory is the user directory. During execution, the user can navigate up or down in the tree to define a different working directory.

8.4

FILE SHARING

In a multiuser system, there is almost always a requirement for allowing files to be shared among a number of users. Two issues arise: access rights and the management of simultaneous access.

Access Rights

The file system should provide a flexible tool for allowing extensive file sharing among users. The file system should provide a number of options so that the way in which a particular file is accessed can be controlled. Typically, users or groups of users are granted certain access rights to a file. A wide range of access rights has been used. The following list is representative [CALI82] of access rights that can be assigned to a particular user for a particular file:

- *None:* The user may not even learn of the existence of the file, much less access it. To enforce this restriction, the user is not allowed to read the user directory that includes this file.
- *Knowledge:* The user can determine that the file exists and who its owner is. The user is then able to petition the owner for additional access rights.
- *Execution:* The user can load and execute a program but cannot copy it. Proprietary programs are often made accessible with this restriction.
- *Reading:* The user can read the file for any purpose, including copying and execution. Some systems are able to enforce a distinction between viewing and copying. In the former case, the contents of the file can be displayed to the user, but the user has no means for making a copy.
- *Appending:* The user can add data to the file, often only at the end, but cannot modify or delete any of the file's contents. This right is useful in collecting data from a number of sources.
- *Updating:* The user can modify, delete, and add to the file's data. Updating normally includes writing the file initially, rewriting it completely or in part, and removing all or a portion of the data. Some systems distinguish among different degrees of updating.
- *Changing protection:* The user can change the access rights granted to other users. Typically, this right is held only by the owner of the file. In some systems, the owner can extend this right to others. To prevent abuse of this mechanism, the file owner is typically able to specify which rights can be changed by the holder of this right.
- *Deletion:* The user can delete the file from the file system.

These rights can be considered to constitute a hierarchy, with each right imply-
ing those that precede it. Thus, if a particular user is granted the updating right
for a particular file, then that user is also granted the following rights: knowledge, execution, reading, and appending.

One user is designated as owner of a given file, usually the person who
initially created the file. The owner has the access rights listed earlier, and may
grant rights to others. Access can be provided to the following classes of users:

- *Specific user:* Individual users who are designated by user ID.
- *User groups:* A set of users who are not individually defined. The system must
  have some way of keeping track of the membership of user groups.
- *All:* All users who have access to this system. These are public files.

Simultaneous Access

When access is granted to append or update a file to more than one user, the
operating system or file-management system must enforce discipline. A brute-
force approach is to allow a user to lock the entire file when it is to be updated.
A finer control is to lock individual records during update. Essentially, this is
the readers/writers problem discussed in Chapter 4. Issues of mutual exclusion
and deadlock must be addressed in designing the capability for shared access.

8.5

RECORD BLOCKING

As indicated in Figure 8.2, records are the logical unit of access to a file, whereas
blocks are the unit of I/O with secondary storage. For I/O to be performed,
records must be organized as blocks.

There are several issues to consider. First, should blocks be of fixed or variable
length? On most systems, blocks are of fixed length. This simplifies I/O, buffer
allocation in main memory, and the organization of blocks on secondary storage.
Next, what should the relative size of a block be, compared to the average record
size? The trade-off is this: The larger the block, the more records that are passed
in one I/O operation. If a file is being processed or searched sequentially, this
is an advantage because the number of I/O operations is reduced by using larger
blocks, thus speeding up processing. On the other hand, if records are being
accessed randomly, and no particular locality of reference is observed, then
larger blocks result in the unnecessary transfer of unused records. However,
combining the frequency of sequential operations with the potential for locality
of reference, we can say that the I/O transfer time is reduced by using larger
blocks. The competing concern is that larger blocks require larger I/O buffers,
making buffer management more difficult.

Given the size of block, the following three methods of blocking can be used:

- *Fixed blocking:* Records of fixed length are used, and an integral number of records are stored in a block. There may be unused space at the end of each block.
- *Variable-length spanned blocking:* Variable-length records are used and are packed into blocks with no unused space. Thus, some records must span two blocks, with the continuation indicated by a pointer to the successor block.
- *Variable-length unspanned blocking:* Variable-length records are used, but spanning is not employed. There is wasted space in most blocks because of the inability to use the remainder of a block if the next record is larger than the remaining unused space.

Figure 8.6 illustrates these methods, assuming that a file is stored in sequential blocks on a disk. The effect would not be changed if some other file allocation scheme were used (see Section 8.6).

Fixed blocking is the common mode for sequential files with records of fixed length. Variable-length spanned blocking is efficient for storage and does not limit the size of records. However, this technique is difficult to implement. Records that span two blocks require two I/O operations, and files are difficult to update, regardless of the organization. Variable-length unspanned blocking results in wasted space and limits record size to the size of a block.

The record blocking technique may interact with the virtual memory hardware if such technique is employed. In a virtual memory environment, it is desirable to make the page the basic unit of transfer. Pages are generally quite small, so that it is impractical to treat a page as a block for unspanned blocking. Accordingly, some systems combine multiple pages to create a larger block for file I/O purposes. This approach is used for VSAM files on IBM machines.

8.6

SECONDARY STORAGE MANAGEMENT

In secondary storage, a file consists of a collection of blocks. The operating system or file management system is responsible for allocating blocks to files. This raises two management issues. First, space on secondary storage must be allocated to files, and second, it is necessary to keep track of the space available for allocation. We shall see that these two tasks are related; that is, the approach taken for allocation of files may influence the approach taken for management of free space. Furthermore, we shall see that there is an interaction between file structure and allocation policy.

We begin this section by looking at alternatives for file allocation on a single disk. Then, we look at the management of free space. Finally, we examine techniques for storing a single file on multiple disks.

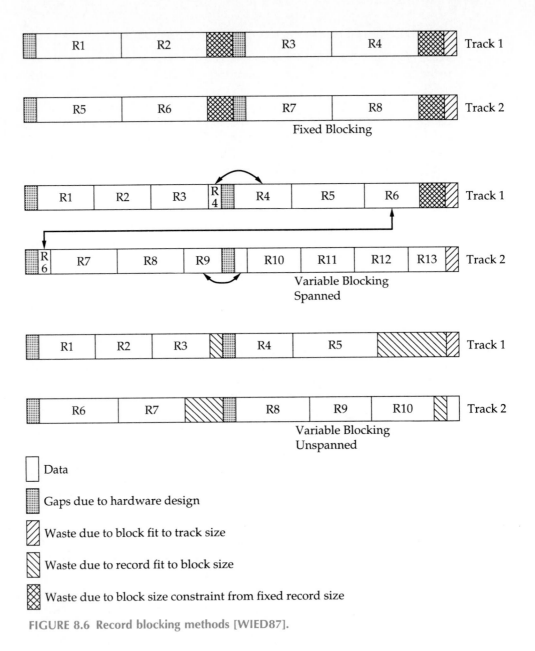

FIGURE 8.6 Record blocking methods [WIED87].

File Allocation

Several issues are involved in file allocation:

1. When a new file is created, is the maximum space required for the file allocated at once?
2. Space is allocated to a file as one or more contiguous units, which we shall refer to as *portions*. The size of a portion can range from a single block to the entire file. What size of portion should be used for allocating files?
3. What sort of data structure or table is used to keep track of the portions assigned to a file? Such a table is typically referred to as a **file allocation table** (FAT).

Let us examine these issues in turn.

Preallocation versus Dynamic Allocation

A preallocation policy would require that the maximum size of a file be declared at the time of the file creation request. In a number of cases, such as program compilations, the production of summary data files, or the transfer of a file from another system over a communications network, this value can be reasonably estimated. However, for many applications, it is difficult if not impossible to reliably estimate the maximum potential size of the file. In those cases, users and application programmers would tend to overestimate file size so as not to run out of space. This clearly is wasteful from the point of view of allocation of secondary storage. Thus, there are advantages in the use of dynamic allocation, which allocates space to a file in portions as needed.

Portion Size

The second issue in the foregoing list is that of the size of the portion allocated to a file. At one extreme, a portion large enough to hold the entire file is allocated. At the other extreme, space on the disk is allocated one block at a time. In choosing a portion size, there is a trade-off between efficiency from the point of view of a single file versus the overall system. [WIED87] lists the following four items to be considered in the trade-off:

1. Contiguity of space increases performance, especially for Retrieve_Next operations, and greatly for transactions running in a transaction-oriented operating system.
2. Having a large number of small portions increases the size of tables needed to manage the allocation information.
3. Having fixed-size portions—for example, blocks—simplifies the reallocation of space.
4. Having variable-size or small fixed-size portions minimizes waste of unused storage caused by overallocation.

Of course, these items interact and must be considered together. The result is that there are two major alternatives:

- *Variable, large contiguous portions:* This will provide better performance. The variable size avoids waste, and the file allocation tables are small. However, space is hard to reuse.
- *Blocks:* Small fixed portions provide greater flexibility. They may require large tables or complex structures for their allocation. Contiguity has been abandoned; blocks are allocated as needed.

Either option is compatible with preallocation or with dynamic allocation. In the first case, a file is preallocated one contiguous group of blocks. This eliminates the need for a file allocation table; all that is required is a pointer to the first block and the number of blocks allocated. In the second case, all the portions required are allocated at one time. This means that the allocation table for the file will remain of fixed size.

With variable-size portions, we need to be concerned with the fragmentation of free space. This issue was faced when we considered partitioned main memory in Chapter 5. Some possible alternative strategies are the following:

- *First fit:* Choose the first unused contiguous group of blocks of sufficient size.
- *Best fit:* Choose the smallest unused group that is of sufficient size.
- *Nearest fit:* Choose the unused group of sufficient size that is closest to the previous allocation for the file to increase locality.

It is not clear which strategy is best. The difficulty in modeling alternative strategies is that so many factors interact, including types of files, pattern of file access, degree of multiprogramming, other performance factors in the system, disk caching, disk scheduling, and so on.

File Allocation Methods

Having looked at the issues of preallocation versus dynamic allocation and portion size, we are in a position to consider specific methods of file allocation. Three methods are in common use: contiguous, chained, and indexed. Table 8.3 summarizes some of the characteristics of each method.

With **contiguous allocation**, a single contiguous set of blocks is allocated to a file at the time of file creation (Figure 8.7). Thus, this is a preallocation strategy, using portions of variable size. The file allocation table needs just a single entry for each file, showing the starting block and the length of the file. Contiguous allocation is the best from the point of view of the individual sequential file. Multiple blocks can be brought in one at a time to improve I/O performance for sequential processing. It is also easy to retrieve a single block. For example, if a file starts at block b, and the ith block of the file is wanted, its location on secondary storage is simply $b + i$. Contiguous allocation presents some problems. External fragmentation will occur, making it difficult to find contiguous blocks of space of sufficient length. From time to time, it will be necessary to

TABLE 8.3   File Allocation Methods

Characteristic	Contiguous	Chained	Indexed	Indexed
Fixed or variable size portions?	Variable	Fixed blocks	Fixed blocks	Variable
Pre-Allocation?	Necessary	Possible	Possible	Possible
Portion size	Large	Small	Small	Medium
Allocation frequency	Once	Low to high	High	Low
Time to allocate	Medium	Long	Short	Medium
File allocation table size	One entry	One entry	Large	Medium

perform a compaction algorithm to free up additional space on the disk (Figure 8.8). Also, with preallocation, it is necessary to declare the size of the file at the time of creation, which can cause the problems mentioned earlier.

At the opposite extreme from contiguous allocation is **chained allocation** (Figure 8.9). Typically, allocation is on the basis of an individual block. Each block contains a pointer to the next block in the chain. Again, the file allocation table needs just a single entry for each file to show the starting block and the length of the file. Although preallocation is possible, it is more common to simply allocate blocks as needed. The selection of blocks is now a simple matter: any free block can be added to a chain. There is no external fragmentation to worry about because only one block at a time is needed. This type of physical organization is best suited to sequential files that are to be processed sequentially.

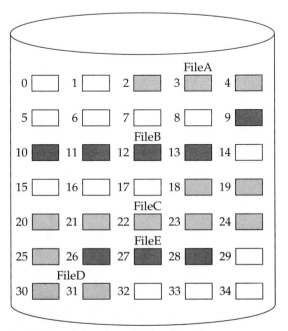

File Allocation Table

File Name	Start Block	Length
FileA	2	3
FileB	9	5
FileC	18	8
FileD	30	2
FileE	26	3

FIGURE 8.7 Contiguous file allocation.

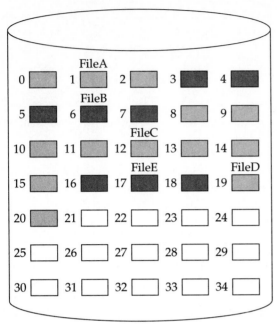

FIGURE 8.8 Contiguous file allocation (after compaction).

File Allocation Table

File Name	Start Block	Length
FileA	0	3
FileB	3	5
FileC	8	8
FileD	19	2
FileE	16	3

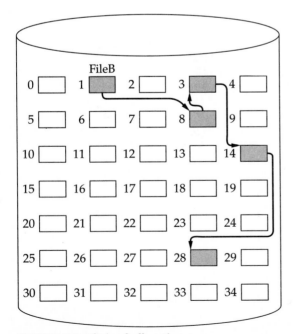

FIGURE 8.9 Chained allocation.

File Allocation Table

File Name	Start Block	Length
...	...	...
FileB	1	5
...	...	...

To select an individual block of a file requires tracing through the chain to the desired block.

One consequence of chaining, as described so far, is that there is no accommodation of the principle of locality. Thus, if it is necessary to bring in several blocks of a file at a time, as in sequential processing, then a series of accesses to different parts of the disk are required. This has perhaps a more significant effect on a single-user system but may also be of concern on a shared system. To overcome this problem, some systems periodically consolidate files (Figure 8.10).

Indexed allocation addresses many of the problems of contiguous and chained allocation. In this case, the file allocation table contains a separate one-level index for each file; the index has one entry for each portion allocated to the file. Typically, the file indexes are not physically stored as part of the file allocation table. Rather, the file index for a file is kept in a separate block, and the entry for the file in the file allocation table points to that block. Allocation may be on the basis of either fixed-size blocks (Figure 8.11) or variable-size portions (Figure 8.12). Allocation by blocks eliminates external fragmentation, whereas allocation by variable-size portions improves locality. In either case, files may be consolidated from time to time. Consolidation reduces the size of the index in the case of variable-size portions but not in the case of block allocation. Indexed allocation supports both sequential and direct access to the file, and thus it is the most popular form of file allocation.

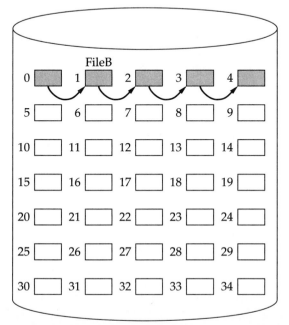

File Allocation Table

File Name	Start Block	Length
...	...	...
FileB	0	5
...	...	...

FIGURE 8.10 Chained allocation (after consolidation).

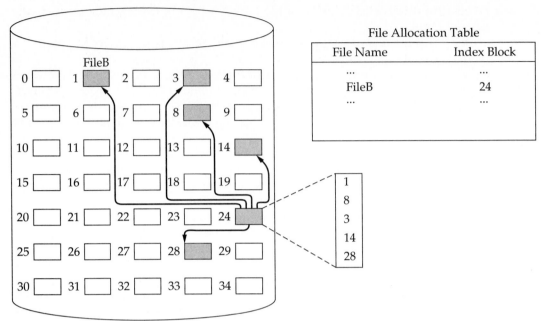

FIGURE 8.11 Indexed allocation with block portions.

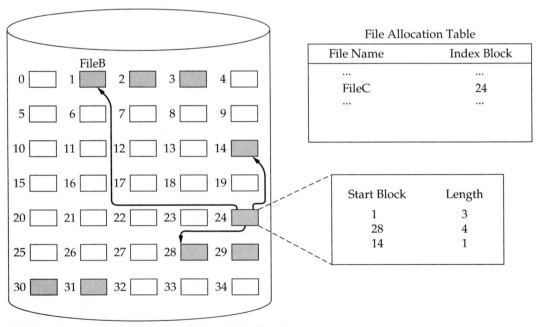

FIGURE 8.12 Indexed allocation with variable-length portions.

Free Space Management

Just as the space that is allocated to files must be managed, so the space that is not currently allocated to any file must be managed. To perform any of the file allocation techniques that have been described, it is necessary to know what blocks on the disk are available. Thus, we need a **disk allocation table** in addition to a file allocation table. Three techniques are in common use: bit tables, chained free portions, and indexing.

Bit Tables

The method of bit tables uses a vector containing 1 bit for each block on the disk. Each entry of a 0 corresponds to a free block, and each 1 corresponds to a block in use. For example, for the disk layout of Figure 8.7, a vector of length 35 is needed, and would have the following value:

00111000011111000011111111111011000

A bit table has the advantage that it is relatively easy to find one or a contiguous group of free blocks. Thus, a bit table works well with any of the file allocation methods we have discussed. Another advantage is that it is as small as possible and can be kept in main memory. This avoids the need to read the disk allocation table into memory every time an allocation is performed.

Chained Free Portions

The free portions may be chained together by using a pointer and length value in each free portion. This method has negligible space overhead because there is no need for a disk allocation table, merely for a pointer to the beginning of the chain and the length of the first portion. This method is suited to all the file allocation methods. If allocation is made a block at a time, simply choose the free block at the head of the chain and adjust the first pointer or length value. If allocation is made by variable-length portion, a first-fit algorithm may be used: The headers from the portions are fetched one at a time to determine the next suitable free portion in the chain. Again, pointer and length values are adjusted.

Indexing

The indexing approach treats free space as a file and uses an index table as has been described in the subsection, "File Allocation Methods." For efficiency, the index should be on the basis of variable-size portions rather than blocks. Thus, there is one entry in the table for every free portion on the disk. This approach provides efficient support for all the file allocation methods.

Reliability

Consider the following scenario:

1. User A requests a file allocation to add to an existing file.
2. The request is granted and the disk and file allocation tables are updated in main memory but not yet on disk.
3. The system crashes and subsequently restarts.
4. User B requests a file allocation and is allocated space on disk that overlaps the last allocation to user A.
5. User A accesses the overlapped portion via a reference that is stored inside A's file.

This difficulty arose because for efficiency the system maintained a copy of the disk allocation table and file allocation table in main memory. To prevent this type of error, the following steps could be performed when a file allocation is requested:

1. Lock the disk allocation table on disk. This prevents another user from causing alterations to the table until this allocation is completed.
2. Search the disk allocation table for available space. This assumes that a copy of the disk allocation table is always kept in main memory. If not, it must first be read in.
3. Allocate space, update the disk allocation table, and update the disk. Updating the disk involves writing the disk allocation table back onto disk. For chained disk allocation, it also involves updating some pointers on disk.
4. Update the file allocation table and update the disk.
5. Unlock the disk allocation table.

This technique will prevent errors. However, when small portions are allocated frequently, the impact on performance will be substantial. To reduce this overhead, a scheme for batch storage allocation could be used, in which case a batch of free portions on the disk is obtained for allocation. The corresponding portions on disk are marked "in use." Allocation using this batch may proceed in main memory. When the batch is exhausted, the disk allocation table is updated on disk and a new batch may be acquired. If a system crash occurs, portions on the disk marked "in use" must be cleaned up in some fashion before they can be reallocated. The technique for cleanup will depend on the characteristics of this particular file system.

Disk Interleaving

In Section 7.5, we discussed the trends in performance that have made disk I/O a serious bottleneck on many systems. Two approaches that have been presented so far in this book for enhancing performance are disk caching and disk scheduling. However, neither of these techniques offers in the foreseeable future a satisfactory solution to the performance problems of maintaining large file or database systems. The disk cache is effective only if the data access pattern follows the principle of locality and if the ratio of Reads to Writes is high. The degree of locality depends on the degree of multiprogramming, the file structure, the file allocation method, and the nature of the application. Thus, although the disk cache is useful, it has not entirely solved the performance problem. Similarly, disk scheduling may improve performance but is unlikely on its own to overcome the performance disparity between disk and computer systems.

In recent years, there has been much interest in the use of multiple disks to store a single file, a technique referred to as *disk interleaving*, or *disk striping* [CHEN90, REDD89, NG88, KATZ89]. A group of disks is interleaved if successive portions of a file are stored on different disks in an array of disks. The granularity of the distribution can be from the block to the byte level. In the former case, successive blocks of a file are stored on successive disks; in the latter, individual bytes of a file are interleaved across disks. In memory, the file is buffered as a set of blocks as usual. To read or write a block, the assignment is:

B_i is stored on disk unit $((B_i - 1) \bmod n) + 1$

where

$B_i = i$th block (block interleaving) or ith byte of the block (byte interleaving)
$n = $ number of disks in the disk array

With disk interleaving, requests for file I/O tend to be uniformly distributed across all the disks in the array, yielding higher throughput and improved response time. This allocation method relieves the system administrator of the tasks of monitoring the system and moving the files to obtain a proper system balance. In addition, the request load will tend to stay balanced under a changing mix of application request patterns.

Three approaches have been studied: independent drives, synchronous arrays, and asynchronous arrays.

With **independent drives** [OLSO89], the granularity of the interleaving is typically at the block level. That is, successive blocks of a file are allocated on successive disks. An overall file index must be maintained for each file. The operating system is responsible for operating the drives in parallel. If the I/O request is for a single block, then the request is queued for the disk containing that block. If a multiple-block request arrives, then that request is broken up into a number of single-block requests and is queued at the corresponding disks, which results in concurrent access to the blocks. This approach also enables multiple single-block requests for different files to be served concurrently.

This approach may be effective when there is a large number of small independent requests, such as in a transaction processing system. However, this approach does not necessarily improve the performance of any single application.

The **synchronous array** approach [KIM86] requires that all disks spin, seek, and transfer in synchronization with one another. Interleaving is at the byte level. The result is that data may be accessed in parallel, reducing data transfer time by a factor of $1/n$, where n is the degree of interleaving. In effect, all the disks together function as a single large disk with n times the transfer rate and n times the capacity of a single disk. Because all the disks are coupled together, each disk sees the same request rate, and hence there is a balanced load on all the disks.

Synchronous arrays do not reduce Seek time or rotational latency, but they provide high bandwidth by transferring to and from all disks simultaneously. For a single large application that is reading or writing a large file, this approach can provide substantial speedup. The disadvantage of synchronous arrays is that they are difficult and expensive to build, and they may not scale readily to arrays with tens or hundreds of disks.

The **asynchronous array** approach [KIM87] simulates the behavior of a synchronous array using unmodified off-the-shelf disk drives in conjunction with a new controller architecture. Again, byte interleaving is used. A Read request is implemented by independent Seeks and transfers from each of the disks to a shared buffer in the controller, which interleaves the data coming from the disk drives. This approach yields most of the performance benefits of a synchronous array with lower hardware costs.

8.7

EXAMPLE SYSTEM—UNIX System V

The UNIX kernel views all files as streams of bytes. Any internal logical structure is application-specific. However, UNIX is concerned with the physical structure of files and distinguishes four types of files as follows:

- *Ordinary:* Consists of files that contain information entered by a user, an application program, or a system utility program.
- *Directory:* Contains a list of file names plus pointers to associated inodes (information nodes) described shortly. Directories are hierarchically organized (Figure 8.4). Directory files are actually ordinary files with special Write protection privileges so that only the file system can write into them, whereas Read access is available to user programs.
- *Special:* Used to access peripheral devices, such as terminals and printers. Each I/O device is associated with a special file, as discussed in Section 7.6.
- *Named:* Consists of named pipes, as discussed in Section 4.7.

In this section, we are concerned with the handling of ordinary files, which correspond to what most systems treat as files.

Inodes

All types of UNIX files are administered by the operating system by means of inodes. An inode (index node) is a control structure that contains the key information needed by the operating system for a particular file. Several file names may be associated with a single inode, but an active inode is associated with exactly one file, and each file is controlled by exactly one inode.

The attributes of the file as well as its permissions and other control information are stored in the inode. Table 8.4 lists the contents.

File Allocation

Files are allocated on a block basis. Allocation is dynamic, as needed. Preallocation is not used. Hence, the blocks of a file on disk are not necessarily contiguous. An indexed method is used to keep track of each file, with part of the index stored in the inode for the file. The inode includes 39 bytes of address information organized as 13 3-byte addresses, or pointers. The first 10 addresses point to the first 10 data blocks of the file. If the file is longer than 10 blocks, then one or more levels of indirection are used as follows:

TABLE 8.4   Information in a UNIX Disk-Resident Inode

File Mode	16-bit flag that stores access and execution permissions associated with the file.
	12–14 File type (regular, directory, character or block special, FIFO pipe)
	9–11 Execution flags
	8 Owner Read permission
	7 Owner Write permission
	6 Owner Execute permission
	5 Group Read permission
	4 Group Write permission
	3 Group Execute permission
	2 Other Read permission
	1 Other Write permission
	0 Other Execute permission
Link Count	Number of directory references to this inode
Owner ID	Individual owner of file
Group ID	Group owner associated with this file
File Size	Number of bytes in file
File Addresses	39 bytes of address information
Last Accessed	Time of last file access
Last Modified	Time of last file modification
Inode Modified	Time of last inode modification

- The eleventh address in the inode points to a block on disk that contains the next portion of the index. This block is referred to as the *single indirect block*. This block contains the pointers to succeeding blocks in the file.
- If the file contains more blocks, the twelfth address in the inode points to a double indirect block. This block contains a list of addresses of additional single indirect blocks. Each of the single indirect blocks in turn contains pointers to file blocks.
- If the file contains still more blocks, the thirteenth address in the inode points to a triple indirect block that is a third level of indexing. This block points to additional double indirect blocks.

All of this is illustrated in Figure 8.13. The total number of data blocks in a file depends on the capacity of the fixed-size blocks in the system. In UNIX System V, the length of a block is 1 KB, and each block can hold a total of 256 block addresses. Thus, the maximum size of a file using this scheme is over 16 GB (Table 8.5).

This scheme has several advantages, as follows:

1. The inode is of fixed size and relatively small and hence may be kept in main memory for long periods.
2. Smaller files may be accessed with little or no indirection, reducing processing and disk access time.
3. The theoretical maximum size of a file is large enough to satisfy virtually all applications.

TABLE 8.5   Capacity of a UNIX File

Level	Number of Blocks	Number of Bytes
Direct	10	10 KB
Single Indirect	256	256 KB
Double Indirect	$256 \times 256 = 65$ K	65 MB
Triple Indirect	$256 \times 65K = 16$ M	16 GB

8.8

SUMMARY

A file-management system is a set of system software that provides services to users and applications in the use of files, including file access, directory maintenance, and access control. The file-management system is typically viewed as a system service that itself is served by the operating system, rather than being part of the operating system itself. However, in any system, at least part of the file-management function is performed by the operating system.

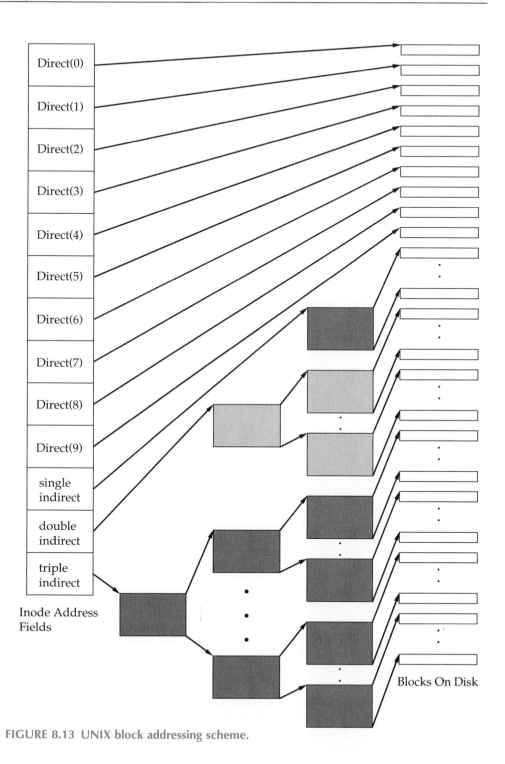

FIGURE 8.13 UNIX block addressing scheme.

A file consists of a collection of records. The way in which these records may be accessed determines its logical organization and to some extent its physical organization on disk. If a file is primarily to be processed as a whole, then a sequential file organization is the simplest and most appropriate. If sequential access is needed but random access to an individual file is also desired, then an indexed sequential file may give the best performance. If access to the file is principally at random, then an indexed file or hashed file may be the most appropriate.

Whatever file structure is chosen, a directory service is also needed to allow files to be organized in a hierarchical fashion. This organization is useful to the user in keeping track of files and is useful to the file-management system in providing access control and other services to users.

File records, even when of fixed size, generally do not conform to the size of a physical disk block. Accordingly, some sort of blocking strategy is needed. A trade-off among complexity, performance, and use of space determines the blocking strategy to be used.

A key function of any file-management scheme is the management of space on disk. Part of this function is the strategy for allocating disk blocks to a file. A variety of methods has been employed, and a variety of data structures has been used to keep track of the allocation for each file. In addition, the space on disk that has not been allocated must be managed. This latter function primarily consists of maintaining a disk allocation table indicating which blocks are free.

8.9

RECOMMENDED READING

There are several good books on file management. The following all focus on file-management systems but also address related operating-system issues. Perhaps the most useful is [WEID87], which takes a quantitative approach to file-management and deals with all the issues raised in Figure 8.2, from disk scheduling to file structure. [LIVA90] emphasizes file structures, providing a good and lengthy survey with comparative performance analyses. [GROS86] provides a balanced look at issues relating to both file I/O and file access methods. It also contains general descriptions of all the control structures needed by a file system. These descriptions provide a useful checklist in assessing the design of a file system. [FOLK87] emphasizes the processing of files, addressing such issues as maintenance, searching and sorting, and cosequential processing. [MART77] addresses database issues, but over half of the book is devoted to file structures, covering much of the material of this chapter.

Surveys of disk interleaving, with an emphasis on performance modeling, can be found in [CHEN90], [REDD89], and [NG88].

8.10

PROBLEMS

8.1 Define:

B = block size
R = record size
P = size of block pointer
F = blocking factor; expected number of records within a block

Give a formula for F for the three blocking methods depicted in Figure 8.6.

8.2 One scheme to avoid the problem of preallocation versus waste or lack of contiguity is to allocate portions of increasing size as the file grows. For example, begin with a portion size of one block, and double the portion size for each allocation. Consider a file of n records with a blocking factor of F, and suppose that a simple one-level index is used as a file allocation table.

(a) Give an upper limit on the number of entries in the file allocation table, as a function of F and n.

(b) What is the maximum amount of the allocated file space that is unused at any time?

8.3 What file organization would you choose to maximize efficiency in terms of speed of access, use of storage space, ease of updating (adding/deleting/modifying), when the data is:

(a) updated infrequently, and accessed frequently in random order?

(b) updated frequently, and accessed in its entirety relatively frequently?

(c) updated frequently and accessed randomly and frequently

8.4 Directories can be implemented either as a "special files" that can only be accessed in limited ways, or as ordinary data files. What are the advantages and disadvantages of each approach?

8.5 Some operating systems have a tree structured file system, but limit the depth of the tree to some small number of levels. What effect does this limit have on users? How does this simplify file system design (if it does)?

8.6 Discuss the merits and demerits of file protection and sharing based on the notion of user groups vs. access lists, where individual users are designated as having specific access privileges to a file. Consider complexity of implementation, ease of use, flexibility, and security in your answer.

8.7 The file organization type (pile, sequential, indexed sequential, indexed and hashed) determines the logical organization. The storage allocation method (continuous, chained, indexed) determines the physical organization of the file on the media. Which combinations of logical and physical organization work well together, and which do not?

8.8 Compare issues of storage allocation in a file system with that of main memory allocation. What are the similarities and differences?

8.9   What are the advantages and disadvantages of disk interleaving, independent of which form of interleaving is used?

8.10 Some systems provide file sharing by allowing several users to access a single copy of a file simultaneously. Other systems provide a copy of the shared file to each user. Discuss the advantages and disadvantages of both approaches.

8.11 A government agency wants a computerized information system to assist them in the preparation of several statistical reports. The data they want to store consists of information about employees of U.S. companies, and the records in the file will contain the following data:

Size of data	Description of data
4 bytes	Employer's identification number
4 bytes	Employee's social security number
4 bytes	Salary
4 bytes	Job description (coded)
1 byte	Sex
1 byte	Age
1 byte	Marital status
1 byte	Ethnic origin

The disk on their computer system has 10,000 blocks, each of which can hold 4000 bytes. Each record contains 20 bytes, and the entire file will contain about one million records.

The file will be accessed occasionally for updating purposes. This includes adding new records, and deleting or modifying existing ones. The main use of the file will be for statistical studies; such accesses are anticipated to occur about 50 times more frequently than updates.

Statistical queries may use any or all of the abovementioned fields except social security number; some examples are given below:

Find the highest and lowest salary of all Caucasian females that work for employer #22452, or

Find the average age of all married employees who earn less than $10,000, or

Print a table that shows how many workers doing job #4522 are male and female, how many are single and married, and how many are in various age categories.

You are to design a method of storing this file on their disk so that the operations described above can be performed most efficiently. You must completely describe the layout of the file system, including (but not limited to) the actual record layout(s), how to keep track of which blocks on the disk belong to the file(s) and their order, how to keep track of the unused blocks, and what method(s) would be used to access the file(s).

8.12 In the past decade the storage capacity of disks has increased by almost an order of magnitude, but the transfer rate has not similarly increased. What effect do you anticipate this will have on file organizations and storage allocation schemes?

CHAPTER 9

Networking and Distributed Processing

With the increasing availability of inexpensive yet powerful personal computers and minicomputers, there has been an increasing trend toward distributed data processing (DDP). The use of DDP, allows processors, data, and other aspects of a data processing system to be dispersed within an organization. Dispersal provides a system that is more responsive to user needs, is able to provide better response times, and may minimize communications costs by comparison to a centralized approach. A DDP system involves a partitioning of the computing function and may also involve a distributed organization of data bases, device control, and interaction (network) control.

In many organizations, there is heavy reliance on personal computers coupled with a large central facility for data processing. Personal computers are used to support a variety of user-friendly applications, such as word processing, spreadsheets, and presentation graphics. The mainframe houses the corporate data base plus sophisticated software for data base management and information systems. Linkages are needed among the personal computers and between each personal computer and the mainframe. Various approaches for the micro-to-mainframe link are in common use, ranging from treating the personal computer as a simple terminal to a high degree of integration between personal computer applications and the mainframe data base.

These application trends have been supported by the evolution of distributed capabilities in the operating system and support utilities. A spectrum of capabilities have been explored, as follows:

- *Communications architecture:* Software that supports a network of independent computers. It provides support for distributed applications, such as electronic mail, file transfer, and remote terminal access. However, the computers retain a distinct identity to the user and to the applications, which must communicate with other computers by explicit reference. Each computer has its own separate operating system, and a heterogeneous mix of computers and operating systems is possible, as long as all machines support the same communications architecture.

505

• *Network operating system:* A configuration in which there is a network of application machines, usually single-user workstations and one or more "server" machines. The server machines provide network-wide services or applications, such as file storage and printer management. Each computer has its own private operating system. The network operating system is simply an adjunct to the local operating system that allows application machines to interact with server machines. The user is aware that there are multiple independent computers and deals with them explicitly. Typically, a common communications architecture is used to support these network applications.

• *Distributed operating system:* A common operating system shared by a network of computers. It looks to its users like an ordinary centralized operating system but provides the user with transparent access to the resources of a number of machines. A distributed operating system may rely on a communications architecture for basic communications functions; more commonly, a stripped-down set of communications functions is incorporated into the operating system to provide efficiency.

The technology of the communications architecture is well developed and is supported by all vendors. The first commercially available communications architecture was IBM's System Network Architecture (SNA), introduced in 1974. Network operating systems are a much more recent phenomenon, but a number of commercial products exist. The leading edge of research and development for distributed systems is in the area of distributed operating systems. Although some commercial systems have been introduced, fully functional distributed operating systems are still at the experimental stage.

In this chapter, we provide a survey of this spectrum of distributed processing capabilities. We begin with an examination of communications architectures, focusing on the most important: the open systems interconnection (OSI) model. Next, we examine some of the key concepts in server software.

The next four sections examine various important aspects of distributed operating systems. Process migration is the ability to move an active process from one machine to another; it has become an increasingly hot topic in distributed operating systems. Next, we look at two techniques for interprocess communication between systems, namely message passing and the remote procedure call. Finally, two key issues in the management of distributed processes are explored: mutual exclusion and deadlock.

9.1

COMMUNICATIONS ARCHITECTURE

The Need for a Communications Architecture

When computers, terminals, and other data processing devices exchange data, the procedures involved can be quite complex. Consider, for example, the transfer of a file between two computers attached to a network. The following are some of the typical tasks to be performed:

1. The source system must inform the network of the identity of the desired destination system.
2. The source system must determine that the destination system is prepared to receive data.
3. The file transfer application on the source system must determine that the file management program on the destination system is prepared to accept and store the file from this particular user.
4. If the file formats used on the two systems are incompatible, one of the two systems must perform a format translation function.

It is clear that there must be a high degree of cooperation between the two computers. Instead of implementing the logic for this cooperation as a single module, the task is broken up into subtasks, each of which is implemented separately. As an example, Figure 9.1 suggests the way in which a file transfer facility could be implemented. Three modules are used. Tasks 3 and 4 in the preceding list could be performed by a file transfer module. The two modules on the two systems exchange files and commands. However, rather than requiring the file transfer module to deal with the details of actually transferring data and commands, each of the file transfer modules relies on a communications service module. This module is responsible for making sure that the file transfer commands and data are reliably exchanged between systems. Among other things, this module would perform task 2. Now the nature of the exchange between systems is independent of the nature of the network that interconnects them. Therefore, rather than building details of the network interface into the communications service module, it makes sense to have a third module, the network access module, that performs task 1 by interacting with the network.

Let us try to summarize the motivation for the three modules in Figure 9.1. The file transfer module contains all the logic that is unique to the file transfer application, such as transmitting passwords, file commands, and file records.

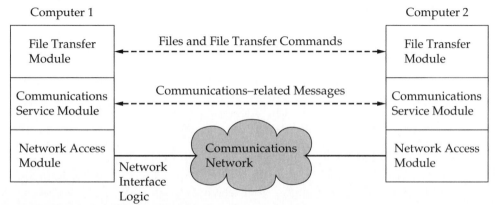

FIGURE 9.1 A simplified architecture for file transfer.

There is a need to transmit these files and commands reliably. However, the same sorts of reliability requirements are relevant to a variety of applications (e.g., electronic mail, document transfer). Therefore, these requirements are met by a separate communications service module that can be used by a variety of applications. The communications service module is concerned with assuring that the two computer systems are active and ready for data transfer and for keeping track of the data that are being exchanged to assure delivery. However, these tasks are independent of the type of network that is being used. Therefore, the logic for actually dealing with the network is separated out into a separate network access module. That way, if the network to be used is changed, only the network access module is affected.

Thus, instead of a single module for performing communications, there is a structured set of modules that implements the communications function. That structure is referred to as a **communications architecture**. In the remainder of this section, we generalize the preceding example to present a simplified communications architecture. Following that, we look at a more complex, real-world example.

A Simple Communications Architecture

In very general terms, communications can be said to involve three agents: applications, computers, and networks. The applications that we are concerned with here are distributed applications that involve the exchange of data between two computer systems; examples are electronic mail and file transfer. These applications and others execute on computers that are multiprogrammed to support multiple concurrent applications. Computers are connected to networks, and the data to be exchanged are transferred by the network from one computer to another. Thus, the transfer of data from one application to another involves first getting the data to the computer in which the application resides and then getting it to the intended application within the computer.

With these concepts in mind, it appears natural to organize the communication task into the following three relatively independent layers:

- Network access layer
- Transport layer
- Application layer

The *network access layer* is concerned with the exchange of data between a computer and the network to which it is attached. The sending computer must provide the network with the address of the destination computer, so that the network may route the data to the appropriate destination. The sending computer may wish to invoke certain services, such as priority, that might be provided by the network. The specific software used at this layer depends on the type of network to be used; different standards have been developed for circuit switching, packet switching, local area networks, and others. For example, X.25 is a standard that specifies the access to a packet-switching network. Thus, it makes sense to separate those functions having to do with network access into a separate layer. By doing this, the remainder of the communications software, above the network access layer, need not be concerned about the specifics of the network to be used. The same higher-layer software should function properly regardless of the particular network to which the computer is attached.

Regardless of the nature of the applications that are exchanging data, there is usually a requirement that data be exchanged reliably. That is, we would like to be assured that all the data arrive at the destination application and that the data arrive in the same order in which they were sent. The mechanisms for providing reliability are essentially independent of the nature of the applications. Thus, it makes sense to collect those mechanisms in a common layer shared by all applications; this is referred to as the *transport layer*.

Finally, the *application layer* contains the logic needed to support the various user applications. For each different type of application, such as file transfer, a separate module is needed that is peculiar to that application.

Figures 9.2 and 9.3 illustrate this simple architecture. Figure 9.2 shows three computers connected to a network. Each computer contains software at the network access and transport layers and software at the application layer for one or more applications. For successful communication, every entity in the overall system must have a unique address. Actually, two levels of addressing are needed. Each computer on the network must have a unique network address to allow the network to deliver data to the proper computer. Each application on a computer must have an address that is unique within that computer, which allows the transport layer to deliver data to the proper application. These latter

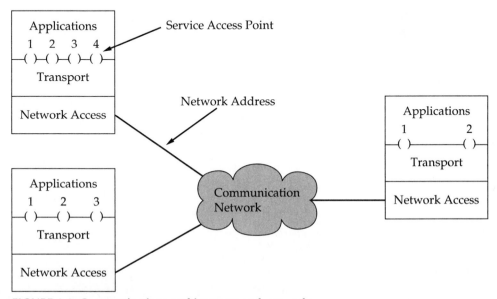

FIGURE 9.2 Communications architectures and networks.

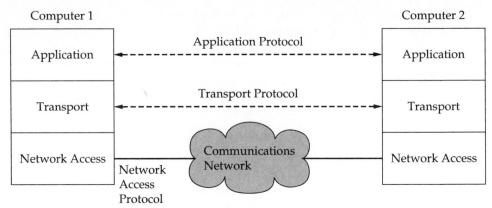

FIGURE 9.3 Protocols in a simplified architecture.

addresses are known as *service access points* (SAPs), connoting the fact that each application is individually accessing the services of the transport layer.

Figure 9.3 indicates the way in which modules at the same level on different computers communicate with each other: by means of a protocol. A *protocol* is the set of rules or conventions governing the way in which two entities cooperate to exchange data. A protocol specification details the control functions that may be performed, the formats and control codes used to communicate those functions, and the procedures that the two entities must follow.

Let us trace a simple operation. Suppose that an application associated with SAP 1 at computer A wishes to send a message to another application associated with SAP 2 at computer B. The application at A hands the message over to its transport layer with instructions to send it to SAP 2 on computer B. The transport layer hands the message over to the network access layer, which instructs the network to send the message to computer B. The network need not be told the identity of the destination service access point. All that it needs to know is that the data are intended for computer B.

To control this operation, control information as well as user data must be transmitted, as suggested in Figure 9.4. Let us say that the sending application generates a block of data and passes it to the transport layer. The transport layer may break this block into two smaller pieces to make it more manageable. To each of these pieces the transport layer appends a transport header, containing protocol control information. The combination of data from the next higher layer and control information is known as a protocol data unit (PDU); in this case, it is referred to as a transport PDU. The header in each transport PDU contains control information to be used by the peer transport protocol at computer B. Examples of items that may be stored in this header include the following:

- *Destination SAP:* When the destination transport layer receives the transport protocol data unit, it must know to whom the data are to be delivered.

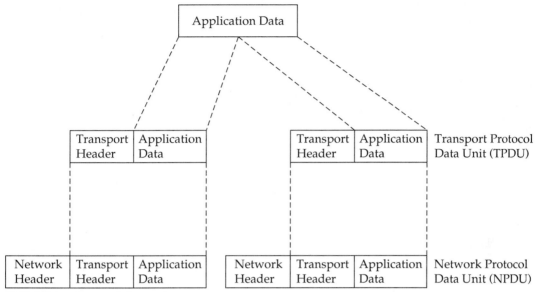

FIGURE 9.4 Protocol data units.

- *Sequence number:* Since the transport protocol is sending a sequence of protocol data units, it numbers them sequentially so that if they arrive out of order, the destination transport entity may reorder them.
- *Error-detection code:* The sending transport entity may calculate and insert an error-detecting code so that the receiver can determine if an error has occurred, discard the PDU, and request its retransmission.

The next step is for the transport layer to hand each PDU over to the network layer, with instructions to transmit it to the destination computer. To satisfy this request, the network access protocol must present the data to the network with a request for transmission. As before, this operation requires the use of control information. In this case, the network access protocol appends a network access header to the data it receives from the transport layer, creating a network-access PDU. Examples of the items that may be stored in the header include the following:

- *Destination computer address:* The network must know to whom (which computer on the network) the data are to be delivered.
- *Facilities requests:* The network access protocol may want the network to make use of certain facilities, such as priority.

Figure 9.5 puts all these concepts together, showing the interaction between modules to transfer one block of data. Let us say that the file transfer module in computer X is transferring a file one record at a time to computer Y. Each record is handed over to the transport layer module. We can picture this action as being in the form of a command or procedure call, A-SEND (application-

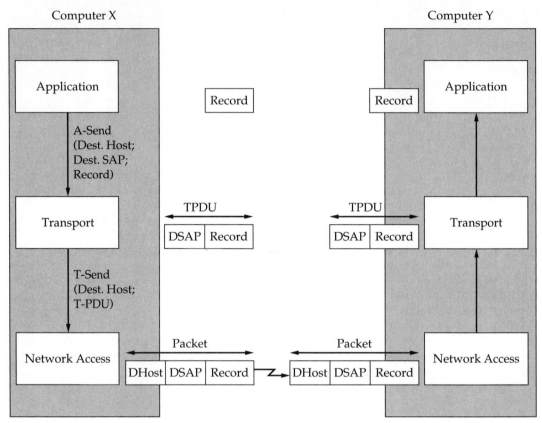

FIGURE 9.5 Operation of a communications architecture.

send). The arguments of this procedure call include the destination computer address, the destination service access point, and the record. The transport layer appends the destination service access point and other control information to the record to create a transport PDU. This is then handed down to the network access layer in a transport-send (T-SEND) command. In this case, the arguments for the command are the destination computer address and the transport protocol data unit. The network access layer uses this information to construct a network PDU. Suppose the network is an X.25 packet-switching network. In this case, the network protocol data unit is an X.25 data packet. The transport PDU is the data field of the packet, and the packet header includes the virtual circuit number for a virtual circuit connecting X and Y.

The network accepts the data packet from X and delivers it to Y. The network access module in Y receives the packet, strips off the packet header, and transfers the enclosed transport protocol data unit to X's transport layer module. The transport layer examines the transport protocol data unit header and, on the basis of the destination SAP field in the header, delivers the enclosed record to the appropriate application, in this case the file transfer module in Y.

This example will repay close study. In the remainder of this section, we look at a more complex communications architecture. However, this architecture is based on the same principles and mechanisms as this simple example.

The OSI Architecture

When communication is desired among computers from different vendors, the software development effort can be a nightmare. Different vendors use different data formats and data exchange protocols. Even within one vendor's product line, different model computers may communicate in unique ways.

As the use of computer communications and computer networking proliferates, a one-at-a-time special-purpose approach to communications software development is too costly to be acceptable. The only alternative is for computer vendors to adopt and implement a common set of conventions. For this to happen, international standards are needed. Such standards would have two benefits:

- Vendors would feel encouraged to implement the standards because of an expectation that, because of wide usage of the standards, their products would be less marketable without them.
- Customers would be in a position to require that the standards be implemented by any vendor wishing to propose equipment to them.

This line of reasoning led the International Organization for Standardization (ISO) to develop a communications architecture known as the **open systems interconnection** (OSI) model. The model is a framework for defining standards for linking heterogeneous computers. The term *open* denotes the ability of any two systems conforming to the architecture and the associated standards to communicate.

The Concept of Open Systems

Open systems interconnection is based on the concept of cooperating distributed applications. In the OSI model, a system consists of a computer, all its software, and any peripheral devices attached to it, including terminals. A distributed application is any activity that involves the exchange of information between two open systems. Examples of such activities include the following:

- A user at a terminal on one computer is logged onto an application such as transaction processing on another computer.
- A file-management program on one computer transfers a file to a file-management program on another computer.
- A user sends an electronic mail message to a user on another computer.
- A process control program sends a control signal to a robot.

The OSI is concerned with the exchange of information between a pair of open systems and not with the internal functioning of each individual system.

Specifically, it is concerned with the capability of systems to cooperate in the exchange of information and in the accomplishment of tasks.

The objective of the OSI effort is to define a set of standards that will enable open systems located anywhere in the world to cooperate by being interconnected through some standardized communications facility and by executing standardized OSI protocols.

An open system may be implemented in any way provided that it conforms to a minimal set of standards that allows communication to be achieved with other open systems. An open system consists of a number of applications, an operating system, and system software such as a data base management system and a terminal handling package. It also includes the communications software that turns a closed system into an open system. Different manufacturers will implement open systems in different ways to achieve a product identity that will increase their market share or create a new market. However, virtually all manufacturers are now committed to providing communications software that behaves in conformance with OSI to provide their customers with the ability to communicate with other open systems.

The OSI Model

A widely accepted structuring technique and the one chosen by ISO is layering. The communications functions are partitioned into a hierarchical set of layers. Each layer performs a related subset of the functions required to communicate with another system. Each layer relies on the next lower layer to perform more primitive functions and to conceal the details of those functions, and it provides services to the next higher layer. Ideally, the layers should be defined so that changes in one layer do not require changes in the other layers. Thus, we have decomposed one problem into a number of more manageable subproblems.

The task of ISO is to define a set of layers and the services performed by each layer. The partitioning should group functions logically and should have enough layers to make each layer manageably small. There should not be, however, so many layers that the processing overhead imposed by the collection of layers is burdensome. The resulting OSI architecture has seven layers, which are listed with a brief definition in Table 9.1.

Figure 9.6 illustrates the OSI architecture. Each computer contains the seven layers. Communication is between applications in the two computers, labeled application X and application Y in the figure. If application X wishes to send a message to application Y, it invokes the application layer (layer 7). Layer 7 establishes a peer relationship with layer 7 of the target computer, using a layer-7 protocol (application protocol). This protocol requires services from layer 6, so the two layer-6 entities use a protocol of their own, and so on down to the physical layer, which actually transmits bits over a transmission medium.

Figure 9.6 also illustrates the way in which the protocols at each layer are realized. When application X has a message to send to application Y, it transfers those data to an application layer module. That module appends an application header to the data; the header contains the control information needed by the

TABLE 9.1   The OSI Layers

Layer	Definition
1 Physical	Concerned with transmission of unstructured bit stream over physical link; involves such parameters as signal voltage level and bit duration; deals with mechanical, electrical, and procedural characteristics to establish, maintain, and deactivate physical link.
2 Data Link	Provides for the reliable transfer of data across the physical link; sends blocks of data (frames) with the necessary synchronization, error control, and flow control.
3 Network	Provides upper layers with independence from the data transmission and switching technologies used to connect systems; responsible for establishing, maintaining, and terminating connections.
4 Transport	Provides reliable, transparent transfer of data between end points; provides end-to-end error recovery and flow control.
5 Session	Provides the control structure for communication between applications; establishes, manages, and terminates connections (sessions) between cooperating applications.
6 Presentation	Performs transformations on data to provide a standardized application interface and to provide common communications services; examples: encryption, text compression, reformatting.
7 Application	Provides services to users of the OSI environment; examples: transaction server, file transfer service, network management.

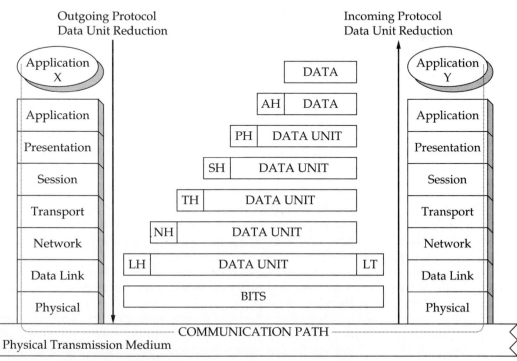

FIGURE 9.6 The OSI environment.

peer layer on the other side. The original data plus the header, referred to as an application PDU, is passed as a unit to layer 6. The presentation module treats the whole unit as data and appends its own header. This process continues down through layer 2, which generally adds both a header and a trailer. This layer-2 protocol data unit, usually called a *frame*, is then transmitted by the physical layer onto the transmission medium. When the frame is received by the target computer, the reverse process occurs. As we ascend the layers, each layer strips off the outermost header, acts on the protocol information contained therein, and passes the remainder up to the next layer.

The OSI Layers

The principal motivation for the development of the OSI model was to provide a framework for standardization. Within the model, one or more protocol standards can be developed at each layer. The model defines in general terms the functions to be performed at that layer and facilitates the process of making standards in two ways:

- Because the functions of each layer are well defined, standards can be developed independently and simultaneously for each layer. This speeds up the process of making standards.
- Because the boundaries between layers are well defined, changes in standards in one layer need not affect already existing software in another layer. This condition makes it easier to introduce new standards.

We now turn to a brief description of each layer and discuss some of the standards that have been developed for each layer.

Physical Layer

The physical layer covers the physical interface between a data transmission device and a transmission medium and the rules by which bits are passed from one to another. The physical layer has four important characteristics:

- *Mechanical:* Pertains to the point of demarcation. Typically, this is a pluggable connector with a specified number of pins to support a number of signal-carrying wires across the interface.
- *Electrical:* Have to do with the voltage levels and timing of voltage changes that define bits. These characteristics determine the data rates and distances that can be achieved.
- *Functional:* Specify the functions that are performed by assigning meaning to various wires. For example, one or more circuits may carry data, and others may carry control signals.
- *Procedural:* Specify the sequence of events for transmitting data. The sequence is based on the functional characteristics. For example, a control signal from one side may be followed by a companion control signal from the other side.

One of the most common physical interface standards is RS-232-C, and its follow-on version, EIA-232-D. The physical interface to a local area network is specified in a set of standards referred to as ISO 8802.

Data Link Layer

The physical layer provides only a raw bit stream. The data link layer attempts to make the physical link reliable and provides the means to activate, maintain, and deactivate the link. The principal services provided by the data link layer to higher layers are those of error detection and error control. Thus, with a fully functional data link layer protocol, the next higher layer may assume error-free transmission over the link.

The approach taken to provide reliability is to communicate control information as well as data over the link. Data are transmitted in blocks, called *frames*. Each frame consists of a header, a trailer, and an optional data field. The header and trailer contain control information used to manage the link.

As an example of a data link layer protocol, we consider HDLC (high-level data link control). HDLC is an ISO standard that is commonly used on computer-to-computer links and on computer-to-terminal links. Most proprietary link standards, such as IBM's SDLC are similar to HDLC. In addition, other data link control standards, such as that for local area networks, are based on HDLC.

With HDLC, three modes of operation are defined, as follows:

- *Normal response mode:* Used for point-to-point links (a link that connects only two stations) and also for multipoint links. The latter are typified by a line that connects a number of terminals to a computer. There are one primary station and one or more secondary stations. The primary station is responsible for initiating activity, controlling the flow of data to and from secondary stations, recovering from errors, and logically disconnecting secondary stations. A secondary station may transmit only in response to a poll from the primary. This mode is ideally suited for a host computer supporting a number of terminals.
- *Asynchronous response mode:* Is similar to the normal response mode, but a secondary station may initiate a transmission without being polled by the primary station. This mode is useful in certain types of loop configurations.
- *Asynchronous balanced mode:* Used only on a point-to-point link. Each station assumes the role of both the primary and secondary stations. This mode is more efficient for point-to-point links because there is no polling overhead and both stations may initiate transmission.

Data are transmitted in frames that consist of six fields (Figure 9.7a):

- *Flag:* Used for synchronization. This field appears at the start and end of every frame.
- *Address:* Indicates the secondary station for this transmission. It is needed in

8 bits	8	8	≤ 0	16	8
Flag	Address	Control	Information	CRC	Flag

(a) Frame format

	1	2	3	4	5	6	7	8
Information	0		N(S)		P/F		N(R)	
Supervisory	1	0	Type		P/F		N(R)	
Unnumbered	1	1	Modifier		P/F		Modifier	

(b) Control field format

FIGURE 9.7 HDLC frame structure.

the case of a multipoint line: a primary may send to one of a number of secondaries and one of a number of secondaries may send to the primary.
- *Control:* Identifies the function of the frame. It is described presently.
- *Information:* This field contains the user data provided by the next higher layer.
- *CRC:* The cyclic redundancy check is a function of the contents of the address, control, and data fields. It is generated by the sender and again by the receiver. If the receiver's result differs from the received CRC field, a transmission error has occurred.
- *Flag:* As was said in first item, this field appears at the end of every frame.

Three types of frames are used, each with a different control field format (Figure 9.7b). Information frames carry user data. Supervisory frames provide basic link control functions, and unnumbered frames provide supplemental link control functions.

The P/F bit is used by a primary station to solicit a response (poll). More than one frame may be sent in response, with the P/F bit set to indicate the last frame (final).

The N(S) and N(R) fields in the information frame provide an efficient technique for both flow control and error control. A station numbers the information frames that it sends sequentially modulo 8, using the N(S) field (Send sequence number). When a station receives a valid information frame, it may acknowledge that frame the next time it sends its own information frame by setting the N(R) field (Receive sequence number) to the number of the next frame that it expects to receive. This is known as *piggybacked acknowledgment* because the acknowledgment rides back on an information frame.

Acknowledgments can also be sent on a supervisory frame. The 2-bit type of field indicates one of four supervisory frames:

* *Receive Ready (RR):* Used to acknowledge correct receipt of information frames up to but not including N(R).
* *Receive Not Ready (RNR):* Used to indicate temporary busy condition. N(R) is used for a possibly redundant acknowledgment.
* *Reject (REJ):* Used to indicate an error in information frame N(R) and to request retransmission of that and all subsequent frames.
* *Selective Reject (SREJ):* Used to request retransmission of a single information frame.

The use of sequence numbers accomplishes three important functions:

* *Flow control:* Once a station has sent seven frames, it can send no more until the first frame has been acknowledged. This prevents the sender from overwhelming the receiver.
* *Error control:* If a frame is received in error, a station can send a REJ or SREJ to specify that the frame was received in error.
* *Pipelining:* More than one frame may be in transit at a time. This allows efficient use of links with a high propagation delay, such as satellite links.

The N(S)/N(R) technique is known as a *sliding-window protocol* because the sending station maintains a window of frames to be sent that gradually shrinks with transmissions and expands with acknowledgments. The process is depicted in Figure 9.8.

The unnumbered frames have no sequence numbers, but they have a 5-bit modifier field to indicate a variety of functions, such as initialize a station, set the mode, disconnect a station, and reject a command.

Network Layer

The network layer provides for the transfer of information between computers across some sort of communications network. It relieves higher layers of the need to know anything about the underlying data transmission and switching technologies used to connect systems. The network service is responsible for establishing, maintaining, and terminating connections across the intervening network. At this layer, the computer system engages in a dialogue with the network to specify the destination address and to request certain network facilities, such as priority.

There is a spectrum of possibilities for intervening communications facilities to be managed by the network layer. At one extreme, there is a direct point-to-point link between stations. In this case, there may be no need for a network layer because the data link layer can perform the necessary function of managing the link.

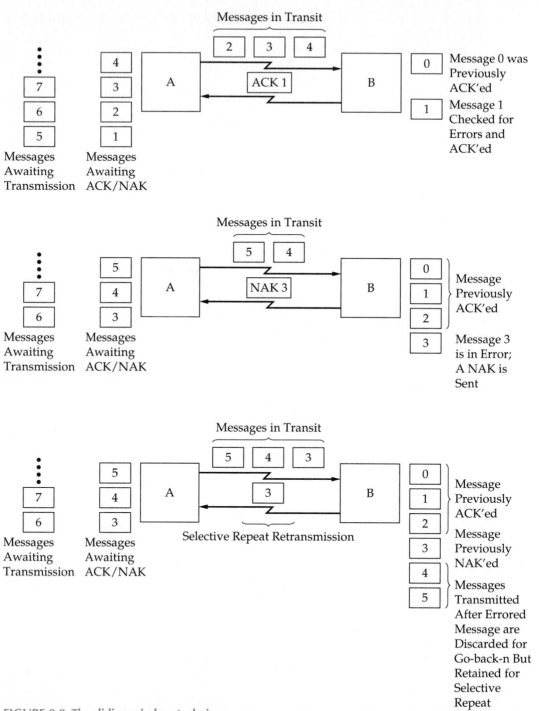

FIGURE 9.8 The sliding-window technique.

Next, the systems could be connected across a single network, such as a circuit-switching or packet-switching network. As an example, the packet level of the X.25 standard is a network layer standard for this situation. Figure 9.9 shows how the presence of a network affects the OSI architecture. The lower three layers are concerned with attaching to and communicating with the network. The packets (layer-3 protocol data units) that are created by the end system pass through one or more network nodes that act as relays between the two end systems. The network nodes implement layers 1 to 3 of the architecture. In the figure, two end systems are connected through a single network node. Layer 3 in the node performs a switching and routing function. Within the node, there are two data link layers and two physical layers, corresponding to the links to the two end systems. Each data link (and physical) layer operates independently to provide service to the network layer over its respective link. The upper four layers are "end-to-end" protocols between the attached computers.

At the other extreme, two stations may wish to communicate but are not even connected to the same network. Rather, they are connected to networks that, directly or indirectly, are connected to each other. This case requires the use of some sort of internetworking technique. In essence, packets are still used, but the logic involved includes functions for routing between networks as well as routing within networks.

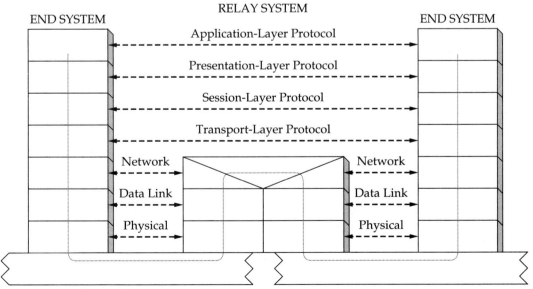

FIGURE 9.9 The use of a relay.

Transport Layer

The transport layer provides a reliable mechanism for the exchange of data between computers. It ensures that data are delivered error-free, in sequence, and with no losses or duplications. The transport layer may also be concerned with optimizing the use of network services and providing a requested quality of service. For example, the session layer may specify maximum delay, priority, and security features.

The mechanisms used by the transport protocol to provide reliability are very similar to those used by data link control protocols such as HDLC: the use of sequence numbers, error-detecting codes, and retransmission after time-out. The reason for this apparent duplication of effort is that the data link layer deals with only a single, direct link, whereas the transport layer deals with a chain of network nodes and links. Although each link in that chain is reliable because of the use of HDLC, a node along that chain may fail at a critical time. Such a failure affects data delivery, and it is the transport protocol that addresses this problem.

The size and complexity of a transport protocol depend on how reliable or unreliable the underlying network and network layer services are. Accordingly, the ISO has developed a family of five transport protocol standards, each oriented toward a different underlying service.

Session Layer

The session layer provides the mechanism for controlling the dialogue between two end systems. In many cases, there is little or no need for session layers, but for some applications, such services are used. The key services provided by the session layer include the following:

- *Dialogue discipline:* This can be two-way simultaneous (full duplex) or two-way alternate (half duplex).
- *Grouping:* The flow of data can be marked to define groups of data. For example, if a retail store is transmitting sales data to a regional office, the data can be marked to indicate the end of the sales data for each department, thus signaling the host computer to finalize running totals for that department and start new running counts for the next department.
- *Recovery:* The session layer can provide a checkpointing mechanism, so that if a failure of some sort occurs between checkpoints, the session entity can retransmit all data since the last checkpoint.

The ISO has issued a standard for the session layer that includes as options services such as those just described.

Presentation Layer

The presentation layer defines the format of the data to be exchanged between applications and offers application programs a set of data transformation services. For example, data compression or data encryption could occur at this level.

Application Layer

The application layer provides a means for application programs to access the OSI environment. This layer contains management functions and generally useful mechanisms to support distributed applications. In addition, general-purpose applications such as file transfer, electronic mail, and terminal access to remote computers are considered to reside at this layer.

9.2

SERVERS

One of the key benefits of a network, especially a local area network (LAN) is the ability to share expensive resources such as secondary storage devices and high-quality printers. A common way in which this is done is to provide one or more servers on the LAN. Figure 9.10 illustrates the concept in the case of a personal computer LAN. On the LAN are a number of personal computers, not necessarily of the same type and not necessarily employing the same operating system. In addition, for each shared resource, there are one or more servers. Users of personal computers have access to the shared resource by means of special software in the personal computer. In this section, we discuss the design of the software needed to support servers, and then we look at several examples.

Server Software Architecture

A LAN server is designed to provide shared access to a resource such as a disk or printer. The various user stations (personal computers, UNIX workstations, etc.) on the LAN are able to access this resource across the LAN.

Figure 9.11 suggests a general architecture for a server. The server is typically a dedicated microcomputer that controls one or more resources. As with other stations on the LAN, it includes a network interface module, which includes the hardware and software for interacting with the LAN. Thus, the appropriate layers of the OSI architecture are present.

The user station also includes a network interface. In addition, it includes some "network logic" that allows it to communicate with the server. This logic is accessed by an application. For example, to write a file to the server disk, the application issues a Write command to the network logic module. This module in turn prepares and sends the appropriate messages to the server.

This architecture is both powerful and flexible. The power of this approach is that it can be used to control virtually any kind of resource. Thus, new servers

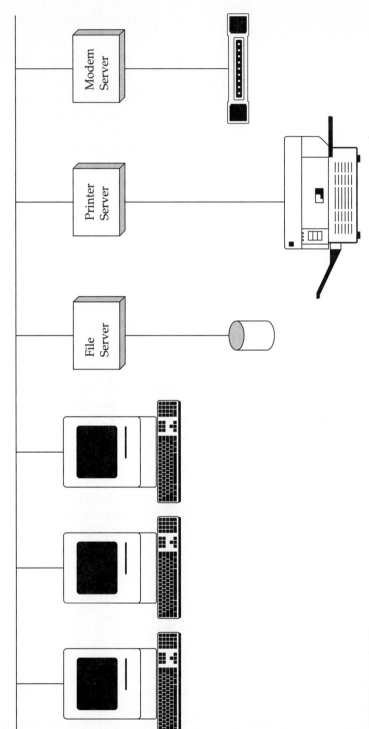

FIGURE 9.10 LAN servers.

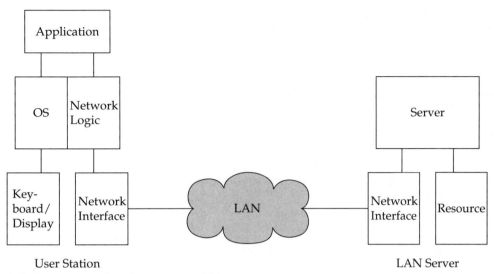

FIGURE 9.11 Workstation-server architecture.

can be added to a LAN at any time. In addition to the server system itself, the appropriate network software must be included in each user station. The flexibility of this approach is that it does not depend on a particular type of computer. Thus, the network logic can be tailored for any type of personal computer or workstation.

An important characteristic of a server capability is the degree to which it is transparent. In the ideal case, a user or application can use the same commands and parameters to access a resource that is locally attached to the user station or remotely attached to a server. For example, a user or application should be able to read a file from or write a file to a disk using the same commands for a local disk as for the remote server disk. In some cases, the user or application will have to select explicitly either the local or remote resource, after which the commands and parameters are identical. In other cases, the decision of whether to use a local or remote resource is made by the network software on the basis of file name or some other implicit designator.

Disk and File Servers

The growth in the use of LANs and in the number of personal computers and workstations on LANs has fueled the growth in interest in file servers. Although it is possible to let each computer on the LAN create and control its own files and to make those files available to others, it is preferable to provide a centralized storage and management facility for those files that are to be shared by a substantial portion of the community. The individual personal computers and workstations, being controlled by their users, cannot be guaranteed to be always available or fully trusted. The solution is to use a file server machine to administer the shared resources and support applications running on the workstations.

A file server is a separate computer (or collection of computers) attached to the LAN that provides a common service to all the other systems on the LAN. Typically, the file server is a microcomputer or, occasionally, a minicomputer. The primary service of the file server is to provide a shared storage space for files. In addition, the server can provide other valuable services, as follows:

- *Automatic backup and recovery:* Backup is the function of periodically copying the contents of a file system onto a backup disk or tape. This is a defense against storage media failure, user error, and viruses. Backup must be performed regularly, and the recovery procedure must be available for use. The average user of a personal computer or workstation should not be burdened with this responsibility.
- *User mobility:* There are several reasons why a user should be able to use different computers at different times:
  1. A computer may fail.
  2. Some people need or desire to work at more than one physical location.
  3. In some cases, workstations are managed as a common pool.
  A file server makes it feasible to provide a working environment independent of the workstation without the necessity of physically transporting the file storage medium (disk or tape).
- *Links to other file servers:* An organization may have a number of LANs in one or more locations, each with a file server. A file transfer facility can be implemented in each file server to allow users to access files on other LANs (Figure 9.12).

The term *file server* has unfortunately been used for devices covering a broad range of capabilities. Two extremes can be identified: shared storage and a shared file-management system.

Many of the file servers on the market simply provide a centralized disk facility that can be used as an extension of local storage by users of personal computers. Such systems are sometimes referred to as *disk servers*. The user simply perceives a much larger disk space than before and may use this disk space to store and retrieve files. There is no file sharing. To send files between users, each user must employ a separate program called a *file transfer facility*. The disk server may provide automatic backup and user mobility. In addition, these systems may provide a cost savings: In general, the larger a storage system, the lower the cost per bit of storage. Thus, centralized shared storage, which is relatively cheap, allows the use of personal computers with very little or no disk storage.

At the other extreme is a file server that provides all the file-management capabilities found on a time-sharing system. Thus, in addition to providing storage space, the file server allows multiple users to have access to files. The server controls concurrent access to files, enforces access rights and restrictions, and provides directory structures that recognize file names and support grouping of files.

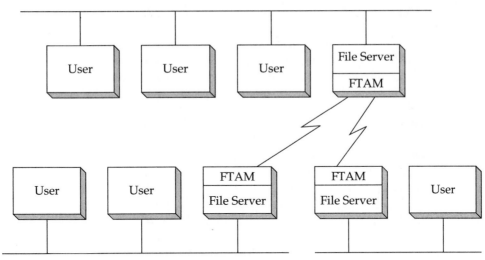

FIGURE 9.12 File servers and multiple LANs.

File Cache Consistency

When a file server is used, performance of file I/O can be noticeably degraded relative to local file access because of the delays imposed by the network. To reduce this performance penalty, individual systems can use file caches to hold recently accessed file records. Because of the principle of locality, use of a local file cache should reduce the number of remote server accesses that must be made.

Figure 9.13 illustrates a typical distributed mechanism for caching files among a networked collection of workstations. When a process makes a file access, the

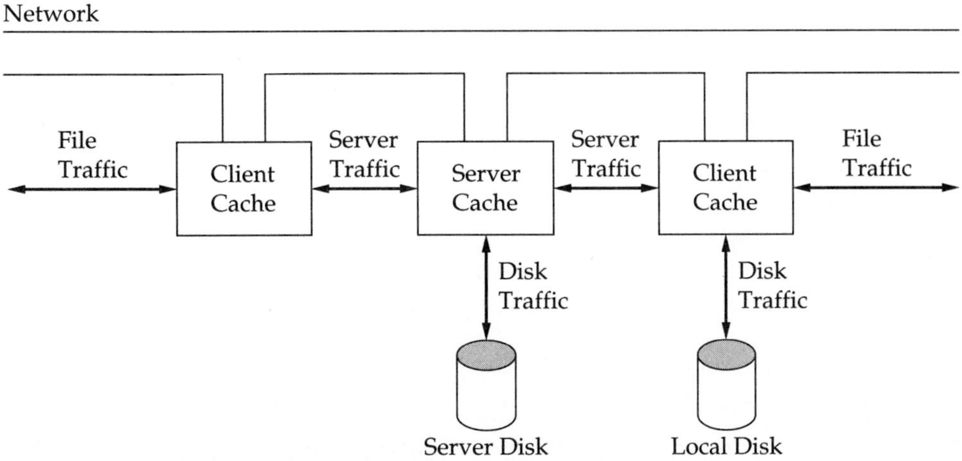

Network
_____

File
Traffic   Client Cache   Server Traffic   Server Cache   Server Traffic   Client Cache   File Traffic

Disk Traffic   Disk Traffic

Server Disk   Local Disk

FIGURE 9.13 Distributed file cacheing in sprite.

request is presented first to the cache of the process's workstation ("file traffic"). If not satisfied there, the request is passed either to the local disk if the file is stored there ("disk traffic"), or to a file server where the file is stored ("server traffic"). At the server, the server's cache is first interrogated, and if there is a miss, then the server's disk is accessed. The dual caching approach is used to reduce communications traffic (client cache) and disk I/O (server cache).

When caches always contain exact copies of remote data, we say that the caches are **consistent**. It is possible for caches to become inconsistent when the remote data are changed and the corresponding obsolete local cache copies are not discarded. This can happen if one client modifies a file that is also cached by other clients. The difficulty is actually at two levels. If a client adopts a policy of immediately writing any changes to a file back to the server, then any other client with a cache copy of the relevant portion of the file will have obsolete data. The problem is made even worse if the client delays writing back changes to the server. In that case, the server itself has an obsolete version of the file, and new file Read requests to the server may obtain obsolete data. The problem of keeping local cache copies up to date to changes in remote data is known as the **cache consistency** problem.

The simplest approach to cache consistency is to use file-locking techniques to prevent simultaneous access to a file by more than one client. This guarantees consistency at the expense of performance and flexibility. A more powerful approach is provided with the facility in Sprite [NELS88, OUST88]. Any number of remote processes may open a file for Read and create their own client cache. But when an open file request to a server requests Write access and other processes have the file open for Read access, the server takes two actions. First, it notifies the Writing process that, although it may maintain a cache, it must write back all altered blocks immediately upon update. There can be at most one such client. Second, the server notifies all Reading processes that have the file open that the file is no longer cacheable.

Printer Servers

A printer server (Figure 9.14) can handle the printing requirements of a number of user workstations. This not only saves money on printing, it can make printing easier and faster.

The printer server makes use of one of the oldest of operating-system techniques, known as spooling. A spool (simultaneous peripheral operation on line) is a combination of hardware and software that redirects I/O requests from the relatively slow printer to a fast disk. As print requests come in, each document or file is first spooled out onto the disk. The files are organized as a first-in, first-out queue. The server retrieves files from the disk one at a time and prints them. The spooling facility overcomes two problems relating to the use of the printer:

• The document to be printed next may be larger than the available space in

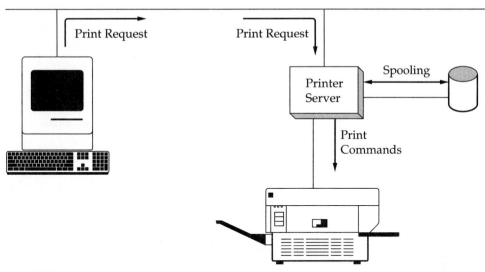

Print Request Print Request

Spooling

Printer
Server

Print
Commands

FIGURE 9.14 Printer server.

main memory. Thus, it can be stored on disk and read in a block at a time
and printed.

• One or more users may issue a print request while the printer is engaged in
printing a file. These requests can be queued up waiting for the printer.

Modem Server

A simple but useful capability to add to a LAN is a modem server. For example,
if a user wishes to access an information-retrieval/electronic-mail system such
as CompuServe, the user needs a modem to connect to an outside telephone
line and to dial into the desired system. As with other hardware resources,
modems are relatively expensive and should be shared. Typically, only a small
fraction of the number of users will need modem access at any one time. Thus,
a small number of modems will suffice to support the LAN user community.
A server with one or a few attached modems and as many telephone lines as
modems will suffice.

A user request to the server requests access to a modem and provides a phone
number. The server activates the modem, dials the number, and reports the
result. If the call is successfully placed, the user is provided a connection. Once
the user has a connection, data can be sent and received as if the user were
using the modem directly. The only difference that may be perceived by the
user is that data coming in via the modem is "packetized." That is, as the data
arrive at the server over the modem, the data are buffered and sent to the user
in packets. Thus, the user may perceive a "bursty" flow of characters onto the
screen.

9.3

PROCESS MIGRATION

Process migration is the transfer of a sufficient amount of the state of a process from one machine to another for the process to execute on the target machine. Interest in this concept grew out of research into ways to do load balancing across multiple networked systems, although the application of the concept now extends beyond that one area.

In the past, only a few of the many papers on load distribution were based on true implementations of process migration, which includes the ability to preempt a process on one machine and reactivate it later on another machine. Experience showed that preemptive process migration is possible, although it resulted in higher overhead and complexity than originally anticipated [ARTS89a]. This cost led some observers to conclude that process migration was not practical. For example, consider the following statement [TANE85]:

> Actually migrating running processes is trivial in theory, but close to impossible in practice.

Such assessments have proved too pessimistic. New implementations, including those in commercial products, have fueled a continuing interest and new developments in this area. This section provides an overview.

Motivation

Process migration is desirable in distributed systems for a number of reasons, including the following [SMIT88, JUL88]:

- *Load sharing:* By moving processes from heavily loaded to lightly loaded systems, the load can be balanced to improve overall performance. Empirical data suggest that significant performance improvements are possible [LELA86, CABR86]. However, care must be taken in the design of load-balancing algorithms. [EAGE86] points out that the more communication necessary for the distributed system to perform the balancing, the worse the performance becomes. A discussion of this issue, with references to other studies, can be found in [ESKI90].
- *Communications performance:* Processes that interact intensively can be moved to the same node to reduce communications cost for the duration of their interaction. Also, when a process is performing data analysis on some file or set of files larger than the process's size, it may be advantageous to move the process to the data rather than vice versa.
- *Availability:* Long-running processes may need to move to survive in the face of faults for which advance notice can be achieved or in advance of scheduled downtime. If the operating system provides such notification, a process that wants to continue can either migrate to another system or ensure that it can be restarted on the current system at some later time.

- *Utilizing special capabilities:* A process can move to take advantage of unique hardware or software capabilities on a particular node.

Process Migration Mechanisms

A number of issues need to be addressed in designing a process migration facility. Among them are the following:

- Who initiates the migration?
- What "portion" of the process is migrated?
- What happens to outstanding messages and signals?

Initiation of Migration

Who initiates migration will depend on the goal of the migration facility. If the goal is load balancing, then some module in the operating system that is monitoring system load is generally responsible for deciding when migration should take place. The module is responsible for preempting or signaling a process to be migrated. To determine where to migrate, the module needs to be in communication with similar modules in other systems so that the load pattern on other systems can be monitored. If the goal is to reach particular resources, then a process may migrate itself as the need arises. In this latter case, the process must be aware of the existence of a distributed system. In the former case, the entire migration function, and indeed the existence of multiple systems, may be transparent to the process.

What is Migrated?

When a process is migrated, it is necessary to destroy the process on the source system and create it on the target system. This is a movement of a process, not a replication. Thus, the process image, consisting of at least the process control block, must be moved. In addition, any links between this process and other processes, such as for passing messages and signals, must be updated. Figure 9.15 illustrates these considerations. Process 3 has migrated out of machine S to become process 4 in machine D. All link identifiers held by processes (denoted in lowercase letters) remain the same as before. It is the responsibility of the operating system to move the process control block and to update link mappings. The transfer of the process of one machine to another machine is invisible to both the migrated process and its communication partners.

The movement of the process control block is straightforward. From a performance point of view, the difficulty concerns the process address space and any open files assigned to the process. Consider first the process address space and let us assume that a virtual memory scheme (segmentation and/or paging) is being used. Two strategies suggest themselves:

1. Transfer the entire address space at the time of migration. This is certainly

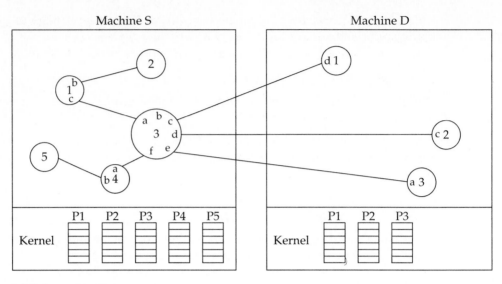

(a) Before migration

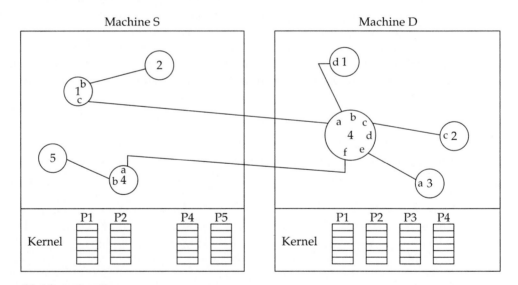

(b) After migration

FIGURE 9.15 Example of process migration.

the cleanest approach. No trace of the process need be left behind at the old system. However, if the address space is very large and if the process is likely to not need most of it, then this approach may be unnecessarily expensive.

2. Transfer only that portion of the address space that is in main memory. Any additional blocks of the virtual address space will be transferred on demand

only. This minimizes the amount of data that is transferred. It does require, however, that the source machine continue to be involved throughout the life of the process by maintaining page and/or segment table entries.

If it is likely that the process will not use much of its nonresident address space (for example, the process is only temporarily going to another machine to work on a file and will soon return), then the second strategy makes sense. On the other hand, if much of the nonresident address space will eventually be accessed, then the piecemeal transfer of blocks of the address space may be less efficient than simply transferring all the address space at the time of migration.

In many cases, it may not be possible to know in advance whether much of the nonresident address space will be needed. However, if processes are structured as threads and if the basic unit of migration is the thread rather than the process, then the second strategy listed would seem to be the best. Indeed, the second strategy is almost mandated, since the remaining threads of the process are left behind and also need access to the address space of the process. Thread migration is implemented in the Emerald operating system [JUL89, JUL88].

Similar considerations apply to the movement of open files. If the file is initially on the same system as the process to be migrated and if the file is locked for exclusive access by that process, then it may make sense to transfer the file with the process. The danger here is that the process may be gone only temporarily and may not need the file until its return. Therefore, it may make sense to transfer the entire file only after an access request is made by the migrated process.

If caching is permitted, as in the Sprite system (Figure 9.13), then an additional complexity is introduced. For example, if a process has a file open for writing, and it forks and migrates a child, the file would then be open for writing on two different hosts. Sprite's cache consistency algorithm dictates that the file be made noncacheable on the machines on which the two processes are executing [DOUG89].

Messages and Signals

The final issue listed earlier, the fate of outstanding messages and signals, is addressed by providing a mechanism for temporarily storing outstanding messages and signals during the migration activity and then directing them to the new destination. It may be necessary to maintain forwarding information at the initial site for some time to assure that all outstanding messages and signals get through.

A Migration Scenario

As a representative example of self-migration, let us consider the facility available on IBM's AIX operating system [WALK89], which is a distributed UNIX operating system. A similar facility is available on the LOCUS operating system [POPE85], and in fact the AIX system is based on the LOCUS development.

The following sequence of events occurs:

1. When a process decides to migrate itself, it selects a target machine and sends a remote tasking message. The message carries a part of the process image and open file information.
2. At the receiving site, a kernel server process forks a child, giving it this information.
3. The new process pulls over data, environment, arguments, and stack information as needed to complete its operation. Program text is copied over if it is impure, and it is demand paged from the global file system if it is pure.
4. The originating process is signaled on the completion of the migration. This process sends a final done message to the new process and destroys itself.

A similar sequence is followed when another process initiates the migration. The principal difference is that the process to be migrated must be suspended so that it can be migrated in a nonrunning state. This procedure is followed in Sprite, for example [DOUG89].

In the foregoing scenario, migration is a dynamic activity involving a number of steps for moving the process image over. When migration is initiated by another process, rather than by self-migration, another approach is to copy the process image and its entire address space into a file, destroy the process, copy the file to another machine using a file transfer facility, and then recreate the process from the file on the target machine. [SMIT89] describes such an approach.

Negotiation of Migration

Another aspect of process migration relates to the decision about migration. In some cases, the decision is made by a single entity. For example, if load balancing is the goal, a load-balancing module monitors the relative load on various machines and performs migration as necessary to maintain a load balance. If self-migration is used to allow a process access to special facilities or to large remote files, then the process itself may make the decision. However, some systems allow the designated target system to participate in the decision, one reason being to preserve response time for users. A user at a workstation, for example, may suffer noticeable degradation in response time if processes migrate to the user's system, even if such migration serves to provide better overall balance.

An example of a negotiation mechanism is that found in Charlotte [FINK89, ARTS89b]. Migration policy (when to migrate which process to what destination) is the responsibility of the Starter utility, which is a process that is also responsible for long-term scheduling and memory allocation. The Starter can therefore coordinate policy in these three areas. Each Starter process may control a cluster of machines. The Starter receives timely and fairly elaborate load statistics from the kernel of each of its machines.

The decision to migrate must be reached jointly by two Starter processes, as illustrated in Figure 9.16. The following steps occur:

1. The Starter that controls the source system (S) decides that a process (P) should be migrated to a particular destination system (D). It sends a message to D's Starter requesting the transfer.
2. If D's Starter is prepared to receive the process, it sends back a positive acknowledgment.
3. S's Starter communicates this decision to S's kernel via service call (if the starter runs on S) or a message to the KernJob (KJ) of machine S, a process used to convert messages from remote processes into service calls.
4. The kernel on S then offers to send the process to D. The offer includes statistics about P, such as its age and processor and communication loads.
5. If D is short of resources, it may reject the offer. Otherwise, the kernel on D relays the offer to its controlling Starter. The relay includes the same information as the offer from S.
6. The Starter's policy decision is communicated to D by a MigrateIn call.
7. D reserves necessary resources to avoid deadlock and flow-control problems, and then sends an acceptance to S.

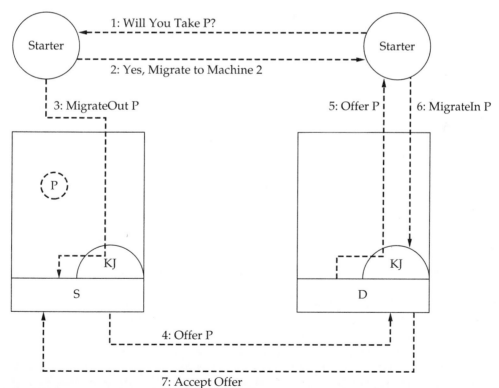

FIGURE 9.16 Negotiation of process migration.

Eviction

The negotiation process allows a destination system to refuse to accept the migration of a process to itself. In addition, it may also be useful to allow a system to evict a process that has been migrated to it. For example, if a workstation is idle, one or more processes may be migrated to it. Once the user of that workstation becomes active, it may be necessary to evict the migrated processes to provide adequate response time.

An example of an eviction capability is that found in Sprite [DOUG89]. In Sprite, which is a workstation operating system, each process appears to run on a single host throughout its lifetime. This host is known as the *home node* of the process. If a process is migrated, it becomes a *foreign process* on the destination machine. At any time the destination machine may evict the foreign process, which is then forced to migrate back to its home node.

The elements of the Sprite eviction mechanism are as follows:

1. A monitor process at each node keeps track of current load to determine when to accept new foreign processes. If the monitor detects activity at the workstation's console, it initiates an eviction procedure on each foreign process.
2. If a process is evicted, it is migrated back to its home node. The process may be migrated again if another node is available.
3. Although it may take some time to evict all processes, all processes marked for eviction are immediately suspended. Permitting an evicted process to execute while it is waiting for eviction would reduce the time during which the process is frozen but also reduce the processing power available to the host while evictions are underway.
4. The entire address space of an evicted process is transferred to the home node. The time to migrate a process may be reduced substantially by retrieving the memory image of a migrated process from its previous host as referenced. However, this compels the former host to dedicate resources and to honor service requests from the evicted process for a longer period than necessary.

9.4

DISTRIBUTED PROCESS COMMUNICATION

It is usually the case in true distributed processing systems that the computers do not share main memory; each is an isolated computer system. Thus, interprocessor techniques that rely on shared memory, such as semaphores and the use of a common area of memory, will not work. Instead, techniques that rely on message passing are used. In this section, we look at the two most common approaches. The first is the straightforward application of messages as they are used in a single system. The second is a separate technique that relies on message passing as a basic function: the remote procedure call.

Message Passing

Figure 9.17 shows the most common model used for distributed message passing, which is referred to as the *client-server model*. A client process requires some service (e.g., Read a file, Print) and sends a message containing a request for service to a server process. The server process honors the request and sends a reply. In its simplest form, only two functions are needed: Send and Receive. The Send function specifies a destination and includes the message content. The Receive function tells from whom a message is desired (including "all") and provides a buffer where the incoming message is to be stored.

Figure 9.18 suggests an implementation approach for message passing. Processes make use of the services of a message-passing module, which is part of the operating system. Service requests can be expressed in terms of primitives and parameters. A primitive specifies the function to be performed, and the parameters are used to pass data and control information. The actual form of a primitive depends on the operating system. It may be a procedure call, or it may itself be a message to a process that is part of the operating system.

The Send primitive is used by the process that desires to send the message. Its parameters are the identifier of the destination process and the contents of the message. The message-passing module constructs a data unit that includes these two elements (compare Figure 9.18). This data unit is sent to the machine that hosts the destination process, using some sort of communications utility such as the OSI communications architecture. When the data unit is received in the target system, it is routed by the communications utility to the message-passing module. This module examines the process Id field and stores the message in the buffer for that process.

In this scenario, the receiving process must announce its willingness to receive messages by designating a buffer area and informing the message-passing module by means of a Receive primitive. An alternative approach does not require such an announcement. Instead, when the message-passing module receives a message, it signals the destination process with some sort of Receive signal and then makes the received message available in a shared buffer.

Several design issues are associated with distributed message passing, and these are addressed in the remainder of this subsection.

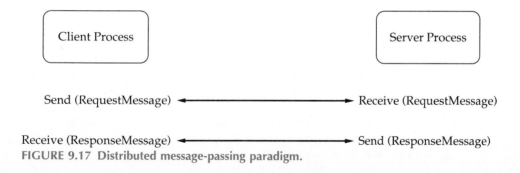

FIGURE 9.17 Distributed message-passing paradigm.

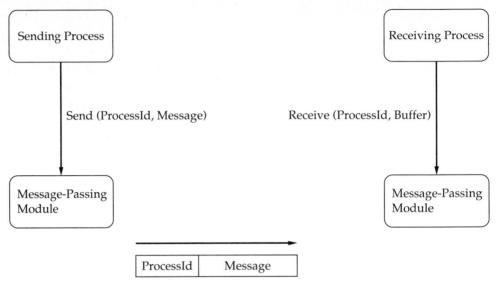

FIGURE 9.18 Basic message-passing primitives.

Reliable versus Unreliable

A reliable message-passing facility is one that guarantees delivery if possible. Such a facility would make use of a reliable transport protocol or similar logic and would perform error checking, acknowledgment, retransmission, and reordering of misordered messages. Because delivery is guaranteed, it is not necessary to let the sending process know that the message was delivered. However, it can be useful to provide an acknowledgement to the sending process so that it knows that delivery has already taken place. In either case, if the facility fails to achieve delivery (e.g., persistent network failure, crash of destination system), then the sending process is notified of the failure.

At the other extreme, the message-passing facility may simply send the message out into the communications network but will report neither success nor failure. This alternative greatly reduces the complexity and the processing and communications overhead of the message-passing facility. For those applications that require confirmation that a message has been delivered, the applications themselves may use Request and Reply messages to satisfy the requirement.

Blocking versus Nonblocking

With nonblocking primitives, a process is not suspended as a result of issuing a Send or Receive. Thus, when a process issues a Send primitive, the operating system returns control to the process as soon as the message has been queued for transmission or a copy has been made. If no copy is made, any changes made to the message by the sending process before or even while it is being transmitted are made at the risk of the process. When the message has been transmitted or copied to a safe place for subsequent transmission, the sending process is interrupted to be informed that the message buffer may be reused. Similarly, a nonblocking Receive is issued by a process that then proceeds to run. When a message arrives, the process is informed by interrupt, or it can poll for status periodically.

Nonblocking primitives provide for efficient, flexible use of the message-passing facility by processes. The disadvantage of this approach is that it is difficult to test and debug programs that use these primitives. As we have seen in our discussion of concurrency, irreproducible, timing-dependent sequences can create subtle and difficult problems.

The alternative is to use blocking primitives. A blocking Send does not return control to the sending process until the message has been transmitted (unreliable service) or until the message has been sent and an acknowledgment received (reliable service). A blocking Receive does not return control until a message has been placed in the allocated buffer.

Remote Procedure Calls

A variation on the basic message-passing model is the remote procedure call, which is now a widely accepted and common method for encapsulating communication in a distributed system. The essence of the technique is to allow programs on different machines to interact using simple procedure call/return semantics, just as if the two programs were on the same machine. That is, the procedure call is used for access to remote services. The popularity of this approach is due to the following advantages:

1. The procedure call is a widely accepted, used, and understood abstraction.
2. The use of remote procedure calls enables remote interfaces to be specified as a set of named operations with designated types. Thus, the interface can be clearly documented and distributed programs can be statically checked for type errors.
3. Since a standardized and precisely defined interface is specified, the communication code for an application can be generated automatically.
4. Since a standardized and precisely defined interface is specified, developers can write client and server modules that can be moved among computers and operating systems with little modification and recoding.

The remote procedure call mechanism can be viewed as a refinement of reliable, blocking message passing. Figure 9.19 illustrates the general architecture, and Figure 9.20 shows the internal program logic. The calling program makes a normal procedure call with parameters on its machine. For example,

CALL $P\ (X,\ Y)$

where

P = procedure name
X = passed arguments
Y = returned values

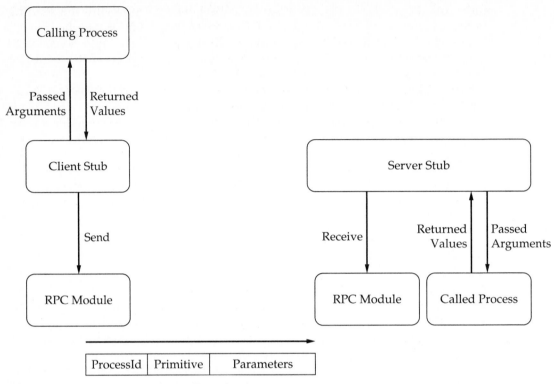

FIGURE 9.19 Remote procedure call mechanism.

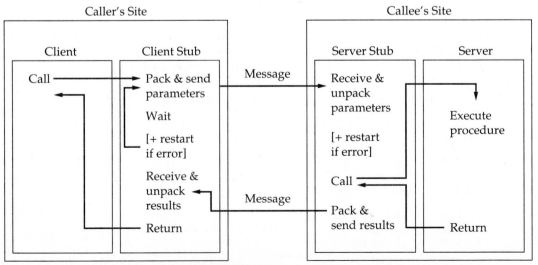

FIGURE 9.20 Remote procedure call logic [KRAK88].

It may or may not be transparent to the user that the intention is to invoke a remote procedure on some other machine. A dummy or stub procedure P must be included in the caller's address space or dynamically linked to it at call time. This procedure creates a message that identifies the procedure being called and includes the parameters. It then sends this message, using a Send primitive, and waits for a reply. When a reply is received, the stub procedure returns to the calling program, providing the returned values.

At the remote machine, another stub program is associated with the called procedure. When a message comes in, it is examined and a local CALL $P(X, Y)$ is generated. This remote procedure is thus called locally, and so its normal assumptions about where to find parameters, the state of the stack, and the like are identical to the case of a purely local procedure call.

Several design issues are associated with remote procedure calls, and these are addressed in the remainder of this subsection.

Parameter Passing

Most programming languages allow parameters to be passed as values (call by value) or as pointers to a location that contains the value (call by reference). Call by value is simple for a remote procedure call: The parameters are simply copied into the message and sent to the remote system. It is more difficult to implement call by reference. A unique, system-wide pointer is needed for each object. The overhead for this capability may not be worth the effort.

Parameter Representation

Another issue is how to represent parameters and results in messages. If the called and calling programs are in identical programming languages on the same type of machines with the same operating system, then the representation requirement may present no problems. If there are differences in these areas, then there will probably be differences in the ways in which numbers and even text are represented. If a full-blown communications architecture is used, then this issue is handled by the presentation layer. However, the overhead of such an architecture has led to the design of remote procedure call facilities that bypass most of the communications architecture and provide their own basic communications facility. In that case, the conversion responsibility falls on the remote procedure call facility (e.g., see [GIBB87]).

The best approach to this problem is to provide a standardized format for common objects such as integers, floating-point numbers, characters, and character strings. Then, the native parameters on any machine can be converted to and from the standardized representation.

Client-Server Binding

Binding specifies how the relationship between a remote procedure and the calling program is to be established. A binding is formed when two applications have made a logical connection and are prepared to exchange commands and data.

Nonpersistent binding means that a logical connection is established between the two processes at the time of the remote procedure call and that as soon as the values are returned, the connection is dismantled. Because a connection requires the maintenance of state information on both ends, it consumes resources. The nonpersistent style is used to conserve those resources. On the other hand, the overhead involved in establishing connections makes nonpersistent binding inappropriate for remote procedures that are called frequently by the same caller.

With **persistent binding**, a connection that is set up for a remote procedure call is sustained after the procedure return. The connection can then be used for future remote procedure calls. If a specified period passes with no activity on the connection, then the connection is terminated. For applications that make many repeated calls to remote procedures, persistent binding maintains the logical connection and allows a sequence of calls and returns to use the same connection.

Determining the Global State of a Distributed System

Global States and Distributed Snapshots

All the concurrency issues that are faced in a tightly coupled system, such as mutual exclusion, deadlock, and starvation, are also faced in a distributed system. Design strategies in these areas are complicated by the fact that there is no global state to the system. That is, it is not possible for the operating system, or any process, to know the current state of all processes in the distributed system. A process can know only the current state of all the processes on the local system, by access to process control blocks in memory. For remote processes, a process can know only state information that is received via messages, which represent the state of the remote process some time in the past. This is analogous to the situation in astronomy: Our knowledge of a distant star or galaxy consists of light and other electromagnetic waves arriving from the distant object, and these waves provide a picture of the object some time in the past. For example, our knowledge of an object at a distance of 5 light-years is 5 years old at the time we receive it.

The time lags imposed by the nature of distributed systems complicate all issues relating to concurrency. To illustrate this, we present an example taken from [ANDR90]. We will use process/event graphs (Figures 9.21 and 9.22) to illustrate the problem. In these graphs, there is a horizontal line for each process that represents the time axis. A point on the line corresponds to an event (e.g., internal process event, message send, message receive). A box surrounding a point represents a snapshot of the local process state taken at that point. An arrow represents a message between two processes.

In our example, an individual has a bank account distributed over two

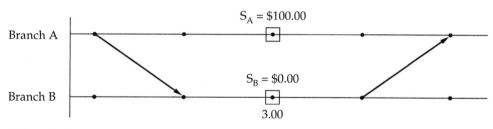

(a) Total = $100.00

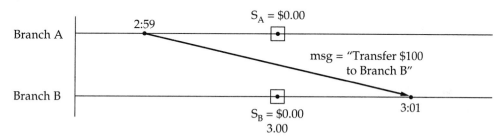

(b) Total = $0.00

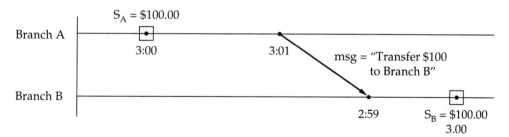

(c) Total = $200.00

FIGURE 9.21 Example of determining global state.

branches of a bank. To determine the total amount in the customer's account, the bank must determine the amount in each branch. Suppose that the determination is to be made at exactly 3:00 P.M. Figure 9.21a shows an instance in which a balance of $100.00 in the combined account is found. But the situation in Figure 9.21b is also possible. Here, the balance from branch A is in transit to branch B at the time of observation; the result is a false reading of $0.00. This particular problem can be solved by examining all messages in transit at the time of observation. Branch A will keep a record of all transfers out of the account, together with the identity of the destination of the transfer. Therefore, we will include in the "state" of a branch account both the current balance and a record of transfers. When the two accounts are examined, the observer finds a transfer that has left branch A destined for the customer's account in branch

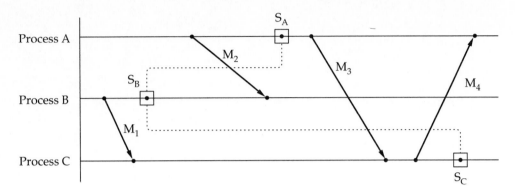

(a) Inconsistent global state

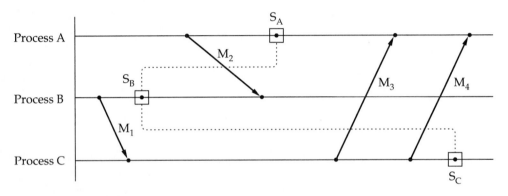

(b) Consistent global state

FIGURE 9.22 Inconsistent and consistent global states.

B. Since the amount has not yet arrived at branch B, it is added into the total balance. Any amount that has been both transferred and received is counted only once, as part of the balance at the receiving account.

This strategy is not foolproof, as shown in Figure 9.21c. In this example, the clocks at the two branches are not perfectly synchronized. The state of the customer account at branch A at 3:00 P.M. indicates a balance of $100.00. However, this amount is subsequently transferred to branch B at 3:01 according to the clock at A but arrives at B at 2:59 according to B's clock. Therefore, the amount is counted twice for a 3:00 P.M.observation.

To understand the difficulty we face and to formulate a solution, let us define the following terms:

- *Channel:* A channel exists between two processes if they exchange messages. We can think of the channel as the path or means by which the messages are transferred. For convenience, channels are viewed as being one-way. Thus, if two processes exchange messages, two channels are required, one for each direction of message transfer.

- *State:* The state of a process is the sequence of messages that have been sent and received along channels incident with the process.
- *Snapshot:* A snapshot records the state of a process. Each snapshot includes a record of all messages sent and received on all channels since the last snapshot.
- *Global State:* The combined state of all processes.
- *Distributed Snapshot:* A collection of snapshots, one for each process.

The problem that we face is that a true global state cannot be determined because of the time lapse associated with message transfer. We can attempt to define a global state by collecting snapshots from all processes. For example, the global state of Figure 9.22a at the time of the taking of snapshots shows a message in transit on the $< A, B >$ channel; one in transit on the $< A, C >$ channel; and one in transit on the $< C, A >$ channel. Messages 2 and 4 are represented appropriately, but message 3 is not. The distributed snapshot indicates that this message has been received but not yet been sent!

We desire that the distributed snapshot record a consistent global state. A global state is consistent if for every process state that records the receipt of a message, the sending of that message is recorded in the process state of the process that sent the message. Figure 9.22b gives an example. An inconsistent global state arises if a process has recorded the receipt of a message but the corresponding sending process has not recorded that the message has been sent (Figure 9.22a).

The Distributed Snapshot Algorithm

A distributed snapshot algorithm that records a consistent global state has been described in [CHAN85]. The algorithm assumes that messages are delivered in the order that they sent and that no messages are lost. A reliable transport protocol (OSI layer 4) satisfies these requirements. The algorithm makes use a a special control message, called a **marker**.

Some processes initiate the algorithm by recording its state and sending a marker on all outgoing channels before any more messages are sent. Each process p then proceeds as follows. Upon the first receipt of the marker (say from process q), a receiving process performs the following steps:

1. p records its local state S_p.
2. p records the state of the incoming channel from q to p as empty.
3. p propagates the marker to all its neighbors along all outgoing channels.

These steps must be performed atomically; that is, no messages can be sent or received by p until all three steps have been performed.

At any time after recording its state, when p receives a marker from another incoming channel (say from process r), it performs the following:

1. p records the state of the channel from r to p as the sequence of messages p has received from r from the time p recorded its local state S_p to the time it received the marker from r.

The algorithm terminates at a process once the marker has been received along every incoming channel.

[ANDR90] makes the following observations about the algorithm:

1. Any process may start the algorithm by sending out a marker. In fact, several nodes could independently decide to record the state, and the algorithm would still succeed.
2. The algorithm will terminate in finite time if every message (including marker messages) is delivered in finite time.
3. This is a distributed algorithm: Each process is responsible for recording its own state and the state of all incoming channels.
4. Once all the states have been recorded (the algorithm has terminated at all processes), the consistent global state obtained by the algorithm can be assembled at every process by having every process send the state data that it has recorded along every outgoing channel and having every process forward the state data that it receives along every outgoing channel. Alternatively, the initiating process could poll all processes to acquire the global state.
5. The algorithm does not affect and is not affected by any other distributed algorithm that the processes are participating in.

As an example of the use of the algorithm (taken from [BEN90]), consider the set of processes illustrated in Figure 9.23. Each process is represented by a node, and each unidirectional channel is represented by a line between two nodes, with the direction indicated by an arrow. Suppose that the snapshot algorithm is run, with nine messages being sent along each of its outgoing channels by each process. Process 1 decides to record the global state after sending six messages, and process 4 independently decides to record the global state after sending three messages. Upon termination, the snapshots are collected from each process; the results are shown in Figure 9.24. Process 2 sent four messages on each of the two outgoing channels to processes 3 and 4 prior to the recording

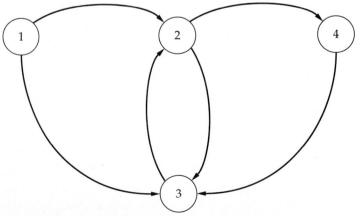

FIGURE 9.23 Process and channel graph.

Process 1
  Outgoing channels
    2 sent 1,2,3,4,5,6
    3 sent 1,2,3,4,5,6
  Incoming channels
Process 2
  Outgoing channels
    3 sent 1,2,3,4
    4 sent 1,2,3,4
  Incoming channels
    1 received 1,2,3,4 stored 5,6
    3 received 1,2,3,4,5,6,7,8
Process 3
  Outgoing channels
    2 sent 1,2,3,4,5,6,7,8
  Incoming channels
    1 received 1,2,3 stored 4,5,6
    2 received 1,2,3 stored 4
    4 received 1,2,3
Process 4
  Outgoing channels
    3 sent 1,2,3
  Incoming channels
    2 received 1,2 stored 3,4

FIGURE 9.24 An example of a snapshot.

of the state. It received four messages from process 1 before recording its state, leaving messages 5 and 6 to be associated with the channel. Check the snapshot for consistency: Each message sent was either received at the destination process or recorded as being in transit in the channel.

The distributed snapshot algorithm is a powerful and flexible tool. It can be used to adapt any centralized algorithm to a distributed environment because the basis of any centralized algorithm is knowledge of the global state. Specific examples include detection of deadlock and detection of process termination (e.g., see [BEN90]). It can also be used to provide a checkpoint of a distributed algorithm to allow rollback and recovery if a failure is detected.

9.5

DISTRIBUTED PROCESS MANAGEMENT—MUTUAL EXCLUSION

Recall that in Chapter 4 we addressed the issues relating to the execution of concurrent processes. The two key problems that arose were those of mutual exclusion and deadlock. That chapter focused on solutions to this problem in the context of a single system having one or more processors and a common main memory. In dealing with a distributed operating system and a collection of processors that do not share common main memory, new difficulties arise and new solutions are called for. Algorithms for mutual exclusion and deadlock must depend on the exchange of messages and cannot depend on access to common memory. In this section and the next, we examine mutual exclusion and deadlock in the context of a distributed operating system.

Distributed Mutual Exclusion

When two or more processes compete for the use of system resources, there is a need for a mechanism to enforce mutual exclusion. Suppose two or more processes require access to a single nonsharable resource such as a printer. During the course of execution, each process will be sending commands to the I/O device, receiving status information, sending data, and/or receiving data. We will refer to such a resource as a *critical resource* and the portion of the program that uses it as a *critical section* of the program. It is important that only one program at a time be allowed in its critical section. We cannot simply rely on the operating system to understand and enforce this restriction because the detailed requirement may not be obvious. In the case of the printer, for example, we wish any individual process to have control of the printer while it prints an entire file. Otherwise, lines from competing processes will be interleaved.

The successful use of concurrency among processes requires the ability to define critical sections and enforce mutual exclusion. This ability is fundamental for any concurrent processing scheme. Any facility or capability that is to provide support for mutual exclusion should meet the following requirements:

1. Mutual exclusion must be enforced: Only one process at a time is allowed into the facility's critical section, among all processes that have critical sections for the same resource or shared object.
2. A process that halts in its noncritical section must do so without interfering with other processes.
3. It must not be possible for a process requiring access to a critical section to be delayed indefinitely: no deadlock or starvation.
4. When no process is in a critical section, any process that requests entry to its critical section must be permitted to enter without delay.
5. No assumptions are made about relative process speeds or number of processors.
6. A process remains inside its critical section for a finite time only.

Figure 9.25 shows a model that we can use for examining approaches to mutual exclusion in a distributed context. We assume some number of systems interconnected by some type of networking facility. We assume that some function or process within the operating system is responsible for resource allocation. Each such process controls a number of resources and serves a number of

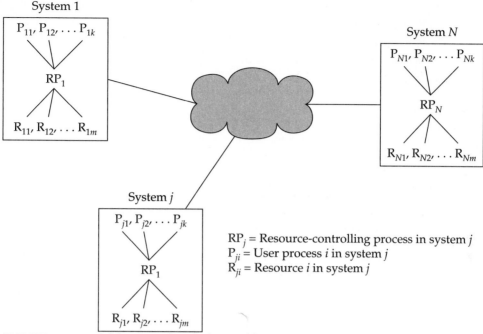

System 1

$P_{11}, P_{12}, \ldots P_{1k}$

RP_1

$R_{11}, R_{12}, \ldots R_{1m}$

System N

$P_{N1}, P_{N2}, \ldots P_{Nk}$

RP_N

$R_{N1}, R_{N2}, \ldots R_{Nm}$

System j

$P_{j1}, P_{j2}, \ldots P_{jk}$

RP_1

$R_{j1}, R_{j2}, \ldots R_{jm}$

RP_j = Resource-controlling process in system j
P_{ji} = User process i in system j
R_{ji} = Resource i in system j

FIGURE 9.25 Model for mutual exclusion problem in distributed process management.

user processes. The task is to devise an algorithm by which these processes may cooperate in enforcing mutual exclusion.

Algorithms for mutual exclusion may be either centralized or distributed. In a fully **centralized algorithm**, one node is designated as the control node and controls access to all shared objects. When any process requires access to a critical resource, it issues a Request to its local resource-controlling process. This process in turn sends a Request message to the control node, which returns a Reply (permission) message when the shared object becomes available. When a process has finished with a resource, a Release message is sent to the control node. Such a centralized algorithm has two key properties:

1. Only the control node makes resource-allocation decisions.
2. All necessary information is concentrated in the control node, including the identity and location of all resources and the allocation status of each resource.

The centralized approach is straightforward, and it is easy to see how mutual exclusion is enforced: The control node will not satisfy a request for a resource until that resource has been released. However, such schemes suffer several drawbacks. If the control node fails, then the mutual exclusion mechanism breaks down, at least temporarily. Furthermore, every resource allocation and deallocation requires an exchange of messages with the control node. Thus, the control node may become a bottleneck.

Because of the problems with centralized algorithms, there has been more interest in the development of **distributed algorithms**. A fully distributed algorithm is characterized by the following properties [MAEK87]:

1. All nodes have an equal amount of information, on average.
2. Each node has only a partial picture of the total system and must make decisions based on this information.
3. All nodes bear equal responsibility for the final decision.
4. All nodes expend equal effort, on average, in effecting a final decision.
5. Failure of a node, in general, does not result in a total system collapse.
6. There exists no system-wide common clock with which to regulate the timing of events.

Points 2 and 6 may require some elaboration. With respect to point 2: Some distributed algorithms require that all information known to any node be communicated to all other nodes. Even in this case, at any given time, some of that information will be in transit and will not have arrived at all of the other nodes. Thus, because of time delays in message communication, a node's information is usually not completely up to date and is in that sense only partial information.

With respect to point 6: Because of the delay in communication among systems, it is impossible to maintain a system-wide clock that is instantly available to all systems. Furthermore, it is also difficult to maintain one central clock and to keep all local clocks synchronized precisely to that central clock; over time, there will be some drift among the various local clocks that will cause a loss of synchronization.

It is the delay in communication, coupled with the lack of a common clock, that makes it much more difficult to develop mutual exclusion mechanisms in a distributed system compared to a centralized system. Before looking at some algorithms for distributed mutual exclusion, we examine a common approach to overcoming the clocking difficulty.

Ordering of Events in a Distributed System

Fundamental to the operation of most distributed algorithms for mutual exclusion and deadlock is the temporal ordering of events. The lack of a common clock or a means of synchronizing local clocks is thus a major constraint. The problem can be expressed in the following manner. We would like to be able to say that at event a at system i occurred before (or after) event b at system j, and we would like to be able to consistently arrive at this conclusion at all systems in the network. Unfortunately, this statement is not precise for two reasons. First, there may be a delay between the actual occurrence of an event and the time that it is observed on some other system. Second, the lack of synchronization leads to a variance in clock readings on different systems.

To overcome these difficulties, a method referred to as *timestamping* has been proposed by Lamport [LAMP78] that orders events in a distributed system without using physical clocks. This technique is so efficient and effective that it is used in the great majority of algorithms for mutual exclusion and deadlock.

The timestamping scheme is intended to order events consisting of the transmission of messages. Each system i in the network maintains a local counter, C_i, which functions as a clock. Each time a system transmits a message, it first increments its clock by 1. The message is sent in the form:

(m, T_i, i)

where
m = contents of the message
T_i = timestamp for this message, set to equal C_i
i = numerical identifier of this site.

When a message is received, the receiving system j sets its clock to one more than the maximum of its current value and the incoming timestamp:

$C_j: = 1 + \max [C_j, T_i]$

At each site, the ordering of events is determined by the following rules. For messages x from site i and y from site j, x is said to precede y if one of the following conditions holds:

1. If $T_i < T_j$, or
2. If $T_i = T_j$ and $i < j$

The time associated with each message is the timestamp accompanying the message, and the ordering of these times is determined by the preceding two rules. That is, two messages with the same timestamp are ordered by the numbers of their sites. Because the application of these rules is independent of site, this approach avoids any problems of drift among the various clocks of the communicating processes.

An example of the operation of this algorithm is shown in Figure 9.26 in which three sites are shown, each of which is represented by a process that controls the timestamping algorithm. Process P_1 begins with a clock value of 0. To transmit message a, it increments its clock by 1 and transmits (a, 1, 1), the first numerical value of which is the timestamp and the second is the identity of the site. This message is received by processes at sites 2 and 3. In both cases, the local clock has a value of 0 and is set to a value of $2 = 1 + \max [1, 0]$. P_2 issues the next message, first incrementing its clock to 3. Upon receipt of this message, P_1 and P_3 must increment their clocks to 4. Then, P_1 issues message b and P_3 issues message j at about the same time and with the same timestamp. Because of the ordering principle, this causes no confusion. After all these events have taken place, the ordering of messages is the same at all sites, namely {a, x, b, j}.

The algorithm works in spite of differences in transmission times between pairs of systems, as illustrated in Figure 9.27, where P_1 and P_4 are shown as issuing messages with the same timestamp. The message from P_1 arrives earlier than that of P_4 at site 2 but later than that of P_4 at site 3. Nevertheless, after all messages have been received at all sites, the ordering of messages is the same at all sites; namely {a, q}.

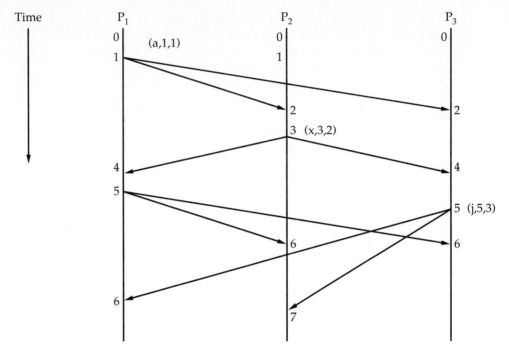

FIGURE 9.26 Example of operation of time-stamping algorithm.

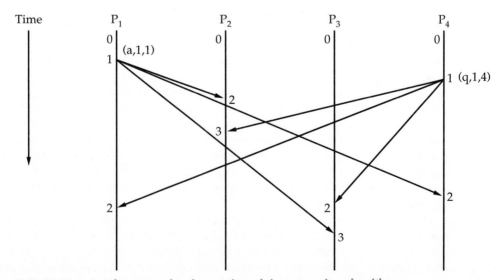

FIGURE 9.27 Another example of operation of time-stamping algorithm.

Note that the ordering imposed by this scheme does not necessarily correspond to the actual time sequence. For the algorithms based on this timestamping scheme, it is not important which event actually happened first. It is important only that all processes that implement the algorithm agree on the ordering that is imposed on the events.

Distributed Queue

First Version

One of the earliest proposed approaches to providing distributed mutual exclusion is based on the concept of a distributed queue [LAMP78]. The algorithm is based on the following assumptions:

1. A distributed system consists of N nodes, uniquely numbered from 1 to N. Each node contains one process that makes requests for mutually exclusive access to resources on behalf of other processes; this process also serves as an arbitrator to resolve incoming requests that overlap in time.
2. Messages sent from one process to another are received in the same order in which they are sent.
3. Every message is correctly delivered to its destination in a finite amount of time.
4. The network is fully connected, which means that every process can send messages directly to every other process without requiring an intermediate process to forward the message.

Assumptions 2 and 3 can be realized by the use of a reliable transport protocol, such as was discussed in Section 9.1.

For simplicity, we describe the algorithm for the case in which each site controls only a single resource. The generalization to multiple resources is trivial.

The algorithm attempts to generalize an algorithm that would work in a straightforward manner in a centralized system. If a single central process managed the resource, it could queue incoming requests and grant requests in a first-in, first-out manner. To achieve this same algorithm in a distributed system, all the sites must have a copy of the same queue. Timestamping can be used to assure that all sites agree on the order in which resource requests are to be granted. One complication arises: Because it takes some finite amount of time for messages to transit a network, there is a danger that two different sites will not agree on which process is at the head of the queue. Consider Figure 9.27. There is a point at which message a has arrived at P_2 and message q has arrived at P_3, but the other message is in transit. Thus, there is a period in which P_1 and P_2 consider message a to be the head of the queue and in which P_3 and P_4 consider message q to be the head of the queue. This could lead to a violation of the mutual exclusion requirement. To avoid a violation, the following rule is imposed: For a process to make an allocation decision that is based on its own queue, it needs to have received a message from all other sites that guarantees that no message earlier than its own head-of-queue message is still in transit.

At each site, a data structure is maintained that keeps a record of the most recent message received from each site (including the most recent message generated at this site). Lamport refers to this structure as a queue; actually it is an array with one entry for each site [LAMP 78]. At any instant, entry q [j] in the local array contains a message from P_j. The array is initialized as follows:

q [j] = (Release, 0, j) $j = 1, \ldots, N$

Three types of messages are used in this algorithm:

- (Request, T_i, i): A request for access to a resource is made by P_i.
- (Reply, T_j, j): Pj grants access to a resource under its control.
- (Release, T_k, k): P_k releases a resource previously allocated to it.

The algorithm is as follows:

1. When P_i requires access to a resource, it issues a request (Request, T_i, i), timestamped with the current local clock value. It puts this message in its own array at q [i], and sends the message to all other processes.
2. When P_j receives (Request, T_i, i), it puts this message in its own array at q [i] and transmits (Reply, T_j, j) to all other processes. It is this action that implements the rule described earlier, that assures that no earlier Request message is in transit at the time of a decision.
3. P_i can access a resource (enter its critical section) when both of the following conditions hold:
   (a) P_i's own Request message in array q is the earliest Request message in the array; because messages are consistently ordered at all sites, this rule permits one and only one process to access the resource at any instant.
   (b) All other messages in the local array are later than the message in q [i]; this rule guarantees that P_i has learned about all requests that preceded its current request.
4. P_i releases a resource by issuing a release (Release, T_i, i), which it puts in its own array and transmits to all other processes.
5. When P_i receives (Release, T_j, j), it replaces the current contents of q [j] with this message.
6. When P_i receives (Reply, T_j, j), it replaces the current contents of q [j] with this message.

It is easily shown that this algorithm enforces mutual exclusion, is fair, avoids deadlock, and avoids starvation:

- *Mutual exclusion:* Requests for entry into the critical section are handled according to the ordering of messages imposed by the timestamping mechanism. Once P_i decides to enter its critical section, there can be no other Request message in the system that was transmitted before its own, for P_i has by then necessarily received a message from all other sites and these messages date from later than its own Request message. We can be sure of this because of the Reply message mechanism; remember that messages between two sites cannot arrive out of order.

- *Fair:* Requests are granted strictly on the basis of timestamp ordering. Therefore, all processes have equal opportunity.
- *Deadlock-free:* Because the timestamp ordering is consistently maintained at all sites, deadlock cannot occur.
- *Starvation-free:* Once P_i has completed its critical section, it transmits the Release message. This has the effect of deleting P_i's Request message at all other sites, allowing some other process to enter its critical section.

As a measure of efficiency of this algorithm, note that to guarantee exclusion, $3 \times (N - 1)$ messages are required: $(N - 1)$ Request messages, $(N - 1)$ Reply messages, and $(N - 1)$ Release messages.

Second Version

A refinement of the Lamport algorithm was proposed in [RICA81]. It seeks to optimize the original algorithm by eliminating Release messages. The same assumptions as before are in force, except that it is not necessary that messages sent from one process to another be received in the same order in which they are sent.

As before, each site includes one process that controls resource allocation. This process maintains an array q and obeys the following rules:

1. When P_i requires access to a resource, it issues a request (Request, T_i, i), timestamped with the current local clock value. It puts this message in its own array at $q[i]$, and sends the message to all other processes.
2. When P_j receives (Request, T_i, i), it obeys the following rules:
   (a) If P_j is currently in its critical section, it defers sending a Reply message (see Rule 4, following)
   (b) If P_j is not waiting to enter its critical section (has not issued a Request that is still outstanding), it transmits (Reply, T_j, j) to all other processes.
   (c) If P_j is waiting to enter its critical section and if the incoming message follows P_j's request, then it puts this message in its own array at $q[i]$ and defers sending a Reply message.
   (d) If P_j is waiting to enter its critical section and if the incoming message follows P_j's request, then it puts this message in its own array at $q[i]$ and transmits (Reply, T_j, j) to P_i.
3. P_i can access a resource (enter its critical section) when it has received a Reply message from all other processes.
4. When P_i leaves its critical section, it releases the resource by sending a Reply message to each pending Request.

The state transition diagram for each process is shown in Figure 9.28.

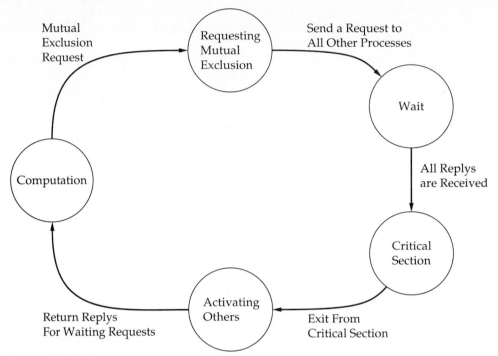

FIGURE 9.28 State diagram for algorithm in [RICA81].

To summarize, when a process wishes to enter its critical section, it sends a timestamped Request message to all other processes. When it receives a Reply from all other processes, it may enter its critical section. When a process receives a Request from another process, it must eventually send a matching Reply. If a process does not wish to enter its critical section, it sends a Reply at once. If it wants to enter its critical section, it compares the timestamp of its Request with that of the last Request received, and if the latter is more recent, it defers its Reply; otherwise Reply is sent at once.

With this method, $2(N-1)$ messages are required: $(N-1)$ Request messages to indicate P_i's intention of entering its critical section, and $(N-1)$ Reply messages to allow the access it has requested.

The use of timestamping in this algorithm enforces mutual exclusion. It also avoids deadlock. To prove the latter, assume the opposite: that it is possible that, when there are no more messages in transit, we have a situation in which each process has transmitted a Request and has not received the necessary Reply. This situation cannot arise because a decision to defer a Reply is based on a relation that orders Requests. There is therefore one Request that has the earliest timestamp and that will receive all the necessary Replies. Deadlock is therefore impossible.

Starvation is also avoided because Requests are ordered. Because Requests are served in that order, every Request will at some stage become the oldest and will then be served.

A Token-Passing Approach

A number of investigators have proposed a quite different approach to mutual exclusion that involves passing a token among the participating processes. The token is an entity that at any time is held by one process. The process holding the token may enter its critical section without asking permission. When a process leaves its critical section, it passes the token to another process.

In this subsection, we look at one of the most efficient of these schemes. It was first proposed in [SUZU82]; a logically equivalent proposal also appeared in [RICA83]. For this algorithm, two data structures are needed. The token, which is passed from process to process, is actually an array, *token*, whose kth element records the timestamp of the last time that the token visited process P_k. In addition, each process maintains an array, *request*, whose jth element records the timestamp of the last Request received from P_j.

The procedure is as follows. Initially, the token is assigned arbitrarily to one of the processes by setting *token_present* to true for that process. When a process wishes to use its critical section, it may do so if it currently possesses the token; otherwise, it broadcasts a timestamped request message to all other processes and waits until it receives the token. When process P_i leaves its critical section, it must transmit the token to some other process. It chooses the next process to receive the token by searching the *request* array in the order $i + 1, i + 2, \ldots,$ 1, 2, ..., $i - 1$ for the first entry *request* [j] such that the timestamp for P_j's last request for the token is greater than the value recorded in the token for P_j's last holding of the token: *request* [j] > *token* [j].

Figure 9.29 depicts the algorithm, which is in two parts. The first part deals with the use of the critical section and consists of a prelude, followed by the critical section, followed by a postlude. The second part concerns the action to be taken upon receipt of a request. The variable clock is the local counter used for the timestamp function. The operation Wait (access, token) causes the process to wait until a message of the type "access" is received. The message contains a token value, which is then put into the variable array *token*.

The algorithm requires either of the following:

- N messages ($N - 1$ to broadcast the request and 1 to transfer the token) when the requesting process does not hold the token.
- no messages if the process already holds the token.

if not token_present **then begin** clock := clock + 1;   [Prelude]
                                        broadcast (request, clock, i);
                                        wait (access, token);
                                        wait (access, token);
                                        token_present := True
                                end;
endif;
token_held := True;
  ⟨critical section⟩
token (i) := clock;   [Postlude]
token_held := False;
for j := i + 1 **to** n, 1 **to** i−1 **do**
  if (request (j) > token (j)) ∧ token_present
    then begin
      token_present := False;
      send (j, access, token)
    end
  endif;

(a) First Part

when received (request, t, j) **do**
  request (j) := max (request (j), t);
  if token_ present ∧ **not** token_held **then**
    ⟨text of postlude⟩
  endif
enddo;

(b) Second Part

Notation:
    send (j, access, token)   send message of type access, with token,
                                     to process j
    broadcast (request, clock, i)   send message from process i of type request,
                                     with timestamp, to all other processes
    received (request, t, j)   receive message from process i of type
                                     request, with timestamp

FIGURE 9.29 Token-passing algorithm (for process P_i).

9.6

DISTRIBUTED PROCESS MANAGEMENT—DEADLOCK

Recall from Chapter 4 that deadlock is the permanent blocking of a set of processes that either compete for system resources or communicate with one another. As with mutual exclusion, deadlock presents more complex problems in a distributed system as compared with a shared-memory system.

We consider two types of deadlock: those that arise in the allocation of resources, and those that arise with the communication of messages.

Deadlock in Resource Allocation

Recall from Chapter 4 that a deadlock in resource allocation exists only if all the following conditions are met:

1. *Mutual exclusion:* Only one process may use a resource at a time.
2. *Hold-and-wait:* A process may hold allocated resources while awaiting assignment of others.
3. *No preemption:* No resource can be forcibly removed from a process holding it.
4. *Circular wait:* A closed chain of processes exists, such that each process holds at least one resource needed by the next process in the chain.

The aim of an algorithm that deals with deadlock is either to prevent the formation of a circular wait or to detect its actual or potential occurrence. In a distributed system, the resources are distributed over various sites, and access to them is regulated by control processes that do not have complete, up-to-date knowledge of the global state of the system and must therefore make their decisions on the basis of local information. Thus, new deadlock algorithms are required.

One example of the difficulty faced in distributed deadlock management is the phenomenon of *phantom deadlock*. An example of phantom deadlock is illustrated in Figure 9.30. The notation $P_1 \rightarrow P_2 \rightarrow P_3$ means that P_1 is halted waiting for a resource held by P_2, and P_2 is halted waiting for a resource held by P_3. Let us say that at the beginning of the example, P_3 owns resource R_a and P_1 owns resource R_b. Suppose now that P_3 issues first a message releasing R_a and then a message requesting R_b. If the first message reaches a cycle-detecting process before the second, the sequence of Figure 9.30a results, which properly reflects resource requirements. If, however, the second message arrives before the first message, a deadlock is registered (Figure 9.30b). This is a false detection, not a real deadlock, and is caused by the lack of a global state, such as would exist in a centralized system.

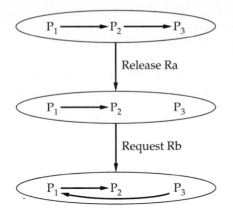

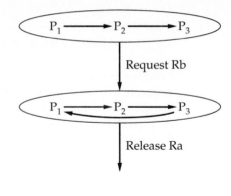

(a) Release arrives before request   (b) Request arrives before release

FIGURE 9.30 Phantom deadlock.

Deadlock Prevention

Two of the deadlock prevention techniques discussed in Chapter 4 can be used in a distributed environment.

1. The *circular wait condition* can be prevented by defining a linear ordering of resource types. If a process has been allocated resources of type R, then it may subsequently request only those resources of types following R in the ordering. A major disadvantage of this method is that resources may not be requested in the order in which they are used; thus, resources may be held longer than necessary.
2. The *hold-and-wait condition* can be prevented by requiring that a process request all its required resources at one time, and by blocking the process until all requests can be granted simultaneously. This approach is inefficient in two ways. First, a process may be held up for a long time waiting for all its resource requests to be filled, when in fact it could have proceeded with only some of the resources. And second, resources allocated to a process may remain unused for a considerable period, during which time they are denied to other processes.

Both of these methods require that a process determine its resource requirements in advance. This is not always possible; an example is a database application in which new items can be added dynamically. As an example of an approach that does not require this foreknowledge, we consider two algorithms proposed in [ROSE78]. These were developed in the context of database work, so we shall speak of transactions rather than processes.

The proposed methods make use of timestamps. Each transaction carries throughout its lifetime the timestamp of its creation, which establishes a strict ordering of the transactions. If a resource R already being used by transaction

T_1 is requested by another transaction T_2, the conflict is resolved by comparing their timestamps. This comparison is used to prevent the formation of a circular wait condition. Two variations of this basic method are proposed by the authors, referred to as the "wait-die" method and the "wound-wait" method [ROSE78].

Let us suppose that T_1 currently holds R and that T_2 issues a request. For the **wait-die method**, Figure 9.31a shows the algorithm used by the resource allocator at the site of R. The timestamps of the two transactions are denoted as $e(T_1)$ and $e(T_2)$. If T_2 is older, it is blocked until T_1 releases R, either by actively issuing a release or by being "killed" when requesting another resource. If T_2 is younger, then T_2 is restarted but with the same timestamp as before.

Thus, in a conflict, the older transaction takes priority. A killed transaction is revived with its original timestamp, so it grows older and therefore gains increased priority. No site needs to know the state of allocation of all resources. All that are required are the timestamps of the transactions that request its resources.

The **wound-wait method** immediately grants the request of an older transaction by killing a younger transaction that is using the required resource, as is shown in Figure 9.31b. In contrast to the wait-die method, a transaction never has to wait for a resource being used by a younger transaction.

Deadlock Detection

With deadlock detection, processes are allowed to obtain free resources as they wish, and the existence of a deadlock is determined after the fact. If a deadlock is detected, one of the constituent processes is selected and required to release the resources necessary to break the deadlock.

The difficulty with distributed deadlock detection is that each site knows about only its own resources, whereas a deadlock may involve distributed resources. Several approaches are possible, depending on whether the system control is centralized, hierarchical, or distributed.

With **centralized control**, one site is responsible for deadlock detection. All Request and Release messages are sent to the central process as well as to the

if $e(T2) < e(T1)$ **then** halt T2 ('wait')
                     else kill T2 ('die')
endif
(a) Wait-die method

if $e(T2) < e(T1)$ **then** kill T1 ('wound')
                     else halt T2 ('wait')
endif
(b) Wound-wait method
FIGURE 9.31 Deadlock prevention methods.

process that controls the particular resource. Because the central process has a complete picture, it is in a position to detect a deadlock. This approach requires a lot of messages and is vulnerable to a failure of the central site. In addition, phantom deadlocks may be detected.

With **hierarchical control**, the sites are organized in a tree structure, with one site serving as the root of the tree. At each node, other than the leaf node, information about the resource allocation of all dependent nodes is collected. This permits deadlocks to be detected at lower levels than the root node. Specifically, a deadlock that involves a set of resources will be detected by the node that is the common ancestor of all sites whose resources are among the objects in conflict.

With **distributed control**, all processes cooperate in detecting deadlocks. In general, this means that considerable information with timestamps must be exchanged. Thus, the overhead is significant. [RAYN88] cites a number of approaches based on distributed control, and [DATT90] provides a detailed examination of one approach.

Deadlock in Message Communication

Mutual Waiting

Deadlock occurs in message communication when each of a group of processes is waiting for a message from another member of the group and there is no message in transit.

To analyze this situation in more detail, we define the dependence set (DS) of a process. For a process P_i that is halted waiting for a message, $DS(P_i)$ consists of all processes from which P_i is expecting a message. Typically, P_i can proceed if *any* of the expected messages arrives. An alternative formulation is that P_i can proceed only after *all* the expected messages arrive. The former situation is the more common and is considered here.

With the foregoing definition, a deadlock in a set S of process can be defined as follows:

1. All the processes in S are halted, waiting for messages.
2. S contains the dependence set of all processes in S.
3. No messages are in transit between members of S.

Any process in S is deadlocked because it can never receive a message that will release it.

In graphic terms, there is a difference between message deadlock and resource deadlock. With resource deadlock, a deadlock exists if there is a closed loop, or cycle, in the graph that depicts process dependencies. In the resource case, one process is dependent on another if the latter holds a resource that the former requires. With message deadlock, the condition for deadlock is that all successors of any member of S are themselves in S; that is, the graph of S is a knot.

Figure 9.32 illustrates the point. In Figure 9.32a, P_1 is waiting for a message from either P_2 or P_5; P_5 is not waiting for any message and so can send a message

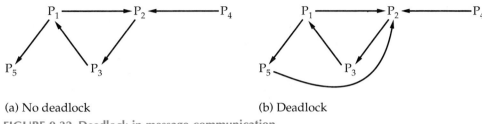

(a) No deadlock   (b) Deadlock

FIGURE 9.32 Deadlock in message communication.

to P_1, which is therefore released. As a result, the links (P_1, P_5) and (P_1, P_2) are deleted. Figure 9.32b adds a dependency: P_5 is waiting for a message from P_2. The graph is now a knot, and deadlock exists.

As with resource deadlock, message deadlock can be attacked by either prevention or detection. [RAYN88] gives some examples.

Unavailability of Message Buffers

Another way in which deadlock can occur in a message-passing system is through the allocation of buffers for the storage of messages in transit. This kind of deadlock is well known in packet-switching data networks [STAL91]. We first examine this problem in the context of a data network and then view it from the point of view of a distributed operating system.

The simplest form of deadlock in a data network is direct store-and-forward deadlock, and it can occur if a packet-switching node uses a common buffer pool from which buffers are assigned to packets on demand. Figure 9.33a shows a situation in which all the buffer space in node A is occupied with packets destined for B. The reverse is true at B. Neither node can accept any more packets because their buffers are full. Thus, neither node can transmit nor receive on any link.

Direct store-and-forward deadlock can be prevented by not allowing all buffers to end up dedicated to a single link. Using separate fixed-size buffers, one for each link, will achieve this prevention. Even if a common buffer pool is used, deadlock is avoided if no single link is allowed to acquire all the buffer space.

A more subtle form of deadlock, *indirect store-and-forward deadlock*, is illustrated in Figure 9.33b. For each node, the queue to the adjacent node in one direction is full, with packets destined for the next node beyond. One simple way to prevent this type of deadlock is to employ a structured buffer pool (Figure 9.34). The buffers are organized in a hierarchical fashion. The pool of memory at level 0 is unrestricted; any incoming packet can be stored there. From level 1 to level N (where N is the maximum number of hops on any network path), buffers are reserved in the following way: Buffers at level k are reserved for packets that have traveled at least k hops so far. Thus, in heavy load conditions, buffers fill up progressively from level 0 to level N. If all buffers up through level k are

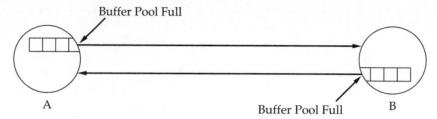

Buffer Pool Full

Buffer Pool Full

A

B

(a) Direct store-and-forward deadlock

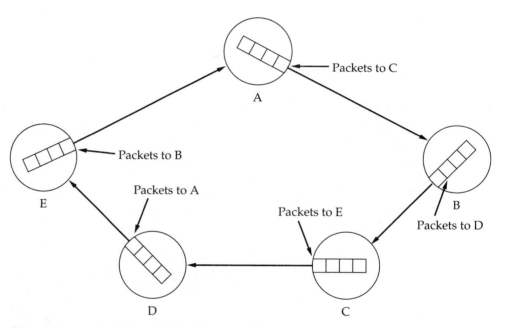

Packets to C

A

Packets to B

Packets to A

Packets to E

E

B

Packets to D

D

C

(b) Indirect store-and-forward deadlock
FIGURE 9.33 Store-and-forward deadlock.

filled, arriving packets that have covered k or fewer hops are discarded. It can be shown [GOPA85] that this strategy eliminates both direct and indirect store-and-forward deadlocks.

The deadlock problem just described would be dealt with in the context of a communications architecture, typically at OSI layer 3 (network layer). The same sort of problem can arise in a distributed operating system that uses message passing for interprocess communication. Specifically, if the *send* operation is nonblocking, then a buffer is required to hold outgoing messages. We can think of the buffer used to hold messages to be sent from process X to process Y to be a communications channel between X and Y. If this channel has finite capacity (finite buffer size), then it is possible for the *send* operation to result in

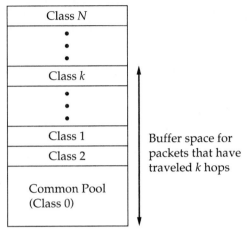

FIGURE 9.34 Structured buffer pool for deadlock prevention.

process suspension. That is, if the buffer is of size n and there are currently n messages in transit (not yet *received* by the destination process), then the execution of an additional *send* will block the sending process until a *receive* has opened up space in the buffer.

Figure 9.35 illustrates how the use of finite channels can lead to deadlock. The figure shows two channels, each with a capacity of four messages, one from process X to process Y and one from Y to X. If exactly four messages are

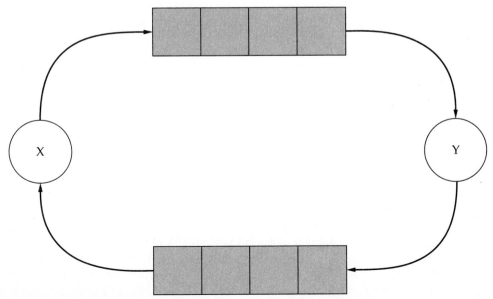

FIGURE 9.35 Communication deadlock in a distributed system.

in transit in each of the channels and if both X and Y attempt a further transmission before executing a Receive, then both are suspended and a deadlock arises.

Now, if it is possible to establish upper bounds on the number of messages that will ever be in transit between each pair of processes in the system, then the obvious prevention strategy would be to allocate as many buffer slots as needed for all these channels. This might be extremely wasteful and, of course, requires foreknowledge. If requirements cannot be known ahead of time or if allocating based on upper bounds is deemed too wasteful, then some estimation technique is needed to optimize the allocation. It can be shown that this problem is unsolvable in the general case; some heuristic strategies for coping with this situation are suggested in [BARB90].

9.7

SUMMARY

Increasingly, computers function not in isolation but as part of a network of computers and terminals. To support such distributed systems, a spectrum of capabilities has been developed, including communications architectures, network operating systems, and distributed operating systems.

A **communications architecture** is the structured set of hardware and software that supports the exchange of data between systems and that supports distributed applications, such as electronic mail and file transfer. The open systems interconnection (OSI) model is a standardized communications architecture designed to allow heterogeneous computers to cooperate. The OSI model consists of seven layers of functionality. Standards have been developed to implement the functions at each layer.

A **network operating system** is not actually an operating system but a distributed set of system software to support the use of servers on a network. The server machines provide network-wide services or applications, such as file storage and printer management. Each computer has its own private operating system. The network operating system is simply an adjunct to the local operating system that allows application machines to interact with server machines. Typically, a common communications architecture is used to support these network applications.

A **distributed operating system** is a common operating system shared by a network of computers. It looks to its users like an ordinary centralized operating system but provides the user with transparent access to the resources of a number of machines. A distributed operating system may rely on a communications architecture for basic communications functions; more commonly, a stripped-down set of communication functions is incorporated into the operating system to provide efficiency.

A distributed operating system may support process migration, which is the transfer of a sufficient amount of the state of a process from one machine to another to enable the process to execute on the target machine. Process migration may be used for load balancing, to improve performance by minimizing communication activity, to increase availability, or to give processes access to specialized remote facilities.

The key function supported by a distributed operating system is interprocess communication. Two techniques are in common use. A message-passing facility generalizes the use of messages within a single system. The same sorts of conventions and synchronization rules apply. Another approach is the use of the remote procedure call, a technique by which two programs on different machines interact using procedure call/return syntax and semantics. Both the called and calling program behave as if the partner program were running on the same machine.

In addition to supporting interprocess communication, a distributed operating system should be responsible for process management. This includes providing facilities for enforcing mutual exclusion and for taking action to deal with deadlock. In both cases, the problems are more complex than those in a single system.

9.8

RECOMMENDED READING

[STAL91] covers communications architectures with emphasis on the technology and design issues. [STAL90b] is a detailed description of the OSI model and of the standards at each layer of the model. [TANE88] also covers the various OSI-related standards.

[ESKI90] and [SMIT88] are useful surveys of process migration mechanisms. [ARTS89a] is a special issue devoted to the mechanisms and policies of process migration.

[TANE85] is a survey of distributed operating systems that covers both distributed process communication and distributed process management. [CHAN90b] provides an overview of distributed message-passing operating systems. [TAY90] is a survey of the approach taken by various operating systems in implementing remote procedure calls, and [MALA90] examines the application of remote procedure calls.

Algorithms for distributed process management (mutual exclusion, deadlock) can be found in [MAEK87] and [RAYN88]. A more formal treatment is contained in [RAYN90]. A collection of recent papers on performance aspects of distributed systems is found in [GELE91].

9.9
_____

PROBLEMS

9.1 Write a program to implement the sliding-window technique for (a) REJ and (b) SREJ.

9.2 Consider a transmission link between stations A and B with a probability of error in a frame of p.

(a) Assume a SREJ protocol and assume that A is sending data (information frames) and B is sending acknowledgments only (RR, SREJ) and that B individually acknowledges each frame. Assume that acknowledgments are never lost. What is the mean number of retransmissions required per frame?

(b) Now assume an REJ protocol and that the link is such that A will transmit three additional frames before it receives RR or REJ for a particular frame. Also assume that acknowledgments are never lost. What is the mean number of retransmissions required per frame?

9.3 List the major disadvantages of the layered approach to protocols.

9.4 Among the principles used by ISO to define the OSI layers were:

(a) The number of layers should be small enough to avoid unwieldy design and implementation but large enough so that separate layers handle functions that are different in process or technology.

(b) Layer boundaries should be chosen to minimize the number and size of interactions across boundaries.

Design an architecture with eight layers that is based on these principles, and make a case for it. Design one with six layers and make a case for it.

9.5 In Figure 9.6, exactly one protocol data unit (PDU) in layer N is encapsulated in a protocol data unit at layer $(N - 1)$. It is also possible to break up on N-level PDU and place it in multiple $(N - 1)$-level PDUs (segmentation) or group multiple N-level PDUs and place them in one $(N - 1)$-level PDU (blocking).

(a) In the case of segmentation, is it necessary that each $(N - 1)$-level PDU contain a copy of the N-level header, or can the N-level PDU simply be chopped into pieces, with one piece going into each $N - 1$ level PDU?

(b) In the case of blocking, is it necessary that each N-level PDU retain its own header, or can the data be consolidated into a single N-level PDU with a single N-level header, and then placed into an $(N - 1)$-level PDU?

9.6 Prove the correctness of the distributed snapshot algorithm by proving the following:

(a) The algorithm does not record an inconsistent global state. Hint: Proof by contradiction.

(b) The algorithm correctly records the state of every channel. That is, for every channel, say from process r to process p, the state of the channel $< r, p >$ is the sequence of messages sent by r up to S_r but not received by p up to S_p. For example, the state of channel $< C, A >$ in Figure 9.22b is $\{M_3, M_4\}$. Hint: Proof depends on the assumption that messages are received in the order that they are sent.

9.7 In Figure 9.27, consider that there is a point in time when site 2 has received message a but not message q, and site 3 has received message q but not message a. Thus, for a time, there is an inconsistent view among the sites. We have seen how Lamport's algorithm overcomes this problem. Does this cause any difficulty with any of the other mutual-exclusion algorithms discussed in Section 9.5?

9.8 For Lamport's algorithm, are there any circumstances under which Pi can save itself the transmission of a Reply message?

9.9 For the mutual-exclusion algorithm of [RICA81]:
(a) Prove that mutual exclusion is enforced.
(b) If messages do not arrive in the order that they are sent, the algorithm does not guarantee that critical sections are executed in the order of their requests. Is starvation possible?

9.10 In the token-passing, mutual-exclusion algorithm, is the timestamping used to reset clocks and correct drifts, as in the distributed queue algorithms? If not, what is the function of the timestamping?

9.11 For the token-passing, mutual-exclusion algorithm, prove that it:
(a) Guarantees mutual exclusion
(b) Avoids deadlock
(c) Is fair

9.12 Assume a distributed system with logical clocks. If process P1's logical clock value is 12 at the time that it sends a message to process P2, and process P2's logical clock value is 8 at the time that it receives P1's message, what will be the value of P2's logical clock at its next local event? If, instead, P2's logical clock value is 15 at the time of reception, what will be the value of P2's logical clock at its next local event?

9.13 In Section 9.5, one of the six requirements listed for distributed mutual exclusion is that a process that halts in its non-critical section must do so without interfering with other processes. Suppose some other process executes an algorithm that sends a message to the halted process and then waits for a reply. How can this deadlock be avoided?

9.14 In part (b) of Figure 9.29, explain why the second line cannot simply read "request (j) := t".

9.15 Heathkit markets a clock kit that receives the time signals broadcast from WWV, driven off a cesium clock maintained by the National Institute of Standards and Technology (NIST), and synchronizes its display accordingly. It even takes into account the propagation delay of the radio signal. This hardware could be used to provide a distributed, synchronized clock. How would this affect the various algorithms discussed in this chapter?

CHAPTER 10

Security

The requirements of **information security** within an organization have undergone two major changes in the last several decades. Prior to the widespread use of data processing equipment, the security of information felt to be valuable to an organization was provided primarily by physical and administrative means. An example of the former is the use of rugged filing cabinets with a combination lock for storing sensitive documents. An example of the latter is personnel screening procedures used during the hiring process.

With the introduction of the computer, the need for automated tools for protecting files and other information stored on the computer became evident. This is especially the case for a shared system, such as a time-sharing system, and the need is even more acute for systems that can be accessed over a public telephone or data network. The generic name for the collection of tools designed to protect data and thwart hackers is **computer security**.

The second major change that affected security was the introduction of distributed systems and the use of networks and communications facilities for carrying data between terminal user and computer and between computer and computer. **Network security** measures are needed to protect data during transmission.

The area of computer and network security is a broad one and encompasses physical and administrative controls as well as automated controls. In this chapter, we confine the discussion to consideration of automated security tools. Figure 10.1 suggests the scope of responsibility of these tools. We begin by examining the types of threats faced by computer communications complexes. Then the bulk of the chapter deals with specific tools that can be used to enhance security. Section 10.2 deals with traditional approaches to computer security that are based on the protection of various computer resources, including memory and data. Next, a relatively new approach to security, *trusted systems*, is examined. This is followed by a discussion of network security. The main body of the chapter closes with a look at a recent and increasingly worrisome type of threat: that posed by viruses and similar mechanisms. Finally, an appendix to this chapter introduces encryption, which is a basic tool used in many security applications.

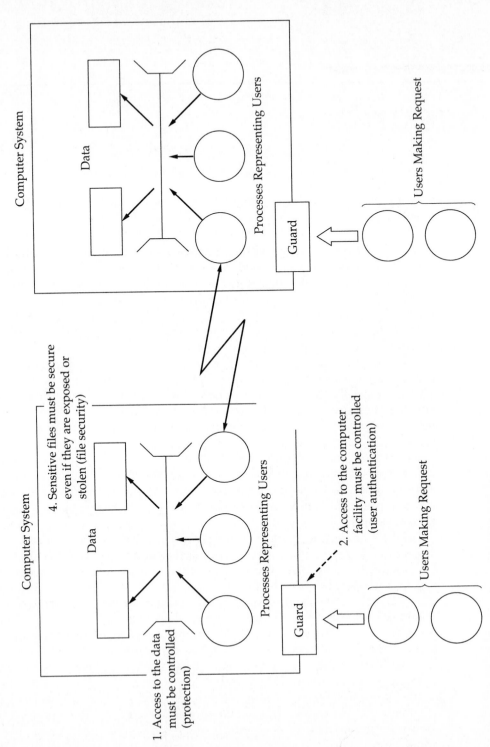

FIGURE 10.1 Scope of system security [MAEK87].

SECURITY THREATS

A publication of the National Bureau of Standards identified some of the threats that stimulated the upsurge of interest in security [BRAN78]:

1. Organized and intentional attempts to obtain economic or market information from competitive organizations in the private sector.
2. Organized and intentional attempts to obtain economic information from government agencies.
3. Inadvertent acquisition of economic or market information.
4. Inadvertent acquisition of information about individuals.
5. Intentional fraud through illegal access to computer data banks with emphasis, in decreasing order of importance, on acquisition of funding data, economic data, law enforcement data, and data about individuals.
6. Government intrusion on the rights of individuals.
7. Invasion of individual rights by the intelligence community.

These are examples of specific threats that an organization or an individual (or an organization on behalf of its employees) may feel the need to counter. The nature of the threat that concerns an organization will vary greatly from one set of circumstances to another. Fortunately, we can approach the problem from a different angle by looking at the generic types of threats that might be encountered.

Security Requirements

Computer and network security address three requirements:

*   *Secrecy:* Requires that the information in a computer system be accessible for reading by authorized parties only. This type of access includes printing, displaying, and other forms of disclosure, including simply revealing the existence of an object.
*   *Integrity:* Requires that computer system assets can be modified by authorized parties only. Modification includes writing, changing, changing status, deleting, and creating.
*   *Availability:* Requires that computer system assets be available to authorized parties.

Types of Threats

The types of threats to the security of a computer system or network are best characterized by viewing the function of the computer system to be providing information. In general, there is a flow of information from a source, such as a file or a region of main memory, to a destination, such as another file or a user.

This normal flow is depicted in Figure 10.2a. The remainder of the figure shows four general categories of threats:

- *Interruption:* An asset of the system is destroyed or becomes unavailable or unusable. This is a threat to **availability**. Examples include destruction of a piece of hardware, such as a hard disk, the cutting of a communication line, or the disabling of the file-management system.
- *Interception:* An unauthorized party gains access to an asset. This is a threat to **secrecy**. The unauthorized party could be a person, a program, or a computer. Examples include wiretapping to capture data in a network and the illicit copying of files or programs.
- *Modification:* An unauthorized party not only gains access but tampers with an asset. This is a threat to **integrity**. Examples include changing values in a data file, altering a program so that it performs differently, and modifying the content of messages being transmitted in a network.

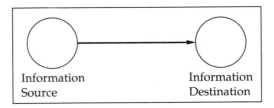

(a) Normal flow

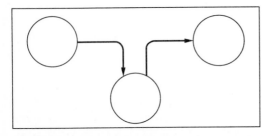

(b) Interruption

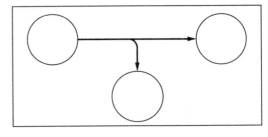

(c) Interception

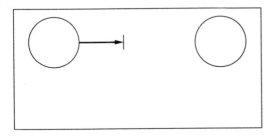

(d) Modification

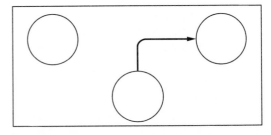

(e) Fabrication

FIGURE 10.2 Security threats.

- *Fabrication:* An unauthorized party inserts counterfeit objects into the system. This is also a threat to **integrity**. Examples include the insertion of spurious messages in a network or the addition of records to a file.

Computer System Assets

The assets of a computer system can be categorized as hardware, software, data, and communication lines and networks. Figure 10.3 and Table 10.1 indicate the nature of the threats faced by each category of asset. Let us consider each of these in turn.

Hardware

The main threat to computer system hardware is in the area of availability. Hardware is the most vulnerable to attack and the least amenable to automated controls. Threats include accidental and deliberate damage to equipment, as well as theft. The proliferation of personal computers and workstations and the increasing use of local area networks increases the potential for losses of this kind. Physical and administrative security measures are needed to deal with these threats.

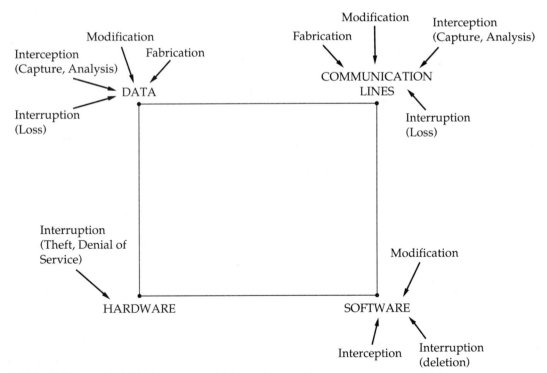

FIGURE 10.3 Security threats and computer system assets.

TABLE 10.1   Security Threats and Assets

Asset	Availability	Secrecy	Integrity
Hardware	Equipment is stolen or disabled, thus denying service.		
Software	Programs are deleted, denying access to users.	An unauthorized copy of software is made.	A working program is modified, either to cause it to fail during execution, or to cause it to do some unintended task.
Data	Files are deleted, denying access to users.	An unauthorized read of data is performed. An analysis of statistical data reveals underlying data.	Existing files are modified or new files are fabricated.
Communication Lines	Messages are destroyed or deleted. Communication lines or networks are rendered unavailable.	Messages are read. The traffic pattern of messages is observed.	Messages are modified, delayed, reordered, or duplicated. False messages are fabricated.

Software

The operating system, utilities, and application programs—the software—are what make computer system hardware useful to businesses and individuals. Several distinct threats need to be considered.

A key threat to software is availability. Software, especially application software, is surprisingly easy to delete. Software can also be altered or damaged to render it useless. Careful software configuration management, which includes making backups of the most recent version of software, can maintain high availability.

A more difficult problem to deal with is software modification that results in a program that still functions but that behaves differently than before. Computer viruses and related attacks fall into this category and are treated later in this chapter.

A final problem is software secrecy. Although certain countermeasures are available, by and large the problem of unauthorized copying of software has not been solved.

Data

Hardware and software security are typically concerns of professionals in computing centers or individual concerns of users of personal computers. A much more widespread problem is data security, which involves files and other forms of data controlled by individuals, groups, and business organizations.

Security concerns with respect to data are broad, encompassing availability, secrecy, and integrity. In the case of availability, the concern is with the destruction of data files, which can occur either accidentally or as a result of malice.

The obvious concern with secrecy, of course, is the unauthorized reading of data files or databases, and this area has been the subject of perhaps more research and effort than any other aspect of computer security. A less obvious secrecy threat involves the analysis of data and is manifest in the use of so-called statistical databases, which provide summary, or aggregate, information. Presumably, the existence of aggregate information does not threaten the privacy of the individuals involved. However, as the use of statistical databases grows, there is an increasing potential for disclosure of personal information. In essence, characteristics of constituent individuals may be identified through careful analysis. To take a simple-minded example, if one table records the aggregate of the incomes of respondents A, B, C, and D and another records the aggregate of the incomes of A, B, C, D, and E, the difference between the two aggregates would be the income of E. This problem is exacerbated by the increasing desire to combine data sets. In many cases, matching several sets of data for consistency at levels of aggregation appropriate to the problem requires a retreat to elemental units in the process of constructing the necessary aggregates. Thus, the elemental units, which are the subject of concerns about privacy, are available at various stages in the processing of data sets. A detailed and thoughtful discussion of these problems is provided in [DUNN74].

Finally, data integrity is a major concern in most installations. Modifications to data files can have consequences ranging from minor to disastrous.

Communication Lines and Networks

Communication systems are used to transmit data. Thus, the concerns of availability, security, and integrity that are relevant to data security apply as well to network security. In this context, threats are conveniently categorized as passive or active (Figure 10.4).

Passive threats are in the nature of eavesdropping on, or monitoring, the transmissions of an organization. The goal of the attacker is to obtain information that is being transmitted. Two types of threats are involved here: release of message contents and traffic analysis.

The threat of *release of message contents* is clearly understood by most observers. A telephone conversation, an electronic mail message, a transferred file may contain sensitive or confidential information. We would like to prevent the attacker from learning the contents of these transmissions.

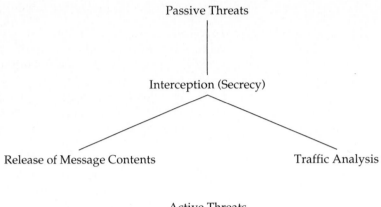

FIGURE 10.4 Active and passive network security threats.

The second passive threat, *traffic analysis,* is more subtle and often less applicable. Suppose that we had a way of masking the contents of messages or other information traffic so that an attacker, even if he or she captured the message, would be unable to extract the information from the message. The common technique for doing masking is *encryption,* discussed at length subsequently. If we had such protection in place, it might still be possible for an attacker to observe the pattern of these messages. The attacker could determine the location and identity of communicating hosts and could also observe the frequency and length of messages being exchanged. This information might be useful in guessing the nature of the communication that was taking place.

Passive threats are very difficult to detect because they do not involve any alteration of the data. However, it is feasible to prevent these attacks from being successful. Thus, the emphasis in dealing with passive threats is on prevention and not detection.

The second major category of threat is **active threats**, which involve some modification of the data stream or the creation of a false stream. We can subdivide these threats into three categories: message-stream modification, denial of message service, and masquerade.

Message-stream modification simply means that some portion of a legitimate message is altered, or that messages are delayed, replayed, or reordered to produce an unauthorized effect. For example, a message meaning "Allow John

Smith to read confidential file *accounts*" is modified to mean "Allow Fred Brown to read confidential file *accounts*."

The *denial of service* prevents or inhibits the normal use or management of communications facilities. This attack may have a specific target; for example, an entity may suppress all messages directed to a particular destination (e.g., the security audit service). Another form of service denial is the disruption of an entire network, either by disabling the network or by overloading it with messages to degrade performance.

A *masquerade* takes place when one entity pretends to be a different entity. A masquerade attack usually includes one of the other two forms of active attack. Such an attack can take place, for example, by capturing and replaying an authentication sequence.

Active threats present the opposite characteristics of passive threats. Although passive attacks are difficult to detect, measures are available to prevent their success. On the other hand, it is quite difficult to absolutely prevent active attacks because prevention would require physical protection of all communications facilities and paths at all times. Instead, the goal with respect to active attacks is to detect these attacks and to recover from any disruption or delays caused by the attacks. The detection has a deterrent effect that may also contribute to prevention.

Design Principles

[SALT75] identifies a number of principles for the design of security measures for the various threats to computer systems. These include the following:

- *Least privilege:* Every program and every user of the system should operate using the least set of privileges necessary to complete the job. Access rights should be acquired by explicit permission only; the default should be "no access."
- *Economy of mechanisms:* Security mechanisms should be as small and simple as possible, aiding in their verification. This requirement usually means that they must be an integral part of the design rather than add-on mechanisms to existing designs.
- *Acceptability:* Security mechanisms should not interfere unduly with the work of users, while at the same time meeting the needs of those who authorize access. If the mechanisms are not easy to use, they are likely to be unused or incorrectly used.
- *Complete mediation:* Every access must be checked against the access control information, including those accesses occurring outside normal operation, as in recovery or maintenance.
- *Open design:* The security of the system should not depend on keeping the design of its mechanisms secret. Thus, the mechanisms can be reviewed by many experts, and users can therefore have high confidence in them.

10.2

COMPUTER SECURITY

The introduction of multiprogramming brought about the ability to share resources among users. Sharing involves not only the processor but also the following:

* Memory
* I/O devices, such as disks and printers
* Programs
* Data

The ability to share resources introduced the need for protection. [PFLE89] points out that an operating system may offer protection along the following spectrum:

* *No protection:* This is appropriate when sensitive procedures are being run at separate times.
* *Isolation:* This approach implies that each process operates separately from other processes, with no sharing or communication. Each process has its own address space, files, and other objects.
* *Share all or share nothing:* The owner of an object (e.g., a file or memory segment) declares it to be public or private. In the former case, any process may access the object; in the latter, only the owner's processes may access the object.
* *Share via access limitation:* The operating system checks the permissibility of each access by a specific user to a specific object. The operating system therefore acts as a guard, or gatekeeper, between users and objects, ensuring that only authorized accesses occur.
* *Share via dynamic capabilities:* This kind of protection extends the concept of access control to allow dynamic creation of sharing rights for objects.
* *Limit use of an object:* This form of protection limits not only access to an object but also the use to which that object may be put. For example, a user may be allowed to view a sensitive document but not print it. Another example: A user may be allowed access to a database to derive statistical summaries but not to determine specific data values.

The foregoing items are listed roughly in increasing order of difficulty to implement but also in increasing order of the fineness of protection that they provide. A given operating system may provide different degrees of protection for different objects, users, or applications.

The operating system needs to balance the need to allow sharing, which enhances the utility of the computer system, with the need to protect the resources of individual users. In this section, we consider some of the mechanisms by which operating systems have enforced protection for these objects.

Protection of Memory

In a multiprogramming environment, protection of main memory is essential. The concern is not security only but also the correct functioning of the various processes that are active. If one process can inadvertently write into the memory space of another process, then the latter process may not execute properly.

The separation of the memory space of various processes is easily accomplished with a virtual memory scheme. Either segmentation or paging, or the two in combination, provides an effective means of managing main memory. If complete isolation is sought, then the operating system must simply assure that each segment or page is accessible only by the process to which it is assigned. This is easily accomplished by requiring that there be no duplicate entries in page or segment tables.

If sharing is to be allowed, then the same segment or page may be referenced in more than one table. This type of sharing is most easily accomplished in a system that supports segmentation or a combination of segmentation and paging. In this case, the segment structure is visible to the application, and the application can declare individual segments to be sharable or nonsharable. In a pure paging environment, it becomes more difficult to discriminate between the two types of memory because the memory structure is transparent to the application.

An example of the hardware support that can be provided for memory protection is that of the IBM System/370 family of machines, on which MVS runs. Associated with each page frame in main memory is a 7-bit storage control key, which may be set by the operating system. Two of the bits indicate whether the page occupying a frame has been referenced and changed; these bits are used by the page replacement algorithm. The remaining bits are used by the protection mechanism: a 4-bit access control key and a fetch protection bit. Processor references to memory and DMA I/O memory references must use a matching key to gain permission to access that page. The fetch protection bit indicates whether the access control key applies to Writes or to both Reads and Writes. In the processor, there is a program status word (PSW), that contains control information relating to the process that is currently executing. Included in this word is a 4-bit PSW key. When a process attempts to access a page or to initiate a DMA operation on a page, the current PSW key is compared to the access code. A Write operation is permitted only if the codes match. If the fetch bit is set, then the PSW key must match the access code for Read operations.

User-Oriented Access Control

Figure 10.5 depicts, generically, the measures taken to control access in a data processing system. They fall into two categories; those associated with the user and those associated with the data.

The control of access by user is, unfortunately, sometimes referred to as *authentication*. Because this term is now widely used in the sense of message

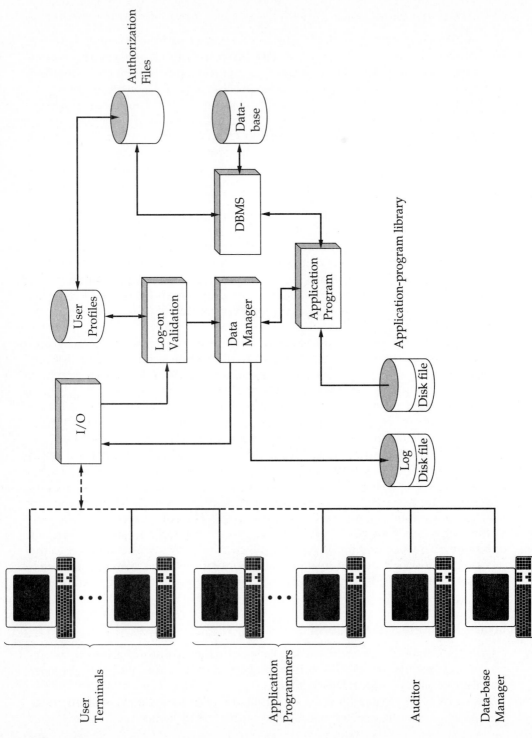

FIGURE 10.5 Data processing system security.

582

authentication, we will refrain from applying it here. You are warned, however, that this usage may be encountered in the literature.

The Use of Passwords

A quite common example of user access control on a time-sharing system is the user log on, which requires both a user identifier (ID) and a password. The system will allow a user to log on only if that user's ID is known to the system and if the user knows the password associated by the system with that ID. This ID/password system is a notoriously unreliable method of user access control. Users can forget their passwords, and they can accidentally or intentionally reveal their password. Hackers have become very skillful at guessing IDs for special users, such as system control and system management personnel. Finally, the ID/password file is subject to penetration attempts.

A number of measures can be taken to improve the security of the password scheme. Three requirements can be stated:

1. There should be a large number of possible password combinations. This reduces an outsider's chances for success from either guessing the codes or using a computer to make repetitive brute-force attempts under program control. It is useful to restrict the passwords to alphanumeric characters and to use pronounceable combinations of characters, so that users can easily remember them and avoid writing them down. A five-character password has more than 60 million possible combinations; even with the restriction to pronounceable combinations, this is a reasonably secure length, provided points 2 and 3 are met.

2. There should be automatic disconnection of the incoming terminal line after a small number of invalid password attempts have been made. The usual limit is three to five attempts. This requires an attacker to hang up and redial after every few tries, increasing the time required to perform a brute-force penetration to a matter of years. The programmed attack favored by hackers is thus rendered useless. A related and very valuable feature is automatic deactivation of a user ID if it is used in multiple, invalid attempts to log on.

3. The operating system should log and report invalid sign-on attempts and other "events" having security implications. These could include, for example, an unauthorized person attempting to run sensitive application programs, such as human resources systems, or using high-powered system utility programs to copy or modify files. This feature will reveal whether attempts at computer vandalism are taking place, so that further, more positive means can be used to report and apprehend the attackers. Security reports can also be used as evidence in police or FBI investigations and in trials.

One interesting related issue is that of who is authorized to create passwords. Some security managers feel that users should not be allowed to assign their own passwords; people tend to use personal names, dates, and other readily guessed information. Others feel that forcing system-selected passwords onto users causes them to write the password down, which is more of a security risk than having them select their own password.

The problem of user access control is compounded over a communication network. The log-on dialogue must take place over the communication medium, and eavesdropping is a potential threat. The approaches discussed under network security later in this chapter must then be employed.

User access control in a distributed environment can be either centralized or decentralized. In a centralized approach, the network provides a log-on service to determine who is allowed to use the network and to whom the user is allowed to connect.

Decentralized user access control treats the network as a transparent communication link, and the usual log-on procedure is carried out by the destination host. Of course, the security concerns for transmitting passwords over the network must still be addressed.

In many networks, two levels of access control may be used. Individual hosts may be provided with a log-on facility to protect host-specific resources and application. In addition, the network as a whole may provide protection to restrict network access to authorized users. This two-level facility is desirable for the common case in which the network connects disparate hosts and simply provides a convenient means of terminal/host access. In a more uniform network of hosts, some centralized access policy could be enforced in a network control center.

More elaborate techniques than a simple ID/password have been proposed for user identification. Exotic techniques such as voiceprints, fingerprints, and hand geometry analysis may be more secure but are at present considered too expensive.

The Password File

If passwords are chosen carefully, if password owners exercise discipline, and if network security measures prevent the reading of transmitted passwords, then most avenues of attack are closed. However, for passwords to be usable, the operating system must maintain a password file, listing legal passwords and the privileges associated with each password. If a hacker succeeds in gaining access to that file, then the system has been defeated.

The password file can be protected using encryption (Figure 10.6; see Appendix 10A). In this case, all the passwords in the password table are stored in encrypted form. When a user enters a password, that password is encrypted and compared with the encrypted passwords in the table for a match. Note that with this technique, the passwords in the password file are never decrypted.

The advantage of this approach is that the password table itself need not be protected. Unless the attacker knows the decryption key, the table is of no use. Furthermore, if an asymmetrical encryption technique is used, in which the

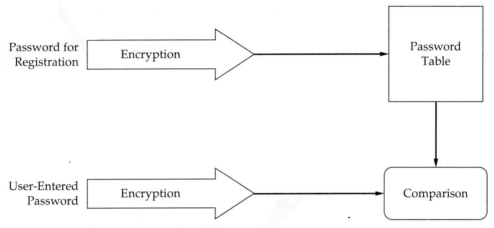

FIGURE 10.6 One-way encryption of passwords.

encryption key and decryption keys are different, then the decryption key need not be stored in the computer system or anywhere else.[1]

Data-Oriented Access Control

Following successful log on, the user has been granted access to one or a set of hosts and applications. This is generally not sufficient for a system that includes sensitive data in its database. Through the procedure for user access control, a user can be identified to the system. Associated with each user, there can be a user profile that specifies permissible operations and file accesses. The operating system can then enforce rules based on the user profile. The database management system, however, must control access to specific records or even portions of records. For example, it may be permissible for anyone in administration to obtain a list of company personnel, but only selected individuals may have access to salary information. The issue is more than just one of level of detail. Whereas the operating system may grant a user permission to access a file or use an application, following which there are no further security checks, the database management system must make a decision on each individual access attempt. That decision will depend not only on the user's identity but also on the specific parts of the data being accessed and even on the information already divulged to the user.

A general model of access control as exercised by a file or database management system is that of an **access matrix** (Figure 10.7a). The basic elements of the model are the following:

---

[1]This technique is used with public-key encryption, for example. See the Appendix to this chapter.

	Program 1	• • •	Segment A	Segment B
Process 1	Read Execute		Read Write	
Process 2				Read
• • •				

(a) Access matrix

Access Control List for Program1: Process1 (Read, Execute)
Access Control List for SegmentA: Process1 (Read, Write)
Access Control List for SegmentB: Process2 (Read)

(b) Access control list

Capability List for Process1: Program1 (Read, Execute) Segment A (Read, Write)
Capability List for Process1: SegmentB (Read)

(c) Capability list

FIGURE 10.7 Access control structures.

- *Subject:* An entity capable of accessing objects. Generally, the concept of subject equates with that of process. Any user or application actually gains access to an object by means of a process that represents that user or application.
- *Object:* Anything to which access is controlled. Examples include files, portions of files, programs, and segments of memory.
- *Access right:* The way in which an object is accessed by a subject. Examples are Read, Write, and Execute.

One axis of the matrix consists of identified subjects that may attempt data access. Typically, this list consists of individual users or user groups, although access can be controlled for terminals, hosts, or applications instead of or in addition to users. The other axis lists the objects that may be accessed. At the greatest level of detail, objects may be individual data fields. More aggregate groupings, such as records, files, or even the entire data base, may also be objects in the matrix. Each entry in the matrix indicates the access rights of that subject for that object.

In practice, an access matrix is usually sparse and is implemented by decomposition in one of two ways. The matrix may be decomposed by columns, yielding **access control lists** (Figure 10.7b). Thus, for each object, an access control list gives users and their permitted access rights. The access control list may contain a default, or public, entry. The default allows users that are not explicitly listed as having special rights to have a default set of rights. Elements of the list may include individual users as well as groups of users.

Decomposition by rows yields **capability tickets** (Figure 10.7c). A capability ticket specifies authorized objects and operations for a user. Each user has a number of tickets and may be authorized to lend or give them to others. Because tickets may be dispersed around the system, they present a greater security problem than do access control lists. In particular, the ticket must be unforgeable. One way to accomplish unforgeability is to have the operating system hold all tickets on behalf of users. The tickets must be held in a region of memory inaccessible to users.

Network considerations for data-oriented access control parallel those for user-oriented access control. If only certain users are permitted to access certain items of data, then encryption may be needed to protect those items during transmission to authorized users. Typically, data-oriented access control is decentralized, that is, controlled by host-based database management systems. If a network database server exists on a network, then data access control becomes a network function.

10.3

TRUSTED SYSTEMS

The techniques we have discussed so far have been concerned with protecting a given message or item from passive or active attack by a given user. A somewhat different but widely applicable requirement is to protect data or resources on the basis of levels of security. This requirement is commonly found in the military, where information is categorized as unclassified (U), confidential (C), secret (S), top secret (TS), or beyond. This concept is equally applicable in other areas, where information can be organized into gross categories and users can be granted clearance to access certain categories of data. For example, the highest level of security might be for strategic corporate-planning documents and data, accessible by corporate officers and their staff only; next might come sensitive financial and personnel data, accessible to administration personnel and corporate officers only, and so on.

When multiple categories or levels of data are defined, the requirement is referred to as **multilevel security**. We first addressed this requirement in the context of a single-computer system and subsequently extended the discussion to networks. We examine the single-system concept in this section.

The general statement of the requirement for multilevel security is that a subject at a high level may not convey information to a subject at a lower or noncomparable level unless that flow of information accurately reflects the will of an authorized user. For implementation purposes, this requirement is in two parts and is simply stated. A multilevel secure system must enforce the following:

- *No Read-up:* A subject can read an object of less or equal security level only. This is referred to in the literature as the **Simple Security Property**.
- *No Write-down:* A subject can write into an object of greater or equal security level only. This is referred to in the literature as the *-**Property** (pronounced *star property*).[2]

These two rules, if properly enforced, provide multilevel security. For a data processing system, the approach that has been taken and that has been the object of much research and development is based on the *reference monitor* concept. This approach is depicted in Figure 10.8. The reference monitor is a controlling element in the hardware and operating system of a computer; it regulates the access of subjects to objects on the basis of security parameters of the subject and object. The reference monitor has access to a file known as the *security kernel database* that lists the access privileges (security clearance) of each subject and the protection attributes (classification level) of each object. The reference monitor enforces the security rules (no read up, no write down) and has the following properties:

- *Complete mediation:* The security rules are enforced on every access, not just, for example, when a file is opened.
- *Isolation:* The reference monitor and database are protected from unauthorized modification.
- *Verifiability:* The reference monitor's correctness must be provable. That is, it must be possible to demonstrate mathematically that the reference monitor enforces the security rules and provides complete mediation and isolation.

These are stiff requirements. The requirement for complete mediation means that every access to data within main memory and on disk and tape must be mediated. Pure software implementations impose too high a performance penalty to be practical; the solution must be at least partly in hardware. The requirement for isolation means that it must not be possible for an attacker, no matter how clever, to change the logic of the reference monitor or the contents of the security kernel data base. Finally, the requirement for mathematical proof

---

[2]The asterisk does not stand for anything. No one could think of an appropriate name for the property during the writing of the first report on the model. The asterisk was a dummy character entered in the draft so that a text editor could rapidly find and replace all instances of its use once the property was named. No name was ever devised, and so the report was published with the asterisk intact.

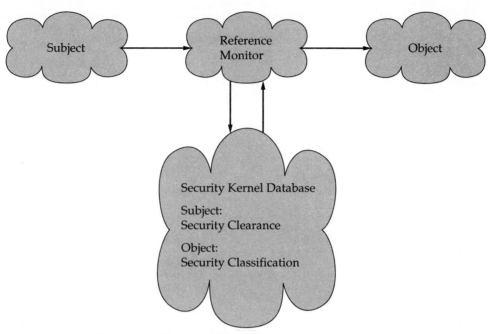

FIGURE 10.8 Reference monitor concept.

is formidable for something as complex as a general-purpose computer. A system that can provide such verification is referred to as a **trusted system**.

In an effort to meet its own needs and also as a service to the public, the U.S. Department of Defense in 1981 established the Computer Security Center within the National Security Agency (NSA) with the goal of encouraging the widespread availability of trusted computer systems. This goal is realized through the center's Commercial Product Evaluation Program. In essence, the center attempts to apply mathematical techniques to verify commercially available products as meeting the security requirements just listed. The center classifies verified products according to the range of security features they provide. The evaluations are needed for Department of Defense procurements but are published and freely available. Hence, they can guide commercial customers in the purchase of commercially available, off-the-shelf equipment.

10.4

NETWORK SECURITY

Network security presents a host of new problems not found in a single-system implementation. In this section, we look at the nature of the problem and some of the approaches that are available. These approaches can be implemented as part of a distributed operating system or as additional utility software supported by the distributed operating system.

Potential Locations for Security Attacks

Figure 10.9 illustrates the variety of places at which an attack can occur by giving an example of the communications path that might be followed between a terminal and a host. Information entered on the terminal by the user must pass along a communications link to a cluster controller. From there it enters a packet-

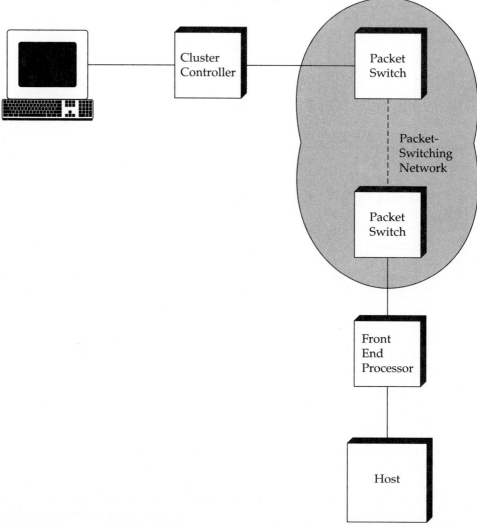

FIGURE 10.9 Typical physical path.

switching network by means of a communications link from the controller to one of the network nodes. Inside the network, the information passes through a number of nodes and links between nodes until it arrives at the node to which the destination service host is connected. In this case, the host is not directly connected to the network. Instead, information first passes to a front-end processor and then through a link to the host.

An attack can take place at any of the communications links. For an active attack, the attacker needs to gain physical control of a portion of the link and be able to insert and capture transmissions. For a passive attack, the attacker merely needs to be able to observe transmissions by tapping into a communications link.

In addition to the potential vulnerability of the various communications links, the processors along the path are themselves subject to attack. An attack can take the form of attempts to modify the hardware or software, to gain access to the memory of the processor, or to monitor the electromagnetic emanations. These attacks are less likely than those involving communications links but are nevertheless a source of risk.

Thus, there are a large number of locations at which an attack can occur. Furthermore, for wide-area communications, many of these locations are not under the physical control of the end user. Even in the case of local area networks, in which physical security measures are possible, there is always the threat of the disgruntled employee.

Location of Encryption Devices

The most powerful and most common approach to countering the threats highlighted in our discussion of Figure 10.9 is encryption. If encryption is to be used to counter these threats, then we need to decide what to encrypt and where the encryption gear should be located. As Figure 10.10 indicates, there are two fundamental alternatives: link encryption and end-to-end encryption.

With link encryption, each vulnerable communications link is equipped on both ends with an encryption device. Thus, all traffic over all communications links is secured. Although this requires a lot of encryption devices in a large network, the value of this approach is clear. One disadvantage of the approach is that the message must be decrypted each time it enters a packet switch; descryption is necessary because the switch must read the address (virtual circuit number) in the packet header to route the packet. Thus, the message is vulnerable at each switch. If it is a public packet-switching network, the user has no control over the security of the nodes.

With end-to-end encryption, the encryption process is carried out at the two end systems. The source host or terminal encrypts the data. The data in encrypted form are then transmitted unaltered across the network to the destination terminal, or host. The destination shares a key with the source and so is able to decrypt the data. This approach would seem to secure the transmission against attacks on the network links or switches. There is, however, still a weak spot.

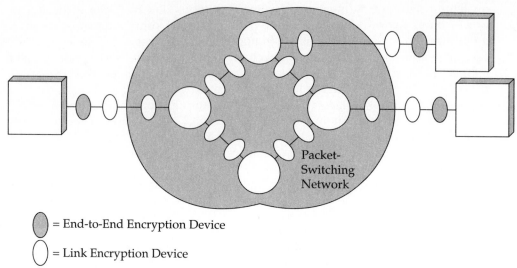

= End-to-End Encryption Device

= Link Encryption Device

FIGURE 10.10 Encryption across a packet-switching network.

Consider the following situation. A host connects to an X.25 packet-switching network, sets up a virtual circuit to another host, and is prepared to transfer data to that other host using end-to-end encryption. Data are transmitted over such a network in the form of packets that consist of a header and some user data. What part of each packet will the host encrypt? Suppose that the host encrypts the entire packet, including the header. This tactic will not work because, remember, only the other host can perform the decryption. The packet-switching node will receive an encrypted packet and be unable to read the header. Therefore, it will not be able to route the packet! It follows that the host may encrypt only that portion of the packet containing the user data and must leave the header in the clear so that it can be read by the network.

Thus, with end-to-end encryption, the user data are secure. However, the traffic pattern is not because packet headers are transmitted in the clear. To achieve greater security, both link and end-to-end encryption are needed, as is shown in Figure 10.10.

Figure 10.11 illustrates the separate and joint effects of the two forms of encryption. When both forms are employed, the host encrypts the user data using an end-to-end encryption key. The entire packet is then encrypted using a link encryption key. As the packet traverses the network, each switch decrypts the packet using a link encryption key in order to read the header and then encrypts the entire packet again for sending it on the next link. Now the entire packet is secure except for the time that the packet is actually in the memory of a packet switch, at which time the packet header is in the clear.

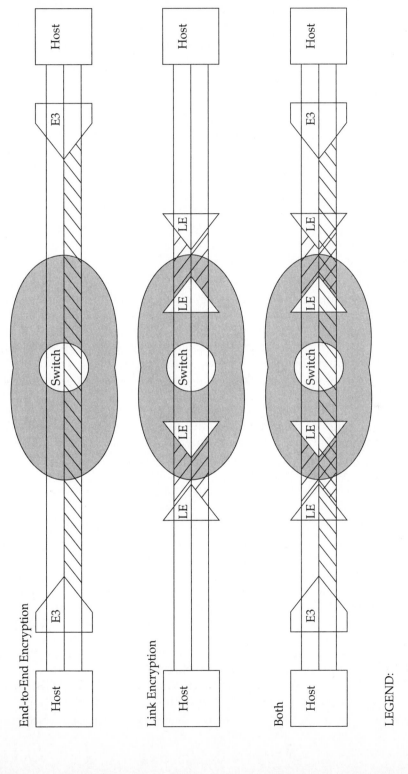

FIGURE 10.11 End-to-end and link encryption.

Key Distribution

For conventional encryption to work, the two parties to an exchange must have the same key, and that key must be protected from access by others. Furthermore, frequent key changes are usually desirable to limit the amount of data compromised if an attacker learns the key. Therefore, the strength of any cryptographic system rests with the *key distribution technique,* a term that refers to the means of delivering a key to two parties that wish to exchange data without allowing others to see the key. Key distribution can be achieved in a number of ways. For two parties A and B:

1. A key can be selected by A and physically delivered to B.
2. A third party can select the key and physically deliver it to A and B.
3. If A and B have previously and recently used a key, one party can transmit to the other the new key, which has been encrypted by using the old key.
4. If A and B each has an encrypted connection to a third party C, C can deliver a key on the encrypted links to A and B.

Options 1 and 2 call for manual delivery of a key. For link encryption, this is a reasonable requirement because each link encryption device is going to be exchanging data with only its partner on the other end of the link. However, for end-to-end encryption, manual delivery is awkward. In a distributed system, any given host or terminal may need to engage in exchanges with many other hosts and terminals over time. Thus, each device needs a number of keys, supplied dynamically. The problem is especially difficult in a wide-area distributed system.

Option 3 is a possibility for either link encryption or end-to-end encryption, but if an attacker ever succeeds in gaining access to one key, then all subsequent keys are revealed. Even if frequent changes are made to the link encryption keys, the changes should be done manually. To provide keys for end-to-end encryption, option 4 is preferable.

Figure 10.12 illustrates an implementation that satisfies option 4 for end-to-end encryption. In the figure, link encryption is ignored, but it can be added or not as required. For this scheme, two kinds of keys are identified:

- *Session key:* When two end systems (hosts, terminals, etc.) wish to communicate, they establish a logical connection (e.g., virtual circuit). For the duration of that logical connection, all user data are encrypted with a one-time session key. At the conclusion of the session, or connection, the session key is destroyed.
- *Permanent key:* A permanent key is a key used between entities for the purpose of distributing session keys.

The configuration consists of the following elements:

- *Access control center:* The access control center determines which systems are allowed to communicate with each other.
- *Key distribution center:* When permission is granted by the access control center

1. Host sends packet requesting connection.
2. Front end buffers packet, asks ACC for session key.
3. ACC approves request, commands KDC.
4. KDC distributes session key to both front ends.
5. Buffered packet transmitted.

FEP = Front-end Processor
ACC = Access Control Center
KDC = Key Distribution Center

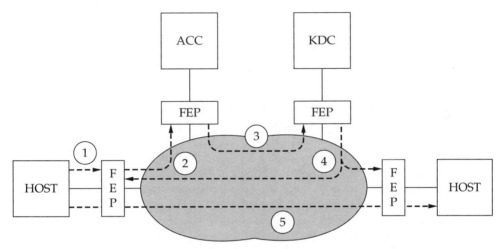

FIGURE 10.12 End-to-end encryption across a network.

for two systems to establish a connection, the key distribution center provides a one-time session key for that connection.

• *Front-end processor:* The front-end processor (FEP) performs end-to-end encryption and obtains session keys on behalf of its host or terminal.

The steps involved in establishing a connection are shown in Figure 10.12. (1) When one host wishes to set up a connection to another host, it transmits a connection request packet. (2) The FEP saves that packet and applies to the access control center for permission to establish the connection. (3) The communication between the front-end processor and the access control center is encrypted, using a permanent key shared by only the access control center and the front-end processor. The access control center has one such unique key for each front-end processor and for the key distribution center. If the access control center approves the connection request, it sends a message to the key distribution center, asking for a session key to be generated. (4) The key distribution center generates the session key and delivers it to the two appropriate front-end processors, using a unique permanent key for each front end. (5) The requesting front-end processor can now release the connection request packet, and a connection is set up between the two end systems. All user data exchanged between the two end systems are encrypted by their respective front-end processors using the one-time session key.

Several variations on the foregoing scheme are possible. The functions of access control and key distribution can be combined into a single system. The separation makes the two functions clear and may provide a slightly enhanced level of security. If we wish to let any two devices communicate at will, then the access control function is not needed at all: When two devices wish to establish a connection, one of them applies to the key distribution center for a session key. Finally, the functions performed by the front-end processor need not be housed in a separate device but can be incorporated into the host system. The advantage of the front-end processor is that it minimizes the impact on the network. From the host's point of view, the FEP appears to be a packet-switching node, and the host interface to the network is unchanged. From the network's point of view, the FEP appears to be a host, and the packet-switching interface to the host is unchanged.

The automated key distribution approach provides the flexibility and dynamic characteristics needed to allow a number of terminal users to access a number of hosts and for the hosts to exchange data with each other.

Of course, another approach to key distribution is public-key encryption (see the Appendix to this chapter). A main disadvantage of public-key encryption compared to conventional encryption is that algorithms for the former are much more complex. Thus, for comparable size and cost of hardware, the public-key scheme provides much lower throughput. One possible application of public-key encryption is to use it for the permanent key portion of Figure 10.12, with conventional keys used for session keys. Since there are few control messages relative to the amount of user data traffic, the reduced throughput should not be a handicap.

Traffic Padding

We mentioned that in some cases users are concerned about security from traffic analysis. With the use of link encryption, packet headers are encrypted, reducing the opportunity for traffic analysis. However, it is still possible in those circumstances for an attacker to assess the amount of traffic on a network and to observe the amount of traffic entering and leaving each end system. An effective countermeasure to this attack is traffic padding, illustrated in Figure 10.13.

Traffic padding is a function that produces ciphertext output continuously, even in the absence of plaintext. A continuous random data stream is generated. When plaintext is available, it is encrypted and transmitted. When input plaintext is not present, the random data are encrypted and transmitted. This makes it impossible for an attacker to distinguish between true data flow and noise, and it is therefore impossible to deduce the amount of traffic.

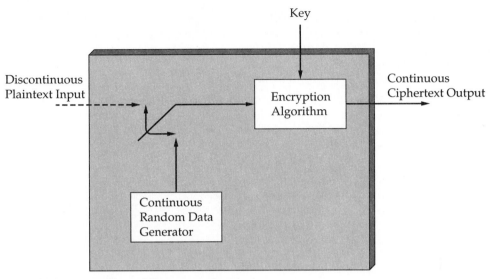

FIGURE 10.13 Traffic padding encryption device.

Multilevel Network Security

The concept of a trusted system can be extended to a network environment. In this case, we wish to enforce the security policy (no Read up, no Write down) among a number of hosts and terminals connected to a network, such as a local area network (LAN).

One approach to this problem is to require that all hosts on the network be trusted systems. Because a trusted system is generally more expensive than an untrusted system, this choice may not be attractive. An alternative is a product that has been announced by several vendors and that is referred to as a **trusted interface unit** (TIU). A TIU attaches to a network, and terminals or hosts attach to the TIU. The TIU accepts data from attached devices and transmits the data in packets on the network. Similarly, incoming packets from the network are delivered to the attached device.

The TIU is designed to operate at an assigned security level. Two functions are required:

- The TIU labels each packet that it transmits with its security label.
- The TIU accepts only packets that are labeled with its own or a lesser security level.

Figure 10.14 depicts the architecture that can be supported by TIUs. Single-level hosts at a given security level connect to the network via a TIU of the same level. The TIU assures that the host receives only those data that are at or below the classification that it is permitted to have. All data transmitted by the host

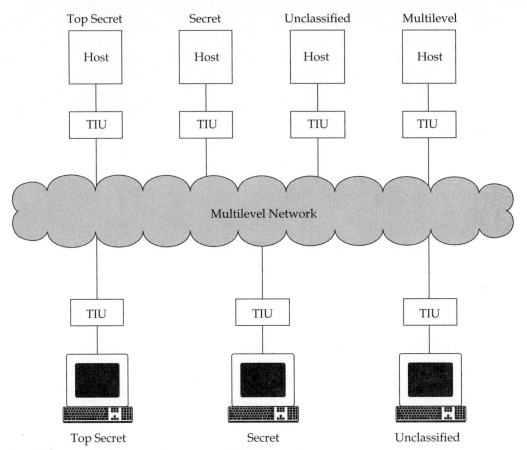

FIGURE 10.14 Application of the trusted interface unit (TIU).

are labeled by the TIU with its security level, thereby ensuring that no end point of a lower classification level can receive the data.

As with hosts, terminals are also connected to the network via TIUs. All terminals connected to the same TIU must operate at the same level.

Unclassified devices require a TIU operating at the unclassified level, not a simple network interface unit (NIU); the latter performs the interfacing function but not the security function. The filtering function is most important for un-classified devices. That is, we must ensure that an unclassified terminal or computer is prevented from receiving classified data.

The TIU approach is attractive because of the relative ease of building a trusted interface unit. The performance penalty is slight: Only a small amount of ad-ditional processing per packet is required. And compared to a general-purpose trusted computer, the TIU is quite simple to verify.

The TIU is one approach to applying the technology of trusted systems to network security. The technology can be applied in a number of other ways.

Any critical security function can be implemented as a separate piece of trusted hardware or as an isolated piece of trusted software within a general-purpose system. For example, the front-end processors, access control center, and key distribution center of Figure 10.12 are good candidates for the technology of trusted systems. Any function, such as public or private key generation done within a host, is a candidate for isolation as a trusted service. Because the technology of trusted systems is so new, it will be some time before all the possible security applications are evident.

10.5

VIRUSES AND RELATED THREATS

Perhaps the most sophisticated security threats are presented by programs that exploit vulnerabilities in computing systems. In this context, we are concerned with application programs as well as utility programs such as editors and compilers. Two kinds of threats can be presented by programs:

- *Information access threats:* Intercept or modify data on behalf of users who should not have access to that data.
- *Service threats:* Exploit service flaws in computers to inhibit use by legitimate users.

Table 10.2 summarizes the key types of threats in each category. We briefly examine each of these in turn.

Information Access Threats

Trapdoor

A trapdoor is a secret entry point into a program that allows someone who is aware of the trapdoor to gain access without going through the usual procedures for security access. Trapdoors have been used legitimately for many years by programmers to debug and test programs. Debugging and testing are usually done when the programmer is developing an application that has an authentication procedure, or a long setup, that requires the user to enter many different values to run the application. To debug the program, the developer may wish to gain special privileges or to avoid all the necessary setup and authentication. The programmer may also want to ensure that there is a method of activating the program should something be wrong with the authentication procedure that is being built into the application. The trapdoor is code that recognizes some special sequence of input, or that is triggered by being run from a certain user ID or by an unlikely sequence of events.

Trapdoors become threats when they are used by unscrupulous programmers to gain unauthorized access. The trapdoor was the basic idea for the vulnera-

TABLE 10.2   Program-Related Threats

Information Access Threats

Trapdoor
  Secret undocumented entry point into a program. Used to grant access without normal methods of access authentication.
Trojan Horse
  Secret undocumented routine embedded within a useful program. Execution of the program results in execution of the secret routine.
Covert Channels
  A hidden means to enable a program to communicate information.

Service Threats

Virus
  Code inserted into a program that causes a copy of itself to be inserted into one or more other programs. In addition to propagation, the virus usually performs some unwanted function.
Worm
  Program that can travel form computer to computer across network connections. May contain a virus or bacterium.
Bacterium
  Program that consumes system resources by replicating itself.

bility portrayed in the movie *War Games* [COOP89]. In a real-life case, auditors discovered a trapdoor in a commercial software product [GOLD85] in which the author's name served as the bypass password. Another example: During the development of Multics, penetration tests were conducted by an Air Force "tiger team" (simulating adversaries). One tactic employed was to send a bogus operating-system update to a site that was running Multics. The update contained a Trojan horse (described later) that could be activated by a trapdoor and that allowed the tiger team to gain access. The threat was so well implemented that the Multics developers could not find it, even after they were informed of its presence [ENGE80].

It is difficult to implement operating-system controls for trapdoors. Security measures must focus on program development and software update.

Trojan Horses

A Trojan horse is a useful or apparently useful program or command procedure containing hidden code that, when invoked, performs some unwanted or harmful function.

Trojan horse programs can be used to accomplish functions indirectly that an unauthorized user could not accomplish directly. For example, to gain access to the files of another user on a shared system, a user can create a Trojan horse program that, when executed, changes the invoking user's file permissions so that the files are readable by any user. The author can then induce users to run the program by placing it in a common directory and naming it so that it appears to be a useful utility. An example is a program that ostensibly produces a listing of the user's files in a desirable format. After another user has run the program, the author can then access the information in the user's files. An example of a Trojan horse program that would be difficult to detect is a compiler that has been modified to insert additional code into certain programs as they are compiled, such as a system login program [THOM84]. The code creates a trapdoor in the log-in program that permits the author to log on to the system using a special password. This Trojan horse can never be discovered by reading the source code of the log-in program.

Another common motivation for using the Trojan horse is data destruction. Although the program appears to be performing a useful function (e.g., a calculator program), it may also be quietly deleting the user's files. For example, a CBS executive was victimized by a Trojan horse that destroyed all information in his computer's memory [TIME86]. The Trojan horse was implanted in a graphics routine offered on an electronic bulletin board system.

One approach to securing against Trojan horse attacks is the use of a secure, trusted operating system. Figure 10.15 illustrates an example taken from [BOEB85]. In this case, a Trojan horse is used to get around the standard security mechanism used by most file-management and operating systems: the access control list. In this example, a user named Doe interacts through a program with a data file containing the critically sensitive character string CPE1704TKS. User Doe has created the file with Read and Write permission provided only to programs executing on his own behalf: that is, only processes that are owned by Doe may access the file.

The Trojan horse attack begins when a hostile user, named Drake, gains legitimate access to the system and installs both a Trojan horse program and a private file to be used in the attack as a "back pocket." Drake gives Read and Write permission to himself for this file and gives Doe Write-only permission (Figure 10.15a). Drake now induces Doe to invoke the Trojan horse program, perhaps by advertising it as a useful utility. When the program detects that it is being executed by Doe, it copies the sensitive character string from Doe's file and copies it into Drake's back-pocket file (Figure 10.15b). Both the Read and Write operations satisfy the constraints imposed by access control lists. Drake then has only to access his file at a later time to learn the value of the string.

Now consider the use of a secure operating system in this scenario (Figure 10.15c). Security levels are assigned to subjects at log-on on the basis of criteria such as the terminal from which the computer is being accessed and the user involved as identified by ID/password. In this example, there are two security levels, sensitive and public, ordered so that sensitive is higher than public. Processes owned by Doe and Doe's data file are assigned the security level of sensitive. Drake's file and processes are restricted to public. Now, if Doe invokes the Trojan horse program (Figure 10.15d), that program acquires Doe's security level. It is therefore able, under the Simple Security Property, to observe the

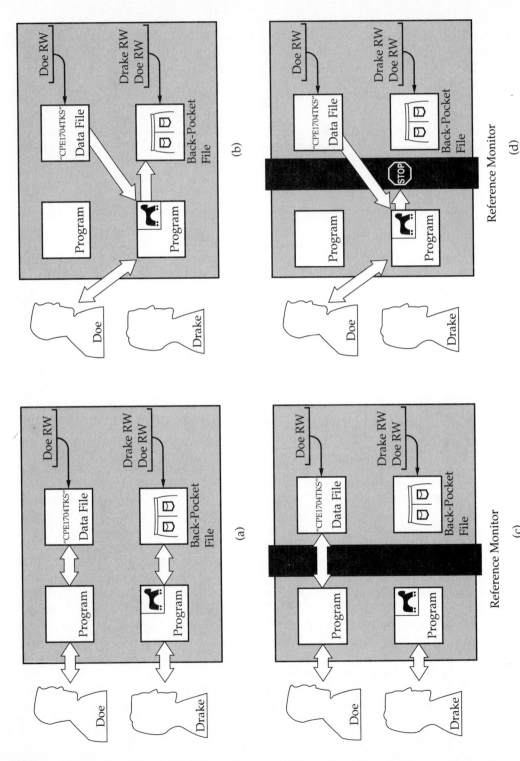

FIGURE 10.15 Trojan horse and secure operating system.

sensitive character string. When the program attempts to store the string in a public file (the back-pocket file), however, the *-Property is violated and the attempt is disallowed by the reference monitor. Thus, the attempt to write into the back-pocket file is denied even though the access control list permits it: The security policy takes precedence over the access control list mechanism.

Covert Channels

Features incorporated in multilevel secure operating systems give assurance that a privileged user will be prevented from sending privileged information to an unprivileged user. A covert channel attempts to transfer the information in an unexpected and subtle way that is not prevented by ordinary multilevel security controls.

For example, a privileged program may have the function of producing an unprivileged summary of a privileged data file. The system can easily check that no sensitive data are printed. However, changing the word TOTAL to TOTALS in a heading would not be noticed, thus creating a 1-bit covert channel. If the word TOTAL or TOTALS appears sufficiently often, useful information can be communicated.

The usefulness of covert channels is limited by the rate of information transfer, which will usually be small.

Service Threats

A new threat has arisen to cause concern to data processing and data communications managers: the virus and its near-relatives, the worm and the bacterium. These software creations range from the harmless to the extremely destructive. What is worrisome to the manager responsible for security is the prevalence of these computer contagions. In the first nine months of 1988, an estimated 250,000 computers, from the smallest laptop machines to the most powerful workstation, have been hit with a virus.[3]

What was once a rare electronic disease has reached epidemic proportions. Across the United States, it is disrupting operations, destroying data, and raising disturbing questions about the vulnerability of information systems everywhere.

Viruses

A virus is a program that can "infect" other programs by modifying them; the modification includes a copy of the virus program, which can then go on to infect other programs.

Biological viruses are tiny scraps of genetic code—DNA or RNA—that can take over the machinery of a living cell and trick it into making thousands of

---

[3]Time Magazine, *Invasion of the Data Snatchers.* September 26, 1988

flawless replicas of the original virus. Like its biological counterpart, a computer virus carries in its instructional code the recipe for making perfect copies of itself. Lodged in a host computer, the typical virus takes temporary control of the computer's disk operating system. Then, whenever the infected computer comes into contact with an uninfected piece of software, a fresh copy of the virus passes into the new program. Thus, the infection can be spread from computer to computer by unsuspecting users who either swap disks or send programs to one another over a network. In a network environment, the ability to access applications and system services on other computers provides a perfect culture for the spread of a virus.

A virus can do anything that other programs do. The only difference is that it attaches itself to another program and executes secretly every time the host program is run. Table 10.3 shows a simple example of how a virus can be implemented in such a way as to spread. This example only indicates the mechanism by which the virus remains hidden and by which it spreads. If this were all there were to viruses, they would not be a cause for concern. Unfortunately, once a virus is executing, it can perform any function, such as erasing files and programs. This is the threat of the virus. Table 10.4 lists some of the more common viruses and indicates the damage that they can do.

During its lifetime, a typical virus goes through the following four stages:

1. A dormant phase, in which the virus is idle. The virus will eventually be activated by some event, such as a date, the presence of another program or file, or the capacity of the disk exceeding some limit. Not all viruses have this stage.

2. A propagation phase, during which the virus places an identical copy of itself into other programs or into certain system areas on the disk. Each infected program will now contain a clone of the virus, which will itself enter a propagation phase. This process is illustrated in Figure 10.16, which shows a virus spreading across 3 user programs.

3. The triggering phase, in which the virus is activated to perform the function

TABLE 10.3   Trail of the Virus

A very simple assembly language virus that does nothing more than infect programs might work something like this:

- Find the first program instruction.
- Replace it with a jump to the memory location following the last instruction in the program.
- Insert a copy of the virus code at that location.
- Have the virus simulate the instruction replaced by the jump.
- Jump back to the second instruction of the host program.
- Finish executing the host program.

Every time the host program is run, the virus infects another program and then executes the host program. Except for a short delay, a user notices nothing suspicious.

TABLE 10.4   Some Common Viruses

IBM PC Viruses

Pakistani Brain

One of the most prevalent viruses, so called because it originated in Pakistan. It infects the boot sector on a PC-DOS disk and replicates, infecting every floppy disk inserted into the system. The virus takes over the floppy disk controller interface. If it sees a Read operation, it pushes the original Read operation aside and attempts to read the boot track. If it determines that the boot is uninfected, it modifies the boot to contain the virus. In some versions, the virus starts to mark areas on your disk as bad even though they are good. Eventually, the disk contains nothing but bad sectors.

Jerusalem Virus

This virus infects executable programs such as .COM or .EXE files. It resides in the memory and infects every program that is executed. It destroys file allocation tables, which makes it impossible to access files on disk, and it scrambles data on the disk. This virus is spread by floppy disks but attacks hard disks as well.

LeHigh Virus

This virus infects the operating system by getting into the command processor. Whenever a disk access is made, it checks to see if the command processor on that disk is infected. If not, the virus is introduced. If so, a counter controlled by the virus is incremented. When the counter reaches four (or ten, in a more recent version), the virus destroys all the data on the hard disk.

Alemeda Virus

This virus infects the system's boot sector. It then infects any floppy disk inserted during reboot and destroys the last track on the disk.

Macintosh Viruses

Scores Virus

This virus is designed to replicate for a specified number of days, followed by several days of dormancy. Thereafter, when the user attempts to save information in a file, the virus will not let it, and crashes the system.

nVIR

This virus comes in a variety of forms, of which at least a dozen have been detected. The technique by which it spreads is especially virulent. It invades the system file; once this crucial resource is infected, every application that is subsequently launched is contaminated.

---

for which it was intended. As with the dormant phase, the triggering phase can be caused by a variety of system events, including a count of the number of times that this copy of the virus has made copies of itself.

4. The execution phase, in which the function is performed. The function may be harmless, such as a message on the screen, or damaging, such as the destruction of programs and data files.

Most viruses carry out their work in a manner that is specific to a particular operating system. Thus, they are designed to take advantage of the details and weaknesses of particular systems.

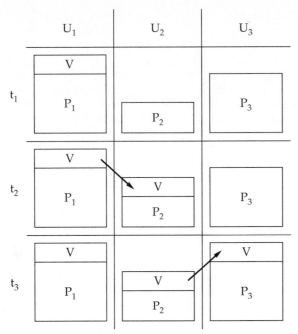

FIGURE 10.16 The spread of a virus.

The ideal solution to the threat of viruses is prevention: Don't allow a virus to get into the system in the first place. In general, this goal is impossible to achieve, although prevention can reduce the number of successful viral attacks. Failing prevention, the next-best approach is to be able to do the following:

- *Detection:* Once the infection has occurred, determine that it has occurred and locate the virus.
- *Purging:* Remove the virus from all infected systems, so that the disease cannot spread further.
- *Recovery:* Recover any lost data or programs.

Even this less ambitious goal may be difficult to achieve. Before discussing specific measures, let us look at a useful classification of viruses developed by the Computer Virus Industry Association.[4] As the name suggests, this is a group of vendors that design and sell products designed to prevent viruses or to achieve recovery from them. The association has defined three classes of viruses:

- Those that infect general-purpose programs. These must attach themselves to a program in order to spread. Most of these are detectable and preventable.

---

[4]"Antivirus Vendors form Industry Regulation Group." *Network World,* July 11, 1988.

- Those that infect operating-system files. These must also attach themselves to a program to spread and execute, but they are more difficult to detect because they have already infected the operating system.
- Those that attack the boot sector. The boot is the first sector of the disk that is used to boot the operating system into main memory when the computer is turned on. These viruses are relatively easy to detect because they cause obvious changes to the boot sector.

Because of the variety of viruses out there, there is no universal remedy. A number of programs have been developed that provide some protection, and a security manager is advised to contact several vendors and assess the various products. Some of the measures that can be taken to ward off viruses are the following:

- *Cryptographic checksum:* A checksum is a value produced by means of a calculation on a block of bits. The value is then stored as part of the block. For example, the binary image of a program can be viewed as a sequence of 16-bit binary integers. The sum of all these words, modulo 2^{16}, is a simple checksum. The advantage of a checksum is that it is a quick way of detecting alterations in a large block of data. If any word or words in the block are changed, the calculated checksum will differ from the stored checksum. To prevent a viral program from modifying both the program and the checksum, an encrypted version of the checksum is stored with the program, with the key maintained separately in a protected manner. Each time the program is to be used or transferred to another disk or computer, the checksum is validated to assure that no modifications have occurred.
- *Program monitor:* A program monitor is triggered by any system interrupt and examines each one for suspicious activity. If the program monitor detects anything considered suspicious by the author of the antiviral program, it interrupts the operation and alerts the user.
- *Virus removal:* Some virus removal programs are specific, looking for the telltale signs in storage of viruses known to the author of the removal program. Others compare snapshots of the system portion of a known clean system with the current system.
- *Backups:* Regular backup of current files is sound practice in any case. Most shared systems (minicomputers, mainframes) provide this service automatically. Unfortunately, most users of personal computers are lazy when it comes to this chore. Aside from its value in the event of a disk crash, it can be used as a tool in combating viruses. This technique can be used in conjunction with virus detection for the purpose of recovery.

The dilemma facing the security manager is this. If sharing programs and data is prohibited, viruses cannot occur, but this defeats the purpose of sharing. However, if sharing is allowed, then viruses can occur and the current repertoire of tools for detecting and preventing viruses is not foolproof.

Worms

Network worm programs use network connections to spread from system to system. Once active within a system, a network worm can behave like a computer virus or bacterium (discussed later), or it can implant Trojan horse programs or perform any number of disruptive or destructive actions.

To replicate itself, a network worm uses some sort of network vehicle. Examples include the following:

- *Electronic mail facility:* A worm mails a copy of itself to other systems.
- *Remote execution capability:* A worm executes a copy of itself on another system.
- *Remote log-in capability:* A worm logs on to a remote system as a user and then uses commands to copy itself from one system to the other.

The new copy of the worm program is then run on the remote system where, in addition to any functions that it performs at that system, it continues to spread in the same fashion.

A network worm exhibits the same characteristics as a computer virus: a dormant phase, a propagation phase, a triggering phase, and an execution phase. The propagation phase generally performs the following functions:

1. Searches for other systems to infect by examining host tables or similar repositories of remote system addresses.
2. Establishes a connection with a remote system.
3. Copies itself to the remote system and causes the copy to be run.

The network worm may also attempt to determine whether a system has previously been infected before copying itself to the system. In a multiprogramming system, it may also disguise its presence by naming itself as a system process or using some other name that may not be noticed by a system operator.

As with viruses, network worms are difficult to counter. However, both network security and single-system security measures, if properly designed and implemented, minimize the threat of worms.

Bacteria

Bacteria are programs that do not explicitly damage any files. Their sole purpose is to replicate themselves. A typical bacteria program may do nothing more than execute two copies of itself simultaneously on a multiprogramming system or perhaps create two new files, each of which is a copy of the original source file of the bacteria program. Both of those programs then may copy themselves twice, and so on. Bacteria reproduce exponentially, eventually taking up all the processor capacity, memory, or disk space, denying users access to those resources.

10.6

SUMMARY

The increasing reliance by business upon the use of data processing systems and the increasing use of networks and communications facilities to build distributed systems have resulted in a strong requirement for computer and network security. Computer security concerns the mechanisms that are inside, and that are related to, a single computer system. The principal object is to protect the data resources of that system. Network security deals with the protection of data and messages that are communicated.

The requirements for security are best assessed by examining the various security threats faced by an organization. The interruption of service is a threat to availability. The interception of information is a threat to secrecy. Finally, both the modification of legitimate information and the unauthorized fabrication of information are threats to integrity.

One key area of computer security involves the protection of memory. This is essential in any system in which multiple processes are active at one time. Virtual memory schemes are typically equipped with the appropriate mechanisms for this task.

Another important security technique is access control. The purpose of access control is to ensure that only authorized users have access to a particular system and its individual resources and that access to and modification of particular portions of data are limited to authorized individuals and programs. Strictly speaking, access control is a problem of computer security rather than of network security. That is, in most cases, access control mechanisms are implemented within a single computer to control the access to that computer. However, because much of the access to a computer is by means of a networking or communications facility, access control mechanisms must be designed to operate effectively in a distributed networking environment.

A relatively new technology with increasing application in military and commercial environments is the trusted system. The trusted system provides a means of regulating access to data on the basis of who is authorized to access what. The key point is that the system is designed and implemented in such a way that the users can have complete trust that the system will enforce the given security policy. The U.S. National Security Agency is engaged in a program of evaluating commercially available products to certify those that are trusted systems with a particular range of capabilities. This evaluation can be useful to the nonmilitary customer.

Network security raises new issues in the protection of information. In this case, the focus is on the protection of the data transmissions. By far the most important automated tool for network and communications security is *encryption*. Encryption is a process that conceals meaning by changing intelligible messages into unintelligible messages. Most commercially available encryption equipment uses conventional encryption, in which the two parties share a single encryption/decryption key. The principal challenge with conventional encryption is the distribution and protection of the keys. The alternative is a public key encryption scheme in which the process involves two keys, one for encryption and a paired key for decryption. One of the keys is kept private by the party that generates the key pair, and the other is made public.

A recent and increasingly worrisome threat is that posed by viruses and similar software mechanisms. These threats exploit vulnerabilities in system software either to gain unauthorized access to information or to degrade system service.

10.7

RECOMMENDED READING

One of the best and most complete treatments of the topics of this chapter is [PFLE89]. A somewhat less technical, more management-oriented text is [COOP89]. A good discussion of operating-system issues is to be found in [MAEK87]. Another excellent book is [DAVI84], which concentrates on networking security. [ABRA87] is a useful collection of papers on security, some of which are virtually unavailable elsewhere. A more recent collection is in [LUNT91]. A good survey article is [SUMM84]. A collection of papers on multilevel security and trusted systems can be found in [AMES83].

Two interesting treatments of viruses and related program threats are [WACK89] and [SPAF89].

10.8

PROBLEMS

10.1 Assume that passwords are selected from 4-character combinations of 26 alphabetic characters. Assume that an adversary is able to attempt passwords at a rate of one per second.
(a) Assuming no feedback to the adversary until each attempt has been completed, what is the expected time needed to discover the correct password?
(b) Assuming feedback to the adversary who is flagging an error as each incorrect character is entered, what is the expected time needed to discover the correct password?

10.2 Assume that source elements of length k are mapped in some uniform fashion into target elements of length p. If each digit can take on one of r values, then the number of source elements is r^k and the number of target elements is the smaller number r^p. A particular source element x_i is mapped to a particular target element y_j.

(a) What is the probability that the correct source element can be selected by an adversary on one try?

(b) What is the probability that a different source element x_k ($x_i \neq x_k$) that results in the same target element, y_j, can be produced by an adversary?

(c) What is the probability that the correct target element can be produced by an adversary on one try?

10.3 A phonetic password generator picks two segments randomly for each six-letter password. The form of each segment is CVC (consonant, vowel, consonant), where V = <a,e,i,o,u> and C = $\overline{V}$.

(a) What is the total password population?

(b) What is the probability of an adversary guessing a password correctly?

10.4 In Figure 10.15 one link of the Trojan horse copy-and-observe-later chain is broken. There are two other possible angles of attack by Drake: Drake's logging on and attempting to read the string directly, and Drake's assigning a security level of sensitive to the back-pocket file. Does the reference monitor prevent these attacks?

10.5 The necessity of the "no read up" rule for a multi-level secure system is fairly obvious. What is the importance of the "no write down" rule?

10.6 Give some examples where traffic analysis could jeopardize security. Describe situations where end-to-end encryption combined with link encryption would still allow enough traffic analysis to be dangerous.

10.7 The need for security and the desirability of sharing data have always been at odds with each other. As more people access computer networks involving thousands of nodes, what are the implications of worms and viruses on this increasing interaction? Consider not only technical ramifications, but also the potential impact on human communication.

10.8 Key distribution schemes using an access control center and/or a key distribution center have central points vulnerable to attack. Discuss the security implications of such centralization.

10.9 Should the protection of users of a network against worms and similar threats be the responsibility of the network itself or the hosts that use it? Defend your answer.

APPENDIX 10A

Encryption

One the most important automated tools for computer security is encryption. Encryption is a process that conceals meaning by changing intelligible messages into unintelligible messages. Encryption can be achieved by means of either a code or a cipher. A code system uses a predefined table or dictionary to substitute a meaningless word or phrase for each message or part of a message. The simplest code substitutes another letter for each letter of the alphabet. A cipher uses a computable algorithm that can translate any stream of message bits into an unintelligible cryptogram. Because cipher techniques lend themselves more readily to automation, it is these techniques that are used in contemporary computer and network security facilities. This Appendix discusses only cipher techniques.

We begin by looking at the traditional approach to encryption, now known as conventional encryption. We then look at a new and quite useful technique known as public key encryption.

10A.1 Conventional Encryption

Figure 10.17a illustrates the conventional encryption process. The original intelligible message, referred to as *plaintext*, is converted into apparently random nonsense, referred to as *ciphertext*.The encryption process consists of an algorithm and a key. The key is a relatively short bit string that controls the algorithm. The algorithm produces a different output, depending on the specific key being used at the time. Changing the key radically changes the output of the algorithm.

Once the ciphertext is produced, it is transmitted. Upon reception, the ciphertext can be transformed back to the original plaintext by using a decryption algorithm and the same key that was used for encryption.

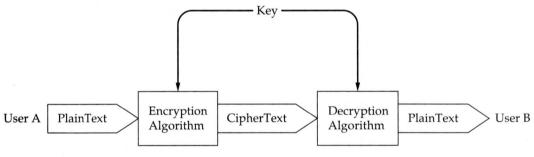

(a) Conventional encryption

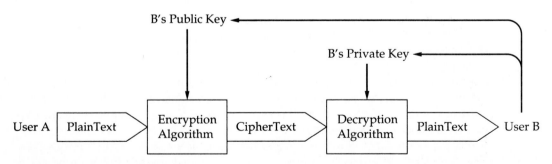

(b) Public-key encryption

FIGURE 10.17 Encryption.

The security of conventional encryption depends on several factors. First, the encryption algorithm must be powerful enough so that it is impractical to decrypt a message on the basis of the ciphertext alone. Beyond that, the security of conventional encryption depends on the secrecy of the key, not the secrecy of the algorithm. That is, it is assumed that it is impractical to decrypt a message on the basis of the ciphertext *plus* knowledge of the encryption/decryption algorithm. In other words, we don't need to keep the algorithm secret; we need only to keep the key secret.

This feature of conventional encryption is what makes it feasible for widespread use. The fact that the algorithm need not be kept secret means that manufacturers can and have developed low-cost chip implementations of data encryption algorithms. These chips are widely available and are incorporated into a number of products. With the use of conventional encryption, the principal security problem is maintaining the secrecy of the key.

The Data Encryption Standard

The most widely used encryption scheme is based on the data encryption standard (DES), adopted in 1977 by the National Bureau of Standards (NBS). For DES, data are encrypted in 64-bit blocks using a 56-bit key. Using the key, the 64-bit input is transformed in a series of steps into a 64-bit output. The same steps, with the same key, are used to reverse the encryption.

The DES has enjoyed increasingly widespread use. Unfortunately, it has also been the subject of much controversy as to how secure the DES is. The main concern is in the length of the key, which some observers consider to be too short. To appreciate the nature of the controversy, let us quickly review the history of the DES.

The DES is the result of a request for proposals for a national cipher standard released by the NBS in 1973. At that time, IBM was in the final stages of a project called Lucifer to develop its own encryption capability. IBM proposed the Lucifer scheme, which was by far the best system submitted. It was, in fact, so good that it considerably upset some people at the National Security Agency (NSA), which until that moment had considered itself comfortably ahead of the rest of the world in the still arcane art of cryptography. The DES, as eventually adopted, was essentially the same as Lucifer, with one crucial difference: Lucifer's key size was originally 128 bits, whereas the final standard uses a key of 56 bits. What is the significance of the 72 dropped bits?

There are basically two ways to break a cipher. One way is to exploit properties of whatever mathematical functions form the basis of the encryption algorithm to make a cryptanalytic attack on it. It is generally assumed that the DES is immune to such attacks, although the role of the NSA in shaping the final DES standard leaves lingering doubts. The other way is a brute-force attack in which you try all possible keys in an exhaustive search. That is, you attempt to decrypt ciphertext with every possible 56-bit key until something intelligible pops out. With only 56 bits in the DES key, there are 2^{56} different keys—a number that is uncomfortably small and that is becoming smaller as computers get faster.

According to David Kahn, author of *Codebreakers* (New York: Macmillan, 1967) and a noted expert on cryptography, Lucifer set off a debate within the NSA. "The codebreaking side wanted to make sure that the cipher was weak enough for the NSA to solve it when used by foreign nations and companies. The codemaking side wanted any cipher it was certifying for use by Americans to be truly good. The resulting bureaucratic compromise was a cipher weak enough for them to read but strong enough to protect the traffic against the casual observer."

Whatever the merits of the case, the DES has flourished in recent years and is widely used, especially in financial applications. Except in areas of extreme sensitivity, the use of the DES in commercial applications should not be a cause for concern by the responsible managers.

Commercial Communications Security Endorsement Program

Although the DES still has a reasonably useful life ahead of it, it is likely that nongovernment organizations will begin to look for replacements for what is seen as an increasingly vulnerable algorithm. The most likely replacement is a family of algorithms developed under the NSA Commercial COMSEC (communications security) Endorsement Program (CCEP). The CCEP is a joint effort by the NSA and industry to produce a new generation of encryption devices that are more secure than the DES, that are of low cost, and that are capable of operating at high data rates. Features of the new CCEP algorithms are the following:

1. The CCEP algorithms are developed by the NSA and are classified. Thus, the algorithms themselves remain secret and are subject to change from time to time.
2. Industry participants will produce chip implementation of the algorithms, but the NSA maintains control over the design, fabrication, and dissemination of chips.

Two types of algorithms come under the CCEP heading. Type I algorithms are designed to protect classified government information. Equipment using type I CCEP will be available to government agencies and their designated contractors only. Type II algorithms are designed to protect sensitive but unclassified information. Type II gear is intended to replace the DES gear. Unlike the type I modules that will handle classified information, the type II equipment is controlled only to the point of sale. Presumably, after a type II module is built into a computer or communication device and sold by a vendor, the customer can do with it whatever he or she pleases—short of exporting it overseas.

Although the purpose of developing the type II equipment, as with the type I equipment, was to provide a means of protecting government information, the type II modules are available for use in nongovernment, private sector applications. As this equipment becomes more widely available, it is likely to become more widely used, at the expense of the DES.

10A.2 Public-Key Encryption

As we have seen, one of the major difficulties with conventional encryption schemes is the need to distribute the keys in a secure manner. A clever way around this requirement is an encryption scheme that, surprisingly, does not require key distribution. This scheme, known as public-key encryption and first proposed in 1976, is illustrated in Figure 10.17b.

For conventional encryption schemes, the keys used for encryption and decryption are the same. This is not a necessary condition. Instead, it is possible to develop an algorithm that uses one key for encryption and a companion but different key for decryption. Furthermore, it is possible to develop algorithms such that knowledge of the encryption algorithm plus the encryption key is not sufficient to determine the decryption key. Thus, the following technique will work:

1. Each end system in a network generates a pair of keys to be used for encryption and decryption of messages that it will receive.
2. Each system publishes its encryption key by placing it in a public register or file. This is the public key. The companion key is kept private.
3. If A wishes to send a message to B, it encrypts the message using B's public key.
4. When B receives the message, it decrypts it using B's private key. No other recipient can decrypt the message because only B knows B's private key.

As you can see, public-key encryption solves the key distribution problem because there are no keys to distribute! All participants have access to public keys, and private keys are generated locally by each participant and therefore need never be distributed. As long as a system controls its private key, its incoming communication is secure. At any time, a system can change its private key and publish the companion public key to replace its old public key.

A main disadvantage of public-key encryption compared to conventional encryption is that algorithms for the former are much more complex. Thus, for comparable size and cost of hardware, the public-key scheme will provide much lower throughput.

Table 10.5 on the following page summarizes some of the important aspects of conventional and public-key encryption.

TABLE 10.5   Conventional and Public-Key Encryption

Conventional Encryption	Public-key Encryption
Needed to Work:	*Needed to Work:*
1. The same algorithm with the same key can be used for encryption and decryption.	1. One algorithm is used for encryption and decryption with a pair of keys, one for encryption and one for decryption.
2. The sender and receiver must share the algorithm and the key.	2. The sender and receiver must each have one of the matched pair of keys.
Needed for Security:	*Needed for Security:*
1. The key must be kept secret.	1. One of the two keys must be kept secret.
2. It must be impossible or at least impractical to decipher a message if no other information is available.	2. It must be impossible or at least impractical to decipher a message if no other information is available.
3. Knowledge of the algorithm plus samples of ciphertext must be insufficient to determine the key.	3. Knowledge of the algorithm plus one of the keys plus samples of ciphertext must be insufficient to determine the other key.

APPENDIX A

Queuing Analysis

In a number of places in this book, especially Chapter 6, reference is made to queuing analysis, and the results based on such an analysis are presented. Indeed, queuing analysis is one of the most important tools for persons involved with computer and network analysis. It can be used to provide approximate answers to a host of questions, such as the following:

- What happens to file retrieval time when disk I/O utilization goes up?
- Does response time change if both processor speed and the number of users on the system are doubled?
- How many lines should a time-sharing system have on a dial-in rotary?
- How many terminals are needed in an on-line inquiry center, and how much idle time will the operators have?

The number of questions that can be addressed with a queuing analysis is endless and touches on virtually every area discussed in this book. The ability to make such an analysis is an essential tool for anyone involved in this field.

Although the theory of queuing is mathematically complex, the application of queuing theory to the analysis of performance is in many cases remarkably straightforward. A knowledge of elementary statistical concepts (means and standard deviations) and a basic understanding of the applicability of queuing theory is all that is required. Armed with this knowledge, the analyst can often make a queuing analysis on the back of an envelope using readily available queuing tables or using simple computer programs that occupy only a few lines of code.

The purpose of this Appendix is to provide a practical guide to queuing analysis. A subset, although a very important subset, of the subject is addressed. In the final section, pointers to additional references are provided. An annex to this Appendix reviews some elementary concepts in probability and statistics.

A.1

WHY QUEUING ANALYSIS?

There are many cases when it is important to be able to project the effect of some change in a design: Either the load on a system is expected to increase or a design change is contemplated. For example, an organization supports a number of terminals, personal computers, and workstations on a 4-Mbps (megabits per second) local area network (LAN). An additional department in the building is to be cut over onto the network. Can the existing LAN handle the increased workload, or would it be better to provide a second LAN with a bridge between the two? There are other cases in which no facility exists, but on the basis of expected demand, a system design needs to be created. For example, a department intends to equip all its personnel with a personal computer and to configure these computers into a LAN with a file server. Based on experience elsewhere in the company, the load generated by each PC can be estimated.

The concern is system performance. In an interactive or real-time application, the parameter of concern is often response time. In other cases, throughput is the principal issue. In any case, projections of performance are to be made on the basis of existing load information or on the basis of estimated load for a new environment. A number of approaches are possible:

1. Do an after-the-fact analysis based on actual values.
2. Make a simple projection by scaling up from existing experience to the expected future environment.
3. Develop an analytic model based on queuing theory.
4. Program and run a simulation model.

Option 1 is no option at all: We will wait and see what happens. This leads to unhappy users and to unwise purchases.

Option 2 sounds more promising. The analyst may take the position that it is impossible to project future demand with any degree of certainty. Therefore, it is pointless to attempt some exact modeling procedure. Rather, a rough-and-ready projection will provide ballpark estimates. The problem with this approach is that the behavior of most systems under a changing load is not what one would intuitively expect. If there is an environment in which there is a shared facility (e.g., a network, a transmission line, a time-sharing system), then the performance of that system typically responds in an exponential way to increases in demand.

Figure A.1 is a typical example. The upper line shows what happens to user response time on a shared facility as the load on that facility increases. The load is expressed as a fraction of capacity. Thus, if we are dealing with an input from a disk that is capable of transferring 1000 blocks per second, then a load of 0.5 represents transfer of 500 blocks per second, and the response time is the amount of time it takes to retransmit any incoming block. The lower line is a simple projection based on a knowledge of the behavior of the system up to a

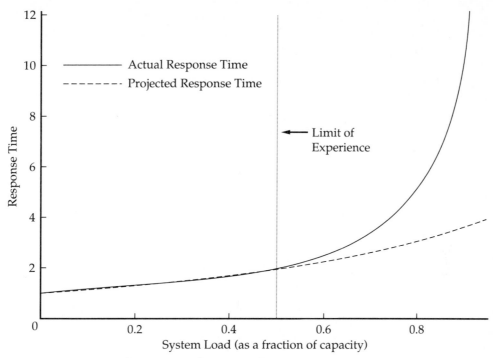

FIGURE A.1 Projected versus actual response time.

load of 0.5.[1] Note that although things appear rosy when the simple projection is made, performance on the system will in fact collapse beyond a load of about 0.8 to 0.9.

Thus, a more exact prediction tool is needed. Option 3 is to make use of an analytic model, which can be expressed as a set of equations that can be solved to yield the desired parameters (response time, throughput, etc.). For computer, operating-system, and networking problems, and indeed for many practical real-world problems, analytic models based on queuing theory provide a reasonably good fit to reality. The disadvantage of queuing theory is that a number of simplifying assumptions must be made to derive equations for the parameters of interest.

The final approach is a simulation model. Given a sufficiently powerful and flexible simulation programming language, the analyst can model reality in great detail and avoid making the many assumptions required of queuing theory. However, in most cases, a simulation model is not needed or at least is not advisable as a first step in the analysis. For one thing, both existing measurements and projections of future load carry with them a certain margin of error.

---

[1]In fact, the lower line is based on fitting a third-order polynomial to the data available up to a load of 0.5.

Thus, no matter how good the simulation model, the value of the results are limited by the quality of the input. For another, despite the many assumptions required of queuing theory, the results that are produced usually come quite close to those that would be produced by a more careful simulation analysis. Furthermore, a queuing analysis can literally be accomplished in a matter of minutes for a well-defined problem, whereas simulation exercises can take days, weeks, or longer to program and run.

Accordingly, it behooves the analyst to master the basics of queuing theory.

A.2

QUEUING MODELS

The Single-Server Queue

The simplest queuing system is depicted in Figure A.2. The central element of the system is a server, which provides some service to items. Items from some population of items arrive at the system to be served. If the server is idle, an item is served immediately. Otherwise, an arriving item joins a waiting line.[2] When the server has completed serving an item, the item departs. If there are items waiting in the queue, one is immediately dispatched to the server.

Figure A.2 also illustrates the parameters associated with a queuing model. Items arrive at the facility at some average arrival rate (items arriving per second) λ. At any given time, a certain number of items will be waiting in the queue (zero or more); the average number waiting is w, and the mean time that an item must wait is t_w. Note that t_w is averaged over all incoming items, including

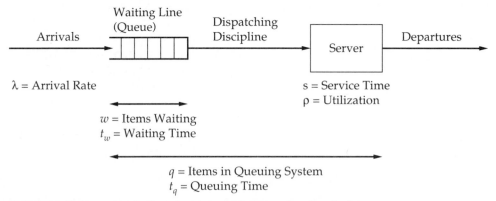

FIGURE A.2 Queueing system structure and parameters for single-server queue.

---

[2]The waiting line is referred to as a queue in some treatments in the literature; it is also common to refer to the entire system as a queue.

those that do not wait at all. The server handles incoming items with an average service time s; this is the time interval between the dispatching of an item to the server and the departure of that item from the server. Utilization is the fraction of time that the server is busy, measured over some interval of time. Finally, there are two parameters that apply to the system as a whole. The average number of items in the system, including the item being served (if any) and the items waiting (if any), is q; and the average time that an item spends in the system, waiting and being served, is t_q.

If we assume that the capacity of the waiting line is infinite, then no items are ever lost from the system; they are just delayed until they can be served. Under these circumstances, the departure rate equals the arrival rate. As the arrival rate, which is the rate of traffic passing through the system, increases, the utilization increases and with it, congestion. The waiting line becomes longer, increasing waiting time. At $\rho = 1$, the server becomes saturated, working 100% of the time.

Thus, the theoretical maximum input rate that can be handled by the system is:

$$\lambda_{max} = \frac{1}{s}$$

However, waiting lines become very large near system saturation, growing without bound when $\rho = 1$. Practical considerations, such as response time requirements or buffer sizes, usually limit the input rate for a single server to 70 to 90% of the theoretical maximum.

To proceed, we need to make some assumption about this model:

- *Item population:* Typically, we assume an infinite population, which means that the arrival rate is not altered by the loss of population. If the population is finite, then the population available for arrival is reduced by the number of items currently in the system; this would typically reduce the arrival rate proportionally.
- *Queue size:* Typically, we assume an infinite queue size. Thus, the waiting line can grow without bound. With a finite queue, it is possible for items to be lost from the system. In practice, any queue is finite. In many cases, this will make no substantive difference to the analysis. We address this issue briefly later.
- *Dispatching discipline:* When the server becomes free and if there is more than one item waiting, a decision must be made as to which item to dispatch next. The simplest approach is first-in, first-out; this discipline is what is normally implied when the term queue is used. Another possibility is last-in, first-out. One that you might encounter in practice is a dispatching discipline based on service time. For example, a packet-switching node may choose to dispatch packets on the basis of shortest first (to generate the most outgoing packets) or longest first (to minimize processing time relative to transmission time). Unfortunately, a discipline based on service time is very difficult to model analytically.

TABLE A.1   Notation Used in This Appendix

λ = mean number of arrivals per second
s = mean service time for each arrival
σ_s = standard deviation of service time
ρ = utilization; fraction of time facility is busy
q = mean number of items in system (waiting and being served)
t_q = mean time an item spends in system
σ_q = standard deviation of q
σ_{tq} = standard deviation of t_q
w = mean number of items waiting to be served
t_w = mean time an item spends waiting for service
t_d = mean waiting time for items that have to wait (not including items with waiting
    time = 0)
σ_w = standard deviation of w
M = number of servers
$m_x(r)$ = the rth percentile; that value of r below which x occurs r % of the time

Table A.1 summarizes the notation that is used in Figure A.2 and introduces some other parameters that are useful. In particular, we are often interested in the variability of various parameters, and this is neatly captured in the standard deviation.

The Multiserver Queue

Figure A.3 shows a generalization of the simple model we have been discussing. In this case, there are multiple servers, all sharing a common waiting line. If an item arrives and at least one server is available, then the item is immediately dispatched to that server. It is assumed that all servers are identical; thus, if more than one server is available, it makes no difference which server is chosen

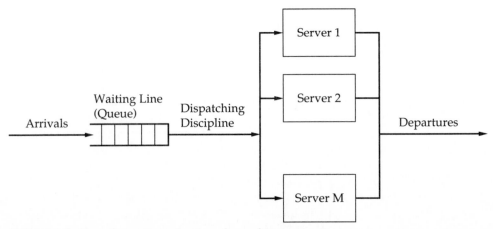

FIGURE A.3 Queueing system structure for multiserver queue.

for the item. If all servers are busy, a waiting line begins to form. As soon as one server becomes free, an item is dispatched from the waiting line, using the dispatching discipline in force.

With the exception of utilization, all the parameters illustrated in Figure A.2 carry over to the multiserver case with the same interpretation. If we have M identical servers, then ρ is the utilization of each server, and we can consider $M\rho$ to be the utilization of the entire system. Thus, the theoretical maximum utilization is $M \times 100\%$, and the theoretical maximum input rate is:

$$\lambda_{max} = \frac{M}{s}$$

Basic Queuing Relationships

To proceed much further, we are going to have to make some simplifying assumptions. These assumptions risk making the models less valid for various real-world situations. Fortunately, in most cases, the results will be sufficiently accurate for planning and design purposes.

There are, however, some relationships that are true in the general case, and these are illustrated in Table A.2. By themselves, these relationships are not particularly helpful.

Assumptions

The fundamental task of a queuing analysis is as follows: Given the following information as input:

- Arrival rate
- Service time

Provide as output information concerning:

- Items waiting
- Waiting time
- Items queued
- Queuing time.

TABLE A.2   Some Basic Queuing Relationships

$\rho = \lambda s$	for a single server
$\rho = \dfrac{\lambda s}{M}$	for multiple servers
$q = \lambda t_q$	Little's formula
$w = \lambda t_w$	
$t_q = t_w + s$	
$q = w + \rho$	for a single server
$q = w + M\rho$	for multiple servers

What specifically would we like to know about these outputs? Certainly we would like to know their average values (w, t_w, q, t_q). In addition, it would be useful to know something about their variability. Thus, the standard deviation of each would be useful (σ_q, σ_{tq}, σ_w, σ_{tw}). Other measures may also be useful. For example, to design a buffer associated with a multiplexer, it might be useful to know what is that buffer size such that the probability of overflow is less than 0.001? That is what is the value of N such that $P_r[q < N] = 0.999$?

To answer such questions in general requires complete knowledge of the probability distribution of the arrival rate and service time. Furthermore, even with that knowledge, the resulting formulas are exceedingly complex. Thus, to make the problem tractable, we need to make some simplifying assumptions.

The most important of these assumptions is that the arrival rate obeys the Poisson distribution, which is equivalent to saying that the interarrival times are exponential. This assumption is almost invariably made. Without it, queuing analysis is impractical. With this assumption, it turns out that many useful results can be obtained if only the mean and standard deviation of the arrival rate and service time are known.

Matters can be made even simpler and more detailed results can be obtained if it is assumed that the service time is exponential or constant.

A convenient notation has been developed for summarizing the principal assumptions that are made in developing a queuing model. The notation is $X/Y/N$, where X refers to the distribution of the interarrival times, Y refers to the distribution of service times, and N refers to the number of servers. The most common distributions are denoted as follows:

G = general independent arrivals or service times
M = negative exponential distribution
D = deterministic arrivals or fixed length service.

Thus, M/M/1 refers to a single-server queuing model with Poisson arrivals and exponential service times.

A.3

SINGLE-SERVER QUEUES

Table A.3a provides some equations for single server queues that follow the M/G/1 model. That is, the arrival rate is Poisson. Making use of a scaling factor, A, the equations for some of the key output variables are straightforward. Note that the key factor in the scaling parameter is the ratio of the standard deviation of service time to the mean. No other information about the service time is needed. Two special cases are of some interest. When the standard deviation is equal to the mean, the service time distribution is exponential. This is the simplest case, and the easiest one for calculating results. Table A.3b shows the simplified versions of equations for σ_q, σ_{tq}, σ_w, and σ_{tw}, plus some other param-

TABLE A.3 Formulas for Single-Server Queues

Assumptions: 1. Poisson arrival rate.
2. Dispatching discipline does not give preference to items based on service times.
3. Formulas for standard deviation assume first-in, first-out dispatching.
4. No items leave the queue (lost calls delayed).

(a) General Service Times (M/G/1)

$$A = \frac{1}{2}\left[1 + \left(\frac{\sigma_s}{s}\right)^2\right] \qquad \text{useful parameter}$$

$$q = \rho + \frac{\rho^2 A}{1 - \rho}$$

$$w = \frac{\rho^2 A}{1 - \rho}$$

$$t_q = s + \frac{\rho s A}{1 - \rho}$$

$$t_w = \frac{\rho s A}{1 - \rho}$$

(b) Exponential Service Times (M/M/1)

$$q = \frac{\rho}{1 - \rho}$$

$$w = \frac{\rho^2}{1 - \rho}$$

$$t_q = \frac{s}{1 - \rho}$$

$$t_w = \frac{\rho s}{1 - \rho}$$

$$\sigma_q = \frac{\sqrt{\rho}}{1 - \rho}$$

$$\sigma_{tq} = \frac{s}{1 - \rho}$$

$$\Pr[q = N] = (1 - \rho)\rho^N$$

$$\Pr[q \le N] = \sum_{i=0}^{N} (1 - \rho)\rho^i$$

$$\Pr[t_q \le t] = 1 - e^{-(1 - \rho)t/s}$$

$$m_{tq}(r) = t_q \times \log_e\left(\frac{100}{100 - r}\right)$$

$$m_{tw}(r) = \frac{t_w}{\rho} \times \log_e\left(\frac{100\rho}{100 - r}\right)$$

(c) Constant Service Times (M/D/1)

$$q = \frac{\rho^2}{2(1 - \rho)} + \rho$$

$$w = \frac{\rho^2}{2(1 - \rho)}$$

$$t_q = \frac{s(2 - \rho)}{2(1 - \rho)}$$

$$t_w = \frac{\rho s}{2(1 - \rho)}$$

$$\sigma_q = \frac{1}{1 - \rho} R$$

$$R = \sqrt{\rho - \frac{3\rho^2}{2} - \frac{5\rho^3}{6} - \frac{\rho^4}{12}}$$

$$\sigma_{tq} = \frac{s}{1 - \rho}\sqrt{\frac{\rho}{3} - \frac{\rho^2}{12}}$$

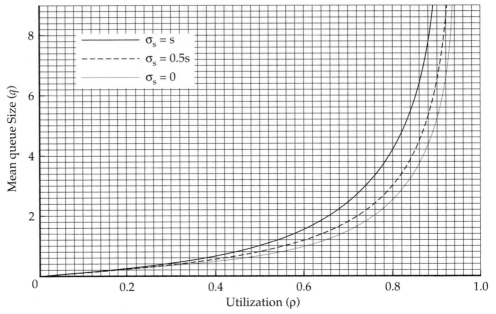

FIGURE A.4 Mean queue sizes for M/G/1 model.

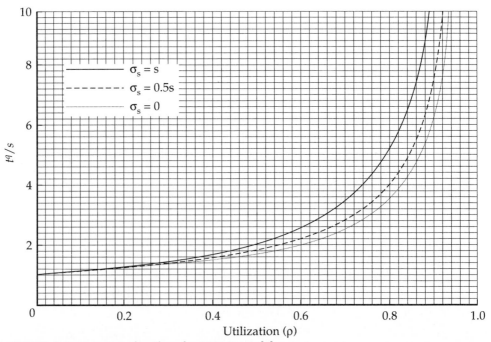

FIGURE A.5 Mean queuing time for M/G/1 model.

eters of interest. The other interesting case is a standard deviation of service time equal to zero, that is, a constant service time. The corresponding equations are shown in Table A.3c.

Figures A.4 and A.5 plot values of average queue size and queuing time versus utilization for three values of σ_s/s. Note that the poorest performance is exhibited by the exponential service time and the best by a constant service time. Usually, one can consider the exponential service time to be a worst case. An analysis based on this assumption will give conservative results. This is nice, since tables are available for the M/M/1 case and values can be looked up quickly.

What value of σ_s/s is one likely to encounter? We can consider four regions:

- *Zero:* This is the rare case of constant service time. For example, if all transmitted messages are of the same length, they will fit this category.
- *Ratio less than· 1:* Since this ratio is better than the exponential case, using M/M/1 tables will give queue sizes and times that are slightly larger than they should be. Using the M/M/1 model will give answers on the safe side. An example of this category might be a data entry application from a particular form.
- *Ratio close to 1:* This is the most common occurrence and corresponds to exponential service time. That is, service times are essentially random. Consider message lengths to a computer terminal: A full screen might be 1920 characters, with message sizes varying over the full range. Airline reservations, file lookups on inquires, shared LAN and packet-switching networks are examples of systems that often fit this category.
- *Ratio greater than 1:* If you observe this, you need to use the M/G/1 model and not rely on the M/M/1 model. The most common occurrence of this is a bimodal distribution, with a wide spread between the peaks. An example is a system that experiences many short processes, many long processes, and few in between.

Incidentally, the same consideration applies to the arrival rate. For a Poisson arrival rate, the interarrival times are exponential, and the ratio of standard deviation to mean is 1. If the observed ratio is much less than 1, then arrivals tend to be evenly spaced (not much variability), and the Poisson assumption will overestimate queue sizes and delays. On the other hand, if the ratio is greater than 1, then arrivals tend to cluster and congestion becomes more acute.

A.4

MULTISERVER QUEUES

Table A.4 lists formulas for some key parameters for the multiserver case. Note the restrictiveness of the assumptions. Useful congestion statistics for this model have been obtained only for the case of M/M/N, where the exponential service times are identical for the N servers.

TABLE A.4   Formulas for Multiserver Queues (M/M/N)

Assumptions: 1. Poisson arrival rate.
              2. Exponential service times
              3. All servers equally loaded
              4. All servers have same mean service time
              5. First-in, first-out dispatching
              6. No items leave the queue

$$K = \frac{\sum_{N=0}^{M-1} \dfrac{(M\rho)^N}{N!}}{\sum_{N=0}^{M} \dfrac{(M\rho)^N}{N!}} \qquad \text{useful parameter}$$

Probability that all servers are busy $= B = \dfrac{1 - K}{1 - \rho K}$

$$q = B\,\frac{\rho}{1 - \rho} + M\rho$$

$$w = B\,\frac{\rho}{1 - \rho}$$

$$t_q = \frac{B}{M}\,\frac{s}{1 - \rho} + s$$

$$t_w = \frac{B}{M}\,\frac{s}{1 - \rho}$$

$$\sigma_{tq} = \frac{s}{M(1 - \rho)}\,\sqrt{B(2 - B) + M^2(1 - \rho)^2}$$

$$\sigma_w = \frac{1}{1 - \rho}\,\sqrt{B\rho(1 + \rho - B\rho)}$$

$$PR[t_w > t] = Be^{-M(1 - \rho)t/s}$$

$$t_d = \frac{s}{M(1 - \rho)}$$

A.5

NETWORKS OF QUEUES

In a distributed environment, isolated queues are unfortunately not the only problem presented to the analyst. Often, the problem to be analyzed consists of several interconnected queues. Figure A.6 illustrates this situation, using nodes to represent queues and the interconnecting lines to represent traffic flow.

Two elements of such a network complicate the methods shown so far:

• The partitioning and merging of traffic, as illustrated by nodes 1 and 5, respectively, in the figure.

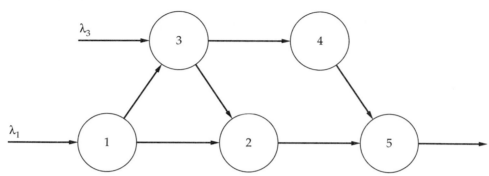

FIGURE A.6 Example of network of queues.

- The existence of queues in tandem, or series, as illustrated by nodes 3 and 4.

No exact method has been developed for analyzing general queuing problems that have the preceding two elements. However, if the traffic flow is Poisson and the service times are exponential, an exact and simple solution exists. In this section, we first examine the two elements listed and then present the approach to queuing analysis.

Partitioning and Merging of Traffic Streams

Suppose that traffic arrives at a queue with a mean arrival rate of λ, and that there are two paths, A and B, by which an item may depart (Figure A.7a). When an item is serviced and departs the queue, it does so via path A with probability P and via path B with probability $(1 - P)$. In general, the traffic distribution of streams A and B will differ from the incoming distribution. However, if the incoming distribution is Poisson, then the two departing traffic flows also have Poisson distributions, with mean rates of $P\lambda$ and $(1 - P)\lambda$.

A similar situation exists for merging traffic. If two Poisson streams with mean rates of λ_1 and λ_2 are merged, the resulting stream is Poisson with a mean rate of $\lambda_1 + \lambda_2$.

Both of these results generalize to more than two departing streams for partitioning and more than two arriving streams for merging.

Queues in Tandem

Figure A.7c is an example of a set of single-server queues in tandem: The input for each queue except the first is the output of the previous queue. Assume that the input to the first queue is Poisson. Then, if the service time of each queue is exponential and the waiting lines are infinite, the output of each queue is a Poisson stream statistically identical to the input. When this stream is fed into the next queue, the delays at the second queue are the same as if the

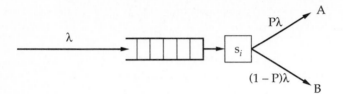

(a) Traffic partitioning

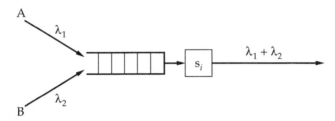

(b) Traffic merging

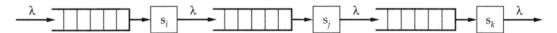

(c) Simple tandem queue

FIGURE A.7 Elements of queuing networks.

original traffic had bypassed the first queue and fed directly into the second queue. Thus, the queues are independent and may be analyzed one at a time. Therefore, the mean total delay for the tandem system is equal to the sum of the mean delays at each stage.

This result can be extended to the case in which some or all of the nodes in tandem are multiserver queues.

Jackson's Theorem

Jackson's theorem can be used to analyze a network of queues. The theorem is based on three assumptions:

1. The queuing network consists of m nodes, each of which provides an independent exponential service.
2. Items arriving from outside the system to any one of the nodes arrive at a Poisson rate.
3. Once served at a node, an item goes (immediately) to one of the other nodes with a fixed probability, or it goes out of the system.

Jackson's theorem states that in such a network of queues, each node is an independent queuing system, with a Poisson input determined by the principles of partitioning, merging, and tandem queuing. Thus, each node may be analyzed separately from the others using the M/M/1 or M/M/N model, and the results may be combined by ordinary statistical methods. Mean delays at each node may be added to derive system delays, but nothing can be said about the higher moments of system delays (e.g., standard deviation).

Jackson's theorem appears attractive for application to packet-switching networks. One can model the packet-switching network as a network of queues. Each packet represents an individual item. We assume that each packet is transmitted separately and that at each packet-switching node in the path from source to destination, the packet is queued for transmission on the next length. The service at a queue is the actual transmission of the packet and is proportional to the length of the packet.

The flaw in this approach is that a condition of the theorem is violated: namely, it is not the case that the service distributions are independent. Because the length of a packet is the same at each transmission link, the arrival process to each queue is correlated to the service process. However, Kleinrock [KLEI76] has demonstrated that, because of the averaging effect of merging and partitioning, assuming independent service times provides a good approximation.

Application to a Packet-Switching Network

Consider a packet-switching network, consisting of nodes interconnected by transmission links, with each node acting as the interface for zero or more attached systems, each of which functions as a source and destination of traffic.[3] The external workload that is offered to the network can be characterized as:

$$\gamma = \sum_{j=1}^{N} \sum_{k=1}^{n} \gamma_{jk}$$

where

γ = total workload in packets per sec

γ_{jk} = workload between source j and destination k

Since a packet may traverse more than one link between source and destination, the total internal workload will be higher than the offered load:

$$\lambda = \sum_{i=1}^{L} \lambda_i$$

where

λ = total load on all the links in the network

λ_i = load on link i

[3]This discussion is based on the development in [MOLL89].

The internal load will depend on the actual path taken by packets through the network. We will assume a routing algorithm is given such that the load on the individual links, λ_i, can be determined from the offered load, γ_{jk}. For any particular routing assignment, we can determine the average number of links that a packet will traverse from these workload parameters. Some thought should convince you that the average length for all paths is given by:

$$E[\text{number of links in a path}] = \frac{\lambda}{\gamma}$$

Now, our objective is to determine the average delay, T, experienced by a packet through the network. For this purpose, it is useful to apply Little's formula (Table A.2). For each link in the network, the average number of items in the queue for that link is given by:

$$q_i = \lambda_i t_i$$

Where t_i is the yet to be determined queuing delay at each queue. Suppose that we sum these quantities. That would give us the average total number of packets waiting in all the queues of the network. Now, it turns out that Little's formula works in the aggregate as well.[4] Thus, the number of packets waiting in the network can be expressed as γT. Combining the two:

$$T = \frac{1}{\gamma} \sum_{i=1}^{L} \lambda_i t_i$$

To determine the value of T, we need to determine the values of the individual delays, t_i. Since we are assuming that each queue can be treated as an independent M/M/1 model, this is easily determined:

$$t_i = \frac{s_i}{1 - \rho_i} = \frac{s_i}{1 - \lambda_i s_i}$$

The service time s_i for link i is just the product of the data rate on the link, in bits per second and the average packet length in bits. To be consistent with commonly used notation we will denote these values as C_i and $1/\mu$, respectively. Then:

$$t_i = \frac{\dfrac{1}{\mu C_i}}{1 - \dfrac{\lambda_i}{\mu C_i}} = \frac{1}{\mu C_i - \lambda_i}$$

Putting all the elements together, we can calculate the average delay of packets sent through the network:

$$T = \frac{1}{\gamma} \sum_{i=1}^{L} \frac{\lambda_i}{\mu C_i - \lambda_i}$$

---

[4]In essence, this statement is based on the fact that the sum of the averages is the average of the sums.

A.6

EXAMPLES

Let us look at a few examples to get some feel for the use of these equations.

Database Server

Consider a LAN with 100 personal computers and a server that maintains a common database for a query application. The average time for the server to respond to a query is 0.6 sec, and the standard deviation is estimated to equal the mean. At peak times, the query rate over the LAN reaches 20 per min. We would like to find the following:

- The average response time ignoring line overhead.
- If a 1.5-sec response time is considered the maximum acceptable, what percentage of growth in message load can occur before the maximum is reached?
- If 20% more use is experienced, will response time increase more or less than 20%?

We will assume an M/M/1 model, with the database server being the server in the model. We ignore the effect of the LAN, assuming that its contribution to the delay is negligible. Facility utilization is calculated as:

$\rho = \lambda s$
$ = (20 \text{ arrivals per min})(0.6 \text{ sec per transmission})/(60 \text{ sec/min})$
$ = 0.2$

The first value, average response time, is easily calculated:

$t_q = s/(1 - \rho)$
$ = 0.6/(1 - 0.2) = 0.75 \text{ sec}$

The second value is more difficult to obtain. Indeed, as worded, there is no answer because there is a nonzero probability that some instances of response time will exceed 1.5 sec for any value of utilization. Instead, let us say that we would like 90% of all responses to be less than 1.5 sec. Then, we can use the equation from Table A.3b:

$m_{tq}(r) = t_q \times \log_e (100/(100 - r))$

$m_{tq}(90) = t_q(\log_e (10)) = \dfrac{s}{1 - \rho} \times 2.3 = 1.5 \text{ sec}$

We have $s = 0.6$. Solving for ρ yields $\rho = 0.08$. In fact, utilization would have to decline from 20 to 8% to put 1.5 sec at the 90th percentile.

The third part of the question is to find the relationship between increases in load and response time. Because a facility utilization of 0.2 is down in the flat part of the curve, response time will increase more slowly than utilization. In this case, if facility utilization increases from 20% to 40%, which is a 100%

increase, the value of t_q goes from 0.75 sec to 1.0 sec, which is an increase of only 33%.

Tightly Coupled Multiprocessor

In Section 6.3, we discussed the use of multiple tightly coupled processors in a single computer system. One of the design decisions had to do with whether processes are dedicated to processors. If a process is permanently assigned to one processor from activation until its completion, then a separate short-term queue is kept for each processor. In this case, one processor can be idle, with an empty queue, while another processor has a backlog. To prevent this situation, a common queue can be used. All processes go into one queue and are scheduled to any available processor. Thus, over the life of a process, the process may be executed on different processors at different times.

Let us try to get a feel for the performance speedup to be achieved by using a common queue. Consider a system with five processors. The average amount of processor time provided to a process while it is in the Running state is 0.1 sec. Assume that the standard deviation of service time is observed to be 0.094 sec. Because the standard deviation is close to the mean, we will assume exponential service time. Also assume that processes are arriving at the Ready state at the rate of 40 per sec.

Single-Server Approach

If processes are evenly distributed among the processors, then the load for each processor is $40/5 = 8$ packets per sec. Thus,

$$\rho = \lambda s$$
$$= 8 \times 0.1 = 0.8$$

The queuing time is then easily calculated:

$$t_q = \frac{s}{1 - r} = \frac{0.1}{0.2} = 0.5 \text{ sec}$$

Multiserver Approach

Now assume that a single Ready queue is maintained for all processors. We now have an aggregate arrival rate of 40 processes per sec. However, the facility utilization is still 0.8 ($\lambda s/M$). To calculate the queuing time from the formula in Table A.4, we need first to calculate B. If you have not programmed the parameter, you can look it up in a table under a facility utilization of 0.8 for 5 servers to yield B = 0.554. Substituting,

$$t_q = (0.1) + \frac{(0.544)(0.1)}{5(1 - 0.8)} = 0.1544$$

So the use of a multiserver queue has reduced average queuing time from 0.5 sec down to 0.1544 sec, which is greater than a factor of 3! If we look at just the waiting time, the multiserver case is 0.0544 sec compared to 0.4 sec, which is a factor of 7.

Although you may not be an expert in queuing theory, you now know enough to be annoyed when you have to wait in a line at a multiple single-server queue facility.

Calculating Percentiles

Consider a configuration in which messages are sent from computers on a local area network (LAN) to systems on other networks. All these messages must pass through a computer that connects the LAN to a wide-area network and hence to the outside world. This linking system is generally referred to as a router, or gateway. Let us look at the traffic from the LAN through the router. Messages arrive with a mean arrival rate of 5 per sec. The average message length is 144 octets, and it is assumed that message length is exponentially distributed. Line speed from the router to the wide-area network is 9600 bps. The following questions are asked:

1. What is the mean queuing time in the router?
2. How many messages are in the router center, including those waiting for transmission and the one currently being transmitted (if any), on the average?
3. Same question as (2), for the 90th percentile.
4. Same question as (2), for the 95th percentile.

λ = 5 msgs/sec
s = (144 octets $\times$ 8 bits/octet)/9600 bps = 0.12 sec
ρ = λs = 5 $\times$ 0.12 = 0.6

Mean queuing time:

$$t_q = s/(1 - \rho) = 0.3 \text{ sec}$$

Mean queue length:

$$q = \rho/(1 - \rho) = 1.5 \text{ packets}$$

To obtain the percentiles, we use the equation from Table A.3b:

$$\Pr[q = N] = (1 - \rho)\rho^N$$

To calculate the rth percentile of queue size, we write the foregoing equation in cumulative form:

$$\frac{r}{100} = \sum_{k=0}^{m(r)} (1 - \rho)\rho^k = 1 - \rho^{1+m(r)}$$

Here $m(r)$ represents the maximum number of messages in the queue expected r % of the time. In the form given, we can determine the percentile for any queue size. We wish to do the reverse: given r, find $m(r)$. So, taking the logarithm to the base 10 of both sides:

$$m(r) = \frac{\log \left(1 - \frac{r}{100} \right)}{\log \rho} - 1$$

If $m(r)$ is fractional, take the next higher integer; if it is negative, set it to 0. For our example, $\rho = 0.6$ and we wish to find $m(90)$ and $m(95)$:

$$m(90) = \frac{\log (1 - 0.90)}{\log (0.6)} - 1 = 3.5$$

$$m(95) = \frac{\log (1 - 0.95)}{\log (0.6)} - 1 = 4.8$$

Thus, 90% of the time there are fewer than four messages in the queue, and 95% of the time there are fewer than five messages. If we were designing to a 95th percentile criterion, a buffer would have to be provided to store at least five messages.

A-7

OTHER QUEUING MODELS

In this Appendix, we have concentrated on one type of queuing model. There are in fact a number of models, based on two key factors:

• The manner in which blocked items are handled
• The number of traffic sources

When an item arrives at a server and finds that server busy, or when it arrives at a multiple-server facility and finds all servers busy, that item is said to be blocked. Blocked items can be handled in a number of ways. First, the item can be placed in a queue awaiting a free server. This method is referred to in the telephone traffic literature as *lost calls delayed*, although in fact the call is not lost. Alternatively, no waiting line is provided. This in turn leads to two assumptions about the action of the item. The item may wait some random amount of time and then try again; this is known as *lost calls cleared*. If the item repeatedly attempts to gain service with no pause, it is referred to as *lost calls held*. The lost calls delayed model is the most appropriate for most computer and data communications problems. Lost calls cleared is usually the most appropriate in a telephone switching environment.

The second key element of a traffic model is whether the number of sources is assumed to be infinite or finite. For an infinite source model, there is assumed to be a fixed arrival rate. For the finite source case, the arrival rate will depend on the number of sources already engaged. Thus, if each of L sources generates arrivals at a rate λ/L, then when the queuing facility is unoccupied, the arrival rate is λ. However, if K sources are in the queuing facility at a particular time, then the instantaneous arrival rate at that time is $\lambda(L - K)/L$. Infinite source models are easier to deal with. The infinite source assumption is reasonable when the number of sources is at least 5 to 10 times the capacity of the system.

A.8

RECOMMENDED READING

Perhaps the most useful reference that you could acquire is [MART72]. Despite the age of this book, it is a valuable practical source. The book provides a number of graphs and tables that can be used to perform quick queuing analyses. It also provides detailed guidance for the application of queuing analysis plus a number of worked-out examples.

In addition to Martin's book, there are several obscure but readily available publications that are of great practical assistance. [IBM71] is an excellent concise treatment of queuing analysis applied to computer and communications problems, with many examples, plus graphs and tables. [FRAN76] is a good collection of tables for various queuing models. An excellent guide to the practical application of statistics is [NBS63]; the book contains tables, formulas, and examples that aid in determining the proper procedure for estimating values from samples and for evaluating the results.

The foregoing references are sufficient for those who wish only to apply queuing analysis. For those who wish to delve more deeply into the subject, a host of books is available. Some of the more worthwhile ones are the following. Good texts that provide a treatment of queuing theory and its application to computers and communications are [MOLL89] and [KOBA78]. [STUC85] is an excellent treatment that focuses on data communications and networking. [COOP81] covers the subject with an emphasis on concepts of telephone traffic analysis. The classic treatment of queuing theory for computer applications, with a detailed discussion of computer networks, is found in [KLEI75] and [KLEI76]. [CONW89] provides a good summary of queuing results, including more recent results; the mathematical treatment, however, makes for rather stiff reading.

ANNEX A

JUST ENOUGH PROBABILITY AND STATISTICS

Measures of Probability

A continuous random variable X can be described by either its distribution or density function:

$$F(x) = \Pr[X \le x] \qquad \text{distribution function}$$

$$f(x) = \frac{d}{dx} F(x) \qquad \text{density function}$$

For a discrete random variable, its probability distribution is characterized by

$$P_X(k) = \Pr[X = k]$$

We are often concerned with some characteristic of a random variable rather than the entire distribution. For example, the mean value:

$$E[X] = \int_{-\infty}^{\infty} x f(x)\, dx \qquad \text{continuous case}$$

$$E[X] = \sum_{\text{all } k} k\, \Pr[x = k] \qquad \text{discrete case}$$

Other useful measures:

Second moment: $\qquad E[X^2] = \int_{-\infty}^{\infty} x^2 f(x)\, dx \qquad\qquad$ continuous case

Second moment: $\qquad E[X^2] = \sum_{\text{all } k} k^2\, \Pr[x = k] \qquad\qquad$ discrete case

Variance: $\qquad\qquad \text{Var}[X] = E[(X - E[X])^2] = E[X^2] - E^2[X]$

Standard deviation $\qquad \sigma_X = \sqrt{\text{Var}[X]}$

The variance and standard deviation are measures of the dispersion of values around the mean.

The Exponential and Poisson Distributions

The exponential distribution (Figures A.8a and A.8b) is given by:

$$F(x) = 1 - e^{-\mu x} \qquad \text{distribution}$$

$$f(x) = \mu e^{-\mu x} \qquad \text{density}$$

The exponential distribution has the interesting property that its mean is equal to its standard deviation:

$$E[X] = \sigma_X = \frac{1}{\mu}$$

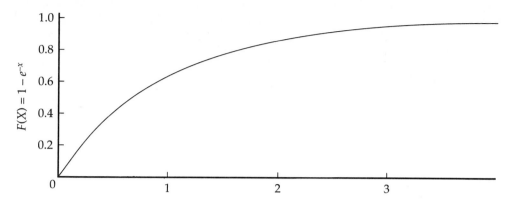

(a) Exponential probability distribution function

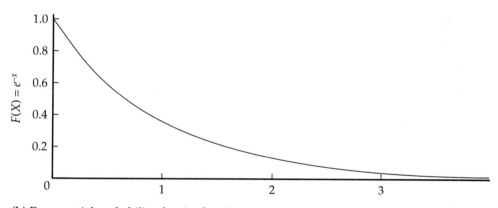

(b) Exponential probability density function

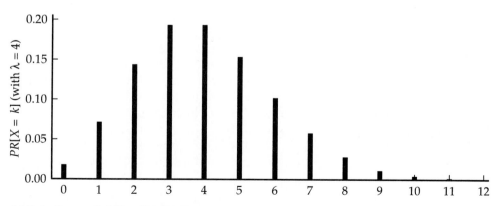

(c) Poission probability distribution

FIGURE A.8 Some probability functions.

When used to refer to a time interval, such as a service time, this distribution is sometimes referred to as a *random distribution*. The reason is that, for a time interval that has already begun, each time at which the interval may finish is equally likely.

This distribution is important in queuing theory because we can often assume that the service time of a server in a queuing system is exponential. In the case of telephone traffic, the service time is the time for which a subscriber engages the equipment of interest. In a packet-switching network, the service time is the transmission time and is therefore proportional to the packet length. It is difficult to give a sound theoretical reason why service times should be exponential, but the fact is that in most cases they are very nearly exponential. This is good news because it simplifies the queuing analysis immensely.

Another important distribution is the Poisson distribution:

$$Pr[X = k] = \frac{\lambda^k}{k!} e^{-\lambda}$$

$$E[X] = \sigma_X = \lambda$$

The Poisson distribution is also important in queuing analysis because we must assume a Poisson arrival pattern to be able to develop the queuing equations. Fortunately, the assumption of Poisson arrivals is usually valid.

The way in which the Poisson distribution can be applied to the arrival rate is as follows. If items are arriving at a queue according to a Poisson process, this situation may be expressed as:

$$Pr[k \text{ items arrive in a time interval } T] = \frac{(\lambda T)^k}{k!} e^{-\lambda T}$$

Expected number of items to arrive in time interval $T = \lambda T$

Mean arrival rate, in items per second $= \lambda$

Arrivals occurring according to a Poisson process are often referred to as *random arrivals* because the probability of the arrival of an item in a small interval is proportional to the length of the interval and is independent of the amount of elapsed time since the arrival of the last item. That is, when items are arriving according to a Poisson process, an item is as likely to arrive at one instant as any other, regardless of the instants at which the other items arrive.

Another interesting property of the Poisson process is its relationship to the exponential distribution. If we look at the times between arrivals of items Ta (called the interarrival times), then we find that this quantity obeys the exponential distribution:

$$Pr[Ta \le t] = 1 - e^{-\lambda t}$$

$$E[Ta] = \frac{1}{\lambda}$$

Thus, the mean interarrival time is the reciprocal of the arrival rate, as one would expect.

Sampling

To perform a queuing analysis, we need to estimate the values of the input parameters, specifically the mean and standard deviations of the arrival rate and service time. If we are contemplating a new system, these estimates may have to be based on judgment and an assessment of the equipment and work patterns likely to prevail. However, it will often be the case that an existing system is available for examination. For example, a collection of terminals, personal computers, and host computers are interconnected in a building by direct connection and multiplexers, and it is desired to replace the interconnection facility with a local area network. To be able to size the network, it is possible to measure the load currently generated by each device.

The measurements are taken in the form of samples. A particular parameter— for example, the rate of packets generated by a terminal or the size of packets— is estimated by observing the number of packets generated during a period.

To estimate a quantity, such as the length of a packet, the following equations can be used:

sample mean:
$$\overline{X} = \frac{1}{n} \sum_{i=1}^{n} X_i$$

sample variance
$$S^2 = \frac{\sum_{i=1}^{n} (X_i - \overline{X})^2}{n - 1}$$
$$= \frac{n \sum_{i=1}^{n} X_i^2 - \left(\sum_{i=1}^{n} X_i\right)^2}{n(n - 1)}$$

sample standard deviation:
$$S = \sqrt{S^2}$$

where

n = sample size
X_i = ith sample

To estimate the arrival rate from a sample, we can use the following:

$$\overline{\lambda} = \frac{n}{T}$$

where n is the number of items observed in a period of duration T. Another approach is to consider each arrival time as a sample and calculate the sample mean and sample standard deviation as was done earlier.

When we estimate values such as the mean and standard deviation on the basis of a sample, we leave the realm of probability and enter that of statistics. This is a complex topic that will not be explored here, except to provide a few comments.

It is important to note that the sample mean and sample standard deviation are themselves random variables. For example, if you take a sample from some population and calculate the sample mean and do this a number of times, the calculated values will differ. Thus, we can talk of the mean and standard deviation of the sample mean, or even of the entire probability distribution of the sample mean.

It follows that the probabilistic nature of our estimated values is a source of error, known as *sampling error*. In general, the greater the size of the sample taken, the smaller the standard deviation of the sample mean, and therefore the closer that our estimate is likely to be to the actual mean. By making certain reasonable assumptions about the nature of the random variable being tested and the randomness of the sampling procedure, you can in fact determine the probability that a sample mean or sample standard deviation is within a certain distance from the actual mean or standard deviation. This concept is often reported with the results of a sample. For example, it is common for the result of an opinion poll to include a comment such as: "The result is within 5% of the true value with a confidence [probability] of 99%."

There is, however, another source of error that is less widely appreciated among nonstatisticians, namely, bias. For example, if an opinion poll is conducted and only members of a certain socioeconomic group are interviewed, the results are not necessarily representative of the entire population. In a communications context, sampling done during one time of day may not reflect the activity at another time of day. If we are concerned to design a system that will handle the peak load that is likely to be experienced, then we should observe the traffic during the time of day that is most likely to produce the greatest load.

Glossary

Some of the terms in this glossary are from the *American National Standard Dictionary for Information Systems* [ANSI90]. These terms are indicated in the glossary by an asterisk.

Access Method*   The method that is used to find a file, a record, or a set of records.

Address Space*   The range of addresses available to a computer program.

Address Translator*   A functional unit that transforms virtual addresses to real addresses.

Asynchronous Operation*   An operation that occurs without a regular or predictable time relationship to a specified event, for example, the calling of an error diagnostic routine that may receive control at any time during the execution of a computer program.

Bacteria   Program that consumes system resources by replicating itself.

Base Address*   An address that is used as the origin in the calculation of addresses in the execution of a computer program.

Batch Processing*   Pertaining to the technique of executing a set of computer programs such that each is completed before the next program of the set is started.

Binary Semaphore   A semaphore that takes on only the values 0 and 1.

Block*   (1) A collection of contiguous records that are recorded as a unit, and the units are separated by interblock gaps. (2) A group of bits that are transmitted as a unit.

Busy-Waiting   The repeated execution of a loop of code while waiting for an event to occur.

Cache Memory   A memory that is smaller and faster than main memory and that is interposed between the processor and main memory. The cache acts as a buffer for recently used memory locations.

Chained List*   A list in which data items may be dispersed but in which each item contains an identifier for locating the next item.

Communications Architecture   The hardware and software structure that implements the communications function.

Compaction   A technique used when memory is divided into partitions of variable size. From time to time, the operating system shifts the partitions so that they are contiguous and so that all the free memory is together in one block. See *External Fragmentation*.

Concurrent*   Pertaining to processes that take place within a common interval of time during which they may have to share common resources alternately.

Consumable Resource   A resource that can be created (produced) and destroyed (consumed). When a resource is acquired by a process, the resource ceases to exist. Examples of consumable resources are interrupts, signals, messages, and information in I/O buffers.

Context Switch   A hardware operation that occurs when the currently executing program is interrupted. The program counter, processor status word, and other registers are saved.

Critical Section*   In an asynchronous procedure of a computer program, a part that cannot be executed simultaneously with an associated critical section of another asynchronous procedure. See *Mutual Exclusion*.

Database*   A collection of interrelated data, often with controlled redundancy, organized according to a schema to serve one or more applications; the data are stored so that they can be used by different programs without concern for the data structure or organization. A common approach is used to add new data and to modify and retrieve existing data.

Deadlock   (1)* An impasse that occurs when multiple processes are waiting for the availability of a resource that will not become available because it is being held by another process that is in a similar Wait state. (2) An impasse that occurs when multiple processes are waiting for an action by or a response from another process that is in a similar Wait state.

Deadlock Avoidance   A dynamic technique that examines each new resource request for deadlock. If the new request could lead to a deadlock, then the request is denied.

Deadlock Detection   A technique in which requested resources are always granted when available. Periodically, the operating system tests for deadlock.

Deadlock Prevention   A technique that guarantees that a deadlock will not occur. Prevention is achieved by assuring that one of the necessary conditions for deadlock is not met.

Demand Paging*   The transfer of a page from auxiliary storage to real storage at the moment of need. Compare *Prepaging*.

Direct Access*   The capability to obtain data from a storage device or to enter data into a storage device in a sequence independent of their relative position, by means of addresses that indicate the physical location of the data.

Direct Memory Address (DMA)   A form of I/O in which a special module, called a DMA module, controls the exchange of data between main memory and an I/O device. The processor sends a request for the transfer of a block of data to the DMA module and is interrupted only after the entire block has been transferred.

Disabled Interrupt   A condition, usually created by the operating system, during which the processor will ignore interrupt request signals of a specified class.

Disk Allocation Table   A table that indicates which blocks on secondary storage are free and available for allocation to files.

Disk Cache   A buffer, usually kept in main memory, that functions as a cache of disk blocks between disk memory and the rest of main memory.

Dispatch*   To allocate time on a processor to jobs or tasks that are ready for execution.

Distributed Operating System   A common operating system shared by a network of computers. The distributed operating system provides support for interprocess communication, process migration, mutual exclusion, and the prevention or detection of deadlock.

Dynamic Relocation*   A process that assigns new absolute addresses to a computer program during execution so that the program may be executed from a different area of main storage.

Enabled Interrupt   A condition, usually created by the operating system, during which the processor will respond to interrupt request signals of a specified class.

Encryption   The conversion of plain text or data into unintelligible form by means of a reversible mathematical computation.

External Fragmentation   Occurs when memory is divided into variable-size partitions corresponding to the blocks of data assigned to the memory (e.g., segments in main memory). As segments are moved into and out of the memory, gaps will occur between the occupied portions of memory.

Field*   (1) Defined logical data that are part of a record. (2) The elementary unit of a record that may contain a data item, a data aggregate, a pointer, or a link.

File*   A set of related records treated as a unit.

File Allocation Table (FAT)   A table that indicates the physical location on secondary storage of the space allocated to a file. There is one file allocation table for each file.

File-Management System   A set of system software that provides services to users and applications in the use of files, including file access, directory maintenance, and access control.

File Organization*   The physical order of records in a file, as determined by the access method used to store and retrieve them.

First-In, First-Out (FIFO)*   A queuing technique in which the next item to be retrieved is the item that has been in the queue for the longest time.

Gang Scheduling   The scheduling of a set of related threads to run on a set of processors at the same time, on a one-to-one basis.

Hash File   A file in which records are accessed according to the values of a key field. Hashing is used to locate a record on the basis of its key value.

Hashing   The selection of a storage location for an item of data by calculating the address as a function of the contents of the data. This technique complicates the storage allocation function but results in rapid random retrieval.

Indexed Access*   Pertaining to the organization and accessing of the records of a storage structure through a separate index to the locations of the stored records.

Indexed File   A file in which records are accessed according to the value of key fields. An index is required that indicates the location of each record on the basis of each key value.

Indexed Sequential Access*   Pertaining to the organization and accessing of the records of a storage structure through an index of the keys that are stored in arbitrarily partitioned sequential files.

Indexed Sequential File   A file in which records are ordered according to the values of a key field. The main file is supplemented with an index file that contains a partial list of key values; the index provides a lookup capability to quickly reach the vicinity of a desired record.

Internal Fragmentation   Occurs when memory is divided into fixed-size partitions (e.g., page frames in main memory, physical blocks on disk). If a block of data is assigned to one or more partitions, then there may be wasted space in the last partition. This will occur if the last portion of data is smaller than the last partition.

Interrupt*   A suspension of a process, such as the execution of a computer program, caused by an event external to that process and performed in such a way that the process can be resumed.

Interrupt Handler   A routine, generally part of the operating system. When an interrupt occurs, control is transferred to the corresponding interrupt handler, which takes some action in response to the condition that caused the interrupt.

Job Control Language (JCL)*   A problem-oriented language that is designed to express statements in a job that are used to identify the job or to describe its requirements to an operating system.

Kernel   A portion of the operating system that includes the most heavily used portions of software. Generally, the kernel is maintained permanently in main memory.

Last-In, First-Out (LIFO)*   A queuing technique in which the next item to be retrieved is the item most recently placed in the queue.

Logical Address   A reference to a memory location independent of the current assignment of data to memory. A translation must be made to a physical address before the memory access can be achieved.

Logical Record*   A record independent of its physical environment; portions of one logical record may be located in different physical records, or several logical records or parts of logical records may be located in one physical record.

Mailbox   A data structure shared among a number of processes that is used as a queue for messages. Messages are sent to the mailbox and retrieved from the mailbox rather than passing directly from sender to receiver.

Main Memory   Memory that is internal to the computer system, is program-addressable, and can be loaded into registers for subsequent execution or processing.

Memory Partitioning*   The subdividing of storage into independent sections.

Message   A block of information that may be exchanged between processes as a means of communication.

Multilevel Security   A capability that enforces access control across multiple levels of classification of data.

Multiprocessing*   A mode of operation that provides for parallel processing by two or more processors of a multiprocessor.

Multiprocessor*   A computer that has two or more processors that have common access to a main storage.

Multiprogramming*   A mode of operation that provides for the interleaved execution of two or more computer programs by a single processor.

Multiprogramming Level   The number of processes that are partially or fully resident in main memory.

Multitasking*   A mode of operation that provides for the concurrent performance or interleaved execution of two or more computer tasks.

Mutual Exclusion   A condition in which there is a set of processes, only one of which is able to access a given resource or perform a given function at any time. See *Critical Section*.

Network Operating System   The software supplemental to the operating system that provides support for the use of common server systems in a network of computers.

Open Systems Interconnection (OSI) Reference Model   A model of communications between cooperating devices. It defines a seven-layer architecture of communication functions.

Operating System*   Software that controls the execution of programs and that provides services such as resource allocation, scheduling, input/output control, and data management.

Page*   In virtual storage, a fixed-length block that has a virtual address and that is transferred as a unit between real storage and auxiliary storage.

Page Fault   Occurs when the page containing a referenced word is not in main memory. This causes an interrupt and requires that the proper page be brought into main memory.

Page Frame*   An area of main storage used to hold a page.

Paging*   The transfer of pages between real storage and auxiliary storage.

Physical Address   The absolute location of a unit of data in memory (e.g., word or byte in main memory, block on secondary memory).

Pipe   A circular buffer allowing two processes to communicate on the producer/consumer model. Thus, it is a first-in, first-out queue, written by one process and read by another. In some systems, the pipe is generalized to allow any item in the queue to be selected for consumption.

Prepaging   The retrieval of pages other than the one demanded by a page fault. The hope is that the additional pages will be needed in the near future, conserving disk I/O. Compare *Demand Paging*.

Privileged Instruction* An instruction that can be executed only in a specific mode, usually by a supervisory program.

Process A program in execution. A process is controlled and scheduled by the operating system. Same as *Task*.

Process Control Block The manifestation of a process in an operating system. It is a data structure containing information about the characteristics and state of the process.

Process Image All the ingredients of a process, including program, data, stack, and process control block.

Process Migration The transfer of a sufficient amount of the state of a process from one machine to another for the process to execute on the target machine.

Process Spawning The creation of a new process by another process.

Protocol Data Unit Information that is delivered as a unit between peer entities of a network and that may contain control information, address information, or data.

Real-Time System An operating system that must schedule and manage real-time tasks.

Real-Time Task A task that is executed in connection with some process or function or set of events external to the computer system and that must meet one or more deadlines to interact effectively and correctly with the external environment.

Record* A group of data elements treated as a unit.

Reentrant Procedure* A routine that may be entered before the completion of a prior execution of the same routine and execute correctly.

Relative Address* An address calculated as a displacement from a base address.

Remote Procedure Call (RPC) A technique by which two programs on different machines interact using procedure call/return syntax and semantics. Both the called and calling program behave as if the partner program were running on the same machine.

Rendezvous In message passing, a condition in which both the sender and receiver of a message are blocked until the message is delivered.

Resident Set That portion of a process that is actually in main memory at a given time. Compare *Working Set*.

Reusable Resource A resource that can be safely used by only one process at a time and is not depleted by that use. Processes obtain reusable resource units that they later release for reuse by other processes. Examples of reusable resources include processors, I/O channels, main and secondary memory, devices, and data structures such as files, databases, and semaphores.

Secondary Memory Memory located outside the computer system itself, including disk and tape.

Schedule* To select jobs or tasks that are to be dispatched. In some operating systems, other units of work, such as input/output operations, may also be scheduled.

Segment In virtual memory, a block that has a virtual address. The blocks of a program may be of unequal length and may even be of dynamically varying lengths.

Segmentation   The division of a program or application into segments as part of a virtual memory scheme.

Semaphore   An integer value used for signaling among processes. Only three operations may be performed on a semaphore, all of which are atomic: initialize, decrement, and increment. Depending on the exact definition of the semaphore, the decrement operation may result in the blocking of a process, and the increment operation may result in the unblocking of a process.

Sequential Access*   The capability to enter data into a storage device or a data medium in the same sequence as the data are ordered, or to obtain data in the same order as they were entered.

Sequential File*   A file in which records are ordered according to the values of one or more key fields, and processed in the same sequence from the beginning of the file.

Server*   In a network, a data station that provides facilities to other stations; for example, a file server, a print server, a mail server.

Session   A collection of one or more processes that represents a single interactive user application or operating-system function. All keyboard and mouse input is directed to the foreground session, and all output from the foreground session is directed to the display screen.

Shell   The portion of the operating system that interprets interactive user commands and job control language commands. It functions as an interface between the user and the operating system.

Spooling*   The use of auxiliary storage as buffer storage to reduce processing delays when transferring data between peripheral equipment and the processors of a computer.

Stack*   A list that is constructed and maintained so that the next data item to be retrieved is the most recently stored item in the list. This method is characterized as last-in, first-out.

Starvation   A condition in which a process is indefinitely delayed because other processes are always given preference.

Swapping*   A process that interchanges the contents of an area of main storage with the contents of an area in auxiliary storage.

Synchronous Operation*   An operation that occurs regularly or predictably with respect to the occurrence of a specified event in another process, for example, the calling of an input/output routine that receives control at a precoded location in a computer program.

Task   Same as *Process*.

Thrashing   A phenomenon in virtual memory schemes in which the processor spends most of its time swapping pieces rather than executing instructions.

Thread   The unit of dispatching. In most operating systems, there is a one-to-one correspondence between process and thread. In some operating systems, the process is the unit of resource ownership, and the thread represents the execution path through one or more programs.

Time Sharing* The concurrent use of a device by a number of users.

Time Slicing* A mode of operation in which two or more processes are assigned quanta of time on the same processor.

Translation Lookaside Buffer (TLB) A high-speed cache used to hold recently referenced page table entries as part of a paged virtual memory scheme. The TLB reduces the frequency of access to main memory to retrieve page table entries.

Trap* An unprogrammed conditional jump to a specified address that is automatically activated by hardware; the location from which the jump was made is recorded.

Trapdoor Secret undocumented entry point into a program, used to grant access without normal methods of access authentication.

Trojan Horse Secret undocumented routine embedded within a useful program. Execution of the program results in execution of the secret routine.

Trusted System A computer and operating system that can be verified to implement a given security policy.

Virtual Address* The address of a storage location in virtual storage.

Virtual Storage* The storage space that may be regarded as addressable main storage by the user of a computer system in which virtual addresses are mapped into real addresses. The size of virtual storage is limited by the addressing scheme of the computer system and by the amount of auxiliary storage available, and not by the actual number of main storage locations.

Virus Secret undocumented routine embedded within a useful program. Execution of the program results in execution of the secret routine.

Working Set The working set with parameter D for a process at virtual time t, $W(t, D)$, is the set of pages of that process that have been referenced in the last D time units. Compare *Resident Set.*

Worm A program that can travel from computer to computer across network connections. May contain a virus or a bacterium.

References

ABRA87 Abrams, M., and Podell, H. *Computer and Network Security.* Los Alamitos, CA: IEEE Computer Society Press, 1987.

AGAR89a Agarwal, A. *Analysis of Cache Performance for Operating Systems and Multiprogramming.* Boston: Kluwer Academic Publishers, 1989.

AGAR89b Agarwal, A., Horowitz, M., and Hennessy, J. "An Analytical Cache Model." *ACM Transactions on Computer Systems,* May 1988.

ALMA89 Almasi, G., and Gottlieb, A. *Highly Parallel Computing.* Redwood City, CA: Benjamin/Cummings, 1989.

AMES83 Ames, S., and Neumann, P. "Special Issue on Computer Security Technology." *Computer,* July 1983.

ANDE89 Anderson, T., Laxowska, E., and Levy, H. "The Performance Implications of Thread Management Alternatives for Shared-Memory Multiprocessors." *IEEE Transactions on Computers,* December 1989.

ANDL90 Andleigh, P. *UNIX System Architecture.* Englewood Cliffs, NJ: Prentice Hall, 1990.

ANDR90 Andrianoff, S. "A Module on Distributed Systems for the Operating System Course." *Proceedings, Twenty-First SIGCSE Technical Symposium on Computer Science Education, SIGSCE Bulletin,* February 1990.

ANSI90 American National Standards Institute. *American National Standard Dictionary for Informatin Systems.* X3-N-1990.

ARDE80 Arden, B., ed. *What Can Be Automated?* Cambridge, MA: MIT Press, 1980.

ARTS89a Artsy, Y., ed. Special Issue on Process Migration. *Newsletter of the IEEE Computer Society Technical Committee on Operating Systems,* Winter 1989.

ARTS89b Artsy, Y. "Designing a Process Migration Facility: The Charlotte Experience." *Computer,* September 1989.

ATLA89 Atlas, A., and Blundon, B. "Time to Reach for It All." *UNIX Review,* January 1989.

ATT87a   AT&T *UNIX System Readings and Examples*, Volume I. Englewood Cliffs, NJ: Prentice Hall, 1987.

ATT87b   AT&T. *UNIX System Readings and Examples*, Volume II. Englewood Cliffs, NJ: Prentice Hall, 1987.

AXFO88   Axford, T. *Concurrent Programming: Fundamental Techniques for Real-Time and Parallel Software Design.* New York: Wiley, 1988.

BACH86   Bach, M. *The Design of the UNIX Operating System.* Englewood Cliffs, NJ: Prentice Hall, 1986.

BAER80   Baer, J. *Computer Systems Architecture.* Rockville, MD: Computer Science Press, 1980.

BARB90   Barbosa, V. "Strategies for the Prevention of Communication Deadlocks in Distributed Parallel Programs." *IEEE Transactions on Software Engineering,* November 1990.

BAYS77   Bays, C. "A Comparison of Next-Fit, First-Fit, and Best-Fit." *Communications of the ACM,* March 1977.

BECK90   Beck, L. *System Software.* Reading, MA: Addison-Wesley, 1990.

BELA66   Belady, L. "A Study of Replacement Algorithms for a Virtual Storage Computer," *IBM Systems Journal,* No. 2, 1966.

BELL71   Bell, C., and Newell, A., editors. *Computer Structures: Readings and Examples.* New York: McGraw-Hill, 1971.

BEN82   Ben-Ari, M. *Principles of Concurrent Programming.* Englewood Cliffs, NJ: Prentice Hall, 1982.

BEN90   Ben-Ari, M. *Principles of Concurrent and Distributed Programming.* Englewood Cliffs, NJ: Prentice Hall, 1990.

BERN89   Bernabeu, J. et al. "The Architecture of Ra: A Kernel for Clouds." *Proceedings, 22nd Annual Hawaii International Conference on System Science,* January 1989.

BERN90   Bernstein, P. "Transaction Processing Monitors." *Communications of the ACM,* November 1990.

BIC88   Bic, L., and Shaw, A. *The Logical Design of Operating Systems, 2nd ed.* Englewood Cliffs, NJ: Prentice Hall, 1988.

BLAC90   Black, D. "Scheduling Support for Concurrency and Parallelism in the Mach Operating System." *Computer,* May 1990.

BOEB85   Boebert, W., Kain, R., and Young, W. "Secure Computing: The Secure Ada Target Approach." *Scientific Honeyweller,* July 1985. Reprinted in [ABRA87].

BOLO89   Bolosky, W., Fitzgerald, R., and Scott, M. "Simple But Effective Techniques for NUMA Memory Management." *Proceedings, Twelfth ACM Symposiun on Operating Systems Principles,* December 1989.

BRAN78   Branstad, D., ed. *Computer Security and the Data Encryption Standard.*

National Bureau of Standards, Special Publication No. 500-27, February 1978.

BREN89 Brent, R. "Efficient Implementation of the First-Fit Strategy for Dynamic Storage Allocation." *ACM Transactions on Programming Languages and Systems*, July 1989.

BROW84 Brown, R., Denning, P., and Tichy, W. "Advanced Operating Systems." *Computer*, October 1984.

BRUM87 Brumm, P., and Brumm, D. *80386: A Programming and Design Handbook.* Blue Ridge Summit, PA: Tab Books, 1987.

CABR86 Cabrear, L. "The Influence of Workload on Load Balancing Strategies." *USENIX Conference Proceedings*, Summer 1986.

CALI82 Calingaert, P. *Operating System Elements: A User Perspective.* Englewood Cliffs, NJ: Prentice Hall, 1982.

CARR81 Carr, R., and Hennessey, J. "WSClock—A Simple and Efficient Algorithm for Virtual Memory Management." *Proceedings of the Eighth Symposium on Operating System Principles*, December 1981.

CARR84 Carr, R. *Virtual Memory Management.* Ann Arbor, MI: UMI Research Press, 1984.

CARR89 Carriero, N., and Gelernter, D. "How to Write Parallel Programs: A Guide for the Perplexed." *ACM Computing Surveys*, September, 1989.

CHAN85 Chandy, K., and Lamport, L. "Distributed Snapshots: Determining Global States of Distributed Systems." *ACM Transactions on Computer Systems*, February 1985.

CHAN88 Chang., A., and Mergen, M. "801 Storage: Architecture and Programming." *ACM Transactions on Computer Systems*, February 1988.

CHAN90a Chang, A. et al. "Evolution of Storage Facilities in AIX Version 3 for RISC System/6000 Processors." *IBM Journal of Research and Development*, January 1990.

CHAN90b Chandras, R. "Distributed Message Passing Operating Systems." *Operating Systems Review*, January 1990.

CHEN90 Chen, P, and Patterson, D. "Maximizing Performance in a Striped Disk Array." *Proceedings, 17th Annual International Symposium on Computer Architecture*, May 1990.

CHU72 Chu, W., and Opderbeck, H. "The Page Fault Frequency Replacement Algorithm." *Proceedings, Fall Joint Computer Conference*, 1972.

CHU76 Chu, W., and Opderbeck, H. "Program Behavior and the Page-Fault-Frequency Replacement Algorithm." *Computer*, November 1976.

CLAR85 Clark, D., and Emer, J. "Performance of the VAX-11/780 Translation Buffer: Simulation and Measurement." *ACM Transactions on Computer Systems*, February 1985.

COFF71 Coffman, E., Elphick, M., and Shoshani, A. "System Deadlocks." *Computing Surveys*, June 1971.

COME84 Comer, D. *Operating System Design: The Xinu Approach.* Englewood Cliffs, NJ: Prentice-Hall, 1984.

CONW63 Conway, M. "Design of a Separable Transition-Diagram Compiler." *Communications of the ACM*, July 1963.

CONW67 Conway, R., Maxwell, W., and Miller, L. *Theory of Scheduling.* Reading, MA: Addison-Wesley, 1967.

CONW89 Conway, A., and Georganas, N. *Queuing Networks—Exact Computational Algorithms: A Unified Theory Based on Decomposition and Aggregation.* Cambridge, MA: MIT Press, 1989.

COOP81 Cooper, R. *Introduction to Queuing Theory, Second Edition.* New York: North Holland, 1981.

COOP89 Cooper, J. *Computer and Communications Security: Strategies for the 1990s.* New York: McGraw-Hill, 1990.

COOP90 Cooper, E., Steenkiste, P., Sansom, R., and Zill, B. "Protocol Implementation on the Nectar Communication Processor." *Proceedings, SIGCOMM '90 Symposium,* September 1990.

CORA88 Coraza, J., editor. *IBM Application System/400 Technology.* IBM SA21-9540, 1988.

CORB62 Corbato, F., Merwin-Daggett, M., and Dealey, R. "An Experimental Time-Sharing System." *Proceedings of the 1962 Spring Joint Computer Conference,* 1962.

CORB63 Corbato, F, et al. *The Compatible Time-Sharing System: A Programmers Guide.* Cambridge, MA: M.I.T. Press, 1963.

CORB68 Corbato, F. "A Paging Experiment with the Multics System," *MIT Project MAC Report MAC-M-384,* May 1968.

COX89 Cox, A., and Fowler, R. "The Implementation of a Coherent Memory Abstraction on a NUMA Multiprocessor: Experiences with PLATINUM." *Proceedings, Twelfth ACM Symposium on Operating Systems Principles,* December 1989.

DASG88 Dasgupta, P., LeBlanc, R., and Appelbe, W. "The Clouds Distributed Operating System: Functional Description, Implementation Details and Related Work." *Proceedings, 8th International Conference on Distributed Computing Systems,* June 1988.

DATT90 Datta, A., and Ghosh, S. "Deadlock Detection in Distributed Systems." *Proceedings, Phoenix Conference on Computers and Communications,* March 1990.

DAVI84 Davies, D., and Price, W. *Security for Computer Networks.* New York: Wiley, 1984.

DAVI87 Davis, W. *Operating Systems: A Systematic View, Third Edition.* Reading, MA: Addison-Wesley, 1987.

DEIT90 Deitel, H. *An Introduction to Operating Systems, Second Edition.* Reading, MA: Addison-Wesley, 1990.

DENN68 Denning P. "The Working Set Model for Program Behavior." *Communications of the ACM,* May 1968.

DENN70 Denning, P. "Virtual Memory." *Computing Surveys,* September 1970.

DENN71 Denning, P. "Third Generation Computer Systems." Computing Surveys, December 1971.

DENN80a Denning, P., Buzen, J., Dennis, J., Gaines, R., Hansen, P., Lynch, W., and Organick, E. "Operating Systems" in [ARDE80].

DENN80b Denning, P. "Working Sets Past and Present." *IEEE Transactions on Software Engineering,* January 1980.

DENN84 Denning, P., and Brown, R. "Operating Systems." *Scientific American,* September 1984.

DESR87 Desrochers, G. *Principles of Parallel and Multiprocessing.* New York: McGraw-Hill, 1987.

DEWA90 Dewar, R., and Smosna, M. *Microprocessors: A Programmer's View.* New York: McGraw-Hill, 1990.

DIJK65 Dijkstra, E. *Cooperating Sequential Processes.* Technological University, Eindhoven, The Netherlands, 1965. (Reprinted in *Programming Languages,* F. Genuys, ed., Academic Press, New York, NY, 1968).

DOUG89 Douglas, F., and Ousterhout, J. "Progress Migration in Sprite: A Status Report." *Newsletter of the IEEE Computer Society Technical Committee on Operating Systems,* Winter 1989.

DUNN74 Dunn, E. *Social Information Processing and Statistical Systems—Change and Reform.* New York: Wiley, 1974.

EAGE86 Eager, D., Lazowska, E., and Zahnorjan, J. "Adaptive Load Sharing in Homogeneous Distributed Systems." *IEEE Transactions on Software Engineering,* May 1986.

ENGE80 Enger, N., and Howerton, P. *Computer Security.* New York: Amacom, 1980.

ESKI90 Eskicioglu, M. "Design Issues of Process Migration Facilities in Distributed Systems." *Newsletter of the IEEE Computer Society Technical Committee on Operating Systems and Application Environments,* Summer 1990.

FALK88 Falk, H. "Deadline Scheduling for Timely Response." *Computer Design,* April 1, 1988.

FEIT90a Feitelson, D., and Rudolph, L. "Distributed Hierarchical Control for Parallel Processing." *Computer,* May 1990.

FEIT90b   Feitelson, D., and Rudolph, L. "Mapping and Scheduling in a Shared Parallel Environment Using Distributed Heirarchical Control." *Proceedings, 1990 International Conference on Parallel Processing*, August 1990.

FERR83   Ferrari, D., and Yih, Y. "VSWS: The Variable-Interval Sampled Working Set Policy." *IEEE Transactions on Software Engineering*, May 1983.

FINK88   Finkel, R. *An Operating Systems Vade Mecum.* Englewood Cliffs, NJ: Prentice Hall, 1988.

FINK89   Finkel, R. "The Process Migration Mechanism of Charlotte." *Newsletter of the IEEE Computer Society Technical Committee on Operating Systems*, Winter 1989.

FOLK87   Folk, M., and Zoellick, B. *File Structures: A Conceptual Toolkit.* Reading, MA: Addison-Wesley, 1987.

FRAN76   Frankel, T. *Tables for Traffic Management and Design.* abc Teletraining (P.O. Box 537, Geneva, IL 60134), 1976

GEHR87   Gehringer, E., Siewiorek, D., and Segall, Z. *Parallel Processing: The Cm* Experience.* Bedford, MA: Digital Press, 1987.

GEHR88   Gehringer, E., Abullarade, J., and Gulyn, M. "A Survey of Commercial Parallel Processors." *Computer Architecture News*, September 1988.

GELE91   Gelenbe, E., editor. "Special Issue on Parallel and Distributed System Performance Methodology." *IEEE Transactions on Software Engineering*, October 1991.

GIBB87   Gibbons, P. "A StubGenerator for Multilanguage RPC in Heterogeneous Environments." *IEEE Transactions on Software Engineering*, January 1987.

GING90   Gingras, A. "Dining Philosophers Revisited." *ACM SIGCSE Bulletin*, September 1990.

GOLD85   Goldstone, B. "A Backdoor Password Problem." *EDPACS*, July 1985.

GOLD89   Goldman, P. "Mac VM Revealed." *Byte*, September 1989.

GOPA85   Gopal, I. "Prevention of Store-and-Forward Deadlock in Computer Networks." *IEEE Transactions on Communications*, December 1985.

GROS86   Grosshans, D. *File Systems: Design and Implementation.* Englewood Cliffs, NJ: Prentice Hall, 1986.

GUTE88   Guterl, F. "Compact Disc." *IEEE Spectrum*, November 1988.

GUPT78   Gupta, R., and Franklin, M. "Working Set and Page Fault Frequency Replacement Algorithms: A Performance Comparison." *IEEE Transactions on Computers*, August 1978.

GUYN88   Guynes, J. "Impact of System Response Time on State Anxiety." *Communications of the ACM*, March 1988.

HAGM89   Hagmann, R. "Comments on Workstation Operating Systems and Virtual Memory. *Proceedings of the Second Workshop on Workstation Operating Systems*, September 1989.

HALD91 Haldar, S., and Subramanian, D. "Fairness in Processor Scheduling in Time Sharing Systems." *Operating Systems Review,* January 1991.

HALL88 Halliday, C., and Shields, J. *IBM PS/2 Technical Guide.* Indianapolis, IN: Howard W. Sams, 1988.

HAMA84 Hamacher, V., Vranesic, Z., and Zaky, S. *Computer Organization,* 2nd ed. New York: McGraw-Hill, 1984.

HANS73 Hansen, P. *Operating System Principles.* Englewood Cliffs, NJ: Prentice Hall, 1973.

HATF72 Hatfield, D. "Experiments on Page Size, Program Access Patterns, and Virtual Memory Performance." *IBM Journal of Research and Development,* January 1972.

HAYE88 Hayes, J. *Computer Architecture and Organization, Second Edition.* New York: McGraw-Hill, 1988.

HENN90 Hennessy, J., and Patterson, D. *Computer Architecture: a Quantitative Approach.* San Mateo, CA: Morgan Kaufmann, 1990.

HENR84 Henry, G. "The Fair Share Scheduler." *AT&T Bell Laboratories Technical Journal,* October 1984.

HOAR85 Hoare, C. *Communicating Sequential Processes.* Englewood Cliffs, NJ: Prentice Hall, 1985.

HOFR90 Hofri, M. "Proof of a Mutual Exclusion Algorithm." *Operating Systems Review,* January 1990.

HOLT72 Holt, R. "Some Deadlock Properties of Computer Systems." *Computing Surveys,* September, 1972.

HONG89 Hong, J., Tan, X., and Towsley, D. "A Performance Analysis of Minimum Laxity and Earliest Deadline Scheduling in a Real-Time System." *IEEE Transactions on Computers,* December 1989.

HORN89 Horner, D. *Operating Systems: Concepts and Aplications.* Glenview, IL: Scott, Foresman, 1989.

HUCK83 Huck, T. *Comparative Analysis of Computer Architectures.* Stanford University Technical Report Number 83-243, May 1983.

HYMA66 Hyman, H. "Comments on a Problem in Concurrent Programming Control." *Communications of the ACM,* January 1966.

IACO88 Iacobucci, E. *OS/2 Programmer's Guide.* Berkeley, CA: Osborne McGraw-Hill, 1988.

IBM71 IBM Corp. *Analysis of Some Queuing Models in Real-Time Systems.* IBM Document GF20-0007, 1971. Available from IBM document distribution centers.

IBM86 IBM National Technical Support, Large Systems. *Multiple Virtual Storage (MVS) Virtual Storage Tuning Cookbook.* Dallas, TX: Dallas Systems Center Technical Bulletin G320-0597, June 1986.

ISLO80 Isloor, S., and Marsland, T. "The Deadlock Problem: An Overview." *Computer,* September 1980.

JOHN89 Johnson, R. *MVS Concepts and Facilities.* New York: McGraw-Hill, 1989.

JONE80 Jones, S., and Schwarz, P. "Experience Using Multiprocessor Systems—A Status Report." *Computing Surveys,* June 1980.

JUL88 Jul, E., Levy, H., Hutchinson, N., and Black, A. "Fine-Grained Mobility in the Emerald System." *ACM Transactions on Computer Systems,* February 1988.

JUL89 Jul, E. "Migration of Light-Weight Processes in Emerald." *Newsletter of the IEEE Computer Society Technical Committee on Operating Systems,* Winter 1989.

KATZ84 Katzan, H., and Tharayil, D. *Invitation to MVS: Logic and Debugging.* New York: Petrocelli, 1984.

KATZ89 Katz, R., et al. "A Project on High Performance I/O Subsystems." *Computer Architecture News,* September 1989.

KAY88 Kay, J., and Lauder, P. "A Fair Share Scheduler." *Communications of the ACM,* January 1988.

KENA88 Kenah, L., Goldenberg, R., and Bate, S. *VAX/VMS Internals and Data Structures.* Bedford, MA: Digital Press, 1988.

KILB62 Kilburn, T., Edwards, D., Lanigan, M., and Sumner, F. "One-Level Storage System." IRE Transactions, April 1962; reprinted in [BELL71].

KIM86 Kim, M. "Synchronized Disk Interleaving." *IEEE Transactions on Computers,* November, 1986.

KIM87 Kim, M., and Tantawi, A. *Asynchronous Disk Interleaving.* Yorktown Heights, NY: IBM T. J. Watson Research Center, Report RC 12497, February 1987.

KIRS89 Kirschen, D. "An Overview of the Mach Operating System." *Newsletter of the IEEE Computer Society Technical Committee on Operating Systems,* Vol 3, No. 2, 1989.

KLEI75 Kleinrock, L. *Queueing Systems, Volume I: Theory.* New York: Wiley, 1975.

KLEI76 Kleinrock, L. *Queueing Systems, Volume II: Computer Applications.* New York: Wiley, 1976.

KNUT71 Knuth, D. "An Experimental Study of FORTRAN Programs." *Software Practice and Experience,* Vol. 1, 1971.

KNUT73 Knuth, D. *The Art of Computer Programming, Volume 1: Fundamental Algorithms, Second Edition.* Reading, MA: Addison-Wesley, 1973.

KOBA78 Kobayashi, H. *Modeling and Analysis: An Introduction to System Performance Evaluation Methodology.* Reading, MA: Addison-Wesley, 1978.

KOGA88   Kogan, M., and Rawson, F. "The Design of Operating System/2." *IBM Systems Journal*, No. 2, 1988.

KRAK88   Krakowiak, S., and Beeson, D. *Principles of Operating Systems.* Cambridge, MA: MIT Press, 1988.

KRAN88   Krantz, J., Mizell, A., and Williams R. *OS/2: Features, Functions, and Applications.* New York: Wiley, 1988.

KRON90   Kron, P. "A Software Developer Looks at OS/2." *Byte*, August 1990.

KUCK78   Kuck, D. *The Structure of Computers and Computations.* New York: Wiley, 1978.

KURZ84   Kurzban, S., Heines, T., and Kurzban, S. *Operating Systems Principles*, 2nd ed. New York: Van Nostrand Reinhold, 1984.

LAMP74   Lamport, L. "A New Solution of Dijkstra's Concurrent Programming Problem." *Communications of the ACM*, August 1974.

LAMP78   Lamport, L. "Time, Clocks, and the Ordering of Events in a Distributed System." *Communications of the ACM*, July 1978.

LAMP86   Lamport, L. "The Mutual Exclusion Problem." *Journal of the ACM*, April 1986.

LAMP91   Lamport, L. "The Mutual Exclusion Problem Has Been Solved." *Communications of the ACM*, January 1991.

LANE89   Lane, M., and Mooney, J. *A Practical Approach to Operating Systems*, Boston, MA: PWS-KENT Publishing Company, 1989.

LARM75   Larmouth, J. "Scheduling for a Share of the Machine." *Software Practices and Experience*, January 1975.

LIVA90   Livadas, P. *File Structures: Theory and Practice.* Englewood Cliffs, NJ: Prentice Hall, 1990.

LEBA84a   Leban, J., and Arnold, J. *IBM I/O Architecture and Virtual Storage Concepts: System/370-Mode and 370-XA-Mode Processors.* New York: Wiley, 1984.

LEBA84b   Leban, J., and Arnold, J. *IBM CPU and Storage Architecture: System/370-Mode and 370-XA-Mode Processors.* New York: Wiley, 1984.

LEBA84c   Leban, J., and Arnold, J. *Introduction to MVS and JCL.* New York: Wiley, 1984.

LEBL87   LeBlanc, T., and Mellor-Crummey, J. "Debugging Parallel Programs with Instant Replay." *IEEE Transactions on Computers*, April 1987.

LEFF88   Leffler, S., McKusick, M., Karels, M., Quartermain, J., and Stettner, A. *The Design and Implementation of the 4.3BSD UNIX Operating System.* Reading, MA: Addison-Wesley, 1988.

LEIB89   Leibfried, T. "A Deadlock Detection and Recovery Algorithm Using the Formalism of a Directed Graph Matrix." *Operating Systems Review*, April 1989.

LELA86 Leland, W., and Ott, T. "Load-Balancing Heuristics and Process Behavior." *Proceedings, ACM SigMetrics Performance 1986 Conference, 1986.*

LERO76 Leroudier, J., and Potier, D. "Principles of Optimality for Multiprogramming." *Proceedings, International Symposium on Computer Performance Modeling, Measurement, and Evaluation, March 1976.*

LETW88 Letwin, G. *Inside OS/2.* Redmond, WA: Microsoft Press, 1988.

LEUT90 Leutenegger, S., and Vernon, M. "The Performance of Multiprogrammed Multiprocessor Scheduling Policies." *Proceedings, Conference on Measurement and Modeling of Computer Systems, May 1990.*

LEVY89 Levy, H., and Eckhouse, R. *Computer Programming and Architecture: The VAX-11, Second Edition.* Bedford, MA: Digital Press, 1989.

LIST88 Lister, A., and Eager, R. *Fundamentals of Operating Systems,* 4th ed. London: Macmillan Education Ltd, 1988.

LIVA90 Livadas, P. File Structures: Theory and Practice. Englewood Cliffs, NJ: Prentice-Hall, 1990.

LUNT91 Lunt, T., and Cooper, D., editors. "Special Section on Computer Security." *IEEE Transactions on Software Engineering, November 1991.*

MAEK87 Maekawa, M., Oldehoeft, A., and Oldehoeft, R. *Operating Systems: Advanced Concepts.* Menlo Park, CA: Benjamin Cummings, 1987.

MAJU88 Majumdar, S., Eager, D., and Bunt, R. "Scheduling in Multiprogrammed Parallel Systems." *Proceedings, Conference on Measurement and Modeling of Computer Systems, May 1988.*

MALA90 Malamud, C. "Sharing the Wealth: RPCs Help Programs Go Places." *Data Communications, June 21, 1990.*

MANO88 Mano, M. *Computer Engineering Hardware Design.* Englewood Cliffs, NJ: Prentice Hall, 1988.

MART72 Martin, J. *Systems Analysis for Data Transmission.* Englewood Cliffs, NJ: Prentice Hall, 1972.

MART77 Martin, J. *Computer Data-Base Organization.* Englewood Cliffs, NJ: Prentice Hall, 1977.

MART88 Martin, J. *Principles of Data Communication.* Englewood Cliffs, NJ: Prentice Hall, 1988.

MASS86 Massie, P. *Operating Systems Theory and Practice.* New York: Macmillan, 1986.

MILE87 Milenkovic, M. *Operating Systems: Concepts and Design.* New York: McGraw-Hill, 1987.

MILL68 Miller, R. "Response Time in Man-computer Conversational Transactions." *Proceedings, Spring Joint Computer Conference, 1968.*

MOLL89 Molloy, M. *Fundamentals of Performance Modeling.* New York: Macmillan, 1989.

MORS87 Morse, S., Isaacson, E., and Albert, D. *The 80386/387 Architecture.* New York: Wiley, 1987.

NBS63 National Bureau of Standards. *Experimental Statistics.* NBS Handbook 91 (Available from Government Printing Office, GPO Stock No. 003-003-00135-0), 1963.

NG88 Ng, S., Lang, D., and Selinger, R. "Trade-Offs Between Devices and Paths in Achieving Disk Interleaving." *Proceedings, 15th International Symposium on Computer Architecture,* June 1988.

NEHM75 Nehmer, J. "Dispatcher Primitives for the Construction of Operating System Kernels." *Acta Informatica,* Vol. 5, 1975.

NELS88 Nelson, M., Welch, B., and Ousterhout, J. "Caching in the Sprite Network File System." *ACM Transactions on Computer Systems,* February 1988.

OLSO89 Olson, T. "Disk Array Performance in a Random I/O Environment." *Computer Architecture News,* September 1989.

OUST85 Ousterhout, J, et al. "A Trace-Drive Analysis of the UNIX 4.2 BSD File System." *Proceedings, Tenth ACM Symposium on Operating System Principles,* 1985.

OUST88 Ousterhout, J, et al. "The Sprite Network Operating System." *Computer,* February 1988.

PAAN86 Paans, R. *A Close Look at MVS Systems: Mechanisms, Performance, and Security.* New York: Elsevier, 1986.

PANW88 Panwar, S., Towsley, D., and Wolf, J. "Optimal Scheduling Policies for a Class of Queues with Customer Deadlines in the Beginning of Service." *Journal of the ACM,* October 1988.

PATT82 Patterson, D., and Sequin, C. "A VLSI RISC." *Computer,* September 1982.

PATT85 Patterson, D. "Reduced Instruction Set Computers." *Communications of the ACM,* January 1985.

PETE81 Peterson, G. "Myths About the Mutual Exclusion Problem." *Information Processing Letters,* June 1981.

PFLE89 Pfleeger, C. *Security in Computing.* Englewood Cliffs, NJ: Prentice Hall, 1989.

PINK89 Pinkert, J., and Wear, L. *Operating Systems: Concepts, Policies, and Mechanisms.* Englewood Cliffs, NJ: Prentice Hall, 1989.

PIZZ89 Pizzarello, A. "Memory Management for a Large Operating System." *Proceedings, International Conference on Measurement and Modeling of Computer Systems,* May 1989.

PLAM89 Plambeck, K. "Concepts of Enterprise Systems Architecture." *IBM Systems Journal,* No. 1, 1989.

POPE85 Popek, G., and Walker, B. *The LOCUS Distributed System Architecture,* Cambridge, MA: MIT Press, 1985.

PRAS81 Prasad, N. *Architecture and Implementation of Large Scale IBM Computer Systems.* Wellesley, MA: Q.E.D., 1981.

PRAS89 Prasad, N. *IBM Mainframes: Architecture and Design.* New York: McGraw-Hill, 1989.

PRZY88 Przybylski, S., Horowitz, M., and Hennessy, J. "Performance Trade-offs in Cache Design." *Proceedings, Fifteenth Annual International Symposium on Computer Architecture,* June 1988.

RASH88 Rashid, R., et al. "Machine-Independent Virtual Memory Management for Paged Uniprocessor and Multiprocessor Architectures." *IEEE Transactions on Computers,* August 1988.

RASH89 Rashid, R., et al. "Mach: A System Software Kernel." *Proceedings, COMPCON Sprint '89,* March 1989.

RAYN86 Raynal, M. *Algorithms for Mutual Exclusion.* Cambridge, MA: MIT Press, 1986.

RAYN88 Raynal, M. *Distributed Algorithms and Protocols.* New York: Wiley, 1988.

RAYN90 Raynal, M., and Helary, J. *Synchronization and Control of Distributed Systems and Programs.* New York: Wiley, 1990.

REDD89 Reddy, A., and Banerjee, P. "An Evaluation of Multiple-Disk I/O Systems." *IEEE Transactions on Computers,* December 1989.

RICA81 Ricart, G., and Agrawala, A. "An Optimal Algorithm for Mutual Exclusion in Computer Networks." *Communications of the ACM,* January 1981 (Corrigendum in *Communications of the ACM,* September 1981).

RICA83 Ricart G., and Agrawala, A. "Author's Response to 'On Mutual Exclusion in Computer Networks' by Carvalho and Roucairol." *Communications of the ACM,* February 1983.

RITC74 Ritchie, D., and Thompson, K. "The UNIX Time-Sharing System." *Communications of the ACM,* July 1974.

RITC78a Ritchie, D., and Thompson, K. "The UNIX Time-Sharing System." *The Bell System Technical Journal,* July-August 1978. This is a revision of RITC74 above.

RITC78b Ritchie, D. "UNIX Time-Sharing System: A Retrospective." *The Bell System Technical Journal,* July-August 1978.

RITC84 Ritchie, D. "the Evolution of the UNIX Time-Sharing System." *AT&T Bell Laboratories Technical Journal,* October 1984.

ROBI90 Robinson, J., and Devarakonda, M. "Data Cache Management Using Frequency-Based Replacement," *Proceedings, Conference on Measurement and Modeling of Computer Systems,* May 1990.

ROSE78 Rosenkrantz, D., Stearns, R., and Lewis, P. "System Level Concurrency Control in Distributed Database Systems." *ACM Transactions on Database Systems,* June 1978.

RUDO90   Rudolph, B. "Self-Assessment Procedure XXI: Concurrency." *Communications of the ACM,* May 1990.

RUSC77   Ruschitzka, M, and Fabry, R. "A Unifying Approach to Scheduling." *Communications of the ACM,* July 1977.

SALT75   Saltzer, J., and Schroeder, M. "The Protection of Information in Computer Systems." *Proceedings of the IEEE,* September 1975.

SAMS90   Samson, S. *MVS Performance Management.* New York: McGraw-Hill, 1990.

SATY81   Satyanarayanan, M. and Bhandarkar, D. "Design Trade-Offs in VAX-11 Translation Buffer Organization." *Computer,* December 1981.

SAUE81   Sauer, C, and Chandy, K. *Computer Systems Performance Modeling.* Englewood Cliffs, NJ: Prentice Hall, 1981.

SCHA62   Schay, G., and Spruth, W. "Analysis of a File Addressing Method." *Communications of the ACM,* August 1962.

SCHL89   Schleicher, D., and Taylor, L. "System Overview of the Application System/400." *IBM Systems Journal,* No. 3, 1989.

SCHN85   Schneider, G. *The Principles of Computer Organization.* New York: Wiley, 1985.

SHAW87   Shae, M., and Shaw, S. *UNIX Internals: A Systems Operations Handbook.* Blue Ridge Summit, PA: Tab Books, 1987.

SHNE84   Shneiderman, B. "Response Time and Display Rate in Human Performance with Computers." *ACM Computing Surveys,* September 1984.

SHOR75   Shore, J. "On the External Storage Fragmentation Produced by First-Fit and Best-Fit Allocation Strategies." Communications of the ACM, August, 1975.

SHUB90   Shub, C. "ACM Forum: Comment of a Self-Assessment Procedure on Operating Systems." *Communications of the ACM,* September 1990.

SIEB83   Sieber, J. *TRIX: A Communications-Oriented Operating System.* M.S. Thesis, M.I.T., September 1983.

SIER90   Sierra, H. *An Introduction to Direct Access Storage Devices.* Boston, MA: Academic Press, 1990.

SILB91   Silberschatz, A., Peterson, J., and Galvin, P. *Operating System Concepts.* Reading, MA: Addison-Wesley, 1991.

SMIT82   Smith, A. "Cache Memories." *ACM Computing Surveys,* September 1982.

SMIT83   Smith, D. "Faster Is Better: A Business Case for Subsecond Response Time." *Computerworld,* April 18, 1983.

SMIT85   Smith, A. "Disk Cache—Miss Ratio Analysis and Design Considerations." *ACM Transactions on Computer Systems,* August 1985.

SMIT88 Smith, J. "A Survey of Process Migration Mechanisms." *Operating Systems Review,* July 1988.

SMIT89 Smith, J. "Implementing Remote *fork*() with Checkpoint/restart." *Newsletter of the IEEE Computer Society Technical Committee on Operating Systems,* Winter 1989.

SPAF89 Spafford, E., Heaphy, K., and Ferbrache, D. *Computer Viruses.* Arlington, VA: ADAPSO, 1989.

STAL90a Stallings, W. *Computer Organization and Architecture,* 2nd ed. New York: Macmillan, 1990.

STAL90b Stallings, W. *Handbook of Computer-Communications Standards, Volume I: The Open Systems Interconnection (OSI) Model and OSI-Related Standards, 2nd ed.* Carmel, IN: Howard W. Sams, 1990.

STAL91 Stallings, W. *Data and Computer Communications, 3rd ed.* New York: Macmillan, 1991.

STAN88 Stankovic, J., and Ramamrithan, K. *Hard Real-Time Systems.* Washington, DC: IEEE Computer Society Press, 1988.

STAN89 Stankovic, J., and Ramamrithan, K. "The Spring Kernel: A New Paradigm for Real-Time Operating Systems." *Operating Systems Review,* July 1989.

STON90 Stone, H. *High-Performance Computer Architecture, 2nd ed.* Reading, MA: Addison-Wesley, 1990.

STRE83 Strecker, W. "Transient Behavior of Cache Memories." *ACM Transactions on Computer Systems,* November 1983.

STUC85 Stuck, B., and Arthurs, E. *A Computer and Communications Network Performance Analysis Primer.* Englewood Cliffs, NJ: Prentice Hall, 1985.

SUMM84 Summers, R. "An Overview of Computer Security." *IBM Systems Journal,* No. 4, 1984. Reprinted in [ABRA87].

SUZU82 Suzuki, I., and Kasami, T. "An Optimality Theory for Mutual Exclusion Algorithms in Computer Networks." *Proceedings of the Third International Conference on Distributed Computing Systems,* October 1982.

TABA90 Tabak, D. *Multiprocessors.* Englewood Cliffs, NJ: Prentice Hall, 1990.

TAMI83 Tamir, Y., and Sequin, C. "Strategies for Managing the Register File in RISC." *IEEE Transactions on Computers,* November 1983.

TANE78 Tanenbaum, A. "Implications of Structured Programming for Machine Architecture." *Communications of the ACM,* March 1978.

TANE85 Tanenbaum, A., and Renesse, R. "Distributed Operating Systems." *Computing Surveys,* December 1985.

TANE87 Tanenbaum, A. *Operating System Design and Implementation.* Englewood Cliffs, NJ: Prentice Hall, 1987.

TANE88 Tanenbaum, A. *Computer Networks.* Englewood Cliffs, NJ: Prentice Hall, 1988.

TANE90 Tanenbaum, A. *Structured Computer Organization.* Englewood Cliffs, NJ: Prentice Hall, 1990.

TAY90 Tay, B., and Ananda, A. "A Survey of Remote Procedure Calls." *Operating Systems Review,* July 1990.

TEVA87 Tevanian, A., et al. "Mach Threads and the Unix Kernel: The Battle for Control." *Proceedings, Summer 1987 USENIX Conference,* June 1987.

TEVA89 Tevanian, A., and Smith, B. "Mach: The Model for Future Unix." *Byte,* November 1989.

THAD81 Thadhani, A. "Interactive User Productivity." *IBM Systems Journal,* No. 1, 1981.

THEA83 Theaker, C., and Brookes, G. *A Practical Course on Operating Systems.* New York: Springer-Verlag, 1983.

THOM84 Thompson, K. "Reflections on Trusting Trust (Deliberate Software Bugs)." *Communications of the ACM,* August 1984.

TIME86 Time, Inc. *Computer Security, Understanding Computers Series.* Alexandria, VA: Time-Life Books, 1986.

TUCK89 Tucker, A., and Gupta, A. "Process Control and Scheduling Issues for Multiprogrammed Shared-Memory Multiprocessors." *Proceedings, Twelfth ACM Symposium on Operating Systems Principles,* December 1989.

TURN86 Turner, R. *Operating Systems: Design and Implementations.* New York: Macmillan, 1986.

WACK89 Wack, J., and Carnahan, L. *Computer Viruses and Related Threats: A Management Guide.* Gaithersburg, MD: National Institute of Standards and Technology, NIST Special Publication 500-166, August 1989.

WALK89 Walker, B., and Mathews, R. "Process Migration in AIX's Transparent Computing Facility." *Newsletter of the IEEE Computer Society Technical Committee on Operating Systems,* Winter 1989.

WARD80 Ward, S. "TRIX: A Network-Oriented Operating System." *Proceedings, COMPCON '80,* 1980.

WATE86 Waters, F, editor. *RT Personal Computer Technology.* IBM SA23-1057, 1986.

WATS70 Watson, R. *Timesharing System Design Concepts.* New York: McGraw-Hill, 1970.

WEIZ81 Weizer, N. "A History of Operating Systems." *Datamation,* January 1981.

WEND89 Wendorf, J., Wendorf, R., and Tokuda, H. "Scheduling Operating System Processing on Small-Scale Microprocessors." *Proceedings, 22nd Annual Hawaii International Conference on System Science,* January 1989.

WIED87 Wiederhold, G. *File Organization for Database Design.* New York: McGraw-Hill, 1987.

WOOD86 Woodside, C. "Controllability of Computer Performance Tradeoffs

Obtained Using Controlled-Share Queue Schedulers." *IEEE Transactions on Software Engineering*, October 1986

WOOD89   Woodbury, P. et al. "Shared Memory Multiprocessors: The Right Approach to Parallel Processing." *Proceedings, COMPCON Spring '89*, March 1989.

ZAHO90   Zahorjan, J., and McCann, C. "Processor Scheduling in Shared Memory Multiprocessors." *Proceedings, Conference on Measurement and Modeling of Computer Systems*, May 1990.

ZHAO89   Zhao, W., ed. Special Issue on Real-Time Operating Systems. *Operating System Review*, July 1989.

ZOBE88   Zobel, D., and Koch, C. "Resolution Techniques and Complexity Results with Deadlocks: A Classifying and Annotated Bibliography." *Operating Systems Review*, January 1988.

Index

ACKNOWLEDGMENTS

Table 1.2: © 1990 Morgan Kaufmann Publishers. Reprinted with permission from David Patterson and John Hennessy, *Computer Architecture: A Quantitative Approach*. Figure 2.3: From A. Silberschatz, J. Peterson, and P. Galvin, *Operating System Concepts*. © 1991, by Addison-Wesley Publishing Company. Reprinted with permission of the publisher. Figures 2.7 and 2.8: Reprinted with permission of Macmillan Publishing Company from *Operating Systems: Design and Implementation* by Raymond W. Turner. Copyright © 1986 by Macmillan Publishing Company, a Division of Macmillan, Inc. Figure 2.14: Reprinted with permission from *Version 4.4 VAX/VMS Internals and Data Structures* by Lawrence J. Kenah, Ruth E. Goldenberg, and Simon F. Bate. Copyright © 1988 Digital Press/Digital Equipment Corporation, 12 Crosby Drive, Bedford, MA. 01730. Figure 2.18: From Maurice J. Bach, *the Design of the UNIX® Operating System*, © 1986, pp. 20. Reprinted by permission of Prentice Hall, Englewood Cliffs, New Jersey. Figure 2.19: Reprinted, by permission, from *Architecture and Implementation of Large Scale IBM Computer Systems*, Second Edition, 1981, QED Information Sciences, Inc., Wellesley, MA. Table 3.2: From James R. Pinkert and Larry L. Wear, *Operating Systems: Concepts, Policies, and Mechanisms*, © 1989, p. 69. Reprinted by permission of Prentice Hall, Englewood Cliffs, New Jersey. Table 3.11: From S. Krakowiak and D. Beeson, *Principles of Operating Systems*. Copyright © Massachusetts Institute of Technology 1988. Published by the MIT Press. Figure 3.14: From Maurice J. Bach, *the Design of the UNIX® Operating System*, © 1986, p. 148. Reprinted by permission of Prentice Hall, Englewood Cliffs, New Jersey. Table 4.4: From S. Isloor and T. Marsland, "The Deadlock Problem: An Overview," *Computer*, September 1980. © 1980 IEEE. Tables 4.7, 4.8, 4.9, and 4.16: From M. Ben-Ari, *Principles of Concurrent Programming*, © 1982, pp. 29, 32, 39, 52. Reprinted by permission of Prentice Hall, Englewood Cliffs, New Jersey. Figure 4.18: From J. Hayes, *Computer Architecture and Organization*, Second Edition. © 1988. Reprinted by permission of McGraw-Hill, Inc. Figure 4.24: From Lubomir Bic and Alan C. Shaw, *The Logical Design of Operating Systems*, 2e., © 1988, p. 78. Reprinted by permission of Prentice Hall, Englewood Cliffs, New Jersey. Figure 4.27: From M. Milenkovic, *Operating Systems: Concepts and Design*. © 1987. Reprinted by permission of McGraw-Hill, Inc. Figure 5.24: From J. Hayes, *Computer Architecture and Organization*, Second Edition. © 1988. Reprinted by permission of McGraw-Hill, Inc. Figure 5.27: From Maurice J. Bach, *The Design of the UNIX® Operating System*, © 1986, p. 287. Reprinted by permission of Prentice Hall, Englewood Cliffs, New Jersey. Figure 5.28: From M. Maekawa, A. Oldehoeft, and R. Oldehoeft, *Operating Systems: Advanced Concepts*. Copyright © 1987. Reprinted by permission of Benjamin/Cummings Publishing Co. Table 6.7: From James Martin, *Principles of Data Communication*. © 1988. Reprinted by permission of Prentice Hall, Englewood Cliffs, New Jersey. Figures 6.14 and 6.15: From Raphael A. Finkel, *An Operating Systems Vade Mecum*, 2e, © 1988, pp. 35 and 36. Adapted by permission of Prentice Hall, Englewood Cliffs, New Jersey. Figure 6.16: From Maurice J. Bach, *The Design of the UNIX® Operating System*, © 1986, p. 257. Reprinted by permission of Prentice Hall, Englewood Cliffs, New Jersey. Figure 6.17: From Charles H. Sauer and K. Mani Chandy, *Computer Systems Performance Modeling*, © 1981, p. 25. Reprinted by permission of Prentice Hall, Englewood Cliffs, New Jersey. Figure 6.23: From Maurice J. Bach, *The Design of the UNIX® Operating System*, © 1986, p. 253. Reprinted by permission of Prentice Hall, Englewood Cliffs, New Jersey. Figure 6.24: From E. Iacobucci, *OS/2 Programmer's Guide*. © 1988. Reprinted by permission of McGraw-Hill, Inc. Tables 7.4 and 8.1 and Figure 8.6: From G. Wiederhold, *File Organization for Database Design*. © 1987, pp. 75, 225, and 420. Reprinted by permission of McGraw-Hill, Inc. Table 7.6: From J. Krantz, A. Mizell, and R. Williams, *OS/2: Features, Functions, and Applications*. © 1988, p. 32. John Wiley & Sons, Inc. Figure 8.1: From Daniel Grosshans, *File Systems: Design & Implementation*, © 1986, p. 395. Adapted by permission of Prentice Hall, Englewood Cliffs, New Jersey. Figure 8.6: From G. Wiederhold, *File Organization for Database Design*. © 1987. Reprinted by permission of McGraw-Hill, Inc. Figure 9.19: From S. Krakowiak and D. Beeson, *Principles of Operating Systems*. Copyright © Massachusetts Institute of Technology 1988. Published by the MIT Press. Figure 10.1: From M. Maekawa, A. Oldehoeft, and R. Oldehoeft, *Operating Systems: Advanced Concepts*. Copyright © 1987. Reprinted by permission of Benjamin/Cummings Publishing Co.

College Division
Macmillan Publishing Company
Front & Brown Streets
Riverside, NJ 08075

ORDER FORM

Ship To: **Bill to:**
(Please print or type)   (If different from shipping address)

Name _____   Name _____

Co. _____   Co. _____

Address _____   Address _____

_____   _____

City _____ St _____ Zip _____   City _____ St _____ Zip _____

Mail your order to the above address or call 800-548-9939 (in New Jersey call
609-461-6500) or Fax 609-461-9265

Shipping Method **(select one)**
_____ UPS ground _____ 2nd Day Air _____ Book Rate

Payment Method **(select one)**	
_____ Check	_____ Visa
_____ Bill Me	_____ MasterCard
_____ Authorized Signature	
_____ _____ Card Number Exp Date	

(continued)

TEAR OUT THIS PAGE TO ORDER OTHER TITLES BY WILLIAM STALLINGS:

SEQ.	QTY.	ISBN NO.	TITLE	PRICE	TOTAL
1	_____	002-415491-1	Computer Organization & Architecture 2/e	$63.00	_____
2	_____	002-415454-7	Data and Computer Communications 3/e	$66.00	_____
3	_____	002-415531-4	Local Networks 3/e	$54.00	_____
4	_____	002-415431-8	Business Data Communications	$43.00	_____
5	_____	002-415475-X	ISDN and Broadband ISDN 2/e	$54.00	_____

Handbooks of Computer Communications Standards

SEQ.	QTY.	ISBN NO.	TITLE	PRICE	TOTAL
6	_____	002-415521-7	Volume 1, The Open Systems Interconnection (OSI) Model and OSI-Related Standards, 2/e	$43.00	_____
7	_____	002-415522-5	Volume 2, Local Area Network Standards, 2/e	$43.00	_____
8	_____	002-415523-3	Volume 3, The TCP/IP Protocol Suite, 2/e	$43.00	_____

GRAND TOTAL _____

A small shipping charge will be added. Prices subject to change without prior notification.

PSR-PSL 350-3500   FC# 1355

ACRONYMS

CPU	Central Processing Unit
CTSS	Compatible Time-Sharing System
DES	Data Encryption Standard
DMA	Direct Memory Access
FAT	File Allocation Table
FCFS	First-Come-First-Served
FIFO	First-In-First-Out
I/O	Input/Output
IBM	International Business Machines Corporation
JCL	Job Control Language
LAN	Local Area Network
LIFO	Last-In-First-Out